IT WAS A
VERY GOOD
YEAR

Martha H. Clark

IT WAS A VERY GOOD

YEAR

A CULTURAL HISTORY OF THE UNITED STATES FROM 1776 TO THE PRESENT

Vincent dePaul Lupiano

AND

Ken W. Sayers

BOB ADAMS, INC.
Holbrook, Massachusetts

Published by Bob Adams, Inc.
260 Center Street, Holbrook, MA 02343

ISBN: 1-55850-419-2

Printed in the United States of America.

J I H G F E D C B A

Library of Congress Cataloging-in-Publication Data
Lupiano, Vincent dePaul.
    It was a very good year : a cultural history of the United States from 1776 to the present /
Vincent dePaul Lupiano and Ken Sayers.
        p.   cm.
Includes index.
ISBN 1-55850-419-2
1. United States–Civilization. I. Sayers, Ken W. II. Title
E169.1.L857   1994
973–dc20   94-33211
                                                                        CIP

*This publication is designed to provide accurate and authoritative information with regard to the subject
matter covered. It is sold with the understanding that the publisher is not engaged in rendering legal, accounting, or other professional advice. If legal advice or other expert assistance is required, the services
of a competent professional person should be sought.*
— From a *Declaration of Principles* jointly adopted by a Committee of the American Bar Association
and a Committee of Publishers and Associations

This book is available at quantity discounts for bulk purchases.
For information, call 1-800-872-5627.

Dedication

To my wife and friend, Nancy Connolly Lupiano, with much love and heart-felt appreciation for her patience and understanding; the anchor on the kite.

— *V. deP. L.*

To my father, William Sayers, who loved history and taught me well.

— *K. S. W.*

Contents

Preface

*T*his is a compilation of the popular culture of America. It makes no pretense at being all–inclusive. Omissions? There are plenty. In a work this broad, each reading will raise questions such as, "Why didn't you include this? How come you omitted that?" In selecting material to be included, albeit subjectively, the authors used "popular" as the operative word and a guide. Thus, the contents are presented as an overall indication of who and what we are as a people; what occupied us; what worried us; what made the nation successful; and, of course, some of the things that brought doubt and tragedy to the country.

Against the history of Europe, we are a very young nation. But that does not diminish our country's complexity, achievements, and flaws. To include all of that in one work would, in our opinion, be impossibly difficult, even with the aid of computers. Thus, we have presented a quick view of our brief history—something you can hold in your hand.

If, in reading this, you experience a sense of delight and revelation, that's due to much effort on the part of many people; if, however, you detect any errors, you can look to the authors alone.

— *Vincent dePaul Lupiano*
— *Ken W. Sayers*

Acknowledgments

*M*uch of the credit for acquiring the rights to this book and the subsequent legal effort goes to our attorney, Ronald Markowitz. Working with a quiet energy over a lengthy period, Ron was a great source of substantial advice and hope, particularly during those frequent moments when the authors felt that the project was a lost cause.

Since the project began, Jill Egleland spent countless hours typing the manuscript, and to her and her skill we are very much indebted.

We would also like to thank Rose Sayers, for her sharp eye and helpful encouragement, support and suggestions; Wendy and Brian Rehnberg for invaluable research assistance; Judy Cornell for her numerous research trips to the library, and for fulfilling last minute requests for odd bits of information; and Richard C. Marshall, for guidance and insights on the value, collection and presentation of information.

Our agent, Carole Abel, was a wellspring of wisdom and advice.

— *Vincent dePaul Lupiano*
— *Ken W. Sayers*

Introduction

*B*etween 1969 and 1973 I was working at the American Broadcasting Company's WPLJ, an FM radio station in New York City, and I wanted very much to leave and start my own business. My ambition was to write and produce a syndicated radio program that would be aired across the nation—a weekly show that would highlight the music and news of the 1930s, '40s, '50s and '60s. I began by looking for a single book that would provide the popular culture of America during that musically and culturally rich period. The search, I thought, would be easy. All I had to do was go to the library and there, on a shelf, would be a single source. Not so.

The library contained not one but dozens of research books which could not be lent. There were numerous books on the political history of the period; books on Broadway shows; charts on the most popular music and books; film histories and lists. But was there a single book that encompassed all these categories? Where would I go, for instance, to find the first year television brought the national conventions of the two major political parties into American homes? (Republican, July 7–12; Democratic, July 21–26; both in Chicago in 1952.) What year did Ned Washington and Victor Young write "My Foolish Heart"? (1949.)

In October of 1973, after a long search, I found what I was looking for on the shelf of the G. Schirmer music store (now Brown's Music) in New York City. I almost passed it but the title caught my eye. I thumbed through it and knew instantly that I had everything I needed in one book. The first edition of the *Variety Music Cavalcade* was written by Julius Mattfeld and published in 1952. I bought the final edition, published in 1971, the same year Mr. Mattfeld died; it covered the years 1880 through 1969.

Julius Mattfeld was an outstanding musicologist, a former Director of the Music Library for the Columbia Broadcasting System. For years he provided the arrangements for the musical backgrounds of many CBS radio and TV shows. He was also a professionally trained librarian, an organist and a composer.

If you looked at the title alone, it would seem that the focus of the book was on music—who wrote what and when. But Mr. Mattfeld—almost incidentally, it seems—also included a synopsis of unusual political events as an adjunct to his listing of songs. If the book was to be judged by its title, no one would ever imagine that Mr. Mattfeld's book contained such a wide range of American pop culture between its covers.

The title, *Variety Music Cavalcade*, was really a misnomer because the book was much more than just a listing of popular music. There, in any given year, was a snapshot of the history, notable deaths, sports events, music, literature, and theatrical highlights of our nation compressed into six or seven succinct pages—grammatical "sound bites." The book was a storehouse of popular, interesting facts that would not only help to launch my programming idea, but would be a valuable resource later on. The book almost immediately inspired a title for the proposed radio program: "It Was a Very Good Year."

But the dream of launching a syndicated radio program never came to fruition. Instead, I moved on, taking Mr. Mattfeld's work with me, which, by then, had become a dependable old friend.

As an IBM speechwriter I used the book constantly. But Mr. Mattfeld's work stopped at 1969 and my single source for comprehensive, cultural information often met a big, frustrating challenge. Over the next few years, I would periodically call the publisher and ask if they had intentions to update the book. "No," was always the reply, along with no awareness of the book itself, or Julius Mattfeld. The more I thought about it, the more I wondered about acquiring the rights and updating the book myself.

In 1991 I left IBM and resumed a writing and communications consulting business. Since then, I have learned that every book is, at its core, an idea. But that idea is either still-born—because it languishes and is repeated over and over in the author's mind—or evolves ultimately, with many tedious twists and turns, into fruition and fulfillment. So it was with this book.

During the course of bringing this project to reality, I was joined by Ken W. Sayers, a friend and former colleague who shared my enthusiasm for preserving and updating Mr. Mattfeld's achievement. And I met Carole Abel, a highly respected New York literary agent, who found us a publisher with the same passion.

— *Vincent dePaul Lupiano*

The illusion that the times that were are better than those that are,
has probably pervaded all ages.

— *Horace Greeley* (1811–1872)
American journalist and political leader

1776

$\mathcal{T}$he first state constitution was adopted (Jan. 5) by the colony of new Hampshire.

Thomas Paine published "Common Sense in Philadelphia" (Jan. 10). The pamphlet, which called for total independence from Britain, sold more than a hundred thousand copies.

Philip Freneau, "poet of the American Revolution," wrote biting satires against the British.

Father Garces, a Spanish priest, reached a Mohave Indian settlement on the Colorado River (Feb. 14).

British troops evacuated (Mar. 17) Boston after continental forces occupied Dorcester Heights.

Fire destroyed most of the old parts of New York City.

John Adams, Benjamin Franklin, Thomas Jefferson, and others were appointed (June 11) to draft a declaration of independence.

The Continental Congress approved (July 4) the document and it was signed (Aug. 2) in Philadelphia by delegates to the Congress. Benjamin Franklin said at the time that "We must all hang together, else we shall all hang separately." The Congress later passed (Sept. 9) a resolution replacing the designation "United Colonies" with "United States."

Father Silvestre Velez de Escalante began (July 29) an expedition to map parts of New Mexico, Utah, Colorado, and Arizona.

Continental Army Captain Nathan Hale was captured (Sept. 21) by the British while operating as a spy on Long Island, and was hanged the next day.

The new U.S. flag was saluted (Nov. 16) for the first time at St. Eustactius in the Dutch West Indies.

The Phi Beta Kappa Society was founded (Dec. 5) at the College of William and Mary in Williamsburg, Virginia.

General George Washington crossed (Dec. 25) the Delaware River and captured (Dec. 26) 1,000 Hessian troops during the Battle of Trenton.

1777

$\mathscr{B}$ritain's General William Howe defeated (Sept. 11) troops led by General George Washington at the Battle of Brandywine in Pennsylvania. That same month, British forces encamped (Sept. 14) at Saratoga, N.Y., and occupied (Sept. 26) Philadelphia. The Americans reversed some of those setbacks the following month when, at the second Battle of Saratoga, General Horatio Gates won (Oct. 7) a key victory over General John Burgoyne of Britain.

The New Testament was published in English for the first time in America.

The Continental Congress, then meeting at York, Pennsylvania, adopted (Nov. 15) the Articles of Confederation. The document required the consent of nine states to all important measures and denied Congress the power to tax or regulate trade.

Some eleven thousand troops, many barefoot and hungry, arrived (Dec. 14) in Valley Forge, Pennsylvania, to spend the winter under the command of General Washington.

Congress specified the design of the U.S. flag: "thirteen strips alternate red and white...thirteen stars of white on a blue field."

1778

$\mathscr{B}$ritish explorer James Cook arrived (Jan. 18) in the Hawaiian Islands and renamed them the Sandwich Islands. Two months later, he reached (Mar. 6) the coast of Oregon while pursuing a search for the Northwest Passage.

France recognized America's fight for independence and signed (Feb. 6) a treaty of alliance with Benjamin Franklin. The treaty was ratified (May 4) by the Continental Congress. A French fleet commanded by Count d'Estaing arrived (July 8) off Delaware and later operated (July 29) off Newport, R.I.

Gotthilf Henry Muhlenberg, botanist, began a systematic study of American plants.

General George Washington's forces, which had declined in number to eight thousand soldiers during the winter encampment at Valley Forge, defeated (June 28) British troops at the Battle of Monmouth.

The Continental Congress appointed (Dec. 10) John Jay as its President and named (Dec. 14) Benjamin Franklin as the U.S. representative to France.

Jonathan Carver's "Travels Through the Interior of North America" contained information on Indian customs and the natural history of the Great Lakes and the upper Mississippi region.

Thomas Jefferson persuaded the Virginia legislature to ban the further importation of slaves.

1779

---

*B*ritish forces captured and burned (May 10) Portsmouth and Norfolk, Virginia.

Billings published "Music in Miniature."

Captain John Paul Jones, commanding a continental Navy squadron of five ships aboard his flagship *Bon Homme Richard* near Britain, successfully fought (Sept. 23) the Royal Navy frigate *Serapis*. When asked if he was surrendering during the engagement, Jones replied, "I have not yet begun to fight."

Under Thomas Jefferson, statesman and author, William and Mary College created schools of medicine, law and modern languages. A system allowing students to choose courses was introduced.

John Adams was appointed (Sept. 27) by the Continental Congress to negotiate an end to the war with Britain.

Sweet corn, well known to the Iroquois Indians, was discovered along the Susquehanna River by Richard Bagnal, an officer serving with General John Sullivan.

The popular sport around Charlottesville, Va., was sprint racing, quarter-mile races between two horses.

1780

The Court of Appeals was established (Jan. 15) by the Continental Congress.

The American Academy of Arts and Sciences was organized and established in Boston.

John Andre, a captured British spy, disclosed (Sept. 23) a plot by American General Benedict Arnold to surrender West Point to forces led by Sir Henry Clinton. The unfortunate Andre was hanged (Oct. 2) for his trouble.

Congress requested (Nov. 4) contributions of flour, hay, and pork from the states to support the continental armies.

North Carolina settler James Robertson built a fort on the Cumberland River that later became the city of Nashville, Tennessee.

The Philadelphia Humane Society was established to teach first aid (how to revive drowning victims). Franklin proposed mouth-to-mouth resuscitation.

An automated flour mill was developed by Oliver Evans, a storekeeper in Delaware.

U.S. population was estimated at 2.7 million.

1781

$\mathcal{T}$he Articles of Confederation were adopted (Mar. 1), including agreements by New York and Virginia to cede their western land claims to the republic.

British forces under General Charles Cornwallis occupied (Aug. 1) Yorktown, Virginia. At the end of the month, a French fleet commanded by Admiral de Grasse arrived off Yorktown and drove (Sept. 5) the British fleet away from Chesapeake Bay. With King George's troops surrounded and under attack, Cornwallis surrendered (Oct. 19) his eight thousand man army, effectively concluding the Revolutionary War. Despite that, however, British soldiers remained in the Carolinas until the following year and did not leave New York until November of 1783.

Virginia commissioned French artist Jean-Antoine Houdon to sculpt a statue of Lafayette.

The Continental Congress chartered (Dec. 31) the Bank of North America at Philadelphia, with an initial capitalization of $400,000.

Spanish settlers established El Pueblo de Nuestra Senora la Reina de los Angeles de Porciuncula, now known simply as Los Angeles.

New Haven, Connecticut, enacted an ordinance prohibiting Sunday work and sales. The regulation was printed on blue paper, leading to the term "blue laws."

A French traveler to Annapolis, Maryland, reported on its splendor. Fine women, elegant horses, coaches, sumptuous dinners and balls were described. He noted that "A French hairdresser is a man of importance…, and it is said, a certain dame here hires one…at a thousand crowns a year salary."

1782

*G*eneral George Washington established (Aug. 7) the Purple Heart as an award for military merit.

J. Hector St. John Crevecoeur published "Letters from an American Farmer," a series of twelve essays about his extensive travels in North America.

John Trumbull published "M'Fingal," his most important work, considered at the time to contain much anti-loyalist propaganda.

Harvard Medical School opened.

Hugh Martin, physician, proposed a cure for cancer—a powder containing arsenic, a common cancer treatment at the time.

Robert Aitken, printer, published the first complete English language Bible in America.

Use of the scarlet letter for adulterers in New England was discontinued.

The Great Seal of the United States was adopted (Sept. 15) by Congress.

Spanish forces completed their defeat of the British in Florida.

The French envoy in Philadelphia gave a party to honor the new republic and served ice cream to his guests.

1783

*S*pain recognized (Feb. 3) the independence of the United States. Other recognition would follow during the year by Sweden, Denmark, and Russia.

The first daily newspaper in the country, the *Pennsylvania Evening Post*, was published (May 30).

The Treaty of Paris was signed (Sept. 3) by Britain, France, Spain, and the United States. The agreement recognized the independence of the thirteen colonies, ceded Florida to Spain, ceded and other territories to the Americans.

General George Washington made (Nov. 2) his farewell address to his officers and men, and officially resigned (Dec. 23) his commission as commander-in-chief of the Continental Army. Departing soldiers were issued script certificates entitling them to land west of the Appalachians.

An economic depression began during the year as the new nation struggled with debt of $6.4 million to France, $1.3 million to Holland, and $174,000 to Spain. At the same time, inflation reduced the value of paper currency issued by Congress. Shoes, for example, sold for $100 a pair.

Lexicographer Noah Webster published "The American Spelling Book," popularly called the "Blue-Backed Speller." It was the first part of "A Grammatical Institute of the English Language." The other parts were a grammar book (1784) and a reader (1785). The work helped standardize spelling of American English.

The population of the U.S. was estimated at 2.4 million. The decrease was due mainly to war deaths and to the departure of Loyalists during the Revolutionary War.

Enrollment at Yale College was 270.

1784

$\mathscr{D}$avid Landreth opened (Jan. 7) the nation's first seed supply business in Philadelphia.

The U.S. Congress, then sitting in Annapolis, ratified (Jan. 14) the Treaty in Paris to formally end the War of Independence.

East Tennessee declared itself the independent state of Franklin (Aug. 23), in honor of Benjamin Franklin. That same year, Mr. Franklin, who was serving as U.S. minister to France, invented bifocal glasses and encouraged the French to adopt daylight savings time, a notion they rejected.

"Gentlemen and Ladies' Town and Country Magazine," one of the first periodicals designed especially for female readers, began publication.

Joel Barlow, poet, established a weekly newspaper, "American Mercury," in Hartford, Ct.

Thomas Jefferson published "Notes on Virginia."

Joseph-Siffred Duplessis, French portraitist, executed a portrait of Benjamin Franklin.

Captain John Greene moored (Aug. 30) his vessel *Empress of China* in Canton, marking the first visit of an American ship to China.

Russian settlers on Kodiak Island established (Sept. 22) their first permanent settlement in Alaska.

The first bales of American cotton were delivered to Britain.

Acadians in Louisiana established Cajun cooking by combining their French Canadian recipes with native American dishes.

1785

*N*ew York City became (Jan. 11) the temporary national capital.

Thomas Jefferson was appointed (March 10) the U.S. minister to France, and Ben Franklin returned to America after nine years in that post.

Congress enacted (May 8) an ordinance providing for the sale of public lands in the Northwest Territories in 640-acre tracts at a minimum cash price of $1 an acre.

John MacPherson in Philadelphia published (Oct. 1) the first city directory.

Congress rejected (Nov. 28) the formation of the state of Franklin. North Carolina reasserted its jurisdiction over the area, which became part of the state of Tennessee when it was admitted to the Union in 1796.

1786

$\mathcal{T}$he Ohio Company was formed (March 1) to acquire land for settlement along the upper Ohio River.

The continuing economic depression sparked a rebellion by farmers led by Daniel Shay in Massachusetts. At one point, state militia troops were used (Sept. 26) to prevent seizure of the Springfield Arsenal by the farmers.

Baseball was first played at Princeton. That same year, Charleston, S.C., clergyman Henry Purcell founded the first American golf club.

Ezekiel Reed of Bridgewater, Massachusetts, patented a nail-making machine. Despite the invention, wooden pegs remained in general use.

Charles Willson Peale, portrait painter, opened the Philadelphia Museum with displays of animals, minerals and art.

John Foulke, physician, flew a small paper balloon.

Peter Carnes paid a thirteen-year-old boy to make America's first manned balloon flight.

Oliver Evans established an automatic production line in a flour mill near Philadelphia.

Jedidiah Morse published "Geography Made Easy" and included descriptions of American plants and animals.

Andrew Ellicot surveyed and extended the Mason-Dixon Line.

The first ice cream was made commercially in New York City.

Pennsylvania Hospital opened an outpatient dispensary, a forerunner of free clinics.

A "golf club" was established at Charleston, S.C.

1787

$\mathscr{C}$ongress called (Feb. 21) for a constitutional convention, which later convened (May 25) in Philadelphia under the leadership of George Washington. Congress later voted (Sept. 28) to submit the proposed constitution to the states for ratification. Delaware became (Dec. 7) the first state to ratify, followed by Pennsylvania (Dec. 12) and New Jersey (Dec. 18).

Congress enacted (July 13) the Northwest Ordinance to establish a government north of the Ohio River and ban slavery there. Five states were later created out of the Northwest Territory.

One of the first nonreligious songbooks, "A Select Collection of the Most Favorite Scots Tunes," was published in the U.S.

John Fitch launched (Aug. 22) a steamboat on the Delaware River.

Publication began (Oct. 27) of "The Federalist Papers," political essays by John Jay, Alexander Hamilton, James Madison, and others.

Oliver Evans developed an automated grain-grinding and flour-sifting process, which lowered milling costs and made white bread widely available in the U.S.

1788

The proposed U.S. constitution was ratified by Georgia (Jan. 2), Connecticut (Jan. 9), Massachusetts (Feb. 6), Maryland (Apr. 8), South Carolina (May 23), New Hampshire (June 21), Virginia (June 25), and New York (July 26).

Riots broke out (April) in New York City in protest against dissections performed on corpses robbed from graves.

Congress adjourned (Nov. 1) under the Articles of Confederation, with no national government in place.

Francis Hopkinson, claiming himself to be the first native-born American composer, published "Seven Songs for the Harpsichord."

"The Federalist" papers were published.

"Cases and Observations," America's first collection of medical papers, was published by the Medical Society of New Haven.

1789

$\mathcal{T}$he first Congress met (Feb. 4) at Federal Hall in New York City. John Adams took (Apr. 21) his seat as the first presiding officer of the Senate.

George Washington was inaugurated (Apr. 30) at Federal Hall as the first president of the United States. John Adams became vice president, Thomas Jefferson was secretary of state, and Alexander Hamilton served as secretary of the treasury.

Congress enacted (July 4) the first Tariff Act, which placed a protective tariff on several imported items.

A six-man Supreme Court was established (Sept. 24) by Congress when it enacted the Federal Judiciary Act.

Congress sent (Sept. 25) ten of the proposed 12 amendments to the Constitution (the Bill of Rights) to the states for ratification.

North Carolina became (Nov. 21) the twelfth state to join the United States. That same year, the University of North Carolina was established (Dec. 11) at Chapel Hill to become the first state university in the country.

North Carolina ceded (Dec. 22) Tennessee to the United States to become a separate state.

Rochester, New York, was founded by Ebenezer Allen, a miller.

Peter and George Lorillard placed the first known U.S. tobacco advertisement.

Baptist minister Elijah Craig distilled the first bourbon whisky in an area that later became Bourbon County, Kentucky.

1790

$\mathscr{A}$lexander Hamilton, the U.S. Treasury secretary, submitted (Jan. 14) his first report on public credit to Congress.

In New York, the Supreme Court held (Feb. 2) its first session.

The Society of Friends (Quakers) sent (Feb. 11) its first emancipation petition to Congress.

Congress enacted (March 1) legislation calling for a regular national census.

The Revenue Marine Service, a predecessor of today's Coast Guard, was established (Apr. 4) by Congress.

Captain Robert Gary became the first American to circumnavigate the globe when he moored (Apr. 10) his ship Columbia in Boston. That same day, Congress passed a law forming the U.S. Patent Office.

Rhode Island ratified (May 29) the Constitution and became the thirteenth state.

President George Washington signed (May 31) the first U.S. copyright law.

The Resident Act was enacted (July 16) by Congress. The legislation designated Washington as the future national capital. President Washington then appointed Pierre Charles L'Enfant, thirty-five, to design the federal city.

Congress approved (Aug. 4) the Funding Act, which permitted the issuing of bonds to finance the national debt.

Near Fort Wayne, Indiana, the Ohio Indians attacked (Oct. 18) an expedition of settlers, marking the start of hostilities in the Northwest Territories.

Philadelphia became (Dec. 6) the nations's second capital.

Samuel Slater, who had earlier brought English textile technology to the United States, began (Dec. 21) production in the first American cotton mill in Pawtucket, R.I.

The U.S. population reached 3.9 million.

Inventor, publisher, and statesman Benjamin Franklin died (Apr. 17) in Philadelphia at age eighty-four.

1791

$\mathscr{P}$resident George Washington signed (Feb. 25) a bill establishing the Bank of the United States. That same day, carpenters in Philadelphia went on strike to force adoption of a twelve-hour day.

Vermont was admitted (March 4) as the fourteenth state in the Union.

Construction began (March 30) on the Knoxville Road, built to link the Wilderness Road with Knoxville south of the Ohio River.

The Cherokee Indians approved (Apr. 26) the Treaty of Holston, which deeded most of their land to the United States.

The Bill of Rights, the first ten amendments to the Constitution, was ratified (Dec. 15) by the states and went into effect.

Congress imposed a nine-cent-a-gallon tax on whiskey.

1792

$\mathcal{T}$homas Pinckney was appointed (Jan. 12) as the first American ambassador to England.

Congress approved (Feb. 2) the Presidential Succession Act.

Dollar coinage was introduced (Apr. 2), and the U.S. Mint at Philadelphia was established.

Congress enacted (May 8) the Militia Act, which authorized the states to draft able-bodied men to fight against the Indians.

Thomas Jefferson founded (May 13) the Democratic-Republican Party.

Local brokers signed (May 17) an agreement to establish the New York Stock Exchange.

Kentucky became (June 1) the fifteenth state of the Union.

Columbus Day was celebrated (Oct. 12) in New York for the first time. The celebration marked the three-hundredth anniversary of Columbus's discovery.

The White House cornerstone was put in place (Oct. 13).

George Washington was reelected president of the United States.

The Farmer's Almanac was published for the first time.

1793

$\mathcal{J}$ean-Pierre Francois Blanchard, a Frenchman, made the first balloon flight (Jan. 9) in America.

Congress approved (Jan. 13) the addition of two more stars and stripes to the American flag to designate Vermont and Kentucky.

The Fugitive Slave Act was passed (Feb. 12) by Congress, giving slave owners the right to recover runaway slaves and making it illegal for anyone to help the slaves escape to freedom.

President George Washington issued (Apr. 22) a U.S. proclamation of neutrality regarding the war between France and England, Holland, Spain, and the Holy Roman Empire. Four months later, the United States asked (Aug. 3) France to recall Citizen Genet, its minister, for compromising U.S. neutrality. Britain threatened the U.S. position by ordering (Nov. 6) the capture of any vessel found to be carrying French goods.

The cornerstone of the Capitol Building was laid (Sept. 18). Designed by William Thornton, the building was eventually completed in 1830.

A yellow fever epidemic that year killed more than four thousand people in Philadelphia and became the worst health disaster to affect an American city up to that point.

1794

*T*he 11th amendment to the Constitution was proposed (March 5). It was intended to prevent suits against a state by citizens of another state or another country.

Eli Whitney of Georgia received (March 14) a patent for his invention the year before of the cotton gin, an innovation that facilitated the rapid growth in cotton exports from the South.

Congress passed (March 22) legislation making it illegal for U.S. citizens to engage in the trading of slaves with other nations. Five days later, it authorized the construction of six ships and the formation of a national navy to consist of fifty-four officers and two thousand sailors.

General "Mad Anthony" Wayne defeated (Aug. 20) Indians at the Battle of Fallen Timbers in Ohio.

A force of fifteen thousand militiamen in western Pennsylvania put down (Sept. 24) a rebellion against a liquor excise tax.

American envoy John Jay signed (Nov. 19) a treaty in England to settle the outstanding issues between the two countries and to secure the territorial integrity of the U.S.

1795

*T*ndian chiefs ceded (Aug. 3) the southeast corner of the Northwest Territories, along with Detroit and Chicago, under the Treaty of Greenville. The Native Americans received annuities valued a $10,000 for the land.

Spain agreed (Oct. 27) under the Treaty of San Lorenzo to give up two Mississippi River forts and open the river to navigation.

The United States paid (Nov. 28) $800,000 and a frigate, and agreed to an annual payment of $25,000, to avoid hostilities with Algiers and Tunis.

1796

$\mathcal{C}$ongress passed (Apr. 18) legislation establishing trading houses for commerce with Indian tribes. The following month, Congress enacted (May 18) the Public Land Act to authorize the sale of federal land in minimum lots of 640 acres each at a cost of $2.00 an acre.

Tennessee was admitted (June 1) as the sixteenth state of the Union.

President George Washington delivered (Sept. 17) his farewell address to the nation in which he warned against permanent alliances with other countries, high public debt, and a large military.

Captain Ebenezer Dorr entered (Oct. 29) Monterey Bay in his ship, the *Otter*. He was the first American to explore the California coast.

John Adams defeated (Nov. 15) Thomas Jefferson for the presidency; Jefferson became vice president. That same day, France, with whom relations had steadily soured, announced it was suspending diplomatic relations with the United States.

1797

*J*ohn Adams was inaugurated (March 4) as the second president of the United States.

In its first-ever special session, Congress convened (May 15) to debate the growing crisis in U.S. relations with France. In the autumn, following the expulsion of the U.S. minister to France, a team of U.S. commissioners arrived (Oct. 4) in Paris to negotiate with the ruling Directory to preserve the peace between the two countries. However, the commissioners refused to give bribes in the so-called XYZ Affair, and returned to the U.S.

The United States launched three new Navy frigates: the *United States* (July 10) in Philadelphia; the *Constellation* (Sept. 7) in Baltimore; and the *Constitution* (Sept. 20), later honored as "Old Ironsides," in Boston.

1798

$\mathcal{T}$he Mississippi Territory was created (Apr. 7) by Congress from land acquired from Spain.

Congress authorized (May 28) President John Adams to order American warships to seize French vessels found to be interfering with U.S. shipping.

Debtors' prisons were abolished (June 6) in legislation passed by Congress.

Alien Acts were approved (June 25 and July 6) by Congress to give President Adams the authority to order any alien from the country and to imprison aliens in time of war. The Sedition Act was enacted (July 14) to suppress editorial criticism of the president and his administration.

The U.S. schooner *Retaliation* was seized (Nov. 20) by the French off the coast of Guadaloupe.

Charles Brockden Brown, the first American professional writer, published "Alcuin: A Dialogue on the Rights of Women."

1799

Congress passed (Jan. 30) the Logan Act, which prohibited private citizens from negotiating with foreign governments.

The U.S. Navy frigate *Constitution* captured the French frigate *L'Insurgente* off the island of Nevis in the quasi-war with France.

John Fries led an armed force of outraged German-Americans in Pennsylvania to protest a federal property tax assessment.

George Washington died at Mt. Vernon, Va., at the age of sixty-seven.

1800

*T*he United States comprised 16 states. The census showed a population of 5,308,483, as against 3,929,214 in 1790. John Adams, Federalist of Massachusetts, second President, was inaugurated in 1797; his opponent, Thomas Jefferson, was Vice President. A state of war existed between the United States and France, created by mutual distrust abroad and partisan interests at home. Although war was undeclared, the United States Navy captured or destroyed 84 French vessels. In Europe, Napoleon was rising to power.

The seat of the national government was transferred from Philadelphia to Washington, D.C., when the north wing of the Capitol was finished.

President Adams and his wife, Abigail, were the first occupants of the uncompleted President's Palace, now the White House.

Congress appropriated $5,000 "for the purchase of such books as may be necessary for the use of Congress at the said City of Washington," thus establishing (Apr. 24) the Library of Congress.

The Sixth Congress, 2nd Session, was the first to convene (Nov. 17) in Washington.

In the national election, Thomas Jefferson and Aaron Burr, who had jockeyed the hitherto unpolitical Tammany Society of New York into a political machine, received equal electoral votes. The House of Representatives, influenced strongly by Alexander Hamilton, the former Secretary of the Treasury who hated Burr, after many ballots chose Jefferson as President and Burr as Vice President.

Mason Locke Weems, Episcopal clergyman of Mt. Vernon, Va., published his "Life and Memorable Actions of George Washington." The subject of this idealized account died the previous year. The celebrated but fictitious cherry-tree episode first appeared in the fifth edition of the book (1806).

William Dunlap was the country's leading playwright.

In Print
American women novelists published a host of romantic best-sellers. Among these authors were Sarah Wentworth Morton, Sarah Sayward, Barrell Keating Wood, Susannah Haswell Rowson, and Hannah Webster Foster, whose novel, *The Coquette*, went through 13 editions.

On Stage

The Mount Vernon Gardens in New York on Broadway and Leonard Street opened (July 9) as a regularly organized summer theater, perhaps the first in the United States.

Music

The American Star, The Wounded Hussar, The Blue Bell of Scotland, Crazy Jane.

1801

$\mathcal{T}$he United States rounded out its first twenty-five years.

Thomas Jefferson, Republican of Virginia, was inaugurated as the third President—the first to be inaugurated in Washington.

Dolley Payne Madison, wife of the newly appointed Secretary of State, James Madison, became the first social leader in the White House as hostess for President Jefferson, a widower since 1782.

To curb piracy and stop the paying of tribute money by American shippers to the Barbary pirates, President Jefferson instituted naval action against their states, Morocco, Algiers, Tripoli, and Tunis. (The operations were carried on intermittently until 1815.)

Governor James Monroe, of Virginia, later fifth President, proposed the founding of a Negro colony in Africa for American slaves. (Monrovia, capital of Liberia, established in 1847, was named after him.)

Woolen-milling was begun in Massachusetts by Arthur Schofield, a leading exponent of the industry. Meantime, the Berkshire Hills region had become noted as a sheep country.

The first United Sates pleasure yacht, a 22-ton sloop called *Jefferson*, was built for Captain George Crowninshield, Jr.

The New York Evening Post was founded by Alexander Hamilton. (Published today as *The New York Post*.)

The completion of the Bank of Pennsylvania (1799-1801), designed by the English-born architect Benjamin Henry Latrobe, set the fashion of Greek temples for bank buildings.

Benedict Arnold, aged 60, died (June 14) in exile in London.

1802

---

*T*he U.S. Military Academy opened (July 4) at West Point, N.Y., with 10 cadets.

Frederick Graff of Philadelphia burned anthracite in a large stove—a startling novelty, inasmuch as anthracite was considered fit for use only by blacksmiths.

In Saratoga, N.Y., a hotel was built, and the spa was started on its career as a society resort.

A public demonstration of an early type of upright piano, called the "cottage piano," was held in Philadelphia at the Franklin Institute. The instrument was patented by John Isaac Hawkins. It is said that President Jefferson was interested in obtaining one for his home in Monticello, Va.

The United States entered its fourth depression since 1790; it lasted three years.

In Print

Nathaniel Bowditch published *The New American Practical Navigator*, commonly called *Bowditch's Navigator*.

Self-styled "Lord" Timothy Dexter, eccentric wealthy landowner of Newburyport, Mass., published a volume, *A Pickle for the Knowing Ones*, remarkable for its absence of punctuation and its queer, phonetic spelling.

1803

Ohio was admitted (March 1) as the 17th state.

Former U.S. Minister to France, James Monroe, together with the then current minister, Robert R. Livingston, exceeded their instructions and purchased (Apr. 31) from Napoleon for the sum of $15,000,000, or about four cents per acre, the entire Louisiana area in North America. This comprised all the French possessions west of the Mississippi. The purchase, ratified (Oct. 31) by Congress, added territory to the United States for 13 subsequent states. The United States took possession (Dec. 30) at New Orleans with a simple ceremony, the simultaneous lowering and raising of the national flags.

John Marshall, Chief Justice of the Supreme Court, in the case of *Marbury vs. Madison*, laid down the principle that the Supreme Court can render an act of Congress void when, in the Court's opinion, it violates the Constitution.

Congress voted $2,500 to Captains William Clark and Meriwether Lewis, the latter being private secretary to President Jefferson, to explore a land route to the Pacific. (They set out from St. Louis with 32 men in May 1804, and returned in Sept. 1806. The journey covered 8,500 miles.)

Robert Fulton, American inventor, launched a primitive steamboat on the Seine in France.

In Print
William Wirt, Virginia lawyer, published *Letters of the British Spy*, ten essays on contemporary Southern life that gained a wide reading public.

Music
He Who His Country's Liv'ry Wears (*The Glory of Columbia, Her Yeomanry*); *When a Woman Hears the Sound of the Drum and Fife.*

1804

$\mathscr{S}$tephen Decatur became a national hero when he recaptured and destroyed the grounded United State frigate *Philadelphia*. It had been seized by Barbary pirates in the harbor of Tripoli.

The 12th Amendment, laying out the procedure of choosing the President and Vice President, was ratified (Sept. 25).

Alexander Hamilton was killed (July 12) in a duel with Aaron Burr on the Palisades above Weehawken, N.J. Hamilton fired into the air. The duel resulted from Hamilton's bitter criticism of Burr during the latter's unsuccessful candidacy for the governorship of New York. With this event duels went into disfavor in this country.

John Stevens, of Hoboken, N.J., experimented with a steamboat equipped with twin-screw propellers.

John James Audubon began drawing and classifying birds and flowers in Kentucky.

Georg Rapp and 600 co-religionists of a pietist sect from Württemberg, Germany, established in Pennsylvania a communal town called Harmony—the forerunner of numerous utopian communities in the United States. (The Rappists also founded settlements at New Harmony on the Wabash, Ind., 1814, and at Economy, Pa., 1825.)

Rhode Island College, founded at Providence in 1764, was renamed Brown University in honor of its benefactor Nicholas Brown.

John Pickering, Judge of the District Court of New Hampshire, became the first man to be removed from office by impeachment when he was found guilty of drunkenness and other charges. (It was the second impeachment—presentation of formal charges against a public official—in American history; the first occurred in 1797.)

Modern printer's ink used for the first time by Jacob Johnston in Philadelphia.

Music
    Canadian Boat Song.

1805

$\mathscr{P}$resident Thomas Jefferson began his second term.

The Pennsylvania Art Academy was founded, but the replica of *Venus de Medici* so shocked viewers that it had to be shown discreetly.

Lorenzo da Ponte, Italian librettist of Mozart's operas *Don Giovanni* and *Cosi fan tutte*, settled in New York City. He engaged in Italian operatic enterprises and became a teacher of Italian at Columbia College, now Columbia University.

In Print

A precocious 14-year-old lad attracted the attention of New York literati with a theatrical journal, *The Thespian Mirror*. He was John Howard Payne, the future poet of *Home, Sweet Home* (1823).

Music

All's Well (The English Fleet in 1342); *The Bay of Biscay O!*; *The Origin of Gunpowder*.

1806

*A*merican shipping was hampered by the divergent sea laws of the warring England and France. However, American blockade runners got such high prices for their wares that they considered the situation tolerable. In retaliation against Great Britain's maritime restrictions, Congress passed a Non-Importation Act limiting the importation of certain British commodities. The Act was never actually enforced.

Pike's Peak was discovered (Nov. 15) by Lieutenant Zebulon Montgomery Pike during an expedition to locate the source of the Mississippi.

An approximately 60-year-long "War of the Dictionaries," chiefly concerned with pronunciation, began between the lexicographers Joseph Worcester and Noah Webster. Webster published a "Compendious Dictionary of the English Language," the forerunner of his monumental two-volume work in 1828. The rivalry finally resolved itself in favor of Webster in 1846, twenty-one years after his death, when a group of scholars published a revised edition of his dictionary.

William Colgate, English-born soapmaker's apprentice, opened a modest soap-making shop in New York.

1807

Widespread resentment prevailed when the British frigate *Leopard* fired a broadside off Cape Henry (June 12) at the American man-of-war *Chesapeake*, which had refused to halt and be searched for deserters from the Royal Navy. Five men were killed and 16 wounded. Of four alleged deserters, three proved to be American citizens and England made full restitution.

In consequence of the French and British interdicts against one another, Congress passed the Embargo Act closing American ports for foreign trade. The Act aroused much indignation, as reflected in Bryant's poem *The Embargo*.

Aaron Burr was arrested in Mississippi for complicity in a plot to establish a Southern empire in Louisiana and Mexico. He went on trial for treason (May 23) at Richmond, Va., but was acquitted (Sept. 1).

Robert Fulton's first practical steamboat, the *Clermont*, made (Aug. 17) a trial run of 154 miles up the Hudson River from New York to Albany in 32 hours. The boat created such curiosity that the New York Legislature passed a bill making it a crime for anyone to tamper with the vessel. (Fulton's undertaking was financed by Robert R. Livingston, of the Louisiana Purchase deal, and gave both men a monopoly on the river's traffic. The steamboat was named after Livingston's estate.)

The first life boat station in the United States was built at Cohasset, Mass.

In Print

A Connecticut poet, Joel Barlow, published an attempt at an American Miltonic epic in 10 "books." The collection was called *The Columbiad*, and recounted in heroic didactic couplets a vision that is unfolded by a "radiant seraph" before the eyes of an imprisoned and dying Columbus. The poem ended with a prophetic picture of universal brotherhood, "all regions in the leagues of peace."

William Hill Brown, author of one of the earliest American novels, (*The Power of Sympathy*, 1789), published his second book of fiction, *Ira and Isabella*, or, *The Natural Children*.

New York City became popularly known as Gotham, named for the imaginary English village known for its follies, in the humorous *Salmagundi* pamphlets written by Washington Irving, William Irving, and James Kirke Paulding.

Music

   Thro' Tara's Halls; Gramachree; Rich and Rare Were the Gems She Wore; The Summer is Coming.

1808

$\mathscr{C}$ongress prohibited the importation of African slaves into the United States; smuggling of Negroes, however, continued. (Great Britain also abolished the slave trade in the same year.)

John Jacob Astor, a German immigrant in 1784, established the American Fur Company which soon acquired a monopoly on Canadian fur.

Wheat dropped from $2 to $0.75 per bushel because of the shipping embargo.

A temperance society was founded at Saratoga, N.Y.

The American Academy of Fine Arts was founded in New York.

On Stage

The Indian Princess, or, *La Belle Sauvage*, a play by James Nelson Barker with music by John Bray, was produced (Apr. 6) in Philadelphia at the New Theater and (June 14) in New York at the Park Theater. A riot ruined the Philadelphia performance because "a large party" or section of the audience objected to the presence in the cast of an actor named Webster. The play was also performed in London in 1820. It is the earliest known dramatization of the story of Pocahontas.

Pepin and Breschard opened (June) in New York their extravagantly advertised *New Circus, Corner of Broadway and Anthony Streets*, which had "received the most unbounded applause and approbation of the inhabitants of Boston."

Music

Believe Me if All Those Endearing Young Charms; *My Lodging Is on the Cold Ground*; *Let Erin Remember the Days of Old*; *The Red Fox*.

1809

---

*J*ames Madison, Republican of Virginia, was inaugurated as the fourth President.

The first inaugural ball was held in Washington, with Dolley Madison presiding.

The unpopular Embargo Act (1807) was repealed and replaced by a Non-Intercourse Act that prohibited commercial shipping to Great Britain and France.

The *Phoenix*, an American steamboat built by John Stevens, sailed (June 8) from New York to Philadelphia.

Some 30 daily newspapers circulated throughout the nation.

Thomas Paine, aged 72, died (June 8) in New York; he was buried on his New Rochelle farm when interment in consecrated ground was refused.

In Print

Washington Irving published his burlesque account, *A History of New York from Beginning of the World to the End of the Dutch Dynasty*, purportedly the work of a Dutch-American scholar, Dietrich Knickerbocker.

On Stage

John Howard Payne, precocious playwriting genius, aged 18, enjoyed a brief and exciting three months' acting career in New York and Boston. He made (Feb. 24) his debut in New York at the Park Theater as the handsome Scottish *Young Norval*, with sword, shield, head plumes, and kilts. He played in quick order roles in *Mahomet, The Mountaineers, Barbarossa, Tancred, Pizarro in Peru, Douglas, Jane Shore, Romeo and Juliet, Hamlet,* and Edgar in *King Lear*.

During Payne's interval in Boston, the Park Theater in New York mounted (March 20) with elaborate scenery and stage machinery a splendid *Arabian Nights* spectacle, *The Forty Thieves*. It played eight nights consecutively, and held the boards for many years in revivals.

1810

---

*A*ccording to the census there were now 109 cotton mills in New England just 20 years after Samuel Slater introduced the first one, and became the father of the modern factory system in the U.S.

John Scudder's long-famed *American Museum*, eventually to become the property of P.T. Barnum, opened (Apr.) in New York. Here were to be seen 12 wax figures including the recently deceased Daniel Lambert, the English Mammoth, who weighed 739 pounds and whose body measured 9 feet 4 inches in circumference; a stuffed tortoise, 7 feet 6 inches long; 70 quadrupeds, 100 preserved reptiles; 150 Indian weapons and articles; 250 stuffed birds; 1,200 submarine objects; besides other curiosa, including an organ.

Fashionable ladies used rouge and pearl powder, and dresses were fuller than they had been.

The population of the United States was 7,239,881.

On Stage

Mary Ann Duff, young English tragedienne, made her American debut as Juliet in Boston. (She was one of the outstanding figures on the American stage until her retirement in 1838. Her husband, John Duff, was a recognized and versatile actor.)

George Frederick Cooke, 54-year-old veteran English actor, came to the U.S. and was hailed during the next two years as a popular tragedian in New York, Boston, Philadelphia, Baltimore, and Providence. He died of alcoholism Sept. 26, 1812, in New York and was buried in the strangers' vault in St. Paul's churchyard. There the great Edmund Kean, during his first New York season (1820-21) erected in Cooke's memory the first monument in the United States to an actor.

William B. Wood made (Nov. 12) his New York debut as an actor at the Park Theater in the popular play *The Foundling of the Forest*. (Born in Montreal and raised in New York, Wood was long an important figure in the American theater as an actor and as a manager in Philadelphia.)

The musical sensation of the year was the Pandean Band of Italian Music "from Drury Lane and Covent Garden," which made (Oct. 29) its first appearance in New York at the Park Theater and was heard in many places of amusement until 1817.

1811

*R*ebellious Indians under Tecumseh, Shawnee chief, organized a conspiracy organized in defiance of the United States government. They were defeated (Nov. 7) during Tecumseh's absence in the disastrous Battle of the Wabash (or Tippecanoe) by William Henry Harrison, governor of Indiana Territory. The victory was celebrated in a popular ballad and earned Harrison the sobriquet "Tippecanoe," which became part of the slogan of his presidential campaign in 1840.

Henry Clay, Virginia-born statesman of Kentucky, was elected to the House of Representatives, and became its prominent Speaker (1811-20, 1823-25).

Earthquakes were reported in the Mississippi Valley in December.

The United States was building up a war fever against Great Britain, fanned by the "war hawk" elements in Congress headed by Henry Clay and John Caldwell Calhoun. Tension was aggravated by the alarms of western farmers who were being harassed by Indians said to be abetted by England through Canada.

Music
The Battle of the Wabash; To Anacreon in Heaven; The Death of Nelson.

1812

$\mathscr{L}$ouisiana was admitted (Apr. 30) as the 18th state.

The enthusiastic efforts of Henry Clay and John C. Calhoun finally led the United States to declare (June 18) its second war on Great Britain, although the latter had withdrawn its maritime restrictions two days earlier. The hostilities gained momentum slowly and lasted officially until Jan. 8, 1815. Throughout, the Americans were more successful on sea than on land. One of their land battles was against the Creek Indians of Alabama, under the Shawnee chief Tecumseh, who had joined ranks with the British.

In New York, a mass meeting was held (Aug. 19) in protest against the war.

The term "gerrymander" came into use when Benjamin Russell, ardent Federalist editor of the *Boston Centinel*, so described the lizard-like appearance of the map of the new voting districts in Essex County, Mass., alleged to have been re-aligned by Democratic Governor Elbridge Gerry to favor his party. The word was coined from "Salamander."

On Stage
The Walnut Street Theater in Philadelphia opened with Sheridan's comedy *The Rivals*. (The building is still standing, the oldest extant theater in the United States.)

Music
The American Star.

1813

$\mathscr{P}$resident Madison began his second term.

The War of 1812 continued. American naval success spread from Newfoundland to Brazil and across the Atlantic to the Azores. On the Thames River in Canada, the Indian chief Tecumseh, now a brigadier general with the enemy, was killed (Oct. 15).

Two historic utterances characterized the war events of the year. Commander James Lawrence, fatally wounded while his frigate *Chesapeake* engaged the British *Shannon* in a bitter 15-minute encounter (June 15) off the shore of Boston, cried: "Don't give up the ship" (though the *Chesapeake* did later surrender with 145 killed and wounded). The words were inscribed on a flag unfurled at the Battle of Lake Erie by Commodore Oliver Hazard Perry, who defeated (Sept. 10) the British navy and announced his victory with the words: "We have met the enemy and they are ours." (The slogans are often incorrectly interchanged.)

The earliest known printed reference to the United States by the nickname "Uncle Sam" is believed to have occurred (Sept. 7) in the *Troy Post*.

The *Boston Daily Advertiser* was founded and became the first successful daily newspaper in New England. (Ceased publication in 1929.)

The Théâtre d'Orléans in New Orleans, La., was rebuilt at a cost of $180,000; it had grilled loges for people in mourning.

General Zebulon Pike died (Apr. 27). Navy Captain James Lawrence died (June 1).

Music
The Minstrel Boy; The Moreen; 'Tis the Last Rose of Summer; The Groves of Blarney.

1814

*T*he War of 1812 entered its final stages. In the North, the Americans frustrated (Sept. 11) an attempted invasion from Canada via Lake Champlain. In the South, however, they were routed (Aug. 24) at Bladensburg, Md., and lost the nation's capital to the British who burned the Capitol, the Library of Congress, the White House, and other public buildings.

The tide of the war turned when the British Chesapeake fleet unsuccessfully bombarded Fort McHenry, near Baltimore, for 25 hours in the night of Sept. 13-14. During the engagement the future national anthem of the United States was created. Francis Scott Key, a 33-year-old Baltimore lawyer, who witnessed the scene from a British man-of-war on which he was detained while on a legal mission, wrote the words of *The Star-Spangled Banner*.

Meanwhile, 26 disgruntled New England merchantmen were meeting in convention (1814-15) at Hartford, Conn., in protest against "Mr. Madison's War." Motions were entertained for secession or a separate peace with England, and against the admission of new States to the Union.

A treaty of peace between the United States and Great Britain, terminating the War of 1812, was signed (Dec. 24) at Ghent, Belgium. The news did not reach the United States until two weeks later.

At Middlebury, Vt., Emma Willard opened a female seminary for the study of philosophy, history, mathematics, and the sciences—subjects hitherto unavailable to women.

In Print
The Massachusetts Historical Society printed the Burwell Papers, a contemporary manuscript account of Bacon's Rebellion (1676). (They are now preserved by the Virginia Historical Society.)

Music
Love Has Eyes; *The Star Spangled Banner*, Francis Scott Key (Tune: *To Anacreon in Heaven*); *Strike the Cymbal*.

1815

$\mathcal{U}$naware that the war with England was terminated, Major General Andrew Jackson fifteen days later (Jan. 8) defeated the powerful British land and naval forces in a needless battle at Chalmette, outside New Orleans, in which 2,000 British were killed. There were seven American fatalities.

As an aftermath of the war (Apr. 6), a guard at Dartmoor Prison, Princetown, England, killed seven and wounded about 60 of 1,700 American naval prisoners confined there during the War of 1812. It was reported that those killed were attempting to escape. England made liberal restitution to the families of the victims. The incident is known as the Dartmoor Massacre.

The United States renewed naval operations against the Barbary States to suppress piracy. Algiers declared war, but capitulated before the speedy action of Admiral Stephen Decatur. At a banquet in his honor, he delivered the famous toast: "Our country! In her intercourse with foreign nations may she be always right; but our country, right or wrong."

President Madison pardoned Jean Lafitte, French-American pirate and smuggler, for his bravery and help at the Battle of New Orleans. (He later resumed piracy, operating out of Galveston, Tex., and was driven away by government troops after his gang had damaged American property.)

To re-establish the Library of Congress, burned by the British in 1814, Congress purchased Thomas Jefferson's library of 6,457 volumes for $23,950.

The Handel and Haydn Society, a now-legendary choral organization, was founded (Mar. 30) in Boston.

The government raised funds by taxing watches, hats, caps, boots, umbrellas, and other consumer goods.

John Singleton Copley, aged about 78, Boston painter, died (Sept. 9) in London. (Copley Square in Boston is named after him. His son John Singleton Copley, Lord Lyndhurst, was three times Lord Chancellor of England.)

In Print
The North American Review was founded in Boston as a monthly literary magazine. Benjamin Franklin's newspaper, *The Pennsylvania Gazette*, started 1792, came to an end.

Music
On the Banks of Allan Water, Lady C.S.

1816

The Second Bank of the United States was established in Philadelphia and chartered for 21 years with $35,000,000 capital. (Its predecessor, chartered in 1791, had failed five years before, and the nation's currency was in virtual chaos with 245 state corporations individually issuing their own money.)

Indiana was admitted (Dec. 11) as the 19th state.

The National Colonization Society of America was organized to settle free American Negroes in Africa. (The first attempt was made south of Sierra Leone in 1820.)

Jacob Hyer and Tom Beasley fought the first ring prizefight in American history.

Of grave concern to the United States was the formation of the Holy Alliance by Russia, Austria, and Prussia at Paris (Sept. 26, 1815) and proclaimed at Frankfort (Feb. 2, 1816). One of its most drastic pronouncements was the demand for the abolition of the republics then being established on the principles of the United States Constitution by the revolting Spanish colonies in South America under Simon Bolivar. This demand led to the formulation of the Monroe Doctrine.

On Stage
Guy Mannering was the hit play of Boston with Mrs. Powell, a popular actress, playing the role of Meg.

1817

*J*ames Monroe, Republican of Virginia, was inaugurated as the fifth President beginning a period that was called the "Era of Good Feeling" by the *Boston Journal.*

The United States and Great Britain signed (Apr. 28-29) the Rush-Bagot Treaty, which eliminated forts and limited naval armaments on the Great Lakes.

Mississippi was admitted (Dec. 10) as the 20th state.

The United States began military operations against the Seminole Indians in Florida, then under Spanish rule.

Thousands of settlers moved west, and the prairies were dotted with log cabins.

The first steamboat appeared in St. Louis.

Harvard University Law School was established.

Benjamin West finished his immense painting (25 feet x 15 feet) *Death on the Pale Horse,* illustrating Revelation, chapter six, in the Pennsylvania Academy, Philadelphia.

In Print

William Cullen Bryant published *Thanatopsis,* written when he was 16, in *The North American Review,* Boston. (The poem lacked the present opening 17 lines and closing 15, which first appeared in the author's collected "Poems," 1821.)

Music

Mary's Tears.

1818

*E*xceeding orders, Andrew Jackson, military hero of the War of 1812, suppressed the uprising (1817-18) of the Seminole Indians in Florida—an act which involved the United States in serious diplomatic exchanges with Spain and Great Britain.

Congress standardized the national flag, prescribing 13 horizontal stripes (7 red and 6 white) and a blue field with one white star for each state. (At the time, the flag contained 15 stripes and 15 stars.)

Illinois was admitted (Dec. 3) as the 21st state.

Charles Bulfinch succeeded Benjamin Latrobe as architect of the Capitol at Washington, D.C. (He held the post until the completion of the building in 1830. Bulfinch's design has been the model for state capitols throughout the United States.)

Pigs were so common in the streets of New York that the *Evening Post* started a crusade against them.

The system of pensioning war veterans and their widows and children was established.

Silversmith and engraver Paul Revere of the historic "midnight ride" died (May 18) in his native Boston. He was 83.

On Stage

The great Edmund Kean performed in London a blank-verse play *Brutus, or The Fall of Tarquin* by a struggling American poet, John Howard Payne.

James William Wallack, the elder, London-born tragedian, made his American debut (Sept. 7) as Macbeth in New York at the Park Theater. Meanwhile T.A. Cooper, member of an English theatrical company in New Orleans, was said to have received the fabulous sum of $333 per night.

Music

Hark! the Vesper Hymn Is Stealing, Russian Air, Oft in the Stilly Night, Silent Night, Holy Night.

1819

$\mathscr{C}$hief Justice John Marshall of the Supreme Court set the precedent in the Dartmouth College Case that the Supreme Court is the tribunal for reviewing laws passed by state legislatures.

On Washington's Birthday, Spain ceded Florida to the United States. No money was paid but the United States assumed and settled American claims against Spain to the amount of $5,000,000.

Alabama was admitted (Dec. 14) as the 22nd state, making now 11 slave states and 11 free states.

The S.S. *Savannah*, a sailing packet of 350 tons, equipped with a steam engine and iron paddle wheels, was the first American vessel to cross the Atlantic mainly under steam propulsion. She sailed (May 22) from Savannah, Ga., for New York and proceeded (July 15) to Liverpool, making the crossing in 26 days, the whole trip in 31 days. (May 22 would be proclaimed National Maritime Day in 1935.)

The University of Virginia at Charlottesville, was founded in accordance with Thomas Jefferson's plans and built according to his architectural designs.

Harvard University Divinity School was established.

Ludwig van Beethoven was already sufficiently known in New England that a choral organization in Portland, Me., called itself the "Beethoven Musical Society." (The great composer was then living in Vienna, writing his 9th Symphony, and still had eight years of life ahead.)

The remains of Thomas Paine were removed from their New Rochelle, N.Y., burial plot by William Cobbett, English journalist and radical, for re-interment in England. (Cobbett's plan to erect a monument was never realized, and the whereabouts of Paine's bones are now unknown.)

The French corset, a two-piece affair laced up the back and considered standard feminine equipment until the 1900s, came into use.

The seventh depression since 1790 set in; like many of its predecessors, it lasted three years.

In Print

Washington Irving's classic *The Sketch Book of Geoffrey Crayon*, containing the stories *Rip Van Winkle* and *The Legend of Sleepy Hollow*, was the literary event of the year.

The Philadelphia Register and National Recorder appeared as a weekly journal. (Subsequently published under various names, it became a monthly called *The Eclectic Magazine*, which ceased publication in 1907.)

Music

Lo! Here the Gentle Lark, (words, William Shakespeare, music, Sir Henry Rowley Bishop); *Sicilian Hymn.*

1820

$\mathcal{M}$aine was admitted (Mar. 15) as the 23rd state.

Congress passed (Mar. 3) Henry Clay's Missouri Compromise bill, permitting slavery in Missouri but in no other state west of the Mississippi and north of 36° 30' north.

President Monroe congratulated the newly established republics in South America (Venezuela, Paraguay, Argentina, Chile, Colombia).

The first American missionaries visited Hawaii.

Men considered watch fobs an essential piece of haberdashery.

Deaths of the year included: Benjamin West, aged 82 (Mar. 11), American painter and second president of the Royal Academy; and Daniel Boone, aged 86 (Sept. 20), quasi-legendary frontiersman.

In the national elections, President Monroe was re-elected, receiving all but one elector's vote, the exception being cast by the staunchly independent Federalist John Quincy Adams of Massachusetts, son of the second President, so that Washington would not be deprived of the honor of being the only unanimously elected President.

The total population of the country now was 9,638,453, with the state of New York assuming the lead it would hold for decades. Westward migrations had shifted the center of the population to Moorfield, W. Va.

In Print

An English translation of Carlo Botta's Italian *History of the War of Independence of the United States of America* (1809) appeared and remained a standard until superseded by George Bancroft's *History of the United States* (1834-76).

On Stage

Edwin Forrest, American tragedian, made his debut in Philadelphia at the Walnut Street Theater.

Edmund Kean, English actor, came to the United States and was acclaimed in New York, Boston, and Philadelphia.

Music

Bid Me Discourse, (words, William Shakespeare, music, Sir Henry Rowley Bishop); *Hail to the Chief*, (words, Sir Walter Scott, music, James Sanderson); *D'ye Ken John Peel.*

1821

*P*resident James Monroe began his second term. He was the first President to be inaugurated on the fifth of March instead of the traditional fourth because the latter date fell on a Sunday.

Missouri was admitted (Aug. 10) as the 24th state.

The Santa Fe Trail, extending from Independence, Mo., to what would become Santa Fe, N.M., was mapped (1821-22) by William Becknell.

Ladies' shoes insinuated themselves into view beneath decidedly shorter skirts; Nile green was a fashionable color; and most jewelry was made of polished steel.

In Print

Connecticut-born James Gates Percival published his *Poems*. He was esteemed by his contemporaries as the nation's premier poet until the ascendancy of William Cullen Bryant. The long Spenserian epic, *Prometheus*, included in the Percival volume, was regarded the equal of Byron's *Childe Harold*.

James Fenimore Cooper published, in the two-volume format usual for the time, his immediately popular novel *The Spy*.

On Stage

In New York the Park Theater was rebuilt, replacing an older structure that had been erected in 1798 and destroyed in 1820. The new theater opened (Sept. 1) its doors to fashionable theatergoers with Mrs. Elizabeth Inchbald's English comedy *Wives as They Were and Maids as They Are*, followed by the American John Howard Payne's charming success, *Therese, the Orphan of Geneva*.

African-Americans were not admitted to white theaters, so Black singers and actors in New York gave several performances at the African Grove Theater. These included a version of *Richard III* with "a dapper wooly-haired waiter at the City Hotel in the role of the king." Neighbors, however, soon objected to the noise, and two of the actors were "taken up by the watch." Undaunted, they resumed their performances at the Pantheon, on the corner of Mercer and Bleecker streets, again giving *Richard III* with an actor named Hewlett, who continued to appear in New York and Brooklyn for a number of years as a singer and impersonator.

Music

Invitation to the Dance.

1822

*S*tephen Fuller Austin of Virginia established the American settlement in Texas, then under Mexican rule, on land inherited from his father.

Daniel Treadwell of Boston constructed the first American printing press to be operated by steam.

The novelist James Fenimore Cooper and his circle of literary friends formed the informal Bread and Cheese Club in New York.

A Grand Orchestra of Androides, consisting of "seven Automaton Figures as large as life, who perform on Twelve different instruments," was an attraction in New York.

Music

The Fortune I Crave (The Deed of Gift); The Cottage on the Moor; The Harp of Love (The Spy).

1823

$\mathscr{P}$resident Monroe, replying to the pronouncements of the Holy Alliance (1816), proclaimed (Dec. 2) the principles known as the Monroe Doctrine, "that the American continents, by the free and independent condition which they have assumed and maintained, are henceforth not to be considered as subjects for future colonization by European powers."

The Virginia was the first steamboat to sail up the Mississippi on a run of 729 miles to Fort Snelling, Minn. The journey took approximately 19 days (Apr. 21-May 10).

In Print

The Troy Sentinel printed (Dec. 23) an anonymous poem, *A Visit from St. Nicholas*, which latter became better known as a book with the title *'Twas the Night Before Christmas* by Clement Clarke Moore, a learned Biblical scholar of New York City.

On Stage

Sir Henry Rowley Bishop's three-act opera *Clari, or The Maid of Milan*, to a libretto by the American poet John Howard Payne, containing *Home, Sweet Home*, was produced in London at Covent Garden Theater, May 8, and given in New York at the Park Theater, Nov. 12.

Equestrian spectacles and dramas, imported from Astley's London Amphitheater, began their long vogue on American stages. Among the outstanding shows of this type were *Timour the Tartar* and *El Hyder*.

Music

Home, Sweet Home; Sicilian Air; Rose of Lucerne, or, *The Swiss Toy Girl.*

1824

*T*he 67-year-old Marquis de Lafayette revisited the United Sates by invitation of Congress, which voted him a gift of $200,000 and a land grant of 24,000 acres and conferred American citizenship on him and his descendants in perpetuity. He made a triumphal tour of all 24 states before returning to France (1825).

The American Sunday School Union came into being. Sunday school, which typically offered both secular and religious instruction, was one of the chief U.S. educational institutions at this time. (In 1872 uniform Sunday school lessons were established, but by that time the Sunday school was mainly religious.)

John Trumbull, American painter, completed his four large pictures (each 12 feet x 18 feet) for the rotunda of the Capitol at Washington, D.C. Begun in 1817, they represent the *Signing of the Declaration of Independence*, *Surrender of Cornwallis*, *Surrender of General Burgoyne*, and *Washington Resigning His Commission*. (Trumbull died in 1825.)

The greatest billiard player in the land was Higham, "The Albany Pony," who appeared in New York City and embarked on a long series of victories.

Johann Nepomuk Maelzel, Bavarian mechanical genius, associated with Beethoven in the performance of the latter's battle symphony *Wellington's Victory* and maker of his ear trumpet, came to New York during this year. His Panharmonicon, a mechanical monstrosity capable of imitating 206 musical instruments, was exhibited (Dec. 14) for some time in a large hall in Reed Street.

In Print
The Springfield Republican was founded as a weekly newspaper in Springfield, Mass.

On Stage
The Camp Street Theater opened (Jan. 1) as the first English-language playhouse in New Orleans.

The veteran actor Joseph Jefferson, the elder, closed (Aug. 5) his glorious stage career in New York at the new Chatham Theater, "over-powered with the good wishes of every one present," as newspapers reported.

The Saw Mill, or A Yankee Trick, an "opera" by Micah Hawkins with music by James Hewitt, was produced (Nov. 29) at the same theater.

1825

*J*ohn Quincy Adams, Republican of Massachusetts, was inaugurated as the sixth President.

In New York State, the Erie Canal, extending from Buffalo to Albany and connecting Lake Erie with the Hudson River, was completed after 32 years at a cost of $7,000,000 and opened (Oct. 26) with appropriate ceremonies by Governor De Witt Clinton. (The first boat sailed from Buffalo on the opening day and arrived in New York City on Nov. 4.)

In Charlestown, Mass., Lafayette laid the cornerstone of the Bunker Hill Monument on the 50th anniversary of the battle (June 17). (The monument was completed in 1843.)

John Elgar built the first American iron steamboat, *Codorus*, in York, Pa.

The first Norwegian immigrants arrived (Oct. 9) on the sloop *Restaurationen*. (The 100th anniversary of the event was celebrated in 1925 by the issuance of two commemorative postage stamps by the United States Post Office Department.)

The murder of Kentucky Solicitor-General Col. Solomon P. Sharp was a nation-wide sensation and became the subject of pamphlets, ballads, plays (*Conrad and Eudora* by Thomas Holley Simms, 1832; *Politian* by Edgar Allan Poe, 1835-36; *Octavia Brigaldi* by Charlotte Barnes, 1837) and novels (*Greyslaer* by Charles Fenno Hoffman, 1840; *Beauchampe* by William Gilmore Simms, 1842). Sharp had seduced Ann Cook, who was married to an attorney, Jeroboam O. Beauchamp. She persuaded her husband to murder Sharp. After several unsuccessful attempts, Beauchamp, in disguise, stabbed Sharp to death (Nov. 5). Beauchamp's trial was marked by perjury and corruption, and resulted in his conviction. During the night before his execution, Ann gained admittance to the jail and both swallowed laudanum. When it failed, they stabbed themselves. Ann died; Beauchamp was carried to the gallows and hanged.

Frances Wright, Scottish-born reformer and author, founded the Nashoba Community, Tenn., for the education and eventual emancipation of Negro slaves. (The rigors of the climate and the hardship of frontier life caused her to abandon the project in 1828. She freed 30 Negroes in her care and settled them in Haiti.)

The United Tailoresses of New York became the first American trade union for women only.

Jefferson Medical College was founded in Philadelphia.

The Kappa Alpha Society, second American college Greek letter fraternity, was founded (Nov. 26). (The first was Phi Beta Kappa, organized Dec. 5, 1776, at William and Mary College, Williamsburg, Va.)

In Print

The Boston Traveler was founded as a daily newspaper.

Gift annuals, containing stories, poetry, and engravings, became the vogue. Contributions from many well-known writers and poets appeared in them. One of the first books of this kind was *The Atlantic Souvenir*, which was issued annually until 1832.

Fitz-Greene Halleck's poem, *Marco Bozzaris*, written on the death of the Greek patriot, was printed in the *New York Review*.

On Stage

Italian opera was introduced (Nov. 29) in the United States at the Park Theater in New York by Manuel Garcia and his 17-year-old daughter Maria Felicita Garcia (later to be the famous singer Malibran). The opening opera was Rossini's *Il Barbiere di Siviglia*, in which Garcia had created the tenor role at the world premiere (Rome, 1816). The performance grossed $2,980. Librettos were sold at the theater (price 37-3/4 cents). Joseph Bonaparte, ex-King of Spain; James Fenimore Cooper, American novelist; and Lorenzo da Ponte, Mozart's librettist, were in the audience. (The season ran to Sept. 30, 1826.)

The Chatham Theater, New York, re-opened (May 6) as the first American playhouse to be illuminated by gas. (It was followed in 1826 by the Lafayette Amphitheater and the Bowery Theater.)

Music

Buy a Broom?; Cherry Ripe, Love's Eyes (The Forest Rose); Roy's Wife; The Meeting of the Waters of Hudson and Erie; A Wet Sheet and a Flowing Sea.

1826

$\mathcal{T}$he United States was 50 years old. Its semicentennial (July 4) was marked by the death of two former Presidents—John Adams, aged 91, and Thomas Jefferson, aged 83.

The American Society for the Promotion of Temperance was founded (Feb. 13) in Boston.

Jedediah Strong Smith, New York-born fur trader, led the first exploring expedition (1826-27) over the Sierra Nevada from Salt Lake along a route that later formed part of the Overland Trail, the traffic artery of the 1849 gold rush.

The first experimental steam locomotive was built by John Stevens of Hoboken, N.J.

Sing Sing, the New York State penitentiary at Ossining on the Hudson, was built by convicts.

American colonists in Texas announced their independence from Mexico and named their settlements the Republic of Fredonia.

The first season of Italian opera in the United States at the Park Theater, New York, ended (Sept. 30) after 10 months of presentation. Some 80 performances of nine operas by Rossini, Mozart, Zingarelli, and Garcia were given. *Il Barbiere di Siviglia* was sung completely 24 times.

In Print

James Fenimore Cooper published his best-seller, *The Last of the Mohicans*, the second of the Leather-Stocking Tales, which derive their name from the long deerskin leggings worn by the hero, Natty Bumppo.

On Stage

Actor James Henry Hackett made (Mar. 1) his stage debut in New York at the Park Theater. He played Justice Woodcock in Arne's well-known ballad opera, *Love in a Village*, with his wife, the former actress Miss Leesugg, whom he married in 1819. He was followed (June 23) at the same theater by a 20-year-old rival, Edwin Forrest, who began his career as a popular American tragedian as Othello.

The first New York performance of Shakespeare's play *A Midsummer Night's Dream* was given (Nov. 9) at the Park Theater.

Music

Araby's Daughter; The Dashing White Sergeant; The Hunters of Kentucky; Meet Me by Moonlight Alone; I'd Be a Butterfly; The Old Oaken Bucket; Jessie, the Flower of Dumblane.

1827

$\mathcal{T}$he United States made an unsuccessful attempt to purchase Texas from Mexico.

The New York State Legislature abolished (July 4) slavery in the State.

In Gurleyville, Conn., the first successful silk mill was established, and a veritable craze developed in the Connecticut and Willimantic valleys for raising mulberry trees to feed the silkworms. The enterprise was never to succeed.

The United States endured its eighth depression since 1790; running true to form, it lasted three years.

In Print

The Youth's Companion was founded in Boston as a weekly magazine for young people. (Long a popular publication to which Tennyson, Hardy, Kipling, Louisa Alcott, Whittier, Theodore Roosevelt, Robert Louis Stevenson, Jules Verne, Jack London, Woodrow Wilson, and many others contributed, it ceased publication after 102 years in 1929.)

Audubon began the publication (1827-38) of his elephant folio edition of drawings, *The Birds of America.*

On Stage

Madame Francisque Hutin, "of the Opera House, Paris," introduced (Feb. 7) French ballet for the first time on the American stage in New York at the Bowery (then New York) Theater, and flabbergasted the first nighters with her flimsy attire. She was followed (Mar. 1) at the same theater by M. and Mme. Achille, also "from the Opera House, Paris," and presently (June 27) by the incomparable Mlle. Celeste, then a young danseuse. The new style of dancing eliminated from the stage the prevalent English style.

French art being the major attraction of the time, the French Opera Company from New Orleans gave seasons of opera in New York, Philadelphia, and other cities.

Music

The Coal Black Rose; The Merry Swiss Boy; The Minstrel's Return from the War; My Long-Tail Blue.

1828

*C*ongress passed an obnoxious tariff bill, raising prices up to 44 percent. Popularly called the Tariff of Abominations, it was beneficial to no one and particularly harmful to the South. It helped to pattern the events that were to lead to the Civil War.

In protest against the tariff, Vice President John Caldwell Calhoun of South Carolina resigned. A defender of slavery and states' rights, he declared in his South Carolina Exposition that the "United States is not a union of the people, but a league or compact between sovereign states, any of which has the right to judge when the compact is broken and to pronounce any law null and void which violates its conditions."

On the nation's anniversary (July 4), President John Quincy Adams turned the first earth of the Chesapeake and Ohio Canal, an artificial waterway 184 miles long from Washington, D.C., to Cumberland, Md. (The construction was competed in 1850.)

On the same day, the Baltimore & Ohio Railroad inaugurated the first passenger service with horse-drawn cars over wooden rails covered with iron.

Varnish was first introduced in the United States. So, too, damask linen and straw paper.

After the collapse of the Nashoba Community (1825-28) in Tennessee, Frances Wright continued to disturb the American peace of mind with her lectures on women's rights, birth control, emancipation of Negroes, equal distribution of wealth, and sundry other then startling topics. (She left the United States in 1830, only to return in 1836 and resume her activities.)

The National Academy of Design was founded in New York by 30 artists with Samuel Morse, later the inventor of the telegraph, as president.

A group of Winnebago Indians visited President Adams at the White House.

In Print
Noah Webster published his mammoth two-volume philological work, *An American Dictionary of the English Language*.

On Stage
The Musical Fund Society, New York, performed Beethoven's Third Symphony *Eroica* as a septet.

Niblo's Garden, a theater in New York that would be identified for more than half a century with seemingly every theatrical artist of significance, was opened (July 4) as the San Souci by the restaurateur William Niblo. (The theater was twice destroyed by fire, in 1846 and in 1848.)

Music

Oh! No, We Never Mention Her; Tyrolese Evening Hymn.

1829

*G*eneral Andrew Jackson, Democrat, of South Carolina, was inaugurated as the seventh President. He was popularly known as "Old Hickory."

Canals opened everywhere in the industrial East. Among them: the Delaware & Chesapeake, the Delaware & Hudson, and the Oswego in New York, the Farmington in Connecticut, and the Cumberland & Oxford in Maine.

Ironmaster Peter Cooper built the first practical American steam locomotive—the "Tom Thumb," so called because of its size. It made (Sept.) a 13-mile trial run in Baltimore on the Baltimore & Ohio's tracks in 1 hour, 12 minutes.

Kit (Christopher) Carson, Kentucky frontiersman, was coming into prominence as a Santa Fe guide for the first overland expeditions to California.

In Print

William Cullen Bryant was appointed editor of the New York *Evening Post*, a position he held for nearly 50 years (until 1878).

Francis Lieber, German-born political writer and educator, began the publication of the *Encyclopedia Americana*. (It was completed in 13 volumes in 1833.)

Sidney Smith, eccentric Episcopalian clergyman and wit, wrote in the *Edinburgh Review*, Jan., 1820: "In the four quarters of the globe, who reads an American book? or goes to an American play? or looks at an American picture or statue?" Nine years later, two industrious Massachusetts writers showed what the young country had to offer in literature. Samuel Kettell edited a three-volume anthology *Specimens of American Poetry* from Cotton Mather to Whittier; and Samuel Lorenzo Knapp published his diffuse and padded *Lectures on American Literature*.

On Stage

Edwin Forrest offered a prize of $500 and the usual half of the third night's proceeds for the "best Tragedy, in five acts, of which the hero, or principal character shall be an aboriginal of this country." The prize-winning play was John Augustus Stone's *Metamora, or, The Last of the Wampanoags*, which was produced (Dec. 15) in New York at the Park Theater, and long remained a popular melodrama on the American stage. (It was parodied in 1847 by John Brougham's highly amusing burlesque, *Metamora, or, The Last of the Pollywogs.*)

Richard Penn Smith, a prolific Philadelphia playwright, this year produced *William Penn, or The Elm Tree*, *The Eighth of January*, *The Disowned*, and *The Sentinels, or The Two Sergeants*.

Music

From Greenland's Icy Mountains; *Missionary Hymn*; *Love's Ritornella* (*The Brigand*); *Serenade*; *There's Nothing True but Heaven.*

1830

---

*T*he U.S. Naval Observatory was established (Dec. 6).

A 21-year-old Harvard graduate named Oliver Wendell Holmes was suddenly catapulted into national prominence. His poem *Old Ironsides* aroused public sentiment to a point which prevented the dismantling of the old, unseaworthy frigate *Constitution* that had been launched in 1797 in Boston and had been a heroic campaigner in the War of 1812.

At the Jefferson Day Dinner, President Jackson, in reply to Calhoun's speech that placed liberty above the Union, reaffirmed national solidarity with the words: "Our Federal Union; it must be preserved!"

The Mormon Church, known officially as "The Church of Jesus Christ of Latter-Day Saints," was organized (Apr. 6) by the Vermont-born prophet Joseph Smith in Fayette, Seneca County, N.Y. Its scriptures, the "Book of Mormon," was published in Palmyra, N.Y.

The "Tom Thumb" (1829) steam locomotive ran (Aug. 25) its famous race with a horse-drawn car. The horse won; the engine, ahead for a while, broke down.

March 16 was the dullest day in New York Stock Exchange history; only 31 shares changed hands.

Cincinnati was called "Porkopolis" because it was the nation's greatest meat-packing center.

The banjo is reputed to have been "invented" about this time by the Negro minstrel Joel W. Sweeny.

The national population was 12,866,020.

In Print

Louis Antoine Godey brought out the first issue of his monthly *Godey's Lady's Book*, the forerunner of women's magazines, incorporating fiction, etiquette, articles on sewing, etc. (It was transferred to New York in 1892 and ceased publication in 1898.)

The word "Hoosier" entered the American vocabulary when John Finley used it for probably the first time in print in his poem *The Hoosier Nest*.

Sarah Josepha Hale published "Mary Had a Little Lamb" in *Poems for Our Children*.

On Stage

The play *Rip Van Winkle* ran in New York at the Park Theater.

As a sample of the magnitude of early theatrical production, an elephant and her calf were introduced on the stage during the performance of *The Forty Thieves* at the Walnut Street Theater in Philadelphia. At the Arch Street Theater in the same city, a living rhinoceros was part of the cast of *The Lover's Test*.

Music

I Know a Bank Where the Wild Thyme Blows (words, William Shakespeare, music, Charles Edward Horn); *Jim Crow*; *My Heart and Lute*; *The Pilgrim Fathers* (also known as: *The Landing of the Pilgrims*; also as *The Breaking Waves Dashed High*); *Sparkling and Bright*.

1831

*I*n the Virginia legislature, a hotly debated bill providing for the colonization of freed slaves and recommending private emancipation was defeated by only one vote. In Boston, the powerful New England Anti-Slavery Society was founded by William Lloyd Garrison. He also began to publish a widely circulated weekly, *The Liberator*, which continued to appear for 34 years (1831-65) despite violent opposition.

Some sixty Negro slaves, headed by Nat Turner, who believed himself divinely appointed to lead his people to freedom, terrorized Southampton County, Va. He and other leaders were finally captured and hanged after 61 whites had lost their lives during the insurrection.

The Mormons began to move westward; some established themselves in Kirtland, Ore., while others settled into Missouri.

The first known transportation of mail by railroad occurred (Nov.) on the South Carolina Railroad.

Train service by steam locomotive was established (Aug. 9) in New York State between Albany and Schenectady by the Mohawk & Hudson Railroad; the "De Witt Clinton" was the first steam locomotive in the state.

The first streetcars in the United States made their appearance in New York; they were horse-drawn.

New York University was founded for male students.

Ex-President James Monroe, age 72, died in New York City. He was the third former President to die on the Fourth of July.

In Print
The *Spirit of the Times* appeared in New York as a journal devoted to "the Turf, Agriculture, Field Sports, Literature, and the Stage." (It ceased publication in 1858.)

On Stage
Delaware dramatist Robert Montgomery Bird wrote his most popular play, *The Gladiator*, for Edwin Forrest, who acted the role of Spartacus more than 1,000 times. The jealous actor, whose partisans were to precipitate the Astor Place riots in New York in 1849, guarded against the publication of the play all his life lest it be performed by a rival. The play was first published in 1919.

1832

President Jackson vetoed the bill for rechartering the second Bank of the United States (1816). The bank closed with the expiration of its charter in 1836.

Congress enacted a new tariff bill that repealed the law of 1828 ("Tariff of Abominations") but left the rates substantially unchanged. In retaliation, the South Carolina Legislature, at the instigation of former Vice President Calhoun, passed (Nov.) an Ordinance of Nullification and threatened to secede from the Union if President Jackson took military measures to enforce the law.

The Black Hawk War (1831-32) ended.

The first national convention for the nomination of a presidential candidate was held. It replaced the Congressional caucus. In the national election President Jackson was re-elected.

Ann McKim, the first clipper ship, was built for the China trade, and a new era in shipbuilding was launched.

The first steam locomotive in the Mississippi Valley was placed (Sept. 17) in operation on the Pontchartrain Railroad that ran from Elysian Fields Street, New Orleans, to Lake Pontchartrain, Milneburg. The engine, the *Pontchartrain*, was built in England.

Bassford, a table maker, opened a billiard parlor in New York with 20 tables, and it was here that pinpool and 15-ball pool were introduced. These superseded the early two-ball pool.

Two fraternal societies of European origin appeared on the American scene—the Ancient Order of Hibernians (from Ireland) and the Ancient Order of Foresters (from England).

In the fall Illinois state elections, young Abraham Lincoln, then 23 years old, ran for his first public office (a seat in the state legislature) and was defeated.

In Print

American readers of Ms. Frances Trollope's new book, *Domestic Manners of the Americans*, published in London, were incensed by her opinions of American culture and business methods, as well as by her anti-slavery sentiments. The press of the country was flooded with bitter rejoinders. Her observations were based on a three years' (1827-30) residence in Cincinnati, where she had operated a fancy-goods shop.

William Dunlap published his *History of the American Theater*, derived largely from personal associations with the stage as a playwright, manager, and actor.

On Stage

The handsome, athletic English actor Charles Kemble and his daughter, Fanny, played to great applause on American stages. Since the days of Malibran (1825-26), no actress had made so profound an impression. The illustrious pair made their debuts in New York at the Park Theater—the 57-year-old father in *Hamlet* (Sept. 17) and his 23-year-old daughter in *Fazio* (Sept. 18). They appeared (Sept. 20) together in *Romeo and Juliet*, in which the father replaced at the last minute an inadequate actor in the part of Romeo.

The second American season of Italian opera opened (Oct. 6) in New York at the Richmond Hill Theater at Varick and Charlton Streets, formerly the residence of Aaron Burr. The company later went to Philadelphia and played at the Chestnut Street Theater, renamed *Italian Opera House*.

Cholera broke out in the East and closed the theaters during the summer months.

Music

America (words, Samuel Francis Smith, tune, *God Save the King*, attributed to Henry Carey); *The Bloom Is on the Rye* (better known as: *My Pretty Jane*); *Rock of Ages, Toplady*; *My Faith Looks Up to Thee*; *Olivet*.

1833

$\mathscr{P}$resident Andrew Jackson began his second term.

Secretary of the Treasury Roger Brooke Taney withdrew the government's deposits from the Bank of the United States after President Jackson vetoed (1832) the bill to recharter it.

The American Anti-Slavery Society was established in Philadelphia by the New England Anti-Slavery Society and other sympathetic groups (1831).

The Academy of Music, Boston, an educational organization that enrolled 2,200 pupils during its first year, was founded by Lowell Mason.

The Improved Order of Red Men was established (Oct. 14) in Baltimore.

In Print

The Sun was founded in New York as a penny daily. (After other mergers, it became *The New York World-Telegram and Sun* in 1950.)

The Knickerbocker Magazine was founded in New York as a monthly literary journal. (It ceased publication in 1865. Its contributors included many prominent American writers and poets.)

On Stage

Tyrone Power, celebrated Irish comedian, made (Aug. 28) his American debut in *The Irish Ambassador* in New York at the Park Theater. In 1841 he sailed from New York on the steamer *President*, which was lost at sea. (He was the grandfather of the American actor of the same name and the great-grandfather of the film actor popular during the 1930's and '40's.)

In Lowell, Mass., a group of players from Boston opened a theater and were promptly thrown into jail for not "pursuing an honorable and lawful profession."

Music

Ching a Ring Chaw; *Long Time Ago* (or, *Shinbone Alley*); *Rise, Gentle Moon*.

1834

*C*yrus Hall McCormick, Virginia-born inventor, patented the practical reaper he had perfected in 1831.

Stephen Fuller Austin, founder of American settlements in Texas which was then under Mexican rule, went to Mexico City to negotiate for their political independence. He was imprisoned for a year by Mexican President Santa Anna.

A new kind of cigar, called the *locofoco* and invented by John Marck of New York, came on the market. It was a self-lighting cigar which, at one end, had a substance that was ignited by friction.

Brooklyn, N.Y., was chartered as a city. (In 1898 it became a borough of Greater New York.)

In Print

Two literary journals that published contributions from Poe, Longfellow, and others were founded—*The Ladies' Companion* in New York, and the *Southern Literary Messenger* in Richmond, Va. (They ceased publication in 1844 and in 1846, respectively.)

The *New Yorker Staats Zeitung* was founded in New York as a German-language weekly. (It became a daily in 1849.)

On Stage

An attempt to establish grand opera permanently in the United States was made in New York with the building of a sumptuous theater: the Italian Opera House opened (Nov. 18) with the first American performance of Rossini's *La Gazza Ladra*. After eight months, the venture was abandoned. The total expenses had been $81,054.98; the receipts, $51,780.89.

Music

Jesus, Lover of My Soul; Martyn, Zip Coon (also known as: *Turkey in the Straw*); *By the Margin of Fair Zurich's Waters (Beulah Spa).*

1835

*R*oger Brooke Taney of Maryland succeeded John Marshall as Chief Justice of the Supreme Court. Taney was a brother-in-law of Francis Scott Key, author of "The Star-Spangled Banner."

Samuel Colt, American inventor, patented the revolver, the "six-shooter" of desperado legends.

The government's attempt to transfer the Seminole Indians of Florida west of the Mississippi started a seven-year conflict, known as the second Seminole War. (The first occurred in 1817-18.)

A mob in South Carolina broke into the United States mails and burned copies of the abolitionist weekly *The Liberator*, along with effigies of its editor, William Lloyd Garrison.

The Liberty Bell in Philadelphia cracked (July 8) as it tolled for the funeral of Chief Justice John Marshall.

Texas officially proclaimed (Nov. 13) its independence from Mexico. It called itself the Lone Star Republic until its admission to the Union in 1845.

Antimonopolistic New York City Democrats were called Locofocos, after the recently (1834) invented self-lighting cigars, when they persisted in conducting one of their meetings by the light of candle and *locofoco* cigars—after the lights in the hall had been extinguished by the regular, or Tammany, Democrats.

A fire in New York destroyed property estimated to be worth $20,000,000. Beginning in a store at Pearl and Merchant (Hanover) Streets, it lasted two days (Dec. 16-17), ravaged 17 blocks (52 acres), and destroyed 674 buildings including the Stock Exchange, Merchants' Exchange, Post Office, and the South Dutch Church.

Oberlin College, Ohio, became the first institution of higher learning to admit Black students.

Phineas Taylor Barnum made his first appearance on the stage as assistant to the magician Signor Vivalla. A few months later Barnum paid $1,000 for the services of an elderly African-American named Joice Heith, whom he billed as "Washington's Nurse," and started his career as an impresario at Niblo's Garden.

Nathaniel Currier, American printer and lithographer, established in New York a firm for making "colored engravings for the people." (He took as a partner in 1850 the artist J. Merritt Ives, but continued to label his prints "N. Currier." The firm was later called Currier & Ives.)

Extremely popular were tall stories about colorful frontiersmen like Daniel Boone, Kit Carson, Mike Fink, Simon Kenton, David (Davy) Crockett, and others.

In Print

The public was agog over an article in *The New York Sun* (Aug.), by Richard Adams Locke, which alleged that the astronomer Sir John Herschel had discovered the existence of men and animals on the moon. It was a publicity stunt, but the hoax brought a group of Yale scientists into the investigation and caused Edgar Allen Poe to abandon the writing of his story "Hans Pfahl."

Poe's story "Berenice" was published in the newly (1834) founded *Southern Literary Messenger* of Richmond, Va.; in December he was appointed editor of the magazine at a salary of $15 per week. (He was forced to resign in 1837 because of his drinking habits, but in that short time his literary contributions and provocative criticisms raised the magazine's subscriptions from 500 to more than 3,500.)

James Gordon Bennett launched *The New York Herald*. Among other things, he initiated society pages in United States newspapers. (*The Herald* merged with *The New York Tribune* in 1924, becoming *The Herald Tribune*.)

On Stage

The 19-year-old Boston-born opera singer Charlotte Cushman made her first stage appearance (Apr. 8) in *The Marriage of Figaro* in Boston. Her debut (Sept. 12) as an actress was made as Lady Macbeth in New York at the Bowery Theater.

Music

Clare de Kitchen (or, *De Kentucky Screamer*); *Long Time Ago* (or, *Shinbone Alley*); *Old Rosin the Beau*; *See, Gentle Patience Smiles on Pain*.

1836

$\mathcal{T}$he Whig Party was formally organized by Henry Clay and Daniel Webster to oppose the Democratic party, which formerly had been called the Republican Party. (The present-day Republican Party evolved from Federalists, through Whigs, into its current form in the early 1850s.)

Arkansas was admitted (June 15) as the 25th state.

Congress passed the "Gag Resolutions" prohibiting petitions against slavery.

Mexican President Santa Anna led 4,000 troops into Texas, then claimed as Mexican territory, to subdue American secessionists and sympathizers. The Mexicans met with stubborn resistance at a Franciscan mission and in a days' siege, massacred 150 of its defenders in a desperate battle (Mar. 6). Some Texans survived the carnage and surrendered, but they were shot down on Santa Anna's orders.

Texas adopted (Mar. 17) a constitution. Samuel (Sam) Houston, Virginia-born soldier, congressman, and former governor of Tennessee, defeated a Mexican army of 3,000 at San Jacinto. Santa Anna now recognized by treaty Texan independence and the Mexico-Texas boundary along the Rio Grande River.

Mount Holyoke College for women was founded in South Hadley, Mass. It is the oldest women's college in the United States.

Henry Wadsworth Longfellow was appointed professor of modern languages and literature at Harvard. (He occupied the chair for nearly 18 years.)

Ralph Waldo Emerson and his friends were meeting informally at his home in Concord, Mass., to discuss philosophy, theology, religion, and literature, calling themselves the Symposium. Outsiders called the group the Transcendental Club. (The meetings continued for seven or eight years.)

Louis Napoleon, later Emperor Napoleon III of France, visited New York.

James Madison, fourth President, died (June 28).

In Print

The first of William Holmes McGuffey's famed *Eclectic Readers* appeared. (Six readers were published between 1836-57. They reached their peak sales from the Civil War period to the end of the century, selling millions of copies; the last copyright on them was taken out in 1900 by the American Book Company.)

The Philadelphia Public Ledger was founded as the first penny daily in that city. In Toledo, Ohio, the *Blade* appeared as a daily newspaper. In Cincinnati, the *Volksblatt* became the first German-language daily in the United States.

Richard Hildreth, Massachusetts-born jurist, published what is believed to be the earliest antislavery novel, *The Slave, or Memoirs of Archy Moore*. (Immensely popular, it was reprinted under the titles, *The White Slave* and *Archy Moore*, and did much to further the abolitionist movement.)

Music

The Carrier Dove; Corn Cobs Twist Your Hair; Yankee Doodle; The Light of Other Days (The Maid of Artois); Rory O'More.

1837

*M*artin Van Buren, Democrat, of New York, was inaugurated as the eighth president. Because Van Buren had been a widower since 1818, his son's wife, Angelica Singleton Van Buren, a cousin of Dolley Madison, acted as White House hostess. (Van Buren was the first President to be born an American citizen.)

Congress stabilized (Jan. 18) the American silver dollar at 412 grains. (Its previous weight, 416 grains, had been fixed by the Act of 1792.)

Michigan was admitted (Jan. 26) as the 26th state.

During the Canadian Rebellion, loyalists crossed the St. Lawrence to the United States and burned the American vessel *Caroline*, which carried supplies to the insurgents. War between the United States and Great Britain was only narrowly averted.

Samuel Morse demonstrated to Congress his electric telegraph. (Morse, a sculptor and painter of portraits and historical scenes abandoned the arts for science when he became interested in telegraphy during a voyage from Havre to New York in 1832.)

In a collision on the Mississippi the steamer *Monmouth* sank with a loss of 234 lives.

The town of Chicago, with an area of 10 square miles and a population of 3,297, was incorporated as a city.

In Print

The Baltimore Sun and *The New Orleans Picayune* were founded as dailies. The latter took its name from an old Spanish coin then in use, worth 6-1/4 cents—the price of the paper. The oldest newspaper in the United States, *The Connecticut Courant*, which had been published as a weekly since 1764, became *The Hartford Daily Courant*.

Music

The Brave Old Oak; *The Friar of the Olden Time*; *Brothers, Hark*; *Woodman! Spare That Tree!*; *A Yankee Ship and a Yankee Crew*.

1838

---

*A*ntislavery supporters were combining their efforts about this time in a movement known as the Underground Railroad, using their homes as "stations" for secretly enabling fugitive slaves to reach freedom in the Northern States or in Canada.

Medical College of Virginia, in Richmond, was founded.

Ralph Waldo Emerson began to attract attention as a public speaker in Boston in consequence of his Phi Beta Kappa oration (1837) and Harvard Divinity School address (1838). The latter speech (which touched on Emerson's own spiritual views) was received with sharply mixed response.

In Print

Joseph Clay Neal published the first of his *Charcoal Sketches, or, Scenes in a Metropolis*, satires on Philadelphians which became popular not only in the United States, but also England where they were reprinted by Dickens.

On Stage

The first known theatrical performance in Chicago was given by the Mackenzie & Jefferson Company.

Music

All Things Love Thee, So Do I; Annie Laurie; Flow Gently, Sweet Afton; Afton Water; Mary of Argyle; 'Tis Home Where'er the Heart Is (Pocahontas); When Stars Are in the Quiet Skies.

1839

$\mathscr{P}$resident Van Buren was empowered by Congress to resist British "invasion" when a boundary dispute along the Aroostook River between Maine and New Brunswick, Canada, nearly precipitated a war between the United States and Great Britain. It was averted by Gen. Winfield Scott.

Henry Clay is reputed to have said, when informed that his political utterances would injure his public career, "I had rather be right than be President." (He was, in fact, for many years a regular candidate for the presidential nomination. Never elected, he was defeated for the last time in 1844 by Polk.)

The Liberty Party, the first political anti-slavery organization in the United States, was formed in the Northern States to oppose William Lloyd Garrison's policy of non-political action. (The party merged in 1848 with the Free Soil Party.)

A German-Swiss military officer, Capt. John Augustus (really Johann August) Sutter was stranded (July) in California on his way from Sitka, Alaska. He established (Aug.) a settlement called New Helvetia on the present site of Sacramento.

The British government awarded James Bogardus, American inventor, a prize for a machine for engraving postage stamps. (England issued its first official postage stamps in Jan., 1840, the first country to do so.)

The Baltimore College of Dental Surgery was established, the first institution of its kind in the world.

Abner Doubleday (later Civil War officer and colonel of the 35th Infantry, United States Army) devised at Cooperstown, N.Y., a game with bases and positions for players, thus beginning modern baseball. His placement of bases, and the distances between them, have never been changed.

In Print

Henry Wadsworth Longfellow brought out his first book of verse, *Voices of the Night*, which at once established his reputation and popularity as a poet. A slender volume, it contained such favorites as *Hymn to the Night*, *A Psalm of Life*, *The Reaper and the Flowers*, *Footsteps of Angels*, and others.

Theodore Dwight Weld, Massachusetts abolitionist and reformer, published a tract, *American Slavery as It Is*, which did much to advance the antislavery cause. (It is said to have inspired Harriet Beecher Stowe's novel, *Uncle Tom's Cabin*.)

On Stage

Beethoven's opera *Fidelio* was performed (Sept. 9) for the first time in the United States in New York at the Park Theater. The performance was in English. Later the opera was frequently played by stock companies.

Edwin Forrest played (Sept. 4) Edward Bulwer-Lytton's *Richelieu* at the National Theater, New York.

Music

Joy to the World; *Antioch* (music from "Handel").

1840

$\mathscr{C}$ommander Charles Wilkes of the first United States Antarctic expedition discovered (Jan.-Feb.) the region later named Wilkes Land.

A widespread slang phrase was "Wake me up when Kirby dies" (from the theatrical hit *The Carpenter of Rouen*).

Showmanship got into politics when the conservative Whigs shouted "Tippecanoe and Tyler too," erected log cabins to typify their "grass-roots" candidate, William Henry Harrison, and served cider to the populace.

John W. Draper is believed to have been the first American to take a photograph.

Ladies were served at special post-office windows and even special bowling alleys to help them avoid the tobacco-chewing male.

Football was played in colleges at this time as a crude game among freshmen and sophomores.

A five-year depression (the eleventh since 1790) got under way. It reached its height in 1843.

The national population was 17,069,453.

In Print

The National Anti-Slavery Standard was founded in New York by the American Anti-Slavery Society. Strongly Union in its sympathies, the magazine advocated immediate abolition and Negro education. (It ceased publication in 1872.)

The Memphis, Tenn., *Commercial Appeal* was founded as a daily newspaper.

Books of the year included *The Pathfinder* by James Fenimore Cooper and *Two Years Before the Mast* by Richard Henry Dana.

Music

Consider the Lilies; Kathleen Mavourneen; The Old Arm Chair; Ole Tare River; The Pesky Sarpent; Rocked in the Cradle of the Deep; Tippecanoe and Tyler Too (to the tune of *Little Pigs*); *The Two Grenadiers; Cracovienne; The Ingle Side; Jim Along, Josey; Springfield Mountain; Whar Did You Cum from?*

1841

$\mathscr{G}$eneral William Henry Harrison, Whig, of Virginia, was inaugurated as the ninth President. He contracted pneumonia at the rainy inaugural ceremonies and died, aged 68, on Apr. 4, after serving only 31 days. He was succeeded by Vice President John Tyler, also a Whig, also of Virginia, who took the oath as the tenth President.

President Tyler vetoed the bill for rechartering the Bank of the United States, and all members of his cabinet, except Daniel Webster, resigned in protest.

A cargo of Negro slaves, en route from Richmond, Va., to New Orleans aboard the American vessel *Creole*, mutinied, seized the ship, and took it to the British port of New Providence in the West Indies, where the local authorities assisted their escape.

A rival to the paddle wheel was found in the screw propeller, probably used for the first time on the USS *Princeton*.

After its inability to cope with the conflagration of 1835, New York City in this year installed a fire engine, built after a recent British model.

Coke ovens were popular in Connellsville, Fayette County, Pa.

Thomas Cole completed his four allegorical pictures *Voyage of Life* (*The Child*, *The Youth*, *The Man*, *The Old Man*), which were to adorn American homes for years to come in a series of popular engravings.

Feminine fashions prescribed high combs.

In Print
The New York Tribune was founded as a daily newspaper by Horace Greeley, who remained its editor until his death in 1872. (The paper merged with the *New York Herald* in 1924, becoming the *Herald Tribune*.)

Across the East River, the *Brooklyn Daily Eagle* was established. (Walt Whitman was editor of the paper from 1846 to 1848.)

The Ladies Repository was founded in Cincinnati as a monthly literary magazine. (Called the *National Repository* after 1876, it ceased publication in 1880.)

Henry Wadsworth Longfellow published his second book of verse, *Ballads and Other Poems*. It contained the now well-known pieces, *The Skeleton in Armor*, *The Wreck of the Hesperus*, *The Village Blacksmith*, *It Is Not Always May*, *The Rainy Day*, and *Excelsior*.

Other literary publications of the year included James Fenimore Cooper's novel *The Deerslayer*, Edgar Allan Poe's story *The Murders in the Rue Morgue*—one of the earliest examples of detective fiction—and Ralph Waldo Emerson's first series of *Essays*. In the racy, popular magazine, *"Spirit of the Times"* appeared the famous tall story of the Southwest, *The Big Bear of Arkansas*, by Thomas Bangs Thorpe, Massachusetts-born humorist.

George Catlin, self-taught painter of Indian scenes, published *Manners and Customs of the North American Indians* in two volumes with 300 handsome engravings. The book was the result of an eight-year sojourn among various tribes from Yellowstone River to Florida. (In 1861 and in 1868 he published two similar books and also exhibited Indian troupes in the East and in Europe.)

On Stage

Dion Boucicault scored (Oct. 11) a popular theatrical success with his often-revived comedy *London Assurance* at the Park Theater, New York.

Donizetti's popular vehicle for operatic coloratura sopranos, *Lucia di Lammermoor*, was performed (Dec. 28) for the first time in the United States at the Théâtre d'Orléans in New Orleans in French. (It was first performed in the United States in the original Italian at Niblo's Garden, New York, Sept. 15, 1843.)

Music

Molly Bawn (Il Paddy Whack in Italia); *My Mother's Bible*; *Niagara Falls*.

1842

$\mathcal{T}$he Webster-Ashburton Treaty between the United States and Great Britain settled the dispute of 1839 over the boundary between Maine and New Brunswick.

General Zachary Taylor subdued the Seminole Indians of Florida, when their chief Osceola was killed, and effected the removal of most of the tribe west of the Mississippi. The war cost $20,000,000; Caucasian deaths totaled 1,500. The number of Indians who were massacred far exceeded that count.

Ether was administered (March) for the first time, in a surgical operation performed at Jefferson, Ga., by Dr. Crawford Williamson Long.

Martial law was invoked (May 18) in Providence, Rhode Island, by newly elected Governor Samuel W. King of the "Landholders" party when Thomas Wilson Dorr, elected to the same office by the opposing "Suffragists" party, attempted to seize the local arsenal. (Dorr fled, but on his return he was arrested and convicted of high treason. In June 1844 he was sentenced to life imprisonment, but he was released in 1845.)

A Massachusetts court ruled that Labor unions were legal organizations and denied that an attempt to establish a "closed shop" was unlawful or evidence of unlawful intent.

John Charles Fremont and Kit Carson made expeditions to California.

P.T. Barnum opened his showplace, the "American Museum," in New York at Broadway and Ann Street, for a cost of $12,000. His main feature was a four-year-old dwarf, two feet tall, billed as "General Tom Thumb," whose real name was Charles Sherwood Stratton. (At maturity Stratton reached 40 inches in height; he died at the age of 45 in 1883.)

The Philharmonic Society was organized (Apr. 2) in New York as a symphonic orchestra by Ureli Corelli Hill. Hill was an American musician who had been a pupil of the celebrated Ludwig Spohr in Cassel, Germany. The orchestra gave its first concert on Dec. 7, 1842, and has been in continuous existence since then.

President John Tyler's invalid wife, Letitia Christian Tyler, died in the White House.

New feminine vogues included mantillas, black varnished leather shoes, lace mitts, small parasols, and large muffs.

In Print

Charles Dickens paid the first of two visits to the United States (Jan.-May), giving lectures in which he advocated international copyright and the abolition of slavery. (He published his unfavorable impressions in *American Notes for General Circulation* on his return to London, and incorporated other American material in his novel *Martin Chuzzlewit*, 1843-44.)

Music

The Blind Boy; *Come, O Come with Me; The Moon is Beaming, Glenmary Waltzes; The Pope He Leads a Happy Life; Widow Machree.*

1843

*T*he Department of the Interior was established (Mar. 3).

The end of the world was at hand! The cosmic cataclysm was to take place between Mar. 21, 1843, and Mar. 21, 1844. The pronouncement was uttered by Preacher William Miller of Pittsfield, Mass. Thousands of his followers, the Millerites, disposed of property, settled accounts, etc., in preparation for Doomsday.

On the death of Pierre Lorillard, wealthy snuff and cigar manufacture and pioneer of the current Old Gold cigarette interests, newspapers coined the word "millionaire."

The Bunker Hill Monument, near Boston, was dedicated on the 68th anniversary (June 17) of the battle which it commemorates. Daniel Webster delivered the dedicatory address.

Before adjourning at midnight, Congress hurriedly granted to Samuel Morse an appropriation of $30,000 for the erection of an experimental electric wire between Washington, D.C., and Baltimore, with which to demonstrate his magnetic telegraph.

Samuel Colt, inventor of the revolver (1835), laid the first submarine cable in New York Harbor.

The B'nai B'rith was founded in New York as a Jewish fraternal organization.

The steady rise in immigration caused the formation of the secret Native American Party by antagonistic citizens. (Of no great importance, the party dissolved soon after its national convention in 1845, but it gave impetus to the Know-Nothing movement around 1850.)

The University of Notre Dame for men, near South Bend, In., was founded.

Henry Wadsworth Longfellow married (July 13) his second wife, Frances Elizabeth Appleton, daughter of wealthy cotton-mill proprietor who presented the couple with Craigie House, in Cambridge, Mass., as a wedding gift.

Deaths of the year included Francis Scott Key, aged 64 (Jan. 11), poet of *The Star-Spangled Banner*, and Noah Webster, aged 85 (May 28), lexicographer.

In Print

Edgar Allan Poe won the $100 prize of the *Dollar Magazine* with his story *The Gold Bug*—largely, according to rumor, because of the author's neat handwriting. Meanwhile, his bizarre murder story, *The Black Cat,* was appearing in *The Saturday Evening Post* and his tale of the Spanish Inquisition, *The Pit and the Pendulum,* in *The Gift.*

William Hickling Prescott published his three-volume *History of the Conquest of Mexico.* (It was followed in 1847 by his two-volume *History of the Conquest of Peru.*)

On Stage

Beethoven's great third (*Eroica*) Symphony received (Feb. 18) its first complete orchestral performance in the United States by the New York Philharmonic Society, in the Apollo Rooms, at the second concert of its first season.

Ole Bull, noted Norwegian violinist, made (Nov. 25) his American debut at the Park Theater in New York. He toured the Eastern States and visited Havana, Cuba, giving over 200 concerts. His receipts were said to have totaled $400,000.

The Virginia Minstrels, the first regularly organized band of Negro minstrels, gave their initial public performance in New York at the Chatham Square Theater. The company was composed of Dan (Daniel Decatur) Emmett, Frank Brower, Bill Whitlock, and Dick Pelham. (The troupe visited England in 1844 and returned in 1846. Pelham remained in England.)

Music

Columbia, the Gem of the Ocean; De Boatman's Dance, Go Call the Doctor; or, Anti-Calomel; The Grave of Bonaparte; The Heart Bow'd Down (The Bohemian Girl); I Dreamt I Dwelt in Marble Halls (The Bohemian Girl); The Lament of the Irish Emigrant; Long, Long Ago; Old Dan Tucker; The Old Granite State; The Old Church Yard; Stop Dat Knocking at My Door; Then You'll Remember Me (The Bohemian Girl).

1844

Samuel Morse successfully demonstrated (May 24) before Congress his electric telegraph by sending a message from the United States Supreme Court room in the Capitol to Baltimore by wire. The message read: "What hath God wrought!" (Mrs. Dolley Madison, widow of the fourth President, dispatched the first personal message.)

Charles Goodyear patented (June 15) his process for vulcanizing rubber, which he invented in 1839.

Dr. Horace Wells, Hartford, Connecticut dentist, used "laughing gas" (nitrous oxide) as an anesthetic to have one of his own teeth extracted. (He had also experimented with ether as early as 1840, before Long, 1842, and Morton, 1846.)

The USS *Princeton* (1841) fired one of its guns, called the Peacemaker, during a pleasure trip on the Potomac. The gun exploded, killing several persons and injuring many. Among those killed were Secretary of State Abel P. Upshur, Secretary of the Navy Thomas W. Gilmer, and David Gardiner of Gardiners Island, New York. President Tyler was aboard the ship and narrowly escaped death. On June 26 Tyler married his second wife, Gardiner's daughter, Julia. He composed for her a song, "Sweet Lady, Awake."

In New York, the ranks of the Democratic Party were again split for a time into opposing factions, the "Hunker," and "Barnburners." The Hunkers represented the conservative element that wanted to keep the local "hunk" of the party in the hands of established patronage. Those who were antagonistic to this policy and were against corporations and the extension of slavery were regarded as radicals and called Barnburners, after the man in the fable who burned his barn to destroy the rats. (Many of the latter group joined the Free-Soil Party in 1848.)

For the national campaign, President John Tyler accepted renomination but withdrew before election. Martin Van Buren ran in Tyler's place on the Democratic ticket but was defeated because of his opposition to the annexation of Texas. His opponent was James Knox Polk, the first "dark horse" nominee, whose platform favored not only the annexation of Texas but, in defiance of Great Britain, the whole of the Oregon Territory, as expressed in the slogan "Fifty-four forty or fight!"

Mormon Joseph Smith died (June 27).

In Print

Moses Yale Beach, owner of The *New York Sun*, published his *Wealth and Biography of Wealthy Citizens of the City of New York*. He listed about 850 persons worth $100,000 or more, among them John Jacob Astor ($44,000,000), Stephen Van Rensselaer ($10,000,000), William B. Astor ($5,000,000), Peter Stuyvesant ($4,000,000), and Cornelius Vanderbilt ($1,200,000).

Edgar Allan Poe joined the staff of the *New-York Mirror* and began his literary attacks, on among others, Henry Wadsworth Longfellow, whom he accused of plagiarism.

On Stage

Michael William Balfe's famous opera *The Bohemian Girl* was introduced (Nov. 25) to American audiences at the Park Theater in New York.

The popular French play *Don Caesar de Bazan* by Philippe Francois Dumanoir and Adolphe D'Ennery was introduced (Dec. 9) in English by Charles Walcot at the Olympic Theater in New York. The play had many revivals and adaptations.

The Hasty Pudding Club, a student body dramatic organization formed in 1770 at Harvard, gave (Dec. 13) its first theatrical production.

Music

The Blue Juniata; God Bless Our Native Land; The Ole Grey Goose; Open Thy Lattice.

1845

*J*ames Knox Polk, Democrat, of North Carolina, was inaugurated as the 11th President. His wife, Sarah Childress Polk, a Methodist educated by the Moravians, prohibited liquor and dancing in the White House.

Retiring President Tyler signed (Mar. 1) the bill for the annexation of Texas. The territory, comprising the present state of Texas and parts of New Mexico, Colorado, and Wyoming, was admitted (Dec. 29) as a state, with the proviso that the area (389,166 square miles) should be divided into no more than five states "of convenient size." But the Texas question was not thereby resolved. Border disputes continued between Americans and Mexicans. To thwart a suspected attempt by the latter to regain the lost territory, President Polk dispatched into the region an armed force under Zachary Taylor—a step that was to lead to the Mexican War.

Congress designated (Jan. 23) the national election day as the first Tuesday after the first Monday in November.

Two more states were admitted to the Union—Florida (Mar. 3) as the 27th and Texas (Dec. 29) as the 28th.

The U.S. Naval Academy was founded (Oct. 10) at Annapolis, Md.

The American steamer *Massachusetts* crossed the Atlantic to Liverpool by means of a screw propeller.

The first set of baseball rules was formulated by the Knickerbocker Club of New York.

Tenpins superseded billiards as a common pastime.

Andrew Jackson, seventh President, died (June 8).

In Print

"Manifest destiny" was a new phrase added to the popular vocabulary when New York editor John L. O'Sullivan coined the words in an article published in his July *United States Magazine and Democratic Review*.

The *Scientific American* was founded in New York as a weekly "illustrated journal of art, science, and mechanics."

The weekly *National Police Gazette*, in its subsequently famous pink covers, made its first appearance in New York.

Edgar Allan Poe's poem *The Raven* was printed in The *American Review* and republished in his volume *The Raven and Other Poems*.

Henry Wadsworth Longfellow's fourth book of verse, *The Belfry of Bruges and Other Poems*, contained *The Arsenal at Springfield, The Bridge, The Arrow and the Song,* and *The Day is Done.*

Dorothy Lynde Dix, who spent her life in the relief of paupers, criminals, and the insane, published *Prisons and Prison Discipline.*

Equally significant was Sarah Margaret Fuller's study *Woman in the Nineteenth Century.*

On Stage

The first grand opera by a native American composer was produced (June 4) in Philadelphia at the Chestnut Street Theater—*Leonora* by William Henry Fry, of Philadelphia. The libretto, in four acts, was written by the composer's brother, Joseph Reese Fry, and based on Edward Bulwer-Lytton's successful play *The Lady of Lyons.* (The opera was performed 16 times, and given in New York at the Academy of Music, Mar. 29, 1858, in Italian.)

Mrs. Anna Cora Mowatt's popular five-act play *Fashion, or Life in New York* opened (Mar. 24) in New York and ran for 20 nights.

German actors began putting on plays in New York beer halls.

Music

Yes! Let Me Like a Soldier Fall (Maritana); Crambambuli; Bright Source of Pleasure; Dennis; Scenes That Are Brightest.

1846

$\mathcal{T}$he successful demonstration of Morse's telegraph before Congress in 1844 led to the establishment of a telegraph line from New York to Washington, D.C. Connections were established between New York and Philadelphia (Jan. 20) and between Philadelphia and Baltimore (June 5). The line of Morse's experiment from Baltimore to Washington completed the circuit.

In consequence of Texan border disputes, Congress debated a bill for the settlement of differences either by boundary treaty or by purchase. During the discussions, David Wilmot introduced a Proviso for the exclusion of slavery for the area, which was passed by the House but rejected by the Senate.

The belligerent atmosphere of "Fifty-four forty or fight," created by the Oregon boundary dispute between the United States and Great Britain, was amicably dispelled by the Webster-Ashburton Treaty compromise. It gave Vancouver to Great Britain and settled the northern limits of the Oregon Territory at the present boundary.

Clashes between American forces under Zachary Taylor and Mexicans in Texas at Palo Alto (May 8) and Resaca de la Palma (May 9) resulted (May 13) in a declaration of war by the United States on Mexico, thus starting the Mexican War (1846-48).

Capt. John Charles Fremont, United States Engineers, took possession of the Mexican province of California and proclaimed (June 14) at Sonoma the Bear Flag Republic.

Monterey was captured by the United States Pacific fleet under Commodore John Drake Sloat (July), and Santa Barbara and San Pedro by his successor Commodore Robert Field Stockton (Aug.). On land, American victories were won at Santa Fe by Stephen Watts Kearney and at El Paso and Chihuahua by Alexander William Doniphan.

In the midst of hostilities, Capt. Fremont, acting as civil governor of California, rashly resisted the superior authority of General Kearney, who had been appointed to organize the local government. Fremont was court-martialed and found guilty of mutiny. His life was saved by order of President Polk.

Iowa was admitted (Dec. 28) as the 29th state.

Ether was administered (Oct. 16) in public at the Massachusetts General Hospital in Boston by Dr. William Thomas Green Morton during an operation performed by Dr. John Collins Warren.

Dr. Morrison of St. Louis devised the "dental engine" or drilling machine.

Congress enacted a law requiring the deposit of one copy of each copyrighted book in the Library of Congress. (Since 1870, the deposit of two copies has been required.)

Maine adopted prohibition—the first state to do so.

The American Missionary Association was formed for the propagation of the Christian religion among the Negroes of the Southern States, Jamaica, and West Africa.

The Smithsonian Institution, Washington, D.C., was founded by an act of Congress in accordance with the terms of a bequest made by an Englishman, James Smithson, Oxford graduate and Fellow of the Royal Society, London. Smithson left the sum of 100,000 pounds for "an establishment for the increase and diffusion of knowledge among men."

A wagon train of emigrants en route to California was caught in the Sierra Nevada by severe snowstorms and encamped amid severe privations on a site now called Donner Lake. Survivors were rescued after resorting to cannibalism.

Two important inventions were introduced during the year—the sewing machine of Elias Howe of Spencer, Mass., and the cylinder rotary press by Richard March Hoe. The latter was installed by the *Philadelphia Public Ledger*. Howe's sewing machine was later improved by Isaac Merritt Singer.

In Hoboken, N.J., the first game of baseball as we know it was played between the Knickerbocker Club of New York and a picked team then calling itself the New York Club.

The potato famine in Ireland was rapidly increasing American immigration.

Ladies' parasols could, for the first time, be folded up.

English journalists and visitors deplored the American male's habit of chewing tobacco.

In Print

The *Boston Herald* was founded as a daily newspaper.

Elijah Kellogg's blank verse classic of schoolboy declamation, *Spartacus to His Gladiators*, appeared in Epes Sargent's *School Reader*.

On Stage

Edwin T. Christy's "original and far-famed band of Ethiopian Minstrels" opened (Apr. 24) at Palmo's Opera House in New York.

The first American performance of the famous ballet *Giselle*, scenario by Théophile Gautier and music by Adolphe Adam, was given (Feb. 2) in New York.

1847

$\mathcal{T}$he Mexican War continued. Notable American victories were won at Buena Vista (Feb. 22-23) by Zachary Taylor, and at Vera Cruz (Mar. 27) and Chapultepec (Sept. 13) by Winfield Scott. Hostilities ended (Sept. 17) with Scott's capture of Mexico City and the capitulation of the Mexican dictator, Santa Anna.

Congress authorized (Mar. 3) the issuance of the first United States adhesive postage stamps in 5 and 10 cent values. The stamps bore portraits of Franklin and Washington, and were light brown and black in color, respectively. The stamps were placed on sale July 1. Diagonal, vertical, or horizontal halves of the 10-cent stamp were often used as a 5-cent value. The stamps were unperforated. Previously, mail had been merely marked "Paid" by postmasters using pen and ink or by hand stamp impressions. (Until 1894 United States postage stamps were printed by private manufacturers for the government.)

New Hampshire became the first state to legalize the ten-hour working day.

Following violent clashes over polygamy in Nauvoo, Ill., a band of Mormons (143 men, 3 women, and 2 children) moved westward into Utah under their leader, Brigham Young, and established (July 24) Salt Lake City.

Telegraph connection was completed (June 27) between New York and Boston.

The immigrant ship *Phoenix* burned on Lake Michigan with a loss of 240 lives.

Maria Mitchell, American astronomer, discovered (Oct. 1) a comet and was elected the same day to the American Academy of Art—the first woman to be so honored. The King of Denmark awarded her a gold medal for her discovery.

Henry Ward Beecher, 34-year-old Congregational minister, father of Harriet Beecher Stowe, was called from Indiana to Brooklyn, N.Y., to take charge of the new Plymouth Church and its congregation of nine families. (He served the church for nearly 40 years, and his zeal and brilliant oratory ultimately built an edifice seating about 3,000 persons.)

John Chapman, aged about 72, Swedenborgian planter of apple trees from Pennsylvania to Illinois and better known as "Johnny Appleseed," died (Mar. 11) of pneumonia in Fort Wayne, Ind.

In Print

The *Chicago Tribune* was founded as a daily newspaper.

The *National Era* was founded as an antislavery magazine in Washington, D.C. (It published Hawthorne's allegorical tale *The Great Stone Face*, Harriet Beecher Stowe's *Uncle Tom's Cabin* in serialization before its appearance in book form, and many of Whittier's writings. It ceased publication in 1860.)

Benjamin Penhallow Shillaber, Boston humorist and printer, created the character of Mrs. Parkington, a Yankee Mrs. Malaprop noted for her amusing misuse of words. (He developed the character in *Life and Sayings of Mrs. Parkington*, 1854, *Mrs. Parkington's Knitting Work*, 1859, *Parkingtonian Patchwork*, 1873, and the posthumous *Mrs. Parkington's Grab Bag*, 1893. The author died in 1890.)

A Dr. Collyer exhibited (Sept. 23) in New York at the Apollo Rooms a tableau of living male and female models "from the Royal Academies of London and Paris." This started a craze for posturing scantily clad "artists" viewed rapturously through "prodigious opera glasses and pocket telescopes." Several hundred fashionable old rakes and ineffable scoundrels about town—some of them bankers and brokers in Wall Street, and over sixty years of age—were finally rounded up by the police (Mar., 1848). A group of drunken devotees climbed on the stage during a performance at the Temple of the Muses and chased the female models into the wings.

On Stage

A frame building erected by John B. Rice was Chicago's first real theater.

Italian opera was in the ascendancy. The Havana Opera Company from the Teatro Tacon began giving operatic seasons in New York, Philadelphia, and Boston under the direction of Luigi Arditi, later the composer of *The Kiss Waltz*. The company introduced Italian opera to Boston at the Howard Athenaeum with a performance (Apr. 23) of Verdi's *Ernani*. In New York, the Astor Place Opera House, the city's first real operatic theater, was opened (Nov. 22) under the management of Sanquirico and Salvatore Patti (father of the subsequently famous Adelina Patti) also with *Ernani*. In fact, the first Verdi operas were being heard in the United States—*I Lombardi* at Palmo's Opera House in New York (Mar. 3), *Ernani* at the Park Theater (Apr. 15), and *I Due Foscari* in Boston (May).

Music

Carry Me Back to Ole Virginny; *The Rainy Day* (words, Henry Wadsworth Longfellow, music, Isaac Baker); *Be Kind to the Loved Ones at Home*; *Footsteps of Angels*; *Row Thy Boat Lightly*.

1848

The Mexican War was terminated by a treaty of peace signed at Guadalupe Hidalgo (Feb. 2; ratified by Congress May 19). Mexico relinquished its claims to Texas and ceded to the United States an area comprising California, Nevada, Utah, Arizona, New Mexico, and part of Colorado, or two-fifths of its territory. The United States paid Mexico an indemnity of $15,000,000 and assumed American claims amounting to $3,000,000. The war caused the death of 13,237 enlisted American men. Among the officers serving in the war were Colonel Jefferson Davis, Captain Robert E. Lee, Captain George B. McClellan, and Lieutenant U.S. Grant.

Wisconsin was admitted to the Union (May 29) as the 30th state.

Gold was discovered (Jan. 24) by James Wilson Marshall at his partner Johann August Sutter's sawmill on the South Fork of the American River, near Coloma, Calif. President Polk incorporated the news in his message (Dec. 5) to Congress, which set off a gold rush the following year.

Pennsylvania became the first state to pass a child labor law fixing the minimum age in commercial pursuits at twelve years (raised to thirteen in 1849).

Women clamoring for the right to vote met in convention (July 19-20) in Seneca Falls, NY, and drafted a Declaration of Sentiments. Among the leaders in the movement were Lucretia Mott and Elizabeth Cady Stanton.

Congress authorized the erection of the Washington National Monument from funds to be raised by public subscription. The cornerstone was laid on July 4. (The monument was completed in 1884.)

The village of Saint Anthony, Minn., now part of Minneapolis, was established. Maine woodsmen and others were attracted to the place because of the plentiful pine forests in the region.

The China clipper *Sea Witch*, built in 1846, became the fastest ship afloat when it made a record trip from Canton to New York in 77 days.

Samuel M. Kier, Pittsburgh druggist, sold petroleum as "a wonderful medical virtue" behind an advertising campaign using imitation bank notes as bait. At this time peddlers generally hawked petroleum as "Seneca oil," with reputed medicinal qualities.

The University of Wisconsin, Madison, Wis., for men and women, and the College of the City of New York, for men, were founded.

Andrew Carnegie, a poor 13-year-old Scottish lad, began work as a "bobbin boy" in a cotton factory in Allegheny, PA.

John Quincy Adams, sixth President (1825-29) and for 17 years thereafter Massachusetts Representative in Congress, was stricken in the House and died (Feb. 23), aged 81, in the Speaker's room.

Giuseppe Garibaldi, Italian patriot, came to the United States as a refugee and worked in Antoni Meucci's candle factory on Staten Island, New York. He remained about two years.

The first locomotive steamed (Oct. 25) out of Chicago - the *Pioneer* of the Galena & Chicago (now Chicago & North Western) Railroad.

Spiritualism began when certain "rappings" were heard in the home of J. D. Fox in Hydesville, Wayne Country, NY. (They ultimately led to the formation of the National Spiritualists' Association, incorporated in 1893 in Washington, D.C.)

John Jacob Astor, aged 85, died (Mar. 29) in New York, leaving a fortune of $40,000,000.

In Print

Mrs. Amelia Jenks Bloomer began publishing her magazine *The Lily*, devoted to temperance and woman suffrage. She became better known, however, as the creator of the "bloomer," a pantaloon or loose-fitting trouser-like dress gathered about the ankles, for women. (*The Lily* ceased publication in 1854.)

The Independent was founded in New York as a weekly religious magazine. (It became a secular periodical under later editors. It ceased publication in 1828.)

William Frederick Poole, Massachusetts librarian, began the publication of his *Alphabetical Index to Subjects Treated in… Periodicals*, the forerunner of the present *Reader's Guide to Periodical Literature*.

On Stage

In Boston, Fanny Kemble, celebrated English actress, gave successful Shakespearean readings, which she repeated elsewhere until her return to England (1851).

Fire destroyed (Dec. 16) the historic Park Theater, New York, opened in 1798.

Monte Cristo, a play by Alexandre Dumas, Sr., was introduced (Dec. 25) at the Broadway Theater, New York, by J. Lester, stage-name of J. Lester Wallack.

Palmo's Opera House in New York reopened (July 10), remodelled and improved, as Burton's Theater, long to remain an important playhouse.

Music

Ben Bolt, or Oh! Don't You Remember; The Cottage of My Mother; The Folks Are All Waiting to See the Fast Streamer (A Glance at New York); Oh! Susanna, Stephen C. Foster; *Old Uncle Ned; 'Twas Off the Blue Canaries, or, My Last Cigar.*

1849

$\mathscr{G}$eneral Zachary Taylor, Whig of Virginia, nicknamed "Old Rough and Ready," was inaugurated as the 12th President.

Gold was on everybody's mind. Congress authorized (Mar. 3) the coinage of gold dollars. More gold was discovered in the Mother Lode, stretching 110 miles along the western foothills of the Sierra Nevada. The *New York Tribune* sent into the region the adventurous Pennsylvania Quaker writer, Bayard Taylor, who fired the imagination of readers with two volumes of descriptions under the fanciful title *El Dorado* (1850). He used the title for a poem in which he referred to "the gold rush." So many prospectors hurried to California (1,200 sailed from the East in three months), and so many perished en route, that wiseacres told departing hopefuls to take tombstones with them. By the end of 1850 San Francisco boasted 34,776 inhabitants. (There were 500 in 1840.) Stay-at-homes in the East had to content themselves with a then popular type of theatrical presentation, a *Panorama of the Gold Mines of California*.

Meanwhile, California embraced the entertainment business at once with the $80,000 Eagle Theater in Sacramento; Stephen C. Massett gave a series of songs and recitations in San Francisco, using the only piano in that section of the country. Hénri Herz, celebrated French pianist, also played in Sacramento, performing before an audience of gold miners on a dilapidated piano. The instrument had only six octaves, with half of the keys out of order. The miners paid their admission at the box office with gold dust which the cashier weighed on a pair of scales. (The story is told in Herz's book *Mes Voyages en Amérique*, Paris, 1866.) Before the year ended there occurred in San Francisco an event often repeated in its history—fire destroyed (Dec. 24) more than a million dollars' worth of property.

In New York, a mob invaded (May 10) the Astor Place Opera House, creating a riot against the English actor William Macready; 22 people were killed and 36 wounded. The magnificent interior of the building was reduced almost to a wreck. The outbreak was in retaliation for the treatment accorded Edwin Forrest, American actor, in London in 1845. The demonstration, said to have been instigated by Forrest himself, was led by the notorious Edward Zane Carroll Judson, who was arrested and sentenced to a year in the penitentiary.

William Lowndes Yancey of Georgia, formulated the Alabama Platform. This asserted that Congress had no constitutional power to abolish slavery and that no territory before it was admitted as a state possessed the right of choice in the question.

Walter Hunt invented the safety pin.

The recently invented saxophone of Adolphe Sax was introduced (Apr.) to American audiences at the New York concerts of the English Distin family (father and four sons). The players, with their instruments, were much in demand.

Edgar Allan Poe, aged 40, died (Oct. 7) a tragic death in Baltimore. Never able to overcome his drinking habits, he was found in a delirious condition outside a saloon that was used as a voting place.

Ladies now puffed their hair over a cushion, a "mouse," atop the head.

Gas light was installed (Dec. 29) in the White House.

James Polk, eleventh President, died (June 15).

In Print

Poe wrote, in this last year of his life, *The Bells*, *Annabel Lee*, and *Eldorado*.

With feminism stirring the country, Rufus Wilmot Griswold published *The Female Poets of America*.

Music

Just as I Am Without One Plea; *Nelly Bly* and *Nelly Was A Lady* (Stephen C. Foster); *Santa Lucia*; *Angelina Baker*; *By the Sad Sea Waves (The Brides of Venice)*; *I've Left the Snow-Clad Hills*; *The Spacious Firmament of High*; *What Are the Wild Waves Saying?*

1850

$\mathscr{P}$resident Zachary Taylor, aged 66, died (July 9) of typhus. He had served only one year and four months and was succeeded (July 10) by Vice President Millard Fillmore, Whig, of New York, who took the oath as the 13th President. Fillmore's daughter, Mary Abigail, was the White House hostess in place of her mother, who suffered from poor health.

Congress passed (Jan. 29) Henry Clay's Omnibus Bill, the Compromise of 1850. Its provisions were attacked by John Calhoun in his "Fourth of March Speech" ("Speech on the Slavery Question") and defended by Daniel Webster in his "Seventh of March Speech" ("For the Union and Constitution"). In supporting the legislation Webster lost prestige in the Northern States, as reflected in Whittier's poem *Ichabod*.

The Clayton-Bulwer Treaty was negotiated by John Middleton Clayton (United States) and Sir Henry Lytton Bulwer (Great Britain) to regulate the interests of both countries in Central America, particularly in regard to the proposed canal across Nicaragua. (The bill was annulled in 1902.)

California was admitted (Sept. 9) as the 31st state.

The woman suffrage movement was spreading rapidly. A convention took place (Apr.) in Salem, Ohio. The first national convention was held in Worcester, Mass., at which the movement assumed definite political character and allied itself with the abolitionist cause. Among the leaders were Susan Brownell Anthony, Carrie Chapman Catt, Abbey Kelly Foster, the Grimke sisters (Angelina and Sarah Moore), Elizabeth Cady Stanton, and Lucy Stone. The first tangible results of the movement were achieved when Indiana adopted a revised state constitution with liberal provisions for women.

Cincinnati organized the first steam fire department when a native son, A. B. Latta, constructed a practical fire engine.

The first building in the United States to be constructed of cast-iron framework was erected in New York by James Bogardus, inventor of a postage stamp engraving machine (1839).

New York merchant Henry Grinnell outfitted at the expense of $30,000 two ships, the *Advance*, 140 tons, and the *Rescue*, 90 tons. These ships sailed (May 23) from New York for the Arctic to join in the search for the "lost" English explorer Sir John Franklin, who had led an expedition of 219 men into the region in 1845. (The rescue party found no trace of Franklin, who had perished in 1847, but discovered the area now called Grinnell Land.)

The American Express Company was organized (Mar. 18) in Buffalo, NY.

Scottish-born Allan Pinkerton, a cooper by trade, was appointed Chicago's first police detective. After uncovering a counterfeiting gang, he opened a detective bureau of his own.

George H. Fox invented an elevator that operated by means of a vertical screw.

Fire damaged San Francisco three times (May 4, June 14, Sept. 17) and destroyed (June 17) the steamer *Griffith* on Lake Erie with a loss of 300 lives.

George Phillips Bond, Harvard astronomer, used (July 17) the 15-inch refractor of the Harvard Observatory telescope to make the first photograph of a star—a daguerreotype of Vega.

James Gordon Bennett, publisher of the daily *New York Herald*, was horsewhipped on Broadway by a defeated candidate for the office of district attorney.

After an unsuccessful venture in Texas, Etienne Cabet's dwindling band of Icarians (1848) established for a time their Utopian community in Nauvoo, IL.

A German socialist Turnverein, a gymnastics club, was started in New York.

The Christadelphians, an American Christian sect with no ordained clergy, was founded by English-born Dr. John Thomas (1805-71); the sect was also known as the Thomasites.

Returning from Italy, Margaret Fuller, the Marquis Angelo Ossoli her husband, and their child lost their lives in a shipwreck during a storm off Fire Island, near New York. Of the victims, only the body of the child was ever recovered.

Mathew B. Brady became famous as a photographer with his "Gallery of Illustrious Americans."

Whist and faro were popular gambling games.

Men wore cutaway coats for morning and evening occasions. The coats had ample pockets in the tails.

According to immigration statistics, 379,466 aliens entered the United States, making a total of 1,173,251 for the decade. Fearing the potential voting power of the foreign-born, alarmed nativists revived the prejudices of the Native American Party (1843) and formed the quasi-secret Know-Nothing movement. "I don't know" was their usual reply to any question concerning their affairs.

The national population was 23,191,876.

In Print

Harper's *New Monthly Magazine* appeared.

Nathaniel Hawthorne published his novel *The Scarlet Letter*.

Fourteen-year-old Jay Gould, later to become a fabulously rich financier, wrote an essay in Beechwood Seminary entitled *Honesty Is the Best Policy*.

On Stage

Theater-going San Franciscans witnessed (Jan. 16) at the Eagle Theater (later Washington Hall) their first real play, *The Wife*, by the English playwright James Sheridan Knowles, and an afterpiece *Charles the Second*. (The play had been given previously in Sacramento.)

Italian opera came to Chicago when Bellini's *La Sonnambula* was performed (July 29) at Rice's Theater.

Tom Maguire, onetime New York cab driver and saloon-keeper, started his California career as a theatrical manager by opening (Oct. 30) the Jenny Lind Theater in San Francisco.

On the New York stage, *Mose the Volunteer Fireman* (1848), was followed (July) by a fire-eater in *The New York Fireman* and the *Bond Street Heiress*, which played at the National Theater.

Music

De Camptown Races (Stephen C. Foster); *Cheer, Boys, Cheer!*; *It Came upon the Midnight Clear; Creation* (words, Joseph Addison, music arranged from Franz Joseph Haydn).

1851

The United States was 75 years old.

International difficulties arising from an insurrection in Cuba (1850-51) almost brought the United States into war with Spain. France and Great Britain intervened and, at the same time, the United States paid $25,000 to Spain for the damage done to its consulate in New Orleans by riotous Cuban sympathizers and agents.

"Go West, young man" wrote Horace Greeley in an editorial in his *New York Tribune*. The phrase, however, had been used earlier in the year by John Babsone Lane Soule in the Terre Haute, Ind., newspaper *Express*.

The United States changed (July 1) letter postage from 5 and 10 cents to 1, 3, 5, and 12 cents. (Other values were added in 1855, 1856, 1860.)

In California, vigilante committees were being organized by citizens to counteract the lawlessness of the gold rush adventurers.

The United States purchased (July 23) territory in western Minnesota from the Sioux Indians.

San Francisco suffered (June 22) its sixth fire.

The new, trim clipper, *Flying Cloud*, made a record trip from New York to San Francisco via Cape Horn in 89 days, 8 hours.

The New York & Lake Erie opened (May 14) service between Piedmont on the Hudson and Dunkirk on Lake Erie with gala ceremonies conducted by President Fillmore. The New York & Hudson River made (Oct. 8) its first run from New York City to Albany. The caboose, or observatory cabin atop the freight car, originated about this time with the New York & Erie Railroad near Suffern, N.Y.

The Wabash-Erie canal, connecting the Ohio River with Lake Erie, was completed.

Sewing machine patents were granted to Isaac Merritt Singer and to A. B. Wilson.

Lorenzo Lorraine Langstroth, American apiarist, designed the modern box beehive.

Cyrus Hall McCormick was awarded a gold medal for his reaper (1834) at the first International Exposition in the Crystal Palace, London.

Fire damaged (Dec. 24) the Library of Congress, reducing its collection of books to 20,000 volumes.

Northwestern University, Evanston, Ill., an institution for both men and women, was founded (Jan. 28) by the Illinois legislature.

William Marcy Tweed was elected alderman to the New York City Common Council. Its 40 members received no pay and were popularly called The Forty Thieves. During the next twenty years Tweed was a notorious figure in the city's corrupt politics; he gained so much power that he was nicknamed "The Boss."

International yacht racing was instituted when the American schooner *America* defeated (Aug. 12) the chief British contender *Aurora* of the Royal Yacht Squadron in the race around the Isle of Wight for the Cup of All Nations. This gave the United States the first victory in what was to evolve into the America's Cup races, which England has never won. (The next race was in 1870.)

Emanuel Leutze, German-born American painter, finished his painting "Washington Crossing the Delaware" at Düsseldorf.

Eben Tourjee, self-taught 17-year-old Boston musician, introduced class instruction in piano playing at Fall River, Mass.

Deaths of the year included: John James Audubon, aged 76 (Jan. 26), and James Fenimore Cooper, aged 62 (Sept. 14).

In Print

Gleason's Pictorial Drawing-Room Companion was founded in Boston as the first illustrated weekly magazine in the United States. (It ceased publication in 1859.)

Two notable dailies, *The New York Times* and *The Sacramento* (Calif.) *Union* were founded. (Both newspapers are still published.)

Harriet Beecher Stowe's novel *Uncle Tom's Cabin*, which lifted her into nation-wide prominence, appeared serially (1851-52) in the *National Era*, an antislavery magazine published in Washington, D.C.

Herman Melville published his whaling classic *Moby Dick*; Hawthorne, his novel *The House of the Seven Gables*.

The *Carpet-Bag* appeared in Boston as a humorous weekly magazine. The issue for May 1 contained a piece, *The Dandy Frightening the Squatter*, by the 16-year-old Samuel Langhorne Clemens, later known as Mark Twain, and an essay by the 17-year-old Artemus Ward. (The magazine ceased publication in 1853.)

On Stage

In the theater, Negro minstrelsy was all the rage. Some groups called themselves "minstrels"; others were "serenaders." Competing with them were female "bloomer" troupes. Amelia Bloomer's fad in women's dress also became the butt of a comedy, *The Bloomers, or, Pets in Pants*, and was the subject of a song, *The Gal with the Bloomers on*.

The abdication of Ludwig I of Bavaria sent his mistress, the Countess of Landsfield, to America. She is better known to history as Lola Montez, an

Irish-born actress whose real name was Maria Dolores Eliza Rosanna Gilbert. She made (Dec. 29) her American debut in *Betley* in New York at the Broadway Theater. She failed to impress her audience, composed mainly of male spectators, but played, nevertheless, a two weeks' engagement.

In the shadow of Jenny Lind, who was appearing in New York in opera, an "infant prima donna" was growing up in the city and singing operatic arias in concerts—Adelina Patti, born eight years previously in Madrid.

Music

Home Again; How Can I Leave Thee!; Hungarian Rhapsody No. 2, Franz Liszt; *Old Folks at Home*, Stephen C. Foster.

1852

$\mathcal{V}$ermont became the second state to adopt prohibition. (The first was Maine in 1846; Connecticut followed in 1854, and New Hampshire and New York in 1855.

Direct railroad service was established (Dec. 31) between New York and Chicago.

William Walker, lawyer and newspaper editor in California, attempted with a small force to establish (Nov.) a republic of his own in the Mexican states of Sonora and Lower California on the pretext of defending the natives from the Apache Indians. (He was arrested and tried in May, 1854, for a violation of the neutrality laws, but was acquitted.)

Ole Bull, renowned Norwegian violin virtuoso, bought a tract of 125,000 acres in Pennsylvania, which he called Oleana. This was to be a colony of his countrymen, "consecrated to freedom, baptized in independence, and protected by the mighty flag of the Union." (The scheme failed, and Ole Bull lost an immense sum of money in the subsequent litigation and through a swindle. To recoup his losses, he gave concerts during the next five years in the United States, reaching California via Panama.)

Ohio became the first state to limit the working hours for women to ten hours a day.

The United States established its second mint in San Francisco. (The first was established in 1792 in Philadelphia.)

The Boston Public Library was established.

The American Geographical Society was founded in New York.

Catherine Sinclair won a bitterly contested divorce from the actor Edwin Forrest in a suit that gained nationwide publicity. (Miss Sinclair went to San Francisco in the following year and became a notable actress and theatrical manageress there. Forrest unsuccessfully appealed the divorce case for sixteen years.)

Fire destroyed (July 27) the steamer *Henry Clay* on the Hudson River, N.Y., with a loss of 70 lives. Andrew Jackson Downing, pioneer American landscape gardener, lost his life while rescuing fellow passengers. (He designed the gardens surrounding the Smithsonian Institution, the Capitol, and the White House.) On Lake Erie, the steamer *Atlantic* sank (Aug. 20) with a loss of 250 lives.

Jenny Lind married (Feb. 5) her pianist and conductor, Otto Goldschmidt, in Boston.

At the Democratic convention, Franklin Pierce was nominated on the 49th ballot over Henry Clay, Stephen Douglas, and James Buchanan. In the national election, Pierce defeated the Whig candidate, General Winfield Scott; it was the last election in which the Whigs would play a major role.

John Howard Payne, aged 61, luckless poet of *Home, Sweet Home!* died (Apr. 10) as American consul in Tunis, Africa.

Other deaths of the year included: Henry Clay, aged 75 (June 29), and Daniel Webster, aged 70 (Oct. 24).

In Print

Harriet Beecher Stowe's novel *Uncle Tom's Cabin* appeared in book form; 300,000 copies were reported to have been sold during the first year.

Nathaniel Hawthorne published his tales for children, *A Wonder Book*, based on Greek myths. (Its sequel, *Tanglewood Tales*, appeared in 1853.)

On Stage

Without the author's consent, George L. Aiken, American actor and playwright, produced (Sept. 27) in Troy, NY, for a run of 100 performances, his popular dramatization of Harriet Beecher Stowe's novel *Uncle Tom's Cabin*.

Dion Boucicault's much-heralded London play *The Corsican Brothers*, a dramatization of Alexandre Dumas's *Les Frères Corses* (1845), was performed (Apr. 21) with spectacular scenic effects at the Bowery Theater in New York.

Music

By the Margin of Fair Zurich's Waters; Lily Dale; The Rock Beside the Sea; Swiss Song; Thou Art Gone from My Gaze; Do They Miss Me at Home?; Thoughts That Have for Years Been Sleeping.

1853

*F*ranklin Pierce, Democrat, of New Hampshire, was inaugurated as the 14th President.

Boundary disputes again arose between the United States and Mexico—this time over the lands acquired by the Guadalupe Hidalgo Treaty (1848) affecting present-day southern Arizona and southwestern New Mexico. James Gadsden, United States minister to Mexico, negotiated for $10,000,000 the purchase of an additional 45,000 square miles to settle the question permanently.

Commodore Matthew Calbraith Perry, United States Navy, brother of Oliver Hazard Perry, hero of the Battle of Lake Erie (1813), arrived with a squadron in Yokohama harbor, Japan. He was formally received (July 14) by the Lord of Toda on Kurikama Beach. The deliberations resulted in a treaty (ratified by Congress Mar. 8, 1854) that opened Japanese ports to American commercial interests.

Stamped envelopes were placed (June) on sale by the Government.

The Know-Nothing movement in New York (1850) was steadily gaining in momentum and causing riots. It was mainly directed against Irish and German Roman Catholics. To check "the power of the Pope," it started to put Bibles in public schools.

The New York Clearing House was established (Oct. 11).

The Crystal Palace, New York, on the present site of the New York Public Library and Bryant Park, was opened (July 14). It was patterned on its elaborate London namesake (1851) which had been "composed of glass, supported by iron," with a dome 148 feet high and "covered five acres."

The steamer *San Francisco*, bound for California and carrying 700 passengers, including 500 members of the Third Regular U.S. Artillery, foundered (Dec. 24) at sea with a loss of 240 lives.

A. J. Watt of Utica, N.Y., introduced an improved method of filling teeth with gold.

A large 1,413-ton packet was launched at Newburyport, Mass. It was called *Dreadnought*, a name that was to be applied years hence to a powerful type of warship.

Some 50 librarians gathered (Sept. 15-17) in New York at their first U.S. convention.

Heinrich Engelhard Steinweg from Germany established (Mar. 5) the present firm of Steinway & Sons in New York for the manufacture of improved square pianos.

A gelding named "Conqueror" ran 100 miles in 8 hours, 55 minutes, 53 seconds, thus winning a $3,000 to $1,000 wager that the stretch couldn't be traversed in nine hours, over the Union Course, Long Island, N.Y.

Clark Mills, self-taught sculptor, created what is believed to be the first equestrian statue in the United States—General Jackson on a rearing horse. His original payment was $12,000, but Congress voted an additional $20,000 in appreciation. The statue was cast from captured British cannon and unveiled in Washington, D.C. (He erected there in 1860 a similar statue of Washington, and cast in 1863 the statue of Freedom which adorns the Capitol.)

Hénri Franconi's newly erected Hippodrome in New York, seating 4,000 opened (May 2) with a new type of amusement. It presented chariot races, aerial equilibrists thirty feet in the air, stag hunts, etc.—all at a price scale of 25 cents to one dollar. A competitor was the Washington Circus that opened (June 15) opposite the Crystal Palace.

The world of feminine fashion avidly copied Empress Eugenie styles after Eugenie became Louis Napoleon's wife and empress.

In Print

The *New York Clipper* was founded in New York as a weekly theatrical journal. (It ceased publication in 1924.)

In answer to the attacks on the plausibility of the story in her novel, Harriet Beecher Stowe published *A Key to Uncle Tom's Cabin*.

On Stage

Pauline, a romantic and long-popular play imported from London and produced (Mar. 7) in New York at Wallack's Lyceum, brought to the stage a new character—the gentleman "crook."

After a mild reception in New York (1851), Lola Montez went to California where she added another chapter to her strange career. She acted (May 26) Lady Teazle in *The School for Scandal* at the American Theater in San Francisco, electrified her audience the next night with her naughty Spider Dance, married a local newspaperman, Patrick Purdy Hall, moved on to Sacramento, challenged there the editor of the *Daily Californian* to a duel either with pistols or with pills (one to be poison—"Pistols or poison" becoming a catch phrase of the time) and retired for two idyllic years to a remote cottage in the mountains of Grass Valley. She had been particularly effective in a dramatic sketch of her life, *Lola Montez in Bavaria*.

Music

My Old Kentucky Home; Good Night and *Old Dog Tray* (Stephen C. Foster); *Haydn's Ox Minuet; The Hazel Dell*.

1854

$\mathscr{C}$ongress passed the Kansas-Nebraska Bill, which opened the territories to slavery on the principle of "squatter sovereignty," i.e., local choice of government. The bill was championed by Stephen Douglas, Vermont-born Democrat of Illinois.

In response to this and other pro-slavery developments, the present Republican Party was organized (July 6) in Ripon, Wis. It evolved as an antislavery party from the dwindling Whig Party and several minor groups. In the national election its first candidate, John Charles Fremont, was defeated (1856) in a stormy campaign.

The United States signed trade agreements with Japan (Mar. 8) and with Great Britain (June 27), the latter regulating commercial relations with Canada.

The Emigrant Aid Society was formed to settle antislavery New Englanders in Kansas. (Some 2,000 went into the territory.)

In less than six years about $300,000 had been raised by public subscriptions toward the erection of the Washington National Monument in Washington, D.C. The contributions now suddenly ceased when a marble block from the Temple of Concord in Rome, presented by Pope Pius IX, disappeared. For nearly a quarter of a century (until 1878) work on the shaft, which had reached a height of 154 feet, was interrupted.

Walter Hunt, who invented the safety pin, now invented the paper collar.

John Mercer Langston, an African American emancipated from slavery in 1833, was admitted to the Ohio bar.

American marine disasters on the Atlantic took a huge toll of lives: 311 were lost on the *Powhatan*, grounded (Apr. 16) off Long Beach, N.Y.; 300 on the *New Era*, wrecked (Nov. 13) below Sandy Hook, N.J.; the United States war sloop *Albany*, sailing (Sept. 29) from Panama disappeared completely. Smaller fatalities occurred elsewhere in United States waters.

P. T. Barnum took his circus troupe on a tour of Europe.

The hoopskirt, a creation supported by steel wires and tape, was the latest in feminine wardrobes.

In Print
The *Chicago Times* was founded as a daily newspaper.

Henry David Thoreau, Concord-born writer of Scottish, Quaker, and Puritan descent, published *Walden*, an account of his experiences while living from July 4, 1845 to Sept. 6, 1847 in a hut at Walden Pond near Concord.

Massachusetts author Maria Suşanna Cummins won national fame with her novel, *The Lamplighter*, a moralistic romance of a Boston orphan girl befriended by a lamplighter.

Timothy Shay Arthur published his melodramatic temperance novel *Ten Nights in a Barroom and What I Saw There*. (The book was dramatized by William W. Pratt in 1858.)

On Stage

The popular Harrison-Pyne Troupe of English singers gave opera in English in New York and elsewhere for the next three years. Their repertory included *La Sonnambula, Maritana, Fra Diavolo, The Crown Diamonds, The Bohemian Girl,* and *Cinderella.*

The Academy of Music in New York, the city's temple of opera for the next 30 years, succeeding the Astor Place Opera House (1847), opened (Oct. 2) with Bellini's *Norma* sung by Giulia Grisi and Giuseppe Mario and conducted by the eminent Luigi Arditi. The building cost $335,000.

After an inauspicious start in *Camille, or The Fate of Coquette* (Broadway theater, New York, Dec. 9, 1853) that apparently failed because of the questionable morality of its story, actress Jean Margaret Davenport returned (Aug. 28) to the same theater in the play and scored a hit with her superb portrayal of Dumas's heroine—the first in a long line of famous Camilles.

Shakespeare's comedy *A Midsummer Night's Dream* was played with Mendelssohn's music at two New York theaters, opening almost simultaneously— at Burton's (Feb. 3) and at the Broadway (Feb. 6).

The old Bowery Amphitheater in New York reopened (Aug.) as German-language playhouse, the Stadt Theater. For the next ten years the theater hosted opera, operetta, drama, comedy, and farce, either imported from Germany or of local origin.

Music

Jeannie with the Light Brown Hair (Stephen C. Foster); *What Is Home Without a Mother?; Ellen Bayne; Hard Times Come Again No More; There's Music in the Air; Willie, We Have Missed You.*

1855

$\mathcal{T}$he first section of the Atlantic cable was laid between Cape Breton, N.S., and Newfoundland by the New York, Newfoundland and London Telegraph Company, which was organized (May 8, 1854) by Cyrus West Field and Peter Cooper.

The Western Union Telegraph Company was founded. One of its directors was Ezra Cornell, later founder of Cornell University (1865).

The Know-Nothing political party claimed 1,500,000 voters.

The Knights of the Golden Circle was founded as a secret organization in the Southern States to aid the cause of slavery. (It was also known as the Order of American Knights; and its membership included "copperheads" or Northern sympathizers with the South.)

James Oliver of Indiana invented the iron plow.

Henry Bessemer, British engineer, patented (Oct. 17) his steel-making process—a great boon to the industry.

The American, Charles Goodyear Jr., patented in England the process of making dental plates of hard rubber.

The locomotive *Hamilton Davis*, coupled to six cars, made 14 miles in 11 minutes on the New York & Hudson River (now New York Central) tracks.

Steinway & Sons (1853) won first prize at the New York Industrial Exhibition for its square pianos.

The suspension bridge at Niagara Falls, connecting the United States and Canada, was completed.

The first bridge to span the Mississippi was built from Rock Island, Il., to Davenport, Iowa. Two weeks after its completion, a 250-foot span collapsed when the steamer *Effie Afton* collided with one of the piers of the bridge. In the ensuing litigation Abraham Lincoln was among the counsel representing the Rock Island railroad. The opposing counsel was the eloquent river-lawyer, Judge Wead, whose final address to the jury occupied nearly two hours. Lincoln's summation took little more than a minute; he won the case.

Lucy Stone married Dr. Henry B. Blackwell and kept her maiden name after marriage (hence "Lucy Stoners," a synonym for feminine independence as well as social reform).

In Print
Washington Irving coined the expression "the Almighty Dollar" in his book of stories and sketches, *"Wolfert's Roost and Miscellanies,"* originally published in *The Knickerbocker Magazine.*

Walt Whitman issued the first edition of his *Leaves of Grass*, containing 12 poems.

The brothers Evert Augustus and George Long Duychinck published the *Cyclopedia of American Literature* (completed in 1866). Other books of the year included the two standard reference books: *Age of Fable* (Thomas Bulfinch) and *Famous Quotations* (John Bartlett).

On Stage
Norwegian violinist, Ole Bull, took over the operatic management of the Academy of Music in New York. He announced a prize of $1,000 for "a grand opera by an American composer on an American subject." The company's singers attacked the impresario in the newspapers and the undertaking was a fiasco.

Verdi's operas *Rigoletto* and *Il Trovatore* received their United States premieres in New York at the Academy of Music (Feb. 19 and May 2, respectively).

Whether or not Ole Bull's prize was an incentive, an American opera by a native composer was forthcoming. It was George Frederick Bristow's *Rip Van Winkle.* The opera was produced (Sept. 27) in New York at Niblo's Garden, and it fared better than Fry's *Leonora* had in 1845.

The New York Philharmonic Orchestra played (Apr. 21) the first American performance of the great overture to Wagner's opera *Tannhauser.* Said the critic in the *Albion* (Apr. 28) " ...it bears the imprint of great, very great talent, united to but little genius."

Wallack's Theater in New York produced (Dec. 24) John Brougham's hilarious burlesque *Po-co-han-tas, or Ye Gentle Savage*, which amused audiences for years.

English actress Laura Keene became the first theatrical manager in the United States when she reopened (Dec. 27) the Metropolitan Theater in New York as Laura Keen's Varieties.

Music
Hark! the Herald Angels Sing (words by Charles Wesley, music, Felix Mendelssohn); *Listen to the Mocking Bird; The Sword of Bunker Hill; Twinkling Starts Are Laughing; Come, Where My Love Lies Dreaming; Rosalie, the Prairie Flower.*

1856

*J*ohn Brown, abolitionist leader, massacred five proslavery adherents in Osawatomie, Kan. In Kansas, proslavery supporters sacked the town of Lawrence.

Henry Ward Beecher, an ardent supporter of the antislavery cause, held (June 1) a public "auction" of a young mulatto named Sarah to dramatize the evils of slavery. The mock auction raised sufficient funds to purchase her freedom and buy her a modest house in Peekskill, N.Y.

Cyrus Roberts of Illinois dramatically improved the Hiram and John Pitts reaper (1837); his design became a forerunner of the modern version.

With about 50 followers, William Walker landed (1855) in Nicaragua, proclaimed (1856) himself president, and attempted to establish a slaveholding state. He was recognized by President Pierce. (The scheme collapsed in 1857 when Walker opposed Cornelius Vanderbilt's mercantile interests there. Walker renewed the attempt in 1860, but was captured and executed by the Honduran government.)

At the Republican state convention in Illinois, Abraham Lincoln became a political personality of national significance.

In the national elections, the newly organized Republican Party ran its first presidential candidate—John Charles Fremont. His opponents were Millard Fillmore, Whig, supported by the American (or Know-Nothing) party, and James Buchanan, Democrat, a former Federalist. The Republican nominee polled 1,391,555 votes. Buchanan won the election by 536,440 votes.

In Print

So popular was Longfellow's new poem *Hiawatha* that public readings were given in eastern cities. It was ridiculed in a funny burlesque by Charles Melton Walcot, entitled *Hiawatha, or Ardent Spirits and Laughing Waters*, which was produced (Dec. 15) in New York at Wallack's Theaters.

Dred, A Tale of the Great Dismal Swamp was Harriet Beecher Stowe's second antislavery novel. Three dramatizations immediately appeared in New York theaters: by C. W. Taylor at the Nation (Sept. 22), by John Brougham at the Bowery (Sept. 29), and by H. J. Conway at Barnum's American Museum (Oct. 16) with the midget General Tom Thumb playing a character not in Mrs. Stowe's book.

John Greenleaf Whittier published his classic of New England childhood, *The Barefoot Boy*, in his collection of verse *The Panorama and Other Poems*. Other books of the year included *The Rise of the Dutch Republic* (John Lothrop Motley) and the fiction, *Prue and I* (George William Curtis) and *The Quadroon* (Thomas Mayne Reid.) The Reid book provided Dion Boucicault with material for his successful play *The Octoroon*, 1859.

On Stage

Verdi's opera *La Traviata* received (Dec. 3) its American premiere in New York at the Academy of Music with the French coloratura Mme. Anna de La Grange and Luigi Brignoli.

Tom Maguire, who had entered the theatrical business in San Francisco in 1850, remodeled the San Francisco Hall. It opened (Nov.) as Maguire's Opera House.

Music

The Arrow and the Song (words by Henry Wadsworth Longfellow); *The Cottage by the Sea; Gentle Annie; The Last Hope; Old Friends and Old Times; Root, Hog, or Die; Stars of the Summer Night.*

1857

*J*ames Buchanan, Democrat, of Pennsylvania, was inaugurated as the 15th President. He was a bachelor; his niece Harriet Lane, daughter of his sister Jane, was the White House hostess.

Chief Justice of the U.S. Supreme Court Roger Brooke Taney delivered (Mar. 6) the momentous Dred Scott decision, 5 to 3, which stated that "Negroes were not citizens," even when they moved into free states, and could not claim any constitutional rights. The case concerned the slave Dred Scott who had been taken to Illinois and Wisconsin territory and who claimed freedom under the Missouri Compromise (1820). There were five Southern judges on the Court.

With the newly organized Atlantic Telegraph Company (formed in 1856), Cyrus West Field began (Aug. 5) the laying of the Atlantic cable between Europe and North America from Ireland. The cable broke 400 miles from the Irish coast.

A wagon train of 120 emigrants was massacred (Sept. 16) in Mountain Meadows, Utah, by a band of Indians alleged to have been abetted by Mormons.

Mardi Gras was first observed in New Orleans.

Philadelphia installed horse-drawn street cars. (They were in operation in New York since 1831.)

A hand-operated fire-extinguishing apparatus, built by Abel Shawk in Cincinnati, shot a 272-foot stream of water.

Elisha Mitchell, state surveyor of North Carolina, was killed (June 27) in a fall from a precipice during a storm while making observations on the highest mountain east of the Rockies. Mt. Mitchell was later named for him and he was buried on its summit.

Paul Morphy, American chess player, won in New York the first chess tournament held in the United States. To make one move, his opponent Louis Paulsen took 14 hours, 28 minutes.

Baseball was raised to the status of a national sport at a convention of delegates from 25 clubs held in New York.

After 12 years of prosperity, largely due to California gold, the United States entered it twelfth depression since 1790. It was particularly felt in the industrial North.

In Print

The Atlantic Monthly was founded in Boston under the editorship of James Russell Lowell and named by Oliver Wendell Holmes.

New England novelist Delia Salter Bacon aroused Shakespeareans with her book *Philosophy of the Plays of Shakespeare Unfolded.* In it she sought to prove that the Bard's plays were written by Bacon, Raleigh, and Spenser, and that they concealed a system of philosophy in cipher code.

Charles Farrar Browne began the publication of *Artemus Ward's Sayings* in the *Cleveland Plain Dealer.*

Republicans and abolitionists distributed *The Impending Crisis of the South: How to Meet It,* by Hinton Rowan Helper. The book, unpopular in the South, emphasized free labor from the economic viewpoint and not in the interests of the slaves. The author was a native of North Carolina.

"Flora M'Flimsey, of Madison Square," New York, spent six weeks shopping in Paris and despite her many purchases had "nothing to wear." The story of her adventures was told anonymously in *Harper's Weekly* in a satirical poem that was copied, imitated, and parodied in both the United States and England. There were several claimants to its authorship. The author was a New York lawyer, William Allen Butler; the title of the poem, *Nothing to Wear.*

On Stage

The economic depression was reflected in the box office receipts at the theaters. According to the *New York Herald* (Nov. 3), fourteen of the city's places of amusement, capable of seating a total of 16,747 persons, took in only $5,910 for one night's business. The receipts at the six largest theaters were Bowery, 2,580 seats, $480; Christy and Woods, 2,000 seats, $500; Broadway, 2,000 seats, $800; Niblo's Garden, 1,800 seats, $650; Burton's, 1,700 seats, $800. The Academy of Music, seating 1,500, fared best with $1,200; Rossini's opera *Semiramide* was sung there with Mme. Elena D'Angri making her American debut.

Philadelphia's opera house, the Academy of Music, opened (Feb. 25) with Verdi's *Il Trovatore.*

John V. McVicker, a popular actor, built, at a cost of $85,000, Chicago's third theater and named it after himself.

Music

Jingle Bells, or, *The One Horse Open Sleigh; Come into the Garden; Maud; Little White Cottage; Lorena; Mrs. Lofty and I; My Grandma's Advice.*

1858

$\mathcal{M}$innesota was admitted (May 11) as the 32nd state.

Cyrus West Field finally laid the Atlantic cable with the help of the British and United States governments. The U.S. Navy's *Niagara*, and the Royal Navy's *Agamemnon*, met (June) in midocean and, after splicing the cable, sailed with the ends in opposite directions, the former to Newfoundland and the latter to Valentia Harbor, Ireland. Although the cable broke three times, communication was established. President Buchanan and Queen Victoria exchanged (Aug. 5) feebly heard messages. The cable went "dead" soon afterward as a result of high voltage.

The first overland mail began (Sept. 16) between St. Louis, Mo., and San Francisco.

Gold was discovered in Colorado.

New York Senator William Henry Seward, Whig governor from 1839 to 1842, (and later Lincoln's Secretary of State) delivered (Oct.) a demagogic speech in which he declared that the slavery question was an "irrepressible conflict between North and South."

"A house divided against itself cannot stand" was the keynote of a convention speech in an Illinois senatorial race that pitted Republican nominee Abraham Lincoln against a mighty Democratic opponent—Stephen Arnold Douglas, known as the "Little Giant" because of his small stature and powerful personality. Douglas was twice a candidate for the presidency. In seven famous debates during the campaign, Douglas upheld the principle of "popular sovereignty." Less oratorical and more realistic, Lincoln analyzed the political issues with his already characteristic terseness and insight. In the election, however, Douglas defeated Lincoln.

Fire destroyed (Oct. 5) the Crystal Palace (1853) in New York.

The remains of the fifth President, James Monroe were removed from their resting place in New York, where he had died in 1831, and interred in Richmond, Va.

The cornerstone of the new St. Patrick's Cathedral (Roman Catholic) in New York was laid (Aug. 5); the ground was bought in 1852 for $59,500.

At the suggestion of Napoleon III of France, an international gift of $80,000 was presented to Samuel Morse for his invention of the telegraph.

In Print

Boston became the "Hub of the Universe" when Oliver Wendell Holmes published a volume of imaginary boarding-house table-talk under the title *The Autocrat of the Breakfast-Table*. In it occurs the line: "Boston State-House is the hub of the solar system." The book also contained the poem *The Chambered Nautilus*.

Henry Wadsworth Longfellow was the nation's leading poet and best seller. *The Courtship of Miles Standish* followed *Hiawatha* and sold 15,000 copies on the day of its simultaneous appearance in Boston and London.

On Stage

At the Academy of Music, New York, the great Italian soprano Maria Piccolomini made (Oct. 20) her American debut in the opera composed expressly for her—Verdi's *La Traviata*. The public "literally botanized (her) with bouquets." The critics praised her acting, but found much fault with her singing.

American theater audiences were introduced to the play which came to be associated with Lincoln's assassination in 1865—Tom Taylor's London hit *Our American Cousin*. The comedy was staged (Oct. 18) in New York at Laura Keene's Theater with the inimitable comedian Joseph Jefferson. It ran for 149 performances.

Music

Wedding March (Felix Mendelssohn); *Bonny Eloise—The Belle of Mohawk Vale; Christmas Song; A Maiden's Prayer; Thou Art So Near and Yet So Far; Warblings at Eve.*

1859

$\mathcal{O}$regon was admitted (Feb. 14) as the 33rd state; gold was also discovered there.

The Territory of Jefferson was established by local vote in what is now the state of Colorado.

With the intention of inciting a slave insurrection in Virginia, abolitionist John Brown led (Oct. 16) a raid on the United States arsenal at Harpers Ferry at the junction of the Shenandoah and Potomac rivers in the northwestern part of the state. Five men were killed. Brown and 21 followers were captured by Col. Robert E. Lee. Brown was tried and hanged (Dec. 2). His dignified bearing during the trial won him admiration as a martyr. In his defense, Henry David Thoreau, who met Brown in 1857 at Emerson's home in Concord, delivered three lectures, "A Plea for Captain John Brown," "The Last Days of John Brown," and "After the Death of John Brown." Brown was also the subject of a popular song, *John Brown's Body* (1861).

The first oil well in the United States was opened (Aug. 28) in Titusville, Pa., by Col. Edward L. Drake.

The celebrated gold and silver lode on the present site of Virginia City, Nev., was discovered (June 11) by H. T. P. Comstock; it came to be known as the Comstock Lode.

Chicago introduced (Apr. 25) its first horse-drawn streetcars.

Cooper Institute was founded in New York City by Peter Cooper, New York inventor, financier, economist, and philanthropist, for the purpose of "giving instruction in branches of knowledge by which men and women earn their daily bread." (The Institute now is called Cooper Union.)

Charles Blondin, a 55-year-old French acrobat known as "The Little Wonder," whose real name was Jean Francois Gravelet, performed daredevil feats over Niagara Falls. He crossed (June 30) on a tightrope in five minutes, then repeated (July 4) the stunt blindfolded, pushing a wheelbarrow, and carrying (Aug. 19) a man on his back. (On Sept. 14, 1860, he walked a tightrope on stilts in the presence of the Prince of Wales.)

Young ladies went about with beaver hats trimmed with ostrich feathers.

The potato beetle was recognized as a new agricultural pest.

Washington Irving, age 76, died (Nov. 28) in Tarrytown, N.Y.

On Stage

Dion Boucicault appeared (Dec. 5) in New York at the Winter Garden with sensational success in his play *The Octoroon, or Life in Louisiana*, based on Mayne Reid's popular novel *The Quadroon* (1856).

In New Orleans, the new French Opera House was completed in five months. Construction was carried on day and night by special permission. The house opened (Dec. 1) with Rossini's *William Tell*.

Music

Ave Maria (Adapted from the First Prelude in J. S. Bach's *The Well-Tempered Clavier*); *Nearer My God, to Thee*; *Bethany*; *Viva l'America: Home of the Free*; *In the Louisiana Lowlands*.

1860

$\mathcal{T}$he first pony express was established (Apr. 3) between St. Joseph, Mo., and Sacramento, Ca., a distance of 1,980 miles. There were 80 riders and 420 horses which were changed every 10 miles at 190 relay stations. (The service was discontinued in 1861.)

The Prince of Wales (later Edward VII) visited the United States.

Elizabeth Palmer Peabody, sister-in-law of Hawthorne and Horace Mann, established the first kindergarten in her home in Boston.

The cabinet organ, long popular in American homes and rural churches, was perfected about this time by the Boston firm Mason & Hamlin.

J. Fitzpatrick and James O'Neil fought the longest bare-knuckle prize-fight in American ring annals—4 hours, 20 minutes—in Berwick, Maine.

The hoopskirt, or crinoline, grew so expansive in perimeter that newspapers were full of stories of accidents caused by the skirts catching fire.

Men started to wear knickers for sports.

The waterfall hairdress—made over a frame of horsehair— was a vogue that lasted until about 1870.

In the national election, the problem of slavery was an acute issue. The antislavery Republican Party nominated as its candidate Abraham Lincoln. The Democratic Party split over the question: the antislavery North chose Stephen Arnold Douglas; the proslavery South selected John C. Breckinridge. The Constitutional Union Party (Whig and Know-Nothing) ran John Bell. Lincoln and Douglas emphasized the preservation of the Union; Breckinridge and Bell supported secession. The Civil War was in the making. At the polls, Lincoln finished first, receiving only 40 percent of the popular vote, and winning the electoral vote, 180 to 123.

The South girded itself for secession. A last-minute effort to prevent secession was made (Dec.) in Congress by John Jordan Crittenden, Kentucky senator and former attorney-general, who proposed five resolutions that were in effect a modified Missouri Compromise. They were disapproved in a Senate committee. South Carolina, a powerful slaveholding state, then seceded (Dec. 20) from the Union—the first direct step toward the Civil War.

The national population had grown to 31,443,321, of which about 4,000,000 were slaves (Virginia had the most slaves, with 491,000).

In Print

Ann Sophia Stephen's paper-covered thriller *Malaeska, the Indian Wife of a White Hunter* started the vogue of the dime novel. It was advertised as "a dollar book for a dime," and started Erastus Beadle on his 30-odd-year career as a publisher of sensational fiction about frontiersmen, Indians, train robbers, desperados, and detectives.

Nathaniel Hawthorne published the romance *The Marble Faun*.

On Stage

Kate Josephine Bateman, already known as a juvenile actress, began (Mar. 19) her adult career in New York at the Winter Garden in her mother's dramatization of *Evangeline*. She was supported by a cast that included the popular Joseph Jefferson. Jefferson began (Dec. 24) at the same theater his lifelong impersonation of the title role of *Rip Van Winkle*.

Dion Boucicault's London Adelphi Theater success, *The Colleen Bawn, or The Brides of Garryowen*, was a hit at its New York premiere (Mar. 29) in Laura Keene's Theater. The company, which took the play on tour with John Drew, was among the earliest to perform on the road a single show instead of repertory.

Music

I Wish I Was in Dixie's Land; *Old Black Joe* (Stephen C. Foster); *The Glendy Burk*; *My Trundle Bed, or Recollections of Childhood*; *Rock Me to Sleep*; *Mother*; *Sweet Spirit, Hear My Prayer (Lurline)*; *'Tis But a Little Faded Flower*; *When the Corn is Waving*; *Annie Dear*.

1861

*A*braham Lincoln, Republican, of Kentucky, was inaugurated as the 16th President. A plot to assassinate Lincoln as he passed on his way through Baltimore to his inaugural was uncovered by Pinkerton detectives.

Kansas was admitted (Jan. 29) as the 34th state.

Following the lead of South Carolina, six other Southern state seceded from the Union in rapid succession—Mississippi (Jan. 9), Florida (Jan. 10), Alabama (Jan. 11), Georgia (Jan. 19), and Texas (Feb. 1). Representatives of the seven states met (Feb. 4-9) in Montgomery, Ala., and formed the "Confederate States of America."

Confederate General Peter Beauregard attacked (Apr. 12) Fort Sumter in the harbor of Charleston, S.C., starting the Civil War. The fort surrendered two days later (Apr. 14). On Apr. 15 President Lincoln issued a call for 75,000 volunteers and offered the Union command to Robert Edward Lee of Virginia. Lee declined. When his home state of Virginia seceded (Apr. 17), he resigned (Apr. 20) his commission in the U.S. Army and became commander of the Virginia troops in the Confederate army. The eight Confederate States now were joined by Arkansas (May 6), North Carolina (May 21), and Tennessee (June 8). The invading Union army was routed (July 21) at Bull Run, 30 miles southwest of Washington, D.C., by Confederate General Thomas Jonathan Jackson who, it was said, checked the Northern forces like a "stone wall," and earned his nickname. In the October Confederate elections, Jefferson Davis, former Senator from Mississippi and former Secretary of War, was elected President of the Confederate States by popular vote. (He was inaugurated Feb. 22, 1862, at Richmond, Va., which became the capital of the Confederate States.)

In consequence of the war, the United States issued (Aug. 17) new postage stamps to replace the series of 1847 and 1851-60. (The new issues remained in use until Feb. 27, 1869.) The Confederate States also issued stamps for letter postage—a 5-cent green and a 10-cent blue.

Richard Jordan Gatling, American inventor, perfected a rapid-firing gun called the Gatling gun, a forerunner of the machine gun. The new weapon discharged 350 rounds per minute.

The Colorado Territory was established by Congress in what is now the state of Colorado, thus dissolving the Territory of Jefferson (see 1859).

Transcontinental telegraph service was established (Oct. 24).

There were now 31,799 miles of railroad in the United States, and the Erie and the New York Central began to rival the Erie Canal in freight tonnage.

Vassar College for women, Poughkeepsie, N.Y. was founded.

Henry Wadsworth Longfellow's second wife was burned to death (July 9) in her home at Cambridge, Mass., when her light summer dress caught fire from a wax paper while she was sealing a letter.

John LaFarge, New York painter, began to attract attention in the art world with a painting of St. John.

The thirteenth United States depression since 1790 set in. It lasted a year, until war prosperity ended it.

Music

Glory, Glory, Hallelujah; Maryland! My Maryland!; Alice Where Art Thou?; Aura Lee; Balm of Gilead; The Bridge; Holy, Holy, Holy!; Lord God Almighty; Jerusalem the Golden; John Brown's Body; The Vacant Chair, or We Shall Meet but We Shall Miss Him.

1862

$\mathcal{T}$he Civil War continued.

The first congress of the Confederate States convened (Feb. 18) in Richmond, Va. Ulysses Simpson Grant won the first encouraging Union victories when he captured Fort Henry (Feb. 6) on the Tennessee River and Fort Donelson (Feb. 16) on the Cumberland River, held the enemy at Shiloh (Apr. 6-7), and defeated the Confederate army at Corinth (Oct. 4) in northern Mississippi. (After the fall of Fort Donelson, he was nicknamed "Unconditional Surrender" Grant because of his terms of surrender to the fort.)

A "cheese box on a raft," constructed by Swedish engineer John Ericsson and a reconditioned frigate made history in a naval engagement (Mar. 9) at Hampton Roads, Chesapeake Bay, Va. They were the ironclads *Monitor* (Union) and *Merrimac* (Confederate, renamed *Virginia*). Congress abolished (Apr. 16) slavery in the District of Columbia. Admiral David Glasgow Farragut captured (Apr. 25) New Orleans with the Union fleet. President Lincoln read (July 22) to his Cabinet the first draft of the Emancipation Proclamation. Robert Edward Lee began (Sept. 5) an invasion of Maryland with the Confederate army and met (Sept. 17) the Union forces at Antietam Creek in a bitter and indecisive battle.

President Lincoln placed Clara Barton, later founder of the American Red Cross, in charge of the search for missing soldiers and the identification of unknown soldiers' graves.

Congress passed the Homestead Act, giving public lands in the West in parcels of 160 acres, free, to all adult citizens and all aliens filing declaratory papers.

Chicago surpassed Cincinnati as the nation's meat center.

John Davison Rockefeller, aged 23, became a partner in an oil refinery in Cleveland.

Treasury notes, or "greenbacks" (so-called because they were printed with green ink), were issued as a war measure for legal tender.

The Wheeling Bridge, in Wheeling, W. Va, spanning the Ohio River, was completed.

At Barnum's American Museum in New York, along with the showing of a living whale and hippopotamus, such specialties were offered as the Connecticut Giantess, "the Handsomest Fat Girl and largest mountain of human flesh ever seen," 18 years old and weighing 618 pounds, as well as one Lizzie

Harris, 676 pounds. By way of contrast, Barnum featured the tiny midgets General Tom Thumb, Commodore Nutt (even smaller that the "General" and to whom he allegedly paid $30,000), and the sisters Lavinia and Minnie Warren. Lavinia was first exhibited, "undoubtedly the smallest woman alive," and was said to be 21 years old, 32 inches in height, and 30 pounds in weight. When Minnie joined the cast, she was found to be even smaller than her sister, being 25 inches in height, and 30 pounds in weight. Lavinia married Tom Thumb in Grace Church on Feb. 10 with Minnie and "Commodore" as bridesmaid and best man.

A Russian naval training ship on a world cruise (1862-65) stopped in New York Harbor. Among the cadets was an 18-year-old, the future composer Nicolai Rimsky-Korsakov, who visited Niagara Falls with his fellow students.

John Tyler, the tenth President, died (Jan. 18). Captain Nathanial Gordon, last pirate to be hanged in U.S., died (Mar. 8). Martin Van Buren, eighth President, died (July 24).

On Stage

Mysterious and much-publicized American actress Adah Isaacs Menken (real name: Dolores Adios Fuertos) appeared (June 16) in New York at the New Bowery Theater in a daring performance, half-nude and strapped to a dashing steed—"a feat never before attempted by any woman"—in a melodrama *Mazeppa*. This started a craze throughout the country for that sort of exhibitionism, duplicated by Kate Fisher, Kate Vance, Kate Raymond, Mlle. Sanyeah, and others. The part also was played by men.

Boston witnessed (Apr. 7) at the Museum (a theater) the production of a comic opera that enjoyed a long popularity, was performed in Europe, and finally passed into the repertory of amateur troupes—*The Doctor of Alcantara* by Julius Eichberg.

Music

Battle Hymn of the Republic (words by Julia Ward Howe, written in 1861); tune: *Glory, Glory, Hallelujah*); *The Bonnie Blue Flag* (song of the Confederate States during the American Civil War); *Evangeline, We've a Million in the Field* (Stephen C. Foster); *Grafted into the Army; Killarney; Kingdom Coming, We Are Coming, Father Abraham; 300,000 More.*

1863

$\mathcal{T}$he Civil War continued into its third year with important battles at Chancellorsville, Va. (May 2-4), Gettysburg, Pa. (July 1-3), Vicksburg, Miss. (July 4), Chickamauga, Tenn. (Sept. 19-20), and Chattanooga, Tenn. (Nov. 23-25).

On New Year's Day, as announced in the previous September, President Lincoln issued the Emancipation Proclamation, in which he declared "free forever" the slaves in Alabama, Arkansas, Florida, Georgia, Louisiana (certain parts excepted), Mississippi, North Carolina, South Carolina, Texas, and Virginia. The proclamation freed about 3,120,000 slaves.

During the battle at Chancellorsville (May 2-4), "Stonewall" Jackson was accidentally shot by his own soldiers. He died shortly thereafter.

West Virginia was admitted (June 20) as the 35th state.

President Lincoln ordered conscription. Opposition to the measures in New York City, abetted by corrupt local politics, broke out (July 13-16) in violent "draft riots," in which about 1,000 persons were killed, including several African-Americans killed by lynching. Some 50 buildings were burned, and shops were looted. Troops from Pennsylvania and West Point finally quelled the mobsters.

The number of U.S. Supreme Court judges was raised from six to nine.

The United States issued (July 6) its first two-cent postage stamp—a black adhesive with a portrait of Andrew Jackson.

At the dedication (Nov. 19) of a national cemetery at Gettysburg, Pa., President Lincoln followed a two-hour speech by the principal orator, Edward Everett, with an address of three short paragraphs. The majority of the audience was not impressed, though Everett acknowledged the powerful words when he congratulated Lincoln. Today, the speech is known as the Gettysburg Address.

President Lincoln revived the observance of Thanksgiving Day (first proclaimed by Washington in 1789).

The steel age came into being when Lyman Holley and William Kelley, working independently, devised methods for converting iron into steel.

In Philadelphia, the American Wood Paper Company began to make paper from wood pulp. Previously it was made of rags and linen.

The bronze statue of Freedom, surmounting the dome of the Capitol, was placed (Dec. 2) in position. The statue weighs 14,985 pounds and was cast from a plaster model made in Rome by Thomas Crawford, father of the novelist Francis Marion Crawford.

In Print

Francis Lieber, German-born American political writer and educator, published *A Code for the Government of Armies*. It was reissued by the War Department as *General Order No. 100*, and is regarded as a standard work on military law.

Edward Everett Hale's classic novelette *The Man Without a Country* appeared in *The Atlantic Monthly*.

On Stage

East Lynne, a popular 1861 novel by the English author Mrs. Henry Wood won even greater success as a play. The story concerns a married woman who is turned out by her husband "never to darken the door again." It was one of the most popular melodramas ever written. No less than three versions were seen simultaneously in New York. Those who wanted to weep over the unjustly suspected wife went to see Matilda Heron in *Edith, or The Earl's Daughter*, adapted by Benjamin E. Woolff, at Niblo's Garden (Dec. 9, 1862), or Lucille Western in *East Lynne*, adapted by Clifton W. Tayleure, at the Winter Garden (Mar. 23, 1863); on the other hand, those who wanted to witness the heroics of the mistakenly injured husband attended the performance of *Edward Eddy*, in an adaptation by J. F. Poole, at the New Bowery Theater (Mar. 6, 1863). Lucille Western's version was first seen (Jan. 6, 1863) at the Brooklyn Academy of Music.

Edwin Booth played (Oct. 12) Victor Hugo's *Ruy Blas* at the Winter Garden, New York.

Gounod's French opera *Faust* was introduced (Nov. 18) to American opera lovers in Philadelphia at the Academy of Music. New York performances followed in the same year at the Academy of Music, first (Nov. 25) in Italian and then (Dec. 18) in German. (The first French rendition was heard in New Orleans, Nov. 20, 1866.)

Music

Babylon Is Fallen!; *The Battle Cry of Freedom*; *Three Kings of Orient*—better known as *We Three Kings of Orient Are*; *Daisy Deane*; *Folks That Put on Airs*; *Johnny Schmoker*; *Just Before the Battle, Mother*.

1864

$\mathcal{T}$he Civil War went into its fourth year.

Ulysses Simpson Grant was appointed (Mar. 12) commander of the Union armies.

William Tecumseh Sherman captured (Nov. 15) Atlanta, Ga., with the Union forces, burned the city after removing the civilian population, and started on his destructive "march to the sea" through Georgia, which ended (Dec. 21) with the fall of Savannah.

Nevada was admitted (Oct. 31) as the 36th state.

Secretary of the Treasury Salmon Portland Chase, at the suggestion of Reverend M. R. Watkinson, introduced the motto "In God We Trust" which has been inscribed on most United States coins since then. The strong religious sentiment during the Civil War inspired the motto, which appeared for the first time on the new bronze two-cent piece, coined in accordance with the Act of Apr. 22, 1864. The bronze Indian-head one-cent piece took the place of the similarly designed copper and nickel penny of 1859. The coin remained in use until it was superseded by the Lincoln-head piece of 1909.

George Mortimer Pullman began the construction of his railroad sleeping cars.

Arlington National Cemetery, Fort Myer, Va., opposite Washington, D.C., was established (June 15) on land that originally belonged to George Washington Parke Custis, adopted son of George Washington, and that was owned before the Civil War by Confederate General Robert Edward Lee.

The Knights of Pythias was founded in Washington, D.C., as a secret fraternal society.

Winslow Homer, Civil War staff artist of *Harper's Weekly*, attracted attention with his first important painting, *Prisoner from the Front*, exhibited in New York.

Deaths of the year included: Stephen Collins Foster, aged 38 (Jan. 13), Nathaniel Hawthorne, aged 60 (May 19), and Confederate raider John Hunt Morgan (Sept. 4).

The Austrian Archduke Ferdinand Maximilian Joseph was crowned (Dec. 6) Emperor of Mexico.

In Print

John Greenleaf Whittier published the poem *Barbara Frietchie* in his collection of verse *In War Time and Other Poems*.

On Stage

Humorist Artemus Ward was entertaining New Yorkers at Dodworth's Hall for consecutive weeks (Oct.-Dec.) with his lecture "Artemus Ward among the Mormons, a pictorial tour from Pier 3, North River, to Salt Lake City."

Music

All Quiet Along the Potomac Tonight; Der Deitcher's Dog—better known as *Where, O Where Has My Little Dog Gone?; When the War Is Over, Mary; Beautiful Dreamer; Take Back the Heart You Gave; Tenting On the Old Camp Ground; Tramp! Tramp! Tramp!; Work, for the Night Is Coming.*

1865

$\mathscr{P}$resident Abraham Lincoln began his second term.

The last shot of the Civil War was fired. Lee surrendered (Apr. 9) to Grant in Appomattox, Va. The death toll of the war was 524,509—359,528 Union and 164,981 Confederate soldiers.

Almost concurrently with the end of the war, President Lincoln was assassinated (Apr. 14) by actor John Wilkes Booth in Washington, D.C., at Ford's Theater during a performance of the comedy *Our American Cousin* (see 1858). Lincoln died the next day, and the nation went into mourning for the first martyred President.

The same day, crowds of people eager to avenge Lincoln's death stormed the lobby of Burnet House in Cincinnati in an attempt to seize the tragedian Junius Brutus Booth, a brother of the assassin. The actor was forced to remain hidden for several days until he could be smuggled out of town. Mass meetings were held to force the closing of theaters. In Boston, Cleveland, and Columbus, actors were hissed off the stage. In New York, a band of street boys pinned an actress against the fence of Trinity churchyard until she was rescued by a policeman and a naval officer.

The President's murderer, John Wilkes Booth, was shot (Apr. 26) by a soldier in a burning barn near Port Royal, Va. He was buried under the floor of a prison in Washington, D.C.; the remains were later returned to relatives and interred in Baltimore. Others involved in the plot were hanged or sentenced to prison.

Vice President Andrew Johnson, of Tennessee, a Democrat elected with Lincoln on the National Union ticket in 1864, was inaugurated (Apr. 15) as the 17th President. His daughter, Martha, wife of Judge D. T. Patterson, acted as White House hostess in place of her invalid mother.

President Johnson proclaimed (May 26) an amnesty to all Confederate States, conditional to their acceptance of the 13th Amendment then before Congress to abolish slavery.

Jefferson Davis, President of the Confederate States, was captured (May 10) in flight at Irwinville, Ga., a month after Lee's surrender. (Davis was confined for two years at Fort Monroe, Va., awaiting trial for treason. He was released on bail in May, 1867, and proceedings against him were dropped in February, 1869.)

The white-robed and hooded Ku Klux Klan was organized in the Southern states to uphold white supremacy, directed specifically against Black voters and "carpetbaggers" arriving from the North.

The 13th Amendment was ratified (Dec. 18).

The shield-bearing nickel five-cent piece came into circulation. (The coin remained in use until it was superseded by the Liberty head design of 1883.)

Thanksgiving Day was observed on Dec. 7—a week late because President Johnson had neglected to proclaim the day.

Cornell University for men and women, Ithaca, N.Y., was founded by Ezra Cornell, founder of the Western Union Telegraph Company.

New York City established a paid fire department to replace volunteers.

There were about 295,000 Indians in the United States. In 1492 there had been an estimated 850,000.

The Harvard Musical Association gave (Dec. 28) its first concert in Boston.

The baseball championship contest between the Brooklyn Atlantics and the Philadelphia Athletics attracted 30,000 spectators and so clogged the infield that the game was postponed after one inning. It was re-played three weeks later with $1 admission, drew 2,000 customers and 6,000 no-payees, and was called in the seventh inning on account of rain. The Athletics led, 31 to 12.

Post-war gaiety marked the social season. It is estimated that in New York alone 600 balls took place.

Mascara and the pork-pie hat came into vogue.

A postwar depression, lasting scarcely a year, broke out. It was the fourteenth since 1790.

Confederate soldier A. Bordunix, the last fatality of the Civil War, died (May 22).

In Print
Mark Twain gained sudden fame with his retelling of an old Californian folk tale, *The Celebrated Jumping Frog of Calaveras County*, which appeared in the *New York Sunday Press*.

On Stage
The $600,000 Crosby Opera House in Chicago opened (Apr. 20).

Vaudeville, called "variety" at this time, was attracting chiefly male audiences. In Paterson, N.J., Tony (Antonio) Pastor tried his hand at "legitimate" vaudeville and opened (Aug. 14) in New York the grandly named Opera House for family enjoyment.

Music
Ellie Rhee, or, Carry Me Back to Tennessee; The Little Brown Church; Marching Through Georgia; Nicodemus Johnson.

1866

$\mathscr{C}$ongress passed (Apr. 9) a Civil Rights act.

Armed bands of Irish sympathizers, numbering from 500 to some 1,500, began (Apr.) a movement to invade Canada and New Brunswick from Maine, Vermont, and New York. They seized Fort Erie (June 1) and St. Armand (June 7). United States troops under George Gordon Meade of Gettysburg fame put an end to the undertaking.

After 30 attempts Cyrus West Field, on the SS *Great Eastern*, succeeded in repairing the Atlantic cable, which had been damaged in 1858 and lost in 1865. Communication was re-established between Ireland and Newfoundland.

George Armstrong Custer, lieutenant-colonel of the 7th U. S. Cavalry, was sent to quell western Indian uprisings under Sitting Bull and Crazy Horse, Sioux chiefs.

Union leaders formed the National Labor Union, which lasted six years and was one of the first attempts at federating labor.

Civil War veterans of the Union army and navy formed the Grand Army of the Republic ("G.A.R.") to perpetuate the memory of fallen comrades and to aid their widows and dependents.

Christian Science was originated by Mary Baker Eddy.

The Young Women's Christian Association (Y.W.C.A.) was founded in Boston.

The American Society for the Prevention of Cruelty to Animals (A.S.P.C.A.) was organized in New York.

Fisk University, Nashville, Tenn., for Negro men and women, was founded.

Croquet was now such a popular game that the *Nation* printed a lengthy set of rules.

In Print

The *New York World* was founded as a penny daily religious newspaper. However, it soon abandoned its character in favor of a more worldly policy. (The paper was bought by Joseph Pulitzer in 1883 and merged in 1891 with the *New York Telegram*, becoming the *New York World-Telegram*.)

On Stage

Great excitement preceded the New York world premiere of the most spectacular, epoch-making melodrama yet seen on an American stage. It was *The Black Crook* by Charles M. Barras, its plot a hodgepodge of German romanticism derived from Weber's opera *Der Freischutz*, Goethe's *Faust*, and other kindred productions. The show opened (Sept. 12) at Niblo's Garden on a stage remodeled at the cost of $25,000, according to the *New York Times*. "It played by easy stages, from 7 o'clock until 1," involved the expenditure of $35,000 to $55,000, and ran until 1868 (Jan. 4)—474 performances in 16 months, the longest run up to that time of any play. While the public rhapsodized over its endless revelations, members of the clergy and a certain section of the press railed against the "immoral" production and its spirited ballet of 100 lightly clad legs devised by David Costa and danced in the leading roles by 15-year-old ballerinas Marie Bonfanti, Rita Sangalli, and Betty Rigl, who later became famous.

Music

We Parted by the River; When You and I Were Young, Maggie; Angel's Serenade; Beautiful Bird; Sing On; Waiting.

1867

"*S*eward's Folly," "Seward's Ice Box," "Icebergia," "Walrussia" were some of the epithets ridiculing the purchase of Alaska from Russia by Secretary of State William H. Seward and Senator Charles Sumner. The purchase price was $7,200,000 and it added 586,400 square miles (at two cents per acre) to United States territory. President Johnson signed the deal Mar. 30; it was ratified by Congress June 20; payment was made Aug. 1, and the transfer took place in New Archangel on the island of Sitka, Oct. 18. This date is now observed as holiday in Alaska.

Congress passed (Mar. 2 and Mar. 23), over the President's veto, the Reconstruction Act "to provide for a more efficient government of the rebel states" under military governors until the states were readmitted to Congress. In carrying out the laws, President Johnson came into conflict with Secretary of War Edwin McMasters Stanton, who opposed the President's conciliatory attitude toward the South. Johnson called for Stanton's resignation, which was refused, and thereupon (Aug. 12) suspended him. General Ulysses S. Grant was appointed as Acting Secretary and performed the functions of the office until the following January. There was agitation in the House of Representatives to impeach the President, but the move failed for the time to gain the necessary support.

In spite of the opposition of the Cabinet, President Johnson extended (Sept. 7) amnesty to all but a few Southern leaders and officials.

Nebraska was admitted (Mar. 1) as the 37th state.

The Pullman Palace Car Company was organized by George Mortimer Pullman and Ben Field for the construction of railroad sleeping cars (1864).

The first elevated railway opened (July 2) in New York, extending from the Battery to 30th Street; it was operated by a cable.

Three Milwaukee men, Carlos Glidden, Samuel Soule, and Christopher Sholes, the first a mechanic, the other two printers, devised the first practical typewriting machine. It could write only capital letters and could only print on tissue paper. (The invention was patented in June, 1868, and placed on the market in 1873.)

Stock tickers were installed, greatly facilitating speculation.

Charles Dickens made the second of his two visits to the United States (Nov. 1867-Apr. 1868), giving well-attended public readings from his works. (The first was in 1842.)

The Benevolent and Protective Order of Elks (B.P.O.E.) was founded for actors and literary men. (It is now a social charitable organization.)

Howard University for men and women, Washington, D.C., was founded by act of Congress. Primarily for Negro students, it was named in honor of General Oliver Otis Howard, head of the Freedman's Bureau (1865).

Baseball was rapidly becoming the national game. In 1867 the greatest contribution to that sport was made by William Arthur Cummings, Brooklyn pitcher, who perfected the curveball. Meanwhile, the National baseball club of Washington made a tour, beating the Columbus Capitals 90 to 10, the Cincinnati Red Stockings 53 to 10, the Indianapolis Western Club 106 to 21, and the St. Louis Union Club 113 to 26.

The Emperor Maximilian (1864) was executed (June 19) in Mexico.

Canada was raised (July 1) to the status of a Dominion.

In Print
Harper's Bazar was founded as a women's weekly magazine.

The first Horatio Alger stories for boys and Elsie books for girls appeared. Horatio Alger, Jr., chaplain of the Newsboys' Lodging House in New York, began the *Ragged Dick* series of success stories, while Martha Farquharson (Finley) brought out the first of the 28 tales (1867-1905) about *Elsie Dinsmore*. (Alger followed the Ragged Dick stories with the *Luck and Pluck*, 1869, and *Tattered Tom*, 1871, series.)

On Stage
Augustin Daly's 5-act melodrama *Under the Gaslight* was produced (Aug. 13) in New York at the Worrel Sisters' Theater. It introduced the episode of a man tied to railroad tracks before an onrushing express train. The fact that the machinery failed on the opening night added to the audience's excitement and assured the play's immediate popularity. (The play ran until Oct. 5, reached the San Francisco Minstrels, and was revived in 1868 and through the years.)

A tragic and disgraceful incident marred the New York Christmas theatrical season. Four well-known actor-managers, Sam Sharpley, his brother Thomas Sharpe, Leon, and Kelly, quarreled on the afternoon of Dec. 11 in front of the Fifth Avenue Theater. During the altercation, Kelly shot and killed Sharpe, and was himself severely wounded by Sharpley. Kelly was tried, but escaped penalty on a legal technicality. Although none of the wranglers was connected with the Fifth Avenue Theater, the brawl closed the famous house for more than a year.

Music
The Blue Danube (Johann Strauss); *Champagne Charley Was His Name*; and *Slave Songs of the United States*, S. Simpson & Co., 1867. This song book is probably the first published collection of Negro spirituals. According to the preface: "The greater part of the music...has been taken down by the editors from

the lips of the colored people themselves. The editors were William Francis Allen, Charles Pickard Ware, and Lucy McKim Garrison. The latter was particularly active in the field of Negro folk song. The song collection included *Roll, Jordan Roll* and *Nobody Knows the Trouble I've Had* [sic].

1868

*D*isagreement over Reconstruction policies in the South widened the breach between President Andrew Johnson and Congress, the radical elements of which favored the reduction of the former Confederate States to a "territorial condition" (words of abolitionist Thaddeus Stevens).

Congress refused (Jan. 13) to concur in the President's suspension of Secretary of War Edwin McMasters Stanton (1867), and Acting Secretary General Ulysses S. Grant resigned. Johnson ordered (Feb. 21) Stanton's removal, appointing in his stead as Secretary ad interim Adjutant-General Thomas who was placed (Feb. 22) under temporary arrest by Stanton. The President's actions were construed a violation of the Tenure of Office Act; and Congress voted his impeachment. The case occupied 32 days of actual trial (Mar. 23-May 26) before the Senate, and resulted in a verdict, 35 for conviction and 19 for acquittal. Conviction was lost for lack of a constitutional two-thirds majority; the Chief Justice therefore entered a verdict of acquittal.

Alabama, Arkansas, Florida, Georgia, Louisiana, North Carolina, and South Carolina were the first of the former Confederate States to be readmitted (June) to Congress. (The remaining four states were readmitted in 1870.)

The 14th Amendment, concerning citizenship, was ratified (July 28). The bells which were rung at its adoption inspired Whittier to write the poem *Laus Deo*!

President Johnson declared (Dec. 25) amnesty to all, without exception, who had taken a part in the late rebellion.

Congress authorized the formation of the Territories of Wyoming and Alaska, and prohibited the killing of fur seals "within the limit of Alaska territory or the waters thereof."

Major John Wesley Powell began surveys of the Grand Canyon and Colorado River.

Jay Gould and James ("Jim") Fisk were at the height of their financial power as dealers in railway securities.

George Westinghouse invented the air brake. A. M. Hills invented the lawn mower.

The University of California at Berkeley, for men and women, was established.

Hampton Normal and Agricultural Institute for Negro men and women was founded at Hampton, Va.

San Francisco suffered (Oct. 21) a severe earthquake. Other regions in California were also affected.

James Buchanan, 15th President, died (June 1).

In Print

The *Atlanta Constitution* was founded as a daily newspaper.

On Stage

George L. Fox's pantomime *Humpty Dumpty*, produced (Mar. 10) in New York at the Olympic Theater, was the dramatic hit of the year, running 483 performances—nine more than *The Black Crook* (1866)—and later going through periodic revivals. (Fox played his role 1,128 times.)

Public interest in pantomimes, however, began to decline because of the advent of "blondes" on the stage. Troupes of blond-haired women were the latest stage attraction in New York; in less than two years they bedazzled the country. The first troupe came from England—the Lydia Thompson burlesque company—(Sept. 28) at Wood's Theater in Francis Cowley Burnand's mythical Greek extravaganza *Ixion, or, The Man at the Wheel*. Lydia herself was described in the press as "a blonde of the purest type, saucy, blue-eyed, golden-haired and of elegant figure." Their appearance marked the beginning of what later became American "burlesque."

When American actress Adah Isaacs Menken failed to appear at a rehearsal in Paris, the management went to court. The officers of the law found that she had been dead for several days in her apartment. She was 33 years old.

Music

The Flying Trapeze; Her Bright Smile Haunts Me Still; Lullaby (Johannes Brahms); *O Little Town of Bethlehem; Tales From the Vienna Woods* (Johann Strauss); *Yield Not to Temptation; Captain Jinks of the Horse Marines; Little Footsteps; The Long Day Closes; St. Louis; Sweet By and By; Whispering Hope.*

1869

---

*U*lysses Simpson Grant, Republican, of Ohio, was inaugurated as the 18th President.

The first transcontinental railway, the Union Pacific and Central Pacific, was completed and a golden spike was driven (May 10) by Gov. Leland Stanford of California at Ogden, Utah, where tracks from the east and west joined. According to legend he missed the first stroke. Regular service began five days later (May 15). (Construction of the road was begun in 1863.)

Cornelius Vanderbilt consolidated the New York Central and the Lake Shore and Michigan Southern railroads, thus connecting New York and Chicago by a direct route.

An Atlantic cable was laid between the United States and France. It extended from Duxbury, Ma., via the island of St. Pierre, south of Newfoundland, to Brest. The undertaking was chartered by Louis Napoleon.

In Chicago, the Washington street railway tunnel under the Chicago River was completed at a cost of $517,000. (Construction began in 1867.)

Christopher Latham Sholes patented the typewriter. (It was placed on the market in 1873.)

Memorial Day (May 30) was first observed.

The National Woman Suffrage Association was formed to bring pressure on the Federal government. Women were admitted to the practice of law in Kansas by an act of legislature, and voting privileges were granted by the legislatures of the Territories of Wyoming (Dec. 10) and Utah. At the First Presbyterian Church in Philadelphia women were ordained as deacons.

The construction of the Brooklyn Bridge in New York was begun. (It was completed in 1883.)

Public interest induced James Gordon Bennett, wealthy newspaper owner of the *New York Herald*, to finance an expedition to Africa under Sir Henry Morton Stanley to find the "lost" explorer and missionary David Livingstone, who had set out in 1865 to discover the sources of the Nile. (Stanley found Livingstone, in terrible condition, Nov. 10, 1871, at Ujiji, Tanganyika, Central Africa. The rescued Livingstone survived until 1873.)

Everyone's curiosity was aroused when a crude statue of a man, 10 feet high, was "unearthed" near Cardiff, N.Y. It was found to have been carved from gypsum. The monstrosity was exhibited (Dec.) in New York at Apollo Hall. The Cardiff Giant, as it was called, turned out to be a hoax.

The American Museum of Natural History was founded in New York.

Matthew B. Brady added to his reputation as a photographer with his famous "National Photographic Collection of War Views," actual pictures of Civil War scenes.

William Frederick Cody became "Buffalo Bill" and a fictional hero—all because he was so named by Colonel Edward Zane Carroll Judson, who met him at this time. Judson was a founder of the Know-Nothing Party, a leader in the New York Astor Place riots, an accused murderer, and an author. He began writing, under the pseudonym of Ned Buntline, some 400 dime novels dealing with imaginary exploits by the colorful pony express rider and frontiersman.

The bicycle (a wooden affair) was put on the American market by the Six Hanlon Brothers. They opened (Jan.) a shop in New York, which they called Velocipede Hall.

The Cincinnati baseball team became the first outright professional club in America, and made a tour without losing a single game.

At Chicago, the victorious Western tour of the Washington baseball team was stopped by the Rockford, Ill., nine, whose pitcher was a 17-year-old named Albert G. Spalding, later one of the influential figures of baseball.

Princeton and Rutgers played (Nov. 6) the first intercollegiate football game.

The hoopskirt finally gave way to the bustle.

George Peabody, aged 74, Massachusetts-born dry goods merchant and philanthropist, died (Nov. 4) in London. His body was conveyed to the United States on a British warship. Peabody's benefactions to educational institutions, libraries, museums, and other worthy causes, totaled between eight and nine million dollars.

The last surviving soldier of the Revolutionary War died—Daniel F. Bakeman, aged 109 years (Apr. 5), in Freedom, Cattaraugus County, N.Y.

Franklin Pierce, the fourteenth President, died (Oct. 8).

The first patent for chewing gum was issued (Dec. 28).

In Print

Mark Twain published his humorous, quasi-autobiographical narrative of foreign travel *The Innocents Abroad, or The New Pilgrim's Progress*.

On Stage

American bandmaster Patrick Sarsfield Gilmore inaugurated (June 15) in Boston his first colossal Peace Jubilee or music festival. He assembled an orchestra of 1,000 players and a chorus of 10,000 singers, and heightened the performances with many sensational features. The purpose of the festival was to celebrate the return of peace after the Civil War. (Similar "jubilees" were held in 1872 in Boston and in 1873 in Chicago.)

Edwin Thomas Booth, brother of Lincoln's assassin, built Booth's Theater in New York (he managed the theater until 1874). It opened (Feb. 3) with a superb revival of *Romeo and Juliet,* which ran for 10 weeks. Seats for the opening performance were sold at auction, the prices scaling from $125 down. Governor Hoffman and Mayor A. Oakley Hall occupied boxes at the performance.

Music

   The Little Brown Jug, Shew! Fly, Don't Bother Me, Wine, Women and Song, Johann Strauss; *Hungarian Dances; Light Cavalry Overture, Now the Day Is Over, Sweet Genevieve.*

1870

$\mathscr{T}$he four remaining former Confederate States of Georgia, Mississippi, Texas, and Virginia were readmitted to Congress.

Congress chartered (May) the Northern Pacific Railroad Company. The Kansas Pacific Railroad from Kansas City, Mo., to Denver, Col., was completed (Aug. 15). Following the boom in railroads, there were 49,168 miles of railway in the country.

Celluloid was patented by John Wesley Hyatt.

The development of Asbury Park, N.J., as a summer resort was begun by James A. Bradley, a New York businessman.

The brothers John Davison and William Rockefeller founded the Standard Oil Company with a capitalization of $1,000,000.

Alfred Ely Beach designed for New York the first American subway. It was 312 feet long, passing under Broadway from Warren to Murray by a compressed-air apparatus called Root's Patent Force Blast Rotary Blower. The car ran on an irregular schedule; at other times the tunnel was used by pedestrians. The subway operated for about three years.

The Metropolitan Museum of Art in New York was incorporated. (It moved to its present quarters in 1880.)

The steamboat *Robert E. Lee* paddled from New Orleans to St. Louis in 3 days, 18 hours, 14 minutes, for a record.

Roman Catholic Bishop Fitzgerald of Little Rock, Ark., cast one of the dissenting votes at the Ecumenical Council in Rome which endorsed, 547 to 2, the adoption of the doctrine of papal infallibility.

In the second competition for the America's Cup, the American yacht *Magic* defeated (Aug. 8) the British contender *Cambria*.

General Robert Edward Lee, aged 63, died (Oct. 12) in Lexington, Va. At the time of his death, he was president of Washington College (now Washington and Lee University), Lexington, Va.

The national population was 38,558,371.

In Print

Bret Harte's story *The Luck of Roaring Camp* appeared in his San Francisco *Overland Monthly*.

On Stage

Bronson Howard, destined to be one of America's foremost playwrights, produced (Dec. 21) his initial effort, a farce comedy entitled *Saratoga*, in New York at Daly's Fifth Avenue Theater. (The play was splendidly staged and ran until Mar. 27, 1871, for 101 performances.)

Music

Rescue the Perishing; Safe in the Arms of Jesus; Looking Back; Pass Me Not, O Gentle Savior.

1871

*M*rs. O'Leary's cow, according to legend, kicked over a lighted lantern in a barn at 137 DeKoven in Chicago on Sunday evening, Oct. 8, and started a fire which, fanned by heavy winds, devastated for two days an area of 2,000 acres, destroyed about 17,500 buildings including the newly renovated Crosby Opera House, rendered some 98,500 people shelterless, caused the death of about 250 people, and inflicted a property loss estimated close to $200,000,000.

On the same day (Oct. 8), one of the greatest forest fires in history occurred in Wisconsin. Starting in the town of Peshtigo in Marinette County, the conflagration spread through six counties and across Green Bay to Williamsville. More than 1,000 lives were lost and 3,000 people were left destitute.

After years of dispute, the United States was awarded $15,500,000 damages in gold against Great Britain by a Court of Arbitration, comprising five commissioners from Italy, Brazil, Switzerland, the United States, and England. The suit arose from United States claims for the depredations inflicted upon American shipping by the confederate raiders *Alabama*, *Florida*, and *Shenandoah*, built and equipped in British ports in violation of treaties. The *Alabama* destroyed between 57 and 65 United States vessels before it was sunk (June 19, 1864) by the U.S.S. *Kearsarge* off Cherbourg, France.

Captain Charles Francis Hall, commanding an Arctic polar expedition on the government ship *Polaris*, became (Aug. 29) the first American explorer to reach the farthest North Latitude, near Thank God Harbor, Greenland.

The hydraulic elevator came into use.

Brigham Young, Mormon leader, was arrested (Oct. 2) for polygamy.

A boiler explosion wrecked (July 30) the New York and Staten Island ferryboat *Westfield*, with a loss of 100 lives.

Smith College, Northampton, Mass., for women, was founded by the bequest of Sophia Smith.

The National Association of Professional Ball Players was organized in New York. It included the Philadelphia Athletics, the Bostons, the Chicago White Stockings, the Brooklyn Eckfords, the Cleveland Forest Citys, the Rockford (Ill.) Forest Citys, the Troy (N.Y.) Haymakers, the Fort Wayne Kekiongas, and the New York Mutuals.

The New York Canoe Club was organized at St. George, Staten Island, N.Y. This led to the formation of similar clubs in the East.

In Print

Books of the year included *The Hoosier Schoolmaster* (Edward Eggleston), *The Passionate Pilgrim* (Henry James), *Pike County Ballads* (John Hay), *Songs of the Sierras* (Joaquin Miller), William Cullen Bryant's translation of *The Odyssey* (1871-72), the first volumes of the *New Variorum Edition* of Shakespeare's plays by Horace Howard Furness (completed posthumously in 1913), and a classic of cooking, *Common Sense in the Household: A Manual of Practical Housewifery* (Marion Harland, pseudonym of Mary Virginia Terhune).

On Stage

New York witnessed the United States premieres of two famous operas—Wagner's *Lohengrin* at the Stadt Theater (Apr. 3) and Ambroise Thomas's French *Mignon* sung in Italian at the Academy of Music (Nov. 22).

P. T. Barnum organized his circus, the *Greatest Show on Earth*. (It merged in 1881 with J. A. Bailey's company to become Barnum & Bailey's Circus.)

Music

Onward, Christian Soldiers (music by Sir Arthur Sullivan); *Reuben and Rachel; Silent Night! Holy Night!; The Little Old Log Cabin in the Lane; Good-bye, Lisa Jane; There Is a Green Hill Far Away.*

1872

The "Congressional Record" was founded by Congress to publish the proceedings of the Senate and the House of Representatives.

Congress abolished the tariff on tea and coffee.

National bonds in the amount of $200,000,000 at 6 percent interest were reduced to 5 percent. Subsequently, the bonds were reduced to 4 and 4 percent.

Yellowstone National Park in Montana and Wyoming Territories was established by act of Congress.

To test the interpretation of the 14th and 15th Amendments in their application to woman suffrage, Susan Brownell Anthony created a sensation by casting a ballot in the New York State and Congressional election at Rochester. She was indicted for illegal voting and sentenced to pay a fine—which was never collected.

New York erected the first elevated railroad, known as the "el".

Pago Pago harbor, Tutuila, Samoan Islands, was ceded by the native king to the United States as a naval base.

The two-masted square-rigged *Marie Celeste* sailed (Nov. 7) from New York for Genoa with a cargo of alcohol. Five weeks later the boat was found adrift, under full sail, unmanned and undamaged, in the Atlantic some 600 miles west of Gibraltar. There is still much speculation about the fate of the crew.

Arbor Day (Apr. 10) was first observed in Nebraska, when a million trees were planted in the state on that day. The idea was conceived by J. Sterling Morton, a native of Nebraska City, Nebraska.

James Abbott McNeill Whistler, American painter, completed in London his "Portrait of My Mother." Whistler had settled permanently in London in 1863.

Luther Burbank developed the Burbank potato in Worcester, Mass.

To settle the old argument as to whether or not all the legs of a running horse are ever off the ground simultaneously, Senator Leland Stanford of California engaged Edward Maybridge, Scottish-American photographer, to set up a row of 24 cameras, before which a horse was run. The results showed that at one point all four legs of a running horse are indeed off the ground.

In the national election, President Grant was re-elected by a 760,000 majority, the largest ever polled by a presidential candidate up to that time. He won all but seven states.

In Print

Francis Samuel Drake published the *Dictionary of American Biography*, containing 10,000 biographies. Mark Twain published *Roughing It*.

On Stage

William Frederick Cody, known as "Buffalo Bill" since 1869, turned actor in Chicago and played the lead in *Scouts of the Plains*, written by his friend Colonel Edward Zane Carroll Judson.

Bandmaster Patrick Sarsfield Gilmore conducted in Boston his second Peace Jubilee, dedicated to "world peace." The undertaking was even larger than the first (1869) and still more unwieldy, featuring an orchestra of 2,000, a chorus of 20,000, the discharge of distant cannon by electricity, marching brigades of local uniformed firemen down the aisles of the auditorium, the clanging of anvils, and other spectacular additions. The Fisk University Jubilee Singers and Johann Strauss, The Waltz King, just arrived from Austria, participated in the performances. Gilmore conducted his huge force with a six-foot baton.

Herr Johann Strauss, celebrated composer of waltzes *The Blue Danube*, *Wine, Women and Song*, *Tales from the Vienna Woods*, and other equally famous works, including the operetta *Die Fledermaus*, made (July 8) his debut as a conductor in New York at the Academy of Music. He conducted four concerts in New York and 14 in Boston.

Anton Rubinstein, Russian piano virtuoso and composer, and Henri Wieniawski, distinguished Polish violinist, gave joint recitals in the United States. They made (Sept. 23) their first appearance in New York at Steinway Hall. Wieniawski extended his tour alone to California. Rubinstein's style of playing was humorously described in Virginia journalist George William Bagby's sketch "Jud Browning's Account of Rubenstein's (sic) Playing."

Music

Come, Ye Faithful; Raise the Strain; I Need Thee Every Hour.

1873

A "trade dollar" was authorized by Congress to facilitate trade with China and Japan. (Its use was discontinued in 1885.)

Bank failures throughout the country resulted in a panic, the effects of which continued to be felt for several years. The crisis was reached when the New York Clearing House suspended (Sept. 20) for 10 days.

One-cent postal cards were placed (May 1) on sale by the Post Office. By act of Congress, free postage to congressmen was rescinded except for public documents.

What was regarded as an insult to the national flag nearly involved the United States in a war with Spain. A sailing vessel, the *Virginius*, flying the American colors, was seized (Oct. 31) by the Spanish war steamer *Tornado*, on the suspicion that it was conveying munitions to Cuban insurrectionists. After sharp diplomatic exchanges, the *Virginius* was surrendered (Dec. 15) to the United States. The demand that Spain should salute the American flag was waived when that country established the fact that the ship was not entitled to sail under the American flag.

Mrs. Belva Ann Lockwood of Washington, D.C., became (Mar. 3) the first woman lawyer admitted to practice before the Supreme Court.

Brigham Young, Mormon leader, renounced (Apr. 10) temporal power over his followers in Utah.

The discovery of silver in Nevada started another rush.

The first typewriter to be placed on the market was the Sholes and Glidden (patented in 1868). It printed only capital letters.

A railway tunnel, 4 miles long, through Hoosac Mountain in Berkshire County, Mass., was completed (Nov. 27). The construction had taken about 15 years. (The first train passed through the tunnel on Feb. 9, 1875.)

The first cable-car system in the United States was introduced in San Francisco by Andrew S. Hallidie when he equipped the Clay Street Railway with a cable that ran in a slot between the rails.

The New York Society for the Suppression of Vice was founded by Anthony Comstock (1844-1915), social reformer. Its influence was reflected in the enactment by Congress of the so-called "Comstock" law, prohibiting the sending of obscene literature and pictures through the mails.

Henry Clay Frick began consolidating his vast coke-manufacturing business. (In 1889 he became manager of the Carnegie properties, and in 1900 the Frick and Carnegie firms merged into the Carnegie Co.)

Indoor marathon walking exhibitions were the latest attractions for the sport-minded. In New York at the Empire City Rink, Edward Payson Weston, the "great American walker" and a familiar figure to subsequent generations, was advertised to walk (May 15) "one hundred miles inside of twenty-two consecutive hours, for a purse of $1,500" and to cover (June 2) 50 miles in 10 hours. A rival, James Smith, was scheduled (June 4) to reduce the distance of 100 miles to 21 hours.

In Print

Bret Harte published his novel *M'liss: An Idyll of Red Mountain*. Thomas Bailey Aldrich featured his short story *Marjorie Daw* in *Every Saturday*, a Boston magazine of which he was the editor.

Among the periodicals founded were *The Delineator*, a monthly magazine for women, by Ebenezer Buttrick in New York; the semi-monthly *Home Companion*, in Cleveland; and the children's monthly *St. Nicholas*, edited by Mary Mapes Dodge. (The *Delineator* merged in 1937 with the *Pictorial Review*. The *Home Companion* became in 1886 the *Ladies' Home Companion* and in 1897, as a monthly, the *Woman's Home Companion*.)

On Stage

Verdi's spectacular Egyptian opera, *Aida*, received (Nov. 26) its United States premiere in New York at the Academy of Music. The opera was sung by Ostava Torriani (Aida), Annie Louise Cary (Amneris), Italo Campanini (Rhadames), and Victor Maurel (The King).

The Negro Jubilee Singers (1871) gave concerts of their songs in England, Scotland, and Ireland. Their campaign to raise funds for Fisk University, Nashville, Tenn., lasted three years, and brought them $90,000.

Bandmaster Patrick Sarsfield Gilmore conducted in Chicago his third and last Peace Jubilee in celebration of the rebuilding of the city after the great fire of 1871.

Gilbert S. Densmore, dramatic critic in San Francisco, dramatized Mark Twain's just-published novel *The Golden Age* without the author's consent. He produced the play at the California Theater (Apr. 22) and was sued for infringement. Densmore also started John T. Raymond on his career as a comic actor, and provided Broadway with one of its brightest successes, *Colonel Sellers* (1874). (Raymond played his role more than a thousand times.)

P.T. Barnum built and opened (Oct. 20) in New York a "Hippodrome" to house his circus, the "Greatest Show on Earth" (1872). It was a large wooden amphitheater, constructed on the site that had been the depot of the New York Central Railroad until 1871 when the railroad moved to its present Grand Central Station. On this site the first Madison Square Garden was erected.

Music

Good Night! Good Night, Beloved!; *Silver Threads Among the Gold* (music by Johann Strauss); *Eileen Allanna*; *Good Sweet Ham*; *Jennie, the Flower of Kildare*; *The Mulligan Guard*; *Seven-fold Amen*.

1874

$\mathscr{P}$resident Grant's daughter Nellie was married (May 21) to Captain Algernon Sartoris in the White House. Mendelssohn's *Wedding March* was played.

Congress feted (Dec. 18) the first royal visitor to the United States— David Kalakaua, King of the Sandwich Islands (now Hawaii).

William Marcy Tweed, political "Boss" of New York, was convicted (Nov. 19) of fraud in the amount of about $6,000,000 and sentenced to 12 years in prison on Blackwells (now Welfare) Island. (He was released in 1875 on a legal technicality, was then convicted in a civil suit, but escaped from jail to Cuba and Spain. He was extradited in 1876, and died in the Ludlow Street jail, New York, Apr. 12, 1878.)

Agitation against the evils of alcohol brought into existence the Women's Christian Temperance Union.

A movement to increase the issuance of the Treasury notes or "greenbacks" used during the Civil War was now advocated. The measure passed through Congress but was vetoed (in April) by President Grant. Dissatisfied supporters of the bill organized the Independent, or Greenback, party. (It held its first convention on Nov. 25.)

As a result of the crusade against "Boss" Tweed, the tiger and the donkey were familiar symbols of Tammany and the Democratic Party. The figures were drawn by cartoonist Thomas Nast and appeared in *Harper's Weekly*. He now added (Nov. 7) a third caricature, the elephant, to represent the Republican Party.

Charles T. ("Pastor") Russell preached that the millennium or the period of the second coming of Christ had begun invisibly this year and would terminate in 1914. His followers were known as Russellites and as Millennial Dawnists (after his book *Millennial Dawn*) and constituted a society called the Internal Bible Students' Association.

The Lambs, a club for actors, was organized in New York.

A Colosseum, modeled after its London namesake, opened (Jan. 10) in New York, presenting cycloramas of London and Paris. From the tower of the building, bells pealed the St. Paul and the Westminster chimes. The house was closed (in Nov.) for arrears in rent, amounting to $18,000, although shows continued to occupy the place into the next year.

Tennis was becoming a popular sport.

The American game of baseball was taken to England and Ireland by the Boston and Philadelphia National Association (predecessor of today's National League) ball clubs. The teams played 14 baseball games and seven cricket matches.

Five years of secondary postwar depression began (the fifteenth since 1790).

On Stage

Die Fledermaus, Johann Strauss's merry operetta, began (Nov. 21) its varied career in America quite mildly in New York at the Thalia Theater, sung in German. (Its initial English production in America took place Mar. 16, 1885, at the Casino, New York.)

Three great New York stage successes were *Colonel Sellers*, Mark Twain's comedy (already seen in San Francisco, 1873), at the Park Theater (Sept. 16); *The Shaugraun*, Dion Boucicault's Irish comedy, at Wallack's Theater (Nov. 14); and *The Two Orphans*, Hart Jackson's adaptation from the French, at the Union Square Theater (Dec. 21).

Music

The Alabama Blossoms; Patrick's Day Parade; I Love to Tell the Story; The Skidmore Guard; Trabling Back to Georgia.

1875

$\mathcal{C}$ongress passed (Jan. 14) the Resumption Act, a return to specie or "hard money," requiring the coinage of silver to replace other forms of currency and the issuance for every $100 of $80 in "greenbacks," which were to be redeemed in coin by Jan. 1, 1879. The measure was unpopular.

An unpopular Civil Rights Bill, meant to remedy discrimination against freedmen in traveling and in places of entertainment, was enacted by Congress (Mar. 1). (Certain sections of the Bill were declared unconstitutional in 1883. Other civil rights bills had been passed in 1866 and in 1870.)

A new Atlantic cable between the United States and Great Britain, called the United States Direct Cable, was laid to compete with that of Cyrus West Field (1866). In consequence, the rate fell first to 50 cents and then to 25 cents per word. The two Anglo-American lines were later united.

The dynamo was invented by Charles G. Brush of Cleveland, Ohio.

John McCloskey, Roman Catholic Archbishop of New York since 1864, became the first American cardinal when he was elevated to that rank by Pope Pius IX.

Luther Burbank established his scientific plant and fruit nursery in Santa Rosa, Calif.

A statue of "Stonewall" Jackson was unveiled (Oct. 26) in Richmond, Va.

The first Kentucky Derby was run at Churchill Downs, Louisville, Ky. It was won by the horse Aristides.

There were over 2,000 baseball organizations, still nine-tenths amateur. Yale boasted the best college team. The National Association of Professional Baseball Players disbanded because of a public scandal created by the dishonesty of players.

Republicans proposed President Grant for a third term, but public sentiment was against breaking the two-term precedent. (He was again considered in 1880.)

Andrew Johnson, seventeenth President, died (July 21).

In Print

Mary Baker Eddy published *Science and Health with Key to the Scriptures*, the only authorized textbook of Christian Science which she founded (1866).

The Chicago *Daily News* was founded; also in the same city the Czech language daily *Svornost* began publication.

Josiah Gilbert Holland, Massachusetts author and editor, published *Seven Oaks*, a novel about an unscrupulous financier and industrial and social conditions in a New England town.

On Stage

New York was enjoying one of its greatest theatrical years. To *Colonel Sellers*, *The Shaugraun*, and *The Two Orphans* of the previous year's fall season were added *The Big Bonanza* (Feb. 17) *Our Boys* (Sept. 18), and *Pique* (Dec. 14) at Daly's Fifth Avenue Theater, *The Mighty Dollar* (Sept. 6) and *Rose Michel* (Nov. 23) at the Union Square. *Henry V* was revived (Feb. 8) with the heroic George Rignold; Edwin Booth played (Sept. 13) a poetic *Hamlet* to enraptured audiences; *Julius Caesar* featured (Dec. 27) a brilliant cast. Even A. Oakey Hall, former Mayor of New York and puppet of "Boss" Tweed, tried the stage as an actor-playwright at the Park with *The Crucible* (Dec. 18) which ran for three weeks, much to the embarrassment of its public. The play dealt with a court action in which an innocent victim (played by Hall) was led off to jail.

In spectacular style, the Kiralfy Brothers (Imre, Bolossy, and Arnold), Hungarian dancers and pantomimists, who came to the United States in 1868, put on (Aug. 28) in New York at the Academy of Music a stage version of Jules Verne's popular novel, *Around the World in Eighty Days*.

Music

All the Way My Savior Leads Me; *The Blue Alsatian Mountains*; *Fully Persuaded*; *Gems of English Song*; *It Was a Dream*; *Let Me Dream Again*; *Nancy Lee*; *Twickenham Ferry*; *The Yeoman's Wedding Song*.

1876

*T*he United States was 100 years old. The event was commemorated by the Centennial Exposition held (May-Nov.) in Philadelphia. It was planned on a grand scale, larger than any previous European or American exhibition, and covered 236 acres. The main structure cost $4,500,000; an electric railway made a circuit of the building for the convenience of the visitors. Congress appropriated $2,000,000, the city of Philadelphia $1,500,000, the state of Pennsylvania $1,000,000. Stocks were issued in the amount of $10,000,000. The general music director was the noted Theodore Thomas, who assumed the musical expenses and lost a personal fortune in the undertaking. It took him 12 years to pay the deficits ("twelve years of sheriffs and scoundrels," he said) and his large orchestral library was sold at auction to meet his obligations. For the occasion—and $5,000—the great German composer Richard Wagner composed a mediocre "Fest Marsch," "dem Festfeier-Frauenverein gewidmet," played on the opening day (May 10) on the arrival of President Grant. Thomas was so disappointed with the piece that he never forgave the master whose works he helped to popularize in this country. Wagner himself wrote: "The best thing about that composition was the money I got for it." On the same program figured Whittier's "Centennial Hymn," with music by John Knowles Paine, sung by a chorus of 150. The celebrated French opera-bouffe composer Jacques Offenbach conducted popular concerts, mostly of his own works. John Philip Sousa was a member of Offenbach's orchestra. Bandmaster Patrick Sarsfield Gilmore of the monster "Peace Jubilee" concerts was also there. The President failed to attend the elaborate July 4th celebration, preferring, as writer James D. McCabe said, "his selfish ease to a little patriotic exertion." The number of exhibits was exceeded only by those of the Paris and Vienna Expositions. Dom Pedro II, Emperor of Brazil, and Prince Oscar of Sweden took part in the functions.

Elisha Graves Otis again exhibited his passenger elevator at the Exposition.

A mechanical Orchestrion, or Electro-Magnetic Orchestra, invented by William F. and H. Schmoele of Philadelphia, was displayed at the Exposition in Horticultural Hall. Paper rolls, similar to those of the later player piano, provided the music.

103 American and Canadian librarians met (Oct. 4-7) and formed the American Library Association. One of the leaders was Melvil Dewey, originator of the Dewey decimal system of classifying and shelving books.

Twenty-nine-year-old Scottish-American inventor Alexander Graham Bell and Prof. Elisha Gray patented independently—and, by coincidence, on the same day, Feb. 14—the American telephone. A German telephone had been devised by Philip Reis of Friedrichsdorf in 1861. The first intelligible words were sent (Mar. 10) by Bell from the top floor of a boarding house in Boston over a two-mile line to Cambridgeport, Mass. Litigation between Bell and Gray followed, but Bell's priority—his patent was granted Mar. 7, 1876—was sustained by the U.S. Supreme Court. (The first commercial use of the telephone in the United States occurred in 1878.) Bell described his invention in his application for the patent as an "improvement in telegraphy."

About 3,000 Sioux Indians, under Sitting Bull, who had been resisting since 1874 the government's attempt to transfer his people from the Black Hills, S.D., to a reservation, killed (June 25) General George Armstrong Custer and 261 men of the Seventh Cavalry and wounded 51 at Little Big Horn, MT. The episode is known as "Custer's Last Stand." Sitting Bull fled toward Canada and was killed near Fort Yates, N.D.

Colorado was admitted (Aug. 1) as the 38th state.

Secretary of War William B. Belknap was impeached on charges of accepting bribes. He was acquitted. The trial began Mar. 3 and ended Aug. 1. It was the seventh impeachment in United States history.

Senator William Henry Blair of New Hampshire introduced (Dec. 12) in Congress a bill proposing federal prohibition of liquor traffic. New Hampshire was a dry state.

Johns Hopkins University, Baltimore, Md., for men, named after its benefactor, was opened; also, the University of Oregon, at Eugene and Portland, for men and women (Oct. 18).

The present national League of Professional Baseball Clubs was organized to replace the National League of Professional Baseball Players (1871) which had disbanded (1875) because of public scandal created by dishonesty of players, contract-jumping, and gambling accusations.

Scandal besmirched the national elections. To all appearances, the Democratic nominee Samuel J. Tilden, who polled a 250,000 popular majority, had defeated the Republican opponent, Rutherford B. Hayes, 184 electoral votes to 163. Not included in either tally were the 12 votes of Florida, Louisiana, Oregon, and South Carolina, which were contested with increasing bitterness. Rash Democrats even threatened to march an army of volunteers to Washington to install Tilden. The dispute was submitted to Congress (in Dec.), which established an Electoral Commission to meet with the Supreme Court. The Commission consisted of five Senators appointed by the Vice President (three Republicans and two Democrats), five Representatives appointed by the Speaker (three Democrats and two Republicans), and five Judges of the Supreme Court. The tribunal of eight Republicans and seven Democrats concluded its business two days before the inaugural date. The members adhered to party politics and ruled the 22 contested votes in favor of the Republican candidate. Hayes was therefore elected by one electoral vote, 185 to 184, and the cry of "Fraud" went up in the land.

Representatives from Columbia, Harvard, Princeton, and Yale universities met (Nov. 26) in convention at Springfield, Mass., and formed the American Intercollegiate Football Association, which developed modern football. The touchdown became the deciding factor in the game. The new rule read: "A match shall be decided by a majority of touchdowns; a goal shall be equal to four touchdowns; but in case of a tie, a goal kicked from a touchdown shall take precedence over four touchdowns."

Lawman James "Wild Bill" Hickok died (Aug. 2).

In Print

The *Svenska Amerikanaen Tribunen* appeared in Chicago as a Swedish-language weekly.

A modest book that had been rejected by publishers, printed at the author's expense, and finally vended by a Chicago book firm, was the *Pocket Manual of Rules of Order for Deliberative Assemblies* by Henry M. Robert, a South Carolina major in the U.S. Army. The volume met with immediate response; the 4,000 copies of the first edition—priced at 75 cents per copy—were sold within six weeks. (Periodically revised, Robert's "Rules of Order" is today the standard guide for parliamentary procedure.)

Mark Twain published his novel *The Adventures of Tom Sawyer*. Equally characteristic of American life were the comic poems by Charles Follen Adams, which appeared under the title *Leedle Yawcob Strauss*, written in the "scrapple English" dialect of the Pennsylvania Dutch. (The poems were collected and printed in 1878 in Boston.)

Walt Whitman issued in two volumes the Author's or Centennial edition of his *Leaves of Grass*. (It was the sixth edition of the collection.)

On Broadway

The Philharmonic Society of New York, under Carl Bergmann, introduced (Apr. 22) Tchaikovsky's overture *Romeo and Juliet* in America.

The saxophone, before it became a jazz instrument, intrigued women players. Etta Morgan, a member of the Berger Family's Ladies' Orchestra, began (Jan. 17) a two week engagement in New York at the Olympic Theater with her saxophone.

Oscar Hammerstein, erstwhile East Side cigarmaker from Germany, entered show business as manager of the German-language Stadt Theater in New York.

In keeping with the Centennial spirit, Augustin Daly gave change in gold at the box office of his Fifth Avenue Theater in New York on the night of the hundredth performance (Mar. 13) of the play *Pique*.

Music

I'll Take You Home Again, Kathleen; Grandfather's Clock; It Is Well with My Soul; My Dearest Heart; The Ninety and Nine; Rose of Killarney; Trusting Jesus; That Is All.

1877

$\mathscr{R}$utherford Birchard Hayes, Republican, of Ohio, was inaugurated as the 19th President. The President and his wife were observers of temperance; no alcoholic beverages were served in the White House. They celebrated their silver wedding anniversary in the executive mansion during the year.

With the election of President Hayes, Reconstruction in the South was considered accomplished. Federal troops were withdrawn from the former Confederate States.

Chief Joseph of the Nez Perce Indian tribes refused to recognize a fraudulent treaty into which his father had been tricked, and led an uprising to win back their lost gold fields. To avoid capture he led his followers on a remarkable 1,000-mile trek to Canada, which ended after a five-day siege, when he was caught near the Canadian border.

Railroad strikes paralyzed the nation, with virtually every major line in a labor battle after 10 percent wage cuts. The difficulties began on the Baltimore & Ohio, spread to the Pennsylvania, Erie, New York Central, and Missouri Pacific, and involved their Western and Southern affiliates. Federal troops and cavalry aided the local police and firemen to quell the disturbances. At least 50 persons were killed and more than 100 wounded. In Pittsburgh, rioters set oil cars afire, burned and pillaged some 2,000 freight cars, and looted the machine shops. Property damage was estimated at upwards of ten million dollars. (The strikes began July 14 and abated around July 27; nearly all railroads were in operation again by July 30.)

Eleven leaders of the Molly Maguires (1865), labor agitators in the Pennsylvania coal-mining regions, were hanged for murder.

Alexander Graham Bell went to England to introduce his newly (1876) invented telephone. Although its demonstration before Queen Victoria met with Her Majesty's approval, Bell was unable to make headway after a year's effort because of British patent difficulties. Meanwhile, in the United States, telephone service developed over private lines so rapidly that by November some 3,000 telephones were in operation.

Thomas Alva Edison invented the talking machine. He used a cylindrical record that was made of tin foil, and reproduced his own recitation of *Mary Had a Little Lamb*. The talking machine was later called the phonograph when it began transmitting music.

The University of Colorado, Boulder, Colo., for men and women opened.

Greco-Roman wrestling was popular in New York.

Brigham Young, aged 76, Mormon leader, died (Aug. 29) in Salt Lake City, Utah, which he had helped to found (1847). He had at various times 19 to 27 wives and was the father of 56 children.

Chief Crazy Horse died (Sept. 5).

In Print

Puck was issued in New York as a weekly magazine of humor and satire. (It ceased publication in 1918.)

On Stage

At the Academy of Music, manager Maurice Strakosch announced (March) a concert "in which numerous melodies performed in Philadelphia will be heard by means of telephonic connection in New York." Whether the advertised event took place is uncertain. At any rate, the brother-in-law of Adelina Patti actually tried the experiment twice in a much smaller auditorium—Steinway hall. At the first concert (Apr. 2), rain made transmission impractical. He then included the doubtful feature in a Brooklyn Academy of Music concert (Apr. 3). But at the second New York concert (Apr. 4), a piano solo played by Frederick Boskovitz in Philadelphia was heard by the New York audience.

Wagner's great music drama *Die Walküre*, the second of the four "Ring" operas, was heard (Apr. 2) for the first time in the United States at the Academy of Music in New York, and fourteen days later (Apr. 16) in Boston. The work was promised as part of a local Wagner "festival," but the other operas had to be postponed for more rehearsals until after the season. The Brunhilde was Mme. Eugenie Pappenheim; Felix Preusser sang Wotan, and Pauline Canissa and Alexander Bischoff were respectively Sieglinde and Sigmund.

"Dime" entertainments in New York at Cooper Institute and at the Y.M.C.A. were a new means of attracting the public.

Music

The Better Land; *Early in de Mornin'*; *I'll Sing Thee Songs of Araby (Lalla Rookh)*; *Roll Out!*; *Heave Dat Cotton*; *Where Is My (Wand'ring) Boy To-night?*

1878

*O*ver President Hayes's veto, Congress passed (Feb. 28) the Bland-Allison silver bill, authorizing the coinage of 2,000,000 silver dollars per month. (The Act was repealed in 1890 by the Sherman Law.)

The newly invented (1876) telephone became a public necessity. The first commercial telephone exchange opened (Jan. 28) in New Haven, Conn. In Massachusetts, a wire was strung (Apr.) from the home of Charles Williams in Somerville to his business office in Boston, three miles away.

Thomas Alva Edison announced (Oct.) the invention of an incandescent platinum lamp. As a result, gas prices fell from twelve to twenty percent. (The lamp was patented in 1880.)

Dissatisfied with the Resumption Act of 1875, the Greenback Party, the National Grange, and other political and labor elements formed the Greenback-Labor Party. (It waned around 1884 and was absorbed in 1891 by the Populist Party.)

Work on the erection of the Washington National Monument, begun 1848 and discontinued 1854, was resumed at government expense.

For the first time in 17 years gold and paper money were (Dec. 18) of equal value.

Tidewater Oil began pumping oil over the Alleghenies in pipes instead of shipping it by barrels.

The American painter James Abbott McNeill Whistler sued in a London court the famous art critic John Ruskin for libel. The latter had written of Whistler's impressionistic painting "Black and Gold—The Falling Rocket," exhibited in 1877: "I have seen and heard much cockney impudence before now, but never expected to hear a coxcomb ask 200 guineas for flinging a pot of paint in the public's face." The trial was replete with repartee. Whistler was vindicated and was awarded one farthing damages and no costs. As a result of the heavy expenses incurred in the prosecution, Whistler was forced into bankruptcy.

An epidemic of yellow fever took an enormous number of lives despite such advised home-remedies as cigars and whiskey.

In Print
Anna Katherine Green set the formula of the modern detective story with her novel *The Leavenworth Case*.

Daisy Miller: A Study established Henry James's reputation as a novelist.

On Stage

Gilbert and Sullivan's comic opera *H.M.S. Pinafore* reached the United States six months after its London premiere (May 25). First heard (Nov. 25) at the Boston Museum (a theater), it was given in San Francisco at the Bush Street Theater (Dec. 23, with Alice Oates in the male role of the hero, Ralph Rackstraw) and in Philadelphia at the South Broad Street Theater (Jan. 6, 1879) before the work came (Jan. 15, 1879) to New York at the Standard Theater. Due to the absence of copyright protection, garbled and unauthorized versions followed at the Lyceum (Jan. 23), at Niblo's Garden, and at the Fifth Avenue Theater (simultaneously, Feb. 10), by a Black troupe at the Globe (Apr. 28), and elsewhere; in fact, the country was overrun with productions by professional and amateur, adult and juvenile companies and church choirs.

San Francisco's Tivoli Opera House, seating a thousand persons, was opened (Dec. 23) with Gilbert and Sullivan's *H.M.S. Pinafore*. (The theater was enlarged in 1880 to accommodate 2,000.)

Bizet's great French opera *Carmen* had (Oct. 23) its initial United States rendition in New York at the Academy of Music, with Minnie Hauk. It was sung in Italian, and was performed two days later (Oct. 25) in Philadelphia at the Academy of Music, also in Italian.

Music

Carry Me Back to Old Virginny; Baby Mine; A Flower from Mother's Grave; The Skidmore Fancy Ball; Sweet Mary Ann, or *Such an Education Has My Mary Ann (Malone's Night Off, or the German Turnverein); Tell Me the Old, Old Story; Where Was Moses When the Light Went Out?*

1879

$\mathcal{C}$ongress passed an army appropriation bill, which was vetoed by President Hayes because a clause provided that no Federal troops should be employed in police duty in the South. The President deemed this a violation of the executive prerogative. At a special session, Congress enacted a new bill retaining the clause. Such Republican legislation helped to create the Democratic "Solid South." An Arrears of Pensions bill, involving the disbursement of about $300,000,000, was also passed to settle rejected claims.

The United States issued its first "postage due" stamps.

William Tecumseh Sherman, Civil War commander, uttered his dictum, "War is hell," in an address to the Michigan Military Academy.

Frank Winfield Woolworth opened (Feb. 22) a five-and-ten cent store in Utica, N.Y.—the first of his subsequent nation-wide chain—thus founding one of America's most fabulous fortunes.

St. Patrick's Cathedral in New York was dedicated (May). The edifice cost $4,000,000 and replaced an older structure.

The first cash register was devised by James Ritty.

George B. Selden applied for a patent on a vehicle powered with an internal-combustion engine—a forerunner of the automobile. (The patent was granted in 1895.)

The Art Institute of Chicago was founded (May 24) for the "founding and maintenance of schools of art and design, the formation and exhibitions of collections of objects of art, and the cultivation and extension of the arts of design by any appropriate means."

The Richmond and Cleveland baseball clubs played the first no-hit game on record.

In Print

Frank R. (Francis Richard) Stockton published his humorous and fantastic novel *Rudder Grange*, the name of an old, anchored canal boat in which a newly married couple decided to live. (Sequels to the book were *The Rudder Grangers Abroad*, 1891, and *Pomona's Travels*, 1894.)

The New York Mirror was founded as a theatrical weekly. (Renamed the *New York Dramatic Mirror* in 1889, it ceased publication in 1922.)

On Stage

The Philharmonic Society of New York performed (Feb. 8) the first Tchaikovsky symphony heard in America—Symphony No. 3 in D.

In San Francisco, the indefatigable manager Tom Maguire once more ventured into the field of opera. He produced at the Baldwin the West Coast premiere of *Carmen* with Marie Rose and Annie Louise Carey, and lost $20,000 in the production.

The unprecedented craze in America for Gilbert and Sullivan's operetta *H.M.S. Pinafore* brought to New York the author and composer, together with a company from London under the management of R. D'Oyly Carte, in an attempt to protect their work against unauthorized performances and mutilations. Sullivan entered (Dec. 1) the orchestra pit of Daly's Fifth Avenue Theater to conduct the true version of the work and Gilbert is said to have appeared on the stage as a member of the sailors' chorus. On Dec. 31 their new operetta, *The Pirates of Penzance*, had its world premiere at the same theater after a copyright performance had been given in Paignton, England, at the Bijou Theater on Dec. 30.

Hearts of Oak by twenty-year-old playwright David Belasco of San Francisco was produced in Chicago.

In New York, the Broadway Theater (formerly Wood's Museum) was remodeled by Augustin Daly and opened (Sept. 17) as Daly's Theater. Another renovated playhouse, the Bowery Theater, reopened (Sept. 11) as the German-language Thalia Theater, with Heinrich Conried, later impresario of the Metropolitan Opera House, as stage manager.

P. T. Barnum's New York Hippodrome (1873), also known as Gilmore's Garden, became Madison Square Garden under Barnum's management. It started (May 31) with a series of summer-night concerts by H. B. Dodworth's Band. (A new structure was built on the site in 1889-90 and demolished in 1925 when a new "Madison Square Garden" was erected farther uptown.)

Music

The Babies on Our Block (The Skidmore Fancy Ball); *Oh! dem Golden Slippers*; *In the Morning by the Bright Light.*

1880

$\mathcal{T}$he discovery of gold on the Gastineau Channel, Alaska, led to a "gold rush" to the region.

Kansas adopted a liquor prohibition law—the first Midwestern state to do so.

Thomas Alva Edison patented (Jan. 27) the incandescent lamp.

The Salvation Army, first organized in England, established American headquarters in New York. At the Battery, Commissioner George Scott Railton and seven women launched the first Salvation Army drive in the United States.

John Pierpont Morgan reorganized the banking firm of Drexel, Morgan & Co. as J. P. Morgan & Co.

Bryn Mawr College for women, near Philadelphia, was founded by the Society of Friends (Quakers).

57.2 percent of public school teachers were now women.

John Philip Sousa was appointed leader of the U. S. Marine Band—a post he held until 1892 when he resigned to form his own band of 100 players. Sousa had been a Marine from 1867 until about 1875.

Hebe, an elephant in the Cooper & Bailey circus, gave birth to the first elephant born in captivity in this country.

At 116th Street and Sixth Avenue, New York, a bullfight was staged. The venture was later dropped for lack of customers.

At the Republican national convention, some 306 delegates through 36 ballots persistently supported former President Grant for a third term. To break the deadlock, his rivals James G. Blaine of Maine and John Sherman of Ohio combined to nominate James A. Garfield.

Scandal once more marred the national elections. A forged letter, alleged to have been written by the Republican nominee James A. Garfield and favoring the importation of Chinese cheap labor, was circulated in the Democratic press. Garfield denied writing the letter. An attempt to connect him with the Credit Mobilier affair (1873) also failed and Garfield defeated his Democratic opponent, Gen. Winfield Scott Hancock, 214 electoral votes to 155.

The national population soared above the fifty million mark to 50,155,783.

In Print

The Dial was founded as a monthly magazine of literary criticism. (It ceased publication in 1929.)

Il Progresso was issued in New York as an Italian-language daily. (The name was later changed to *Il Progresso Italo-Americano*. It is still published.)

Ben-Hur, a Tale of the Christ by Indiana author Lew Wallace was the novel of the year.

On Stage

When the Park Theater, New York, staged (Jan. 31) the farcical comedy *The Wedding March* by Sullivan's librettist William Schwenck Gilbert, the management announced that seats could be procured by telephone.

David Belasco left San Francisco with a play *La Belle Russe*, in his portfolio, and came to New York to enter its theatrical world.

The great French actress, the "divine" Sarah Bernhardt, made (Nov. 8) her American debut in *Adrienne Lecouvreur* in New York at Booth's Theater. Seven days later (Nov. 15) she appeared in her famous role of *La Dame aux Camellias*, which was then (1880-81) being played in English by Clara Morris and Helen Modjeska, in German by Marie Geistinger, and in French by Mlle. Rhea and Eugenie Legrand. (Bernhardt revisited the United States in 1887, 1891, 1896, 1900, 1911, 1913.)

The Madison Square Theater, New York, opened (Feb. 4) with Steele Mackaye's *Hazel Kirke*. A fire destroyed (Feb. 26) the drop curtain while the audience was assembling. Thanks to the latest fire-fighting devices the performance followed on schedule. *Hazel Kirke* was the play of the year. (It closed late in May, 1881, after an unprecedented run of 486 performances.)

Music

Cradle's Empty; Baby's Gone; The Five Cent Shave; Never Take the Horse Shoe From the Door (The Mulligan Guards' Surprise); Why Did They Dig Ma's Grave So Deep?; The Full Moon Union (The Mulligan Guards' Surprise); Hide Thou Me; Locked Out After Nine (The Mulligan Guards' Picnic); Songs My Mother Taught Me.

1881

$\mathcal{J}$ames Abram Garfield, Republican, of Ohio, was inaugurated as the 20th President.

President Garfield was in office only three months and two days when he was shot (July 2) in the back when entering the Baltimore & Ohio railroad station in Washington, D.C., on his way to his home in Elberon, N.J., to visit his invalid wife. The assassin was a mentally unbalanced, disappointed office-seeker named Charles J. Guiteau, who claimed to have been inspired by God, as he later testified at his trial, to "remove Garfield" for the peace of the country. The President was transferred (Sept. 6) from the White House to Franklyn cottage, his home in Elberon, where he died (Sept. 19). The body was returned to Washington to lie in state and removed to Cleveland, Ohio, for burial. The demonstration of grief was nationwide, even greater than at Lincoln's assassination, for the South was friendly to Garfield. Mrs. Garfield was the recipient of a $364,000 fund raised by her husband's admirers, and Congress voted her his salary for the remainder of the year.

Vice President Chester Alan Arthur, Republican from Vermont, was inaugurated (Sept. 19) upon Garfield's death, as the 21st President. He was a recent widower (his wife died in 1880), and his sister Mary, wife of John E. McElroy of Albany, N.Y., was the White House hostess.

The U.S. Naval vessel *Jeanette*, which had sailed from San Francisco in 1879 (June 2) in search of the North Pole, was crushed (June 12) by ice 500 miles from the Siberian coast. It had been outfitted for the United States Exploring Expedition by James Gordon Bennett, owner of the *New York Herald*. The 33 members of the crew dragged three boats across the ice region and discovered (July 29) new land—Bennett Island, named after their sponsor. They reached Simoutki Island and sailed (Sept. 10) together, but were separated by gales. Capt. George Washington DeLong, U.S.N., and all but two of his crew died of starvation and exposure. Lieutenant Chipp and his associates disappeared entirely. Engineer G. W. Melville and 11 surviving members were rescued.

The American Red Cross was organized (May 21) by Clara Barton of Civil War fame, as a branch of the Red Cross of the Geneva, Switzerland, Convention. She was the American organization's first president.

Edward Muybridge invented the zoopraxiscope, an early form of the motion-picture projector, by means of which animals in motion were reproduced on a screen.

Adolph Strasser and Samuel Gompers, cigar makers, united the dissatisfied elements of the old Knights of Labor (1869) and other workingmen's groups into the American Federation of Labor ("A.F. of L."), eventually an organization of trade unions of the United States, Canada, Puerto Rico, and Panama. (Gompers was its president from the start until his death in 1924.)

The education of African Americans was enhanced by the founding of Tuskegee Normal and Industrial Institute for men and women, in Alabama. The founder, Booker Taliaferro Washington, was the 25-year-old son of a Negro slave and a white father.

Augustus Saint-Gaudens, Irish-born American sculptor, unveiled his first public statue—the Farragut Monument in Madison Square, New York.

The Boston Symphony Orchestra was established by Major Henry Lee Higginson. The first concert was given on Oct. 22.

Barnum & Bailey's Circus was organized by a merger of enterprises.

Outlaw William "Billy the Kid" Bonner died (July 14).

In Print

Jefferson Davis, former President of the Confederate States, who believed until his death (1889) that he had fought for justice and the right, published his two-volume history *The Rise and Fall of the Confederacy*.

Harriet Mulford Stone Lothrop published, under the pseudonym Margaret Sidney, the children's story *Five Little Peppars and How They Grew*.

Joel Chandler Harris brought out in book form his first collection of *Uncle Remus* verses and stories based on Black folklore, which had previously appeared separately in periodicals.

New periodicals included *The Critic*, a weekly literary review; *The Century Illustrated Monthly Magazine*; and *Judge*, a weekly comic and rival of *Puck* (1877). (They ceased publication in 1906, 1930, and 1939, respectively.)

On Stage

Gilbert and Sullivan's latest product *Patience, or, Bunthorne's Bride* had (July 28) its American premiere in St. Louis and came two months later (Sept. 22) to New York at the Standard Theater.

Music

I Am Coming, Paddy Duffy's Cart (Squatter Sovereignty); All on Account of Eliza (Billie Taylor); Good-Bye; Tell It Out Among the Nations (Heathen) That the Lord is King; The Torpedo and the Whale (Olivette); Wait Till the Clouds Roll By.

1882

A report by special inspectors disclosed (Jan.) extensive frauds on what were known as Star Routes of the postal service. No fewer than 296 illegal contracts had been issued, involving a sum in excess of $8,000,000. The Star Route trials occupied the courts for more than six months. Several contractors were arrested for perjury, but ultimately, after 18 months of prosecution, the trials came to naught.

Congress prohibited immigration to Chinese laborers and required those leaving the United States to obtain certificates of identification for use on re-entry.

Congress also disfranchised and declared ineligible to office all polygamists.

Charles J. Guiteau, assassin of President Garfield, was hanged (June 30). He had been arraigned in Washington, D.C. His trial lasted about 10 weeks, with conflicting testimony by experts concerning his mental condition. His flippant and freakish behavior added to the annoyance of the court. The jury, however, convicted him (Jan. 25).

The first Labor Day parade was held (Sept. 5) in New York.

On Pearl Street, New York, the first Edison electric lighting station opened.

Jesse James, notorious Western robber and murderer, was killed (Apr. 3) while in hiding by one of his accomplices.

The Roman Catholic benevolent organization Knights of Columbus was organized in New Haven, Conn. by the Rev. J.C. McGinley.

Harvard University opened a school of higher education called the Society for the Collegiate Instruction for Women. It was renamed Radcliffe College in 1894 after Ann Radcliffe, Lady Mowlson (died about 1661), wife of the donor of a scholarship to the University.

Oscar Wilde, English author, lectured in the United States on art and literature.

John L. Sullivan was adjudged the loser in a prizefight bout (July 17) at New York's Madison Square Garden when he failed to knock out Joseph Collins (Tug Wilson), the English champion. However, Sullivan was said by many observers to have out-fought Collins.

Jumbo, the elephant, arrived from England and was promptly exhibited (Apr. 10) by Barnum.

Deaths of the year included: Henry Wadsworth Longfellow, aged 75 (Mar. 24), and Ralph Waldo Emerson, aged 79 (Apr. 27).

In Print

Fiction readers were buying the November issue of the new *Century Illustrated Monthly Magazine* for the short story, *The Lady or the Tiger*, by Frank Stockton, which became immensely popular. (It was published as a book in 1884 and was turned into an operetta in 1888.)

Mark Twain published his novel *The Prince and the Pauper*, a story of Tudor England under Edward VI.

Ignatius Donnelly, Philadelphia-born politician, journalist, and essayist, printed his account of *Atlantis* in which he endeavored to prove that the fabulous island mentioned in Plato's *Timaeus* had actually existed as the seat of civilization.

On Stage

The 2,500th performance of *The Mighty Dollar* took place in New York at the Grand Opera House.

Esmeralda was the play of the year, a sweet and charming dramatization of a story by Frances Hodgson Burnett and William H. Gillette. First staged at the Madison Square Theater, New York, in Oct., 1881, it ran for about a year, rivaling *Hazel Kirke* in popular appeal, and raising its lead, Annie Russell, to stardom.

La Belle Russe introduced (May 8) David Belasco as a playwright to New York audiences at Wallack's Theater. He sold the play for $1,500, a return railroad ticket to San Francisco, and $100 expenses to his friend Tom Maguire's nephew, Frank L. Goodwin, by arrangement with whom was produced this "new and powerful drama by David Belasco, Esq."

New York and London shared the world premiere of Gilbert and Sullivan's operetta *Iolanthe, or The Peer and the Peri*, given (Nov. 25) simultaneously at the Standard Theater here and at the Savoy overseas.

Music

I Never Drank Behind the Bar (The McSorleys); *The Holy City*; *I'll Be Ready When the Great Day Comes*; *The Market on Saturday Night*; *McNally's Row of Flats*; *When the Clock in the Tower Strikes Twelve*.

1883

*T*o curb political corruption and favoritism in the appointment of government employees, Congress passed (Jan. 16) Ohio Senator Pendleton's bill, creating the Civil Service Commission. Later in the year, Congress lowered letter postage to 2 cents, introduced (Sept.) the postal money-order, and removed the internal revenue tax on nearly all commodities except tobacco and spirits.

At the International Conference in Washington, D.C., American railroads adopted four standards of time, namely, Eastern, Central, Mountain, and Pacific.

The East River or Brooklyn Bridge, New York, was opened (May 24). Six days later (May 30), twelve persons were trampled to death in a panic on the bridge. (The work was begun Jan. 3, 1870, and cost $16,000,000. Twenty workmen lost their lives during its construction. The structure was designed by John Augustus Roebling, builder of similar suspension bridges at Niagara Falls, 1855, and at Cincinnati, 1867. After his death in 1869, his son Washington Augustus Roebling carried on the work.)

The Northern Pacific railroad was completed (Aug. 22). Train service began on Sept. 8.

The Liberty-head five-cent piece went into circulation and remained in use until the appearance of the Indian-head or buffalo nickel in 1913.

Hiram Stevens Maxim, an American inventor living in England, changed the nature of warfare with his invention of the machine gun which bears his name. It fired 11 shots per second, an improvement over the Gatling gun of 1861.

"General Tom Thumb," stage name of Charles Sherwood Stratton, Barnum's famous dwarf, aged 45, died (July 15) in Middleborough, Mass. He was 40 inches tall. Queen Victoria added the "General" to his name in 1854.

The remains of John Howard Payne, writer of *Home, Sweet Home*, who died at Tunis, Africa, in 1852, were removed to Washington, D.C.

In Print

Joseph Pulitzer, Hungarian-born German newspaper editor and owner bought the English *New York World* from Jay Gould. Pulitzer immediately began to campaign against the prevailing plutocracy. His newspaper's flamboyant editorials and style of reporting helped to develop what came to be called "yellow" journalism, a term which originated about 1896.

The year saw the publication of George Wilbur Peck's book *Peck's Bad Boy and His Pa* (first of the series); John Hay's anonymous novel *The Bread-Winners*; the first of Kate Greenaway's *Almanacks*, illustrated in color (issued until 1897); Ella Wheeler Wilcox's *Poems of Passion* (containing *Solitude*, with its famous opening line: "Laugh and the world laughs with you") which were called "immoral" because of their eroticism; and the first installment of Francis James Child's *English and Scottish Popular Ballads* (completed in 1898 in five volumes).

Among periodicals founded were the *Ladies' Home Journal*, in Philadelphia; *The Etude*, a musical educational monthly, in Lynchburg, Va. (removed in 1884 to Philadelphia), and *Life*, in New York, a comic weekly, as a rival to *Puck* (1877) and *Judge* (1881). (*Life* became a monthly in 1933. The title was bought by Time, Inc., for a new weekly pictorial magazine with complementary text.)

On Stage

The Metropolitan Opera House in New York was opened (Oct. 22) with a performance of Gounod's French opera *Faust*, sung in Italian by Christine Nilsson (Marguerite), Sofia Scalchi (Siebel), Italo Campanini (Faust), Franco Novaro (Mephistopheles), and Giuseppe Del Puente (Valentine). The house seated 3,045 and cost $1,732,978.71. After a few weeks, the seating capacity was increased by the removal of the third-tier boxes and the substitution of a dress circle. At the Oct. 24 performance, the management presented its first new star, the incomparable Polish lyric soprano Marcella Sembrich, in *Lucia di Lammermoor*. On Dec. 20 the American premiere (Dec. 20) of Ponshielli's *La Gioconda* was presented. There were two American singers in the company— Franco Novaro, whose real name was Frank Nash, and Baltimore-born soprano Alwina Valleria.

Vaudeville, as distinct from the variety show, began in Boston. Benjamin Franklin Keith, who started his managerial career in the theater by exhibiting a midget called "Baby Alice," opened Keith's Theater in partnership with Colonel Williams Austin. They revolutionized the existing entertainment business by introducing the all-day performance of variety acts, or "continuous vaudeville."

Buffalo Bill (William Frederick Cody) launched his "Wild West" shows in partnership with Major John M. Burke and Dr. W. F. Carver.

Helen Modjeska introduced, in Louisville, Ky., Ibsen's tragic play *A Doll's House* under the title *Thora*, and with a happy ending.

Music

My Dad's Dinner Pail (Cordelia's Aspirations); *There's a Tavern in the Town*; *Forget-Me-Not*; *Marguerite*; *Strolling on the Brooklyn Bridge*; *When the Mists Have Rolled Away*; *When the Robins Nest Again*.

1884

$\mathcal{T}$he Greely Arctic expedition had started out in the summer of 1881 to make scientific observations at circumpolar stations and had not been heard from. A relief expedition sent out in May, 1883, under Lieutenant E. A. Garlington of the Cavalry Service, had been unsuccessful and had returned with great difficulty after having lost one of its tow ships in the ice. A second relief expedition was now equipped under Commander Winfield Scott Schley. It sailed in May from the Brooklyn Navy Yard, New York, and succeeded (June 28) in locating Lieutenant Adolphus Washington Greely and six survivors beyond Brevoort Island. Two of the latter died soon after Schley's arrival. Eighteen other members of the Greely party had perished from starvation shortly before aid arrived. (Greely died in 1935.)

A financial panic developed in New York, causing the failure of former President Grant's banking firm, Grant & Ward, among others.

The Washington National Monument, Washington, D.C., was completed at the cost of $1,300,000 when the capstone, weighing 3,300 pounds, was set (Dec. 6) in place. (The monument, begun in 1848, was dedicated on Feb. 21, 1885.)

Richmond, Va., became the first city in the world to boast a practical electric streetcar system when Frank J. Prague built 13 miles of electric railway.

Lewis Edson Waterman in this year, and Paul E. Wirt in 1885, introduced the fountain pen.

A World's Fair was opened (Dec. 16) in New Orleans by President Arthur pressing an electric button in Washington, D.C. European countries, as well as Mexico and other Central and South American republics, were represented. (The Fair continued until June, 1885, was re-opened in the winter of that year, and closed in May, 1886.)

The American Historical Society was founded in Saratoga, N.Y. (It was incorporated in 1889 with headquarters in Washington, D.C.)

A Bostonian, Russell Montague, and three Scots, George Grant, and Alexander and Roderick McLeod, built in the West Virginia Mountains near Green Brier a nine-hole golf course which they called the Oakhurst Golf Club.

The Equal Rights Party was formed after the Democratic and Republican parties refused to support woman suffrage in the national elections of the year. The party nominated (Aug. 23) in San Francisco the first women candidates for the highest executive offices in the nation—Mrs. Belva Ann Lockwood (1879) of Washington, D.C., for President, and Mrs. Marietta L. B. Stow of San Francisco for Vice President. They polled only a small vote.

Nasty campaigning in the national elections hurt the candidacy of the Republican nominee, James G. Blaine. A violent phrase, "Rum, Romanism, and Rebellion," hurled at the Democratic Party by a New York clergyman, S. D. Burchard, alienated the party's Irish Catholic vote. Equally offensive was a new epithet, "mugwump," of Algonquin Indian origin, applied to a bolter from the ranks. Dissatisfaction with Republican politics caused prominent independent Republicans such as George W. Curtis, Carl Schurz, and others, to bolt the party. It also lost the support of influential Republican newspapers, such as the *New York Times, Boston Herald,* and *Springfield (Mass.) Republican.* The abusive language greatly aided the election of the Democratic candidate, New York Governor Grover Cleveland, who received 219 electoral votes to 182—the first Democrat since the fifteenth President, Buchanan (1857-61), twenty-four years before. Cleveland carried every southern state, besides New York, New Jersey, Connecticut, Delaware, Maryland, and Indiana. The popular vote was over 10,000,000—the largest ever cast—Cleveland polling 4,911,000 votes, a plurality of 62,000 over Blaine.

In Print

Mark Twain published *The Adventures of Huckleberry Finn.*

On Stage

Gilbert and Sullivan's new operetta *Princess Ida, or Castle Adamant* was performed (Feb. 11) simultaneously in new York at the Fifth Avenue Theater and in Boston at the Museum Theater. The piece was not a success; it ran only a month in New York.

Music

Always Take Mother's Advice; My Ideal; Plum Pudding; The Sea Hath Its Pearls; Welcome, Sweet Springtime!; White Wings.

1885

$\mathcal{G}$rover Cleveland, Democrat, of New Jersey, was inaugurated as the 22nd President.

The U.S. Post Office issued by act of Congress (Mar. 3) for the first time a "special postal delivery stamp," a blue 10-cent adhesive with the picture of a running mail carrier.

By special legislation Congress restored Ulysses Simpson Grant to the rank of general, a post he resigned when he became 18th President.

Following the lead of Richmond, Va. (1884), Baltimore replaced (Aug. 10) its horse-drawn streetcars with an electric streetcar railway.

There were now 128,967 miles of railroad in the country.

The American Telephone and Telegraph Company was organized.

Ottmar Mergenthaler, German-American inventor, patented the linotype machine, the type-casting mechanism that eliminated hand-setting and gave a powerful stimulus to mass publications.

Dr. Chichester A. Bell and Charles S. Tainter invented the wax cylinder graphophone, the phonograph.

Stanford University, Palo Alto, Calif., for men and women, was founded by Leland Stanford. Stanford, a founder of the Union Pacific railroad and a governor of California, established the university in memory of his son, who died in boyhood.

Skiing became an American sport at a tournament held among the Norwegian settlers of Wisconsin and Minnesota.

Death claimed two Civil War commanders—Gen. Ulysses Simpson Grant, aged 63 (July 23), in Mt. McGregor, N.Y., and Major General George Brinton McClellan, aged 59 (Oct. 29), in Orange, N.J. Multimillionaire William Henry Vanderbilt, aged 64, who had nearly doubled his father's fortune, died (Dec. 8) in New York. He had uttered the sentiment: "The public be damned."

In Print

William Dean Howells published his novel of Vermont nouveau riche, *The Rise of Silas Lapham*.

The first volume of former President Grant's two-volume *Personal Memoirs* came off the press of Mark Twain's publishing firm, Charles L. Webster and Company, Hartford, Ct. (The second volume was issued in 1886. The memoirs, completed four days before Grant's death, realized over $450,000.)

On Stage

Benjamin Franklin Keith and E. F. Albee combined their vaudeville enterprises into a nationwide chain of theaters.

Gilbert and Sullivan's newest operetta *The Mikado, or The Town of Titipu* achieved even greater popularity in the United States than their *H.M.S. Pinafore*, again due in part to the lack of copyright protection. *The Mikado* swept the country as perhaps no similar piece has ever done. Curiously, the important work was first heard in the United States in a garbled version put on (June 29) by a small company in Chicago at the Museum Theater. The first real performance took place (July 6) in the same city at the Grand Opera House, and the production was brought (July 20) to the Union Square Theater, New York, for one performance. This was given in violation of an injunction, issued by Judge Wheeler, and landed the producer, Sydney Rosenfeld, in jail. The D'Oyly Carte Company from London then staged (Aug. 19) the operetta at the Fifth Avenue Theater for a run of 250 performances.

Music

At the Cross; The Gum Tree Canoe; Poverty's Tears Ebb and Flow (Old Lavender); Remember, Boy, Your're Irish (Shane na Lawn); Sleep, Baby, Sleep; Irene's Lullaby; Still as the Night.

1886

$\mathscr{P}$resident Cleveland married (June 2) at the White House Miss Frances Folsom, daughter of his law partner in Buffalo, N.Y.

Congress passed (Jan.) Senator George Hoar's bill regulating the succession of the members of the cabinet to the presidency in the historical order of the establishment of their departments in the event of the death, resignation, removal, or disability of the President and the Vice President. The measure grew out of the situation that seemed likely to develop between the time of death of President Garfield in September, 1881, and the meeting of the first session of the next Congress in December, during which period his successor, President Arthur, was in imminent danger of death. It was felt that the previous statutes naming in order the President of the Senate and the Speaker of the House, either of whom might represent an opposite party to the President's, was contrary to the people's choice at election.

Vice President Thomas A. Hendricks died (Nov. 25).

Alcatraz, an island fortress in San Francisco Bay, became a military prison. (It was converted in 1934 to a federal penitentiary.)

Geronimo, leader of the Apache Indians against the whites of the southwest, was subdued by Gen. George Crook but escaped. (Geronimo surrendered later, was removed to a reservation in Oklahoma, and died in 1909.)

On the evening of May 4 in Chicago's Haymarket Square, a bomb exploded during a mass meeting advocating the eight-hour work day and protesting the suppression of strikes by the police. A riot started which increased in violence when the police fired into the crowd. Seven policemen were killed and 66 persons were wounded. Eight anarchist Internationalists were arrested and convicted; four were hanged, one committed suicide, and three were sent to jail. (Their trials, however, failed to adduce evidence that the accused were implicated. Seven years later Governor John Peter Altgeld pardoned the prisoners. The event is the subject of a novel, *The Bomb*, by Frank Harris, 1908.)

The American Federation of Labor, a consolidation of trade and industrial unions, was organized with Samuel Gompers as the first president.

The United Mine Workers was established.

The United Labor Party was organized to advocate the single-tax theory of Henry George (1879).

Charles Martin Hall invented, contemporaneously with Paul Heroult of France, a process for making aluminum.

Robert Edwin Peary started his first polar expedition to the Arctic.

New York saloon keeper Steve Brodie gained instantaneous notoriety when he claimed he jumped (July 23), as a stunt, from the Brooklyn Bridge into the East River. He became immortalized in American English by such everyday phrases as to "do a brodie," or "pull a brodie." (Brodie went on the stage in 1891.)

Charleston, S.C., suffered a disastrous earthquake with a loss of 40 lives.

Chester A. Arthur, 21st President, died (Nov. 18).

In Print

The first issue of *The World Almanac and Book of Facts* went on sale. (It has been published annually ever since.)

Little Lord Fauntleroy, a novel by Frances Hodgson Burnett, and *Triumphant Democracy* by Andrew Carnegie were published.

The *Cosmopolitan* and *The Forum* were founded as monthly magazines. (The former started in Rochester, N.Y., and moved in 1887 to New York City.)

On Stage

The Madison Square Theater, New York presented (Nov. 1) one of the outstanding successes of the stage—Sir Charles Young's social drama *Jim, the Penman* with Frederic Robinson and (Mrs.) Agnes Booth.

Victor Herbert, grandson of Samuel Lover, Irish novelist, settled in New York as first violoncellist in the Metropolitan Opera House Orchestra.

The Norfolk, Litchfield County, Ct., music festivals were started.

The Metropolitan Opera House, New York, produced the American premiere of Wagner's two mighty music dramas, *Die Meistersinger von Nurnberg* (Jan. 4) and *Tristan und Isolde* (Dec. 1). Delibes's very French Hindu opera, *Lakme*, was staged (Mar. 1) in English by the rival Academy of Music, with Pauline L'Allemand in the title role singing *The Bell Song*.

Music

At Midnight on My Pillow Lying (Erminie); Darkest the House; Dear Mother, in Dreams I See Her; Forever with the Lord; The Gladiator March; The Letter That Never Came; Maggie, the Cows Are in the Clover; Never Take No for an Answer; Soldier's Life; What the Dicky-Birds Say.

1887

$\mathscr{C}$ongress passed (Feb. 4) the Inter-State Railway Law, creating the Interstate Commerce Commission.

The Dawes Act bestowed United States citizenship on American Indians and allotted them land in individual holdings.

The Progressive Labor Party was organized to oppose the United Labor Party (1886) and the single-tax theory of Henry George.

A hundred years had elapsed since the signing of the Constitution of the United States, and the event was duly observed with a Centenary Celebration (Sept. 15-17).

The world's highest statue, "Liberty Enlightening the World"—the Statue of Liberty, 305 feet, 6 inches, in bronze—by the Alsatian sculptor Frederic Auguste Bartholdi, had been presented to the United States by France in 1876 and erected on Bedloe Island in New York harbor. It was dedicated (Oct. 28) by President Cleveland in the presence of the sculptor and 1,000,000 spectators.

Emil Berliner, German-American inventor, patented the disk phonograph. (It was first publicly demonstrated in 1888 in Philadelphia.)

The Columbia Phonograph Company was founded in Bridgeport, Conn., by a group that acquired the patents of Dr. Chichester A. Bell and Sumner Tainter (1885).

West Street, New York, boasted a line of 90-foot telephone poles each with 25 crossarms.

The American yachts *Coronet* and *Dauntless* started (Mar. 12) a race across the Atlantic. For the eighth consecutive time, the United States won the America's Cup in international yacht racing when the *Volunteer* defeated the British *Thistle* in two races (Sept. 27 and 30).

In Print

Elizabeth Cochrane Seaman, journalist on the *New York World*, wrote under the pseudonym Nelly Bly about abuses in social employment, politics, and penal institutions. She had herself committed to Blackwells (now Welfare) Island, New York, by feigning insanity, and exposed the horrible conditions there in *Ten Days in a Mad House*.

Louis Keller began publishing the *Social Register*, the blue book of American society.

Scribner's Magazine was founded in New York as a monthly. (It ceased publication in 1939.)

On Stage

The Metropolitan Opera House, New York, produced (Nov. 9) the third of Wagner's four *Ring* operas, *Siegried*, for the first time in America.

A month after production in London at the Savoy Theater, Gilbert and Sullivan's comic opera *Ruddigore, or The Witch's Curse* reached (Feb. 21) the Fifth Avenue Theater, New York. Alfred Cellier's popular London Gaiety Theater success, *Dorothy*, came (Nov. 5) to the Standard Theater, New York.

Richard Mansfield played T. R. Sullivan's dramatization of Robert Louis Stevenson's *Dr. Jekyll and Mr. Hyde* in Boston, and created such a sensation by his changes from one character to another that he achieved stardom at its initial performance. He was seen (Mar. 12) in New York at the Madison Square Theater in his gruesome and unforgettable impersonation.

David Belasco and H. C. DeMille scored another success with their play *The Wife* (Lyceum, Nov. 1). With Mrs. G. H. Gilbert and John Drew, Ada Rehan won more laurels, including the praise of Ellen Terry, in *The Railroad of Love* (Daly's Nov. 1).

Music

Away in a Manger, or, Luther's Cradle Hymn; Calvery; Happy Birds; I Will Sing the Wond'rous Story; If the Waters Could Speak as They Flow; If You Love Me, Darling, Tell Me with Your Eyes; Petersbourgh Sleighride; Rock-a bye Baby; The Song That Reached My Heart; Wait Till the Tide Comes In.

1888

---

*T*he formation of monopolies, called "trusts," was a new subject of debate in Congress, which appointed a Committee on Manufactures to investigate the methods of "big business."

Congress created (June 13) a Department of Labor, and passed (Aug.) a Chinese Prohibition Bill (Chinese Exclusion Act) stopping immigration from China. Congress also signed its largest Pension Appropriation Bill up to that time—$80,280,000.

Mrs. Belva Ann Lockwood (1879, 1884) was again the presidential candidate of the Equal Rights Party.

The adoption of formal European dress by the ladies of the Imperial Japanese Court drew a letter of remonstrance from a group of American women headed by Mrs. Grover Cleveland and Mrs. James A. Garfield.

The 25th anniversary of the battle of Gettysburg was observed (July 4) with patriotic ceremonies on the historic spot by 20,000 survivors. Many Confederate soldiers participated.

The Washington National Monument (1848) was opened (Oct. 9) to the public.

The International Council of Women met (Mar. 26) in convention in Washington, D.C.

Steam and hydraulic passenger elevators were being replaced by the electric elevator.

Severe blizzards raged (beginning Jan. 12) through the Northwest and abated only with the coming of spring. In the East, the Atlantic coast, basking in warm early-spring weather, was suddenly chilled by a 60-mile-per-hour gale which swept in (Mar. 11-14) a blizzard that is still one of New York's most vivid memories. Telegraphic communications along the Eastern seaboard were disrupted, business halted, and food prices soared. More than 200 persons perished from cold and exposure. New York was buried (Mar. 12) in a snowfall that piled up as high as the first stories of apartment houses.

The cornerstone of the Catholic University, Washington, D.C., was laid (May 24).

The National Geographic Society, Washington, D.C., and the American Folk-Lore Society, Boston were established.

In Print

Casey at the Bat, a mock-heroic ballad about baseball, by Ernest Lawrence Thayer, was printed (June 3) in the *San Francisco Examiner*. Actor DeWolf Hopper, a baseball fan, is said to have recited the poem for the first time in Wallack's Theater, New York, and so started its enormous popularity.

Collier's was founded in New York as a weekly magazine.

Looking Backward, 2000-1887, a Utopian romance by Massachusetts journalist and novelist Edward Bellamy, and *The American Commonwealth*, a two-volume study of "the nation of the future," by James Bryce, were published.

On Stage

The Metropolitan Opera House, New York, staged (Jan. 25) the fourth and last of Wagner's mighty *Ring* operas, *Gotterdammerung*, for the first time in America. Also heard (Apr. 16) for the first time was Verdi's opera *Otello* at the Academy of Music.

Music

Semper Fidelis; *Where Did You Get That Hat?*; *The Whistling Coon*; *Anchored!*; *The Convict and the Bird*; *Drill, Ye Tarriers, Drill*; *The Mottoes Framed upon the Wall*; *Oh!, that We Two Were Maying*; *Where Did You Get That Hat?*; *With All Her Faults I Love Her Still*.

1889

*B*enjamin Harrison, Republican, of Ohio, was inaugurated as the 23rd President. He was the great grandson of Benjamin Harrison, a signer of the Declaration of Independence, and the grandson of 9th President William Henry Harrison.

Outgoing President Cleveland had vetoed during his term of office 312 bills—175 more than the combined total of his twenty-one predecessors.

Four stars were added to the national flag by the admission of North and South Dakota (Nov. 2), Montana (Nov. 8), and Washington (Nov. 11), respectively, as the 39th, 40th, 41st, and 42nd state.

An outcome of the Grange movement (1867) was the establishment (Feb. 9) of the Department of Agriculture by Congress.

The proposed construction, at an estimated cost of $50,000,000, of a canal across Nicaragua that would reduce travel from ocean to ocean to twenty-eight hours found support in Congress which established (Feb. 7) the Maritime Canal Company.

The Territory of Oklahoma was opened (Apr. 22) to homesteaders. So great was the rush of waiting settlers that towns of two or three thousand inhabitants at once came into existence. Oklahoma was represented this year at the Republican National Convention by a delegate who was a full-blooded Indian.

The United States purchased 11,000,000 acres from the Sioux Indians in Dakota Territory for $14,000,000.

Financial difficulties in the building of the Panama Canal by France (begun in 1882 by Viscount Ferdinand Marie de Lesseps, promotor of the Suez Canal) caused uneasiness in Congress. A Sundry Civil Bill appropriating $250,000 to the President for the protection of American interests on the Isthmus and a resolution protesting against French control of the canal were passed.

Secretary of Navy Benjamin Franklin Tracy outlined a program that included the construction and completion by the close of 1903 of 92 war vessels, aggregating 488,450 tons, at an estimated cost of $268,500,000.

A tidal wave in the Samoan Islands damaged (Mar. 16) the anchored German and American warships; the U.S. flagship *Trenton*, the *Vandalla*, and the *Nipsic* were washed ashore.

Free mail delivery to the home was introduced (Nov. 9) in cities of 5,000 or more inhabitants.

Steady rains in Pennsylvania burst (May 31) the reservoir dams above Johnstown, sending down the Conemaugh Valley a flood in which 2,209 persons perished and many towns were wiped out. The fury subsided about 18 miles below the city. The flood had its Paul Revere in Daniel Periton, son of a local merchant, who lost his life while alerting the inhabitants of the region when a railroad bridge collapsed under him and his bay horse. His cry during the unequal race was: "Run for your lives to the hills! Run to the hills! The dam is bursting!"

An elaborate Washington Centenary was celebrated (Apr. 30-May 2) in New York, commemorating the inauguration of George Washington as the first President of the Untied States. A colorful water pageant in New York Harbor and a parade, including governors of 29 States, foreign consuls, judges, and countless other notables, re-enacted with President Harrison and his official family the scene of the arrival of Washington. The surpliced choir of Trinity Church sang the hymn *Before the Lord We Bow* and the *Doxology* on the stairway of the Equitable Building when the President reached the place of reception. The Centennial Banquet and Ball at the festooned and metamorphosed Metropolitan Opera House that night was a brilliant social affair. Former Presidents Hayes and Cleveland were present. The fact that President Harrison was a descendant of a signer of the Declaration of Independence gave the ceremonies an historical connection with the original event. During a thanksgiving service, the hymn *Rise, Crowned with Light, Imperial Salem, Rise*, was sung. It was said that all the known relics of Washington, including his flute, were on display in New York.

There were now over 200 electric street railways in the United States, with 2,400 cars, operating on the Thomson-Houston and the Sprague systems.

The "Kodak" or hand camera was advertised in *Scribner's Magazine* by the Eastman Kodak Company, Rochester, N.Y., as a simple, snap-shooting device. Thus began the vogue of amateur photography.

The first practical electric elevators were installed in the Demarest Building, New York, by Otis Brothers and Company.

The great cantilever railroad bridge spanning the Hudson River at Poughkeepsie, N.Y., was completed.

Baldwin Brothers advertised "double balloon ascensions with parachute descents."

The last heavyweight boxing championship bout fought with bare knuckles took place (July 8) in Richburg, Missouri, between John L. Sullivan and Jack Kilrain. Kilrain was defeated in 75 rounds.

Jefferson Davis, aged 80, president of the former Confederate States, died (Dec. 11) in New Orleans.

In Print

Books of the year included Mark Twain's novel *A Connecticut Yankee in King Arthur's Court*, William Henry Herndon's three-volume biography *Herndon's Lincoln: The True Story of a Great Life*, Theodore Roosevelt's history *The*

Winning of the West (completed in 4 volumes in 1896), and *Three Men in a Boat* by Jerome K. Jerome.

On Stage

The Metropolitan Opera House, New York, staged (Mar. 4, 5, 8, 11) the first complete American performance of Wagner's four-opera cycle *Der Ring des Nibelungen*.

Music

Down Went McGinty; *Oh Promise Me*; *The Thunderer*; *The Washington Post*; *They Kissed, I Saw Them Do It!*; *Thy Sentinel Am I*.

1890

*I*daho (July 3) and Wyoming (July 10) were admitted as states.

Congress enacted (July 2) the Sherman Anti-Trust Act, as a result of the investigations of the Committee on Manufacturers (1888); established (Oct. 1) the Weather Bureau; and passed, on the same day, Ohio Representative William McKinley's high tariff bill "to protect infant industries." This bill placed sugar, among other articles, on the free list and safeguarded the woolen industry by a heavy duty on imported wool.

Failures in business were widespread. The government closed (Feb.) the First National, the Lenox Hill, and the Equitable banks in New York, suspended the Bank of America in Philadelphia, and arrested the president of the Sixth National Bank. Three Wall Street failures amounted to $10,000,000.

The state prison at Auburn, N.Y., was (Aug. 6) the scene of the first execution of a criminal in the United States by electricity. The electrocution was badly managed at the first attempt, and a second charge of current was required to accomplish its purpose. The victim was William Kemmler, convicted of the murder of Tillie Ziegler at Buffalo. Public sentiment urged repeal of electrocution, but it was upheld by the Court of Appeals.

Telegraphic communication with Europe was possible by means of seven Atlantic cables.

The business of the country was seriously affected for several days when a million-dollar fire damaged (July 18) the building of the Western Union Telegraph Company in New York.

Ellis Island in New York Harbor replaced (Dec. 31) Castle Garden as a port of entry for immigrants.

The Mormons in Utah renounced (Oct. 6) polygamy.

The Daughters of the American Revolution ("D.A.R.") was founded in Washington, D.C., by women descendants of persons who gave "material aid to the cause of independence."

The Woodmen of the World ("W.O.W.") was established in Omaha, Nebr., as a fraternal and benevolent society.

The General Federation of Women's Clubs was formed.

The Blue and the Gray, former Confederate soldiers, assembled (May 26) at a reunion in Vicksburg, Mississippi, the scene of a Civil War battle in 1863.

An influenza epidemic started (Jan.) in the East and spread westward and into Canada and Mexico, taking a large toll of lives.

Feminine fashions came back to the hour-glass figure, leg-of-mutton sleeves, and the gored skirt.

The old high bicycle gave way to the "drop frame" model, equipped with pneumatic tires. The new bicycles were thought to be safer for women who had taken up the sport.

The national population was 62,979,766. The Bureau of Statistics of the Treasury Department reported (June 30, 1891) that the total number of immigrants from 1820 to 1890 was 15,641,688, of whom 5,246,613 had entered during the past ten years. The largest numbers during the 70-year period came from Germany (4,551,719), Ireland (3,501,683), and England (2,460,034).

In Print

"Nelly Bly" (*New York World* journalist Elizabeth Cochrane Seaman) completed a tour of the world, sponsored by the newspaper, in 72 days, 6 hours, 10 minutes, 58 seconds (Nov. 14, 1889-Jan. 25, 1890), bettering Jules Verne's imaginary trip of 80 days. She published an account of the journey, entitled *Nelly Bly's Book: Around the World in Seventy-Two Days*. Her time was reduced later in the year by George Francis Train, who made the trip in 67 days, 12 hours, 3 minutes.

The *Literary Digest* was founded in New York as a weekly magazine. (It ceased publication in 1938.)

Lippincott's Monthly Magazine published (July) simultaneously with its London edition Oscar Wilde's novel *The Picture of Dorian Gray*.

On Stage

A new and magnificent Madison Square Garden—including a reproduction of the Giralda Tower of Seville, soon to be crowned by Augustus Saint-Gauden's statue of Diana—was financed by some of Wall Street's most noted tycoons. It was erected to replace the older structure of the same name that was demolished in 1889. The auditorium was opened (June 16) with a series of orchestral concerts, including two ballets, conducted by Eduard Strauss, brother Johann Strauss, the "Waltz King." The architect was Stanford White.

Exactly a month after its production at the Savoy Theater, London, Gilbert and Sullivan's new comic opera *The Gondoliers, or The King of Barataria* was heard (Jan. 7) in New York at the Park Theater.

Reginal DeKoven's still-popular light opera *Robin Hood* was premiered (June 9) in Chicago at the Grand Opera House, and given (Sept. 20) in London at Camden Town Park Hall. The work was performed in Boston (Music Hall, Sept. 22), in New York (Standard Theater, Sept. 28), and elsewhere on tour. Jessie Bartlett Davis, playing Allan-a-Dale, sang the hit song *O Promise Me*. Since *Erminie* (1886), no operetta had achieved comparable popularity.

Joseph Arthur's rural melodrama *Blue Jeans* (New York, 14th Street Theater, Oct. 6) drew capacity audiences because of its thrilling scene featuring the hero strapped to a threatening buzzsaw.

Music

Annie Rooney; The Birthday of a King; I've Come Here to Stay; The Irish Jubliee; Jolly Commodore; Love Will Find a Way; Maggie Murphy's Home (Reilly and the 400); Passing By; Scheherazade; Still as the Night; Taking in the Town; Tell Mother I'll Be There; Tenderly Calling; Throw Him Down, McCloskey; Thy Beaming Eyes; True-Hearted, Whole-Hearted; Peal Out the Watch-word!

1891

*A*fter several decades of agitation, Congress passed (Mar. 4) the International Copyright Act. The Forest Reserve Act for the protection of forest lands was also enacted.

A war with Chile was a much-discussed topic in the press when that country failed to make proper amends for the killing in Valparaiso of two sailors from the U.S. cruiser *Baltimore*, the wounding of other bluejackets, and the imprisonment of 35 members of the crew. (Chile apologized belatedly in Jan., 1892, and later paid an indemnity of $75,000 to the wounded sailors and to the families of the two who lost their lives.)

The Washington home of Benjamin Franklin Tracy, Secretary of the Navy, was destroyed (Feb. 3) by fire, resulting in the death of Mrs. Tracy, her daughter, and a woman servant, and in injury to other members of the family. The Secretary himself was unconscious when removed from the building and was revived only with difficulty.

Two men wrecked (Dec. 4) the Wall Street, New York, office of financier Russell Sage with a dynamite bomb after demanding $1,200,000. Sage was unharmed, but the bomb blew both men to pieces, killed three other persons, and injured several others.

New Orleans citizens rose (Mar. 14) in arms when a local jury acquitted six of nineteen Italians suspected of the murder (Oct. 15, 1890) of Chief of Police David C. Hennessy. The Italians were believed to be members of a Sicilian secret society called the Mafia, which had been terrorizing the city for years and which feared a Hennessey investigation. An immense armed mob stormed the city jail, dragged forth eleven of the Italian prisoners, and either shot or hanged them from lampposts. The Italian government protested to Secretary of State James G. Blaine, who asked the Governor of Louisiana to bring the lynchers to justice. The request was ignored; and a grand jury in New Orleans whitewashed the perpetrators, among whom were many prominent citizens.

Thomas Alva Edison patented the forerunner of the motion-picture camera—the kinetograph, or kinetoscope, a lantern for projecting moving pictures on a screen. (The invention was first publicly exhibited Apr. 15, 1892, in New York.)

Edward Goodrich Acheson discovered carborundum.

James Naismith, an instructor in the Y.M.C.A. Training School at Springfield, MA, devised the game of basketball.

The first international continuous six-day bicycle race was won by the American "Plugger Bill" Martin in New York at Madison Square Garden.

One Zoe Gayton arrived in New York, claiming to have walked all the way from San Francisco—3,395 miles.

Deaths of the year included: Phineas Taylor Barnum, aged 81 (Apr. 7), and Herman Melville, aged 72 (Sept. 28), author of *Moby Dick*.

In Print

Isaac Kauffman Funk, clergyman, publisher, and lexicographer, began the publication of *A Standard Dictionary of the English Language* (1891-93, 1903, 1910-12).

The *Review of Reviews* was founded as a monthly magazine. (It ceased publication in 1937.)

On Stage

The Russian composer Peter Ilich Tchaikovsky arrived (Apr. 27) in New York for a month's visit. He conducted four concerts in New York in connection with the dedication of Carnegie Music Hall, one in Philadelphia (May 18), and one in Baltimore.

Elaborate ceremonies dedicated (May 5) the Carnegie Music Hall in New York, built by Andrew Carnegie for the Oratorio Society of which he was president (1888-1918). Tchaikovsky shared conducting honors with Walter Damrosch, director of the Oratorio Society.

Theodore Thomas established the Chicago Symphony Orchestra.

New York saloon keeper Steve Brodie, famed jumper from the Brooklyn Bridge (1886), now repeated his stunt from a stage bridge in Steele MacKaye's melodrama *Mad Money* (Niblo's Garden, Feb. 22). Brodie also went on the road with MacKaye's play, was exhibited as a wax figure at Huber's Palace Museum, New York, Aug. 21-26, 1893, and played in a show entitled *On the Bowery*, which reached the California Theater in San Francisco, in 1896.

Sarah Bernhardt introduced (Feb. 5) Victorian Sardou's powerful five-act drama *La Tosca* at the Garden Theater in New York. The play was to furnish the subject for Puccini's Italian opera of the same name in 1900.)

Music

American Patrol; Death and Transfiguration; Little Boy Blue; The Pardon Came Too Late; Actions Speak Louder than Words; Happy Day; Hats Off to Me; Hey, Rube!; Kiss and Let's Make Up; Knights of the Mystic Star; The Last of the Hogans; Life's Railway to Heaven; The Picture That's Turned Toward the Wall; A Pretty Girl; Scarf Dance; Take a Day Off, Mary Ann; Ta-ra-ra-bom-der-e; Whosoever Will May Come.

1892

*S*ocial leader Samuel Ward McAllister is reported to have declared in New York's exclusive Union League Club that there were "only about four hundred people in New York society." He named society's elite on the occasion of a great ball tendered (Feb. 1) by Mrs. William Astor when no more than that number of guests could be accommodated in her ballroom. (The phrase seems already to have been current in 1890; it figured in the title of a popular comedy, *Reilly and the Four Hundred*, which Edward Harrigan wrote and introduced Dec. 29 of that year at his new 35th Street Theater.)

The United States launched its first armored battleship, the *Texas*.

The empty buildings of the Columbian Exposition in Chicago were dedicated (Oct. 21) on the 400th anniversary of the discovery of America. The formal opening took place in the next year.

Lieutenant Robert Edwin Peary explored the Greenland coast.

The cornerstone of the Cathedral of St. John the Divine (Episcopal) in New York was laid on St. John's Day (Dec. 27).

The horseless buggy or self-propelled carriage, now called the automobile, was becoming a mechanical reality in America. German engineer Karl Benz had already exhibited an automobile in 1885, but tinkering American inventors hadn't heard of it. William Morrison of Des Moines, Ia., built an electric automobile, while the brothers Charles E. and J. Frank Duryea, bicycle makers, displayed a gasoline-driven car on the streets of Springfield, Mass.

Direct telephone service between New York and Chicago was established (Oct. 18).

Steam-powered elevated trains began running (June 29) in Chicago.

The notorious Dalton Boys, who for five years had been the nation's top-ranking public enemies, were wiped out by the citizens of Coffeyville, Ks., while they were attempting to rob a couple of banks.

Lizzie Borden became a sensational figure when she was accused on circumstantial evidence of hacking to death her step-parents (Aug. 4) in their home in Fall River, Ma. (She was acquitted at her trial the next year, and became the subject of popular ballads and fiction.)

James J. ("Gentleman Jim") Corbett became the first heavyweight boxing champion according to the Marquis of Queensberry rules when he defeated John L. Sullivan in 21 rounds at New Orleans.

Deaths of the year included: Walt Whitman, aged 73 (Mar. 27), and John Greenleaf Whittier, aged 85 (Sept. 7).

In Print

Rudyard Kipling, English poet and writer, settled for several years in Brattleboro, Vt. Here he wrote, with his brother-in-law Wolcott Balestier, *The Naulahka*, 1892, a novel about a California speculator in India. *Captains Courageous*, 1897, is Kipling's only novel dealing with America.

On Stage

John Philip Sousa, leader of the U.S. Marine Corps band, resigned (Aug. 1) his post to organize his own band of 100 players, which played for many years in the United States and Canada. (The band undertook European tours in 1900, 1901, 1903, 1905, and made a world tour in 1910-11.)

England's Poet Laureate, Lord Tennyson, wrote a play about Robin Hood but because of the vogue of DeKoven's light opera of the same name was compelled to call it *The Foresters*. The poetical play was acted and sung (Mar. 17) with Sir Arthur Sullivan's music in New York at Daly's Theater.

If Chicago's Columbian Exposition was a year late in opening its commemoration of the 400th anniversary of Columbus's discovery, Boston was able to greet the historic event at the Globe Theater with a timely extravaganza, *1492*, book by Robert Ayres Barnet and music by Carl Pflueger, that proved extremely popular.

Other New York plays were *Captain Lettarblair*, *The Masked Ball*, *Diplomacy*, and *Americans Abroad*.

Music

Daddy Wouldn't Buy Me a Bow-Wow; The Man That Broke the Bank at Monte Carlo; My Sweetheart's the Man in the Moon; The Nut-Cracker Suite—(1) Miniature Overture; (2) March; (3) Dance of the Sugar-Plum Fairy; (4) Trepak; (5) Arabian Dance; (6) Chinese Dance; (7) Dance of the Mirlitons; (8) Waltz of the Flowers; Push Dem Clouds Away (A Trip to Chinatown).

1893

$\mathscr{G}$rover Cleveland, Democrat of New Jersey, was inaugurated for a second term—the only President to serve two non-consecutive terms. He was the 22nd and 24th president of the United States.

Congress enacted a law requiring American consuls at foreign ports to register intending immigrants and to deny entry to the United States of persons who were insane, destitute, illiterate, criminal, or physically unfit. Another enactment was the repeal of the Sherman Silver Purchase Act.

Thomas Francis Bayard of Wilmington, Del., lawyer and senator, was appointed the first United States Ambassador to Great Britain (1893-97). Hitherto the American representative there held the rank of Minister Plenipotentiary.

A revolt in Hawaii (Jan.), instigated by its foreign-born and English-speaking inhabitants, deposed the ruling Queen Liliuokalani and set up a provisional government which made overtures to the United States for annexation. Outgoing President Harrison recommended the annexation to the Senate, but his successor, President Cleveland, withdrew the proposal and recalled the United States minister. (Hawaii carried on under a Republican government until its annexation in 1898 on a more formal basis.)

William Jennings Bryan, Representative from Nebraska, became a significant national figure after his eloquent three-hour speech (Aug. 16) in Congress in defense of silver coinage.

The Columbian Exposition, celebrating the 400th anniversary of Columbus's discovery of America, was formally opened (May 1) in Chicago. In connection with the celebration, the U.S. Post Office placed (Jan. 2) on sale its first commemorative postage stamps, and a brilliant naval display in New York City featured war vessels representing the United States, Great Britain, Russia, France, Italy, Spain, Germany, Holland, Brazil, and the Argentine Republic. Foreign powers were careful not to send any vessel, as Nugent Robinson noted in *A History of the World*, "which would by comparison put to shame our own little navy, which then was without battleships." Norway's unique contribution, a Viking ship propelled by oars and a single sail, arrived too late and was exhibited in Chicago. The festivities were saddened (Oct. 28) by the assassination at his residence of the Mayor of Chicago, Carter H. Harrison, Sr., by a man who fired five shots from a revolver. The trial court refused to entertain the plea of insanity.

Twenty-five government employees were killed and many others were seriously injured in the collapse of Ford's Theater, Washington, D.C., the building in which Lincoln was assassinated in 1865. (The old structure was occupied by the Records Division of the War Department.)

New York Central locomotive Engine No. 999, pulling four heavy cars (as the "Empire Express"), made 112-1/2 miles per hour between Crittenden and Wende, N.Y., with Engineer C. Hogan at the throttle. New speeds were also achieved by the U.S. Navy with the gunboat *Detroit*, the commerce destroyer *Columbia*, and the cruiser *New York*—all new vessels.

The Great Northern Railroad, connecting St. Paul, Minn., and the Northwest, was completed.

There were 170,607 miles of railroad in the country.

Various types of automobiles were being tested, among them Henry Ford's. The automobile of this period was usually a one-cylinder gasoline-driven wagon, resting on high wheels, with the engine placed under a seat for two persons. The vehicle was then called a motorcycle, and was capable of traveling seven or eight miles per hour.

Sandow, the strong man who permitted ladies to feel his muscles, was a theatrical attraction at the Columbian Exposition. He was managed by a young, Florenz Ziegfeld, Jr.

The international yacht race for the America's Cup was run for the first time in American waters off New York Harbor. The American *Vigilant* defeated the British *Valkyrie II* in all three races (Oct. 7, 9, 13), thus winning the coveted trophy for the ninth consecutive time since 1851.

T. Bowen and J. Burke, at New Orleans, fought the longest prize-fight in which gloves were used—7 hours, 18 minutes, 10 seconds. It went 110 rounds and ended in a draw.

A panic and a two-year depression marked the seventeenth United States financial calamity since 1790.

Rutherford B. Hayes, the nineteenth President, died (Jan. 17).

In Print

Among new literary periodicals were *McClure's Magazine*, a monthly (which ceased publication in 1929), and *The Outlook*, a weekly (which ceased publication in 1935), in New York.

Henry Blake Fuller published *The Cliff-Dwellers*, a realistic novel about Chicago.

On Stage

New operas heard for the first time in the United States were Camille Saint-Saens's *Samson et Dalila* (New Orleans, French Opera House, Jan. 4; already sung in concert form by the New York Oratio Society, Carnegie Hall, Mar. 25, 1892); Leoncavallo's *Pagliacci* (Philadelphia, Grand Opera House, June 15; New York, Metropolitan Opera House, Dec. 11, in Italian); Bizet's *Les Pecheurs des Perles* (Philadelphia, Grand Opera House, Aug. 25).

Anton Dvorak's Fifth Symphony, called *From the New World*, received (Dec. 15) its world premiere in New York at Carnegie Hall. Anton Seidl conducted the Philharmonic Society in the presence of the composer. Dvorak was at this time artistic director of the National Conservatory in New York.

Lionel Barrymore made his stage debut in Richard Brinsley Sheridan's (1775) comedy *The Rivals* in Philadelphia.

Oscar Hammerstein tried his hand at a one-act comic opera, writing both the book and the music. Entitled *Koh-I-Noor*; it was put on (Oct. 30) in New York at Koster and Bial's Theater.

Films

Thomas Alva Edison built in West Orange, N.J., the first movie studio in America, "The Kinetographic Theater." It was a weird, black structure, costing $637.37, and was popularly called The Black Maria. At this studio, comedian Fred Ott, generally regarded as the first movie actor, recorded portrayed on film a man in the act of sneezing—and *Fred Ott's Sneeze* became a classic phrase.

Music

Happy Birthday to You; The Cat Came Back; December and May; Do, Do, My Huckleberry, Do; The Fatal Wedding; From the New World; Good-Morning to All; Song Stories for the Kindergarten; I Long to See the Girl I Left Behind; Love Me Little, Love Me Long; Mamie! Come Kiss Your Honey; Say "Au Revoir," but Not "Goodbye"; See, Saw, Margery Daw; They Never Tell All What They Know; Little Girls in Blue; The Volunteer Organist; When the Roll Is Called Up Yonder; Won't You Be My Sweetheart?

1894

$\mathscr{T}$he United States recognized the newly established Republic of Hawaii (1893).

Congress designated the first Monday in September as Labor Day.

The Bureau of Engraving and Printing of the Treasury Department took over (July 1) from private manufacturers the printing of United States postage stamps.

The last of the noted war vessels of the Civil War, the *Kearsarge*, foundered on a reef in the Caribbean Sea and was wrecked by pounding breakers after thirty years of service.

The United States government was compelled twice this year to borrow money, each time $50,000,000 in gold—a reflection of the political and labor unrest in the country.

The financial depression that started in 1893 created so much unemployment that Jacob Sechler Coxey, owner of sand quarries and a racing stable, organized an "army"—without weapons—of some 500 laborers, one of several "Industrial Armies," and marched with this followers to Washington to present "a petition in boots" to Congress for relief legislation. The marchers were supplied with sustenance along the route by individuals and communities. Coxey himself rode in a buggy drawn by his $40,000 pacer "Acolyte," while his second-in-command, Carl Browne, sat astride Coxey's $7,500 stallion. The famous march at first alarmed the country, but it soon became an object of ridicule. In Washington, a mild demonstration took place (Apr. 29) on the steps of the Capitol. Coxey and other leaders were arrested by the police for walking on the grass and spent 20 days in jail for the offense. Coxey at the time had been nominated for Congress by an Ohio district, but he was defeated in the fall elections. (Coxey led a second "army" to Washington in 1944. He died May 18, 1951, at the age of 97, in Massillon, Ohio.)

The largest meteorite, weighing 37 tons and called the Ahnighito (The Tent), was found by Lieutenant Robert Edwin Peary, later discoverer of the North Pole, near Melville Bay in northern Greenland. It was eventually placed on permanent exhibition under the arch to the entrance of the Museum of Natural History, New York.

On Broadway, Thomas Alva Edison publicly exhibited (Apr. 14) his motion-picture machine, the kinetoscope.

The Kinetoscope Exhibition Company on Nassau Street, New York, found a new way of making money with the latest (screenless) moving-picture mechanism by showing in separate machines each of the six rounds of a prize fight between Michael Leonard, "Beau Brummell of the prize ring," and Jack Cushing. The fight was staged and photographed in Edison's "Black Maria" studio (1893) in West Orange, N.J. A similar boxing match was photographed between the heavyweight champion James. J. ("Gentleman Jim") Corbett and Pete Courtney of Trenton, N.J.

In Print

An unprofitable investment of $200,000 brought Mark Twain's publishing firm Charles L. Webster and Company, of Hartford, Conn., into bankruptcy. To recoup his losses, Twain went on a lecture tour of the world. (He published his experiences in *Following the Equator*, in 1897.)

Books of the year included Mark Twain's stories *The Tragedy of Pudd'nhead Wilson* and *Tom Sawyer Abroad, by Huck Finn, edited by Mark Twain*; the novels *The Honorable Peter Sterling* by Paul Leicester Ford; and *Katherine Lauderdale* by Francis Marion Crawford; and Henry Demarest Lloyd's trenchant study *Wealth against Commonwealth*.

The Billboard, a theatrical weekly journal, was founded in Cincinnati.

On Stage

Fifteen-year-old Ethel Barrymore made her stage debut in Montreal in Richard Brinsley Sheridan's (1775) comedy *The Rivals*, the same play in which her brother Lionel had debuted the preceding year. Subsequently she appeared in New York at the Empire Theater.

When George Edwardes transferred (Sept. 18) from the Gaiety Theater, London, to Daly's Theater, New York, he "streamlined" his bevy of chorines in *A Gaiety Girl*, replacing the statuesque, padded "Lydia Thompson" blondes of 1868 with more slender women. Soon there were to be the Florodora Girls, the Follies Girls, the Nell Brinkley Bathing Beauties, and others, leading ultimately to the "tall-stemmed roses" of the Billy Rose productions.

Music

And Her Golden Hair Was Hanging Down Her Back; *Comrades, Forgotten*; *Her Eyes Don't Shine Like Diamonds*; *Her Last Thoughts Were of You*; *The Honeymoon March*; *Humoresque*; *I Don't Want to Play in Your Yard*; *Kathleen, My Friend, the Major*; *Prayer of Thanksgiving*; *She May Have Seen Better Days*; *The Sidewalks of New York*; *Sweet Bunch of Daisies*; *Take a Seat, Old Lady*; *Would God I Were a Tender Apple Blossom*; *You Can't Play in Our Yard Any More*.

1895

$\mathscr{C}$ongress passed an income tax law, which was declared unconstitutional by the U.S. Supreme Court.

The U.S. Post Office established rural free delivery.

George Baldwin Seldon patented a gasoline-driven automobile. So keen was the interest in the speeds developed by the various types of automobiles that Herman Kohlsaat, a Chicago newspaper owner, sponsored an endurance contest. Six contestants participated in the event over a 53-1/2 mile course. The Duryea Wagon Motor Company won the race in 10 hours, 23 minutes.

A serious trolley car strike inconvenienced Brooklynites for four weeks. The militia was brought out to maintain order. Other labor strikes occurred elsewhere throughout the year.

Amateur pianists became parlor virtuosi when the automatic player-piano came upon the market. Among the earliest forms of the mechanism were the angelus, autopiano, pianolo, and ampico.

D. D. Palmer began to practice chiropracty.

The Carnegie Institute was founded in Pittsburgh.

In Newport, R.I., the first open golf championship match ever held in the United States took place and was won by Horace Rawlins, with a card showing 173 strokes for 36 holes. At the same time, the first championship for women was held at Meadowbrook, L.I., the victor Mrs. C. S. Brown, who carded 132 strokes for 18 holes. During this year the number of United States golfing clubs increased from about 40 to 100.

In Print

William Randolph Hearst, already owner of the *San Francisco Journal*, now acquired the *New York Journal*, thereby establishing his newspaper chain.

Gelett Burgess's famous quatrain "The Purple Cow" appeared in his magazine *The Lark*. (He also invented the Goops, circle-faced children who did naughty and ill-mannered things, and words such as "bromide," a person who utters platitudes, and "blurb," a brief written expression of praise or admiration.)

On Stage

The New York Metropolitan Opera House produced (Feb. 4) the American premiere of Verdi's *Falstaff*.

Humperdinck's fairy-tale opera *Hansel and Gretel* was produced (Oct. 8) for the first time in the United States in New York at Daly's Theater in English.

Dramatizations of two recent (1894) English novels, *Trilby* and *The Prisoner of Zenda*, were successful on the New York stage. *Trilby*, adapted from George DuMaurier and staged (Apr. 15) at the Garden Theater, started a wild craze across the country. As the reminiscing Amelia Ransome Neville wrote: "The Trilby craze was terrific. We wore Trilby hats, Trilby coats, Trilby slippers, and what not; ate Trilby chocolates, played Trilby waltzes, and developed a 'Trilby type' in beauty." *The Prisoner of Zenda*, derived from Anthony Hope (Hawkins) and produced (Sept. 4) at the Lyceum Theater, provided Edward Hugh Sothern with a new romantic role.

Film

A prize fight between Young Griffo and Battling Barnett on the roof of Madison Square Garden, New York, was filmed. It was publicly exhibited (May 20) on a screen by a projecting machine invented in the preceding year by Woodville Latham.

Music

America, the Beautiful; Materna; The Band Played On; The Hand That Rocks the Cradle; The Afternoon of a Faun; Don't Go Out To-night, Boy; A Dream; Just Tell Them That You Saw Me; My Best Girl's a New-Yorker; The Same Sweet Girl To-day; There'll Come a Time; We Were Sweethearts for Many Years; When Your Love Grows Cold.

1896

$\mathcal{U}$tah was admitted (Jan. 4) as the 32nd state.

The discovery of gold in Alaska and the Yukon territory of northwestern Canada started the Klondike gold rush (1897-99).

The first American subway was built in Boston.

Emile Berliner, German-American inventor, patented the disk phonograph and record.

The first commercial automobile appeared (Mar. 6) on Detroit streets.

Man's attempts to fly were being slowly realized. Otto Lilienthal, a German engineer, had been experimenting for five years in flights with a glider plane near Berlin. In the United States this year, Octave Chanute, assisted by Herring and Avery, completed (June) several successful flights in a glider over the sand dunes of northern Indiana.

The Volunteers of America was founded (Nov. 6) in New York as a religious and philanthropic organization.

The College of New Jersey, founded in 1746, was renamed Princeton University after the town of its location.

William Ashley ("Billy") Sunday, professional baseball player (1883-90) and assistant secretary at the Y.M.C.A. in Chicago (1891-95), embarked on his career as an evangelist.

William Jennings Bryan delivered his "cross-of-gold" speech, outlining his silver money policy, at the Democratic national convention in Chicago, and was nominated the party's presidential candidate at 36. In the bitterly-fought national elections, he was defeated by his Republican opponent William McKinley, who favored the gold standard and high protective tariff.

Agitation for free coinage of silver created a depression which lasted a year—the eighteenth since 1790.

In Print

R. F. Outcault, whose newspaper series of comic pictures, "Hogan's Alley," had been appearing in the *New York World* since 1894, joined the staff of William Randolph Hearst's *Journal*. Both papers printed "Yellow Kid" serials.

Books of the year included Mark Twain's *Personal Recollections of Joan of Arc*, Paul Lawrence Dunbar's *Lyrics of Lowly Life*, John Kendrick Bang's farcical stories *The Houseboat on the Styx*, the novel *The Damnation of Theron Ware* by Harold Frederic, *In His Steps* by Charles Monroe Shelden; *The Little Regiment* by Stephen Crane, and *The Story of the Other Wise Man* by Henry Van Dyck. William Gilbert Patten began the publication of the first of his approximately 200 *Frank Merriwell* tales.

On Stage

New York's Academy of Music produced (Nov. 13) the American premiere of Giordano's opera *Andrea Chenier.*

Bandmaster John Philip Sousa scored his first real success as a composer of operettas with *El Capitan* (Boston, Tremont Theater, Apr. 13; New York, Broadway Theater, Apr. 20, and elsewhere in the United States; performed in London, Lyric Theater, July 10, 1899, as well as in Paris).

Films

Vaudeville theaters began to show motion pictures, but they were still considered a novelty.

Peep-shows, penny arcades, and nickelodeons were showing a film version of the latest stage success, *The Widow Jones*, starring a matronly May Irwin and a fatherly John C. Rice. In the film, they indulged in a protracted kiss that was assailed as "a lyric of the stockyards" by some clergy. The film drew capacity crowds. Another shocker was the action short *The Empire State Express*, featuring a train that rushed full speed toward the audience. So realistic was the effect that spectators in the front rows were said to have jumped to get out of its way. To placate patrons who shied at the darkness in motion-picture houses, T. L. Tally erected, in the lighted area of his new Phonograph and Vitascope Parlor in Los Angeles, a partition through which to view the screen.

Music

El Capitan; A Hot Time in the Old Town; Don't Give Up the Old Love for the New; Elsie from Chelsea; I Wonder if She'll Ever Come Back to Me; Laugh and the World Laughs with You; Love Makes the World Go 'Round; My Gal Is a High Born Lady; Sweet Rosie O'Grady; You're Not the Only Pebble on the Beach.

1897

*W*illiam McKinley, Republican, of Ohio, was inaugurated as the 25th President.

Steam-powered elevated railway trains started running (Oct. 19) in a circuit around the business center of Chicago; thereafter, that part of the city was called "The Loop."

The Library of Congress was transferred from the Capitol to a building of its own, erected at a cost of $6,347,000.

The remains of Gen. Ulysses Simpson Grant, eighteenth President of the United States, were removed from a temporary vault on Riverside Drive, New York, on the bank of the Hudson River, and interred (Apr. 27) with an impressive all-day ceremony in a large vault erected on the site. The Tomb was built by popular subscription; 90,000 citizens contributed $600,000 of the cost, no person being permitted to subscribe more than $5,000.

Bob Fitzsimmons defeated (Mar. 17) James J. ("Gentleman Jim") Corbett in 14 rounds at Carson City, Nev., for the heavyweight boxing championship. The bout was filmed for motion-picture theaters, but the screen version was marred by a continuous copyright notice.

In Belleville, Ill., Jacob Wainwright added a new thrill to the bicycle era when he pedaled backwards 440 yards in 37-7/8 seconds, and 880 yards (also backwards) in 51-3/5 seconds.

In Print
Books of the year included Mark Twain's travel account *Following the Equator*, John Luther Long's story *Madame Butterfly*, and a number of novels: *The Choir Invisible* by James Lane Allen—published in 1893 under the title *John Gray*; *Hugh Wynne, Free Quaker* by Silas Weir Mitchell; *Soldiers of Fortune* by Richard Harding Davis; *What Maisie Knew* by Henry James; and *Wolfville* by Alfred Henry Lewis, the first of his six *Old Cattleman's* tales, published under the pseudonym Dan Quin.

"Yes, Virginia, there is a Santa Claus," declared the *New York Sun* in its editorial (Sept. 21), "Is There a Santa Claus?" in response to a letter from young Virginia O'Hanlon of New York. The famous editorial was written by associate editor Francis Pharcellus Church.

On Stage

Theodore Thomas conducted (Feb. 5) his Chicago Orchestra in the first American performance of Richard Strauss's tone poem *Also sprach Zarathustra*.

The Boston Symphony Orchestra played (Apr. 17) the first American rendition of Rimsky-Korsakoff's symphonic suite *Scheherazade*.

John J. McNally's musical farce *The Good Mr. Best* featured (Aug. 3) in its third act the new "cinematograph" in New York at the Garrick Theater.

Gustave Kerker's musical comedy, *The Belle of New York*, was (Sept. 18) the hit of the Casino Theater.

Music

Asleep in the Deep; Beautiful Isle of Somewhere; Break the News to Mother; Cupid and I (The Serenade); If You See My Sweetheart; I've Just Come Back to Say Goodbye; Just for the Sake of Our Daughter; On the Banks of the Wabash Far Away; The Stars and Stripes Forever; Take Back Your Gold; There's a Little Star Shining for You; Wedding of the Winds, Dear.

1898

$\mathscr{A}$ revolt in Cuba against Spain, begun in 1895, caused increasing concern to the United States. For the protection of American interests, the United States dispatched (Jan.) the battleship *Maine* to the harbor at Havana. An explosion of undetermined origin wrecked (Feb. 15) the ship with a loss of 260 lives. The pro-war press was greatly aroused and Congress appropriated (Mar. 9) the sum of $50,000,000 for eventualities. Spain, long irked by America's pro-insurgent sympathy, declared war (Apr. 24) against the United States. The defeat of the Spanish fleets at Manila in the Philippines (May 1) by Admiral George Dewey and at Santiago, in Cuba (July 3), by Rear-Admiral William Thomas Samson and Commodore Winfield Scott Schley, along with American victories on the island, brought about (Aug. 12) an armistice. "Rough Riders," recruited by Lieutenant Colonel Theodore Roosevelt, aided in the battle at El Caney (July 1) and in the highly publicized assault on San Juan Hill (July 3). The treaty of peace was signed (Dec. 10) in Paris; the United States acquired all Spanish claims on Puerto Rico and Guam, paid $20,000,000 for the Philippine Islands, and undertook the supervision of Cuba until 1934. 6,472 American soldiers and sailors lost their lives in the war.

The United States annexed (July 7) the Hawaiian Islands, which became the Territory of Hawaii by act of Congress June 14, 1900.

A New York legislative act (signed May 11, 1896, and effective Jan. 1, 1898) created the city of "Greater New York," combining the five boroughs of Manhattan, Brooklyn, the Bronx, Richmond, and Queens.

The National Institute of Arts and Letters was founded as an American equivalent to the Academie Francaise, with 250 members representing art, literature, and music.

In Print
Popular novels of the year were *David Harum, A Story of American Life* by Edward Noyes Westcott, and *When Knighthood Was in Flower* by Charles Major.

On Stage
Victor Herbert was appointed musical conductor of the Pittsburgh Symphony Orchestra. He scored his first major comic opera success with *The Fortune Teller* (Buffalo, Star Theater, Sept. 19; New York, Wallack's, Sept. 26, and elsewhere on tour). The cast included Alice Nielsen, Marguerite Sylva,

Eugene Cowles, Joseph Cawthorn, and Joseph Herbert. (The London performance of the operetta in 1901 started Alice Nielsen on her operatic career. She made her grand opera debut in 1903 in Naples.)

Way Down East, a play by Lottie Blair Parker, started (Feb. 7) its long run with Phoebe Davis and Howard Kyle at the Manhattan Theater, New York.

Edmond Rostand's play *Cyrano de Bergerac* was seen (Oct. 3) in English versions simultaneously in New York (Garden Theater) with Richard Mansfield, Margaret Anglin, and William Courtney; and in Philadelphia with Ada Rehan and Charles Richman.

Music

Baby's Prayer; Because; The Boy Guessed Right; Every Night There's a Light; Gold Will Buy Most Anything but a True Girl's Heart; Gypsy Love Song; I Guess I'll Have to Telegraph My Baby; Just As the Sun Went Down; Just One Girl; Little Birdies Learning How to Fly; 'Mid the Green Fields of Virginia; The Moth and the Flame; My Old New Hampshire Home; The Path That Leads the Other Way; She Is the Belle of New York; She Was Bred in Old Kentucky.

1899

*R*eleased from the yoke of Spain (1898), the Philippine Islands now clamored for independence from the military government of the United States and commenced (Feb. 4) guerrilla warfare (1899-1901). (The leader of the insurgents, Emilio Aquinaldo, was captured Mar. 23, 1901, by Brigadier General Frederick Funston. The rebellion ended officially Apr. 30, 1902; military governorship was terminated July 4 of that year.)

Under a tripartite treaty with Great Britain and Germany, the United States acquired (Nov.) the Samoan island Tutuila, its four adjacent islets (Aunu'm, Ofu, Olosega, and Ta'u) and the Manua Islands, including the atoll Rose Island.

The "open-door policy," advocating equal commercial opportunities for all nations in China, was announced in September by Secretary of State John Milton Hay in a note to the foreign powers.

The automobile was barred from Central Park in New York.

Residents of Medicine Lodge, Kansas, were startled by an irate woman who began smashing up the local saloons with a hatchet. She was Carry Amelia Nation, formerly the wife of an intemperate clergyman named Gloyd and remarried since 1877.

Mount Rainier National Park, Wash, was established (Mar. 2) by act of Congress.

Martha Place was the first woman to be put to death in the electric chair. The execution took place at Sing Sing, N.Y.

Sir Thomas Lipton made his first attempt to take the America's yacht trophy back to England, which had never won it, with his boat *Shamrock*, but the American *Columbia* defeated the Lipton entry three times in a row (Oct. 16, 17, 20).

James J. Jeffries won (June 9) the heavyweight boxing championship from Robert ("Bob") Fitzsimmons in 11 rounds at Coney Island, New York. In the same arena Jeffries defended (Nov. 3) his newly won title against Tom Sharkey in 25 rounds, and William A. Brady filmed the first indoor fight pictures for the movies.

In Print

Everybody's magazine began publication as a house organ of Wanamaker's Department Store. (It became an independent magazine in 1903 and merged with *Romance* in 1928.)

Books of the year included Thorstein Veblen's analysis of the wealthy, entitled *The Theory of the Leisure Class*; Edwin Markham's collection of verse *The Man with the Hoe and Other Poems*; George Ade's sketches *Fables in Slang*; and the novels *The Awkward Age* by Henry James; *The Gentleman from Indiana* by Booth Tarkington; *McTeague* by Frank Norris; *Janie Meredith* by Paul Leicester Ford; *The Man that Corrupted Hadleyburg* by Mark Twain; and *Richard Carvel* by Winston Churchill. Elbert Hubbard published *A Message to Garcia*, an inspirational essay on an episode in the Spanish-American War, which so appealed to business executives that they distributed copies of the booklet among their employees. Arthur M. Winfield (Edward Stratemeyer) brought out the first of his long *Rover Boys* series.

On Stage

New York plays included *Zaza* with Mrs. Leslie Carter (Garrick, Jan. 9); *The Man in the Moon* with Sam Bernard, Marie Dressler, and Christie MacDonald (New York Theater, Apr. 24); *Becky Sharpe* with Minnie Maddern Fiske (Fifth Avenue Theater, Sept. 12); *Barbara Frietchie* with Julia Marlowe (Criterion, Oct. 23); *Sherlock Holmes* with William Gillette (Garrick, Nov. 6); *Ben Hur* with Edward Morgan in the name part and William S. Hart as Messala (Broadway Theater, Nov. 29). Alice Nielsen appeared in Victor Herbert's comic opera *The Singing Girl* (Casino, Oct. 23). Anna Held sang Reginald DeKoven's *Papa's Wife* (Manhattan Theater, Nov. 13). Ex-heavyweight boxing champion James J. ("Gentleman Jim") Corbett did a prizefight scene in a revue entitled *Around New York in Eighty Minutes*.

Music

Absent; Always; Hands Across the Sea; Hearts and Flowers; I Wonder Where She Is Tonight; I'd Leave My Happy Home for You; In Good Old New York Town; Maple Leaf Rag; The Mosquitos' Parade; My Little Georgia Rose; My Wild Irish Rose; One Night in June; A Picture No Artist Can Paint; Stay in Your Own Back Yard; The Story of the Rose; We Came from the Same Old State; Where the Sweet Magnolias Grow.

1900

$\mathscr{C}$ongress standardized (Mar. 14) the gold dollar as the unit of monetary value in the United States, and raised (June 14) the status of the Hawaiian Islands to that of a Territory.

Two thousand U.S. Marines aided the British in the capture (Aug. 14) of Peking, China, terminating the Boxer uprising.

William Goebel, Governor of Kentucky, was assassinated (Jan. 30).

Booklets of postage stamps were placed (Apr. 16) on sale by the U.S. Post Office.

Drs. Walter Reed, Aristides Agramonte, Jesse Lazear, and James Carroll began an intensive study at Camp Lazear, Cuba, to eradicate yellow fever ("yellow jack").

Fire destroyed (June 30) the docks of the North German Lloyd and Hamburg American steamship companies, and the ocean liners, the *Main*, *Bremen*, *Saale*, and other ships, in Hoboken, N.J., with a loss of 145 lives. The property damage amounted to $10,000,000.

The Associated Press news service was founded (May 23) in New York.

The Carnegie Institute of Technology was established in Pittsburgh, Pa., with a fund of $1,000,000 (later increased to $4,000,000 for equipment and $7,000,000 for endowment) from Andrew Carnegie.

The Hall of Fame, New York City, was originated by New York University as a memorial to famous Americans with places for 150 commemorative tablets and busts. Five great names are chosen every five years for inclusion in the memorial.

A tornado and tidal wave wreaked havoc (Sept. 8) in Galveston, Tex., killing 6,000 persons and causing untold property damage. Victor Herbert conducted a gigantic concert with 420 players in Madison Square Garden, New York, for the benefit of the sufferers.

The Western League of baseball clubs assumed the name American League.

Dwight Filley Davis, American diplomat, donated the Davis Cup tennis trophy, awarded annually since then to the winning men's team in international matches.

William Jennings Bryan made his second bid for the presidency in the national elections on the Democratic ticket, and was again defeated by William McKinley.

The national population was 76,303,387.

Engineer Casey Jones died (Apr. 30).

Railroad executive Collis P. Huntington died (Aug. 14).

In Print

The first issue of *Who's Who in America* made its appearance.

World's Work was founded as a monthly magazine. (It merged in 1932 with the *Review of Reviews*.)

Cartoonist Frederick Burr Opper began the comic strip, Happy Hooligan and His Mule Named Maud, which appeared regularly in American newspapers for more than 30 years.

Books of the years included Theodore Roosevelt's essays *The Strenuous Life*; the first volume of Josiah Royce's University of Aberdeen lectures *The World and the Individual;* Jack London's Yukon stories, *The Son of the Wolf;* and the novels *Alice of Old Vincennes* by Maurice Thompson; *Eben Holden* by Irving Bacheller; *Monsieur Beaucaire* by Booth Tarkington; *Sister Carrie* by Theodore Dreiser; *To Have and To Hold* by Mary Johnson; *Unleavened Bread* by Robert Grant; and *The Wonderful Wizard of Oz* by Lyman Frank Baum.

On Stage

Clyde Fitch's adaptation of Alphonse Daudet's novel *Sapho* opened (Feb. 5) in New York at Wallack's Theater with Olga Nethersole. The play was condemned as immoral; the theater was closed (Mar. 6). Miss Nethersole's cause was taken up by the women suffragists and the ladies of the "smart world," as well as by writers like Arthur Brisbane, Samuel Untermyer, and Harriet Hubbard Ayer. A petition was sent to the Mayor of the city and the front pages of the newspapers covered the story. Through all the hubbub, the creator of the "Nethersole kiss" retained the dignity she imparted to her "courtesan" roles on the stage. The "Sapho" trial lasted three days (Apr. 3-6). Miss Nethersole was duly cleared and resumed the play, which ran for 86 performances. It was revived (Nov. 12) at the same theater for 28 additional performances.

David Belasco turned John Luther Long's story of *Madame Butterfly* (1897) into a successful one-act play (New York, Herald Square Theater, Mar. 5) with Blanche Bates, as an afterpiece to his farce *Naughty Anthony. Madame Butterfly* had 24 performances.

Maude Adams played (Oct. 23) Sarah Bernhardt's famous role in Edmond Rostand's play *L'Aiglon* when it was first produced in New York at the Knickerbocker Theater in Louis N. Parker's English version. The "divine Sarah" herself performed the play in French a month later.

Outstanding New York successes included Augustus Thomas's *Arizona* (Herald Square Theater, Sept. 10), *Richard Carvel* (Empire, Sept. 11), *David Harum* (Garrick, Oct. 1), and the musical productions *The Casino Girl* (Casino, Mar. 19), *Fiddle-dee-dee* (Weber and Fields Music Hall, Sept. 6), and *San toy* (Daly's, Oct. 1). By all odds—and the production ran 505 performances—the

New York theatrical hit was Owen Hall and Leslie Stuart's musical comedy *Florodora* (Casino Theater, Nov. 10, 1900, New York Theater, Jan. 25, 1902) with its sextette of "typewriter girls," as typists then were called.

Music

Absence Makes the Heart Grow Fonder; A Bird in a Gilded Cage; The Bridge of Sighs; Strike Up the Band—Here Comes a Sailor; The Tale of the Kangaroo; You Can't Keep a Good Man Down.

1901

$\mathcal{T}$he United States was 125 years old.

President William McKinley began his second term.

The Pan-American Exposition was held (May 1-Nov. 2) in Buffalo, N.Y. President McKinley, returning from a tour of the West, visited the celebration. While receiving callers, he was shot (Sept. 6) and fatally wounded by an anarchist, Leon Czolgosz, who concealed a pistol in his right hand which was covered by a handkerchief. The President lingered for eight days. His last words were: "It is God's way. His will, not ours, be done." The assassin was executed.

Following President McKinley's death (Sept. 14), Vice President Theodore Roosevelt, Republican, of New York, was inaugurated as the 26th President. He was 43 years old—the youngest man ever to hold the office.

The Hay-Pauncefote Treaty between the United States and Great Britain established American supremacy in the Caribbean by removing the restrictions of the Clayton-Bulwer Treaty (1850) against the construction of a canal through the Isthmus of Panama.

In the campaign to eradicate yellow fever, Dr. Henry Rose Carter discovered that the disease was transmitted by mosquitoes.

Wireless telegraphy (radio) became (Dec. 12) a reality when Guglielmo Marconi, Italian electrician and inventor, could hear with his apparatus at St. Johns, Newfoundland, the three dots of the letter "S" transmitted without wires across the Atlantic from Wales.

Andrew Carnegie retired (Jan.) from business, selling his steel interests to the U.S. Steel Corporation for $250,000,000, to carry out the principle set forth in his book *The Gospel of Wealth* (1900) that rich men should be "trustees" of wealth for public benefit.

The steamer *Islander*, carrying $3,000,000 in gold, struck (Aug. 14) an iceberg in Steven's Passage, Alaska, and sank, with a loss of 70 lives.

The Junior League of the City of New York was founded. (The national organization came into being 20 years later.)

Chicagoan Charles Fitzmorris, later Chief of Police, traveled around the world in a new record time of 60 days, 13 hours, 29 minutes.

William Sydney Porter, Texan journalist, came to New York after having served two and one half years in the Ohio State Penitentiary for alleged embezzlement in a carelessly conducted bank in Austin, Tex., and started his career as a short-story writer under the pseudonym O. Henry.

Connie Mack (Cornelius McGillicuddy) became manager of the Philadelphia Athletics baseball club—a post he held until 1950.

The Three-I League class B baseball clubs, Bloomington and Decatur, played (May 31) the longest game on record—26 innings. Decatur won by a score of 2 to 1. (The record was equaled May 1, 1920, in the National League when Boston and Brooklyn battled to a 1-1 tie score in a game that was stopped by darkness after 3 hours, 50 minutes of play.)

Chicago stockyard developer Philip Armour died (Jan. 6). Benjamin Harrison, twenty-third President, died (Mar. 13).

In Print

Books of the year included the autobiographies *The Making of an American* by Jacob Riis and *Up from Slavery* by Booker T. Washington; the first volume of *The Jewish Encyclopedia* (completed in 12 volumes in 1909); and the novels *The Crisis*, Winston Churchill; *Graustark*, George Barr McCutcheon; *The Octopus*, Frank Norris; and *Mrs. Wiggs of the Cabbage Patch*, Alice Hegan Rice.

On Stage

The Metropolitan Opera House, New York, gave (Feb. 4) the American premiere of Puccini's *Tosca*, produced a year earlier in Rome.

Theodore Thomas introduced (Dec. 7) in America the music of the Finnish composer Jan Sibelius with a performance by his Chicago Orchestra of two excerpts from the *Kalevala* suite.

In New York's Savoy Theater, *The Governor's Son* featured The Four Cohans (Jerry J., Helen F., and their children George M. and Josephine) in their first musical comedy appearance. The production was written and composed by George M. Cohan.

Popular New York plays included *When Knighthood Was in Flower* with Julia Marlowe; *Captain Jinks of the Horse Marines*; *Under Two Flags*; *On the Quiet*; *A Message from Mars*; *Quality Street* with Maude Adams; and *Monsieur Beaucaire*; *Du Barry* with Mrs. Leslie Carter.

Popular musical productions included: *The Girl from Up There* with Edna May; *The Strollers* with Francis Wilson; *The Messenger Boy*; *The Liberty Belles*; and *The Little Duchess* with Anna Held.

Music

Any Old Place I Can Hang My Hat Is Home Sweet Home to Me; *Blaze Away!* *When the Birds Have Sung Themselves to Sleep*; *When the Blue Sky Turns to Gold*; *Where the Silv'ry Colorado Wends Its Way*; *You're as Welcome as the Flowers in May*.

1902

$\mathcal{T}$he United States established civil government in the Philippines.

The American occupation of Cuba ended (May 20) with the establishment of the Republic of Cuba.

Congress passed the Reclamation Act, creating the Reclamation Service, a bureau of the Department of the Interior, for the purpose of improving American desert areas by irrigation and other means.

Maryland passed the first workingmen's state compensation law.

The first radio message was transmitted (Dec. 17) across the Atlantic.

Admiral Robert Edwin Peary discovered Ellesmere Island in the Arctic.

John J. McGraw became manager of the New York National League Giants baseball club. (He managed the team until 1932, and won 10 National League pennants and 3 world series championships, 1905, 1921, 1922.)

Deaths of the year included author Bret Harte (May 5), suffragette Elizabeth Cady Stanton (Oct. 26), former speaker Thomas B. Reed (Dec. 6), and cartoonist Thomas Nast (Dec. 7).

In Print

Books of the year included *A History of the American People* (5 vols.) by Woodrow Wilson; Admiral Robert Edwin Peary's *Northward over the 'Great Ice'* (2 vols.); James Gibbons Huneker's satirical sketches *Melomaniacs,* and the novels *Brewster's Millions,* George Barr McCutcheon; *The Leopard's Spots,* by Thomas Dixon; *The Little Shepherd of Kingdom Come,* by John Fox; *The Valley of Decision,* by Edith Wharton; and *The Virginian, A Horseman of the Plains,* by Owen Wister.

On Stage

Claude Debussy's orchestral work *Prelude a l'Apres-midi d'un Faune* was performed (Apr. 1) for the first time in America by the Orchestral Club of Boston.

In Los Angeles, a theater was opened by Thomas J. Talley exclusively for the showing of motion pictures.

David Belasco opened (Sept. 29) his first New York playhouse, the Belasco Theater (formerly the Republic), with a revival of his play *Du Barry* (1901). Mrs. Leslie Carter again performed in the piece.

George Bernard Shaw's play *Mrs. Warren's Profession* was given (Oct. 27) in New Haven, Conn., for the first time in America. Its first New York performance was in 1905.

At least ten musical comedies ran over 100 performances: *Twirly Whirly* went to 244; *A Chinese Honeymoon* reached 376. Notable plays included: *The Ninety and Nine,* based on Ira D. Sankey's hymn, "Mary of Magdala" with Minnie Maddern Fiske; Hall Caine's dramatization of his novel *The Eternal City* with Viola Allen; *The Darling of the Gods* with Blanche Bates; and *The Girl with the Green Eyes.*

Music

Because; Bill Bailey, Won't You Please Come Home?; In the Good Old Summer Time; In the Sweet Bye and Bye; Pomp and Circumstance; Where the Sunset Turns the Ocean's Blue to Gold.

1903

$\mathcal{C}$ongress established (Feb. 14) the Department of Commerce and Labor.

The United States signed (May 22) a Treaty of Relations with Cuba and leased (July 2) for an annual rental of $2,000 the Cuban coastal city of Guantanamo as a naval base.

The United States extended (Nov. 8) recognition to the newly created Republic of Panama, which established (Nov. 3) its independence from Columbia. Panama then negotiated (Nov. 18) with the United States a treaty for the construction of a canal through the Isthmus from Cristobal on the Atlantic to Balboa on the Pacific Ocean. The Canal Zone was created, a strip of land five miles on each side of the proposed canal and about fifty miles in length. For the privilege of using this zone the United States paid $10,000,000 and agreed to an annual rental of $250,000 in gold (changed in 1936, because of the devaluation of the dollar, to 430,000 balboas in Panamanian currency. In 1904 the United States purchased the uncompleted De Lesseps canal for $40,000,000.)

Wisconsin became the first State to introduce the direct primary.

Direct wireless communication between Europe and America was established near Wellfleet, Cape Cod, Mass; President Roosevelt sent the first message to King Edward VII.

Women's agitation for union rights resulted in the formation of the National Women's Trade Union League.

The popular Prince Heinrich Albert Wilhelm of Prussia, brother of the Kaiser, made the second of his two visits to the United States. The first was in 1882-84.

Two Americans set records for 'round-the-world travel: J. W. Willis Sayre of Seattle, Wash., in 54 days, 9 hours, 42 minutes; and Henry Frederick in 54 days, 7 hours, 2 minutes.

Denis Dougherty was consecrated in Rome by Pope Pius X as the first American Roman Catholic Bishop of the Philippines.

Dr. H. Nelson Jackson and Sewell K. Crocker made the first transcontinental automobile trip from San Francisco to New York in 70 days (May 23-Aug. 1).

Henry Ford withdrew from the Detroit Automobile Company and organized the Ford Motor Company in that city.

Emma Lazarus's poem *The New Colossus*, cast in a tablet, was set in place (May) on the inside of the base of the Statue of Liberty in New York Harbor.

Wilbur and Orville Wright, who had been experimenting with glider planes, installed a light motor in their equipment and launched (Dec. 17) from Kill Devil Hill, near Kittyhawk, N.C., the first successful mechanical airplane. On the craft's first flight, Orville Wright traveled 120 feet in 12 seconds. On the fourth attempt that day Wilbur Wright covered 852 feet in 59 seconds.

William Butler Yeats, Irish poet, toured the United States as a lecturer.

In baseball, the World Series, was played for the first time. Boston (American League) beat Pittsburgh (National League) five games to three.

What the well-dressed woman should wear for bicycling, outings, and such included: a shirtwaist, a skirt, a straw sailor hat, and a stiff collar with a bow tie.

"Calamity Jane" died. The name was the sobriquet of Martha Jane Burke, born about 1852, a noted frontier character, who frequented mining camps in South Dakota dressed in man's attire. Since she was a crack shot, she threatened "calamity" on anyone who attempted to molest her.

Machine gun inventor Richard Jordan Gatling died (Feb. 26). Naturalist Josiah W. Gibbs died (Apr. 28). Painter James Abbot McNeill Whistler died (July 17). Former Iowa Governor Francis Marion Drake died (Nov. 20).

In Print

Books of the year included Jack London's graphic picture of London slum life *The People of the Abyss*; William DuBois's study, *The Souls of Black Folk*; and the novels *The Ambassadors*, by Henry James; *The Bar Sinister*, by Richard Harding Davis; *The Call of the Wild*, by Jack London; *The Pit, A Story of Chicago*, by Frank Norris, published posthumously; and *Rebecca of Sunnybrook Farm*, by Kate Douglas Wiggin. Charles Evans began the publication of his monumental chronological catalogue *American Bibliography* (completed in 12 volumes in 1934).

On Stage

Phonograph recordings of operatic arias, sung by celebrated artists to piano accompaniment, began to be issued by the Columbia Company, a pioneer in the industry.

Enrico Caruso, famous Italian tenor, made (Nov. 23) his American debut as the Duke in *Rigoletto* in New York at the Metropolitan Opera House.

John Barrymore, younger son of Maurice Barrymore and Georgiana Drew Barrymore, made his stage debut in Herman Sundermann's play *Magda* in Chicago at the Cleveland Theater.

George M. Cohan made (Apr. 27) his debut in a production of his own, a musical comedy entitled *Running for Office*, in New York at the 14th Street Theater. The cast included his father Jerry J. Cohan, his mother Helen F. Cohan, his sister Josephine Cohan, and his wife Ethel Levey.

New York plays included *Mice and Men; The Earl of Pawtucket; Under Cover; Her Own Way; Raffles; The Admirable Crichton; The County Chairman; Candida; Sweet Kitty Bellairs; Merely Mary Ann;* and *The Other Girl.* Musical productions included *The Wizard of Oz* with Fred Stone and Dave Montgomery; *The Runaways; Whoop-Dee-Doo; Babes in Toyland; The Girl from Kay's Square;* and *Mother Goose.*

Films

Progress was made in the motion-picture field with the filming of the silent movie *The Great Train Robbery,* featuring G. M. Anderson, later of *Broncho Billy* fame. Pictures were shown in nickelodeons.

Music

Ain't It Funny What a Difference Just a Few Hours Make?; Always in the Way; Always Leave Them Laughing When You Say Good-bye; The Boys Are Coming Home To-day; I'm on the Water Wagon Now; I Can't Do the Sum; Lincoln; Grant or Lee; The March of the Toys; Your Dad Gave His Life for His Country.

1904

*A*merican occupation of the Canal Zone, Panama, began (May 4); the construction of the Panama Canal was undertaken under Colonel George Washington Goethals. The maintenance of sanitary conditions was entrusted to Surgeon General Dr. William Crawford Gorgas.

The United States established its third mint, in Denver, Colo. (The first was established in 1792 in Philadelphia; the second in 1852 in San Francisco.)

The St. Louis Exposition, celebrating the 100th anniversary of the Louisiana Purchase, opened (May 1).

The 22-floor, 280-foot high Fuller office building (known as the Flatiron Building because of its shape) was completed in New York—at that time the tallest building in the world. Its construction was begun in 1902.

The New York subway opened (Oct. 27).

The steamer *General Slocum*, carrying (June 15), about 1,400 persons, mostly women and children, up the East River in New York on an excursion sponsored by St. Mark's Lutheran Church, caught fire and collapsed in midstream. The disaster took the lives of 1,021 aboard the vessel.

Fire destroyed (Feb. 7) 2,500 buildings in Baltimore.

Helen Adams Keller, who lost her sight, hearing, and speech in infancy, was graduated from Radcliffe College. She was to become a noted American writer and lecturer.

The Olympic games were held for the first time in the United States in St. Louis, Mo. The marathon honors went for the first time to an American runner, T. J. Hicks, who ran the distance in 3 hours, 28 minutes, 53 seconds.

The New York National League baseball champion Giants refused to play the Boston American League champions in the second World Series.

The "rich man's" depression of 1904 was the 19th financial setback since 1790; it lasted one year.

In the national elections, President Theodore Roosevelt won by a majority of nearly 2,000,000 votes, the largest number yet received by any candidate.

Daniel Decatur Emmett, aged 89, composer of *Dixie*, *Old Dan Tucker*, and other minstrel songs, died (June 28) in Mt. Vernon, Ohio.

Brewer Frederick Pabst died (Jan. 2).

In Print

Books of the year included: *The History of the Standard Oil Company*, by Ida Tarbell (2 vols.); and the fiction, *Cabbages and Kings*, by William Sydney Porter; *The Crossing*, by Winston Churchill; *Freckles*, by Gene Stratton-Porter; *The Law of the Land*, by Emerson Hough; and *The Sea-Wolf*, by Jack London.

On Stage

The highly publicized American premiere (Dec. 24, 1903) of Wagner's *Parsifal* and its subsequent ten performances at the Metropolitan Opera House led to other productions of the opera in America in forms which the composer had never imagined, the masterpiece being uncopyrighted in the United States.

Richard Strauss, German composer of symphonic works and operas, visited the United States for the first time, conducting (Mar. 21) the world premiere of his *Symphonia Domestica* in New York at Carnegie Hall with the Hermann Wetzler Symphony Orchestra, organized for the composer's benefit. (Strauss made a second visit in 1922.)

New York plays included *The Virginian* with Dustin Farnum; *The Secret of Polichinelle*; *The Dictator*; *Mrs. Wiggs of the Cabbage Patch*; *The Duke of Killicrankie*; *The College Widow*; and *Leah Freschna*. Long-run musical productions included *The Yankee Consul*; *Piff! Paff! Pouf!* with Eddie Foy; *The School Girl*; *The Sho-gun*; *Higgledy-Piggledy*; *Humpty Dumpty*; *Woodland*; and *It Happened in Nordland*.

Music

Absinth Frappe; *Al Fresco*; *Alexander, Don't You Love Your Baby No More?*; *Back, Back, Back to Baltimore*; *Blue Bell*; *Come, Take a Trip in My Airship*; *Fascination*; *Give My Regards to Broadway*; *The Man with the Ladder and the Hose*; *Meet Me in St. Louis, Louis*; *The Yankee Doodle Boy*.

1905

---

*P*resident Theodore Roosevelt began his second term.

Congress discontinued the coinage of gold dollars, minted since 1849.

President Roosevelt mediated (Sept. 5) at Portsmouth, N.H., the treaty of peace terminating the Russo-Japanese War (1904-05).

The Lewis and Clark Centennial American Pacific Exposition and Oriental Fair was held (June 1-Oct. 15) in Portland, Ore.

Frank Steunenberg, former Governor of Idaho, was assassinated (Dec. 30). Clarence Seward Darrow defended William D. Haywood, accused of instigating the murder.

The remains of John Paul Jones (his real name was John Paul), Scottish seaman and naval hero in the American Revolutionary War who died in 1792 in Paris, were removed to Annapolis, Md.

The Staten Island ferry opened (Oct. 25) in New York.

Orville Wright accomplished (Sept. 26) the first officially recorded airplane flight at Dayton, Oh. He flew 11.12 miles in 18 minutes, 9 seconds. Orville Wright and his brother Wilbur again demonstrated (Oct. 5) their airplane in a flight of about 25 miles, covering the distance in 38 minutes.

The first of the Rotary International businessmen's luncheon clubs was founded in Chicago.

The last surviving soldier of the War of 1812 died (May 13)—Hiram Crouk, aged 105, in Ava, N.Y.

Tyrus Raymond ("Ty") Cobb joined the Detroit Tigers as an outfielder. Although he hit only .240 the first year, his batting average thereafter never fell below .320. He continued to terrorize opposing pitchers and established a record of having hit safely in 40 consecutive games that would stand for years.

Christopher ("Christy") Mathewson, baseball pitcher of the New York Giants club, pitched three shutouts in the World Series.

Industrialist Meyer Guggenheim died (Mar. 16).

In Print

Variety was founded in New York as a weekly journal of the theater, developing a unique literary style of its own. The periodical included in its scope movies, radio, and television, as these came along.

Books of the year included: *The Life of Reason*, by George Santayana, a philosophical treatise, 5 vols., 1905-06; *Iconoclasts, A Book of Dramatists*, by

James Gibbons Huneker; *The War of the Classes,* by Jack London and the fiction, *The Clansman,* by Thomas Dixon; *The Game,* by Jack London; and *The House of Mirth,* by Edith Wharton.

On Stage

At Harvard University Prof. George Pierce Baker founded his "47 Workshop," a student theater for the writing and production of plays. (He transferred his activities in 1925 to Yale. Among his students were George Abbott, Philip Barry, Samuel Nathaniel Behrman, John Dos Passos, Sidney Howard, Eugene O'Neill, Edward Sheldon, John V. A. Weaver, and Thomas Wolfe.)

Abandoning piano accompaniments for operatic arias on phonograph records, companies now issued recordings with specially adapted orchestral backgrounds. (The use of the composer's original orchestration was a later development.)

At the Metropolitan Opera House, New York, the stage bridge in Act I of *Carmen* collapsed (Jan. 7) during the public performance of the opera. The curtain was lowered, and after eight injured members of the chorus were removed to a hospital, the performance continued.

Will Rogers began his stage career at Hammerstein's Roof Garden theater in New York.

R. F. Outcault's *New York Herald* comic cartoons of Buster Brown were transferred to the stage (New York, Majestic Theater, Jan. 24; 95 performances) in a two-act comedy with Master Gabriel as Buster Brown and George Ali as the dog Tige.

George Bernard Shaw's play *Man and Superman* was produced (Sept. 5) in New York at the Hudson Theater.

Arnold Daly presented (Sept. 11-Nov. 11) in New York at the Garrick Theater a cycle of George Bernard Shaw's plays—*Candida, The Man of Destiny, How He Lied to Her Husband, You Never Can Tell, John Bull's Other Island,* and *Mrs. Warren's Profession.* The police stopped the latter as an immoral play after the first night (Oct. 23) and arrested Daly and Mary Shaw (the Mrs. Warren of the production) on a technical charge of disorderly conduct. The actors were released on bail, resumed their season, and were acquitted eight months later.

New York plays included *Adrea; Mrs. Leffingwell's Boots; Zira; The Walls of Jericho; The Man on the Box; The Squaw Man; Peter Pan; The Girl of the Golden West;* and a new long-run play *The Lion and the Mouse* (686 performances). Musical productions included *Fantana; The Duchess of Dantzic; Sergeant Brue; The Rollicking Girl; The Catch of the Season;* and *The Earl and the Girl.*

Music

Claire de Lune (Claude Debussy); *Daddy's Little Girl; If a Girl Like You, Loved a Boy Like Me; In My Merry Oldsmobile; Jim Judson-from the Town of Hackensack; My Gal Sal; Rufus Rastus Johnson Brown; Wait 'Til the Sun Shines; Nellie; A Woman Is Only a Woman but a Good Cigar Is a Smoke.*

1906

℘resident Theodore Roosevelt was awarded the Nobel prize of $40,000 for efforts in terminating the Russo-Japanese War (1904-05)—the first American to receive a Nobel prize. He contributed a sizable part of the money to the endowment of the Foundation for the Promotion of Industrial Peace.

Upton Sinclair's exposure in his novel *The Jungle* of conditions in the Chicago meat-packing industry led President Roosevelt to institute a Congressional investigation, which culminated (June 30) in the passage of the Federal Food and Drug Act by Congress.

Theodore Roosevelt became the first United States President to set foot on foreign soil when he visited Panama.

Congress passed (June 8) "An Act for the preservation of American antiquities," empowering the President to set aside historic landmarks and phenomena of nature, within the jurisdiction of the United States, as national monuments. During the same session, Congress passed (June 29) the Hepburn Act, supplementing the Interstate Commerce Act (1887) for the regulation of rates and transportation of certain products (chiefly coal).

The Cherokee, Chickasaw, Choctaw, Creek, and Seminole Indians of Oklahoma, known as the Five Civilized Nations or Tribes, were granted citizenship.

Admiral Robert Edwin Peary on his dash to the North Pole reached (Apr. 21) the farthest north latitude—87° 6'.

Alice Lee Roosevelt, daughter of President Theodore Roosevelt, married Congressman Nicholas Longworth in the White House. The bride started the vogue for Alice Blue.

Already familiar with earthquakes for nearly half a century, San Francisco experienced (Apr. 18 at 5:15 a.m.) its worst catastrophe. The violent tremors tumbled down houses, hotels, office buildings, churches, theaters, and structures of every kind, and split pavements asunder. The ensuing fire added to the devastation. The lives of 452 persons were lost in the disaster, 1,500 were injured, 265,000 made homeless. 60,000 buildings were destroyed, hundreds of city blocks were burned, and property damage amounted to $350,000,000. Insurance companies paid $132,823,067.21.

Pace Institute, New York, was founded as one of the earliest schools of accountancy and business administration.

Reginald Aubrey Fessenden, American physicist and inventor, experimenting in wireless telephony (radio), succeeded in transmitting (Dec. 24) a musical program from Brant Rock, Mass., to Plymouth, 11 miles away. A steamer about 12 to 15 miles at sea also heard the broadcast.

Roy Knabenshue upset the schedule of both Houses of Congress when he sailed a dirigible around the dome of the Capitol.

Stanford White, noted architect and designer of Madison Square Garden, New York, was shot (June 25) by Harry K. Thaw, heir to a Pittsburgh fortune, at the opening of its roof garden theater during a professional performance of a former Columbia University revue, *Manzelle Champagne*. At the trial the defense counsel coined a term when he said that Thaw had "a brainstorm."

Upton Sinclair, who was much in the limelight at this time, and 40 associates, mostly literary people, established the communal Helicon Home Colony in Englewood, N.J. The enterprise was ridiculed in the press and was abandoned the next year when a fire destroyed the main building.

Picture hats with ostrich plumes were the latest feminine headgear.

In Athens, Greece, the United States won the Olympic Games with 75 points. England trailed in second place with 41.

The Philadelphia and Boston American League baseball clubs battled (Sept. 1) twenty-four innings at Boston in a major league record game that ended, after 4 hours, 47 minutes of play, in favor of Philadelphia 4 to 1. (The record was broken in the National League in 1920.)

Deaths of the year included suffragette Susan B. Anthony (Mar. 13), circus executive James Bailey (Apr. 11), architect Stanford White (June 15), and barbed wire inventor Joseph Glidden (Oct. 9).

In Print

The American Magazine was founded as a continuation of *Frank Leslie's Popular Monthly* (1876).

Books of the year included *With Walt Whitman at Camden*, vol. 1, (Horace Traubel, one of the poet's executors; the work, a diary, was completed in 3 volumes in 1914); *The Cynic's Word Book*, by Ambrose Bierce; and the fiction, *The Awakening of Helena Ritchie*, by Margaret Deland; *Coniston*, by Winston Churchill; *The Jungle*, by Upton Sinclair; *White Fang*, by Jack London; *The Spoilers*, by Rex Beach.

On Stage

Victor Herbert's comic opera *Babes in Toyland* was playing at the Columbia Theater in San Francisco. The New York Metropolitan Opera Company was in the city on tour and had performed *Carmen* the preceding night with Caruso in the cast. In New York, Victor Herbert conducted a monster concert at the Hippodrome for the benefit of the sufferers.

Italian opera composer Ruggiero Leoncavallo came to America from Milan with an opera troupe called *La Scala*. He made (Oct. 8) his American debut as a conductor at Carnegie Hall, New York, and toured the United States and Canada, giving performances of his operas *Pagliacci* and (a new work) *La Jeunesse de Figaro*. The latter proved unsuccessful and was never produced in Europe.

Oscar Hammerstein invaded the field of grand opera and opened (Dec. 3) his Manhattan Opera House in New York with Bellini's *I Puritani*. The celebrated Italian tenor Alessandro Bonci made his American debut on this occasion.

In New York George M. Cohan produced with Fay Templeton his *Forty-five Minutes from Broadway* (New Amsterdam Theater, Jan. 1) and, with his family, the flag-waving *George Washington, Jr.* (Herald Square Theater, Feb. 12).

George Bernard Shaw's play *Caesar and Cleopatra* with Johnston Forbes-Robertson and Gertrude Elliott was produced (Oct. 30) at the New Amsterdam Theater, New York.

The New York stage carried over many of its previous year's successes and offered a rich choice of musical comedies. Among long-run plays were *The Hypocrites* with Richard Bennett and Doris Keane; *The Chorus Lady* with Rose Stahl; *His House in Order* with John Drew and Margaret Illington; *The Great Divide; The Rose of the Rancho* with Frances Starr and Charles Richman; and *The Man of the Hour*. Of the numerous popular musical comedies none equaled the success or longevity of Victor Herbert's operetta *The Red Mill* with Fred A. Stone and David Montgomery; the first New York run totaled 274 performances.

Music

    Anchors Aweigh; In Old New York—The Streets of New York; The Isle of Our Dreams; A Lemon in the Garden of Love; What's the Use of Loving If You Can't Love All the Time?; You're a Grand Old Flag.

1907

$\mathcal{O}$klahoma was admitted (Nov. 16) as the 46th state.

Alabama and Georgia adopted liquor prohibition.

The first round-the-world cruise was made by a United States battle fleet, 16 ships under the command of Admiral Robley Dunglison Evans. (The flotilla left Hampton Roads, Va., Dec. 16, 1907, and returned Feb. 22, 1909.)

In reaction to a scandal over the Honduras Lottery, lotteries in the United States came to an end.

The second Hague Peace Conference convened at the suggestion of President Theodore Roosevelt.

Judge Kenesaw Mountain Landis, later the commissioner of baseball, became a national figure when he sentenced the Standard Oil corporation to a fine of $29,240,000. (The decision was reversed subsequently by higher courts.)

The United Press news service was established in New York.

Lee De Forest demonstrated (Mar. 5) in New York a radio broadcast from Tellharmonic Hall, playing the "William Tell" overture from a phonograph record. During the summer he used phonograph records of celebrated opera singers in testing the wireless telephone transmitters to be installed on Admiral Evans' world-touring fleet.

The latest craze was the game of "diabolo"—a piece of wood tossed around by a cord attached to two sticks.

The shirtwaist was enhanced with perforations, embroidery was attached to the edges, and it became the daring "peek-a-boo" shirtwaist. Feather boas were also quite stylish.

The United States went through its twentieth depression since 1790.

Deaths of the year included Augustus Saint-Gaudens, America's renowned sculptor, aged 59 (Aug. 3), and editor Wendell P. Garrison (Feb. 27).

In Print

Books of the year included *The Education on Henry Adams, A Study of Twentieth Century Multiplicity,* by Henry Adams; *The American Scene,* by Henry James; *Christian Science,* by Mark Twain; *Pragmatism: A New Name for Some Old Ways of Thinking,* by William James; and the fiction, *The Iron Heel,* by Jack London. *The Shepherd of the Hills,* by Harold Bell Wright; *Three Weeks,* by Elinor Glyn; *The Traitor,* by Thomas Dixon; and *The Trimmed Lamp,* by O. Henry.

The first two volumes of *The Catholic Encyclopedia* were issued (completed in 15 volumes in 1914).

On Stage

Richard Strauss's one-hour German opera *Salome*, based on Oscar Wilde's French play of the same name, created a vast scandal in New York when its American premiere was staged (Jan. 22) by Heinrich Conried at the Metropolitan Opera House with Olive Fremstad in the title role. The board of directors immediately forbade its repetition on moral grounds. Mlle. Bianca Froelich of the Corps de Ballet performed the *Dance of the Seven Veils*. A program of vocal music preceded the opera. Not long afterwards vaudeville was overrun by Salome dancers. When Mme. Fremstad sang the Paris premiere on May 8, she was decorated by the French government. (Oscar Hammerstein revived the opera in 1909, in French, at his Manhattan Opera House, New York. Performances followed in Chicago and Milwaukee in 1910 and in St. Louis in 1911. The opera later was reinstated at the Metropolitan and is still in the repertory.)

Ibsen's *Peer Gynt* with Edward Grieg's incidental music was performed (Feb. 25) in New York at the New Amsterdam Theater for 22 performances with actor-producer Richard Mansfield (Peer Gynt), Emma Dunn (Ase), Adelaide Nowak (Solveig), and Irene Prahar (Anitra).

The enterprising Florenz Ziegfeld, son of a Chicago music conservatory director, renamed the roof of the New York Theater the Jardin de Paris, and staged (July 8) a modest revue patterned after the Follies Bergere. This production, which cost only $13,000, inaugurated the Ziegfeld Follies that developed in subsequent years into lavish spectacles of "the most beautiful girls in the world."

New York plays included *Brewster's Millions*; *Caught in the Rain*; *The Road to Yesterday*; *My Wife* with John Drew and Billie Burke; *A Grand Army Man* with David Warfield; *The Warrens of Virginia* (in which the youthful Mary Pickford made her New York debut); and *Polly of the Circus*. The outstanding long-run play was *The Thief* with Kyrle Bellew and Margaret Illington.

Musical comedy dominated the stage although, with the exception of *The Girl Behind the Counter* (260 performances), no show could vie in popularity with *The Merry Widow*, which amassed a total of 416 performances. The romantic Donald Brian and a previously unknown soprano, Ethel Jackson, sang and danced the operetta to its American success. Lehar's music captured the public since some of the music was uncopyrighted and was reprinted in cheap editions; and the famous stage waltz introduced to America a more intimate and appealing type of dance.

There were more than 400 nickelodeons in the country. Song slides were popular as a screen feature and a way of "plugging" the latest songs. David Wark Griffith became a motion picture director and William N. Selig transferred a company of movie actors from Chicago to Los Angeles, thus launching the city as a motion-picture center.

Music

Budweiser's a Friend of Mine; Every Little Bit Added to What You've Got Makes Just a Little Bit More; The Glow-Worm; If I'm Going to Die I'm Going to Have Some Fun; The Merry Widow Waltz; and School Days.

1908

The Federal Bureau of Investigation was established.

Immigration from Japan was restricted by "gentleman's agreement."

Admiral Robert Edwin Peary sailed for the Arctic in a specially constructed 184-foot, 600-ton steamer, the *Roosevelt*, on his sixth and, as it proved, last expedition to find the North Pole. He established (Sept.) his winter camp at Cape Sheridan, Ellesmere Island. His expedition comprised 66 members. In the Arctic 49 Eskimos and 246 dogs were added to the party.

Movements against drinking of liquor and smoking began in earnest. The Henry C. Frick Co., U.S. Steel subsidiary, ordered its employees to be total abstainers both on and off the premises. Likewise, the Baltimore & Ohio Railway, which issued a similar order for all employees running or directing trains. There was a great deal of pressure to stop women from smoking.

Orville Wright made another successful flight in his flying machine, remaining in the air 1 hour, 14 minutes.

Charles D. Herrold, a San Jose, Calif., wireless experimenter, opened (Jan. 16) a local radio station, a pioneer in the field. (The call letters KQW were assigned to the station Dec. 9, 1921.)

The U.S. Post Office placed (Feb. 18) coils of postage stamps on sale.

The manufacture of automobiles passed the 50,000 mark. The limousine, a motorcar with a glass-enclosed body, came into use.

Six automobiles undertook a round-the-world race from New York to Paris, traveling westward. From Seattle, Wash., the cars were shipped to Kobe, Japan. Only one, the American E. R. Thomas "Speedway Flier," completed (July 30) the journey.

At the Polo Grounds, New York, Fred Merkle committed the historic baseball play involving the question of whether or not he touched second base. The game was a crucial battle between the New York Giants and the Chicago Cubs. When the game was declared a tie, it nearly provoked a major riot. After this incident, "bonehead" and "boner" came into baseball and general slang.

In Sydney, Australia, Black boxer Jack Johnson defeated (Dec. 26) Tommy Burns in 14 rounds to gain the heavyweight championship title. The police had stopped the bout before it was officially over.

In the national elections, President Theodore Roosevelt declined to run for a third term and favored William Howard Taft, Republican, who was elected over William Jennings Bryan in Bryan's third and last bid for the presidency.

The Gibson Girl, so-called from Charles Dana Gibson drawings, was considered the ideal of American womanhood.

George MacManus, creator of *Maggie and Jiggs*, was cartooning *The Newlyweds* and appearing in vaudeville.

Women were wearing sheath gowns slit to the knee, large *Merry Widow* hats bedecked with bird wings, artificial flowers, dotted veils, and high buttoned or laced shoes.

Former President Grover Cleveland died (June 24).

In Print

Books of the year included: *The Philosophy of Loyalty*, by Josiah Royce; *The Scarecrow*, by Percy MacKaye; and the fiction, *The Bomb*, by Frank Harris; *The Circular Staircase*, by Mary Roberts Rinehart; *Mr. Crewe's Career*, by Winston Churchill; and *The Tail of the Lonesome Pine*, by John Fox.

On Stage

Gustav Mahler, famous German conductor and symphonic composer, made (Jan. 1) his American debut conducting *Tristan and Isolde* at the Metropolitan Opera House, New York.

Arturo Toscanini, renowned Italian opera conductor, gave (Nov. 16)) his first American performance conducting *Aida* at the Metropolitan Opera House, New York.

Oscar Hammerstein built his second operatic theater—the Philadelphia Opera House—which opened (Nov. 17) with Bizet's *Carmen*.

Isadora Duncan was performing interpretative dances in barefoot Greek style and flowing gowns. After displaying her art in Budapest (1903), Berlin (1904), and in London, she came back to America.

The Dixieland Jazz Band was organized in New Orleans.

The New York stage was crowded with successes: *The Honor of the Family* with Otis Skinner; *Paid in Full*; *The Servant in the House* with Walter Hampden; *The Traveling Salesman*; *The Man from Home*; *Jack Straw*; *A Gentleman from Mississippi* with Thomas A. Wise and Douglas Fairbanks; *The Blue Mouse*; *The Battle* with Wilton Lackaye; and *What Every Woman Knows* with Richard Bennett and Maude Adams. Ferenc Molnar's uncopyrighted Hungarian play, *The Devil*, opened (Aug. 18) simultaneously at the Belasco with George Arliss and at the Garden with Edwin Stevens.

Outstanding among New York musical comedies were *A Waltz Dream*; *The Soul Kiss*; *Nearly a Hero*; *Three Twins* with Bessie McCoy; *The Girls of Gottenburg*; *Little Nemo* by Victor Herbert; *The Boys and Betty*; *Miss Innocence* with Anna Held; *The Queen of the Moulin Rouge* with Frank X. Bushman.

Vaudeville headliners included Eva Tanguay, Irene Franklin, Bert Leslie, Cecilia Loftus, James J. Corbett, Louise Dresser, Ed Wynn, Leon Errol, and Annette Kellerman, who was said to have a perfect figure.

Films

Motion pictures, still tail-enders for vaudeville shows, were becoming longer: *Bobby's Kodak* (518 feet); *Dr. Skinum* (592 feet); *The Snow Man* (717 feet). *The Lonely Villa* featured an unknown, a sweet little actress known only as Little Mary. To later generations she was Mary Pickford. As an experiment in higher drama, the movies offered Shakespeare's *Romeo and Juliet.* The films, of course, were silent.

Music

Love Is Like a Cigarette; She Sells Sea-Shells; Shine On, Harvest Moon; Sweet Violets; Sweetest Maid of All; Take Me Out to the Ball Game; When You First Kissed the Last Girl You Loved; You're in the Right Church, but the Wrong Pew.

1909

---

*W*illiam Howard Taft, Republican of Ohio, was inaugurated as the 27th President.

Former President Theodore Roosevelt, with his son Kermit, undertook an extensive hunting trip in East Africa.

The Stars and Stripes were planted (Apr. 6) in the cold sunlight of the Arctic on the northernmost point of the earth. "The Pole at last...Mine at last" wrote Admiral Robert Edwin Peary in his diary. On this, his sixth attempt, after 20 years of effort, Peary achieved his goal and claimed the discovery of the North Pole. He was accompanied on the last dangerous leg of the journey by only his Black attendant, Matthew Henson, four Eskimos—Egingwah, Ooqueah, Ootah, and Seegloo—and 40 dogs. Peary stayed 30 hours at the Pole. The news of the discovery reached the world exactly five months later (Sept. 6). Five days earlier Frederick Albert Cook, a physician who had accompanied Peary on a previous expedition, startled the world with the announcement that he had discovered the North Pole on Apr. 21, 1908. He was royally entertained in Europe and America but when Peary got back and heard of Dr. Cook's claim, he said, "He has simply handed the public a gold brick." Peary's claim was later established by the National Geographic Society and Dr. Cook's tale was exposed as a fraud, as was his claim of having climbed Mt. McKinley. Subsequently Cook was convicted of a mail fraud and spent seven years in a federal penitentiary. In 1911 Peary received the congratulations of Congress and the rank of rear-admiral for his achievement.

In Seattle, Washington, from June to October, the Alaska-Yukon-Pacific Exposition celebrated the development of the territory. In New York, from September to November the Hudson-Fulton Celebration commemorated the tercentenary of the discovery of the Hudson River and the centennial of its first navigation by steam. The U.S. Post Office issued commemorative postage stamps commemorating these events and Lincoln's birthday. At the same time, the Lincoln-head penny came into circulation, replacing the Indian head-cent piece after half a century of use (1859). The coin was designed by Victor D. Brenner and was the first one-cent piece to bear the motto "In God We Trust."

The National Kindergarten Association was founded in New York for the educational advancement of children.

The Queensborough and Manhattan bridges, each spanning the East River, New York, were opened on Mar. 30 and Dec. 31, respectively.

Mass production of automobiles began with Henry Ford's Model T, thus inaugurating the gasoline era. (15,000,000 cars of this design were built by 1928 when a new type was adopted.)

Three hundred and ninety-three miners lost their lives in the St. Paul Mine at Cheery, Ill.

Edward Payson Weston walked from New York to San Francisco in 105 days.

The hobble skirt was a popular fashion for women. The very name would now be anathema.

Publisher Peter Collier died (Apr. 24).

In Print

Books of the year included: *The Wine of the Puritans,* Van Wyck Brooks; *Egoists: A Book of Supermen,* James Gibbons Huneker; *Personae* and *Exultations,* by Ezra Pound; and the fiction, *A Girl of the Limberlost,* by Gene Stratton-Porter; *54-40 or Fight!,* by Emerson Hough; *Martin Eden,* by Jack London; *Three Lives,* by Gertrude Stein; and *The White Sister,* by Francis Marion Crawford.

On Stage

Sergei Rachmaninoff, Russian piano virtuoso and composer of the popular *Prelude in C sharp minor,* gave his first concert in the United States.

The New York stage presented *The Easiest Way; The Girl from Rector's; The Third Degree; The Climax; Is Matrimony a Failure?; Arsene Lupin; The Fortune Hunter; The Melting Pot; The Passing of the Third Floor Back;* and *The Lottery Man.* Among musical productions that ran over 250 performances were *Havana; The Midnight Sons; The Dollar Princess;* and *The Chocolate Soldier.* The Hippodrome staged (Sept. 4) two presentations daily of a spectacle *A Trip to Japan* and achieved 447 performances. The *Ziegfeld Follies of 1909* burlesqued former President Theodore Roosevelt, teeth and all, and his historic African hunting trip. The production also introduced the Nell Brinkley Bathing Girls.

Films

Ten thousand drawings made possible the first animated cartoon—*Gertie the Dinosaur* by artist Winsor McKay of the daily newspaper *New York American.*

When a William N. Selig cameraman was unable to accompany the Roosevelt African expedition, the company simply relied on its imagination and filmed the travelogue *Hunting Big Game in Africa* indoors with the aid of tropical scenery. Audiences believed their eyes.

A film version of Dumas' novel *The Count of Monte Cristo* also was being shown.

The first colored motion pictures (scenes and short subjects) were exhibited (Dec. 11) in New York.

Music
    By the Light of the Silvery Moon; Come After Breakfast; Bring 'Long Your Lunch and Leave 'Fore Supper Time; I've Got a Pain in My Sawdust; I Wonder Who's Kissing Her Now; My Own United States; The Wiffenpoof Song, and *You Taught Me How to Love You; Now Teach Me to Forget.*

1910

$\mathcal{C}$ongress passed the White Slave Act (June 25), known also as the Mann Act after Illinois Representative James Robert Mann. The law prohibited interstate transportation of women and girls for immoral purposes; also the Mann-Elkins Act (June 18), which placed telephone, telegraph, and cable companies under the control of the Interstate Commerce Commission.

Former President Theodore Roosevelt returned (June 18) from his hunting trip in East Africa and his subsequent triumphal lecture tour of Europe.

New York Governor Charles Evans Hughes was appointed (Apr. 25) associate justice of the U.S. Supreme Court by President Taft.

Woodrow Wilson, president of Princeton University, resigned (Oct. 20) to enter on a political career.

New York Mayor William Jay Gaynor was shot (Aug. 9) by a discharged Dock Department employee while he was boarding a steamer for Europe. The Mayor recovered but suffered thereafter from the effects of the wound.

Halley's comet, discovered in 240 B.C., reappeared in 1910 and caused considerable alarm. (It had previously appeared in 1835 and would be visible again in 1985.) Earlier in the year a new comet, 1910A, was discovered.

New York's St. Patrick's Cathedral, Roman Catholic, was consecrated (Oct. 5).

The Camp Fire Girls of America was founded by Dr. and Mrs. Luther Halsey Gulick.

The Boy Scouts of America was incorporated (Feb. 8) by the union of Dan C. Beard's Sons of Daniel Boone and Ernest Seton-Thompson's Woodcraft Indians, thus becoming the American equivalent of the English organization founded in 1908 by Sir (now Baron) Robert Stephenson Smyth Baden-Powell.

The Carnegie Endowment for International Peace was established (Dec. 14) by a gift of $10,000,000 from Andrew Carnegie.

Glenn Hammond Curtis won (May 29) the $10,000 prize of the New York newspaper *The World* for the first continuous airplane flight from Albany to New York, traveling 137 miles in 2 hours, 32 minutes. Shortly thereafter (June) he accomplished a successful airplane landing on water at Hammondsport, Steuben County, N.Y. Later in the year (Sept. 12) Ralph Johnston flew a distance of 101 miles in 3 hours, 14 minutes.

Walter Wellman made (Oct. 15-18) an unsuccessful attempt to fly the Atlantic in a dirigible. He traveled about 1,000 miles.

Undefeated heavyweight boxing champion James J. ("Jim") Jeffries returned to the ring after five years of retirement (1905) and lost his title when he was knocked out (July 4) in 15 rounds at Reno, Nev., by the African-American challenger Jack Johnson. Jeffries was impressive physically at 227 pounds, but slow of movement; Johnson was perfectly trained at 208 pounds, tall, sleek, and agile. The sun, which poured down on the open arena, was so hot that Jeffrie's second held a huge parasol over him between rounds. The bout was filmed. The gate drew $270,775. Jeffries received $66,666 and Johnson $50,000. Their total receipts from all sources was $192,066 and $145,000, respectively. The fight was originally scheduled for San Francisco but was transferred to Reno after official objections were made by Governor Gillet of California. Racial riots broke out after the fight.

The American balloon, "America II," won a 1,171-mile race to capture the James Gordon Bennett cup. The balloon had won a 695-mile race for the cup in 1909.

The United States suffered its twenty-first depression since 1790. It lasted one year.

Deaths of the year included Mark Twain (Samuel Clemens), aged 75 (Apr. 21); philosopher William James (Aug. 26); and Julia Ward Howe, author of *The Battle Hymn of the Republic* and other works, aged 91 (Oct. 17).

The national population was 93,402,151.

In Print

The Russian language newspaper *Novoye Russkoy Slovo* was founded in New York.

Books of the year included *Twenty Years at Hull House*, by Jane Addams; *The Growth of Socialism*, by Eugene Victor Debs; *The North Pole*, by Adm. Robert Edwin Peary; *Shakespeare and His London Associates As Revealed in Recently Discovered Documents*, by Charles William Wallace; and the fiction, *Franklin Winslow Kane*, by Anne Douglas Sedgwick; *Hopalong Cassidy*, by Clarence Mulford; *A Modern Chronicle*, by Winston Churchill. Charles William Eliot, former president of Harvard University, published *The Harvard Classics*, a series of 50 volumes with selections from the literature of the world popularly known as *Dr. Eliot's Five-Foot Shelf of Books*.

On Stage

The first experimental radio broadcast from the stage of the New York Metropolitan Opera House took place. Lee De Forest had erected antennae on the roof of the building and, by means of radiophones, broadcast (Jan. 13) portions of the night's twin bill, *Cavalleria Rusticana* and *Pagliacci*. Emmy Destinn, Riccardo Martin, Dinh Gilly, Jeanne Maubourg, and Marie Mattfeld sang in the former; Enrico Caruso, Bella Alten, and Pasquale Amato sang in the latter. The broadcast was reported to have been tuned in by amateurs at Bridgeport, Conn., and picked up at sea by the S.S. *Avon*.

Oscar Hammerstein's lavish expenditures at his Manhattan Opera House, New York, forced him to sell (Apr.) his interests to the rival Metropolitan Opera House for $2,000,000.

The Metropolitan Opera House, New York, produced (Mar. 18) for the first time an opera by an American composer—*The Pipe of Desire* by Frederick Shephard Converse. It had been previously heard in Boston at Jordan Hall, Jan. 31, 1906. The opera had two performances.

In the presence of the composers, the famous house gave the world premieres of Giacomo Puccini's *La Fanciulla del West* (The Girl of the Golden West) with Caruso, Emmy Destinn, and Pasquale Amato (Dec. 10) and Engelbert Humperdinck's *Die Konigskinder* with Geraldine Farrar (Dec. 28). At Hammerstein's Manhattan Opera House, Richard Strauss's German one-act opera *Elektra*, with Marietta Mazarin received (Feb. 1), in French, its first American performance.

John Philip Sousa's band of 100 players (1892) made a 14-months' concert tour (1910-11) of the world.

The Philadelphia-Chicago Opera Company was formed with the former Metropolitan Opera House tenor Andreas Dippel as manager.

Victor Herbert's operetta *Naughty Marietta* featured (Nov. 7) at the New York Theater two recruits from the operatic stage—the soprano Emma Trentini of the Manhattan Opera House and the tenor Orville Harrold of the Metropolitan Opera House. The familiar song *Ah, Sweet Mystery of Life* was originally an instrumental entr'acte in the work and was converted into a vocal number for the tenor at the suggestion of Orville Harrold. The operetta ran 136 performances.

Fanny Brice, a burlesque house singer, started on her road to success in the *Ziegfeld Follies of 1910* (Jardin de Paris, June 20) at an initial salary of $18 a week, singing a character song *Good-bye, Becky Cohen*. In the same show, Bert Williams, who had been playing in Negro musical comedies, made the first of his many Follies appearances.

New York plays included *Alias Jimmy Valentine*; *Madame X*; *The Commuters*; *The Country Boy*; *Get-Rich-Quick Wallingford*; *The Blue Bird* by Maurice Maeterlinck; *Rebecca of Sunnybrook Farm*; *The Concert*; *The Gamblers*; *Nobody's Widow*; *Pomander Walk*. Musical productions included *The Arcadians*; *The Summer Widowers*; *Madame Sherry*; *Hans, the Flute Player*; *He Came from Milwaukee*; *Alma, Where Do You Live*; and *The Spring Maid*.

Films

Censorship of films was widespread. In San Francisco, the board of censors clamped down on 32 releases as "unfit for public exhibition." They included *Saved by a Sailor; In Hot Pursuit; The Black Viper;* and *Maggie, the Dock Rat*.

Music

    Ah, Sweet Mystery of Life; Come, Josephine, in My Flying Machine; Down By the Old Mill Stream; I'm Looking for a Nice Young Fellow Who Is Looking for a Nice Young Girl; I've Got the Time—I've Got the Place, But It's Hard to Find the Girl; You Remind Me of the Girl That Used to Go to School with Me!

1911

The United States Supreme Court dissolved the Standard Oil and the American Tobacco companies as monopolies (May 15 and May 30, respectively).

The postal bank system was introduced (Aug. 1) in New York, Chicago, St. Louis, and Boston.

The New York Court of Appeals declared the Workmen's Compensation Law unconstitutional.

Admiral Robert Edwin Peary received (Mar. 3) the congratulations of Congress and promotion to the rank of Rear Admiral for his discovery of the North Pole (1909).

Charles Franklin Kettering invented the automobile self-starter in Dayton, Ohio.

John Murphy Farley, Roman Catholic Archbishop of New York, was made (Nov. 27) cardinal by Pope Pius X, the fourth American to be so honored.

The New York Public Library, New York City, was dedicated (May 23) by President Taft.

The Great Lakes Naval Training Station, North Chicago, Ill., opened (July 1).

Fire destroyed (Mar. 25) the Triangle shirtwaist factory in New York, with a loss of 145 lives. Many victims jumped from the windows and were impaled on the iron spike fence in front of the building.

Glenn Hammond Curtis invented the hydro-airplane. Aviator McCurdy flew (Jan. 29) from Key West, Fla., to a landing near Havana, Cuba, a distance of 100 miles in two hours. Earl Ovington transported airmail on Long Island, New York, from the Nassau Boulevard Airdrome to Mineola. C. P. Rodgers made (Sept. 17-Nov. 4) the first transcontinental flight from New York, reaching Pasadena, Calif., after several forced landings in 84 hours, 2 minutes flying time.

Ty Cobb wound up the baseball season with a batting average of .385, bettering his previous year's average of .377. (Between 1910 and 1919 there was only one year in which he wasn't American League batting champion—1916, when Tris Speaker topped the league with .386.)

Temperance crusader Carrie Nation died (June 9) and Merchant Abraham Abraham died (June 28).

In Print

Books of the year included: *The Children of the Poor,* by Victor Eugene Debs; and the fiction, *Ethan Frome,* by Edith Wharton; *The Iron Woman,* by Margaret Deland; *Jennie Gerhardt,* by Theodore Dreiser; *The Long Roll,* by Mary Johnson; *The Ne-er Do-Well,* by Rex Beach; *Queed,* by Henry Sydnor Harrison; *Stover at Yale,* by Owen Johnson; *Tante,* by Anne Douglas Sedgwick; and *The Winning of Barbara Worth,* by Harold Bell Wright.

On Stage

Piano music was very lucrative for the music publishing business, especially after the five-and-ten-cent stores put their wares on the counters and engaged piano players to stimulate sales. Ragtime produced a batch of new dance steps. Most popular was the Turkey Trot, which had originated in Denver vaudeville circles in 1883. Variations on the Turkey Trot included the Crab Step, Kangaroo Dip, Fish Walk, the Texas Tommy, the Snake, and the Grizzly Bear. The waltz and the two step, however, were still popular.

Oscar Hammerstein transferred his activities to London and erected in Kingsway an opera house for French opera. It opened (Nov. 13) with Nougues's *Quo Vadis?* The venture was unsuccessful, and Hammerstein sold the house, which became the Stoll Picture Theater.

New York plays included *The Deep Purple; The Piper; Excuse Me; Everywoman; As a Man Thinks; Maggie Pepper; Disraeli* with George Arliss; *The Woman; Bought and Paid For; Bunty Pulls the Strings; The Return of Peter Grimm* with David Warfield; *The Garden of Allah; Kismet* with Otis Skinner. Musical productions included *The Slim Princess; The Hen-Pecks* with dancer Vernon Castle; *The Balkan Princess; The Pink Lady; The Siren; The Little Millionaire; The Quaker Girl; The Red Widow; Little Boy Blue;* and *Jumping Jupiter* presenting Edna Wallace Hopper, Jeanne Eagles of later (1922) *Rian* fame, Helen Broderick, and Ina Claire, late of vaudeville. The stately Valeska Suratt displayed herself in innumerable gorgeous costumes of her own design in *The Red Robe* (Globe, June 22). She was later imitated by female impersonator Julian Eltinge in *The Fascinating Widow* (Liberty, Sept. 11).

Films

To film a screen version of the Gospel with an authentic background, American motion-picture cameras were taken to the Holy Land to photograph *From the Manger to the Cross.* The film cost $35,000 to make and grossed nearly a million dollars' profit. R. Henderson Bland portrayed the white-robed Christ.

Music

Alexander's Ragtime Band; All Alone; Everybody's Doing It Now; I Want a Girl—Just Like the Girl That Married Dear Old Dad; Oh You Beautiful Doll; There'll Come a Time; When I Was Twenty-one and You Were Sweet Sixteen; Woodman, Woodman, Spare That Tree!

1912

*N*ew Mexico (Jan. 6) and of Arizona (Feb. 14), were admitted as the 47th and the 48th states, respectively.

Massachusetts was the first state to establish a minimum wage for women and children.

The palatial $7,500,000 White Star liner *Titanic* on its maiden voyage from Southhampton, England, to New York struck (Apr. 14-15) an iceberg off Cape Race, Newfoundland, and sank. The ship carried 2,223 persons. The catastrophe took the lives of 1,517, of whom 103 were women and children. Seven hundred and six persons were rescued. Among the prominent Americans who were drowned were John Jacob Astor, Isidor Straus, and Francis D. Millet, the painter.

New York Governor William Sulzer was impeached (Oct. 16) and removed (Oct. 18) from office.

The Girl Scouts of the United States of America was founded (Mar. 12) in Savannah, Ga., by Juliette Low, a friend of Lieutenant General Robert Stephenson Smyth Baden-Powell, as an American equivalent of the latter's Boy Scouts (1908) and his sister Agnes's "Girl Guides" (1910). The name of the organization originally was "Girl Guides" but was changed the following year to "Girl Scouts."

Hadassah, the Women's Zionist Organization of America, was founded in New York.

Nobel prizes were awarded to America's Elihu Root for peace and to Dr. Alexis Carrel for medicine and physiology.

September Morn, a painting of a nude woman bathing at sunrise, by the French artist Paul Emile Chabas, was the talk and scandal of the time.

The memorial for the Oscar Wilde tomb in Pere Lachaise Cemetery, Paris, sculptured by New York-born Jacob Epstein, created such a furor over its alleged indecency that the monument was kept covered with tarpaulins for months.

Jim Thorpe, an American athlete with Indian ancestors, won the pentathlon and the decathlon at the Olympic games in Stockholm, Sweden, thereby gaining acclaim as the world's greatest all-around athlete. Two months after his return to the United States he was shorn of his honors by the Amateur Athletic Union of the United States when it was discovered that he had played professional baseball in 1909, thus eliminating him from amateur standing. The A.A.U. apologized to the International Olympic Committee and Thorpe was compelled to relinquish his trophies.

Dr. Hudson Stuck and H. P. Karstens ascended Mt. McKinley (20,300 feet), Alaska; Miss Dora Keen, traveler and social worker, made the ascent of Mt. Blackburn (16,140 feet), Alaska.

Regarding the conservative tendencies of President Taft as harmful to liberal policies, former President Theodore Roosevelt and former Indiana Senator Albert Jeremiah Beveridge organized (June 22) the Progressive Party and adopted the Bull Moose as its symbol. The name is said to have originated from a remark of Roosevelt's: "I feel as fit as a bull moose." As a result of this Republican split, the national election was won by Woodrow Wilson, Democrat, former president of Princeton University.

Deaths of the year included geologist Clarence E. Dutton (Jan. 4), American Red Cross founder Clara Barton (Apr. 12), aviator Wilbur Wright (May 30), and first American woman pilot Harriet Quimby.

In Print

Books of the year included *The Autobiography of an Ex-Colored Man,* by James Weldon Johnson; and the fiction, *Daddy Long Legs,* by Jean Webster (sequel, *Dear Enemy,* 1914); *The Financier,* by Theodore Dreiser; *Riders of the Purple Sage,* by Zane Grey; and *Smoke Bellew,* by Jack London.

On Stage

Leopold Stokowski was appointed musical director of the Philadelphia Symphony Orchestra. (He held the post until 1926.)

New York plays that ran 175 or more performances included *The Butterfly on the Wheel; Officer 666; Within the Law; Fanny's First Play; Milestones; Broadway Jones; Little Women; Peg o' My Heart; The Argyle Case;* and *Years of Discretion.* Max Reinhardt and his company from the Deutsches Theater, Berlin, brought *Sumurun,* a wordless play in nine tableaux, to America for 62 performances. Belasco reproduced an exact duplicate of a New York Childs restaurant in *The Governor's Lady. The Yellow Jacket* ran for 82 performances. *Julius Caesar,* with William Faversham, had 32 performances. *Hamlet,* with John E. Kellerd, achieved a record-breaking run. Musical productions included: *Whirl of Society; A Winsome Widow; The Rose Maid; The Count of Luxembourg; Oh! Oh! Delphine; The Lady of the Slipper* by Victor Herbert; and *The Firefly* with Emma Trentini. The first *Passing Show* revue opened at the Winter Garden. These shows were for many years summer rivals of the *Ziegfeld Follies.* The Minsky brothers took over the National Winter Garden theater and their bawdy burlesque productions became notorious.

Films

The flourishing motion-picture industry made great technical strides and began to rely on the star system. "This is my one chance of immortality," said the "divine" Sarah Bernhardt, and she acted the elaborate and silently screened *Queen Elizabeth* before the cameras of Louis Mercanton in France. The film was first shown publicly (July 12) in America in New York at Daniel Frohman's Lyceum Theater, and established Adolph Zukor in the motion-picture industry. The picture was artistically ahead of the times, and it was also one of the first long films—a "four-reeler." Douglas Fairbanks was starting his movie career; William Faversham and Julia Opp, were appearing in a film version of *Julius Caesar*. Mack Sennett, via the Keystone Company, was displaying bathing beauties on the screen.

Music

It's a Long, Long Way to Tipperary; Moonlight Bay; My Melancholy Baby; Waiting for the Robert E. Lee; When Irish Eyes Are Smiling.

1913

*W*oodrow Wilson, Democrat, of Virginia, was inaugurated as the 28th President.

Outgoing President Taft vetoed (Feb. 14) an immigration bill which would impose a literacy test for the admission of aliens.

Two amendments were added to the Constitution—the 16th (Feb. 25) establishing income taxes, and the 17th (May 13) regulating the election of senators by popular vote.

Congress passed the Webb-Kenyon Act (Mar. 1) prohibiting the interstate shipment of liquor, and the Owen-Glass Federal Reserve Act (Dec. 23) establishing the Federal Reserve Bank System.

The presidential cabinet was strengthened by the addition of a Secretary of Labor; the first Secretary was William B. Wilson, ex-officer of the United Mine Workers' Union and Congressman from Pennsylvania.

The United States Post Office established (Jan. 1) parcel post service.

President Wilson created the Teapot Dome, Natrona County, Wyo., the government naval oil reserve that was to figure in a 1924 national scandal.

Former President William Howard Taft was appointed professor of constitutional law at Yale (1913-21).

The Indian head or buffalo nickel came into circulation—the first five-cent piece since the Liberty head of 1883. The new coin was designed by James E. Fraser who used as model for the animal, the bison "Black Diamond" in the New York Zoological Gardens.

President Wilson refused to recognize Mexican dictator General Victoriano Huerta's "government by assassination," set up after the midnight shooting (Feb. 23-24) of President Francisco Indalecis Madero and Vice President Jose Pino Suarez. Wilson sent (Nov. 2) a note requesting Huerta's resignation from office.

The Gatun locks on the Panama Canal were completed (June 14).

Floods in Ohio, Indiana, and Texas took more than 1,200 lives; the property damage was enormous.

The Rockefeller Foundation was established by John D. Rockefeller, Sr., with an endowment of $165,281,624 for the study of medical sciences.

The Actors' Equity Association was founded in New York.

The 60-floor Woolworth office building in New York was completed—the tallest contemporary building in the world.

John Henry Mears traveled around the world in a new record time of 35 days, 21 hours, 36 minutes.

Harry Kendall Thaw, who had fatally shot (1906) the architect Stanford White in the Madison Square Garden Roof Theater, New York, and had been adjudged insane at his second trial, escaped (Aug. 17) from Matteawan Asylum. He was taken into custody (Aug. 19) in Coaticook, Que., deported to Vermont, and arrested in Colebrook, N.H.

A mine disaster at Dawson, N. Mex., took the lives of 258 miners. (In 1923, another disaster there killed 120 miners.)

Queen Mary's turbans started a vogue in America.

Modern art created a sensation in New York and the country at large the international exhibition held in the Armory of the 69th Regiment and sponsored by the Association of American Painters and Sculptors. Marcel Duchamp's representation of a "Nude Descending a Staircase" received the most attention.

Ping-pong was a new indoor game.

Deaths of the year included merchant Benjamin Altman (Oct. 7), brewer Adolphus Busch (Oct. 10), and merchant Montgomery Ward (Dec. 7).

In Print

Reedy's Mirror was founded in St. Louis by Missouri journalist William Marion Reedy as a liberal magazine. During the seven years of its existence, it brought before the public many new writers and published Edgar Lee Master's free-verse poems *Spoon River Anthology.*

Books of the year included *A Boy's Will,* by Robert Frost; *General Booth Enters into Heaven and Other Poems,* by Vachel Lindsay; *Mr. Faust,* by Arthur Davison Ficke; *Old Fogy,* by James Gibbons Huneker; and the fiction, *His Great Adventure,* by Robert Herrick; *The Inside of the Cup,* by Winston Churchill; *The Iron Trail,* by Rex Beach; *John Barleycorn* and *The Valley of the Moon,* by Jack London; *O Pioneers!,* by Willa Cather; *Rolling Stones,* by O. Henry (published posthumously); *Virginia,* by Ellen Glasgow.

On Stage

The first American-made orchestral phonograph records were manufactured by the Columbia Company, Bridgeport, Conn., with Felix Weingartner conducting a shortened version of the *Liebestod* from *Tristan und Isolde* and his own arrangement of Weber's *Invitation to the Dance.*

Arturo Toscanini made (Apr. 13) his first American appearance as a symphonic conductor at the Metropolitan Opera House, New York, in Beethoven's Ninth Symphony.

Exotic dancer Roshanara (her real name was Olive Craddock) organized a troupe and toured the United States performing Eastern dances.

"Class" dancers had their advent in hotels: Mr. and Mrs. Vernon Castle's salary was reported at $1,000. Meantime dansants, matinee dances at public places, were bitterly condemned because of "male idlers."

New York plays included *A Good Little Devil*; *Joseph and His Brethren*; *The Poor Little Rich Girl*; *Romance* with Doris Keane; *The Lure*; *Potash and Perlmutter*; *The Temperamental Journey*; *Nearly Married*; *Madame President* with Fannie Ward; *Seven Keys to Badpate*; *Today*; *Grumpy*; *The Misleading Lady*; *The Secret*; and *The Philanderer*.

Musical productions included *The Honeymoon Express*, *The Purple Road*, *All Aboard*, *Sweethearts* by Victor Herbert, *The Little Cafe*, and *High Jinks* by Rudolph Friml. Paul Rubens's musical comedy *The Sunshine Girl* introduced a new singing star, Julia Sanderson, and the husband-and-wife dancing team of Vernon and Irene Castle. Their dancing of the turkey trot and tango set a vogue for dances of Western origin. Joseph Cawthorn's song *You Can't Play Every Instrument in the Band* always stopped the show. All this led to a run of 160 performances—in spite of the fact that its story was about soap.

Films

The motion-picture serial began about this time; one of the earliest was *What Happened to Mary*. The vamp also made her appearance on the screen in a silent film entitled *The Vampire*, starring Alice Hollister as the first of the type which later included Lucille Younge, Theda Bara, and others. D. W. Griffith produced a four reeler, *Judith of Bethulia*. Charlie (Charles Spencer) Chaplin entered the movies. Minnie Maddern Fiske acted a screen version of her stage success *Tess of the D'Urbervilles* for Zukor's Famous Players film company. Other screen stars included William Faversham, Mabel Taliafero, and Florence Nash. The present Paramount Pictures, Inc., was founded in Hollywood, by Jesse Lasky under the name Jesse L. Lasky Feature Play Company. Their first picture was *The Squaw Man*, followed by *Brewster's Millions*, both of which were hits. (Lasky's group merged in 1916 with Zukor's Famous Players Company.) *Cabiria*, a spectacular Italian production, also came out this year.

Music

Ballin' the Jack; *Danny Boy*; *Do You Take This Woman for Your Lawful Wife?*; *It Takes a Little Rain with the Sunshine to Make the World Go Round*; *Low Bridge!—Everybody Down, or, Fifteen Years on the Erie Canal*; *When You're All Dressed Up and No Place to Go*; *You Made Me Love You—I Didn't Want to Do It*.

1914

*T*he Mexican political situation, which had grown more chaotic and violent since 1910, was now considered by some to be a menace to American life and property. President Wilson removed (Feb. 3) the embargo on munitions to Mexico and continued his "watchful waiting" policy. This policy was severely criticized (Mar. 9) in the Senate by New Mexico Senator Albert Bacon Fall who cited between seventy and eighty outrages against Americans in Mexico. The arrest by Tampico soldiers of seven sailors form the U.S. gunboat *Dolphin*, while they were loading (Apr. 9) gasoline into a whaleboat, brought the United States almost to the verge of war. Admiral Henry Thomas Mayo demanded an apology, punishment of the officer in charge of the arrest, and a 21-gun salute to the American flag. The conditions were reported (Apr. 10) to have been carried out but it turned out that the salute was withheld. After a United States note (Apr. 18), was refused (Apr. 19) by the Mexican President General Victoriano Huerta, the American Atlantic fleet, under Admiral Frank Friday Fletcher, was ordered into Mexican waters. Under the fire of Mexican snipers, Marines and sailors landed (Apr. 21) at Vera Cruz and seized the custom house and part of the city. Nineteen Americans were killed. In an effort to prevent further bloodshed, Argentina, Brazil, and Chile undertook (Apr. 25) to mediate a peace. Meanwhile, the 5th Brigade, U.S.A., under General Frederick Funston arrived (Apr. 28) to occupy Vera Cruz. In the United States, public funeral services for the dead were held (May 11) in New York. Honors also were paid (May 13) in Philadelphia, Chicago, Cambridge, Ma., and elsewhere. While the peace conference was meeting (May 20-July 1) in Niagara Falls, Ont., the political situation in Mexico changed. General Alvaro Obregon captured (July 9) Guadalajara; Provisional President Huerta resigned (July 15) and escaped to Jamaica; Venustiano Carranza succeeded to the presidency; the rebel General Francisco (Pancho) Villa, loomed as a new threat, and sharp fighting developed between Carranzistas and Villistas. American troops were withdrawn (Nov. 23) from Vera Cruz.

Congress passed Alabama Representative Henry D. Clayton's Anti-Trust Act (Oct. 14), supplementing the Sherman Anti-Trust Act (1890) and the Harrison Anti-Narcotic Act (Dec. 31).

For the first time citizens had to pay income tax, following the 16th Amendment to the Constitution, which 42 of the 48 states had ratified.

(Three states—Connecticut, Rhode Island and Utah—rejected it.) Individual payments amounted to $28,263,535.

President Wilson established national observance of Mother's Day on the second Sunday in May. The day was originated by Anna Jarvis of Philadelphia and was first celebrated May 10, 1908, in the churches of that city.

The Panama Canal was opened (Aug. 15) to commercial traffic. The *Cristobal* was the first steamship to pass through the waterway but frequent landslides and war conditions interfered for several years with its operation. (The canal was declared officially opened July 12, 1920.)

Former President Theodore Roosevelt again was on an exploring expedition—this time in the jungles of Brazil where he discovered, with Col. Candido Rondon, Brazilian explorer, an uncharted 940-mile tributary of the Amazon. The discovery occasioned much ridicule and though it was popularly called the "river of doubt," it was renamed Rio Roosevelt by the Brazilian government.

Secretary of the Treasury William Gibbs McAdoo married (May) his second wife, Eleanor B. Wilson, second daughter of President Wilson. (They later divorced.)

President Wilson's first wife, Mrs. Ellen Louise Axson Wilson, died (Aug. 6) in the White House.

For the second time Jacob Sechler Coxey of Ohio led an "army" of unemployed to Washington, D.C.

Theodore William Richards was awarded the Nobel prize for chemistry—the first American to be so honored in that field.

The erection of the Lincoln Memorial in Potomac Park, Washington, D.C., at a cost of $2,594,000, was begun on his birthday (Feb. 12).

The new Roman Catholic Cathedral in St. Louis, Mo., was dedicated. (The building was begun in 1907 and replaced the edifice of 1834.)

Detroit manufacturer Henry Ford set a new standard for labor wages when he fixed a five-dollar minimum for an eight-hour day.

A sweeping fire devastated (June 25) a large section of Salem, Mass., making many thousands homeless and destroying property to the extent of $12,000,000.

An Atlantic tidal wave again inundated (Aug. 17) the coastal city of Galveston, Tex., brought death to 275 persons and caused great property damage.

The American Society of Composers, Authors and Publishers (A.S.C.A.P.) was formed by five composers, Silvio Hein, Victor Herbert, Louis A. Hirsch, Raymond Hubbell, and Gustave Kerker; one librettist, Glen MacDonough; and three publishers' representatives, Nathan Burkan, George Maxwell, and Jay Witmark to protect the licensed public performances of musical compositions.

The New York Giants baseball club defeated (July 17) the Pittsburgh Pirates, 3 to 1, in the first 21-inning game in their league.

The assassination (June 28) of the Archduke Franz Ferdinand, heir to the Austrian throne, and his wife, Duchess of Hohenberg, by a Serbian terrorist in Sarejevo, Bosnia, started what became World War I. As an ally of Austria, Germany declared (Aug. 1) war on Russia, ally of Serbia; Great Britain, as an ally of Russia, issued (Aug. 4) a declaration of war against Germany. President Wilson immediately proclaimed (Aug. 4) the United States' neutrality.

Engineer George Westinghouse died (Mar. 12).

In Print

The New Republic was founded in New York as a weekly magazine, "less to inform or entertain its readers than to start little insurrections in the realm of their convictions."

The Little Review appeared in Chicago as a monthly devoted to "extreme" tendencies in art and aesthetics. (It later was published in San Francisco and in New York, and was issued as a quarterly in Paris, 1924-29. Ceased publication in 1929.)

Books of the year included *Other People's Money,* by Louis Dembitz Brandeis; *Progressive Democracy,* by Herbert Croly; and the fiction, *The Auction Block,* by Rex Beach; *Clark's Feild,* by Robert Herrick; *Penrod,* by Booth Tarkington (sequels *Penrod and Sam,* 1916, and *Penrod Jashber,* 1929); *The Rise of Jennie Cushing,* by Mary Watts; and *Vandover and the Brute,* by Frank Norris. American poetry showed signs of rebirth with the publication of *The Congo and Other Poems,* by Vachel Lindsay; *North of Boston,* by Robert Frost; *the Single Hound,* by Emily Dickinson, printed posthumously by her niece Martha Dickinson Bianshi; *Songs of the New Age,* by James Oppenheim; *Sword Blades and Other Poems,* by Amy Lowell; and *Trees and Other Poems,* by Joyce Kilmer.

On Stage

Oscar Hammerstein, having sold his unsuccessful London opera house, in violation of his 1910 Metropolitan Opera House contract, erected his second New York operatic theater—the American Opera House, his fourth venture in the field. The Metropolitan secured an injunction that prevented the opening of the Opera House and compelled him to adhere to the agreement. The building became the Lexington Theater.

Black dance band leader, Jim Reese Europe, gave (Mar. 11) a jazz concert at Carnegie Hall in New York.

Alice Brown's play, *Children of the Earth,* selected from 2,640 manuscripts, won the $10,000 prize offered by New York theatrical manager Winthrop Ames for the best play by a native writer on a local subject. (The play was staged Jan. 12, 1915, at the Booth Theater, and ran 39 performances.)

New York enjoyed an unprecedented season of long-run plays; among those that played 200 or more performances were *Kitty Mackay; Too Many Cooks; A Pair of Sixes; The Dummy; Twin Beds; On Trial; Under Cover; It Pays to Advertise; Daddy Long-Legs; The Law of the Land; A Pair of Silk Stockings;* and *Experience.* Musical productions included *The Whirl of the World; Sari; The Girl from*

Utah; Wars of the World; Dancing Around; Chin-Chin; The Lilac Domino; The Only Girl by Victor Herbert; *Watch Your Step;* and *Hello Broadway. H.M.S. Pinafore* was revived for 89 performances with two complete casts, the operetta being given twice daily. New as the movies were at this time, they already supplied the theater with material for musical comedies—*The Girl on the Film,* imported from George Edwardes's London Gaiety Theater, and *The Queen of the Movies,* adapted from the German *Die Kino-Konigin.*

Films

Motion picture houses sprang up everywhere, just as music halls had 30 years before. Samuel Rothafel ("Roxy") took charge of the Strand Theater, New York, and an era of de luxe houses began. Meantime, Theda Bara was "vamping" not only her fellow players on the screen but also her audiences in films with such lurid titles as *Destruction* and *A Fool There Was.*

Music

By the Beautiful Sea; By the Waters of Minnetonka; Fido Is a Hot Dog Now; On the 5:15; Play a Simple Melody; Rebecca of Sunny-Brook Farm; St. Louis Blues; This Is the Life; Tip-Top Tipperary Mary.

1915

World War I continued. The Central Powers comprised Germany, Austria-Hungary, Turkey, and Bulgaria; the Allies comprised Russia, Great Britain, France, Belgium, Serbia, Montenegro, Japan and Italy. American sentiment began turning against the Central Powers when the German armies introduced (Apr. 23-28) poison gas at Ypres; German "atrocities" in Belgium were reported; German U-boats attacked and sank American vessels; the Cunard Line steamer *Lusitania*, bound from New York to England, was torpedoed (May 7) and sank off Old Head of Kinsale, Ireland, with a loss of 1,198 lives (including 124 Americans, among them Alfred Gwynne Vanderbilt, Mr. and Mrs. Elbert Hubbard, the playwright Charles Klein, and the theatrical producer Charles Frohman). The British Red Cross nurse Edith Cavell was shot (Oct. 12) as a spy.

Secretary of State William Jennings Bryan resigned (June 8) in protest against President Wilson's aggressive notes to Germany over the sinking of the *Lusitania*. Robert Lansing was appointed (June 23) to succeed Bryan.

In New York, 25,000 women marched (Oct. 23) in a suffrage parade.

One hundred years of Anglo-American peace were celebrated (Jan. 8) in New Orleans on the centennial of General Andrew Jackson's victory over the British in the battle at nearby Chalmette. As part of the commemoration, a statue of Jackson was unveiled amid the formal exchange of greetings between British and American representatives.

Fires, storms, floods, mine explosions, and marine disasters caused millions of dollars' worth of damage and loss of life in the United States and Alaska. The U.S. submarine F-4 sank (Mar. 25) in Honolulu Harbor, Hawaii, with the loss of its commanding officer and a crew of twenty. In the Chicago River, the steamer *Eastland* capsized (July 24) and 812 excursionists were drowned. A mine explosion at Layland, W.Va., took the lives of 111 miners.

The legislatures of Wisconsin and Minnesota attempted to abolish by state law the giving or receiving of "tips" or gratuities in public places. In Wisconsin the bill was vetoed by Gov. Philipp as interfering with personal liberty, was then passed over his veto, but was disapproved by the state senate. In Minnesota a similar measure failed to secure the approval of the senate committee on general legislation.

The first New York-to-San Francisco telephone line was opened. Alexander Graham Bell, inventor of the telephone (1876), took part in the inaugural ceremonies.

Progress also was being made in wireless telephony (radio). Speech was transmitted experimentally from Arlington, Va., to Honolulu and to Paris (Sept. 30) and across the Atlantic (Oct. 22).

President Wilson married (Dec. 18) his second wife, Mrs. Edith Bolling Galt, widow of a Washington jeweler. (The President's first wife died in 1914 at the White House.)

Some 80 American women, headed by Jane Addams of Hull House, Chicago, attended the Women's Peace Conference (Apr. 27–May 1) at The Hague, Holland, to protest the war and attempt to restore peace in Europe. Certain representatives from the wronged nations voiced sentiments that were more national than universal.

The first businessmen's Kiwanis Club was formed in Detroit.

The Victor phonograph company, Camden, N.J., introduced in American public schools its record playing machine known commercially as the Victrola.

The St. Louis Cardinals bought second baseman Rogers Hornsby for $400. He became one of the great figures in the game and was seven times National League batting champion.

Jess Willard knocked out (Apr. 5) the Black heavyweight boxing champion Jack Johnson after 26 rounds in Havana, Cuba, thus winning the title.

The United States loaned (Oct. 15) $500,000,000 to Great Britain and France.

Congress created the U.S. Coast Guard (Jan. 28) and the U.S. Naval Reserve (Mar. 3), and re-established the ranks of Admiral and Vice-Admiral.

The United States extended (Oct. 19) recognition to the government of Venustiano Carranza in Mexico, and placed an embargo on arms to other revolutionary leaders including Francisco (Pancho) Villa.

Deaths of the year included sculptor Anne Whitney (Jan. 23), publisher Simon Bretano (Feb. 15), Engineer Frederick W. Taylor (Mar. 21), politician Nelson Aldrich (Apr. 16), and publisher John B. Putnam (Oct. 8).

In Print

The Musical Quarterly was founded in New York as the first American periodical to be devoted to musicological studies.

Books of the year included *America's Coming-of-Age*, by Van Wyck Brooks; *Ivory, Apes and Peacocks*, by James Gibbons Huneker; and the fiction, *The Bent Twig*, by Dorothy Canfield; *The 'Genius'*, by Theodore Dreiser; *The Gray Dawn*, by Stewart Edward White; *The Harbor*, by Ernest Poole; *Old Judge Priest*, by Irvin Cobb; *Ruggles of Red Gap*, by Harry Leon Wilson; *The Song of the Lark*, by Willa Cather; and the poetry, *Rivers to the Sea*, by Sara Teasdale; *The Song of Hugh Glass*, by Hohn Neihardt; and *Spoon River Anthology*, by Edgar Lee Masters.

On Stage

Alexander Scriabin's symphony *Prometheus*, which utilized a "color keyboard" to project color on a screen, was performed (Mar. 20) for the first time in the United States at Carnegie Hall in New York by the Russian Symphony Orchestra under Modest Altschuler.

Paul Whiteman organized an orchestra to play what he called "syncopation" but what was commonly referred to as "jazz."

New York plays that ran more than 175 performances included *The Boomerang*, *Common Clay*, *The House of Glass*, *Hit-the-Trail Holiday*, *The Unchastened Woman*, *Potash and Perlmutter in Society*, *The Great Lover* with Leo Ditrichstein; and *Treasure Island*. The Washington Square Players gave their first season of one-act plays. Musical productions included *The Blue Paradise*, *The Princess Pat*, *Alone at Last*, *Katinka*, *Very Good, Eddie*, and *Stop! Look! Listen!*. The spectacle at the Hippodrome (Sept. 30) was called *Hip-Hip-Horray*. The members of Sousa's band were among the many performers. The show grossed $37,600 in one week and ran 425 performances.

Films

David Wark Griffith produced the silent movie classic *The Birth of a Nation*, starring Lillian Gish and Henry B. Walthall, with specially composed music by Joseph Carl Breil. The film was based on Thomas Dixon's Ku Klux Klan novel, *The Clansman* (1905), and was first shown publicly (Feb. 8) in Los Angeles at Clune's Auditorium.

Music

Auf Wiedersehen; M-O-T-H-E-R, a Word That Means the World to Me; Ragging the Scale.

1916

*W*orld War I continued.

The German submarine U-53 *Deutschland* crossed the Atlantic twice to the United States for medical supplies (July 9, to Norfolk, Va., and Nov. 1, to New London, Conn.) and each time eluded British naval vigilance and returned safely to its European base. American tension was increased further when the liner Sussex was torpedoed (Mar. 24) in the English Channel. The Spanish composer Enrique Granados, whose opera *Goyescas* had just been performed at the Metropolitan Opera House, New York, was among the victims. German saboteurs allegedly caused (July 30) the "Black Tom" explosion at the docks of Jersey City, N.J., killing two persons and creating a property damage of $22,000,000, thus adding to American tension. Nevertheless, President Wilson made efforts to bring about a cessation of hostilities, suggesting (Dec. 18) to the warring powers "peace without victory." The offer was scorned.

A near panic of stock selling developed in New York following Secretary of State Robert Lansing's warning that the United States was being drawn into the European conflict.

In retaliation against American recognition (1915) of the Carranza government in Mexico, the Chihuahua revolutionary leader Francisco (Pancho) Villa shot (Jan. 10) eighteen Americans in Santa Isabel, Mex., and raided (Mar. 9) the city of Columbus, Luna County, N.M., where he killed 17 persons. The United States sent (Mar. 15) General John Joseph Pershing with 12,000 troops into Mexico in pursuit of Villa. Fighting took place (Apr. 12) at Parral, Durango. Villa, whose real name was Doroteo Arango, eluded capture.

American marines landed in Nicaragua and in Santo Domingo (Dominican Republic).

The Liberty-winged head or "Mercury" dime and the Liberty-standing half dollar went into circulation. Both coins were designed by A. A. Weinman.

The U.S. cruiser *Memphis* was wrecked (Aug. 29) at Trujillo City (then Santo Domingo), Dominican Republic, with a loss of 33 lives.

The National Research Council was established by the National Academy of Sciences, Washington, D.C., at the suggestion of President Wilson, to co-ordinate all branches of scientific study for national defense.

The luxatone, a keyboard instrument projecting color on a satin screen in conjunction with music, was demonstrated by its inventor, Dr. H. Spencer Lewis, in San Jose, Calif.

Charles Evans Hughes resigned from the U.S. Supreme Court to run as Republican presidential candidate against President Wilson in the national elections. The voters returned to bed after an exciting day at the polls believing that Hughes had captured the election, only to wake up the next morning and learn that President Wilson had won by a bare 600,000 votes on the slogan, "He kept us out of war."

Hetty Green, aged 82, the world's wealthiest woman, often called "The Witch of Wall Street," died (July 3) in New York and left a fortune of one hundred million dollars.

Deaths of the year also included railroad executive J. J. Hill (May 28), painter Thomas Eakins (June 25), and painter William Chase (Oct. 25).

In Print

Books of the year included the fiction, *Cappy Ricks*, by Peter Bernard Kyne; *Casuals of the Sea*, by William McFee; *The Dwelling Place of Light*, by Winston Churchill; *The Leatherwood God*, by William Dean Howells; *Seventeen*, by Booth Tarkington; *Xingu*, by Edith Wharton, *You Know Me, Al; A Busher's Letters*, by Ring Lardner; and the poetry, *Chicago Poems*, by Carl Sandburg; *Heap o' Livin'*, by Edgar Guest; *The Man Against the Sky*, by Edwin Arlington Robinson; *Men, Women, and Ghosts*, by Amy Lowell; and *Spectra*, by Witter Bynner and Arthur Davison Ficke.

On Stage

New York plays that ran for more than 150 performances included *Erstwhile Susan*; *Cheating Cheaters* with Marjoree Rambeau; *Turn to the Right!*; *The Man Who Came Back*; *Upstairs and Down*; *Come Out of the Kitchen*; *Keeping Up Appearances*; *The Yellow Jacket* with Mr. and Mrs. Charles Coburn; *The Thirteenth Chair*; and *A Kiss for Cinderella* with Maude Adams. Notable also were John Galsworthy's *Justice* and *Good Gracious Annabelle*. Stuart Walker's Portmanteau Theater presented its first New York season of short plays. Lewisohn Stadium of City College hosted (May 24) *Caliban of the Yellow Sands* by Percy MacKaye. The dramatic spectacle boasted elaborate scenery and music by Arthur Farwell. Top Broadway stars were featured and a colorful array of national folk groups was introduced. Musical productions included *Sybil*; *Robinson Crusoe, Jr.*; *Pom-Pom*; *The Big Show*; *Flora Bella*; *Miss Springtime*; *The Century Girl* by Victor Herbert and Irving Berlin; and *Her Soldier Boy*.

The Metropolitan Opera House, New York, produced (Jan. 28) the world premiere of Enrique Granados's *Goyescas* in the Spanish language.

Films

The movies, still silent, were in their heyday, showing *The Daughter of the Gods* with swimming champion Annette Kellerman; *The Dumb Girl of Portici* with ballerina Anna Pavlova; *The Fall of a Nation* (with original music by Victor Herbert); *The Foolish Virgin* with Clara Kimball Young; *The Good Bad Man* with Douglas Fairbanks; *Intolerance* (produced by David Wark Griffith); *Less Than the Dust* with Mary Pickford; *Pearl of the Army* with Pearl White; *Rose of the South* with Peggy Hyland and Antonio Moreno; *The Vixen* with Theda Bara; *War Brides* with Alla Nazimova and introducing a later star, Richard Barthelmess; *Wharf Rat* with Mae Marsh; and *The Witching Hour* with C. Aubrey Smith. Other films stars of the time included Richard Bennett, Billie Burke, Francis X. Bushman, Marie Empress, Harry Fox, Anita Stewart, and Norma and Constance Talmadge.

Music

Bugle Call Rag; Colonel Bogey; He May Be Old, but He's Got Young Ideas; I Can Dance with Everyone but My Wife; If I Knock the "L" Out of Kelly; Put on Your Slippers and Fill Up Your Pipe; When the Black Sheep Returns to the Fold; Where Did Robinson Crusoe Go with Friday on Saturday Night?; You Can't Get Along with 'Em or Without 'Em.

1917

*P*resident Woodrow Wilson began his second term.

After 11 months (Mar., 1916-Feb., 1917) of fruitless search in northern Mexico for the revolutionary leader Francisco (Pancho) Villa, the American punitive army under Gen. John Joseph Pershing was withdrawn.

World War I continued. When Germany instituted (Feb. 1) unrestricted submarine warfare, the United States recalled (Feb. 2) its ambassador to the German Empire, James Watson Gerard, and began (Mar. 12) to arm merchant ships. A declaration of war on Germany followed (Apr. 6, Good Friday). Congress enacted (May 18) the Selective Military Conscription Bill, passed (June 15) the Espionage Act, and created the War Industries Board. The government took over the control of all American railroads. American troops, the American Expeditionary Force, arrived (June 26) in France and entered (Oct. 27) into the conflict. The United States declared (Dec. 7) war on Germany's ally, Austria-Hungary. The teaching of the German language in the New York public schools was abolished and the Metropolitan Opera House, New York, banned German opera.

With America's entry into the world war, windows displayed flags starred with the number of men from each family serving in the army and navy. Churches, colleges, and business firms erected tablets bearing the names of their soldiers. Meatless, wheatless, and fuel-less days were observed to conserve food and fuel for the armed forces.

To meet the expenditures of the war, Congress authorized (Apr. 24) the first Liberty Loan and War Savings Certificates.

Engineers in the U.S. War Department designed the 12-cylinder automotive "Liberty motor," capable of delivering up to 400 horsepower.

The Liberty-standing 25-cent piece, designed by Herman A. MacNeil, went into circulation.

President Wilson rejected former President Theodore Roosevelt's offer to organize a volunteer division to help the Allies against Germany.

The Browning machine gun was adopted by the U.S. Army.

The United States purchased (Jan. 25) from Denmark for $25,000,000 the Danish West Indies, later called the Virgin Islands, a group of about 25 islands east of Puerto Rico.

The Lansing-Ishii Agreement, was signed (Nov. 2), recognizing Japan's special interest in China and reaffirming the open-door policy (1899). (The Agreement was annulled Apr. 14, 1932.)

Mt. McKinley National Park, Alaska, was established.

The Hell Gate Bridge, New York, spanning the East River, was completed. A mine disaster at Hastings, Colo, took the lives of 121 miners.

The Rosenwald Fund was established for the furtherance of the philanthropies "in Negro education" of Julius Rosenwald, president of the mercantile firm Sears, Roebuck Company, Chicago, Ill.

The International Association of Lion Clubs was formed to promote national and international welfare.

The first of the Civitan Clubs ("Builders of Good Citizenship") was organized in Birmingham, Ala. The movement spread in the United States and into Canada.

James Buchanan—"Diamond Jim"—Brady, aged 61, symbol of New York's *Gay 90s*, died (Apr. 13).

Deaths of the year also included Navy Admiral George Dewey (Jan. 16), pianist and composer Scott Joplin (Apr. 1), and first American saint Frances X. Cabrini (Dec. 22).

In Print

The first Pulitzer prize in Journalism and Letters were awarded. The awards went to: the *New York Tribune* for editorial writing; Herbert Bayard Swope of the *New York World* for reporting; Jean Jules Jusserand for history for his book *"With Americans of Past and Present Days"*; Laura E. Richards and Maude House Elliott, assisted by Florence Howe Hall, for their *"Julia Ward Howe"* biography.

Books of the year included *A Book of Prefaces*, by Henry Mencken; *The Cambridge History of American Literature*, 4 vols., 1917-21; *Love Songs*, by Sara Teasdale; *The Unpublished Memoirs*, by Abraham Rosenbach; and the fiction, *The Cream of the Jest*, by James Branch Cabell; *The Dwelling Place of Light*, by Winston Churchill; *Fanny Herself*, by Edna Ferber; *Bullible's Travels*, by Ring Lardner; *His Family*, by Ernest Poole (Pulitzer prize 1918); *Parnassus on Wheels*, by Christopher Morley; *Susan Lenox: Her Fall and Rise*, by David Graham Phillips; and *The Three Black Pennys*, by Joseph Hergesheimer.

On Stage

Phonograph recordings of the Chicago, Cincinnati, and New York Philharmonic orchestras under their respective conductors, Frederick Stock, Dr. Ernst Kunwald, and Josef Stransky, were issued by the Columbia Company, Bridgeport, Conn.

Arnold Volpe established the Lewisohn Stadium Summer Concerts in New York at the College of the City of New York.

Paul Whiteman conducted a 40-piece band in the U.S. Navy.

Jascha Heifetz, 16-year-old Russian violin virtuoso, made (Oct. 27) his American debut in New York in a recital at Carnegie Hall.

Rope-twirling "cowboy philosopher" Will Rogers joined the *Ziegfeld Follies of 1917* (New York, New Amsterdam Theater, June 12).

New York plays that ran for 200 or more performances included *Business Before Pleasure, A Tailor Made Man, Polly with a Past, Lombardi, Ltd.; Tiger Rose, Parlor, Bedroom and Bath.* Jesse Lynch Williams's social comedy *Why Marry?* was the first play to be awarded a Pulitzer prize (1918). Musical productions included *Canary Cottage, You're in Love, Oh, Boy, Hitchy-Koo* with Raymond Hitchcock and Irene Bordoni; *Maytime* with Peggy Wood; *Chu Chin Chow* with Tyrone Power; *Flo-Flo; Going Up.*

In vaudeville Lou Holtz appeared with a blackface act. Blossom Seeley, Benny Fields, and Benny Davis had an act called "Seeley's Syncopated Studio".

Films

Douglas Fairbanks starred in *A Modern Musketeer.* Bespectacled comedian Harold Lloyd and 15-year-old Bebe Daniels started their movie careers together in a comedy entitled *Just Nuts.* Soprano Mary Garden took time out from grand opera to do a silent film version of the opera *Thais.* Ince Productions now had a roster including William S. Hart, Dorothy Dalton, Charles Ray, and Enid Bennett. Other film names of the year included William Desmond, Polly Moran, Fatty Arbuckle, Mae Murray, and Harry Carey.

Music

The Bells of St. Mary's; Come and Have a Swing with Me; The Darktown Strutters' Ball; For Me and My Gal; Hail, Hail, the Gang's All Here; I Don't Know Where I'm Going, but I'm On My Way; MacNamara's Band; Nobody Knows de Trouble I've Seen; Oh Johnny, Oh Johnny; Oh!, Over There; When Yankee Doodle Learns to Parlez Vous Francais; Where Do We Go from Here?; The Songs My Mother Never Taught Me.

1918

*W*orld War I entered its final year. President Wilson delivered (Jan. 8) before Congress his "Fourteen Points of Peace" speech. Russia moved (Mar. 9) its capital from Petrograd to Moscow. The collapse of the German armies along a battle-line extending across Europe led (Oct. 20) to an acceptance of defeat. A revolution in Kiel and Hamburg (Nov. 7) and the establishment of a republic in Bavaria (Nov. 8) resulted in the abdication of the German emperor Wilhelm II (Nov. 9). The armistice was signed (Nov. 11, at 11 a.m.) in a railway car, near Compiegne, France. The United States had mobilized 4,355,000 men; casualties amounted to 126,000 killed in action, 234,000 wounded, 4,500 prisoners or missing.

A wild and noisy public demonstration in the United States greeted both the premature and the real announcement of the armistice. In New York alone, 150 tons of paper and ticker tape were swept off the streets. Signs on shop doors read: "Closed for the Kaiser's funeral" and "Too happy to work; come back tomorrow."

The United States adopted daylight savings time, first used as an economy measure by England and Germany during the war.

The 19,300-ton U.S.S. *Cyclops* sailed (Mar. 4) from Barbados, W.I., and disappeared without a trace.

Commercial aviation began in the United States when air mail was established (May 15) between New York, Philadelphia, and Washington, D.C. The postage rate was fixed at 24 cents per ounce or fraction thereof; the Post Office Department accordingly had issued (May 13) a distinctive postage stamp.

A subway wreck in Brooklyn, New York, in the Malbone Street tunnel of the Brighton Beach line, killed (Nov. 2) 97 persons and injured 100 others.

The St. Louis Municipal Outdoor Theater, seating 10,000, was built.

The bellboy hat—a towering affair turned down over one eye—commanded feminine attention.

Norwegian-born Knute Kenneth Rockne was appointed head football coach at the University of Notre Dame, near South Bend, Ind. (During his 13 years there, Notre Dame teams won 105 games, lost 12, and tied 5.)

Charles Pores, long-distance runner, won (Sept. 21) at Great Lakes, Ill., the Amateur Athletic Union five-mile outdoor foot race in 24 minutes, 36.8 seconds, setting a world's record for that distance.

Deaths of the year included historian Hubert H. Bancroft (Mar. 2); historian Henry Adams (Mar. 27); publisher James Gordon Bennett, Jr. (May 14); former Vice President Charles W. Fairbanks (June 4); and Army Private Harry Gunther, last American killed in World War I (Nov. 11).

In Print

Books of the year included *Cornhuskers*, by Carl Sandburg (special Pulitzer prize 1919); *The Education of Henry Adams*, by Henry Adams (Pulitzer prize 1919); and the fiction, *Biltmore Oswald*, by Thorne Smith; *Birth*, by Zona Gale; *Dere Mable: Love Letters of a Rookie*, by Edward Streeter; *Java Head*, by Joseph Hergesheimer; *The Magnificent Ambersons*, by Booth Tarkington (Pulitzer prize, 1919); *My Antonia*, by Willa Cather; *The Passing of the Frontier*, by Emerson Hough; *The Restless Sex*, by Robert Chambers; and *Treat 'Em Rough*, by Ring Lardner.

On Stage

The Victor Company, Camden, N.J., began to issue phonograph recordings for the Boston Symphony Orchestra.

The Metropolitan Opera House, New York, produced, among other new operas, Rimsky-Korsakoff's *Le Coq d'Or* (Mar. 6); Charles Wakefield Cadman's American work *Shanewis* (Mar. 23); and Puccini's operatic triptych *Il Tabarro*, *Suor Angelica*, and *Gianni Schicchi* (Dec. 14). A feature of the production of *Le Coq d'Or* was the use of a ballet to mime the action while the singers sang from positions on both sides of the stage.

The Berkshire, Mass., festivals of chamber music began.

The New York theatrical season was high lighted by the production of *Lightnin'*—a dramatization of the novel by its author and Frank Bacon. With the latter heading the cast, the play achieved the unprecedented run of 1,291 New York performances, the first play in American stage history to pass the one thousand mark. By the time Bacon died in 1922, he had acted the leading role more than 2,000 times. Other long-run plays included *Seventeen*, *Friendly Enemies* with Louis Mann and Sam Bernard; *Three Faces East*, *Daddies*; *Forever After*, *Tea for Three*, *Redemption* by Tolstoy; *Three Wise Fools*; *East Is West*, *A Little Journey*. Musical productions included *Oh, Lady, Lady*; *Sinbad*; *The Rainbow Girl*; *Fancy Free*; *The Girl Behind the Gun*; *Sometime* with Mae West; *Oh My Dear!*; *Listen Lester*; and *Somebody's Sweetheart*. The Century Theater presented (Aug. 19) 32 performances of *Yip Yip Yaphank*, a "musical mess cooked up for the boys of Camp Upton by Sergeant Irving Berlin."

Films

Motion-picture patrons saw David Wark Griffith's *Hearts of the World*, with Mary Miles Minter, Tom Mix, Anna Q. Nilsson, and Wallace Reid.

Music

After You've Gone; I'm Always Chasing Rainbows; I'd Like to See the Kaiser with a Lily in His Hand; If He Can Fight Like He Can Love; Good Night Germany!; Ja-Da; Just Like Washington Crossed the Delaware, General Pershing Will Cross the Rhine; K-K-K-Katy; Keep Your Head Down; "Fritzie Boy"; Oh! How I Hate to Get Up in the Morning; Rock-a-Bye Your Baby With a Dixie Melody; We Don't Want the Bacon—What We Want Is a Piece of the Rhine; When Alexander Takes His Ragtime Band to France; Would You Rather Be a Colonel with an Eagle on Your Shoulder, or a Private with a Chicken on Your Knee?

1919

$\mathscr{T}$he 18th Amendment prohibiting liquor was ratified (Jan. 16). As an instrument for its enforcement, Congress passed Minnesota Representative Andrew Joseph Volstead's National Prohibition Act, known more commonly as the Volstead Act. President Wilson vetoed the bill and it passed (Oct. 28) over the veto. (The Amendment, called the "noble experiment," was repealed Dec. 5, 1933, by the 21st Amendment.)

The World War Peace Conference opened (Jan. 18) in Paris; the peace treaty was signed (June 28) in Versailles. President Wilson attended—the first American President to set foot on European soil. He returned to the United States in disappointment at the results of the conference, his idealism crushed by the national prejudices of the European representatives. Wilson presented the treaty (July 10) to the Senate, which rejected it (Nov. 19). President Wilson, however, was awarded the Nobel prize for peace.

The United States Post Office issued (Mar. 3) a three-cent purple Victory postage stamp to commemorate the successful conclusion of the World War.

The American Legion was formed (Mar. 15-17) as a national organization of men and women war veterans. The organization was chartered (Sept. 16) by Congress and met (Nov. 10-12) in Minneapolis, Minn., at its first national convention.

Almost every city and community in the country held parades for returning soldiers.

President Wilson collapsed (Sept. 25) in Pueblo, Colo., while on a strenuous speaking tour, and several days later suffered a stroke that left him incapacitated for life.

A race riot broke out (July 27) in Chicago, causing the death of 31 persons and injury to about 500 others.

Haiti revolted against occupation by the United States (1914). More than 1,800 Haitians lost their lives in the conflict with American marines.

During this year some 4,100,000 employees went on strike, walked out, or were locked out, affecting all major industries. An actors' strike shut down 12 legitimate shows and caused a precarious season.

Massachusetts Republican Governor Calvin Coolidge came into national prominence when he suppressed (Sept. 9) a strike of the Boston police. He wired Samuel Gompers, president of the American Federation of Labor:

"There is no right to strike against the public safety by anybody, anywhere, anytime."

Eight cigars per minute, or 4,000 per day, were turned out by the first cigar-making machine operated in Newark, N.J.

Henry Ford sued the *Chicago Tribune* for $1,000,000 libel, charging that in an editorial the newspaper had made him seem an anarchist. The trial ran four months, resulted in several million words of testimony, and terminated when the jury, after nine ballots, awarded Ford six cents in damages and costs.

Captain E. F. White made (Apr. 19) a nonstop flight from Chicago to New York. Lieutenants W. B. Maynard and Alexander Pearson completed (Oct. 8-18) the first transcontinental round-trip flight from New York to San Francisco and back.

Bobbed hair timidly made its social beginnings. Skirts were now six inches off the ground and women's hats were adorned with very large brims and fussy, fragile decorations.

Jack Dempsey, "the Manassa Mauler," became (July 4) the heavyweight boxing champion when title holder Jess Willard failed to answer the bell in the 4th round of their title bout at Toledo, Oh.

Deaths of the year included Theodore Roosevelt, aged 61 (Jan. 6), author L. Frank Baum (May 6), Andrew Carnegie, aged 82 (Aug. 11), and union leader John Mitchell (Sept. 9).

In Print

Books of the year included *The American Language,* by Henry Mencken; *The Life of John Marshall,* by Albert Jeremiah Beveridge (Pulitzer prize 1920); *Ten Days That Shook the World,* by John Reed; *Twelve Men,* by Theodore Dreiser; *The War with Mexico,* by Justin H. Smith (Pulitzer prize 1920); and the fiction, *The Builders,* by Ellen Glasgow; *Dr. Jonathan,* by Winston Churchill; *Humoresque,* by Fannie Hurst; *Jurgen,* by James Branch Cabell; *Lad: A Dog,* by Albert Payson Terhune; *Linda Condon,* by Joseph Hergesheimer; *The Sagebrusher,* by Emerson Hough; and *Winesburg, Ohio,* by Sherwood Anderson. No Pulitzer prize was awarded for the year's fiction.

On Stage

Fire destroyed the New Orleans Opera House.

Deems Taylor's suite of five musical pictures, *Through the Looking Glass,* after Lewis Carroll, was played (Feb. 18) by the New York Chamber Music Society for the first time.

An open-air opera performance of Verdi's *Aida* was given (Aug. 16) at Sheepshead Bay Speedway in New York.

The Washington Square Players, New York (1915), reorganized as The Theater Guild and produced (Apr. 19) as their first play *The Bonds of Interest* at the Garrick Theater. (The Guild opened its own theater in 1925.)

The Yiddish Art Theater was founded in New York by the Russian-American actor Maurice Schwartz. The first production was Hershbein's play *An Abandoned Nook* at the Irving Place Theater.

New York plays that ran more than 200 performances included *Up in Mabel's Room*; *Scandal* with Francine Larrimore; *Adam and Eve*; *Clarence* with Alfred Lunt; *The Gold Diggers* with Ina Claire; *The Storm*; *Declassee*; *His Honor*; *Abe Potash*; *The Son-Daughter* with Lenore Ulric; and *My Lady Friends*. John and Lionel Barrymore played an English adaptation of Sem Benelli's *La Cena delle Beffe* as *The Jest*. John Drinkwater's *Abraham Lincoln* with Frank McGlynn ran 193 performances. Musical productions included *The Velvet Lady* by Victor Herbert; *Good Morning, Judge*; *Tumble In*; *La, La Lucille*; *Happy Days*; *Apple Blossoms*; *The Little Whopper*. The Winter Garden show *Whirl of Society* (Mar. 5) provided Blossom Seeley and her chorus girls an opportunity for 136 performances to run up and down the aisles of the theater from the stage over a runway across the pit. The first of George White's *Scandals* was staged. Henri Fevrier's French opera *Aphrodite* was a spectacular perversion of the original with additional Broadway music. *Elsie Janis and Her Gang* played 55 performances "in a bombproof revue" of acts selected from the entertainments she gave for the soldiers in France.

Films

Motion-picture actors Mary Pickford and Douglas Fairbanks, Charles ("Charlie") Chaplin, and producer David Wark Griffith formed the United Artists Company. Griffith's film this year was *Broken Blossoms*. *The Miracle Man* made stars of Lon Chaney, Betty Compson, and Thomas Meighan.

Music

Alice Blue Gown; *Baby, Won't You Please Come Home*; *The Big Brown Bear*; *How Ya Gonna Keep 'Em Down on the Farm?*; *I'm Forever Blowing Bubbles*; *I'll Remember You*; *Indian Summer*; *A Pretty Girl Is Like a Melody*; *Swanee*.

1920

$\mathcal{A}$fter the passage of the 18th amendment and the Volstead Act, the United States went dry and began (Jan. 16) "the noble experiment" of national prohibition of liquor.

The 19th Amendment, giving women the right to vote, became (Aug. 26) the law of the land after nearly 75 years of agitation.

Congress abolished (May 29) the Subtreasury (1836). Its functions were assumed by Federal Reserve Banks.

The government distributed about 4,265,000 bronze "Victory" medals to soldiers, sailors, nurses, and others who participated in military service during the World War.

The League of Nations held (Feb. 11) its first meeting, in London.

The telephone dial system was introduced.

Food prices were extremely high and the term "high cost of living" was on everyone's lips.

Following the wave of strikes and various other post-war disturbances, a great "red scare" arose out of which the Ku Klux Klan, officially defunct since 1869, re-emerged.

Transcontinental air mail service was established between New York and San Francisco.

The Panama Canal was officially opened (July 12). The canal cost $366,650,000.

The Arlington Memorial Amphitheater, opposite Washington, D.C., was dedicated (May 15).

John Llewellyn Lewis was elected president of the United Mine Workers' Union.

A bomb explosion (Sept. 16) in Wall Street, New York, killed 30 persons, wounded 100, and caused a $2,000,000 property damage.

Four U.S. Army aviators, under Lieutenant Street, flew (July 15-Aug. 24) from New York to Nome, Alaska.

The radio compass was used (July 27) for the first time to direct the navigation of aircraft.

Lee De Forest installed (Mar.) a transmitter on the roof of the California Theater in San Francisco. The *Detroit News* began (Aug. 20) the operation of station WWJ. In Pittsburgh the Westinghouse Company launched KDKA, which reported (Nov. 2) to listeners the returns of the Harding-Cox presidential election. Westinghouse also launched its station WJZ in Newark, N.J. later in the month.

Mah-jongg, a Chinese game of 136 ivory tiles, and the Ouija board were popular pastimes.

New York state legalized (Sept.) public prize fighting by the adoption of the Walker Law, sponsored by James J. Walker then Speaker of the state senate and later (1926) Mayor of New York City.

Rogers Hornsby, second baseman of the St. Louis Cardinals, began his six-year reign as National League batting champion.

The Brooklyn and Boston National League baseball clubs battled (May 1) 26 innings at Boston in the longest major league game on record. The game ended in a tie score, 1-1, after 3 hours, 50 minutes. It was called on account of darkness.

The race horse "Man o' War was clocked at 2 minutes, 14-1/5 seconds at Belmont Park, New York, for a $1\frac{3}{8}$ mile stretch. The horse won stakes totaling $166,140.

A Chicago grand jury brought indictments against eight members of the 1919 Chicago White Sox, on the grounds that they had "thrown" the World Series to the Cincinnati Reds. Although the jury eventually voted acquittal, baseball put its house in order by appointing (1921) Judge Kenesaw Mountain Landis as "czar," or supreme arbiter.

The United States entered its twenty-third depression since 1790. It lasted two years and was severe.

The national population soared to 105,710,620.

Deaths of the year included explorer Robert Peary (Feb. 20), and novelist William Dean Howells (May 11).

In Print

Books of the year included *The Americanization of Edward Bok*, by Edward William Bok (Pulitzer prize 1921); *Smoke and Steel*, by Carl Sandburg; *Steeplejack*, by James Gibbons Huneker; *The Tiger in the House*, by Carl Van Vechten; *The Victory at Sea*, by William Sowden Sims and Burton J. Hendrick (Pulitzer prize in 1921); and the fiction, *The Age of Innocence*, by Edith Wharton (Pulitzer prize 1921); *Main Street*, by Sinclair Lewis; *Miss Lulu Bett*, by Zona Gale; *Moon-Calf*, by Floyd Dell; *Painted Veils*, by James Gibbons Huneker; *Poor White*, by Sherwood Anderson; *The Third Woman*, by Anne Douglas Sedgwick; and *This Side of Paradise*, by Francis Scott Fitzgerald.

On Stage

Enrico Caruso made (Dec. 24) the last appearance of his career in New York at the Metropolitan Opera House in Halevy's *La Juive*. (He died in Naples, Italy, Aug. 2, 1921.)

Reginald DeKoven's opera *Rip van Winkle* was produced at the Auditorium Chicago (Jan. 2; New York, Lexington Theater, Jan. 30). At the Metropolitan Opera House, New York, Henry Kimball Hadley's *Cleopatra's Night* was performed (Jan. 31). A Bohemian opera, *V Studni*, by Wilhelm Blodek, was sung (Mar. 6) in its native language at the Jan Huss Neighborhood House, New York.

Music lovers heard the first American performance of Elgar's *Enigma Variations* (Philadelphia Symphony, Feb. 13), Sibelius's symphonic poem *Finlandia* (Metropolitan Opera House orchestra, Dec. 24, conducted by Arturo Vigna), and Holst's symphony *The Planets* (Chicago Symphony, Dec. 31).

New York plays that ran 200 or more performances included *Ladies' Night*, *Enter Madame*, *Spanish Love*, *The Bat*, *The Bad Man*, *The Woman of Bronze*, *Little Old New York*, *Welcome Stranger*, *The Tavern*, *Three Live Ghosts*, *The Meanest Man in the World*, *The First Year*, *The Emperor Jones*, *Rollo's Wild Oat*, *Miss Lulu Bett* (Pulitzer prize 1921). Eugene O'Neill's *Beyond the Horizon* was the Pulitzer prize play of 1920. Musical production included *As You Were*, *The Night Boat*, *My Golden Girl*, *Cinderella on Broadway*, *Poor Little Ritz Girl*, *Good Times*, *Tickle Me*, *Honey-dew*, *Mecca*, *Tip Top*, *Mary*, *Afgar*, *Lady Bill*, and *Sally*.

Films

This year's films included Will Rogers in *Jes' Call Me Jim*; Mary Pickford in *Pollyanna*; and Charlie Chaplin with the child star Jackie Coogan in *The Kid*.

Music

Avalon; *I Lost the Best Pal That I Had*; *Rose of Washington Square*; *Who Ate Napoleons with Josephine When Bonaparte Was Away?*.

1921

*W*arren Gamaliel Harding, Republican, of Ohio, was inaugurated as the 29th President.

The United States officially ended World War I by concluding separate peace agreements with Germany and Austria-Hungary.

The Tomb of the Unknown Soldier in Arlington National Cemetery was dedicated on Armistice Day (Nov. 11) by President Harding, whose speech was broadcast to the nation by radio.

The tercentenary of the landing of the Pilgrims was celebrated with pageantry at Plymouth, Mass. The U.S. Post Office issued (Dec. 18) three commemorative postage stamps for the occasion.

For the centennial (1919) of Alabama's admission to the Union, a commemorative silver half dollar was minted. It bore the busts of W. W. Bibb, first governor of the state, and T. E. Kilby, incumbent at the time of the celebration—the first instance of a living person's portrait on a United States coin. The piece was designed by Laura Gardin Fraser.

A trial (May-June) of two alleged murderers in Dedham, Mass., engaged widespread public attention. The proceedings furnished the subject matter for Maxwell Anderson's plays *Gods of the Lightning* (1928) and *Winterset* (1935), Upton Sinclair's novel *Boston* (1928), poems, and documentary surveys by Felix Frankfurter (1927), by Eugene Lyons (1927), and others. A paymaster and his guard who were carrying the payroll of a Massachusetts shoe company were shot (Apr. 15) in Braintree, Mass., by two men who were said to be anarchists. Nicola Sacco, 29, fish peddler, and Bartolomeo Vanzetti, 32, shoe factory employee, were arrested as perpetrators of the crime. Both men were found to be armed with concealed pistols and to have owned the automobiles said by the police to have been connected with the murders. Vanzetti had a previous conviction for a holdup. A Sacco-Vanzetti Defense Committee raised $50,000 for the accused. The men were convicted and sentenced to death by Judge Webster Thayer on what some thought was inadequate evidence. Legal maneuvers to set aside the verdict failed, even though, during the course of the case, a jailed murderer testified to the commission of the crime and exonerated Sacco and Vanzetti. At the request of prominent citizens, Massachusetts Governor Alvan T. Fuller appointed a committee of eminent persons to review the case, but they concurred in the conviction. Sacco and Vanzetti were executed Aug. 22, 1927, in Charlestown, Mass. (In 1931 a bomb wrecked Judge Thayer's home at Worcester.)

The 18th Amendment was in force for one year and inaugurated an era of bootlegging and gangsterism. Outside the three-mile limit along the Atlantic seaboard stretched a row of speed boats with contraband liquor ready for smuggling. It came to be known as "Rum Row." Luxury liners also made brief excursions to sea to appease patrons' cravings.

The Limitation of Armaments Conference met (Nov. 11-Feb. 6, 1922) in Washington, D.C.

The collapse and explosion of the dirigible balloon ZR-2 over Hull, England, caused (Aug. 24) the death of 62 persons, of whom 17 were U.S. Naval representatives.

Former President William Howard Taft was appointed Chief Justice of the United States Supreme Court.

Denie Dougherty, Roman Catholic Archbishop, was made (Mar. 7) cardinal by Pope Benedict XV, the fifth American to be so honored.

Atlantic City, N.J., held its first "Miss America" bathing beauty contest as part of a pageant organized by local hotelmen to promote business after Labor Day. One result was the growing popularity of the form-fitting one-piece bathing suit.

Radio broadcasting stations had mushroomed so rapidly in America that conflicts of all sorts, technical, personal, and otherwise, arose among the broadcasters and threatened to bring about a chaotic condition on the air. The United States Government sought to regulate the affairs of the new industry and began (Sept.) the practice of licensing broadcasting stations.

The American Birth Control League was organized by Margaret Sanger, leader of the movement in the United States.

Plastic surgeons were advertising heavily in trade journals about the wonders they could work on actors' faces.

Newspaper ballyhoo helped to stimulate the first million-dollar gate in prize fighting when heavyweight champion Jack Dempsey fought (July 2) the French challenger Georges Carpentier at Boyle's Thirty Acres, Jersey City, N.J. The bout went four rounds before Dempsey kayoed the Frenchman. It was the first major prize fight to be broadcast by radio.

Deaths of the year included naturalist John Burroughs (Mar. 29), gunman and writer Bat Masterson (Oct. 25), and the first ordained American woman pastor, Rev. Dr. Antoinette L. Brown Blackwell (Nov. 5).

In Print

Books of the years included *The American Novel*, by Carl Van Doren; *Collected Poems*, by Edwin Arlington Robinson (Pulitzer prize 1922); *A Daughter of the Middle Border*, by Hamlin Garland (Pulitzer prize 1922); *The Founding of New England*, by James Truslow Adams (Pulitzer prize 1922); and the fiction, *Alice Adams*, by Booth Tarkington (Pulitzer prize 1922); *The Big Town*, by Ring Lardner; *Eric Dorn*, by Ben Hecht; *The Grey Room*, by Eden Phillpotts; *Messer*

Marco Polo, by Brian Oswald Donn-Byrne; *The Old Soak*, by Don Marquis; *Scaramouche*, by Rafael Sabatini; *Three Soldiers*, by John Dos Passos; and *The Triumph of the Egg*, by Sherwood Anderson.

On Stage

The American Orchestral Society was founded in New York by Mrs. E. H. Harriman.

New York plays that ran 175 or more performances included *The Champion*; *The Green Goddess* with George Arliss; *Dulcy* with Lynn Fontanne; *Six-Cylinder Love*; *The Circle* with Mrs. Leslie Carter returning after an absence of seven years' retirement in France; *Thank You*; *The Demi-Virgin* with Hazel Dawn; *Anna Christie* by Eugene O'Neill; *Kiki* with Lenore Ulric; *The Dover Road*; *Captain Applejack*. Musical productions included *Shuffle Along*; *Tangerine* with Julia Sanderson; *Blossom Time* with Bertram Peacock; *Bombo* with Al Jolson; *Good Morning*; *Dearie*; *The Perfect Fool* with Ed Wynn. John Charles Thomas and Fred Astaire appeared in the brief run of *The Love Letter*.

Will Rogers, after two and a half years in motion pictures, went into vaudeville. He joked that he was the only movie actor who so far had come out of Hollywood with the same wife.

Films

Motion-picture patrons saw Mary Pickford in *Little Lord Fauntleroy*, shuddered at the horrors of *The Cabinet of Dr. Calagari*, enjoyed *Bunty Pulls the Strings*, and went into raptures over a new romantic star—Rudolph Valentino in *The Sheik* and *The Four Horsemen of the Apocalypse*. Other films were *Cappy Ricks*; *Cup of Life*; *East Lynne*; *The Golem*; *Heart of the North*; *Jim the Penman*; and *Tol'able David*.

Music

Ain't We Got Fun?; *April Showers*; *Ma—He's Making Eyes at Me*; *Second Hand Rose*; *The Sheik of Araby*; *Wabash Blues*.

1922

The United States, Great Britain, France, Italy, and Japan signed (Feb. 6) at the Washington Conference the Five-Power Treaty limiting naval armament (Great Britain 22 capital ships, the United States 18, France, Italy, and Japan 10 each).

The Lincoln Memorial, Potomac Park, Washington, D.C., costing $2,940,000, was dedicated (May 30).

Lieutenant James H. Doolittle flew (Sept. 5-6) an airplane from Jacksonville, Fla., to San Diego, Calif., in 21 hours, 18 minutes, in two hops. At Hampton, Va., the dirigible balloon *Roma*, built for the United States in Italy, exploded, with a loss of 34 lives. In San Antonio, Tx., the blimp *C-2* blew up, but no one was killed.

Mrs. Rebecca L. Felton of Georgia became (Oct. 3) the first woman appointed to the U.S. Senate.

Protestant Episcopal bishops voted to eliminate the word "obey" from the marriage ceremony.

An American, Howard Carter, was with Lord Carnarvon as assistant when the latter opened the tomb of King Tutankhamen of the XVIIIth dynasty in Egypt.

The construction of the Holland tunnel, connecting New York and Jersey City under the Hudson River, was begun (Oct. 26).

The roof of the Knickerbocker Theater, a movie theater, in Washington, D.C., collapsed (Jan. 28), killing 98 persons.

Frederick William MacMonnies's fountain statue "Civic Virtue" was unveiled (Apr. 21) in City Hall Park, New York, and thoroughly offended the citizenry, especially its womenfolk, for its alleged obscenity. The statue represented a nude, robust, club-carrying male, Virtue, standing with one foot on the neck of a prostrate female (Vice). (The monument was removed on Oct. 7, 1941, to the lawn of Queens Borough Hall, New York.)

Radio station KGU, Honolulu, Hawaii, was opened (May 11). In New York, the American Telephone and Telegraph Company began (July) its radio station WEAF and radio turned commercial when the station broadcast the first advertisement—a program sponsored by a real estate firm, the Queensborough Corporation. At the same time, the A.T. & T. utilized its telephone facilities to broadcast programs and reports of events from places of origin outside its studios. Among the earliest such long-distance relays was the football game played by the universities of Chicago and Princeton at Chicago. The description of the game was telephoned from the scene of the contest to New York, nearly 1,000 miles away, and broadcast. In a similar manner, the program of the Bond Club of Chicago was conveyed to twenty stations forming a circuit that extended via New York to Havana, Cuba, and San Francisco, Calif. A feature of the broadcast was that twelve stations of the circuit contributed parts to the program.

George Herman "Babe" Ruth, who began his baseball career as a pitcher and was bought in 1919 from the Boston Red Sox by the New York Yankees club for a reputed price of $125,000, became an outfielder for his club, and displayed such phenomenal hitting ability that he soon was called "Sultan of Swat."

Alexander Graham Bell, aged 75, inventor of the telephone, died (Aug. 2) on his estate near Boddeck, Nova Scotia.

Merchant Jacob Gimbel died (Nov. 7).

In Print

Books of the year included: *American Songs and Ballads*, by Louise Pound; *The Life and Letters of Walter H. Page*, by Burton J. Hendrick (Pulitzer prize 1923); *The Supreme Court in United States History*, by Charles Warren (Pulitzer prize 1923); *The Waste Land*, by Thomas Stearns Eliot; and the fiction, *Babbitt*, by Sinclair Lewis; *The Beautiful and the Damned*, by Francis Scott Fitzgerald; *Birthright*, by Thomas Stribling; *The Covered Wagon*, by Emerson Hough; *The Enormous Room*, by Edward Estlin Cummings; *One of Ours*, by Willa Cather (Pulitzer prize 1923); *Peter Whiffle*, by Carl Van Vechten; *Vandermark's Folly*, by Herbert Quick; and *Where the Blue Begins*, by Christopher Morley).

On Stage

The comedy *Abie's Irish Rose* established a new record with 2,532 performances. The play, by Anne Nichols, was about Jewish and Irish life on New York's Lower East Side. Other plays that ran 175 or more performances included: *Lawful Larceny; The Cat and the Canary; Whispering Wires; The Old Soak; So This Is London; Loyalties; The Fool; The Last Warning; Seventh Heaven; Rain; Merton of the Movies.* Other plays of the year included 'George Bernard Shaw's philosophical fantasy *Back to Methuselah*; Eugene O'Neill's *The Hairy Ape*; Capek's melodrama *R.U.R.*; Pirandello's *Six Characters in Search of an Author*; and Claudel's mystery *The Tidings Brought to Mary*. David Warfield played Shylock in *The Merchant of Venice* and Fritz Lieber appeared in *Macbeth, Julius Caesar,* and *Romeo and Juliet*. Musical productions included *The Blue Kitten; The Blushing Bride;* and *The Gingham Girl*.

Films

In consequence of a sensational series of manslaughter trials involving Roscoe C. ("Fatty") Arbuckle, the Motion Picture Producers and Distributors of America, Inc., was organized in New York, with branches in Hollywood,

Washington, D.C., and Paris. Its president was Will H. Hays, former Postmaster General of the United States under President Harding, and its purpose was to improve and regulate standards of production. (The name of the group was changed in 1945 to the Motion Picture Association of America, Inc.)

Motion pictures included *Blood and Sand* with Rudolph Valentino, Lila Lee, and Nita Naldi; *Grandma's Boy* with Harold Lloyd and Mildred Davis; *Nanook of the North, Oliver Twist* with Jackie Coogan; *Orphans of the Storm* with Lillian and Dorothy Gish (produced by David Wark Griffith); *The Prisoner of Zenda; Robin Hood* with Douglas Fairbanks; *Smilin' Through* with Norma Talmadge; *When Knighthood Was in Flower* with Marion Davies.

Music

I Wish I Could Shimmy Like My Sister Kate; Somebody Stole My Gal; Toot, Toot, Tootsie!; and *'Way Down Yonder in New Orleans.*

1923

$\mathcal{P}$resident Harding visited Alaska late in June. On his return he became seriously ill and died (Aug. 2) in San Francisco. The following day Vice President Calvin Coolidge, Republican, of Vermont, was sworn into office as the 30th President at his home in Plymouth, Vt., by his father, a justice of the peace, and again (Aug. 17) before Justice A. A. Hoehling of the Supreme Court of the District of Columbia.

The U.S. Post Office issued (Sept. 1) a two-cent black commemorative postage stamp bearing the portrait of the late President as a tribute to his memory.

As a result of national prohibition, some 5,000 "speakeasies"—a new word—operated in New York City alone. Champagne was $25 a quart, and Scotch of questionable merit went for $20 a quart. Bathtub gin and needle beer sold for whatever the market would bear in any particular community.

"Day by day in every way I'm getting better and better" was on the tip of everybody's tongue. The rage was initiated by Emile Coue, who claimed that his system of "auto-suggestion" would cure mental and physical ailments.

Dr. Frederick Albert Cook, who claimed to have discovered the North Pole before Admiral Robert Edwin Peary (1909), was convicted of a mail fraud in Texas, fined $12,000 and costs, and sentenced to 14 years, 9 months in a Federal prison. (He was released on parole in 1930, discharged from parole in 1935, and pardoned and restored to civil rights by President Franklin Delano Roosevelt in 1940.)

Robert Andrews Millikan, president of the California Institute of Technology, was awarded the Nobel prize for physics—the first American to be so honored in that field.

Trinity College, Durham, N.C., chartered in 1841, was renamed Duke University after its benefactor James Buchanan Duke, tobacco manufacturer.

The Charleston, a new, fast fox-trot introduced by Cecil Mack and Jimmy Johnston in a Black revue, captured the fancy of ballroom dancers.

Radio station KDKA, Pittsburgh, Pa., successfully sent (Dec. 31) a "short-wave" program to England.

Women now preferred the cape-line hat—a wide-brimmed affair curving down on either side of the face.

Mrs. F. I. Mallory lost the National Women's Tennis championship to Helen Wills, who retained it through 1929 with the exception of one year—1926.

Robert T. Jones, Jr., won the National Open golf championship (and again in 1926, 1929, and 1930).

In Print

Time was founded in New York as a weekly magazine.

Books of the year included *Damaged Souls*, by Gamaliel Bradford; *From Immigrant to Inventor,* by Michael Pupin (Pulitzer prize 1924); *New Hampshire,* by Robert Frost (Pulitzer prize 1924); *The Story of the Bible,* by Hendrik Willem van Loon; and the fiction, *The Able McLaughlins,* by Margaret Wilson (Pulitzer prize 1924); *Black Oxen,* by Gertrude Atherton; *The Hi-Jackers,* by Robert Chambers; *Impromptu,* by Elliot Paul; *A Lost Lady,* by Willa Cather; and *Streets of Night,* by John Dos Passos.

On Stage

Siegfried Wagner, conductor and composer, son of the great Richard Wagner, visited the United States to raise funds for the reopening of the famous Festspielhaus at Bayreuth, Bavaria, which was closed in consequence of World War I.

The League of Composers was organized in New York for the performance of "modern" music.

Night clubs were evolving out of the old-style cabarets.

New York plays that ran 175 or more performances included: *Little Miss Bluebeard; Tarnish; The Nervous Wreck; For All of Us; The Shame Woman; The Swan; Cyrano de Bergerac; White Cargo; Spring Cleaning; Meet the Wife; The Potters;* and *Saint Joan* by George Bernard Shaw. *Icebound* won the Pulitzer prize in 1924. Musical productions included *Wildflower; Go-Go; Helen of Troy; New York; Little Jessie James;* and *Artists and Models.*

Films

Motion pictures included *The Covered Wagon* with Lois Wilson, Ernest Torrence, and J. Warren Kerrigan; *Down to the Sea in Ships; The Green Goddess* with George Arliss; *The Hunchback of Notre Dame* with Lon Chaney; *Little Old New York* with Marion Davies; *The Merry-Go-Round; Rosita* with Mary Pickford; *Safety Last* with Harold Lloyd, Mildred Davis; *Scaramouche;* and *The Ten Commandments.*

Music

Charleston; I Cried for You; I Won't Say I Will but I Won't Say I Won't; That Old Gang of Mine; and *Yes! We Have No Bananas.*

1924

$\mathscr{C}$ongress passed the Soldiers' Bonus Bill over President Coolidge's veto.

A Congressional investigating committee uncovered questionable practices in the granting obtaining of leases at the Elks Hills, Calif., and the Teapot Dome, Wyo. (1913) government oil reserves. The disclosures created a national scandal and involved Secretary of the Navy Edwin Denby, Secretary of the Interior Albert Bacon Fall, Attorney-General Harry M. Daughterty, Edward Doheny of the Doheny Oil Company, and Harry F. Sinclair of the Mammoth Oil Company. Denby, Fall, and Daugherty resigned under the pressure of public opinion. (Fall was sentenced in 1929 to a $100,000 fine and a prison term of one year.)

The Dawes Reparation plan, drafted by General Charles Gates Dawes, Vice President of the United States and chairman of the Reparation Committee, to stabilize German currency and insure the payment of 2,500 million marks, about $595,000,000, by Germany to the Allies as reparation for World War I, was accepted (Aug. 16) by both sides.

J. Edgar Hoover became head of the Federal Bureau of Investigation.

In Chicago, the disappearance (May 22) of 13-year-old Bobby Franks led to kidnapping and murder charges against N. F. Leopold, Jr., and Richard Loeb, both 19, who pleaded (July 19) guilty at their trial. The noted Clarence Darrow, their attorney, saved them from the gallows. The sentence was life imprisonment plus 99 years. (Loeb was killed in 1936 by a fellow convict.)

Pope Pius XI elevated (Mar. 24) two American Roman Catholic Archbishops to the cardinalate, Patrick Joseph Hayes of New York and George William Mundelein of Chicago.

The Bear Mountain and the Castleton bridges, N.Y., spanning the Hudson River, were completed.

Four U.S. Army transport airplanes set out on a round-the-world flight from Seattle, Wa., travelling westward. Two completed the journey, a distance of 27,553 miles, in 371 hours, 11 minutes' flying time (14 days, 15 hours) over a period of 175 days (Apr. 6-Sept. 28). Lieutenant Russell Maughan carried out (June 23) a transcontinental "dawn-to-dusk" flight from New York to San Francisco. A successful aeronautical experiment was conducted (Oct. 3) over Dayton, Oh., where an airplane was launched from a dirigible and continued on its course under its own power. Hugo Echner's Zeppelin R-3 flew (Oct. 12-

15) from Friedrichshafen, Germany, to Lakehurst, N.J., where the U.S. Navy took it over 5,066 miles in 81 hours, 17 minutes.

The crossword puzzle appeared and took the nation by storm. Recognizing the crossword puzzle's popularity, the Baltimore & Ohio Railroad put dictionaries in its mainline trains.

New York's municipal radio station WNYC went (July 8) on the air.

Twenty-seven radio stations combined (Nov. 3) in a coast-to-coast network to broadcast a speech by President Coolidge.

Bobby Jones took the National Amateur golf championship, and repeated the feat in 1925, 1927, 1928, and 1929. Babe Ruth of the New York Yankees topped all American League baseball batting averages of the year with .378. At Notre Dame University the "Four Horsemen" made their school and their coach, Knute Rockne, the giants of football.

A new Progressive Party was organized by the forceful Wisconsin Senator Robert Marion La Follette, who ran as its presidential candidate in the fall elections. He polled 4,822,319 votes. His opponents were President Coolidge, Republican, and John W. Davis, Democrat. The nation, however, re-elected President Coolidge by a landslide of 15,718,789 votes. Radio announcers, political commentators, and analysts kept the people informed of the election trends.

In the State elections of the year (Nov. 9), women were elected for the first time in American history to the gubernatorial office: they were Nellie Taylor Ross of Wyoming and Miriam ("Ma") Ferguson of Texas.

A short-lived, but sharp, depression was the 24th since 1790.

Deaths of the year included painter Maurice Prendergast (Feb. 1), politician Charles F. Murphy (Apr. 25), composer Victor Herbert (May 26), and Senator Henry Cabot Lodge (Nov. 9).

In Print

The American Mercury was founded in New York as a monthly magazine "to attempt a realistic presentation of the whole gaudy, gorgeous American scene."

The Daily Worker appeared as a continuation of the New York weekly *The Worker*, a radical socialist paper.

Books the year included *Autobiography*, by Mark Twain; *Black Cameos*, by R. Emmet Kennedy; *The Man Who Died Twice*, by Edwin Arlington Robinson (Pulitzer prize 1925); *Seven Lively Arts*, by Gilbert Seldes; *A Story Teller's Story*, by Sherwood Anderson; and the fiction, *The Avalanche*, by Ernest Poole; *Cowboys, North and South*, by Will James; *The Green Bay Tree*, by Louis Bromfield; *Hopalong Cassidy Returns*, by Clarence Mulford; *In Our Time*, by Ernest Hemingway; *The Little French Doll*, by Anne Douglas Sedgwick; *Mother of Gold*, by Emerson Hough; *Old New York*, by Edith Wharton; *So Big*, by Edna Ferber (Pulitzer prize 1925); and *Waste*, by Robert Herrick.

On Stage

Paul Whiteman, conductor of "symphonic jazz," gave (Feb. 12) a concert in Aeolian Hall, New York. He performed, for the first time, George Gershwin's *Rhapsody in Blue*, with the composer playing the piano part. Later in the year Whiteman and his orchestra toured Europe.

New York plays that ran 175 or more performances included *The Show-Off*; *Dancing Mothers*; *Pigs*; *What Price Glory?*; *My Son*, *The Guardsman*; *The Firebrand*; *Desire under the Elms*; *The Student Prince* (with Al Jolson); and *Topsy and Eva*, a jazz version of *Uncle Tom's Cabin*.

Films

Motion pictures included *Abraham Lincoln*, with George Billings and Louise Fazenda; *America*, with Carol Dempster and Lionel Barrymore; *Beau Brummel*, with John Barrymore; *Girl Shy*, with Harold Lloyd; *Monsieur Beaucaire*, with Rudolph Valentino; *The Sea Hawk*, with Milton Sills, Enid Bennett, and Wallace Berry; *Secrets*, with Norma Talmadge; and *The Thief of Bagdad*, with Douglas Fairbanks. The handsome German shepherd dog Rin-Tin-Tin was also appearing in motion pictures.

Music

All Alone; *California*; *Here I Come*, *Charley, My Boy*; *Does the Spearmint Lose Its Flavor on the Bedpost Over Night?*; *Drinking Song*; *Everybody Loves My Baby, but My Baby Don't Love Nobody but Me*; *Fascinating Rhythm*; *Hinky Dinky Parlay Voo*; *I Want to Be Happy*; *Indian Love Call*; *King Porter Stomp*; *The Man I Love*, *Tea for Two*; *What'll I Do*.

1925

$\mathscr{P}$resident Calvin Coolidge began his second term.

Nellie Taylor Ross was installed (Jan. 5) as Governor of Wyoming—the first woman to hold such an office. Miriam ("Ma") Ferguson was installed fifteen days later (Jan. 20) as Governor of Texas.

Congress passed (Feb. 28) the Postal Service Act raising postage rates and the Post Office issued a 1-cent and a half-cent stamp, a 25-cent "special handling" stamp, two 15- and 20-cent "special delivery" stamps, and a half-cent "postage due" stamp. Events in American history were also commemorated with adhesives: the 150th anniversary of the Battle of Lexington and Concord, the 100th anniversary of the arrival of the sloop *Restaurationen*, which transported the first group of Norwegian immigrants to the United States. A black 17-cent ordinary postage stamp bearing the portrait of former President Woodrow Wilson completed the year's new issues.

Commander J. Rogers, U.S.N., accomplished (Aug. 31) a nonstop flight in a seaplane from San Francisco to Honolulu, Hawaii.

A severe thunderstorm over Ava, Oreg., tore (Sept. 3, 5 a.m.) to pieces the U.S.N. dirigible *Shenandoah* which was on its way from Lakehurst, N.J., to St. Paul, Minn. Lieutenant Commander Zachary Lansdowne and 13 members of the crew lost their lives.

The trial of a high school teacher in Dayton, Tenn., attracted so much attention that part of it had to be held outdoors. The point of issue was the teaching of the theory of evolution, in contradiction of fundamentalist church doctrine. The case provoked discussion throughout the country. Clarence Darrow was counsel for the defendant John Thomas Scopes; William Jennings Bryan represented the prosecution. Scopes was found guilty (July 24) and fined $100 and costs.

Vice President Charles Gates Dawes was awarded the Nobel prize for peace for his work in helping to stabilize postwar international finances.

The annual Guggenheim Fellowships were established by the John Simon Guggenheim Memorial Foundation, New York, to foster creative talent and research in various fields.

Florida was enjoying a land boom that sent real estate prices skyrocketing and helped establish Coral Gables and Miami.

In Washington, D.C., the last U.S. fire engine drawn by a span of three horses made its final appearance.

Women's skirts were knee length, disclosing flesh-colored silk stockings. Hats were close-fitting.

The "police dog" now was a household pet; one, Rin-Tin-Tin, was a movie star.

The Louisville, Ky., newspaper *Courier-Journal* organized the first National Spelling Bee.

Telephotography was introduced by the American Telephone and Telegraph Company.

The latest development in radio sets for the home was the all-electric mechanism that eliminated cabinets full of batteries or the earlier crystal sets equipped with earphones.

Radio station WEAF, New York, began weekly broadcasts for standard operas. The operas were sung in their original languages by experienced singers and performed by a medium-size orchestra under the direction of Cesare Sodero.

In New York, a new Madison Square Garden sports arena, about two and one-half miles north of its historic predecessor, opened (Dec. 15).

Harold Edward ("Red") Grange, the football star of the University of Illinois, had scored 31 touchdowns in 20 games. In the fall of this year he became a professional player and joined the Chicago Bears football club—a controversial move that created much heated discussion.

Deaths of the year included author George Washington Cable (Jan. 31), automobile inventor Elwood Haynes (Apr. 13), baseball executive Charles H. Ebbets (Apr. 18), photographer Clarence H. White (July 7), and pitcher Christy Mathewson (Oct. 7).

In Print

The New Yorker was founded in New York as a humorous weekly magazine for "caviar sophisticates."

Books of the year included *History of the United States*, by Edward Channing (Pulitzer prize 1926); *The Life of Sir William Osler*, by Dr. Harvey Cushing (Pulitzer prize 1926); *Seventy Years of Life and Labor*, by Samuel Gompers; the poetry, *Roan Stallion*, by Robinson Jeffers; *What's O'Clock?*, by Amy Lowell (Pulitzer prize 1926); and the fiction, *An American Tragedy*, by Theodore Dreiser; *Arrowsmith*, by Sinclair Lewis (Pulitzer prize 1926, but declined by the author); *Barren Ground*, by Ellen Glasgow; *Dark Laughter*, by Sherwood Anderson; *Drums*, by James Boyd; *Gentlemen Prefer Blondes*, by Anita Loos; *The Great Gatsby*, by Francis Scott Fitzgerald; *The Making of Americans*, by Gertrude Stein; *Manhattan Transfer*, by John Dos Passos; *Porgy*, by DuBose Heyward; *The Professor's House*, by Willa Cather; *Pluck and Luck*, by Robert Benchley; and *Thunder on the Left*, by Christopher Morley.

On Stage

Russian composer Igor Stravinsky toured in the United States as pianist and conductor. He played (Jan. 23) the world premiere of his Concerto for Piano and Wind Instruments with the Boston Symphony Orchestra.

Open-air performances of opera were given in the baseball park Ebbets Field, Brooklyn, New York. *Aida* (Aug. 1), *Cavalleria Rusticana* and *Pagliacci* (Aug. 5), and *Faust* (Aug. 8) were performed and broadcast by the municipal radio station.

New York plays that ran 200 or more performances included *Is Zat So?*; *Cradle Snatchers*; *The Jazz Singer*; *The Green Hat*; *The Butter and Egg Man*; *Craig's Wife* (Pulitzer Prize 1926); *The Enemy*; *Young Woodley*; *Laff That Off*; *The Last of Mrs. Cheyney*. Musical productions included *George White's Scandals*; *Artists and Models*; *Earl Carroll Vanities*; and *No! No! Nanette*.

Films

Motion pictures included *The Big Parade*, with John Gilbert and Renee Adoree; *Don Q, Son of Zorro*, with Douglas Fairbanks; *The Freshman*, with Harold Lloyd; *The Gold Rush*, with Charlie Chaplin; *Kiss Me Again*, with Marie Prevost and Monte Blue; *The Last Laugh*, with Emil Jannings; *The Lost World*, with Bessie Love and Lewis Stone; *The Merry Widow*, with Mae Murray and John Gilbert; *The Phantom of the Opera*, with Lon Chaney; and *The Son of the Sheik* with Rudolf Valentino (his last picture).

Music

Alabamy Bound; Does Your Mother Know You're Out, Cecilia?; Five Foot Two, Eyes of Blue; I'm Sitting on Top of the World; If You Knew Susie—Like I Know Susie; Show Me the Way to Go Home; Sleepy Time Gal; Sunny; Sweet Georgia Brown; Who Takes Care of the Caretaker's Daughter While the Caretaker's Busy Taking Care?; Yes Sir, That's My Baby.

1926

$\mathscr{T}$he United States was 150 years old. In celebration of the event, the Sesquicentennial Exposition was held (May 31-Nov. 30) in Philadelphia. The United States Post Office issued (May 10) a red two-cent commemorative postage stamp for the occasion.

Nearly 2,000 violators of the prohibition law died of poisoned liquor. Bootleg prices pegged Scotch at $48 a case; rye, $85; champagne, $95; beer, $38.

Brigadier General William Lendrum ("Billy") Mitchell, one of the outstanding American air force heroes of World War I and a dynamic, outspoken critic of the government's policies in aviation, was haled before a court-martial and accused of violating the 96th Article of War—acting "to the prejudice of good order and military discipline." Mitchell had declared that the loss of the dirigible *Shenandoah* in 1925 was the result of "incompetence, criminal negligence, and almost treasonable administration of the national defense by the War and Navy departments." He was sentenced—the court said, with leniency, because of his military record—to suspension from the service for five years and forfeiture of all pay and allowances. President Coolidge upheld the sentence but mitigated it to give General Mitchell half pay. Mitchell, who had reverted to his permanent rank of colonel, resigned (Feb. 1). (He was posthumously restored in 1942 to the rank of major general. Mitchell died in 1936.)

Illinium, a chemical element (atomic no. 61), was discovered by B. S. Hopkins of the University of Illinois. (Two Italian chemists, L. Fernandez and L. M. Rolla, had claimed the discovery two years earlier, and named the element "florentium," after the city of Florence.)

Lieutenant Commander Richard Evelyn Byrd and Floyd Bennett became the first aviators to fly (May 9) over the North Pole on a flight financed by the United States Government. They left from Svalbard, Greenland, and returned in 15 hours after covering a distance of 1,360 miles. Norway, the United States, and Italy sponsored the Amundsen-Ellsworth-Nobile dirigible expedition which also left from Svalbard, flew over the Pole and, after being lost in the Arctic for 78 hours, landed (May 12) at Barrow, Alaska.

Transatlantic radiotelephone was established (Mar. 7) on the 50th anniversary of Alexander Graham Bell's telephone patent.

The Delaware River bridge, connecting Philadelphia, Pa., and Camden, N.J., was opened to traffic.

Florida and the Gulf States were swept (Sept. 18) by a hurricane that caused the death 372 persons and destroyed some 5,000 buildings and homes.

Gertrude Ederle, a New Yorker from the Bronx, was the first woman swimmer to conquer (Aug. 6) the English Channel; her time was 14 hours, 31 minutes.

White-robed evangelist "Sister" Aimee Semple McPherson of the Angelus Temple, Los Angeles, Calif., disappeared (May 18) from the bathing beach at Venice, Calif.; she later returned to a great deal of newspaper attention.

Annie Oakley, famed crack shot, died. Her name has become synonymous in theater language with a free pass or "punched paper" to a show, and in carnival terminology with a meal ticket.

Rudolph Valentino, idol of motion-picture fans, died (Aug. 23) in New York at 31. Hysterical crowds flocked to the funeral parlor to view his remains. His full name was Rudolpho Alfonzo Raffaelo Pierre Filibert Guglielmi di Valentina d'Antonguolla.

A statue of Captain John Ericsson, builder of the *Monitor* (1862), was unveiled (May 29) in Washington, D.C. by the Crown Prince of Sweden.

The younger generation was referred to as "flaming youth."

The Rev. A. Mark, Austrian-born American Congregational minister, gave (Apr. 4) an Easter sunrise presentation of a modest pageant in two tableaux and 13 characters on a hillside outside Medicine Park, near Lawton, OK. With the help of a government (W.P.A.) grant, this occasion led to the establishment of an American equivalent of Oberammergau, the "Holy City" (dedicated Mar. 31, 1935), located west of Fort Sill in the Wichita Mountains.

Contract bridge was supplanting auction bridge around the country.

A new dance, black bottom, introduced in *George White's Scandals* (New York, Apollo Theater, June 14), vied with the Charleston for popularity.

There now were 536 licensed radio stations in the country.

Thirty-eight radio stations combined (Sept. 15) in a network extending from coast to coast to broadcast the musical program and the address of Vice President Charles Dawes from the Radio Industries banquet in New York.

The National Broadcasting Company (NBC), New York, was inaugurated (Nov. 15) with an unusual program: Mary Garden sang from her studio in Chicago; Will Rogers enlivened the proceedings from Kansas City; and an elaborate program in New York included the comedians Weber and Fields, the baritone Titta Ruffo, the New York Symphony Orchestra, the Oratorio Society chorus, and the pianist Harold Bauer, who had arrived from Europe in New York that very day and was hurried ashore by a special boat.

Gene Tunney won (Sept. 23) by decision Jack Dempsey's heavyweight boxing title in Philadelphia after ten rounds. The gate was $1,900,000.

Deaths of the year also included Luther Burbank, aged 77 (Apr. 11), publisher Edward W. Scripps (Mar. 13), and inventor John Moss Browning (Nov. 26).

In Print

Books of the year included *Abraham Lincoln: The Prairie Years*, by Carl Sandburg; 2 vols.; *Fiddler's Farewell*, by Leonora Speyer (Pulitzer prize 1927); *George Washington*, by Rupert Hughes; 3 vols., 1926-30; *The Mauve Decade*, by Thomas Beer; *Microbe Hunters*, by Paul de Kruif; *Our Times: the United States, 1900-1925*, by Mark Sullivan; 6 vols., 1926-36; *Pinckney's Treaty*, by Samuel Flagg Bemis (Pulitzer prize 1927); *Whitman*, by Emory Holloway (Pulitzer prize 1927); and the fiction, *Early Autumn*, by Louis Bromfield (Pulitzer prize 1927); *Her Sons's Wife*, by Dorothy Canfield; *Nigger Heaven*, by Carl Van Vechten; *Preface to a Life*, by Zona Gale; *Show Boat*, by Edna Ferber; *The Romantic Comedians*, by Ellen Glasgow; *The Silver Stallion*, by James Branch Cabell; *Soldier's Pay*, by William Faulkner; *The Sun Also Rises*, by Ernest Hemingway; *Teeftallow*, by Thomas Stribling; *The Time of Man*, by Elizabeth Maddox Roberts; and *Topper*, by Thorne Smith.

On Stage

Arturo Toscanini was guest conductor of the New York Philharmonic Orchestra.

Frank Harling's opera *Deep River* with the Negro baritone Julius Bledsoe (of later *Show Boat* fame) was staged (Oct. 4) in New York at the Imperial Theater for 32 performances.

New York plays that ran 175 or more performances included *The Great God Brown*; *Lulu Belle*; *The Little Spitfire*; *Two Girls Wanted*; *Broadway*; *Gentlemen Prefer Blondes*; *An American Tragedy*; *The Noose*; *The Ladder*; *Caponsacchi*; and *The Play's the Thing*. Musical productions included *A Night in Paris*; *Americana*; *Earl Carroll's Vanities*; *Castles in the Air*; *Queen High*; *Countess Maritza*; *The Ramblers*; *Honeymoon Lane* ; *Criss Cross*; *Oh Kay*; *The Desert Song*; and *Peggy-Ann*.

Films

The first talking motion picture was publicly exhibited (Aug. 6) in New York at the Warner Theater: *Don Juan*, with John Barrymore and a synchronized orchestral accompaniment. The "talkies," as they were called, or sound film, quickly made the silent pictures obsolete. Among the latter this year were *Beau Geste*, with Ronald Colman and Noah Berry; *Ben Hur*, with Ramon Novarro and Francis X. Bushman; *Black Pirate*, with Douglas Fairbanks; *La Boheme*, with Lillian Gish and John Gilbert; *It*, with Clara Bow (who originated that wonderful "it"); *Sea Beast*, with John Barrymore; *Stella Dallas*, with Belle Bennett and Ronald Colman; *Variety*, with Emil Jannings; *Volga Boatman*, with William Boyd; and *What Price Glory?* Among popular screen stars were Mary Astor, Mary Brian, Dolores Costello, Joan Crawford, Dolores Del Rio, Janet Gaynor, and Fay Wray.

Music

The Birth of the Blues; Bye Bye Blackbird; Charmaine; Gimme a Little Kiss, Will Ya, Huh?; It All Depends on You; Looking at the World Through Rose Colored Glasses.

1927

---

*T*he United Stated dispatched 600 marines to Nicaragua (Jan. 6) and 1,000 to China (Mar. 5) to protect United States citizens and American property. The Standard Oil plant in Nanking was burned (Mar. 23) by Chinese insurgents.

As a result of the Teapot Dome disclosures (1924), the United States Supreme Court voided the Doheny oil leases as fraudulent and ordered the return of the properties to the government. President Coolidge thereupon canceled all other contracts connected with the deals.

President Coolidge uttered (Aug. 2) his famous decision: "I do not choose to run for President in 1928." Republicans had sought to nominate him for the coming national election.

Transatlantic radio telephony was established between New York and London.

The hand-set telephone replaced the wall-set transmitter.

Captain Charles Augustus Lindbergh, United States air mail pilot, won the $25,000 prize offered by Raymond Orteig and made the first solo New York-to-Paris, nonstop airplane flight. Flying alone in his monoplane *Spirit of St. Louis*, Lindbergh left (May 20, 7:52 a.m.) from Roosevelt Field, Long Island, N.Y., and arrived (May 21, 10: 21 p.m., Paris time) at Le Bourget air field, Paris. He had covered 3,610 miles in 33 hours, 29 minutes, 30 seconds. He and his plane thereafter returned to the United States on the cruiser "Memphis." Captain Lindbergh was received (June 11) by President Coolidge in Washington and raised to the rank of colonel. New York tendered (June 13) Colonel Lindbergh one of its wildest receptions. The populace tore up close to 2,000 tons of ticker tape and telephone books for confetti as Lindbergh rode in an automobile up Broadway. To commemorate the flight, the United States Post Office issued (June 18) a special 10-cent blue air mail postage stamp that pictured the "Spirit of St. Louis" and temporarily replaced the regular stamp of 1926.

Also in aviation news was the nonstop flight (June 4-5) of Clarence D. Chamberlin and Charles Levine from Mineola, N.Y., to Eisleben, Germany, covering 3,911 miles in 42 hours, 31 minutes. In the same month (June 28-30) Commander Richard Evelyn Byrd, U.S.N., and three others flew from New York to France. In the fog they missed Paris and landed at Versur-Mer. Later in the year (Aug. 27-Sept. 14) W. S. Brock and E. F. Schlee took off at Harbor Grace, Newfoundland, and reached Kasamingara, Japan. Meanwhile L. H.

Maitland and Albert Hegenberger flew form Oakland, Calif., to Honolulu, Hawaii.

The Holland vehicular tunnel, connecting New York City and Jersey City, N.J., was opened (Nov. 13). Its construction was begun in 1920.

Sculptor Gutzon Borglum began carving gigantic figures of Washington, Jefferson, Lincoln, and Theodore Roosevelt in the granite of Mt. Rushmore, Black Hills, N.D.

Television was the "newest of sciences." It already had been demonstrated experimentally in England, Germany, and France and was being studied in the United States. This year the Radio Corporation of America conducted (Apr. 7) a successful demonstration by telecasting a program of speakers and performers from Washington, D.C., which was visible and audible on receiving sets in New York.

The Columbia Broadcasting System (CBS), New York, was inaugurated (Sept. 18).

An ominous rivalry broke out among radio broadcasters, some going so far as to pirate the wave length, or air space, in which another station was operating. Congress established the Federal Radio Commission, comprised of five members appointed by the President, to arbitrate and re-allocate the positions of the stations on the air. The number of stations was reduced from over 1000 to 708.

Operatic excerpts from the stage of the Auditorium, Chicago, became a regular radio feature after the garden scene from *Faust*, sung by the Chicago Civic Opera, was broadcast (Jan. 21) by means of 15 microphones installed in the theater. Subsequently, a manufacturer of radio supplies sponsored the broadcasting of complete acts of operas from the Auditorium through 19 associated stations.

Right fielder Babe Ruth hit 60 home runs for the New York Yankees, and slammed out two more during the world series against the Pittsburgh Pirates.

At Soldiers Field, Chicago, former heavyweight boxing champion Jack Dempsey attempted (Sept. 22) to regain his lost title in a second match with Gene Tunney. The latter got the decision after 10 rounds, and sport fans forever after discussed the pros and cons of the so-called "long count" when Dempsey, having floored Tunney, was slow in returning to a neutral corner. The fight set an all-time gate record in prize-fight history—$2,650,000 with an attendance of 104,943 spectators. Millions more listened to the fight descriptions over the radio, and it was claimed that five persons dropped dead of heart failure during the seventh round when Tunney fell to the canvas.

Deaths of the year included Isadora Duncan, noted American interpretive dancer, aged 49 (Sept. 14), killed in an automobile accident in Paris; historian Brooks Adams (Feb. 13); Army General Leonard Wood (Aug. 7); and movie pioneer Sam L. Warner (Oct. 5).

In Print

Books of the year included *The American Orchestra and Theodore Thomas*, by Charles Edward Russell (Pulitzer prize 1928); *The American Songbag*, by

Carl Sandburg; *Main Currents in American Thought,* by Vernon Louis Parrington (Pulitzer prize 1928); *The Rise of American Civilization,* by Charles and Mary Beard; 2 vols.; *Tristram,* by Edwin Arlington Robinson (Pulitzer poetry prize 1928); *Trumpets of Jubilee,* by Constance Rourke; and the fiction, *The Lives and Times of archy and mehitabel,* by Don Marquis; *Black April,* by Julia Peterkin; *Blue Voyage,* by Conrad Aiken; *The Bridge of San Luis Rey,* by Thornton Wilder (Pulitzer prize 1928); *Captain Blood: His Odyssey,* by Rafael Sabatini; *Death Comes for the Archbishop,* by Willa Cather; *Elmer Gantry,* by Sinclair Lewis; *Forever Free,* by Honore Willsie Morrow; *Giants in the Earth,* by Ole Rolvaag; *The Grandmothers,* by Glenway Westcott; *Marching On,* by James Boyd; *Me Without Women,* by Ernest Hemingway; and *Twilight Sleep,* by Edith Wharton.

On Stage

After ten years the Metropolitan Opera House, New York, again produced (Feb. 17) an opera by an American composer—*The King's Henchman* by Deems Taylor. The libretto was furnished by the poet Edna St. Vincent Millay.

An open-air performance of Shakespeare's *A Midsummer Night's Dream,* with Mendelssohn's incidental music, was given (June 26) at the Tennis Stadium, Forest Hills, Long Island, N.Y., for the Actors' Fund of America.

New York plays that ran 200 or more performances included *Tommy; The Barker; Burlesque; The Trial of Mary Dugan; The Command to Love; The Shannons of Broadway; Jimmie's Women; Dracula; Porgy; Interference; The Ivory Door; Coquette; Excess Baggage;* and *The Royal Family. The Taming of the Shrew* had a successful revival. Musical productions included *The Circus Princess; Hit the Deck; A Night in Spain; Good News;* and *The Connecticut Yankee.*

Films

The Academy of Motion Picture Arts and Sciences was founded in Los Angeles, Calif., and conferred an annual award (an "Oscar") for outstanding performances in various branches of the industry. The first awards went, among others, to Emil Jannings for *The Way of All Flesh;* Janet Gaynor for *Seventh Heaven;* and to the film *Wings.* Special awards were presented to Charlie Chaplin for *The Circus* and to Al Jolson for *The Jazz Singer,* a part-sound Warner production. Among silent films were *Chang; Flesh and the Devil,* with John Gilbert; *King of Kings,* with H. B. Warner and Joseph and Rudolph Schildkraut; *Resurrection; Sorrell and Son,* with H. B. Warner and Alice Joyce; *Sunrise,* with George O'Brien and Janet Gaynor; and *Underworld.*

Music

Back in Your Own Back Yard; The Best Things in Life Are Free; Funny Face; My Heart Stood Still; The Song Is Ended—but the Melody Lingers On; Strike Up the Band; 'Swonderful; Thou Swell.

1928

$\mathcal{T}$he Kellogg-Briand Anti-War Pact, negotiated by American Secretary of State Frank Billings Kellogg and French Minister of Foreign Affairs Aristide Briand, was signed (Aug. 27) in Paris by fifteen nations. The Pact outlawed war and agreed that the settlement of international differences "shall never be sought except by pacific means." (The treaty was ratified Jan. 25, 1929, by the United States Senate and proclaimed in effect July 24 by President Hoover, with 62 nations now subscribing to its principles.) Kellogg was awarded the Nobel prize for peace.

Transatlantic flyer Charles Augustus Lindbergh received (Mar. 19) the Woodrow Wilson Medal and the $25,000 peace award. Congress presented (Oct. 20) a gold medal to Thomas Alva Edison.

John Henry Mears again made a round-the-world trip from New York, reducing his former (1913) record of 35 days, 19 hours, 42 minutes, 38 seconds to 23 days, 15 hours, 21 minutes, 3 seconds (June 29-July 22). He was accompanied by Captain C.B.D. Collyer. They traveled by steamer and airplane.

Ship-to-shore telephone service was established (Dec. 8); the first ship to be so equipped was the SS *Leviathan.*

The St. Francis dam north of Los Angeles, Calif., burst (Mar. 13) and flooded the region. About 700 houses were washed away and some 450 people lost their lives.

A violent hurricane from the West Indies swept over Florida (Sept.), causing the death of more than 2,000 persons and a property damage of $25,000,000.

A new aviation endurance record was set (Jan. 1-7) by five U.S. Army officers when they remained aloft 150 hours, 40 minutes by refueling in flight. Amelia Earhart became the first woman to cross the Atlantic in a plane when she flew (June 17-18) in the "Friendship," piloted by Wilmer Stultz and Louis Gordon, from Trepassy Bay, Newfoundland, to Burry Port, Wales. Capt. Frank W. Hawkes made (June 27-29) a record trip from New York to Los Angeles in 19 hours, 10 minutes. Dale Jackson and Forrest O'Brine accomplished (July 13-30) another endurance record in their "St. Louis Robin" which remained aloft 420 hours, 21 minutes over St. Louis.

The National Broadcasting Company organized the NBC Symphony Orchestra with Walter Damrosch as conductor. It gave weekly concerts of broadcast music for schools and colleges and the radio audience of the United States and Canada.

Gene Tunney, heavyweight boxing champion, retired from the ring. The title remained vacant until 1930 when it was annexed by Max Schmeling of Germany.

In the national elections, the popular New York Governor Alfred E. Smith, Franklin Delano Roosevelt's "Happy Warrior," ran as Democratic candidate against the Republican nominee Herbert C. Hoover. 106 radio stations across the country familiarized the nation with the election returns; about 25,000 miles of telephone wires formed the network of inter-connection, and some 48,000 miles of telegraph circuits served as an auxiliary means of communication. Smith lost to Hoover by 6,375,747 votes.

Deaths of the year included dancer Loie Fuller (Mar. 3), automobile pioneer James W. Packard (Mar. 20), hotel executive Ellsworth Statler (Apr. 16), and illustrator Richard ("Buster Brown") Outcault (Sept. 25).

In Print

Books of the year included *Dictionary of American Biography*, completed in 20 vols. in 1936; *The Happy Warrior: Alfred E. Smith*, by Franklin Delano Roosevelt; *John Brown's Body*, by Stephen Vincent Benet (Pulitzer prize 1929); *The New Russia*, by Dorothy Thompson; *The Organization and Administration of the Union Army, 1861-65*, by Fred A. Shannon (Pulitzer prize 1929); *The Rediscovery of America*, by Waldo Frank; *The Training of an America: The Earlier Life and Letters of Walter Hines Page*, by Burton J. Hendrick; and the fiction, *Bad Girl*, by Vina Delmar; *Boston*, by Upton Sinclair; *Mary Todd Lincoln*, by Honore Willsie Morrow; *Ol' Man Adam 'n' His Chillun*, by Roark Bradford; *A President Is Born*, by Fannie Hurst; *Scarlet Sister Mary*, by Julia Peterkin (Pulitzer prize 1929).

On Stage

The New York Philharmonic Society and the New York Symphony Society orchestras merged to become the New York Philharmonic-Symphony Society of New York. Walter Damrosch was the conductor of the newly organized body of players.

The first performance of George Gershwin's tone poem *An American in Paris*, using taxihorns as an orchestral effect, was played (Dec. 13) by the New York Philharmonic-Symphony Society under Walter Damrosch.

New York plays that ran 200 or more performances included *Strange Interlude* by Eugene O'Neill (Pulitzer prize 1928); *The Silent House; The Spider; The Bachelor Father; The Road to Rome; The Front Page; Courage; Little Accident; Holiday.* Mae West played *Diamond Lil.* Musical productions included *Rosalie; Rain or Shine; The Three Musketeers; Blackbirds of 1928; George White's Scandals; Earl Carroll's Vanities; Good Boy; The New Moon;* and *Animal Crackers.*

Films

Silent black and white motion pictures gave way to sound and animation. The new sound pictures included *Abie's Irish Rose; Four Sons*, with H. B. Warner; *Lights of New York; The Patriot*, with Emil Jannings; and *The Singing Fool*, with Al Jolson. Silent films included *The Crowd*, with James Murray and Elinore Boardman; *The Last Command*, with Emil Jannings; *Sadie Thompson*, with Gloria Swanson; and *Street Angel*, with Janet Gaynor and Charles Farrell. *Plane Crazy* was 27-year-old Walt Disney's first animated cartoon.

Music

Button Up Your Overcoat; Constantinople; A Garden in the Rain; I'm Wild about Horns on Automobiles That Go "Ta-Ta-Ta-Ta; I Can't Give You Anything But Love; I Wanna Be Loved By You; Love Me or Leave Me; Lover, Come Back to Me; Makin' Whoopee!; Manhattan Serenade.

1929

$\mathcal{H}$erbert Clark Hoover, Republican, of Iowa, was inaugurated as the 31st President.

"Coolidge prosperity" suddenly collapsed with dire effects. The worst stock market crash since "Black Friday" of 1869 occurred (Oct. 29) when 16,400,000 shares in declining values exchanged hands in a single day's selling rush. The ticker barely caught up with transactions by nightfall, and some stocks plunged over 35 points in a day. The New York Stock Exchange closed for three days. By the end of the year, $14,000,000,000 had vanished. It was testified before the Senate investigating committee that 25,000,000 persons had been affected by this financial catastrophe—the twenty-fifth in U.S. history since 1790, and by far the most disastrous, far-reaching, and protracted.

Commodore Richard Evelyn Byrd conducted explorations in the Antarctic. He reported (Feb. 20) the finding of new regions, and discovered (Nov. 29) the South Pole while flying in the tri-motored airplane *Floyd Bennett* accompanied by Bernt Balchen, pilot, Harold I. June, radio operator, and Capt. Ashley C. McKinley, photographer. For this feat, Commodore Byrd was raised to the rank of Rear Admiral.

Charles Augustus Lindbergh married Anne Spencer Morrow, daughter of Dwight Morrow, U.S. Ambassador to Mexico.

The German dirigible balloon "Graf Zeppelin," commanded by Dr. Hugo Eckener, made (July 31-Aug. 10) a trip from Friedrichshafen, Germany to Lakehurst, N.J., and back. The airship then proceeded eastward with 20 passengers on a journey around the world, stopping enroute at Lakehurst.

A strike of textile workers in Gastonia, N.C., caused the death of several persons. A number of strikers were arrested and convicted of homicide. (The episode furnished the material of Mary Vorse's *Strike—A Novel of Gastonia*, 1930, and Grace Lumpkin's novel *To Make My Bread*, 1932, dramatized by Albert Bein as *Let Freedom Ring*, 1936.)

Bridges that were completed this year included the Ambassador, connecting Detroit, Mi., and Canada; the Bristol-Portsmouth, R.I., spanning Mt. Hope Bay, and the Cooper River, Charleston, S.C.

In Chicago, gangsterism reached its height when several of the O'Banion gang were mowed down by machine-gun fire. The occasion became known as the St. Valentine's Day massacre.

The Museum of Modern Art, was founded in New York.

Television in color was demonstrated (June) in Bell laboratories.

Cornelius "Connie Mack" McGillicuddy, manager of the Philadelphia American League "Athletics" baseball club, was awarded the $10,000 Edward W. Bok prize for distinguished service to the city—an honor previously bestowed only on scientists, educators, artists, and philanthropists.

Deaths of the year included Congressman Oscar W. Underwood (Jan. 25), and automobile pioneer David D. Buick (Mar. 6).

In Print

Books of the year included *Are We Civilized?*, by Robert Heinrich Lowie; *The Modern Temper*, by Joseph Wood Krutch; *A Preface to Morals*, by Walter Lippmann; *The Raven*, by Marquis James (Pulitzer prize 1930); *Selected Poems*, by Conrad Aiken (Pulitzer prize 1930); *Sound Off!*, by Edward Arthur Dolph; *The War of Independence*, by Claude H. Van Tyne (Pulitzer prize 1930); and the fiction, *Dodsworth*, by Sinclair Lewis; *A Farewell to Arms*, by Ernest Hemingway; *The Fugitive's Return*, by Susan Glaspell; *Is Sex Necessary?*, by James Thurber and E. B. White; *Laughing Boy*, by Oliver La Farge (Pulitzer prize 1930); *Look Homeward, Angel*, by Thomas Wolfe; *Magnificent Obsession*, by Lloyd Douglas; *Mamba's Daughters*, by DuBose Heyward; *Peder Victorious*, by Ole Rolvaag; *The Roman Hat Mystery*, by Ellery Queen, pseudonym of Frederick Danny and Manfred B. Lee; *She Stooped to Folly*, by Ellen Glasgow; and *The Sound and the Fury*, by William Faulkner. Erich Maria Remarque's German war novel *Im Westen nichts Neues* was popular in its English translation *All Quiet on the Western Front*. (It was made into a movie the following year.)

On Stage

"Amos 'n Andy" started (Aug. 19) its radio career. The two amusing characters were impersonated by Freeman Gosden (Amos) and Charles Correll (Andy).

New York plays that ran 175 or more performances included *Street Scene* (Pulitzer prize 1929); *My Girl Friday*; *Journey's End*; *Bird in Hand*; *Camel Through the Needle's Eye*; *It's a Wise Child*; *Houseparty*; *Strictly Dishonorable*; *Subway Express*; *The Criminal Code*; and *June Moon*. Musical productions included: *Follow Thru*; *The Little Show*; *A Night in Venice*; *Hot Chocolates*; *Earl Carroll's Sketch Book*; *Sweet Adeline*; *Street Singer*; and *Sons o' Guns*.

Films

Motion pictures included *The Broadway Melody; Bulldog Drummond*, with Ronald Coleman; *The Cock-eyed World; Coquette*, with Mary Pickford; *Disraeli*, with George Arliss; *Gold Diggers of Broadway; Hallelujah; In Old Arizona*, with Warner Baxter; *The Innocents of Paris*, with Maurice Chevalier and Jeanette MacDonald; *The Last of Mrs. Cheyney*, with Norma Shearer; *Madame X*, with Ruth Chatterton; *Rio Rita*, with Hons Boles and Bebe Daniels; and *Sunny Side Up*.

Music

Ain't Misbehavin'; Am I Blue?; Happy Days Are Here Again; Honeysuckle Rose; Just You, Just Me; Singin' in the Rain; Tip-toe Through the Tulips With Me; Wedding Bells Are Breaking Up That Old Gang of Mine; Without a Song; You Do Something to Me.

1930

*F*inancial gloom resulting from the stock market crash of the preceding year kept spreading. On indication of the prevailing economic condition was the appearance of apple vendors on street corners in New York and elsewhere.

Bootleg liquor prices were high. American bourbon sold for $100 per case; Canadian bourbon, $150; gin, $35 and $50; champagne, $110; Scotch, $110, and cordials, $120.

Joseph F. Crater, Justice of the State Supreme Court in New York City, mysteriously disappeared (Aug. 6); nothing has ever been heard of him.

Captain Frank W. Hawkes successfully carried out (Mar. 30-Apr. 6) an aeronautical experiment by flying from San Diego, Calif., to New York in a glider towed by an airplane. Later (Aug. 3) he flew from Los Angeles, to New York and reduced his previous (1929) New York-to-Los Angeles record form to 12 hours, 25 minutes.

A meteor, visible in several states, fell (Feb. 17) near Paragould, Ark. It split into fragments, one of which weighed 820 pounds.

The Mid-Hudson Bridge at Poughkeepsie, N.Y. was completed.

Lynchings suddenly increased throughout the United States; 30 occurred during the year.

Sinclair Lewis was awarded the Nobel prize for literature, the first American to be so honored in that field.

A Five-power naval conference opened (Jan. 21) in London. The inaugural address by His Majesty George V, spoken into a gold microphone, was broadcast by more than twenty-five European radio stations and rebroadcast in the United States, Japan, Australia via Manila, and India. It was estimated that 100,000,000 people listened to the speeches of the King and the delegates. Premier Ramsay MacDonald said: "Truly, we are living in times of great miracles."

To a nation in mourning, radio brought (early March) the funeral services of William Howard Taft from Washington, D.C.; it carried into millions of homes the prayers, the music, and descriptions of the solemn cortege as it passed from the Capitol to Arlington Cemetery; at midnight it brought from London a tribute to the late former President and Chief Justice by one of England's notable statesmen, Viscount Cecil.

On the same day, partial success attended a round-the-world broadcast. Two speakers, 10,000 miles apart, addressed each other over the air and the radio public was privileged to eavesdrop on a conversation between Rear Admiral Richard Evelyn Byrd, speaking from Dunedin, New Zealand, on his return from the Antarctic, and Adolph Ochs, owner of the *New York Times* newspaper, facing a microphone at Schenectady, New York. It was 1 a.m., March 12 when Rear Admiral Byrd spoke to America, and 7:30 a.m., Mar. 11, in New York when Mr. Ochs greeted the explorer. Communication between the two points was maintained for forty-five minutes. Unfortunately the voice of Byrd was distorted by static and at times unintelligible.

Although television still was in its experimental stages, radio station WEEI, Boston, televised daily programs for local receivers.

Max Schmeling of Germany claimed the heavyweight boxing title vacated in 1928 by Gene Tunney when he was fouled (June 12) by Jack Sharkey in the fourth round of their bout at Boston.

The national population was 122,776,046.

Deaths for the year included movie star Mabel Normand (Feb. 23), publisher Charles Scribner (Apr. 19), speedboat racer Henry Seagrave (June 13), aviator Glenn H. Curtiss (July 23), actor Lon Chaney (Aug. 26), and chemical manufacturer Herbert Dow (Oct. 15).

In Print

Books of the year included: *Charles W. Eliot,* by Henry James (Pulitzer prize 1931); *Collected Poems,* by Robert Frost (Pulitzer prize 1931); *The Coming of the War, 1914,* by Bernadotte E. Schmitt (Pulitzer prize 1931); *The Strange Death of President Harding,* by Gaston Bullock Means; and the fiction, *The Adventures of Ephraim Tutt,* by Arthur Train; *Alison's House,* by Susan Glaspell (Pulitzer prize 1931); *Arundel,* by Kenneth Roberts; *Cimarron,* by Edna Ferber; *The 42nd Parallel,* by John Dos Passos; *Flowering Judas,* by Katherine Anne Porter; *The Great Meadow,* by Elizabeth Madox Roberts; *Jews without Money,* by Michael Gold; *North of Suez,* by William McFee; and *Tiger! Tiger!,* by Honore Willsie Morrow). The first volume of the *Encyclopedia of Social Sciences* appeared (it was completed in 1935).

On Stage

Arturo Toscanini made a triumphal tour of Europe with the New York Philharmonic-Symphony Society orchestra.

The Columbia Broadcasting System, New York, began (Oct. 5) its Sunday broadcasts of the concerts of the New York Philharmonic-Symphony Society. The first broadcast concert was conducted by Erich Kleiber.

New York plays that ran 200 or more performances included *The Last Mile; Apron Stings; The Green Pastures* by Marc Connelly (Pulitzer prize 1930); *Stepping Sisters; Lysistrata; Once in a Lifetime; The Greeks Had a Word for It; Mrs. Moonlight; Grand Hotel; Tonight or Never;* and *The Vinegar Tree.* Mei Lan-Fang, China's greatest actor, appeared in a program of five traditional one-act plays (49th Street, Feb. 17; 41 performances). The 1931 Pulitzer prize was awarded to *Alison's House* by Susan Glaspell. Musical productions included *Strike Up the*

Band; Flying High; Earl Carroll's Vanities; Nina Rosa; Fine and Dandy; Girl Crazy; Three's a Crowd; Sweet and Low; The New Yorkers; and *Meet My Sister.*

Films

Motion pictures of the year included *Abraham Lincoln; All Quiet on the Western Front; Anna Christie,* with Greta Garbo; *The Big House; Blushing Brides,* with Joan Crawford; *Caught Short,* with Marie Dressler and Polly Moran; *Common Clay,* with Constance Bennett; *Divorce,* with Norma Shearer; *Hell's Angels,* with Jean Harlow; *Holiday,* with Ann Harding; *Journey's End,* with Colin Clive; *King of Jazz; Love Parade,* with Maurice Chevalier; *Morocco,* with Marlene Dietrich; *The New Moon,* with Grace Moore; *Old English,* with George Arliss; *The Rogue Song,* with Lawrence Tibbett; *The Vagabond King,* with Dennis King and Jeanette MacDonald; and *With Byrd at the South Pole.*

Music

The Battle of Jericho; Bidin' My Time; Body and Soul; Can This Be Love?; Dancing on the Ceiling; Exactly Like You; Georgia on My Mind; Get Happy; I'm Confessin' That I Love You; I Got Rhythm; It Happened in Monterey; Just a Gigolo; Love for Sale; On the Sunny Side of the Street; St. James Infirmary; Ten Cents a Dance; Them There Eyes; Three Little Words; Time on My Hands; Walkin' My Baby Back Home; What Is This Thing Called Love?; You Brought a New Kind of Love to Me.

1931

The Star-Spangled Banner was declared (Mar. 3) the national anthem of the United States by act of Congress. Most of those who opposed the adoption of the anthem favored *America, the Beautiful*.

In the wake of the stock market crash of 1929, some 2,300 banks failed. Even bootleg liquor sales fell off, and prices went down.

Massachusetts Congressmen presented (Mar. 13) the first resolution to repeal or amend the prohibition Amendment.

President Hoover rededicated (June 17) the remodeled tomb of Abraham Lincoln in Oak Ridge Cemetery, Springfield, Ill.

Radio telephone service was established between the Pacific Coast and Far East.

Infantile paralysis was a prevalent disease in many states.

Dr. Nicholas Murray Butler and Jane Addams were awarded the Nobel prize for peace.

Rockefeller Center, New York, started rising from the ground when work was begun (Sept.) on the erection of the RKO building. The project ultimately embraced 15 structures, including Radio City.

The Tennessee House of Representatives upheld (June 10), 58 to 14, its statute that prohibited the teaching of the theory of evolution in schools maintained wholly or in part by state funds. The verdict of the Scopes evolution case (1925) was thereby reaffirmed.

The remains of Myles Standish, military leader of the "Mayflower" Pilgrims who died in 1656, were removed (Apr. 25) from their wooden coffin, transferred to a metal casket, and interred in the cemetery in Duxbury, Mass. Traces of his iron-gray hair were said to have been still visible.

The tomb of former President Warren Gamaliel Harding was dedicated (June 16) in Marion, Ohio, by President Hoover.

Newly completed bridges included the Bayonne N.J., over the Kill van Kull; the George Washington, over the Hudson, from New York to New Jersey; the Maysville, Ky., over the Ohio; and the Willamette, in Portland, Oreg.

The Ford Motor Company, Detroit, Mich., turned out (Apr. 14) its 20,000,000th automobile. Henry Ford and his son, Edsel, drove the car to his museum in Dearborn and parked it alongside car No. 1, which was constructed in 1893.

Theodore Dreiser twice slapped Sinclair Lewis across the face at a dinner (Mar. 19) of American writers in honor of the Russian novelist Boris Pilnyak at the Metropolitan Club, New York.

The Empire State office building, New York, tallest in the world—102 floors, 1,449 feet—was opened (May 1). The structure cost $54,000,000.

An armada of 597 airplanes of the First Air Division, United States Army Air Corps, dedicated in New York (May 23) the Municipal Airport at North Beach—which eventually became LaGuardia Airport—and Rentschler Field in Hartford, Conn. (May 24). The planes flew over New England in army maneuvers, and repulsed (May 27) a mythical enemy over the New Jersey coast. They then circled (May 30) over Arlington National Cemetery, Va.

The new 47-floor Waldorf Astoria Hotel, on Park Avenue in New York was completed.

Jack ("Legs") Diamond, gangster boss, was shot to death (Dec. 18) in a boarding house in Albany, N.Y., after having been acquitted of a kidnapping charge.

Iowa, Nebraska, and South Dakota were overrun (July) by hordes of grasshoppers.

Nine Black men were accused by two white girls of rape on a freight train in Alabama and brought to a trial in Scottsboro, Ala. Death sentences were pronounced on eight of the accused. The conduct and verdict of the trial aroused nationwide criticism; an appeal was taken to the United States Supreme Court, which ordered (1932) a new trial. (At the second trial, one of the girls recanted her testimony. This time only one of the young men was sentenced to death. Again appealed to the Supreme Court, the verdict was set aside because of the exclusion of African-Americans from the jury. At the retrial, four defendants were sentenced to life imprisonment and the rape charges against the five others were dropped. The case had its echo in literature, notably in the plays *Scottsboro Limited* by Langston Hughes, 1932, and *They Shall Not Die* by John Wexley, 1934.)

The nation played bridge and more bridge. The Culbertson and Lenz methods were focal points for argument and tournaments.

Women wore stockings of transparent mesh, and the Empress Eugenie hat remained in fashion.

Knute Rockne, noted football coach of Notre Dame University, South Bend, Ind., was killed (Mar. 31) in an airplane crash near Bazaar, Kan.

Rogers "Rajah" Hornsby, star second baseman of the St. Louis Cardinals, hit three home runs in one game.

Deaths of the year included physicist A. A. Michelson (Oct. 9), jazz musician Bix Beiderbecke (Aug. 7), banker and diplomat Dwight Morrow (Oct. 5), Thomas Alva Edison, aged 84 (Oct. 18), jazz musician Charles "Buddy" Bolden (Dec. 26), and decimal system inventor Melvil Dewey (Dec. 26).

In Print

The Pulitzer heirs sold (Feb. 24) the daily newspapers *The World* and *The Evening World*, along with *The Sunday World*, to the Scripps-Howard newspaper organization.

Ballyhoo, a magazine, mocked advertising and built an enormous circulation over night.

Books of the year included *Autobiography*, by Lincoln Steffens; *Classic Americans*, by Henry Seidel Canby; *The Flowering Stone*, by George Dillon (Pulitzer prize 1932); *How to Write*, by Gertrude Stein; *My Experiences in the World War*, by Gen. John Joseph Pershing (Pulitzer prize 1932); *Theodore Roosevelt*, by Henry P. Pringle (Pulitzer prize 1932); and the fiction, *Ambrose Holt and Family*, by Susan Glaspell; *Back Street*, by Fannie Hurst; *Black Daniel*, by Honore Willsie Morrow; *The Forge*, by Thomas S. Stribling; *The Good Earth*, by Pearl Buck (Pulitzer prize 1932); *The Limestone Tree*, by Ernest Hemingway; *The Night Life of the Gods*, by Thorne Smith; *Sanctuary*, by William Faulkner; *Shadows on the Rock*, by Willa Cather; and *Their Father's God*, Ole Rolvaag.

On Stage

American radio stations broadcast (Feb. 12) the Latin speech of Pope Pius XI dedicating the Vatican radio station HVJ on the ninth anniversary of his coronation. In some sections of the world, the papal address was marred by signals sent out by the Russian Soviet station. Later, on the same day, in celebration of Lincoln's Birthday, President Hoover delivered a radio speech from the room in which the Emancipator had signed the Emancipation Proclamation.

The long-popular radio program, *Lady Esther Serenade*, began (Sept. 27).

The first radio broadcast of a complete stage performance of an opera from the Metropolitan Opera House, New York, took place (Dec. 25) when Humperdink's *Hansel und Gretel* was transmitted by the National Broadcasting Company.

Experimental television was being pursued with improved results. In New York, the Columbia Broadcasting System established a television station W2XAB which was the first to maintain a daily schedule of aural and visual transmission. Vocalists and performers such as Kate Smith, the Boswell Sisters, and others of radio fame were featured. Meanwhile John Logie Baird, internationally known British television engineer, came (Oct.) to New York to negotiate with radio station WMCA for the use of the telecasting machinery of his company, Baird Television Corp., Ltd., London. However, the Federal Radio Commission denied the application of WMCA for a license as "in violation of the section of the Radio Law prohibiting alien ownership or directorates of Companies holding wavelength privileges in the United States."

Martha Graham appeared in *Primitive Mysteries*, her own choreographic composition. (She later gained a wider public when she was the mysterious "Miss Hush" of radio whose voice was to be identified in a guessing contest.)

Maude Adams returned (Nov. 3) to the stage, after an absence of 13 years, in *The Merchant of Venice* in Cleveland, Ohio, at the Ohio Theater.

New York plays that ran 175 or more performances included *Tomorrow and Tomorrow; Private Lives; The Barretts of Wimpole Street; Cynara; Counsellor at Law; Reunion in Vienna;* and *Springtime for Henry.* Eugene O'Neill's *Mourning Becomes Electra* was staged. Musical productions included *You Said It; America's Sweetheart; The Band Wagon; Ziegfeld Follies, 1931; Earl Carroll's Vanities; George White's Scandals; Everybody's Welcome; The Cat and the Fiddle;* and *The Laugh Parade. Of Thee I Sing,* with a book by George S. Kaufman and Morrie Ryskind, lyrics by Ira Gershwin, and music by George Gershwin won the Pulitzer prize for 1932, the first musical production to receive such an award.

Films

Motion pictures of the year included *Bad Girl,* with James Dunn and Sally Eilers; *Charlie Chan Carries On,* with Warner Oland; *Cimarron,* with Irene Dunne and Richard Dix; *City Lights,* with Charlie Chaplin; *Daddy Long Legs,* with Janet Gaynor and Warner Baxter; *Five Star Final; Flowers and Trees* (Walt Disney's first Technicolor film); *A Free Soul,* with Norma Shearer; *The Front Page; Min and Bill,* with Marie Dressler and Wallace Beery; *The Sin of Madelon Claudet; Skippy,* with Jackie Cooper; *The Smiling Lieutenant,* with Maurice Chevalier; *Street Scene;* and *Trader Horn.*

Music

All of Me; Between the Devil and the Deep Blue Sea; Dancing in the Dark; Dream a Little Dream of Me; Goodnight, Sweetheart; I Apologize; I Found a Million Dollar Baby—In a Five and Ten Cent Store; Lady of Spain; Life Is Just a Bowl of Cherries; Love Letters in the Sand; Mood Indigo; Penthouse Serenade; Prisoner of Love; River, Stay 'Way from My Door; The Thrill Is Gone; Till the Real Thing Comes Along; When I Take My Sugar to Tea; When the Moon Comes Over the Mountain; Where the Blue of the Night Meets the Gold of the Day; While Hearts Are Singing; You're My Everything.

1932

$\mathcal{I}$n commemoration of the 200th anniversary of George Washington's birth, the U.S. Post Office issued (Jan. 1) a special series of twelve postage stamps, each displaying a portrait of Washington at a different age. Also, a Washington-head 25-cent piece went (Aug. 1) into circulation; the coin was designed by New York sculptor John Flanagan after the bust modeled by Jean Antoine Houdon, who visited Washington at Mount Vernon in 1785.

The financial depression, dating from 1929, still afflicted the country. In an effort to stimulate business, Congress established (Jan. 22) the Reconstruction Finance Corporation ("R.F.C.") to make federal loans to banks and insurance, mortgage, loan, and credit companies. President Hoover declared (June 20) a moratorium on reparations and war debt payments. Meanwhile a movement began in Minnesota instituting a moratorium on mortgage foreclosures; if rapidly spread to other states. As in the time of Coxey (1894), an "army" converged on Washington, D.C.—the veteran's Bonus Army, which camped in the mud flats near the city.

The United States and Canada negotiated a treaty for the development of a waterway for ocean-going ships between the Great Lakes and the Atlantic.

The Federal Bureau of Investigation established a laboratory for the scientific examination of evidence in criminal cases.

Radio telephone service was established between New York and Mexico City.

The term "forgotten man" passed into popular usage when Franklin Delano Roosevelt used (Apr. 7) the words in a presidential campaign speech. The expression had already been coined by William Graham Sumner, a former Yale professor of political science, as the title of a book *The Forgotten Man and Other Essays* (1919).

Nineteen-month-old Charles Augustus Lindbergh, Jr., son of Col. Charles A. Lindbergh and Anne Morrow Lindbergh, disappeared (Mar. 1) from his crib in his parents' home at Hopewell, N.J., near Princeton. While a wide search for the infant and its abductor was in progress, John F. Condon, a Bronx, New York, public school principal, obtained $50,000 ransom money from Lindbergh to contact an alleged agent of the kidnapping. Wealthy Mrs. Evalyn Walsh McLean was swindled out of $100,000 by Gaston Bullock Means on his promise to restore the child. Means later went to prison for the fraud.

The lifeless body of the baby, reduced almost to a skeleton, was located (May 12) in a bush on the roadway between Hopewell and Princeton, less than five miles from the Lindbergh house. A marked ransom banknote was presented at a gasoline filling station in the Bronx, New York City, and the police took into custody the passer of the note, Bruno Richard Hauptmann, a paroled German convict who had entered the country illegally in 1923. In the garage at Hauptmann's Bronx home was discovered more than $14,000 of the ransom money. The excessive publicity given the tragic case drove the Lindberghs to seek peace of mind in England (1935-38) and in France (1939). (In consequence of the case, Congress passed the Patterson Act, known generally as the Lindbergh Act, making the transportation of a kidnapped person across state boundaries punishable with life imprisonment. The act was amended in 1934 to include the death penalty for failure to return the victim unharmed, unless the jury recommends clemency.)

Amelia Earhart (now Mrs. George Palmer Putnam) became the first woman to make a solo flight across the Atlantic when she flew (May 20-21) from Harbor Grace, Newfoundland, to Londonberry, Ireland, a distance of 2,026 miles in 14 hours, 50 minutes.

The air mail rate was changed (July 6) to eight cents, and the U.S. Post Office accordingly issued (Sept. 26) an olive-green postage stamp of the denomination.

The Tomb of the Unknown Soldier in the National Cemetery, Arlington, Va., was dedicated on Armistice Day (Nov. 11).

The Radio City Music Hall, New York, opened (Dec. 27) as the largest indoor theater in the world with a seating capacity of 6,200.

Jack Sharkey brought the heavyweight boxing championship back to America when he defeated (June 21) in New York the German title holder, Max Schmeling, in a 15-round decision. (Sharkey lost to Schmeling on a foul in 1930.)

For the second time (the first was in 1904), the Olympic games were held in the United States; they took place (July 30-Aug. 14) in Los Angeles, Calif.

Deaths of the year included businessman George Eastman (Jan. 5) and poet Hart Crane (Apr. 27).

In Print

Books of the year included *Conquistador,* by Archibald MacLeish (Pulitzer prize 1933); *Earth Horizon,* by Mary Austin; *Grover Cleveland,* by Allan Nevins (Pulitzer prize 1933); *The Liberation of American Literature,* by Victor Francis Calverton; *Life Begins at Forty,* by Walter Boughton Pitkin; *Mark Twain's America,* by John Dos Passos; *The Significance of Sectionalism in American History,* by Frederick Jackson Turner (Pulitzer prize 1933); and the fiction, *Beyond Desire,* by Sherwood Anderson; *The Bishop's Jaegers,* by Thorne Smith; *Bright Skin,* by Julia Peterkin; *The End of Desire,* by Robert Herrick; *The Harbourmaster,* by William McFee; *In Tragic Life,* by Vardis Fisher; *Mutiny on the Bounty,* by Charles Bernard Nordhoff and James Norman Hall; *The Sheltered*

Life, by Ellen Glasgow; *State Fair,* by Philip Duffield Stong; *The Store,* by Thomas S. Stribling (Pulitzer prize 1933); *The Thin Man,* by Dashiell Hammett; *Tobacco Road,* by Erskine Caldwell; and *Young Lonigan,* by James Farrell.

On Stage

New York columnist Walter Winchell started (Dec. 4) his radio program.

New York plays that ran 175 or more performances included *The Animal Kingdom; That's Gratitude; When Ladies Meet; Dinner at Eight; Dangerous Corner; The Late Christopher Bean; Autumn Crocus; Biography;* and *Goodbye Again.* La Compania Dramatica Espanola from Madrid played Spanish repertory (40 perf.). Shakespeare's *Troilus and Cressida* had its first professional presentation in America (8 perf.—the only other known production was by the Yale Dramatic Society). Musical productions included: *Through the Years; Face the Music; Hot-Cha!; Flying Colors; Music in the Air; Take a Chance; The Gay Divorcé;* and *Walk a Little Faster. Show Boat* was revived.

Puppet shows enjoyed a sudden and unprecedented revival in New York in the productions of Tony Sarg, Sue Hastings, the Yale Puppeteers, the Marionette Guild, and Vittorio Podrecca's Teatre dei Piccoli from Italy, which traveled across the country to San Francisco and arrived in Hollywood to take part in the film *I Am Suzanne.*

Films

The double bill became common in motion picture theaters. Films of the year included *Arrowsmith,* with Ronald Coleman and Helen Hayes; *Back Street,* with Irene Dunne and John Boles; *Bill of Divorcement,* with John Barrymore and Katharine Hepburn; *The Champ,* with Wallace Beery and Jackie Cooper; *Dr. Jekyll and Mr. Hyde,* with Frederic March; *Emma,* with Marie Dressler; *Grand Hotel,* with Greta Garbo, John and Lionel Barrymore, Joan Crawford, and Wallace Beery; *The Guardsman,* with Alfred Lunt and Lynn Fontanne; and *Scarface,* with Paul Muni.

Music

Alone Together; April in Paris; Brother, Can You Spare a Dime; Eres Tu; Forty-Second Street; How Deep Is the Ocean?; I'm Gettin' Sentimental over You; I Gotta Right to Sing the Blues; I've Told Ev'ry Little Star; I Surrender, Dear; In a Shanty in Old Shanty Town; It Don't Mean a Thing; Let's Call It a Day; Let's Have Another Cup o' Coffee; Let's Put Out the Lights; Night and Day; Rise 'n Shine; A Shine on Your Shoes; Shuffle Off to Buffalo; The Song Is You; Speak to Me of Love; Willow Weep for Me; You're an Old Smoothie.

1933

*F*ranklin Delano Roosevelt, Democrat of New York, was inaugurated as the 32nd President.

The 20th Amendment was proclaimed (Feb. 6) as ratified. Known as the "lame duck" amendment, it set the date of the beginning of the terms of the President and the Vice President as Jan. 20 and those of the Senators and Representatives as Jan. 3. It also regulated the meeting of Congress and the succession to the Presidency.

Prohibition in the United States came to an end when Utah, as the necessary 36th state, ratified (Dec. 5) the 21st Amendment that repealed the 18th Amendment.

Drastic steps were taken to break the nation's economic depression, now in its fourth year. A local "bank holiday" of eight days (Feb. 14-22) was instituted by Minnesota Governor W. A. Comstock. President Roosevelt proclaimed a national "bank holiday" of ten days (Mar. 4-14). A movement to ferret out "hoarded gold" in private possession began. Gold exports were banned (Apr. 19) by the President. The United States went off the gold standard and started (Oct.) to buy domestic and foreign gold above the market price. Congress passed the Agricultural Adjustment Act (signed May 12) and the National Industrial Recovery Act (signed June 16), commonly known as the N.R.A. Its operations were directed by Gen. Hugh Johnson. (Both enactments were voided by the U.S. Supreme Court—the N.R.A. in 1935; the A.A.A. in 1936.)

President Roosevelt began (Mar. 12) his "fireside chats" over the radio.

"New Deal" and "brain trust" were phrases added to the vocabulary. The first referred to the policies of the Roosevelt administration; the second, to its body of advisers, comprised mostly of college professors.

Federal public assistance went into effect in May.

Congress created the Tennessee Valley Authority (May 18) to develop the water power of the Tennessee River and to prevent floods. The Civilian Conservation Corps was established as a government agency to recruit unemployed youth for service on public works. (It was disbanded June 30, 1943.)

The Century of Progress Exposition was held (May 27-Nov. 12) in Chicago.

The United States extended (Nov. 18) official recognition to the Union of Soviet Socialist Republics.

U.S. Marines, sent to Nicaragua in 1927, were withdrawn.

Lynchings again engaged public attention. Maryland Governor Richie called out (Oct.) the National Guard to protect Black prisoners. California Governor Rolph shocked many when he condoned (Nov.) a lynching in San Jose. In Missouri, a Black man was the victim of lynching in spite of the presence of troops.

The United States established a post office in Little America at the camp of the Byrd Antarctic Expedition; the Post Office Department issued (Oct. 9) a special three-cent navy blue postage stamp. The mail was transported through the facilities of the Expedition because the government had no other means of conveyance.

Thomas H. Morgan was awarded the Nobel prize for medicine and physiology.

The colorful and dynamic Fiorello Henry LaGuardia, popularly called "the Little Flower," was elected (Nov. 7) mayor of New York City on the Fusion (anti-Tammany) ticket. (He was re-elected repeatedly until 1945, when ill health forced his withdrawal.)

Radio City, a towering 70-floor office building in Rockefeller Center, New York, was opened (Nov.) with an exhibition showing the first thirteen years of radio progress.

Albert Einstein, internationally known German-Swiss physicist and discoverer of relativity, settled in Princeton, N.J., as professor of mathematics at the Institute for Advanced Study.

The world's largest dirigible balloon *Macon* was launched (Mar. 11). Less than a month later (Apr. 4), a storm off Barnegat, N.J., destroyed the U.S. Navy dirigible balloon *Akion*; 73 of the personnel, including the Aviation Chief Rear Admiral W. A. Moffett, were drowned. With great national pride, Italy sent to the Chicago Century of Progress Exposition an armada of 24 seaplanes in formation carrying 96 men under the command of General Italo Balbo. In a flight around the world (July 15-22), Wiley Post covered 15,596 miles in 7 days, 18 hours, 49 minutes. Flying for the Pan-American Airways Company, Col. and Mrs. Charles Augustus Lindbergh completed a 29,081 mile survey of transoceanic air routes over Greenland, Iceland, Russia, the Azores, West Africa, and South America.

In major league baseball, the All-Star game was originated; the first was played (July 6) in Chicago, the American League defeating the National League 4 to 2.

Adolf Hitler came (Jan. 30) to power in Germany as Chancellor of the Third Reich. The next year he became *Der Führer*.

Deaths of the year included Calvin Coolidge, 30th President (Jan. 5) and cartoonist Pat ("Felix the Cat") O'Sullivan (Feb. 25).

In Print

Books of the year included *Autobiography of Alice B. Toklas*, by Gertrude Stein; *Collected Verse*, by Robert Hillyer (Pulitzer prize 1934); *Every Man a King,* by Huey Long; *John Hay,* by Tyler Dennett (Pulitzer prize 1934); *The People's Choice,* by Herbert Agar (Pulitzer prize 1934); and the fiction, *Anthony Adverse,* by Hervey Allen; *God's Little Acre,* by Erskine Caldwell; *Lamb in His Bosom,* by Caroline Miller (Pulitzer prize 1934); *No Castle in Spain,* by William McFee; *One More Spring,* by Robert Herrick; *Stranger's Return,* by Philip Stong; and *Winner Take Nothing,* byErnest Hemingway.

On Stage

The Metropolitan Opera House, New York, produced (Jan. 7) the world premiere of Louis Gruenberg's American opera *Emperor Jones,* based on Eugene O'Neill's play (1920). The opera had seven performances.

Tobacco Road, a play by John Kirkland based on the novel of the same name by Erskine Caldwell, opened. It was to run for 3,182 performances—855 more than the 2,327 of its runner-up *Abie's Irish Rose* (1922), and was later topped by *Life with Father* (1939). Maxwell Anderson's *Both Your Houses* won the 1933 Pulitzer prize. New York plays that ran over 200 performances included *One Sunday Afternoon; Another Language; Men in White* by Sidney Kingsley (Pulitzer prize 1934); *Sailor, Beware!; Ah, Wilderness!; The Pursuit of Happiness; Her Master's Voice; She Loves Me Not;* and *Mary of Scotland.* Musical productions included *Murder at the Vanities; As Thousands Cheer; Let 'Em Eat Cake;* and *Roberta.*

Among popular radio programs that began were *Romance of Helen Trent* (July 24), *The Woman in White* (Sept. 11), and *The Lone Ranger* (Nov.).

Films

Motion pictures of the year included *Cavalcade; A Farewell to Arms; Flying Down to Rio,* with Fred Astaire and Ginger Rogers; *Forty-Second Street,* with Warner Baxter, Bebe Daniels, George Brent, and Ruby Keeler; *Gold Diggers of 1933,* with Dick Powell, Ruby Keeler, Joan Blondell, and Warren Williams; *I Am a Fugitive from a Chain Gang; King Kong; Lady for a Day; Madchen in Uniform* (foreign); *Morning Glory,* with Katharine Hepburn; *The Private Life of Henry VIII,* with Charles Laughton; *Rasputin and the Empress,* with John, Ethel, and Lionel Barrymore; *She Done Him Wrong,* with Mae West; *State Fair,* with Janet Gaynor, Will Rogers, and Lew Ayres; *Three Little Pigs* (Walt Disney cartoon); and *Tugboat Annie,* with Marie Dressler and Wallace Beery.

Music

The Boulevard of Broken Dreams; Did You Ever See a Dream Walking; Don't Blame Me; Easter Parade; Everything I Have Is Yours; Flying Down to Rio; The Gold Diggers' Song—We're in the Money; Heat Wave; I Cover the Waterfront; Inka Dinka Doo;, It Isn't Fair; It's Only a Paper Moon; It's the Talk of the Town; Lazybones; Let's Fall in Love; Lovely; Lover; Maria Elena; Smoke Gets in Your Eyes; Sophisticated Lady; Stormy Weather—Keeps Rainin' All the Time; Who's Afraid of the Big Bad Wolf?

1934

$\mathcal{C}$ongress devalued (Jan. 31) the dollar by reducing its gold content 40.94 percent. It passed (Mar. 22) the Tydings-McDuffie Act providing for Philippine independence in 1946, established (June) the Federal Housing Administration under the Federal Housing Act, prohibited (June 28) the exportation of silver, created (July 9) the National Labor Relations Board, and set up the Federal Communications Commission ("F.C.C.") of seven commissioners appointed by the President to replace the Federal Radio Commission of five members.

From Long Beach, Calif., came an idea for a national pension plan of $200 per month for every United States citizen 60 years of age or older. It was proposed by Francis Townsend and was known as the Townsend Plan. The proposal gained nationwide following for a number of years and was discussed in the 74th Congress. Subsequent legislation nullified the scheme.

To fight infantile paralysis (polio) President Roosevelt, who suffered from the effects of the disease, launched for the Warm Springs, Georgia, Foundation a fund-raising campaign that developed (Jan. 3, 1938) into the March of Dimes.

Alcatraz, an island fortress in San Francisco Bay, became a Federal penitentiary.

John Dillinger, leader of a notorious band of bank robbers, was shot (July 22) to death in front of a motion picture theater in Chicago by Department of Justice agents after he had escaped twice from prison. Others of his gang were shot in the round-up.

As a tribute to the mothers of America, a special three-cent purple postage stamp was issued (May 2), reproducing James Abbott McNeill Whistler's famous painting "Portrait of My Mother."

Air mail was reduced (July 1) to six cents and a new orange postage stamp of that denomination appeared.

Adm. Richard Evelyn Byrd established a solitary base in the Antarctic 120 miles from his headquarters at Little America to record daily meteorological observations.

The Ford Motor Company began growing and cultivating soy beans.

Fire destroyed (Sept. 8) the American cruise liner *Morro Castle* off Asbury Park, N.J., with a loss of 134 lives. The ship was returning from Havana, Cuba, to New York and carried 318 passengers and a crew of 231.

Four Americans were awarded Nobel prizes—H. C. Urey for chemistry, and G. R. Minot, W. P. Murphy, and G. H. Whipple for medicine and physiology.

Major W. E. Kepner, Captain O. A. Anderson, and Captain A. W. Stevens ascended (July 28) in a balloon at Rapid City, S. Dak. They reached a height of 60,613 feet before a tear in the bag forced them down at Loomis, N.B.

The Mutual Broadcasting System became the third American broadcasting chain.

Deaths of the year included baseball great John McGraw (Feb. 25) and philanthropist Otto Kahn (Mar. 29).

In Print

Books of the year included *American Ballads and Folk Songs*, by John Lomax; *Bright Ambush*, by Audrey Wurdemann (Pulitzer prize 1935); *The Colonial Period of American History*, by Charles Andrews; vol. 1 (Pulitzer prize 1935); *Robert E. Lee*, by Douglas Southall Freeman; 4 vols.; 1934-35; *Wine from These Grapes*, by Edna St. Vincent Millay; *Stars Fell on Alabama*, by Carl Carmer; and the fiction, *The Daring Young Man on the Flying Trapeze*, by William Saroyan; *The Folks*, by Ruth Suckow; *The Land of Plenty*, by Robert Cantwell; *The Native's Return*, by Louis Adamic; *Now in November*, by Josephine Johnson (Pulitzer prize 1935); and *So Red the Rose*, by Stark Young.

On Stage

Virgil Thomson's surrealistic opera *Four Saints in Three Acts*, to a libretto by Gertrude Stein, received (Feb. 7) its first stage performance in Hartford, Conn., at the opening of the Avery Memorial Theater of the Wadsworth Athenaeum. It was presented with an all-Black cast by the Society of Friends and Enemies of Modern Music.

The Metropolitan Opera House, New York, gave (Feb. 10) the world premiere of another American opera—*Merry Mount* by Dr. Howard Hanson, director of the Eastman School of Music, Rochester, N.Y. The opera had six performances.

In an obscure hall of 23rd Street, a Negro group calling itself the Unity Theater Study staged (May 7) a unique African "dance-opera" entitled *Kykunkor, the Witch* by Asadata Dafora Horton. The composer was a native of Sierra Leone. The production aroused sufficient interest to warrant more than 100 performances in various auditoriums and on Broadway.

Andre Kostelanetz and his orchestra began (Oct. 1) the long-popular Chesterfield radio program with its distinctive orchestral arrangements.

New York plays included *No More Ladies, Dodsworth; The Distaff Side; Personal Appearance; The Children's Hour; Post Road;* and *Accent on Youth*. Musical productions included *Ziegfeld Follies; Life Begins at 8:40; The Great Waltz; Anything Goes; Revenge with Music;* and *Thumbs Up*.

Films

Motion pictures of the year included *The Barretts of Wimpole Street*, with Norma Shearer, Fredric March and Charles Laughton; *Berkeley Square*, with Leslie Howard; *The Bowery*, with Wallace Beery, George Raft, and Jackie Cooper; *The Count of Monte Cristo*, with Robert Donat and Elissa Landi; *Dinner at Eight*, with Marie Dressler, John Barrymore, Wallace Beery, Jean Harlow, and Lionel Barrymore; *The House of Rothschild*, with George Arliss; *I'm No Angel*, with Mae West; *It Happened One Night*, with Claudette Colbert and Clark Gable; *Judge Priest*, with Will Rogers; *Little Women*, with Katharine Hepburn; *One Night of Love*, with Grace Moore; *The Orphans' Benefit*, (Walt Disney cartoon, introducing "Donald Duck" in an inconspicuous part); *The Thin Man*, with William Powell and Myrna Loy; and *Viva, Villa!*, with Wallace Beery. Government morals experts were mulling over (as they still did in 1951) the admission to the American screen of the Czechoslovakian film *Ecstasy* which featured nude scenes by Hedy Lamarr.

Music

All I Do Is Dream of You; All Through the Night; Blue Moon; The Continental; Cocktails for Two; La Cucaracha; For All We Know; I Only Have Eyes for You; The Object of My Affection; On the Good Ship Lollipop; P.S. I Love You; Stars Fell on Alabama; Stay As Sweet As You Are; Tumbling Tumbleweeds; The Very Thought of You; Wagon Wheels; Winter Wonderland; With My Eyes Wide Open I'm Dreaming; You and the Night and the Music; You Oughta Be in Pictures.

1935

$\mathscr{C}$ongress voted (Apr. 5) an economic relief program involving $4,880,000,000, which established (May 6) the Works Progress Administration, and passed (Aug. 14) the Social Security Act. The public debt stood at $28,700,000,000, or $225.71 per capita. Under the W.P.A., various public works as well as literary, musical, theatrical, and artistic projects were sponsored.

The federal dole (1933) was discontinued (Nov. 29); $3,694,000,000 had been expended in this program since May, 1933.

The United States Supreme Court voided the Railroad Pension Act (May 6) and the National Recovery Act, or N.R.A., of 1933 (May 27).

Congress authorized (Aug. 30) the construction of the Bonneville Dam, Oreg.

Louisiana Senator Huey P. Long was assassinated (Sept. 8) in Baton Rouge, La. His assailant was shot on the spot by Long's bodyguards.

The Committee for Industrial Organization (C.I.O.) was formed by some dissident officials of the American Federation of Labor under the chairmanship of John Llewellyn Lewis.

The Huey P. Long Bridge, spanning the Mississippi River at New Orleans, was completed.

The Hayden Planetarium, New York, named in honor of its donor Charles Hayden, was opened (Oct. 3).

Mrs. Fletcher M. Johnson of Gainesville, Ga., became the first American Mother of Year to be selected by the Golden Rule Foundation Mothers' Committee, New York.

The $4,000,000 U.S. Navy dirigible balloon *Macon* suffered a disaster over the Pacific and sank (Feb. 13) off Point Sur, CA; 83 of the 85 persons aboard were rescued.

Humorist Will Rogers and aviator Wiley Post were killed (Aug. 15) near Point Barrow, Alaska, when Post's rebuilt airplane crashed in a fog.

Lincoln Ellsworth explored (Nov. 23-Dec. 15) the Antarctic regions by airplane.

Amelia Earhart (Mrs. George Palmer Putnam) became the first person to fly alone from Hawaii to California. She flew (Mar. 23) from Pearl Harbor, Hawaii, to San Francisco. The Pan American Airways company began (Nov.) regular passenger service across the Pacific from San Francisco to Manila, P.I., with the super-plane "China Clipper," making landings at Honolulu, Midway Island, Wake Island, and Guam.

Popular radio programs that began this year included *Vox Pop* (Feb. 7), *One Man's Family* (Apr. 3), *Fibber McGee and Molly* (Apr. 16), *Your Hit Parade* (Apr. 20), *Lum and Abner* (Sept. 19), *Phil Baker* (Sept. 29), and *Metropolitan Opera Auditions of the Air* (Oct. 18).

The first night game in major league baseball was played (May 23) between the Cincinnati and Philadelphia National League clubs.

Deaths of the year included poet Edwin Robinson (Apr. 6), feminist Jane Addams (May 21), Justice Oliver Wendell Holmes, Jr. (June 6), and feminist Charlotte Perkins Gilman (Aug. 17).

In Print

Books of the year included *Constitutional History of the United States*, by Andrew C. McLaughlin (Pulitzer prize 1936); *Strange Holiness*, by Robert Coffin (Pulitzer prize 1936); *The Thought and Character of William James*, by Ralph B. Perry; 2 vols. (Pulitzer prize 1936); *War Is a Racket*, by Major General Smedley Darlington Butler; and the fiction, *Absalom, Absalom!*, by William Faulkner; *Honey in the Horn*, by H. L. Davis (Pulitzer prize 1936); *It Can't Happen Here*, by Sinclair Lewis; *Life with Father*, by Clarence Day; *Of Time and the River*, by Thomas Wolfe; *Tortilla Flat*, by John Steinbeck; and *The Vein of Iron*, by Susan Glaspell.

On Stage

The Colonial Theater in Boston hosted (Sept. 30) at the first performance of George Gershwin's opera *Porgy and Bess*. (The opera was given in New York at the Alvin Theater, Oct. 10, 1935, and had 124 performances.)

New York plays that ran 175 or more performances included *The Petrified Forest; The Old Maid* by Zoe Akins; *Fly Away Home; Three Men on a Horse; Awake and Sing; Night of January 16; Winterset; Mulatto; Dead End; Pride and Prejudice; First Lady; Boy Meets Girl; One Good Year;* and *Victoria Regina*. Lynn Fontanne and Alfred Lunt revived *The Taming of the Shrew*. Musical productions included *Earl Carroll's Sketch Book; At Home Abroad; May Wine*.

Films

Motion pictures of the year included *Anna Karenina*, with Greta Garbo; *Broadway Melody of 1936*, with Jack Benny and Eleanor Powell; *China Seas*, with Clark Gable, Jean Harlow, and Wallace Beery; *Curly Top*, with Shirley Temple; *Dangerous*, with Bette Davis; *David Copperfield*, with Freddie Bartholomew, W. C. Fields, and Lionel Barrymore; *G Men*, with James Cagney, Margaret Lindsay, Ann Dvorak, and Robert Armstrong; *The Informer*, with Victor McLaglen; *Lives of a Bengal Lancer*, with Gary Cooper; *Les Miserables*, with Frederic March, Charles Laughton, and Cedric Hardwicke; *Mutiny on the Bounty*, with Clark Gable, Charles Laughton, and Franchot Tone; *Ruggles of*

Red Gap, with Charles Laughton and Mary Boland; and *Top Hat*, with Fred Astaire and Ginger Rogers.

Music

What a year it was for popular music! Songs included *Begin the Beguine; Bess, You Is My Woman; Cheek to Cheek; East of the Sun—and West of the Moon; Eeny Meeny Miney Mo; I'm Gonna Sit Right Down and Write Myself a Letter; I'm in the Mood for Love; I'm Shooting High; I Feel a Song Comin' On; I Got Plenty o'Nuttin'; In a Sentimental Mood; Isn't This a Lovely Day—to Be Caught in the Rain?; It Ain't Necessarily So ; Just One of Those Things; Lights Out; Lullaby of Broadway; Lulu's Back in Town; Mad About the Boy; Maybe; Moon Over Miami; The Music Goes 'Round and Around; My Romance; Red Sails in the Sunset; Stairway to the Stars; Summertime; You Are My Lucky Star;* and *Zing! Went the Strings of My Heart.*

1936

*S*ocial security or job insurance, established by Congress the preceding year, went into effect (Jan. 1).

The United States Supreme Court voided (Jan. 6) the Agricultural Adjustment Act.

The United States withdrew (Mar. 2) its guarantee of the independence of Panama, and signed (Mar. 25) with Great Britain and France a treaty limiting naval armaments for a period of six years.

Congress authorized (May 15) a commemorative half-dollar with the head of Phineas Taylor Barnum for the 150th anniversary of the incorporation of the city of Bridgeport, Conn., where Barnum was born. The coin was designed by Henry Kreiss.

The head of Stephen Collins Foster, "American Troubadour," composer of "My Old Kentucky Home," "Way Down Upon the Swanee River," and other favorites, also appeared on a commemorative half-dollar to celebrate the 50th anniversary of Cincinnati as a center of music. The coin was designed by Constance Ortmayer.

The city of Cleveland, Ohio, celebrated its centennial of the founding with the Great Lakes Exposition.

Woman suffrage had fought a long battle from 1848 to recognition in 1920, and now, sixteen years later, the United States commemorated one of the pioneer leaders in the movement, Susan Brownell Anthony (1830-1906), by placing her portrait on a three-cent purple postage stamp.

At the invitation of Nazi Field Marshal Hermann Goering, Colonel Charles Augustus Lindbergh made a tour of inspection of Germany's aviation centers. On his return, he warned the world of that country's growing air power. The message was looked upon disfavorably. German pro-Nazi "Bund" societies made their appearance in the United States under the name *Amerika-deutscher Volksbund*, ostensibly devoted to social and athletic pursuits.

The Boulder (now Hoover) Dam, situated about 25 miles southeast of Las Vegas, Nev., on the Colorado River, was completed by the Bureau of Reclamation. The dam was the largest in the world, at 726 feet high, 1,244 feet long, 45 feet wide at the top, and 650 feet wide at the bottom.

The $60,000,000 Triborough Bridge, spanning the East River, New York, was opened (July 11).

Newspaper reporter H.R. Elkins of the *New York World-Telegram*, using six airplane routes, made a trip around the world of approximately 25,654 miles in 18 days, 11 hours, 14 minutes, 33 seconds (Sept. 30-Oct. 19).

In an effort to unionize the automobile industry, the United Workers of America went (Dec. 30) on strike in Flint, Mich.

Bruno Richard Hauptmann, who had been convicted of kidnapping the Lindbergh baby (1932), was put to death (Apr. 3) in the electric chair in the prison at Trenton, N.J.

Nobel prizes were awarded to Carl D. Anderson for physics and to Eugene O'Neill for literature.

With television still in the laboratory, radio enjoyed a profitable year. Kate Smith, Easy Aces, and newscaster Boake Carter were top personalities. New programs were *Gang Busters* (Jan. 15) and *Major Bowes' Amateur Hour* (Sept. 17). The Columbia Broadcasting System inaugurated (July 18) the Columbia Workshop, a radio theater for the production of experimental forms of broadcast drama.

The "candid" camera craze hit the country and production in the industry jumped 157 percent.

The Democrats ran President Franklin Delano Roosevelt for a second term. The Republicans nominated an unknown—Kansas Governor Alfred Landon, whom many expected to defeat the President. *The Literary Digest*, which for years had been conducting straw votes on a huge scale, predicted an overwhelming victory for Landon, but Jim Farley, Roosevelt's campaign manager, declared the President would carry every state but Maine and Vermont. Farley was right, and the old political adage "As Maine goes, so goes the Nation" became "As Maine goes, so goes Vermont." Roosevelt polled 27,476,673 votes; Landon, 16,679,583.

Hitler's armies marched unopposed into the demilitarized Rhineland as Mussolini completed his Ethiopian campaign with the seizure of Addis Ababa. Germany signed pacts with Italy and with Japan, and established General Francisco Franco in power in Spain. In Great Britain, Edward VII succeeded to the throne and abdicated less than eleven months later, in a farewell speech heard by millions of radio listeners the world over. After his abdication, he was proclaimed His Royal Highness, Duke of Windsor, and married (June 3, 1937) Mrs. Wallis Simpson, an American divorcee of Baltimore, Md., for whom he had renounced the throne.

Former Vice President Charles Curtis died (Feb. 8).

In Print

Life was founded in New York as a weekly pictorial magazine, using the name of an older but totally dissimilar publication (1883).

Books of the year included *Enjoyment of Laughter*, by Max Eastman; *The Flowering of New England*, by Van Wyck Brooks (Pulitzer prize 1937); *Green Laurels: The Lives and Achievements of the Great Naturalists*, by Donald Culross Peattie; *Hamilton Fish*, by Allan Nevins (Pulitzer prize 1937); *How to Win*

Friends and Influence People, by Dale Carnegie; *Inside Europe,* by John Gunther; *Listen for the Lonesome Drum,* by Carl Carmer; *Works,* by George Santayana; 14 vols., 1936-37; the poetry, *A Further Range,* by Robert Frost (Pulitzer prize 1937); *Not So Deep as a Well,* by Dorothy Parker; *The People, Yes,* by Carl Sandburg; and the fiction, *The Big Money,* by John Dos Passos; *Drums Along the Mohawk,* by Walter Dumaux Edmonds; *In Dubious Battle,* by John Steinbeck; *The Last Pilgrim,* by George Santayana; and *Gone with the Wind,* by Margaret Mitchell, which sold a million copies in the first six months (Pulitzer prize 1937).

On Stage

The Federal Theater Project of the Works Progress Administration relief program, organized under Mrs. Hallie Flanagan of Vassar College, set up theatrical production centers in Atlanta, Boston, Chicago, Denver, Los Angeles, New Orleans, New York, Philadelphia, San Francisco, and Seattle that had long-term effect on American drama. (The project ended July 31, 1939)

New York plays included *Call It a Day; Idiot's Delight* by Robert E. Sherwood (Pulitzer prize 1936); *Pre-Honeymoon; Tovarich; Stage Door; You Can't Take It with You* by Moss Hart and George S. Kaufman (Pulitzer prize 1937); *Brother Rat;* and *The Women. Hamlet* was revived by John Gielgud and by Leslie Howard. Musical productions included *On Your Toes; White Horse Inn; Red, Hot and Blue;* and *The Show Is On.*

Films

Motion pictures of the year included *Anthony Adverse,* with Frederic March; *Dodsworth,* with Walter Huston, Ruth Chatterton, and David Niven; *The Garden of Allah; The Great Ziegfeld,* with Luise Rainer, William Powell, and Myrna Loy; *The Green Pastures; A Midsummer Night's Dream,* with James Cagney, Joe E. Brown, and Dick Powell; *Mr. Deeds Goes to Town,* with Gary Cooper; *Modern Times,* with Charlie Chaplin; *One Hundred Men and a Girl,* with Deanna Durbin and Leopold Stokowski; *Romeo and Juliet,* with Leslie Howard, Norma Shearer, Basil Rathbone, John Barrymore, and Edna May Oliver; *San Francisco,* with Clark Gable and Jeanette MacDonald; *The Story of Louis Pasteur,* with Paul Muni; and *A Tale of Two Cities,* with Ronald Colman.

Music

I Can't Get Started with You; I've Got You Under My Skin; It's a Sin to Tell a Lie; It's D'lovely; Let's Face the Music and Dance; Let Yourself Go; There's a Small Hotel; There Is No Greater Love; The Touch of Your Lips; Twinkle, Twinkle, Little Star; Until the Real Thing Comes Along; The Way You Look To-night; The Whiffenpoof Song; You.

1937

$\mathscr{P}$resident Franklin Delano Roosevelt began his second term.

The U.S. gunboat *Panay*, stationed on the Yangtze River near Nanking, China, and several American oil carriers were sunk by Japanese gunfire. A number of lives were lost. The United States issued a vigorous protest; Japan apologized for the "accidental" destruction and made financial restitution.

The United States Supreme Court ruled (Dec. 20) that "tapped" telephone conversations could not be made public.

Nylon was patented by Wallace Hume Carothers, chemist of the Du-Pont Company, Wilmington, Del. (The patents were granted posthumously in 1938; Carothers died in 1937.)

A new transcontinental airplane speed record was established (Jan. 19) when Howard Hughes flew from Los Angeles to New York in 7 hours, 28 minutes.

Amelia Earhart (Mrs. George Palmer Putnam) and Fred Noonan undertook an airplane flight around the world and were lost (their last message was radioed July 2) in the mid-Pacific between New Guinea and Howland Island. No trace of either the aviators or their plane was found, in spite of intensive searches and investigations. (During a stopover at Hawaii by the two aviators, a plaque has been dedicated to Miss Earhart. When originally set in place, the stone bearing the plaque broke from the foundation and fell face downward, arousing superstition among Hawaiians that the flier would never return to the islands.)

The *Hindenburg*, the world's largest dirigible balloon and the pride of Germany, exploded and burst into flames while approaching (May 6) its mooring mast at the U.S. Naval Air Station in Lakehurst, N.J., after a successful Atlantic crossing. Thirty-six of the 97 persons aboard died in the disaster that was witnessed by a horrified throng who had gathered to welcome the historic arrival. The tragedy occurred at night; the flames were seen miles away. Radiocasters dramatically reporting the slow approach of the majestic airship found themselves compelled to change to broadcasting details of a catastrophe.

Sitdown strikes were a new C.I.O. weapon in the glass and automobile industries. The strike of the United Automobile Workers of America against the General Motors Corp. at Flint, Mich., which began in the preceding year, won (Feb. 11) a wage increase of five cents an hour. The Little Steel Strike, at the Republic Steel Plant, flared into violence in the "South Chicago Riot" on Memorial Day; ten were killed, 90 wounded.

The Golden Gate Bridge, spanning the entrance to San Francisco Bay, was completed.

The south tube of the Lincoln Vehicular Tunnel, connecting New York City and Weehawken, N.J., under the Hudson River, was opened (Dec. 21).

An explosion of natural gas wrecked (Mar. 18) the Consolidated Public School, New London, Tex., and caused the death of 294 persons.

Floods inundated the Allegheny, Mississippi, and Ohio River regions. About 300 persons were drowned in Arkansas, Illinois, Kentucky, Missouri, and Tennessee.

Dance-conscious Carolina students worked out the steps of The Big Apple, a modified square dance, which was taken up avidly by young people all over the country.

Benny Goodman, "King of Swing," opened at the Paramount Theater in New York. By 6 a.m., 3,000 assembled, most of them high school students. By 7:30, the crowd was so large that 10 mounted policemen were assigned to control the eager patrons. There was frenzied dancing in the aisles of the theater by these teen-age "jitterbugs" or "alligators," who were adding to the American vocabulary such expressions as "in the groove," "spank the skin," "schmaltz," "boogie woogie," "jam session," and "killer-diller."

In baseball, center fielder Joe DiMaggio of the New York Yankees hit .347 and became the batting and fielding hero of his league. He was extremely popular during his career and after his retirement in 1951.

Skiing, once the pastime of Scandinavian settlers of Minnesota and Wisconsin and later the sport of the privileged few, was taken up by the masses.

Joe Louis, the "Brown Bomber," kayoed (June 22) the heavyweight boxing champion James J. Braddock in eight rounds in Chicago to win the title that he held until his retirement in 1949.

John Davison Rockefeller, aged 98, regarded as the world's richest man, died (May 23) at Ormond Beach, Fla. His fortune was estimated at $1,000,000,000 and was believed to have been exceeded only by that of Aga Khan.

Hitler repudiated (Jan. 30) the Versailles Treaty of World War I. In Spain, the armies of General Francisco Franco besieged Madrid, and the "non-intervention" policy of the rest of the world smoothed the road for Mussolini to help the Spanish dictator. In midsummer, the Japanese began systematic attacks upon China.

George VI and his wife Elizabeth were crowned (May 12) King and Queen of Great Britain in succession to Edward VIII who had abdicated in the preceding year (Dec. 11, 1936). (George had been king for the past six months.)

Deaths of the year included former Secretary of State Elihu Root (Feb. 6), inventor Frederick Louis Maytag (Mar. 26), and composer George Gershwin (July 11).

In Print

Books of the year included *Andrew Jackson*, by Marquis James (Pulitzer prize 1938); *Cold Morning Sky*, by Marya Zaturenska (Pulitzer prize 1938); *Damien the Leper*, by John Farrow; *The Fall of the City*, by Archibald MacLeish; *The Life and Death of a Spanish Town*, by Elliot Paul; *Pedlar's Progress*, by Odell Shephard (Pulitzer prize 1938); *The Road to Reunion: 1865-1900*, by Paul H. Buck (Pulitzer prize 1938); and the fiction, *The Citadel*, by Archibald Joseph Cronin; *The Late George Apley*, by John Philip Marquand (Pulitzer prize 1938); *Northwest Passage*, by Kenneth Lewis Roberts; *Of Mice and Men*, by John Steinbeck; *The Rains Came*, by Louis Bromfield; *Slogum House*, by Mari Sandoz; and *To Have and Have Not*, by Ernest Hemingway.

On Stage

The Columbia Broadcasting System, New York, performed six commissioned orchestral works by American composers: *Lenox Avenue* by William Grant Still (May 23); *Concertino for Piano and Orchestra* by Walter Piston (June 20); *Music for Radio* by Aaron Copland (July 25); *Time Suite* by Ron Harris (Aug. 8); *Third Symphony* by Howard Hanson (Sept. 19; three movements; the fourth was added later); *Green Mansions*, a radio opera, by Louis Gruenberg (Oct. 17).

Arturo Toscanini was appointed musical director of the reorganized NBC Symphony Orchestra. He conducted his first program on Christmas Day (Dec. 25). The audience of about 1,000 was supplied with satin programs so that the maestro would not be distracted by the rustling of paper.

New York plays included *High Tor; Behind Red Lights; Yes, My Darling Daughter; Having a Wonderful Time; Room Service; The Star-Wagon; Susan and God; Amphitryon 38; Golden Boy*. Revivals of classics included Orson Welles in Marlowe's *Dr. Faustus;* Maurice Evans in *Richard II;* and a modern-dress version of a Fascist *Julius Caesar.* The Bulgarian National Theater Company of Sofia toured the country in native dramas before being heard in New York. Musical productions included *The Eternal Road; Naughty Naught '00; Babes in Arms; I'd Rather Be Right; Hooray for What!; Three Waltzes. Pins and Needles* was produced by the International Ladies' Garment Workers' Union Players, none of whom was paid more than $55 a week. A plea for the cause of unions, the show startled Broadway by surviving until 1939 and breaking all previous musical show endurance records with 1,108 performances. Equally proletarian in character was Marc Blitzstein's *The Cradle Will Rock.* It was performed without scenery and with piano accompaniment to overcome certain union restrictions. (Venice Theater, June 16; after three performances, the work was banned by the W.P.A. Federal Theater on an order from Washington, D.C., moved to the Mercury Theater, Dec. 5, and finally staged at the Windsor Theater, Jan. 3, 1938, for 108 performances.)

Popular radio programs which began this year were *Myrt and Marge* (Jan. 4); *The Goldbergs* (Sept. 13); *Voice of Experience* (Sept. 13); *Tony Wons and His Scrapbook* (Sept. 27); *Kate Smith's Bandwagon* (Sept. 30); *The March of Time* (Oct. 14); *The Voice of Niagara* (Carborundum Hour, Oct. 16). Ventriloquist Edgar Bergen and his dummy Charlie McCarthy leaped (May 9) into national publicity as features of the Chase and Sanborn coffee program.

Films

Motion pictures of the year included *The Awful Truth*, with Irene Dunne and Cary Grant; *Captains Courageous*, with Freddie Bartholomew, Spencer Tracy, and Lionel Barrymore; *Dead End*, with Sylvia Sidney and Joel McCrea; *The Firefly*, with Jeanette MacDonald and Allan Jones; *The Good Earth*, with Luise Rainer; *The Life of Emile Zola*, with Paul Muni; *Lost Horizon*, with Ronald Colman; *A Star Is Born*, with Janet Gaynor and Fredric March; *Waikiki Wedding; Wake Up and Live;* and *Winterset*, with Burgess Meredith.

Music

Bei Mir Bist du Schön—Means That You're Grand; Blue Hawaii; Bob White—Whatcha Gonna Swing Tonight?; A Foggy Day; Harbor Lights; I Can Dream, Can't I?; I've Got My Love to Keep Me Warm; In the Still of the Nigh; Johnny One Note; Lambeth Walk; Let's Call the Whole Thing Off; Nice Work if You Can Get It; September in the Rain; So Rare; Sweet Leilani; That Old Feeling; Whistle While You Work.

1938

*T*he House Committee Investigating Un-American Activities was formed (May) under the chairmanship of Texas Democratic Representative Martin Dies.

The Jefferson-head nickel five-cent piece, designed by Felix Schlag, went into circulation. The design won a $1,000 prize in a competition among some 390 artists.

The March of Dimes was organized (Jan. 3) as a fund-raising institution to fight infantile paralysis.

A container made of indestructible metal containing phonograph records and other examples of contemporary culture was buried (Sept. 23) in the New York World's Fair grounds, to be opened five thousand years hence—A.D. 6938. (The fair opened the following year.)

Howard Hughes and four technical assistants made (July 10) a remarkable airplane flight around the world, flying eastward from New York, in 91 hours (3 days, 19 hours, 8 minutes, 10 seconds). Douglas G. Corrigan left Floyd Bennett Field, Brooklyn, New York, in his nine-year-old plane without permit or passport, and landed 28 hours, 13 minutes later at Baldonel Airfield, Dublin (July 17-18).

Pearl Buck was awarded the Nobel prize for literature.

Thomas Mann, noted German novelist and essayist, settled in the United States.

Bingo became the most popular money game in the United States, and one which met with the approval of churches.

Radio station WOR, New York, of the Mutual Broadcasting System began weekly broadcasts of Johann Sebastian Bach's cantatas.

Information Please, a radio quiz program with John Kieran, Franklin P. Adams, and Clifton Fadiman as quizmaster, was extremely popular, as were the new programs *Dick Tracy* (Jan. 3) and *True or False* (Jan. 3).

War of the Worlds, a radio drama, was so realistically enacted (Oct. 30) by Orson Welles and his cast over the Columbia Broadcasting System network that a public uproar, quite unknown to the actors, occurred during the presentation. The script dealt with a supposed invasion of the earth by the inhabitants of Mars. When the fictitious Martians attacked the 15-mile Pulaski Skyway bridge in New Jersey near New York, people in the surrounding areas became panic-stricken. A section of the listening public excitedly telephoned the station from all parts of the country; the police had to be summoned to calm an anxious crowd gathered in front of the broadcasting building. (A similar "Martian" broadcast in Quito, Ecuador, Feb. 13, 1949, resulted in a riot in which 21 persons were killed.)

Twenty-year-old Bobby (Robert) Feller, pitcher of the Cleveland Indians, struck out (Oct. 2) 18 batters in a game with the Detroit Tigers.

Deaths of the year included tire manufacturer Harvey Firestone (Feb. 7), lawyer Clarence Darrow (Mar. 23), painter William Glackens (May 22), Justice Benjamin Cardozo (July 9), and financier Samuel Insull (July 16).

In Print

Books of the year included *Alone,* by Admiral Richard Evelyn Byrd; *Benjamin Franklin,* by Carl Van Doren (Pulitzer prize 1939); *A History of American Magazines,* by Frank L. Mott (Pulitzer prize 1939); *Listen! the Wind,* by Anne Morrow Lindbergh; *A Prairie Grove,* by Donald Culross Peattie; *Selected Poems,* by John Gould Fletcher (Pulitzer prize 1939); and the fiction, *Action at Aquilla,* by Harvey Allen; *All This, and Heaven Too,* by Rachel Lyman Field; *And Tell of Time,* by Laura Lettie Kay; *Concert Pitch,* by Elliot Paul; *Dynasty of Death,* by Janet Taylor Caldwell; *The First Forty-Nine Stories,* by Ernest Hemingway; *The Long Valley,* by John Steinbeck; *My Son, My Son,* by Howard Spring; and *The Yearling,* by Marjorie K. Rawlings (Pulitzer prize 1939).

On Stage

The Scarlet Letter, an American opera by Philadelphia-born composer Vittorio Giannini, had (June 2) its world premiere at the State Opera House in Hamburg, Germany. The composer's sister Dusolina sang the principal role.

The Society for the Preservation and Encouragement of Barber Shop Quartet Singing in America was founded.

The Carnival of Swing, at Randall's Island, New York, featuring 25 bands, drew more than 23,000 jitterbugs who listened for five and three-quarter hours with such unrestrained enthusiasm that police and park officers had all they could do, according to a report in *The New York Times,* to protect the players from "destruction by admiration."

In Chicago at the Great Northern Theater an all-Black jazz version of Gilbert and Sullivan's operetta *The Mikado* was staged (Sept.) with smashing success by the local W.P.A. Federal Theater unit. (The show was taken to New York the next year.)

New York plays included *Bachelor Born; Shadow and Substance; On Borrowed Time; Our Town* (Pulitzer prize 1938); *What a Life; Kiss the Boys Good-Bye; Oscar Wilde; Abe Lincoln in Illinois* (Pulitzer prize 1939, declined by the author); *Outward Bound.* Musical productions included *I Married an Angel; The Fireman's Flame; Hellzapoppin; Leave It to me; The Boys from Syracuse.*

Films

Motion pictures of the year included *The Adventures of Robin Hood*, with Errol Flynn; *Alexander's Ragtime Band*, with Tyrone Power, Alice Faye, and Don Ameche; *Boys Town*, with Spencer Tracy and Mickey Rooney; *The Citadel*, with Robert Donat and Rosalind Russell; *The Hurricane*, with Dorothy Lamour, Jon Hall, and Mary Astor; *In Old Chicago*, with Tyrone Power, Alice Faye, and Don Ameche; *Jezebel*, with Bette Davis and Fay Bainter; *Kentucky*; *The Lady Vanishes*; *Love Finds Andy Hardy*, with Mickey Rooney, Lewis Stone, Judy Garland, and Cecilia Parker; *Marie Antoinette*, with Norma Shearer and Tyrone Power; *Pygmalion*, with Leslie Howard and Wendy Hiller; *Snow White and the Seven Dwarfs* (Walt Disney's first full-length color cartoon); *Three Comrades*, with Margaret Sullavan; and *You Can't Take It with You*, with Jean Arthur, Lionel Barrymore, James Stewart, and Edward Arnold. Walt Disney's *Snow White* was "the happiest thing that has happened in the world since the Armistice," according to columnist Westbrook Pegler. The charming fantasy set the whole country humming *Heigh Ho—Heigh Ho* and *Whistle While You Work* and was a boon to toy manufacturers at a time when economic recession was at its worst. More than 3,000,000 Disney toys were sold, and the Sieberling-Latex factory near Akron, Ohio, couldn't keep up with the demand for rubber reproductions of the seven dwarfs, even by working 24 hours a day.

Music

A-Tisket A-Tasket; Change Partners; Chiquita Banana; Falling in Love With Love; The Flat Foot Floogie; Get Out of Town; Heigh-Ho; I Married an Angel; I'll Be Seeing You; Jeepers Creepers; Love Walked In; Music, Maestro, Please?; My Heart Belongs to Daddy; Semper Paratus; September Song; This Can't Be Love; Two Sleepy People; You Go to My Head; You Must Have Been a Beautiful Baby.

1939

*T*he year marked the beginning of World War II. Adolf Hitler proclaimed (Sept. 1, 1939) war on Poland. Great Britain and France declared (Sept. 3) war on Germany By the end of the year Germany had begun to bomb British towns from the air.

Congress passed the Hatch Act prohibiting the participation of government employees in political activity.

Two great expositions took place a continent apart—the Golden Gate International Exposition in San Francisco (Feb. 18-Oct. 29) and the New York World's Fair (Apr. 30-Oct. 31; May 11-Oct. 21, 1940). The latter was a stupendous, colorful affair, in which sixty nations took part. Germany was not represented. The National Broadcasting Company, New York, telecast the opening ceremonies.

King George VI and Queen Elizabeth of Great Britain visited (June 7-11) the United States, via Canada. They were received (June 8-9) at the White House, made (June 10) a triumphal tour of New York City amid great jubilation, visiting the World's Fair, and were entertained by President Roosevelt at his home in Hyde Park, N.Y., American style with hot dogs.

The $18,000,000 Bronx-Whitestone Bridge, New York spanning the East River, was completed.

Mrs. Clara Adams of New York became the first woman to make a trip around the world by airplane. The journey was accomplished in 16 days, 19 hours, 4 minutes (June 18-July 15).

Captain James W. Chapman, Jr., U.S. Army Air Corps, made a round-trip flight by plane from Washington, D.C., to Moscow and back in 5 days, 1 hour, 55 minutes' flying time.

E. O. Lawrence was awarded the Nobel prize for physics.

Erich Maria Remarque, German author of *All Quiet on the Western Front* and other novels, came to the United States.

Alexander Gretchaninov, Russian composer, settled in the United States.

Baseball was 100 years old, according to the reckoning of Cooperstown, N.Y. experts. The U.S. Post Office honored the centennial by issuing (June 12) a three-cent commemorative postage stamp.

Writer Zane Grey died (Oct. 23).

In Print

Books of the year included *Abraham Lincoln: The War Years*, by Carl Sandburg (Pulitzer prize); *America in Midpassage*, by Charles and Mary Beard; *Collected Poems*, by Mark Van Doren (Pulitzer prize 1940); *Hardly a Man Is Now Alive*, by Daniel Carter Beard; *I'm a Stranger Here Myself*, by Ogden Nash; *Woodrow Wilson*, by Ray Stannard Baker; vols. 7-8 (Pulitzer prize 1940); and the fiction, *Adventures of a Young Man*, by John Dos Passos; *The Bridegroom Cometh*, by Waldo Frank; *Children of God*, by Vardis Fisher; *Claudia*, by Rose Franken; *Disputed Passage*, by Lloyd Cassel Douglas; *The Grapes of Wrath*, by John Steinbeck (Pulitzer prize 1940); *Kitty Foyle*, by Christopher Morley; *The March of the Hundred*, by Manuel Komroff; *The Nazarene*, by Sholem Asch; *Peace, It's Wonderful*, by William Saroyan; *Song of Years*, by Bess Streeter Aldrich; *Tommy Gallagher's Crusade*, by James Farrell; *The Web and the Rock*, by Thomas Wolfe; and *Wickford Point*, by John Phillips Marquand.

On Stage

Marian Anderson, noted Black contralto, was barred by the Washington, D.C. chapter of the Daughters of the American Revolution from giving a concert in Constitution Hall. She performed (Apr. 9) instead in Lincoln Memorial Park to an audience of 75,000 people an open-air concert that was sponsored by many eminent political leaders, among them Secretary of State Harold Leclaire Ickes and Mrs. Franklin Delano Roosevelt.

Unfavorable testimony before the House Committee Investigating Un-American Activities during June led (July 31) to the disbandment of the Federal Theater Project of the Works Progress Administration relief program. The Project had give employment to more than 13,000 actors and other workers in the theatrical profession, and had produced about 1,200 plays.

The New York stage again produced a play that broke all existing box office records, topping both *Tobacco Road* (1933; 3,182 performances) and *Abie's Irish Rose* (1922; 2,327 performances). The play, *Life with Father*, was adapted from Clarence Day's novel by Howard Lindsay and Russel Crouse. When the show closed nearly eight years later (July 12, 1947), it had run up a total of 3,224 performances. Other plays that ran 175 or more performances included *The American Way; I Must Love Someone; The Little Foxes; No Time for Comedy; See My Lawyer; Skylark; The Man Who Came to Dinner; The Time of Your Life* (Pulitzer prize 1940); *Margin for Error*. Musical productions included *Stars in Your Eyes; Street of Paris; Yokel Boy; Too Many Girls; DuBarry Was a Lady*. Jazz versions of Gilbert and Sullivan's operetta *The Mikado* were heard as *The Swing Mikado* (62 perf.; originally produced in Chicago in Sept. 1938 by the Chicago W.P.A. Federal Theater) and as *The Hot Mikado* (85 perf.). A similar treatment of Shakespeare's *A Midsummer Night's Dream* was unsuccessful as *Swingin' the Dream* (13 perf.).

Films

Motion pictures of the year included *Broadway Melody of 1940; Dark Victory*, with Bette Davis); *Gone With the Wind*, with Clark Gable and Vivien Leigh; *Goodbye, Mr. Chips*, with Robert Donat and Greer Garson; *Juarez*, with Paul Muni; *Mr. Smith Goes to Washington*, with Jean Arthur and James Stewart; *The Old Maid*, with Bette Davis; *Stanley and Livingstone*, with Spencer Tracy, Nancy Kelly, and Richard Greene; *The Ugly Duckling* (Walt Disney cartoon); *The Wizard of Oz*, with Judy Garland, Frank Morgan, Ray Bolger, Bert Lahr, and Jack Haley; *The Women*, with Norma Shearer, Joan Crawford, and Rosalind Russell; and *Wuthering Heights*, with Merle Oberon and Laurence Olivier.

Music

All the Things You Are; Beer Barrel Polka; Brazil—Aquarela do Brasil; Darn That Dream; Do I Love You?; God Bless America; I Concentrate on You; I Didn't Know What Time it Was; I'll Never Smile Again; The Lamp Is Low; Lilacs in the Rain; My Prayer; Over the Rainbow; South of the Border; Three Little Fishies.

1940

*W*orld War II continued. The year saw German troops invade Denmark and Norway, the violation of the neutrality of Belgium, Luxembourg, and the Netherlands, with the subsequent surrender of the Dutch and Belgian armies after enormous casualties. The British were driven from the Continent, and some 300,000 British and French soldiers were taken in small private boats from the beaches of Dunkirk in the most heroic rescue of the war. Most of the armament was lost in the retreat, and Britain faced the future nearly helpless to ward off invasion. The Germans almost reached Paris, Italy declared war on Great Britain and France, and the latter sued (June 17) for an armistice. Italy extended the war to the Balkans by attacking Greece; Germany came to Italy's assistance, overran Greece and Yugoslavia, and brought Hungary, Bulgaria, and Rumania under German control.

Hitler's conquests, unequaled since the days of Napoleon, challenged America's isolationist stand. Congress enacted (Aug. 27) a law requiring alien residents to register and passed the Selective Service and Training Act (signed by President Roosevelt Sept. 16), inaugurating the first peace-time military draft in United States history. October 16 was the appointed day for the registration of all male citizens to age thirty-five—16,313,240 received registration cards. Secretary of War Henry Lewis Stimson set the draft in motion by drawing, blind-folded, the card of the first selectee from a glass bowl in the War Department Auditorium in Washington, D.C. To impress further upon the public the necessity of adequate national defense, the Post Office Department issued on that fateful day (Oct. 16) three special postage stamps to replace temporarily the regular issues. The new adhesives pictured the Statue of Liberty (one cent), and anti-aircraft gun (two cents), and an uplifted torch (three cents), each bearing the words "For Defense."

In exchange for 50 old destroyers, the United States obtained from Great Britain naval and air bases in American waters.

"I Am an American Day" (third Sunday in May) was proclaimed (May 3) by Act of Congress.

The Pan American Airways *Yankee Clipper* flew (Apr. 1-2) from New York to Lisbon, Portugal, in a record time of 18 hours, 35 minutes, and made the return trip in 25 hours, 1 minute.

John Llewellyn Lewis, boss of the United Mine Workers Union, who had been noted chiefly for his dictatorial and obstructive ways and who had become unpopular with many of the mine workers he led, resigned (Nov. 18) as president of the Congress of Industrial Organizations (C.I.O.). He had founded the organization in 1935.

The $58,000,000 Manhattan-Queens, Midtown, vehicular tunnel under the East River, New York, was opened (Nov. 15).

The Columbia Broadcasting System, New York, gave (Sept. 4) a public demonstration of television in color over its station W2XAB.

On Mar. 10 the first telecast of an opera in the New York area was broadcast by the National Broadcasting Company. The opera was a tabloid version of *Pagliacci*, sung at Radio City by Metropolitan Opera singers. (The British Broadcasting Company had telecast opera and ballet in London in 1937-38.)

Staticless radio, F.M. or Frequency Modulation, was demonstrated (Jan. 5) by Major Edwin H. Armstrong from station WIXOJ in Worcester, Mass.

Harry James, trumpeter, left the Benny Goodman orchestra to form his own band, and took on a young, unknown vocalist—Frank Sinatra.

The national population was 131,669,275.

Deaths of the year included feminist Emma Goldman (May 14), black nationalist Marcus Garvey (June 10), automobile manufacturer Walter P. Chrysler (Aug. 18), reformer Lillian Wald (Sept. 1), and writer James Welch (Nov. 18).

In Print

Books of the year included *Arena*, by Hallie Flanagan; *The Atlantic Migration*, by Marcus Lee Hansen (Pulitzer prize 1941, awarded posthumously); *Dictionary of American History*, by James Truslow Adams; 6 vols.; *Jonathan Edwards*, by Ola Elizabeth Winslow (Pulitzer prize 1941); *New England: Indian Summer*, by Van Wyck Brooks; *Sunderland Capture*, by Leonard Bacon (Pulitzer prize 1941); *Trojan Horses in America*, by Martin Dies; and the fiction, *For Whom the Bell Tolls*, by Ernest Hemingway; *How Green Was My Valley*, by Richard Llewellyn; *My Name Is Aram*, by William Saroyan; *Native Son*, by Richard Wright; *Pal Joey*, by John O'Hara; *Sapphira and the Slave Girl*, by Willa Cather; *World's End*, by Upton Sinclair; and *You Can't Go Home Again*, by Thomas Wolfe. No Pulitzer prize was awarded for this year's fiction.

On Stage

New York plays included *The Male Animal; Separate Rooms; There Shall Be No Night* (Pulitzer prize 1941); *Johnny Belinda; Charley's Aunt; George Washington Slept Here; The Corn Is Green;* and *My Sister Eileen*. Helen Hayes revived *Twelfth Night*. Musical productions included *Louisiana Purchase; Boys and Girls Together; It Happens on Ice; Panama Hattie;* and *Pal Joey*.

Films

Motion pictures of the year included *Abe Lincoln in Illinois*, with Raymond Massey; *All This, and Heaven Too*, with Bette Davis and Charles Boyer; *Boom Town*, with Clark Gable, Spencer Tracy, and Claudette Colbert; *Foreign*

Correspondent, with Joel McCrea and Laraine Day; *The Grapes of Wrath*, with Henry Fonda and Jane Darwell; *The Great Dictator*, with Charlie Chaplin; *Kitty Foyle*, with Ginger Rogers; *The Mortal Storm*, with Margaret Sullavan and James Stewart; *Ninotchka*, with Greta Garbo; *Northwest Passage*, with Spencer Tracy and Robert Young; *Our Town*, with William Holden; *The Philadelphia Story*, with Katharine Hepburn, Cary Grant, and James Stewart; *Pinocchio;* and *The Westerner. Fantasia*, the spectacular Walt Disney cartoon with musical accompaniments by Leopold Stokowski and a large symphony orchestra, was first shown in New York in the Broadway Theater on Nov. 13.

Music

All or Nothing at All; The Breeze and I; Cabin in the Sky; Fools Rush In; How High the Moon; Imagination; It's a Big, Wonderful World; The Last Time I Saw Paris; The Nearness of You; Taking a Chance on Love; This Is My Country; When You Wish upon a Star; You Are My Sunshine; You Stepped Out of a Dream.

1941

*W*orld War II continued.

President Franklin Delano Roosevelt began his third term—the first American President to be so elected, breaking the tradition against a third term that was established by George Washington. Roosevelt also was the first President to be inaugurated on Jan. 20 (rather than in March) in accordance with the 20th Amendment.

A seven-billion-dollar Lend-Lease Act was signed by President Roosevelt on Mar. 10 to provide aid to the Allies. The Office of Price Administration ("O.P.A.") was set up (Apr. 11), and the Office of Civilian Defense on May 20. President Roosevelt declared (May 21) "an unlimited state of national emergency," pledged assistance to all nations engaged in resisting Nazi aggression, and ordered (June 14) the "freezing" of the assets of Germany and Italy in the United States, the seizure of their vessels in American ports, and the closing of the German consulates. The President enunciated (July 6) four principles of human liberty, known collectively as the "four freedoms," namely, freedom of speech and expression, freedom of worship, freedom from want, and freedom from fear.

U.S. Marines were landed (July 7) in Iceland at the request of its government; President Roosevelt and Prime Minister Winston Churchill of Great Britain met (Aug. 12-14) at an undisclosed spot in the North Atlantic and drafted the eight principles of a document called the Atlantic Charter. By executive order, under Lend-Lease, the sum of $1,000,000,000 was made (Nov. 6) available to Russia under the plan. In Washington, a conference on the situation in the Far East was held (Nov. 17) with Japanese envoys concerning their country's invasion of Thailand, the Malay Peninsula, and the Burma Road. In Havana, representatives of Latin-American republics and the United States met in a Pan American conference to consolidate economic and military co-operation for the defense of the Western hemisphere.

Without warning, after President Roosevelt had addressed (Dec. 6) a personal appeal to Emperor Hirohito of Japan to avoid further conflict in the Pacific, Japanese warplanes blasted (Dec. 7) the port of Pearl Harbor, near Honolulu, the Philippines, and Wake and Guam islands. At Pearl Harbor five battleships were sunk or beached, three more badly damaged, 10 smaller warships destroyed or heavily hurt, and the bomber command at Clark Field in the Philippines was destroyed. The United States declared war on Japan on

Dec. 8. As allies of Japan, Germany and Italy declared (Dec. 11) war on the United States. Churchill again visited (Dec. 23) the United States to participate in a second conference with President Roosevelt.

In defiance of President Roosevelt's "national emergency" proclamation, the United Mine Workers President John Llewellyn Lewis called (Oct. 25) a strike in the coal mines of seven large steel companies that would involve more than 50,000 miners. President Roosevelt succeeded in delaying the strike pending negotiation, but irreconcilable union officials were determined on the strike, set for Nov. 16. It was called off (Nov. 22) by Lewis when President Roosevelt again intervened with a proposal of arbitration.

The old U.S. submarine 0-9 sank (June 13) with a loss of 33 men during a deep-sea diving test in the Atlantic about 24 miles east of Portsmouth, N.H.

The National Gallery of Art, Washington, D.C., was opened. The marble building cost $15,000,000, provided by Andrew William Mellon, Pittsburgh capitalist and Secretary of the Treasury under President Harding, Coolidge, and Hoover.

Joe DiMaggio, center fielder of the New York Yankees, set a record when he hit safely in 56 games.

Deaths of the year included writer Sherwood Anderson (Mar. 8), baseball great Lou Gehrig (June 2), automobile manufacturer Louis Chevrolet (June 6), jazz musician Jelly Roll Morton (July 10), and Justice Louis Brandeis (Oct. 5).

In Print
Books of the year included *Berlin Diary*, William Lawrence Shirer; *Crusader in Crinoline*, by Forrest Wilson (Pulitzer prize 1942); *The Dust Which Is God*, by William Rose Benet (Pulitzer prize 1942); *James Madison*, by Irving Newton Brant, Vol. 1; *The Oxford Companion to American Literature*, by James D. Hart; *Reveille in Washington*, by Margaret Leach (Pulitzer prize 1942); and the fiction, *H.M. Pulham, Esq.*, by John Phillips Marquand; *In This Our Life*, by Ellen Glasgow (Pulitzer prize 1942); *The Keys of the Kingdom*, by Archibald Joseph Cronin; and *The Strange Woman*, by Ben Ames Williams.

On Stage
New York plays included *Arsenic and Old Lace; Mr. and Mrs. North, Claudia; Watch on the Rhine; Blithe Spirit; Spring Again; Junior Miss;* and *Angel Street.* Maurice Evans revived *Macbeth.* Musical productions included *Lady in the Dark; Best Foot Forward; Let's Face It; High Kickers; Sons o' Fun.*

Films
Motion pictures of the year included *Blossoms in the Dust,* with Greer Garson; *Citizen Kane,* with Orson Welles; *Here Comes Mr. Jordan,* with Robert Montgomery; *How Green Was My Valley,* with Walter Pidgeon and Maureen O'Hara; *Kings Row,* with Ann Sheridan, Robert Cummings, Ronald Reagan, and Betty Field; *The Little Foxes,* with Bette Davis; *The Man Who Came to Din-*

ner, with Monty Woolley, Bette Davis, and Ann Sheridan; *Meet John Doe*, with Gary Cooper and Barbara Stanwyck; *Sergeant York*, with Gary Cooper; and *Suspicion*, with Cary Grant and Joan Fontaine.

Music
The Anniversary Waltz; Bewitched; Blues in the Night; Chattanooga Choo; Deep in the Heart of Texas; Don't Take Your Love from Me; How About You?; I Don't Want to Walk Without You; I Don't Want to Set the World on Fire; I Got It Bad and That Ain't Good; I'll Remember April; Jersey Bounce; There! I've Said It Again; This Is New; Waltzing Matilda; The White Cliffs of Dover.

1942

*T*he Japanese landed (Jan. 2) in Manila, Philippine Islands, forced (Apr. 9) the surrender of the American-Filipino forces at Bataan, and, after overcoming stiff resistance, captured Corregidor Fortress in Manila Bay. American troops arrived (Jan. 26) in northern Ireland. The United States began (Mar. 23) the removal of Japanese-American residents from the western coastal states to inland areas. Lieutenant Colonel James H. Doolittle and 79 airmen, with a large squadron of Army B-25 bombers, raided (Apr. 18) the Japanese coastal cities of Tokyo, Yokohama, Kobe, Nagoya, and Osaka. Japan occupied (June 7-8) several of the Aleutian Islands. American army and naval forces began (Aug. 7) the attack on Guadalcanal in the Solomon Islands and finally defeated (Nov. 12-15) the Japanese in a great naval battle. Allied and American forces under General Dwight David Eisenhower, Commander in Chief of the Allied armies, invaded (Nov.) northern Africa. In Naples, the U.S. Air Forces commenced (Dec. 5) the bombardment of Italian cities.

Rationing of food, clothing, and other articles went into effect under the Office of Price Administration. Gasoline was placed on ration in the Eastern states (May 15) and later in the West (Dec. 1).

Air raid sirens were installed and periodic blackout drills were introduced.

President Roosevelt requested 60,000 planes, 45,000 tanks, 20,000 anti-aircraft guns, and 8,000,000 deadweight tons of merchant shipping.

The following government agencies were established: the War Production Board (Jan. 16), the War Manpower Commission (Apr. 18), the U.S. Employment Service (1941), and the Office of War Information ("O.W.I.") (June 13).

Congress voted (Nov. 14) the conscription of boys of eighteen years of age and over for military service.

Wendell Lewis Willkie, "The Barefoot Boy of Wall Street" and unsuccessful Republican presidential candidate in 1940, made (Sept. 2-Oct. 25) a tour of England, the Near East, the Soviet Union, and China as emissary for President Roosevelt.

The Works Progress Administration (1935) was terminated (Dec. 4).

The United States Supreme Court voided (Jan. 12) the 40-year-old Georgia Contract Labor Law as violation of the anti-slavery Amendments, and upheld (Dec. 21) the validity of Nevada's six-weeks-residence divorce decrees.

Capt. Edward "Eddie" Vernon Rickenbacker, American aviator and World War I ace, was found with seven Army men (Nov. 13) in the Southern Pacific after drifting 23 days on a life raft. Rickenbacker's plane had been forced down while on a special government mission. The discovery climaxed one of the greatest rescue hunts in history.

Representatives of 26 nations at war with the Axis powers formed (Jan. 1) in Washington, D.C., the nucleus of the U.N., or United Nations (1945).

Joseph E. Widener presented the priceless Widener Collection of paintings and sculpture to the National Gallery of Art, Washington, D.C., which had been opened in the preceding year.

The National Geographic-Palomar Observatory Sky Survey, a project to photograph 500,000,000 stars, was begun (July 1) at Mt. Palomar, Calif. under the joint auspices of the National Geographic Society and the California Institute of Technology.

The French luxury liner *Normandie* burned (Feb. 9) at her pier in New York and sank.

Boston's Coconut Grove fire horrified the entire nation. The night club had been jammed (Nov. 28) with 800 people after the Boston College—Holy Cross football game. A busboy lit a match and an artificial palm tree went up in flames; 491 persons perished and scores were injured.

Deaths of the year included painter Grant Wood (Feb. 12), sculptor Gertrude Vanderbilt Whitney (Apr. 18), and actor John Barrymore (May 29).

In Print

Books of the year included *Admiral of the Ocean Sea*, by Samuel Eliot Morison (Pulitzer prize 1943); *Lee's Lieutenants*, by Douglas Southall Freeman, 3 vols. 1942-44; *Paul Revere and the World He Lived In*, by Esther Forbes (Pulitzer prize 1943); *A Witness Tree*, by Robert Frost (Pulitzer prize 1943); and the fiction, *Dragon's Teeth*, by Upton Sinclair (Pulitzer prize 1943); *The Robe*, by Lloyd Cassel Douglas; and *See Here, Private Hargrove*, by Marion Hargrove.

On Stage

New York plays included *Guest in the House; Uncle Harry; Janie; The Eve of St. Mark; The Skin of Our Teeth* (Pulitzer prize 1943); *Counsellor-at-Law; The Pirate*, and *The Doughgirls*. Musical productions included: *Porgy and Bess; Priorities of 1942; By Jupiter; Star and Garter; Stars on Ice; This Is the Army; Show Time;* and *Rosalinda*.

Films

Motion pictures of the year included *In Which We Serve*, with Noel Coward; *Mrs. Miniver*, with Greer Garson and Walter Pidgeon; *One Foot in Heaven*, with Frederic March and Martha Scott; *The Pied Piper*, with Monty Woolley and Roddy McDowall; *The Pride of the Yankees*, with Gary Cooper and Teresa Wright; *Random Harvest*, with Ronald Colman and Greer Garson; *Wake Island*, with Brian Donlevy, Robert Preston, and Macdonald Carey; *Woman of the Year*, with Katharine Hepburn and Spencer Tracy; and *Yankee Doodle Dandy*, with James Cagney.

Music

Be Careful! It's My Heart; Don't Get Around Much Anymore; I'm Old Fashioned; I Had the Craziest Dream; I Left My Heart at the Stage Door Canteen; Paper Doll; Praise the Lord and Pass the Ammunition!; Serenade in Blue; This Is the Army, Mr. Jones; Warsaw Concerto; When the Lights Go on Again; White Christmas; You'd Be So Nice to Come Home To.

1943

*P*resident Roosevelt and Prime Minister Churchill conferred (Jan. 14-20) at Casablanca, Morocco, on the "unconditional surrender of Germany, Italy, and Japan." The British and American armies captured (Mar. 13) the German-held cities of Tunis and Bizerte. Premier Benito Mussolini of Italy resigned (July 25), Italy ended (Sept. 8) hostilities with the United States, severed relations with Germany, and declared (Oct. 13) war on its former ally. General Dwight David Eisenhower was appointed (Dec. 24) Supreme Commander of the Anglo-American forces for the invasion of Europe. Commenting on the American war effort, British observer, D. W. Brogan, remarked, "To the Americans, war is a business, not an art."

The cost of the war staggered everyone's imagination. World War I, which lasted less than two years, cost about $35,000,000,000. By mid-year of '43, World War II was costing $8,000,000,000 per month.

The "Wacs," the Women's Army Corps of the U.S. Army, was established (July 1). Soon there were "Waves," Women Appointed for Volunteer Emergency Service, "Spars," Women's Reserve of the U.S. Coast Guard Reserve, and "Wasps," Women's Air Force Service Pilots of the U.S. Army Air Forces.

On July 1, wage earners and salaried employees had 20 percent deducted from their pay in compliance with the pay-as-you-go income tax law, signed by President Roosevelt on June 10.

The F.B.I. captured eight Nazi spies and saboteurs who landed at Amagansett, N.Y. and Jacksonville, Fla. All were convicted and died in the electric chair.

A War Bond rally auction was held in the basement of Gimbel's department store in New York with 750 persons on hand to bid for such precious items as Jefferson's Bible and George Washington's letters. Orchestra leader Jack Benny's violin, a $75 imitation Amati nicknamed "Old Love in Bloom," was put on the block and one Julius Klorfein bought it for $1,000,000. Mr. Klorfein turned out to be president of the Garcia Grande Cigar Company.

When more than half a million coal miners of the United Mine Workers persisted in their strike (1941), Secretary of the Interior Harold L. Ickes assumed (Nov. 1) control of the mines by order of President Roosevelt.

The United Nations Relief and Rehabilitation Administration ("U.N.R.R.A.") was organized (Nov. 9) by 44 nations to supply food, clothing, medicine, and other necessities to the newly liberated peoples of the world.

Anti-Communist and anti-Fascist newspaper editor Carlo Tresca was assassinated (Jan. 11) in New York by Soviet O.G.P.U. agent Carlos Contreras.

Race riots broke out in Detroit (June 21) and in New York (Aug. 1). In Detroit, 34 persons were killed, 700 were injured, and more than 1,000 arrested. In Harlem, an unfounded rumor caused the destruction of about $1,000,000 worth of property and the death of 6 Negroes.

Chicagoans rode (Oct. 16) in a subway for the first time.

The Pentagon, the world's largest office building, covering 34 acres outside Washington, D.C., was completed (Jan. 25) at a cost of about $64,000,000.

The Thomas Jefferson Memorial, East Potomac Park, Washington, D.C., was dedicated (Apr. 13) by President Roosevelt on the 200th anniversary of Jefferson's birth.

The Pan American Airways plane *Yankee Clipper*, whose passenger list included stars of the entertainment world going abroad to perform for GI's, crashed (Feb. 22) in the Tagus River near Lisbon, Portugal. Twenty-four persons were drowned. Among the survivors were radio singer Jane Froman and night club accordionist Gypsy Markoff; among the dead, Tamara ("Smoke Gets in Your Eyes"), and foreign correspondent Ben Robertson.

Lessing J. Rosenwald presented his rare collection of prints and drawings to the National Gallery of Art, Washington, D.C.

Radio Station WRGB of the General Electric Company, Schenectady, N.Y., televised Offenbach's operetta *The Marriage by the Lantern* (May) and a full-length opera, Humperdinck's *Hansel und Gretel* (Dec. 20).

Frank Sinatra captivated bobby-soxers of both sexes: thirty thousand of Sinatra's fans reacted so violently during his appearance at the Paramount Theater in New York that a riot call was sent out, and 421 policemen, 20 policewomen, and 20 patrol cars responded. No less vocally appealing was Dinah Shore, a dark-haired singer who charmed audiences with her rendition of *One Dozen Roses*.

There was much chuckling over the true story of a hoarder who filled her cellar with canned goods. A rainstorm flooded the cellar and washed all the labels off the cans.

Deaths of the year included automobile executive Edsel Ford (May 26) and lyricist Lorenz Hart (Nov. 22).

In Print

Books of the year included *The American Leonardo: The Life of Samuel F.B. Morse*, by Carlton Mabee (Pulitzer prize 1944); *The Growth of American Thought*, by Merle Curtis (Pulitzer prize 1944); *One World*, by Wendell Lewis Willkie; *Western Star*, by Stephen Vincent Benet (Pulitzer prize 1944); and the fiction *The Apostle*, by Sholem Asch; *The Fountainhead*, by Ayn Rand; *The Human Com-*

edy, by William Saroyan; *Journey in the Dark,* by Martin Flavin (Pulitzer prize 1944); and *A Tree Grows in Brooklyn,* by Betty Smith.

On Stage
William Schuman was awarded the Pulitzer music prize for his *Secular Cantata No. 2, A Free Song*—the first award in that field.

New York plays included *Dark Eyes; The Patriots, Harriet; Kiss and Tell; The Two Mrs. Carrolls; Tomorrow the World; Lovers and Friends;* and *The Voice of the Turtle. Othello* was revived by the Negro actor Paul Robeson. Musical productions included *Something for the Boys; Oklahoma!; Ziegfeld Follies; Early to Bed; The Merry Widow; One Touch of Venus; Winged Victory;* and *Carmen Jones.*

Films
Motion pictures of the year included *Casablanca,* with Humphrey Bogart and Ingrid Bergman; *For Whom the Bell Tolls,* with Gary Cooper and Ingrid Bergman; *A Guy Named Joe,* with Spencer Tracy, Irene Dunne, and Van Johnson; *The Human Comedy,* with Mickey Rooney and Frank Morgan; *So Proudly We Hail!,* with Claudette Colbert, Paulette Goddard, and Veronica Lake); *Stage Door Canteen; This Gun for Hire,* with Alan Ladd; *This Is the Army;* and *Watch on the Rhine,* with Paul Lukas and Bette Davis.

Music
Amor; Besame Mucho—Kiss Me Much; Comin' in on a Wing and a Prayer; Do Nothin' Till You Hear from Me; I Couldn't Sleep a Wink Last Night; I've Heard That Song Before; I'll Be Seeing You; A Lovely Way to Spend an Evening; Mairzy Doats; Oh What a Beautiful Mornin'; Oklahoma; People Will Say We're in Love; Pistol Packin' Mama; Speak Low; Star Eyes; Sunday, Monday, or Always; The Surrey with the Fringe on Top.

1944

$\mathcal{T}$he carefully planned invasion of German-held western Europe—D-Day—was successfully carried out in Normandy (June 6) and in southern France (August). The assault broke (Nov. 25) the supposedly impregnable Siegfried Line of German defense west of the Rhine.

Congress approved (Dec. 15) the appointment of the first five-star generals (Arnold, Eisenhower, MacArthur, Marshall) and the first five-star admirals (King, Leahy, Nimitz).

The United States Supreme Court upheld in two decisions (Apr. 3 and May 8) the right of African-Americans to vote in state primaries.

The national debt was $260,000,000,000 when President Roosevelt affixed (June 10) his signature to a bill setting that limit.

Representatives of 44 Allied nations met (July 1-22) at Mount Washington Hotel, Bretton Woods, N.H., and set up the International Bank for Reconstruction and Development, known as the World Bank. (Its operation began June 25, 1946, with a capital of $10,000,000.)

The United Nations was established (Aug. 21-Oct. 7) in a conference at Dumbarton Oaks, on the outskirts of Washington, D.C., by delegates from the United States, Great Britain, Soviet Russia, and China.

President Roosevelt was elected (Nov. 7) to an unprecedented fourth term.

Ninety-year-old "General" Jacob Sechler Coxey of Ohio finally achieved the ambition of his life—he delivered (May 1) from the steps of the Capitol the speech he had been barred from giving when he was leader of an "army" of unemployed in 1894.

The *Flying Ace*, a 30-ton American Export Airlines plane, made a nonstop flight from Foynes, Ireland, to New York, a distance of 3,329 miles, in 15 hours, 30 minutes. It arrived May 1.

A tornado passed (June 23) through western Pennsylvania, West Virginia, and Maryland, causing the death of 153 persons.

The worst circus fire in history occurred (July 6) at Hartford, Conn., when the big top tent of the Ringling Brothers and Barnum & Bailey Circus caught fire during a performance. The conflagration and panic claimed 107 lives and injured 412 persons.

Explosions took the lives of 322 persons at Port Chicago, Calif. (July 17), and of 135 in Cleveland, Ohio.

Nobel prizes were awarded to Isador Isaac Rabbi for physics, and to James Erlanger and Herbert S. Gasser for medicine and physiology.

Horse racing in the U.S. was banned (Dec. 21) on account of the war.

Politician Wendell Willkie died (Oct. 8).

In Print

Books of the year included *George Bancroft: Brahmin Rebel,* by Russell Baline Nye (Pulitzer prize 1945); *Unfinished Business,* by Stephen Bonsal (Pulitzer prize 1945); *V-Letter and Other Poems,* by Karl Shapiro (Pulitzer prize 1945); *Forever Amber,* by Kathleen Winsor; and *Leave Her to Heaven,* by Ben Ames Williams.

On Stage

Howard Hanson was awarded the Pulitzer music prize for this Symphony No. 2, op. 34—the second such award.

The National Negro Opera Company presented performances of *La Traviata* in Chicago, Pittsburgh, New York, and Washington, D.C.

New York plays included *Over 21; Ramshackle Inn; Wallflower; Jacobowsky and the Colonel; Chicken Every Sunday; Pick-Up Girl; Ten Little Indians; The Searching Wind; School for Brides; Catherine Was Great; Anna Lucasta; Soldier's Wife; I Remember Mama; Harvey* (Pulitzer prize 1945); *The Late George Apley; A Bell for Adano;* and *Dear Ruth.* Musical productions included *Mexican Hayride; Follow the Girls; Hats Off to Ice; Song of Norway; Bloomer Girl; Seven Lively Arts; Laffing Room Only;* and *On the Town.*

Films

To commemorate the 50th anniversary of motion pictures, the U.S. Post Office issued (Oct. 31) a three-cent purple postage stamp.

Motion pictures of the year included *Dragon Seed,* with Katharine Hepburn and Walter Huston; *Gaslight,* with Ingrid Bergman; *Going My Way,* with Bing Crosby; *Jane Eyre,* with Joan Fontaine and Orson Welles; *Lifeboat,* with Tallulah Bankhead and William Bendix; *Madame Curie,* with Greer Garson and Walter Pidgeon; *None but the Lonely Heart; See Here, Private Hargrove; Since You Went Away; The Song of Bernadette,* with Jennifer Jones; *The Story of Dr. Wassell,* with Gary Cooper and Laraine Day; and *The White Cliffs of Dover,* with Irene Dunne and Alan Marshall.

Music

Ac-cent-tchu-ate the Positive; Candy; Don't Fence Me in; Dream; Ev'rytime We Say Goodbye; Going My Way; I Should Care; It Could Happen to You; Lilli Marlene; Long Ago and Far Away; Rum and Coca-Cola; Sentimental Journey; Spring Will Be a Little Late This Year; Swinging on a Star; Twilight Time.

1945

President Franklin Delano Roosevelt began (Jan. 20) his fourth term. He served only 96 days before he succumbed (Apr. 12) to a cerebral hemorrhage in Warm Springs, Ga. Vice President Harry S. Truman, Democrat, of Missouri, was inaugurated as the 33rd President.

World War II entered its last year. The American invasion of the Philippines began (Jan. 9), leading to the recapture (Mar. 2) of the islands. Gen. George S. Patton's American Third Army invaded Germany and crossed the Rhine (Mar. 7). U.S. Marines landed in Iwo Jima and suffered heavy losses in the capture (Mar. 16) of this important air base. (In 34 days of fighting there were 20,196 casualties, 4,305 deaths.) President Roosevelt, Prime Minister Churchill, and Premier Stalin conferred (Feb. 3-11) at Yalta in Crimea on the Black Sea. More than 1,000 American planes began (Feb. 3) nightly bombings of Berlin, and Allied planes dropped 12,400 explosives and 650,000 fire bombs on the city. Deposed Premier Mussolini of Italy was captured (Apr. 28) by Italian partisans in the village of Dongo on Lake Como and shot by a firing squad. Russian forces advancing from the East captured (Apr. 30) the Reichstag building of the German government in Berlin. That same day Hitler committed suicide in a bunker of the ruined structure. Totally defeated, Germany capitulated (May 6) and its representatives signed (May 8, V-E Day) the articles of surrender in Berlin.

Meanwhile, in the Far East, the largest armed fleet ever assembled was ready to begin the invasion of Japan. The fleet was not used. Instead, President Harry S. Truman, ordered that an atomic bomb be dropped (Aug. 6) on Hiroshima, Japan. It completely wiped out the city; five days later (Aug. 11) a second bomb destroyed Nagasaki. Japan sued (Aug. 10) for peace and surrendered (Sept. 1; V-J Day) aboard the USS *Missouri* in Tokyo Bay. American forces occupied (Sept. 3) Korea and General Douglas MacArthur became (Sept. 9) the military governor of Japan.

A Japanese sniper's bullet killed (Apr. 18) Ernie Pyle during the battle on the Pacific island of Iow Jima and the country mourned the loss of the nation's most beloved war correspondents.

The F.B.I. reported that it had rounded up 1,500 Axis spies in North and South America during the war.

President Truman attended (July 17—Aug. 2) the Potsdam Conference with Premier Stalin of Soviet Russia and Premier Attlee of Great Britain.

Rationing of meat, butter, and other commodities ended (Nov. 23).

Representatives of 50 nations met (Apr. 25-June 26) in San Francisco and established the United Nations Conference on International Organization (U.N.). A charter was signed on the last day of the session (effective Oct. 24). The signatories pledged "to save succeeding generations from the scourge of war…to maintain international peace and security…to employ international machinery for the promotion of the economic and social advancement of all people."

The United States Supreme Court, which had upheld (1942) the validity of Nevada's six-weeks-residence divorce law, now affirmed (May 21) the right of each state to recognize or reject a Nevada divorce decree.

New York Governor Thomas E. Dewey abolished (Mar. 12) discrimination in employment on account of race, creed, color, or national origin in his state.

Round-the-world airplane service was inaugurated (Sept. 28) when the *Globester* of the U.S. Army Transport Command left the National Airport, Washington, D.C., and completed (Oct. 4) a global trip of 23,279 miles in 149 hours, 44 minutes. An A-26, piloted by Colonel Joseph R. Holzapple and flying westward, circumnavigated the globe in a flight covering 24,859 miles in 96 hours, 50 minutes.

An Army B-25 bomber airplane, flying from New Bedford, Mass., to Newark, N.J., crashed (July 28) headlong into the tower of the 102-floor Empire State office building in New York, 915 feet above street level. The tragedy killed three occupants of the plane and 10 persons in the building, and turned the upper structure into a huge torch. The plane was piloted by a war veteran unfamiliar with the New York area.

Portal-to-portal pay for coal miners was upheld (May 7) by the United States Supreme Court. Pennsylvania anthracite miners again went on strike (May 1). By executive order, Secretary of the Interior Harold L. Ickes seized (May 3) the mines and the miners returned (May 21) to work.

Former Secretary of State Cordell Hull was awarded the Nobel prize for peace.

Ezra Pound, the American poet who was indicted for treason for broadcasting pro-Axis propaganda from Italy during the war, was committed to a mental hospital in Washington, D.C.

Novelist Ellen Gloasgow died (Nov. 21).

In Print

Books of the year included *The Age of Jackson*, by Arthur M. Schlesinger, Jr. (Pulitzer prize 1946); *Son of the Wilderness*, by Linnie Marsh Wolfe (Pulitzer prize 1946); and the fiction, *The Black Rose*, by Thomas Bertram Costain; *Captain from Castile*, by Samuel Shellabarger; *Daisy Kenyon*, by Elizabeth Janeway; *The Egg and I*, by Betty MacDonald. No Pulitzer prizes were awarded for this year's fiction or poetry.

On Stage

Aaron Copland was awarded the Pulitzer music prize for his ballet *Appalachian Spring*. (It was performed for the first time in Washington, D.C., Oct. 30, 1944, by Martha Graham and her dancers.)

New York plays included *The Hasty Heart, The Overtons; Dark of the Moon; The Glass Menagerie; Deep Are the Roots; State of the Union* (Pulitzer prize 1946); and *Dream Girl. The Tempest* was revived in a streamlined version. Maurice Evans presented his GI version of *Hamlet*, which he played in the South Pacific during World War II. Musical productions included *Up in Central Park; Carousel; The Red Mill; Are You with It?;* and *Billion Dollar Baby.*

Films

Motion pictures of the year included *Anchors Aweigh*, with Frank Sinatra, Kathryn Grayson, and Gene Kelly; *The Bells of St. Mary's*, with Bing Crosby and Ingrid Bergman; *The Corn Is Green*, with Bette Davis; *The Keys of the Kingdom*, with Gregory Peck; *Laura*, with Gene Tierney, Dana Andrews, and Clifton Webb; *Leave Her to Heaven*, with Gene Tierney and Cornel Wilde; *The Lost Weekend*, with Ray Milland and Jane Wyman; *Mildred Pierce*, with Joan Crawford; *National Velvet*, with Elizabeth Taylor and Mickey Rooney; *Saratoga Trunk*, with Gary Cooper and Ingrid Bergman; *A Song to Remember,* with Paul Muni and Merle Oberon; *Spellbound*, with Ingrid Bergman and Gregory Peck; *State Fair; The Story of G.I. Joe,* with Burgess Meredith; *A Tree Grows in Brooklyn*, with Dorothy McGuire, Joan Blondell, and James Dunne; *The Valley of Decision*, with Greer Garson and Gregory Peck; and *Wilson*, with Alexander Knox.

Music

Cruising Down the River; Dig You Later—A Hubba-Hubba-Hubba; For Sentimental Reasons; Give Me the Simple Life; If I Loved You; It's a Grand Night for Singing; It Might as Well Be Spring; June Is Bustin' Out All Over; Laura; Let It Snow! Let It Snow! Let It Snow!; The More I See of You; On the Atchison, Topeka and the Santa Fe.

1946

The League of Nations (1920) disbanded (Apr. 18) at Geneva, Switzerland, and assigned its assets to the United Nations.

James Caesar Petrillo, president of the American Federation of Musicians, tried to force radio stations to replace recorded music with live music. The increasing use of mechanical music during the previous two decades was reflected in the decline in the employment of musicians. Petrillo's efforts were stymied by Congress which passed the Lea "anti-Petrillo" act, signed by President Truman Apr. 16 and later upheld by the United States Supreme Court.

The International Court of Justice of the United Nations, successor to the League of Nations' Permanent Court of International Justice, elected (Feb. 6) its first judges, fifteen in number. The first session was held Apr. 18 in The Hague, the permanent seat of the court.

A loan of $1,400,000,000 to France was negotiated in Washington between Secretary of State James Francis Byrnes and Leon Blum, special French emissary.

Atomic bomb tests were carried out at Bikini Atoll in the Pacific. The fourth bomb ever to be exploded was dropped (June 30) from a super-fortress airplane on an assortment of old battleships and vessels, among them several German warships, with animal life aboard; the fifth was set off (July 25) under water. Radio broadcast the sound of the explosions and the descriptions of the events by eye-witnesses.

Following the United States Supreme Court ruling (1944), Black people voted (July 2) for the first time in Mississippi Democratic primaries.

The Philippine Islands became a self-governing country, independent of the United States, with the establishment (July 4) of the Republic of the Philippines.

The late President Franklin Delano Roosevelt was absolved (July 20) of blame, by a vote of 8 to 2, by a Congressional investigating committee that was probing alleged American unpreparedness in the Japanese assault on Pearl Harbor.

Secretary of State James Francis Byrnes assailed (Aug. 15) at the Paris Peace Conference the "repeated abuse and misrepresentation" of the United States by Soviet Russia.

Two unarmed U.S. Army transport airplanes, flying from Austria to Italy, were shot down as they passed over Yugoslavia. Five American airmen were killed in the attack; others of the crews were arrested. The United States sent (Aug. 21) a 48-hour ultimatum to Belgrade demanding an explanation. No sooner were the surviving Americans released (Aug. 22) than a similar fate befell (Aug. 23) another unarmed United States plane of the same type. The Yugoslav government expressed its regrets over the incidents and promised indemnity for the lost lives and the damage.

In a speech in New York Secretary of Commerce Henry Agard Wallace censured (Sept. 12) the "get tough with Russia" policy; eight days later (Sept. 20) President Truman requested the Secretary's resignation. (Wallace resigned—and ran for President in 1948.)

General Pulaski Memorial Day (Oct. 11) was authorized by President Truman in honor of the Polish hero who died in 1779 from wounds received during the siege of Savannah.

The Damon Runyon Memorial Fund for Cancer Research was founded (Dec.) in New York. (Incorporated Feb. 18, 1947.)

John D. Rockefeller, Jr., offered (Dec. 11) the United Nations a six-block area, valued at $8,500,000, along the East River in New York as a site for the headquarters of its capital. The United Nations committee accepted (Dec. 12) the offer by a vote of 37 to 7.

The end of World War II was officially proclaimed (Dec. 31) by President Truman.

The Franklin Delano Roosevelt dime went into circulation. The coin was designed by John R. Sinnock. During World War II, nickel had been eliminated from the Jefferson-head five-cent piece and it was now composed of copper (56 percent), silver (35 percent), and manganese (9 percent).

Commemorative half-dollars were coined in honor of the African American educator Booker Taliaferro Washington. The coin bore the inscription "From Slave to Hall of Fame."

Pope Pius XII elevated (Feb. 18) three American Roman Catholic Archbishops to be cardinals: John Glennon of St. Louis, Francis Joseph Spellman of New York, and Samuel Stritch of Chicago. The pope also canonized (July 17) Frances Xavier Cabrini, American Roman Catholic nun of Italian birth who had died in Chicago, Dec. 22, 1917). She was the first American to be raised to sainthood.

Telephone service was installed on railroad trains.

Fire destroyed the La Salle Hotel, Chicago (June 25), with a loss of 61 lives, and the 15-floor Winecoff Hotel, Atlanta, Ga. (Dec. 7), with a loss of 121 lives.

An Army C-45 airplane crashed (May 20) into the 58th floor of the Bank of Manhattan building in Wall Street, New York, and killed five persons.

John L. Lewis's United Mine Workers union was readmitted (Jan. 25) to the American Federation of Labor.

President Truman predicted a prosperous year "if workers stay on their jobs," but strikes were plentiful throughout the year.

The American Mother of the Year, selected by the Golden Rule Foundation Mothers' Committee, was Mrs. Emma Clarissa Clement of Louisville, Ky. She was the granddaughter of a slave and the first of her race to be so honored.

Nobel prizes were awarded to six Americans: Percy W. Bridgman for physics; Dr. James B. Sumner, Dr. Wendell K. Stanley, and John H. Northrop for chemistry; Herman J. Muller for medicine and physiology, and John R. Mott for peace.

The Cincinnati and Brooklyn National League baseball clubs battled (Sept. 11) 19 innings at Brooklyn, New York, in a scoreless game that was terminated after 4 hours, 40 minutes because of darkness.

Deaths of the year included poet Countee Cullen (Jan. 9), Chief Justice Harlan F. Stone (Apr. 22), novelist Booth Tarkington (May 19), photographer Alfred Stieglitz (July 13), Army General Joseph Stilwell (Oct. 12), former New York Mayor Jimmy Walker (Nov. 18), and comedian W. C. Fields (Dec. 25).

In Print

Books of the year included *The Autobiography of William Allen White* (Pulitzer prize 1947); *Lor Weary's Castle*, by Robert Lowell (Pulitzer prize 1947); *Peace of Mind*, by Joshua Loth Liebman; *Scientists Against Time*, by Dr. James Phinney Baxter 3rd (Pulitzer prize 1947); and the fiction, *All the King's Men*, by Robert Penn Warren (Pulitzer prize 1947); *The Dark Wood*, by Christine Weston; *Foxes of Harrow*, by Frank Yerby; *The Miracle of the Bells*, by Russell Janney; and *The Snake Pit*, by Mary Jane Ward.

On Stage

The RCA Victor recording company pressed its one billionth phonograph record, John Philip Sousa's march, *Stars and Stripes Forever*.

Leo Sowerby was awarded the Pulitzer music prize for his choral composition *The Canticle of the Sun*.

Igor Stravinsky, the Russian composer who became an American citizen in Dec., 1945, had written a piece called *Ragtime* in 1920. He now produced what he called an *Ebony Concerto* for clarinet and swing band which received (Mar. 25) its premiere by Woody Herman's Band in New York at Carnegie Hall.

New York plays included *O Mistress Mine; Born Yesterday; Call Me Mister; Lady Windermere's Fan; Joan of Lorraine; Another Part of the Forest; Years Ago;* and *Burlesque*. Laurence Olivier and the Old Vic Theater Company of London appeared in repertory in *Henry IV, Parts I-II*, and other plays. Webster's Elizabethan play *The Duchess of Malfi* was revived. There was no 1947 Pulitzer prize for this year's drama. Musical productions included *Three to Make Ready; Annie Get Your Gun; Icetime;* and *Happy Birthday*.

Films

Motion pictures of the year included *Anna and the King of Siam*, with Irene Dunne and Rex Harrison; *The Best Years of Our Lives*, with Myrna Loy and Fredric March; *Caesar and Cleopatra*, with Claude Rains and Vivien Leigh; *The Green Years*, with Charles Coburn and Tom Drake; *Henry V*, with Laurence Olivier; *The Jolson Story*, with Larry Parks and William Demarest; *Notorious*, with Cary Grant, Ingrid Bergman, and Claude Rains; *The Postman Always Rings Twice*, with Lana Turner and John Garfield; *To Each His Own*, with Olivia de Havilland and John Lund; and *The Yearling*, with Gregory Peck and Jane Wyman.

Music

Come Rain or Come Shine; Five Minutes More; The Girl That I Marry; I Got the Sun in the Morning; Old Devil Moon; The Old Lamp-Lighter; Ole Buttermilk Sky; Tenderly; There's No Business Like Show Business; Zip-a-Dee-Do-Dah.

1947

$\mathscr{F}$or the first time in 14 years, Republicans controlled Congress, the 80th. The proceedings on the opening day (Jan. 3) were immediately halted by Republican opposition to the seating of Mississippi Democratic Senator-elect Theodore G. Bilbo on the grounds that he had won his election in a campaign based on white supremacy. Bilbo died (Aug. 31) in New Orleans and was never seated.

A new member was added (Jan. 6) to the Presidential Cabinet—a Secretary of Defense, unifying the Army and Navy commands. President Truman named (July 26) James Forrestal to the post.

President Truman appointed (Jan. 8) General George Catlett Marshall as Secretary of State in succession to James Francis Byrnes who had resigned.

The Speaker of the House of Representatives was designated (July 18) by Act of Congress in line of succession to the Presidency "if, by reason of death, resignation, removal from office, inability, or failure to qualify, there is neither President nor Vice President."

Disclosures before the House Investigating Committee on Un-American Activities were creating concern over the spread of Communist ideology in the United States. President Truman ordered (Mar. 22) an examination into the loyalty of all government employees. In testimony by Hollywood producers Louis B. Mayer, Jack Warner, and by director Sam Wood before the same Committee, it was claimed (Oct. 20) that at least a score of persons, chiefly writers, harbored Communist sympathies. The witnesses said that, nevertheless, motion pictures had not been used for subversive purposes.

Congress passed (June 20 by the House, June 23 by the Senate) over President Truman's veto (June 20) the Taft-Hartley Labor Act, a bill that restricted the power of organized labor.

Secretary of State Marshall announced (June 5) in a speech at Harvard University a government plan to aid the economic and military rehabilitation of Europe and China. This plan materialized as the Economic Co-operation Administration (Apr. 3, 1948) and was known as the Marshall Plan.

The Freedom Train, symbol of the 160th anniversary of the signing of the Constitution, was dedicated in Philadelphia before starting its 33,000 mile tour of the country. It contained 100 documents relating to the birth of the Republic.

The charred hulk of the old battleship *Oklahoma*, bombed first at Pearl Harbor, Hawaii, and later in atomic tests at Bikini Atoll, sank in the Pacific Ocean while it was being towed to Oakland, Calif., to be scrapped.

The United Nations adopted (Oct. 20) a flag at Flushing Meadow, New York. A blue field with a white polar map of the world embraced in twin olive branches, the ensign was first flown (Oct. 21) at the organization's temporary headquarters at Flushing Meadow and Lake Success, N.Y.

The first bodies of the American dead in World War II arrived in the United States—3,028 from the Pacific in San Francisco (Oct. 10); 6,248 from Europe in New York (Oct. 26).

As a result of a complicated election (Jan. 15) situation, Georgia had two governors; the incumbent, Ellis G. Arnall, and Herman Talmadge, son of the late Governor-elect Eugene Talmadge. To resolve the dilemma, Arnall resigned (Jan. 19) and the Georgia Supreme Court designated Lieutenant Governor Melvin E. Thompson to the office.

Strikes by public employees and schoolteachers were outlawed in New York State by Governor Thomas E. Dewey (Mar. 27) with the penalty of dismissal for violations.

The last streetcars in Manhattan, New York City, stopped running; they were replaced by diesel-engine buses.

The annual convention of the American Legion in New York was climaxed by a parade of 52,000 veterans of World War I down Fifth Avenue. The procession, seen by 2,000,000 persons, took 12 hours to pass.

The Superior Court in Atlanta, Ga., revoked (June 13) the national charter of the Ku Klux Klan.

"Flying saucers" were seen in the sky during the summer in various parts of the United States. They have continued to appear from time to time ever since.

A strike of 2,400 teachers for higher salaries closed the public schools of Buffalo, N.Y., for seven days (Feb. 24-Mar. 3).

More than 300,000 telephone workers in 39 states walked out in the first country-wide strike in the industry's history. Long-distance service was cut 80 percent, but local service remained almost normal. The strike lasted 23 days (Apr. 7-30).

"We disaffiliate," wired (Dec. 12) John Llewellyn Lewis of the United Mine Workers to President William Green of the American Federation of Labor.

Rear-Admiral Richard Evelyn Byrd, while making his second flight over the South Pole, dropped (Feb. 16) the flags of all the United Nations. (His first flight was in 1929.)

In a converted twin-engine Army bomber plane Captain William P. Odom made (Apr. 12-16) a global trip of 20,000 miles from New York, flying via Paris, Cairo, Calcutta, Tokyo, Alaska, and Canada, in 78 hours, 55 minutes, 12 seconds. Captain Odom later completed a solo flight of 19,645 miles around the world in 63 hours, 15 minutes.

Grace Moore, American opera, radio, and screen star, and Prince Gustaf Adolf, second in line to the throne of Sweden, were among 22 killed when a KLM Royal Dutch airliner crashed (Jan. 26) and exploded outside Copenhagen, Denmark. A four-engine DC-4 burst (May 29) into flames at LaGuardia Field airport, New York, bringing death to 43 passengers and crew. Another DC-4 met (May 30) a similar fate at Port Deposit, Md., killing 53 passengers and members of the crew. A third DC-4 enroute from Chicago to Washington, D.C. crashed (June 14) in the Blue Ridge Mountains, W.Va.; all persons aboard lost their lives. An Army B-17 dropped (Aug. 17) into the Pacific causing the death of 10 persons, including George Atcheson, Jr., chairman of the Allied Control Commission in Japan and adviser to General Douglas MacArthur. A Los Angeles-New York bound United Air Lines plane plunged (Oct. 24) in flames into Bryce Canyon, Utah; all 52 passengers met their death. A private plane crash deprived (Oct. 29) Oregon of Governor Earl Snell, Senate President Marshall Cornett, and Secretary of State Robert S. Farrell, Jr.

A cyclone crossed (Apr. 10) the western part of Texas and Oklahoma killing 134 persons and injuring 1,300. A severe hurricane swept (Sept. 16-19) over Florida, Louisiana, and Mississippi, and took the lives of 100 persons. The Missouri River overflowed and inundated nearly a million acres of farmland. A heavy snowfall of 25.8 inches, the worst experienced in New York since the blizzard of 1888, blanketed (Dec. 27) the Eastern states from Maine to Washington, D.C., and halted railroad, airplane, and bus service.

President John L. Lewis of the United Mine Workers union closed (Mar. 29) all soft coal mines for six days in memory of the 111 miners who died (Mar. 25) in a gas-filled chamber as a result of a mine explosion in Centralia, Ill.

The waterfront and surrounding area of Texas City, Tex., was devastated (Apr. 16) when a nitrate-laden French freighter exploded at its wharf. Five hundred and twelve persons were killed, and property damage amounted to $50,000,000.

A sweeping forest fire destroyed (Oct. 23) a large section of Bar Harbor, Maine, and the surrounding country causing an estimated $30,000,000 property damage.

The signature of President Truman changed the name Boulder Dam to Hoover Dam in honor of the 31st President.

Colonel Jack W. Durant was sentenced to 15 years at hard labor and cashiered out of the Army by a U.S. Military Court in Frankfurt am Main, Germany, for his part in the theft of the $1,500,000 Hesse crown jewels in 1945.

The $6,450,000 damage suit by writer Konrad Bercovici against actor Charlie Chaplin for plagiarism was dismissed when the latter agreed to pay $95,000.

The "new look" in feminine fashions consisted of unusually full dresses that reached nearly to the wearer's ankles.

The Nobel prize for peace was awarded jointly to the American Friends Service Committee (Quakers) and the Friends Service Council, London.

Dr. A. S. W. Rosenbach, rare book dealer, paid $151,000 for a copy of the *Bay Psalm Book*, the first book printed in English colonies in America.

The Library of Congress opened (July 26) to the public the collection of 18,350 letters and documents of Abraham Lincoln bequeathed by his son Robert Todd Lincoln in 1926.

Additions to the National Gallery of Art, Washington, D.C., included 113 paintings, chiefly American, through the A. W. Mellon Educational and Charitable Trust, and loans and gifts from the Chester Dale Collection.

Mrs. Mildred "Babe" Didrickson Zaharias, champion golfer from Texas, defeated Jacqueline Gordon of London, in Scotland. She thus became the first American ever to win the British women's amateur golf championship.

In New York, more than 58,000 baseball fans roared a tribute to Babe Ruth, who was honored at Yankee Stadium in ceremonies attended by Francis Cardinal Spellman and Baseball Commissioner A. B. "Happy" Chandler.

Rocky Graziano, middleweight prize fighter, told a New York County grand jury that he had been offered $100,000 to throw a fight.

The New York Giants baseball team set a record of 221 home runs for a season.

Henry Ford, aged 83, died (Apr. 7) in Dearborn, Mich. He left an estate estimated between five and seven hundred million dollars.

Deaths of the year also included gangster Al Capone (Jan. 25) and New York Mayor Fiorello LaGuardia (Sept. 20).

In Print

Books of the year included *Across the Wide Missouri*, by Bernard DeVoto (Pulitzer prize 1948); *The Age of Anxiety*, by Wystan Hugh Auden (Pulitzer prize 1948); *Columbia Dictionary of Modern European Literature*, by Horatio Smith; *Forgotten First Citizen: John Bigelow*, by Margaret Clapp (Pulitzer prize 1948); *Geoffrey Chaucer of England*, by Marchette Chute; *Inside U.S.A.*, John Gunther; and the fiction, *The Apple Orchard*, by Jahn Kafka; *The Bishop's Mantle*, by Agnes Sligh Turnbull; *Came a Cavalier*, by Frances Parkinson Keyes; *Drums of Destiny*, by Graham Montague Jeffries; *Gentleman's Agreement*, by Laura Hobson; *House Divided*, by Ben Ames Williams; *Kingsblood Royal*, by Sinclair Lewis; *Lydia Bailey*, by Kenneth Roberts; *Marry for Money*, by Faith Baldwin; *The Moneyman*, by Thomas Bertram Costain; *Prince of Foxes*, by Samuel Shellabarger; *Tales of the South Pacific*, by James A. Michener (Pulitzer prize 1948); *Unconquered*, by Neil Harmon Swanson; *The Wayward Bus*, by John Steinbeck; *The Vixens*, by Frank Yerby; and *Yankee Pasha*, by Edison Marshall.

On Stage

Margaret Truman, daughter of the president, made her professional singing debut with the Detroit Symphony Orchestra.

New York plays included *All My Sons; John Loves Mary; A Young Man's Fancy; The Heiress; Command Decision; Man and Superman; Medea; The Winslow Boy; For Love or Money;* and *A Streetcar Named Desire* (Pulitzer prize 1948).

Katharine Cornell revived *Antony and Cleopatra*. Musical productions included: *Finian's Rainbow; Sweethearts; Brigadoon; Inside U.S.A.; High Button Shoes; Allegro; Angel in the Wings*.

Films

Motion pictures of the year included *Boomerang; Crossfire; Great Expectations; Life with Father*, with William Powell and Irene Dunne; *Miracle on 34th Street*, with Maureen O'Hara; and *Odd Man Out*.

Music

Almost Like Being in Love; But Beautiful; The Gentleman Is a Dope; Open the Door, Richard.

1948

$\mathscr{P}$aul G. Hoffman, president of the Studebaker automobile company, a Republican, was appointed (Apr. 5) Administrator of the Marshall Plan. Within nine hours after this confirmation, $21,000,000 was authorized for the relief of France, Italy, Greece, Austria, and the Netherlands. At a conference in Paris of the Foreign Ministers of Great Britain, France, and Russia, the Soviet Union attacked (July 2) the Marshall Plan as a scheme to gain control over smaller nations.

The military draft was renewed when Congress passed (June 12) the Selective Service Act.

The Senate unanimously approved the State Department's request for additional funds to enlarge the "Voice of America" radio programs that were designed to counteract Soviet Union propaganda.

The House Un-American Activities Committee reported that microfilm copies of "documents of tremendous importance" had been removed from state Department files and given to "Russian communist agents." The microfilms were found in a hollowed-out pumpkin at the Westminster, Md. farm of Whittaker Chambers, New York magazine editor, who previously had accused Alger Hiss, former State Department official, of passing the documents to him. (The Hiss case has been a source of controversy in the news to the present day.)

Indictments were brought (July 30) in New York against William Z. Foster, national chairman of the American Communist Party, and 11 party leaders on charges of conspiring to overthrow the U.S. government. The case against Foster was dropped because he was ill. The others were convicted on Oct. 14, 1949, after a nine-month jury trial before Federal Judge Harold R. Medina in New York. All but one were sentenced to five years in prison. The last, a war veteran, received three years.

The U.S. Post Office issued twenty-nine separate three-cent postage stamps in honor of noted American historical events and national movements. Americans so honored were Dr. George Washington Carver, Elizabeth Stanton, Carrie Chapman Catt, Lucretia Mott, William Allen White, Francis Scott Key, Harlan Fiske Stone, Clara Barton, Juliette Gordon Low, Will Rogers, Moina Michael (founder of the Memorial Poppy movement), and Joel Chandler Harris (author of the Uncle Remus stories). The Gold Star Mothers of America also were honored.

The third anniversary of the death (Apr. 12) of Franklin Delano Roosevelt was observed in London with the unveiling by his widow of a statue in Grosvenor Park. The entire Royal Family and Winston Churchill attended.

A Russian schoolteacher who was sought as a witness by the House Un-American Activities Committee leaped (Aug. 12) from the third-floor window of the Soviet Consulate in New York. The woman accused Soviet Consul General Jacob M. Lomakin of confining her in the building as a prisoner. The State Department demanded (Aug. 20) the recall of the Consul General for violation of his diplomatic privileges.

New York City's traditional five-cent subway fare was raised to 10 cents.

President Walter P. Reuther of the United Automobile Workers (C.I.O.) union was seriously wounded (Apr. 20) by a blast from a shotgun fired through the kitchen window of his house in Detroit. Rewards aggregating $117,000 were offered, but the assailant was not found.

On the same day, President John Llewellyn Lewis of the United Mine Workers and his union were fined by a Federal court for ignoring an injunction against a strike (Mar. 15-Apr. 22) by 350,000 soft coal miners.

In commemoration of the first New York-to-Washington air mail flight in 1918, which had taken 194 minutes, two jet-propelled P-80 Shooting Star fighter planes, flying in opposite directions, covered the same route in 27 minutes.

On Kitty Hawk Day, the 45th anniversary of the first flight by the Wright brothers in a heavier-than-air flying machine, Lawrence D. Bell, producer of the rocket plane X-1, the first plane to fly faster than sound, predicted that in the near future planes two or three times as fast as the X-1 would be built. The X-1 attained speeds exceeding 700 miles per hour, the speed of sound at sea level.

The world's largest telescope, on Mt. Palomar, 66 miles north of San Diego, Calif., was dedicated (June 3) and named the Hale Telescope in honor of the astronomer, George Ellery Hale.

The 4,900-acre International Airport at Idlewild, Queens County, N.Y., was dedicated (July 31) by President Truman.

The ban placed by James C. Petrillo, president of the American Federation of Musicians, on the making of commercial master recordings went into effect at midnight, Jan. 1, when the contract with 771 recording companies expired. "We're never going to make records, ever," said Petrillo. (He was forced to reverse himself 15 months later.)

Dr. Peter Goldmark of the Columbia Broadcasting System, Inc., New York, demonstrated (June 21) his "long-playing" (LP) microgroove phonograph record.

Babe Ruth made (July 26) his last public appearance, at the initial showing in New York of the motion picture *The Babe Ruth Story*. He died (Aug. 16) of cancer in Memorial Hospital, New York.

Citation was the race horse of the year, winning 25 of his 27 races, including the Kentucky Derby, the Preakness, and the Belmont Stakes. In the Pimlico Special, he galloped alone around the track; no other horse was regarded his equal.

In the national elections, President Truman opposed New York Governor Thomas E. Dewey and, as in the Roosevelt-Landon campaign of 1936, all predictions pointed to the defeat of the Democratic incumbent and the election of the Republican nominee. Again the polls reversed expectations. President Truman carried 28 states with 304 electoral votes; Dewey 16 States with 189 electoral votes. Dewey ran 36,213 votes behind his 1944 campaign against Roosevelt.

Deaths of the year included aviator Orville Wright (Jan. 30), Army General John Pershing (July 15), film director D. W. Griffith (July 23), Chief Justice Charles Evans Hughes (Aug. 27), and historian Charles Beard (Sept. 1).

In Print

Books of the year included *Crusade in Europe*, by General Dwight David Eisenhower; *The Disruption of American Democracy*, by Roy F. Nichols (Pulitzer prize 1949); *How to Stop Worrying and Start Living*, by Dale Carnegie; *Jefferson, the Virginian*, by Dumas Malone, Vol. 1; *The Life and Times of the Shmoo*, by Al Capp; *Roosevelt and Hopkins*, by Robert E. Sherwood (Pulitzer prize 1949); *The Seven Story Mountain*, by Thomas Merton; *Terror and Decorum*, by Peter Viereck (Pulitzer prize 1949); *Wine, Woman and Words*, by Billy Rose; and the fiction, *The Big Fisherman*, by Lloyd Cassel Douglas; *Dinner at Antoine's*, by Frances Parkinson Keyes; *The Golden Hawk*, by Frank Yerby; *Guard of Honor*, by James Gould Cozzens (Pulitzer prize 1949); *The Naked and the Dead*, by Norman Mailer; *Pilgrim's Inn*, by Elizabeth Goudge; *Raintree County*, by Ross Franklin Lockridge; *Shannon's Way*, by Archibald Joseph Cronin; *Tomorrow Will Be Better*, by Betty Smith; and *The Young Lions*, by Irwin Shaw.

On Stage

New York plays that ran over 200 performances included *Strange Bedfellows; The Respectful Prostitute; Mister Roberts; The Play's the Thing; Edward, My Son; Private Lives; Life with Mother; Goodbye, My Fancy; Light Up the Sky; The Silver Whistle; Anne of the Thousand Days;* and *The Madwoman of Chaillot.* Musical productions included *Make Mine Manhattan; Inside U.S.A.; Howdy, Mr. Ice!; Love Life; Where's Charley?; As the Girls Go; Lend an Ear;* and *Kiss Me, Kate.*

Films

Motion pictures of the year included *Apartment for Peggy; Easter Parade; A Foreign Affair; Hamlet,* with Laurence Olivier; *I Remember Mama; Johnny Belinda,* with Jane Wyman and Lew Ayres; *Paisan; Portrait of Jenny; Red River; The Snake Pit; Sorry, Wrong Number;* and *Treasure of the Sierra Madre,* with Humphrey Bogart.

Television

All four networks provided (Nov. 2) election coverage for the first time, and ABC produced (Nov. 29) a live broadcast from the New York Metropolitan Opera. *The Ed Sullivan Show* (CBS), *Philco Television Playhouse* (NBC) and Milton Berle (NBC) made their debuts that season. *Pantomime Quiz Time* on KTLA won an Emmy for the most popular TV program.

The first telecast of a major American Symphony orchestra took place (Mar. 20). By coincidence, the Philadelphia Symphony under Eugene Ormandy at the Academy of Music, Philadelphia, was put on the air by cable to New York on WCBS-TV at 5:30 p.m.; the NBC Symphony, in an all-Wagner program under the 81-year-old Arturo Toscanini, went on the air in New York on WNBC an hour later, at 6:30 p.m.

Opera was televised (Nov. 29) for the first time from the stage of the Metropolitan Opera House, New York, when the National Broadcasting Company transmitted Verdi's *Otello*, performed on the opening night of the season.

Music

"A"—*You're Adorable; Baby, It's Cold Outside; Buttons and Bows; Enjoy Yourself—It's Later Than You Think; It's Magic; Manana—Is Soon Enough for Me; Once in Love with Amy; Tennessee Waltz; You're Breaking My Heart.*

1949

$\mathscr{P}$resident Truman began his second term. For the first time the nation was able not only to hear the inaugural address by radio but to see the parade and ceremonies (Jan. 20) on television.

In appreciation of the gift-laden Friendship Train shipped to France in the preceding year by the American people, the French sent a Gratitude Train of 49 provisioned boxcars, one for each state and the District of Columbia. A rousing welcome in New York greeted (Feb. 2) the arrival of the freighter *Magellan*, which transported the train.

A temporary period of coffee hoarding began (Oct. 26) when imports of the commodity sharply declined because of crop failures in Central and South American countries.

Mildred E. Gillars, "Axis Sally," who had broadcast Nazi propaganda from Germany to the United States and to GI's in Europe and Africa during World War II, was sentenced (Mar. 25) to prison for 10 to 30 years and fined $10,000 for treason.

A referendum in Kansas resulted (June 6) in the repeal of the state constitution's 69-year-old prohibition amendment.

A December shortage of water in New York made it necessary for inhabitants to observe shaveless and bathless days. The flushing of sidewalks and the washing of automobiles were banned by the city's legislators.

A 16-ton truck that was illegally transporting carbon disulphide exploded (May 13) in the Holland Tunnel under the Hudson River. Sixty-three persons suffered injuries, and 23 trucks and vehicles were damaged.

An arsonist caused (Sept. 13) a $250,000 damage to the "Million Dollar Pier" in Atlantic City, N.J.

The American airlift into Berlin set a new record by flying in 12,940 short tons of supplies on 1,398 flights during a 24-hour period. The previous record was 8,246 tons.

According to the United States Weather Bureau, the country was hit by 290 tornadoes—the highest number in American history. Severe blizzards isolated 2,000,000 cattle and sheep in snowbound areas in Western states. The U.S. Air Force instituted (Jan. 24) "Operation Haylift," sending seventeen C-82 "Flying Boxcars" over the territory to drop five tons each of hay to the stranded livestock. Large sections of New England, New York, and New Jersey were inundated by the flooding of swollen rivers. Damage was estimated at $2,500,00 and several hundred families were left homeless. A record freezing spell with temperatures down to 14 degrees hit Southern California and destroyed one-fifth of the $100,000,000 citrus fruit crop.

Albert Schweitzer, philosopher, medical missionary, organist, and writer, made a brief visit from Equatorial Africa to the United States to deliver a lecture on Goethe at Aspen, Colo., at a celebration of the 200th anniversary of the great German poet's death.

Vaudeville returned (May 19) to the Palace Theater, New York, after an absence of 14 years.

Ralph Kiner, left fielder of the Pittsburgh Pirates, had his best season as a batsman, hitting 54 home runs.

Joe Louis, undefeated heavyweight boxing champion, retired from the ring. Louis, whose real name was Joseph Barrow, was the victor in 60 bouts, of which he won 51 by knockouts and 9 by decision.

Deaths of the year included actor Wallace Beery (Apr. 15), Justice Wiley Rutledge (Sept. 10), and former Secretary of State Edward Stettinius (Oct. 31).

In Print

Books of the year included *John Quincy Adams and the Foundations of American Foreign Policy*, by Samuel Flagg Bemis (Pulitzer prize 1950); *Annie Allen*, by Gwendolyn Brook (Pulitzer prize 1950); *Art and Life in America*, by O. W. Larkin (Pulitzer prize 1950); *Father Flanagan of Boys Town*, by Fulton and Will Oursler; *Peace of Soul*, by Fulton John Sheen; *Shakespeare of London*, by Marchette Chute; *This I Remember*, by Eleanor Roosevelt; and the fiction, *The Brave Bulls*, by Tom Lea; *The Chain*, by Paul Iselin Wellman; *Cutlass Empire*, by Van Wyck Mason; *The Egyptian*, by Mika Waltari; *Father of the Bride*, by Edward Streeter; *The Greatest Story Ever Told*, by Fulton Oursler; *High Towers*, by Thomas Bertram Costain; *Kinfolk*, by Pearl Buck; *Let Love Come Last*, by Taylor Caldwell; *Mary*, by Sholem Asch; *Point of No Return*, by John Phillips Marquand; *Pride's Castle*, by Frank Yerby; *A Rage to Live*, by John O'Hara; *The Road Between*, by James Thomas Farrell; and *The Way West*, by A. B. Guthrie, Jr. (Pulitzer prize 1950).

On Stage

Virgil Thomson was awarded the Pulitzer music prize for his orchestral suite from his incidental music to the motion picture *Louisiana Story*.

Troubled Island, an opera by William Grant Still, received (Mar. 31) its premiere in New York at the City Center of Music and Drama.

Roland Petit's Les Ballets de Paris (Winter Garden, Oct. 6) featured a bold, sensual dance version of Bizet's opera *Carmen*. The Sadler's Wells Ballet from the Royal Opera House, London (Metropolitan Opera House, Oct. 9-Nov. 6) also performed.

New York plays included *Diamond Lil; Death of a Salesman* (Pulitzer prize 1949); *Detective Story; I Know My Love;* and *Clutterbuck*. Musical productions included *Along Fifth Avenue; South Pacific* (Pulitzer prize 1950); *Miss Liberty; Touch and Go; Lost in the Stars; Texas Li'l Darlin';* and *Gentlemen Prefer Blondes.* Daniel Cordoba's *Seven Years in Spain* was also performed in New York.

Television

The first televised charity fund raiser, *The Damon Runyon Memorial Fund,* was hosted (Apr. 9) by Milton Berle. KTTV's *The Ed Wynn Show* won an Emmy for the best live program, and *Texaco Star Theater* was the top rated show.

Films

Motion pictures of the year included *All the King's Men,* with Broderick Crawford and Mercedes McCambridge; *The Barkleys of Broadway; The Champion,* with Kirk Douglas; *Dancing in the Dark; Francis,* with Donald O'Connor; *The Hasty Heart; The Heiress,* with Olivia de Havilland; *I Was a Male War Bride,* with Cary Grant and Rosalind Russell; *Letter to Three Wives,* with Linda Darnell, Ann Sothern, and Jeanne Crain; *On the Town; Samson and Delilah,* with Victor Mature and Hedy Lamarr; *Sands of Iwo Jima,* with John Wayne; *The Stratton Story,* with James Stewart; *They Live by Night;* and *Twelve O'Clock High,* with Gregory Peck.

Music

Bali Ha'i; Bibbidi-Bobbidi-Boo; The Cry of the Wild Goose; Daddy's Little Girl; Dear Hearts and Gentle People; Diamonds Are a Girl's Best Friend; Don't Cry, Joe; I've Got a Lovely Bunch of Coconuts; Mule Train; My Foolish Heart; Some Enchanted Evening; Rudolph the Red-Nosed Reindeer.

1950

*O*n June 24, armed forces of the People's Republic of Korea invaded the Republic of Korea. The United Nations Security Council declared the action a breach of the peace and called upon all its members for support. General of the U.S. Army Douglas MacArthur was appointed (July 8) commander of all U.N. forces in Korea. After 83 days of losses, a powerful offensive, supported by American and British warships and planes, pushed the enemy north, beyond the 38th Parallel. There they were joined (Nov.) by the Communist troops of the People's Republic of China.

President Truman authorized (Jan. 31) the continuation of work by the Atomic Energy Commission on a new bomb, the "H" or hydrogen bomb. Twelve leading American physicists protested (Feb. 4) in New York against the use of atomic energy as "a weapon of war."

Two Puerto Rican Nationalists attempted (Nov. 1) to assassinate President Truman at Blair House in Washington, D.C. They were immediately shot down, but not before one of the President's guards was killed and two others were seriously injured.

The United States severed diplomatic relations (Feb. 21) with Communist-ruled Bulgaria over indignities inflicted on members and employees at the American legation in Sofia.

Russians shot down (Apr. 8) an unarmed U.S. Navy Privateer airplane in the Baltic while the plane was on a training flight from Wiesbaden, Germany, to Copenhagen, Denmark. The Russian government contended that the plane flew over Latvia "to photograph Soviet defense installations." The United States vigorously denied the allegation and conferred (Apr. 25) the Distinguished Flying Cross posthumously on the 10 lost members of the plane.

After 64 years, the federal tax on oleomargarine was repealed (Jan. 18) by the Senate.

The National Capitol was 150 years old. In honor of the event, the U.S. Post Office issued (Apr. 20, June 12, and Nov. 23) three special commemorative postage stamps.

Congress passed (Sept. 23), over President Truman's veto, the Internal Security Act, compelling Communists and totalitarians to register with the Department of Justice, excluding them from Federal and defense employment, and denying them passport privileges.

The Senate, after a closely contested vote (35 to 35, broken by Vice President Alben W. Barkley), formed (May 3) a five-man committee under the chairmanship of Tennessee Senator Estes Kefauver to investigate organized interstate crime; $150,000 was appropriated for the purpose. When the committee began (Oct. 12) its inquiry into crime in the New York area, sensational disclosures implicated persons in high positions as well as police officials, racketeers, and gangsters.

United Nations Day was designated (Oct. 24) by President Truman.

Prime Minister Liaquat Ali Khan of Pakistan and his wife, the Begum Shaiba, visited the United States. They were received (May 3) in Washington by President Truman.

Dr. Wallace E. Howell, director of Mt. Washington Observatory, N.H., was engaged (Mar. 14) at a fee of $100 per day to conduct a six-month experiment in artificial rain-making over the Catskill reservoir area. In the first attempt (Apr. 12), the clouds were "seeded" with 100 pounds of dry ice; in the second attempt (Apr. 13), they were sprayed with silver iodide and a five-hour snowstorm occurred (Apr. 14). Dr. Howell disclaimed credit for this act of nature.

The U.S. Post Office issued (Jan. 27) a special three-cent purple postage stamp with the portrait of the noted labor leader Samuel Gompers.

The fastest ocean-going passenger ship ever to be built in the United States, the 26,000-ton liner *Independence*, was launched (June 3) at Quincy, Mass.

New York City's worst railroad wreck occurred on Thanksgiving eve, Nov. 22, when an eastbound express train of the Long Island Railroad plowed into a stalled passenger train in Richmond Hill, Queens, L.I. It was 6:26 p.m. and the trains were carrying about 2,000 homeward-bound commuters; 78 persons were killed and hundreds injured. Previously (Feb. 17), a head-on collision on the same railroad near Rockville Center caused the death of 32 persons and injury to 100.

A Pan American World Airways Stratocruiser set (Apr. 28) a new transatlantic record from New York to London, flying 3,565 miles in 9 hours, 16 minutes.

Connie Mack (born Cornelius McGillicuddy), manager of the Philadelphia Athletics, retired (Oct. 18) after 67 years in the sport, 50 of which he spent with the Philadelphia club. He won nine American League championships and five World Series.

Joe Louis, undefeated heavyweight boxing champion who had retired form the ring in the preceding year, attempted a comeback and was defeated (Sept. 27) by Ezzard Charles in 15 rounds in New York—Louis's first defeat since winning the title.

George Bernard Shaw, aged 94, died (Nov. 2) in Ayot St. Lawrence, England.

The national population was 150,697,361. The five largest cities were: New York, 7,835,099; Chicago, 3,606,436; Philadelphia, 2,064,794; Los Angeles, 1,957,692; and Detroit, 1,838,517.

Deaths of the year also included Air Force General Henry Arnold (Jan. 15), engineer Karl Jansky (Feb. 14), physiologist George R. Minot (Feb: 25), writer Edgar Lee Masters (Mar. 5), poet Edna St. Vincent Millay (Oct. 19), Secretary of War Henry L. Stimson (Oct. 20), and singer Al Jolson (Oct. 23).

In Print

Books of the year included *John C. Calhoun: American Portrait,* by Margaret Louise Colt (Pulitzer prize 1951); *Complete Poems,* by Carl Sandburg (Pulitzer prize 1951); *Kon-Tiki; Across the Pacific by Raft,* by Thor Heyerdahl; *Listen for a Lonesome Drum,* by Carl Lamson Carmer; *Roosevelt in Retrospect,* by John Gunther; and the fiction, *The Cardinal,* by Henry Morton Robinson; *The Disenchanted,* by Budd Schulberg; *Floodtide,* by Frank Yerby; *Joy Street,* by Frances Parkinson Keyes; *The Little Princesses,* by Marion Crawford; *River of the Sun,* by James Ramsey Ullman; *The Town,* by Conrad Richter (Pulitzer prize 1951); *Valley Forge,* by Van Wyck Mason; and *The Wall,* by John Richard Hersey.

On Stage

A surprise run of the year was the revival of Shakespeare's *As You Like It* with film star Katharine Hepburn, whose legs were much-photographed in stories about the play. The ballroom of the Hotel Edison was converted into a theater and opened (May 31) as New York's first theater-in-the-round or arena theater—a type of production new to the city but already familiar in Texas and the West. Long-run New York plays included *The Member of the Wedding; The Cocktail Party; The Happy Time; Peter Pan; Affairs of State;* and *Season in the Sun.* Musical productions included *Tickets, Please; Michael Todd's Peep Show; Call Me Madam;* and *Guys and Dolls.*

Films

Motion pictures of the year included *All About Eve,* with Bette Davis and Anne Baxter; *The Blue Angel,* with Marlene Dietrich; *Born Yesterday,* with Judy Holliday, William Holden, and Broderick Crawford; *Cyrano de Bergerac,* with Jose Ferrer; *The Halls of Montezuma, Kim,* with Errol Flynn and Dean Stockwell; *Kind Hearts and Coronets,* with Alec Guiness; *King Solomon's Mines,* with Deborah Kerr, Stewart Granger, and Richard Carlsen; *Macbeth,* with Orson Welles; *Mr. Music,* with Bing Crosby; *The Mudlark,* with Irene Dunne and Alec Guinness; *Pagan Love Song,* with Esther Williams and Howard Keel; *Rio Grande,* with John Wayne and Maureen O'Hara; *Stromboli,* with Ingrid Bergman; and *Vendetta,* with Faith Domergue.

Television

DuMont broadcast (Sept. 3) the *Miss Television U.S.A. Contest*, which was won by Edie Adams.

Comedian Jack Benny made his TV debut (Oct. 28), with Ken Murray as his first guest. *The Colgate Comedy Hour* on NBC and *Burns and Allen* on CBS made their debuts on the 1950-1951 schedule.

Walt Disney's first TV production, *One Hour In Wonderland* with Edgar Bergen and Charlie McCarthy, was shown (Dec. 25) on NBC. Groucho Marx on KNBH won an Emmy for most outstanding personality, and *Texaco Star Theater* was again the top-rated program.

The Federal Communications Commission, after several years of debate between the Columbia Broadcasting System and the Radio Corporation of America, granted (Oct. 11) the former the right to broadcast its form of color television. RCA then obtained (Nov. 25) a temporary restraining order from the Federal District Court in Chicago.

Music

Bolero; Autumn Leaves; A Bushel and a Peck; C'est Si Bon; Goodnight, Irene; If I Knew You Were Comin' I'd 'Ave Baked a Cake; It's So Nice to Have a Man Around the House; A Marshmallow World; Rag Mop; Sam's Song; The Third Man Theme; La Vie en Rose.

1951

*M*ilitary operations in Korea continued. Divergent views in the conduct of the war caused President Truman to relieve (Apr. 11) the outspokenly critical General Douglas MacArthur of his command—an act which raised a great deal of controversy—and to appoint General Matthew B. Ridgeway to the post.

General MacArthur made a "grand tour" on his way back home and spoke (Apr. 9) before the Senate and House of Representatives. His address was carried by television and radio to a nationwide audience. In his retirement speech he recalled from his days at West Point "the refrain of one of the most popular barracks ballads of that day, which proclaimed, most proudly, that old soldiers never die; they just fade away."

The 22nd Amendment (limiting the presidency to two terms) was added (Feb. 27) to the Constitution.

World War II ended officially for the United States with the signing of peace treaties with Japan (Sept. 8) and Germany (Oct. 19).

Four United States fliers were forced down (Nov. 19) in Hungary and arrested for border violation; they were released (Dec. 28) after the United States paid $120,000 in fines.

Julius Rosenberg, 35 and his wife Ethel, 37, were sentenced (Apr. 6) to death for treason, as spies, for supplying atom bomb information to Russia. After a great deal of public debate and legal maneuvering, they were executed on June 19, 1953, at Sing Sing Prison, Ossining, N.Y.

The United States Army ended (Feb. 9) a railroad strike by ordering the trainmen either to return to work or lose their jobs; pleading guilty to a "sick-out," the trainmen were fined $75,000.

Thirty-two year old San Diego, Calif., swimmer Florence Chadwick swam (Sept. 11) the English Channel from England to France. She was the first woman to swim both ways—she swam from France to England in 1950.

In an attempted comeback, former heavyweight boxing champion Joe Louis engaged in eight bouts, winning seven victories, but was TKO'd (Oct. 26) in New York by the rising Rocky Marciano in the eighth round, ending an outstanding ring career.

Deaths of the year included writer John Erskine (June 2), salt manufacturer Mark Morton (June 25), composer Arnold Schoenberg (July 13), and director Robert Flaherty (July 23).

In Print

Popular among books of fiction were *The Caine Mutiny,* by Herman Wouk (Pulitzer prize 1952); *The Catcher in the Rye,* by J. D. Salinger; *The Cruel Sea,* by Nicholas Monsarrat; *From Here to Eternity,* by James Jones; *God's Men,* by Pearl S. Buck; *Joy Street,* by Frances Parkinson Keyes; *Melville Goodwin, U.S.A.,* by John Marquand; *Moses,* by Scholem Asch; and *Requiem for a Nun,* by William Faulkner. Nonfiction best sellers included *The Man Called Peter,* by Catherine Marshall; and *The Sea Around Us,* by Rachel L. Carson. The first of Walt Kelly's series of *Pogo* books appeared.

The United States government, through the Government Printing Office, issued nearly half a billion copies of its publications. The best seller was the 15-cent booklet *Infant Care,* which passed the seven million mark. Runner-up was another 15-cent pamphlet, *Prenatal Care,* which sold four million copies. In third place was *Your Child—One to Six,* price 20 cents. A five-cent publication, *The Sex of Watermelons,* was completely sold out.

On Stage

The New York stage presented the plays *The Rose Tattoo; The Moon Is Blue; Stalag 17; The Fourposter; Gigi; I Am a Camera; Point of No Return; Two on the Aisle; Top Banana;* and *Paint Your Wagon.*

Films

Among motion pictures, the top-grossing film was *David and Bathsheba,* with Gregory Peck and Susan Hayward. Other pictures included *Showboat,* with Kathryn Grayson and Howard Keel; *An American in Paris,* with Gene Kelly; *The Great Caruso,* with Mario Lanza; *A Streetcar Named Desire,* with Vivien Leigh and Marlon Brando; and *Quo Vadis?,* with Deborah Kerr and Robert Taylor.

Television

CBS and NBC began (May 14) live coverage of the Kefauver Crime Commission hearings. President Truman's speech at the Japanese Peace Treaty Conference in San Francisco was covered (Sept. 4) by all four networks in the nation's first coast-to-coast telecast. The first network coverage of a National Football League championship game was provided (Dec. 23) by Du-Mont. NBC aired (Dec. 24) the first production of Gian Carlo Menotti's *Amahl and the Night Visitors. I Love Lucy* made its debut on CBS. Sid Caesar and Imogene Coca won Emmys for best actor and actress, and *Arthur Godfrey's Talent Scouts* was the most popular program.

CBS televised (June 25) the first full hour commercial program in color; the program was sponsored by sixteen national advertisers. (The telecasts were suspended on Oct. 19 at the request of the Director of Defense Mobilization "to conserve critical materials.")

The first transcontinental demonstration of a major heart operation on a 20-year-old youth, was telecast (Dec. 7) by CBS Color Television. The operation was performed successfully in Los Angeles by Dr. John C. Jones.

Music

Because of You; Come on-a My House; Cry; Half as Much; Hello, Young Lovers; I Talk to the Trees; I Whistle a Happy Tune; In the Cool, Cool, Cool of the Evening; Kisses Sweeter Than Wine; The Little White Cloud That Cried; Mockin' Bird Hill; My Truly, Truly Fair; On Top of Old Smokey; Please, Mr. Sun; Shrimp Boats; Sound Off; Sparrow in the Tree Top; Tell Me Why; Tennessee Waltz; Too Young; Undecided; Unforgettable; We Kiss in a Shadow.

1952

$\mathcal{T}$he war in Korea continued.

To prevent a strike by 60,000 C.I.O. steel workers, President Truman, ignoring the Labor Management Relations Act of 1947 (Taft-Hartley Act), ordered (Apr. 8) the Government's seizure and operation of the mills. The action was declared (Apr. 30) unconstitutional by the U.S. District Court, whereupon the workers walked out. They returned two days later when the U.S. Supreme Court accepted jurisdiction and restored the mills to Government control, pending its decision. By a vote of 6 to 3, the Supreme Court ruled (June 2) the seizure illegal and in violation of Article I of the Constitution—the first time that the Supreme Court passed on the inherent constitutional powers of a President. Following the ruling, the workers again walked out. United Mine Workers President John L. Lewis set up (June 18) a $10,000,000 fund for the support of the strikes, repayable "when you have achieved victory and convenience permits." The strike lasted 53 days, until July 25.

The Mississippi and Missouri rivers ravaged (Apr. 14) eight Midwestern States, driving more than 65,000 persons from their homes.

The U.S. Supreme Court ruled (May 26) that radio broadcasts to "captive" audiences on public buses are not an invasion of privacy.

A shortage of potatoes prevailed (May-June) throughout the country. Black market prices ranged from $5 to $8 per 100-lb. bag.

A late June heat wave topped local records everywhere, particularly in the East; in New York the thermometer rose to 104 degrees, causing the deaths of seven persons in one day. The heat struck Texas in August, taking a toll of 18 lives and costing about $68,000,000 in the destruction of crops.

President Truman approved (July 3) the newly framed constitution of Puerto Rico; the territory became (July 25) the first commonwealth of the United States.

Southern California suffered (July 21) its severest earthquake in 46 years, the effects of which were felt inland as far as Las Vegas, Nev., and Phoenix, Ariz. The mountain town of Tehachapi, Calif., where 11 persons were killed, was the focal point of the disaster, causing the Southern Pacific Railroad tunnel in the 7,000-foot-high Tehachapi Mountains to cave in.

The United States resumed diplomatic relations with Germany by signing (Aug. 2) a treaty of peace with the new West German Republic.

The nation's most treasured documents, the Declaration of Independence and the United States Constitution, were removed (Dec. 13) from the Library of Congress to their permanent home in the National Archives Building, in accordance with the Federal Records Act (1950). (The Bill of Rights had been transferred in 1938.)

The Chesapeake Bay Bridge, Md., was opened (July) as the world's third longest expressway, 4.3 miles in length.

The 53,300 ton, 990-foot long Atlantic superliner SS *United States*, costing $70,000,000, made (July 7) a record crossing on its maiden trip from New York to Le Havre in 3 days, 10 hours and 40 minutes, reducing by 10 hours and 2 minutes the 14-year-old record of the British Cunard liner Queen Elizabeth. The *United States* made the return trip on July 11 in the record time of 3 days, 12 hours and 12 minutes.

The New York Central railroad ran (Sept. 11) its last steam locomotive in passenger service.

American scientists of the Atomic Energy Commission conducted (Nov. 1) a thermonuclear test in the Marshall Islands, exploding a hydrogen bomb which tore a cavity in the floor of the Pacific measuring a mile in diameter and 175 feet in depth at its lowest point. The blast completely obliterated the Eniwetok atoll.

In cooperation with the American Medical Association, as part of its sixth annual clinical session in Denver, NBC televised (Dec. 2) the Caesarean birth of a baby.

Mars Hill (N.C.) College honored the slave, Joe, who in 1856 was posted as collateral for the final $1,000 of the school's building debt. His remains were moved to a resting place on the campus.

The year marked the quincentenary of the printing of the first Guttenberg Bible. To commemorate the event, the United States Post Office issued (Sept. 30) a special three-cent purple postage stamp. Two new English versions of the Bible for Catholics were published as well as the Old Testament in the National Council of Churches' Revised Standard Version.

The popular radio program *Amos 'n' Andy*, begun in 1929, reached (Nov. 16) its 10,000th broadcast.

"Overture to the Dedication of a Nuclear Reactor" by Arthur Roberts, Associate Professor of Physics at the University of Rochester and a graduate of the Manhattan School of Music in New York, was played (Mar. 19) by the Oak Ridge, Tenn., Symphony Orchestra under Waldo Cohn, its conductor and a biochemist. (The principal theme, played by clarinets with oboes as Geiger counters, was derived from the atomic number of uranium; plutonium was delineated by scale steps of nine and four, its atomic number 94; the Atomic Energy Commission was represented by the notes of its initials.)

Some 50,000 boxing fans in New York's Yankee Stadium saw (June 25) "Sugar" Ray Robinson, holder of the middle weight and welterweight titles, so exhausted and dazed by the extreme heat of the night that he was unable to respond to the bell in the 14th round of his bout with the light-heavyweight title holder, Joey Maxim. Robinson was attempting to become a triple-crown champion, a distinction held previously only by Robert "Bob" Fitzsimmons and Henry Armstrong. Referee Ruby Goldstein succumbed to the heat in the 10th round and was replaced by Ray Miller—the first time such an incident occurred.

In Philadelphia, "Rocky" Marciano defeated (Sept. 23) "Jersey Joe" Walcott in the 13th round for the heavyweight boxing championship. The bout was televised in a closed circuit to 125,000 paying spectators in 50 motion picture theaters across the country.

The United States maintained its supremacy in international sports events at the XVth Olympiad, held in Helsinki, Finland, by collecting 614 points in the face of strong opposition from 69 nations, especially from the Soviet Union. The Soviets, competing for the first time, achieved second place with 553 points.

For the first time television brought into American homes the national conventions of the two major political parties, each of which was held in Chicago (Republican, July 7-12; Democratic, July 21-26).

General Eisenhower retired from the United States Army after 37 years of service on July 18, and was free to accept the nomination for President. The Republican slogan was "I Like Ike." The Republicans broke (Nov. 5) the Democratic Party's 20-year hold on the White House, with Eisenhower's victory over Illinois Governor Adlai E. Stevenson. 61,547,861 citizens went to the polls—the largest number in history—giving Eisenhower a comfortable margin of 6,616,233 votes.

In accordance with his campaign promise, President-elect Eisenhower flew (Dec. 17) to Korea to review the military situation as a preliminary step to "bring the boys home."

Deaths of the year included former Interior Secretary Harold Ickes (Feb. 3), psychoanalyst Karen Horney (Deb. 4), producer William Fox (May 8), union leader William Green (Nov. 21), and restaurateur James "Dinty" Moore (Dec. 25).

In Print

Fiction was represented by *East of Eden*, by John Steinbeck; *Giant*, by Edna Ferber; *The Gown of Glory*, by Agnes Sligh Turnbull; *The Houses in Between*, by Howard Spring; *My Cousin Rachel*, by Daphne Du Maurier; *The Old Man and the Sea*, by Ernest Hemingway (Pulitzer prize 1953); *The Saracen Blade*, by Frank Yerby; and *The Silver Chalice*, by Thomas Costain. Prominent among nonfiction were such diverse publications as *Anne Frank: The Diary of a Young Girl; The Power of Positive Thinking*, by Norman Vincent Peale; *Show Biz*, by Abel Greene and Joe Laurie, Jr.; *U.S.A. Confidential*, by Jack Lait and Lee Mortimer; and *Witness*, by Whittaker Chambers.

On Stage

Broadway offerings included *The Shrike* (Pulitzer prize 1952); *Mrs. McThing; The Male Animal; The Time of the Cuckoo; Dial 'M' for Murder;* and *The Seven-Year Itch*. Beatrice Lillie entertained in an *Evening with Beatrice Lillie*. Competing with the long-running musicals *South Pacific, Guys and Dolls*, and *The King and I*, were *Pal Joey* and *Wish You Were Here*.

Distinguished foreign-language productions were provided by the Madeleine Renaud-Jean Louis Barrault Company of Paris and by Katina Paxinou's National Theater of Greece.

Under Government sponsorship, Gershwin's opera *Porgy and Bess* was performed in Europe on a tour which opened (Sept. 7) in Vienna.

Films

Among motion pictures, *The Greatest Show on Earth*, with Betty Hutton and Cornel Wilde proved to be the top money-grossing film. Other pictures included *Ivanhoe*, with Robert Taylor and Elizabeth Taylor; *The Snows of Kilimanjaro*, with Gregory Peck and Susan Hayward; *The African Queen*, with Humphrey Bogart and Katharine Hepburn; *Hans Christian Andersen*, with Danny Kaye; and *Come Back, Little Sheba*, with Shirley Booth and Burt Lancaster. The British film version of Offenbach's opera *The Tales of Hoffman*, starring Moira Shearer, was shown in theaters and on television.

Cinerama, a three-dimensional motion picture projection, was exhibited (Sept. 3) by its inventor Fred Waller in New York at the Broadway Theater. It had been used during World War II for training gunnery students in the Air Corps, and was then known as the Waller Flexible Gunnery Trainer.

Paying viewers in 31 motion picture houses in 27 American cities from coast to coast witnessed (Dec. 21) a closed-circuit telecast of a full-length presentation of Bizet's opera *Carmen* at the Metropolitan Opera House in New York.

Television

President Truman was seen and heard (May 3) on television by an estimated 30,000,000 people in a twenty-minute impromptu piano performance from the East Room of the White House. He played Mozart's Ninth Sonata. The event, an unexpected feature of a television tour of the Executive Mansion, was broadcast by the three major networks. The President had violated no union regulations—he had been made an honorary member of the American Federation of Musicians by its president James C. Petrillo several years before.

The first live coverage of the Kentucky Derby was broadcast (May 3) by CBS.

The four networks aired live coverage of the Republican National Convention (July 7-11) and Democratic National Convention (July 21-24).

Republican vice presidential candidate Richard Nixon appeared (Sept. 24) on CBS and NBC to give his "Checkers" speech.

The first of many operatic specials was broadcast when *NBC Opera Theater* presented (Oct. 19) "Billy Budd."

The Jackie Gleason Show made its debut on CBS, as did *The Adventures Of Ozzie and Harriet* on ABC.

Dragnet on NBC won an Emmy for best mystery, action or adventure program, and *See It Now* on CBS won an Emmy as the best public affairs program.

CBS's *I Love Lucy* was the top-rated program.

Music

Because You're Mine; The Blacksmith Blues; Blue Tango; Botch-a-Me; Count Your Blessings Instead of Sheep; Delicado; Don't Let the Stars Get in Your Eyes; The Gandy Dancers' Ball; Glow-Worm; A Guy Is a Guy; Here in My Heart; High Noon— Do Not Forsake Me; I Saw Mommy Kissing Santa Claus; Jambalaya—on the Bayou; Pretend; Takes Two to Tango; Till I Waltz Again with You; Wheel of Fortune; Why Don't You Believe Me; Wish You Were Here; You Belong to Me; Your Cheatin' Heart.

1953

$\mathcal{D}$wight David Eisenhower, Republican of Texas, was inaugurated as the 34th President.

The war in Korea entered its final stages. After repeated delays and disagreements, an armistice was signed (July 26, EST). According to the Department of Defense, 5,720,000 Americans were involved in the conflict. The total number of casualties in the four branches of the American armed services amounted to 157,530 (33,629 killed in action; 20,617 dead from other causes; 103,284 wounded).

Republican Senator Joseph Raymond McCarthy of Wisconsin, as chairman of the Senate Permanent Investigating Subcommittee, became a ruthless seeker of possible Communist connections of prominent Americans. His methods gave rise to the term "McCarthyism."

To rectify an 1803 oversight, the House Interior Committee voted (May 5) "to admit Ohio to the union."

The House Un-American Activities Committee subpoenaed (Nov. 6) ex-President Truman to answer Attorney General Herbert Brownell's charge that Truman had appointed the late Harry Dexter White—whom the FBI claimed was a spy for the Soviet Union—to be executive director of the International Monetary Fund. President Eisenhower opposed (Nov. 11) the subpoena, on the basis that Truman would not knowingly have committed an act detrimental to the United States. Truman rejected (Nov. 12) the subpoena, contending that the order was an invasion of Presidential powers by a "trespassing" Congress. Official records showed that the appointment had been confirmed without debate by the Senate in 1946.

An eleven-day strike of about 400 photoengravers in New York caused (Nov. 28-Dec. 9) six major metropolitan newspapers to suspend publication; about 20,000 other newspaper workers refused to cross the picket lines.

The Bureau of the Mint issued a commemorative half-dollar piece in honor of Booker Taliaferro Washington and George Washington Carver.

Sagamore Hill, the summer home of the 26th President, Theodore Roosevelt, at Oyster Bay, Long Island, N.Y., was dedicated (June 14) as a national shrine by President Eisenhower.

General George C. Marshall received the Nobel prize for peace.

The game "Scrabble," devised about 20 years earlier by Alfred Butts, was now a popular pastime.

Be defeating the Brooklyn Dodgers, four games to two, the New York Yankees became the first baseball team to win five successive world championships.

Deaths of the year included: singer Hank Williams (Jan. 1); society leader Mrs. Cornelius Vanderbilt (Jan. 7); former heavyweight boxing champion James J. "Jim" Jeffries, 77 (Mar. 3); athlete Jim Thorpe (Mar. 28); Senator Robert F. Wagner (May 4); tennis star "Big Bill" Tilden (June 5); Julius and Ethel Rosenberg (June 19); actress Maude Adams 80 (July 17); Army General Jonathan Wainwright (Sept. 2); Chief Justice Frederick M. Vinson (Sept. 8); painter John Marin (Oct. 1); America's leading playwright Eugene Gladstone O'Neill 65 (Nov. 27); novelist Majorie Kinnan Rawlings (Dec 14); and physicist Robert Millikan (Dec. 19).

Joseph V. Stalin, Premier of the Soviet Union, died (Mar. 5), aged 73, in the Kremlin in Moscow and was buried beside his predecessor, Lenin, in the latter's tomb in Red Square. Known as the "Man of Steel," he was dictator for 29 years.

In Print

Among books, continuing as best sellers from the previous year, were *The Power of Positive Thinking; A Man Called Peter; The Silver Chalice;* the new Revised Standard Version of the Bible; *Life Is Worth Living,* by Fulton J. Sheen; and *The Greatest Faith Ever Known,* by Fulton Oursler—the sales of the last three then carried over into the following year. Fiction included *Battle Cry,* by Leon M. Uris; *Beyond This Place,* by A. J. Cronin; *The Bridges of Toko-Ri,* by James Michener; *Come, My Beloved,* by Pearl S. Buck; *Desiree,* by Annemarie Selinko; *The High and the Mighty,* by Ernest K. Gann; *The Robe,* by Lloyd Douglas; *Too Late the Phalarope,* by Alan Paton; *Time and Time Again,* by James Hilton; and *The Unconquered,* by Ben Ames Williams.

On Stage

The New York Metropolitan Opera House produced (Feb. 14) the American premiere of Igor Stravinsky's English opera *The Rake's Progress.*

The Broadway stage produced, among other plays *The Fifth Season; Picnic* (Pulitzer prize 1953); *My Three Angels; Tea and Sympathy; The Teahouse of the August Moon* (Pulitzer prize 1954); *The Solid Gold Cadillac; Sabrina Fair; Oh Men! Oh, Women!;* and *The Remarkable Mr. Pennypacker.* An off-Broadway production to enjoy a run was *The World of Sholom Aleichem.* The musicals included *Hazel Flagg; Wonderful Town; Can-Can; Me and Juliet; Kismet;* and *John Murray Anderson's Almanac.* Pianist Victor Borge delighted audiences with his one-man show *Comedy in Music* until Jan. 21, 1956. A revival of Gershwin's *Porgy and Bess* featured the soprano Leontyne Price of future New York Metropolitan Opera fame.

Films

In films, following Cinerama (1952), the motion picture industry exhibited other processes of wide-screen projection, in *Bwana Devil* (3-dimension

Natural Vision), *The Man in the Dark* (3-D film), and *The Robe* (CinemaScope). *The Robe*, with Richard Burton, Jean Simmons, and Victor Mature, based on the year's best selling novel, rose to top money in films. Other pictures included: *The Band Wagon*, with Fred Astaire; *Call Me Madam*, with Ethel Merman; *From Here to Eternity*, with Montgomery Clift, Burt Lancaster, Deborah Kerr, and Frank Sinatra; *Gentlemen Prefer Blondes*, with Marilyn Monroe and Jane Russell; *How to Marry a Millionaire*, with Marilyn Monroe, Betty Grable, and Lauren Bacall; *Julius Caesar*; *Lili*, with Leslie Caron; *Moulin Rouge*, with Jose Ferrer; *Peter Pan* (Walt Disney cartoon); *Shane*, with Alan Ladd and Van Heflin; and *Victory at Sea*. The Lutheran-sponsored *Martin Luther*, with Niall MacGinis was quite controversial.

Television

ABC and CBS broadcast (Mar. 1) *Answer The Call*, a special appeal by the American Red Cross featuring President Eisenhower and a number of celebrities.

A few weeks later, NBC presented (Mar. 19) the first coast-to-coast broadcast of the Academy Awards, with Bob Hope as host.

CBS and NBC covered (June 2) the coronation of Queen Elizabeth II.

Edward R. Morrow hosted (Nov. 15) a tour of Television City, CBS's new West Coast production facility.

Make Room For Daddy began its run on ABC and won an Emmy for best new program, as did *The U.S. Steel Hour* on ABC. *I Love Lucy* took its second consecutive Emmy for best situation comedy and was the nation's top-ranked program.

The controversy over the transmission of color resolved itself in favor of the "compatible" color system of RCA, when CBS withdrew (Mar.) its process. The CBS method required a special mechanism for transforming color into black and white in television sets unequipped to receive color; that of RCA made reception available either in color or in black and white.

Music

And This Is My Beloved; April in Portugal; Baubles, Bangles and Beads; C'est Magnifique; Change Partners; Crying in the Chapel; Dragnet; Ebb Tide; Eh, Cumpari!; Hi-Lili, Hi-Lo; I Believe; I Love Paris; Istanbul; It's All Right with Me; No Other Love; Oh! My Pa-pa; Rags to Riches; Rock Around the Clock; Ruby; Say You're Mine Again; Secret Love; The Song from Moulin Rouge—Where Is Your Heart; Stranger in Paradise; That Doggie in the Window; That's Amore; Vaya con Dios; You, You, You.

1954

$\mathcal{T}$he United States launched the world's first atom-powered submarine (Jan. 21)—the 2,800 ton 300-foot *Nautilus*, at Groton, Conn., as well as the world's largest war vessel (Dec. 11)—the 59,650-ton aircraft carrier *Forrestal*, at Newport News, Va.

Four terrorists, three men and a woman, of the Puerto Rican "Nationalist" independence movement, fired (Mar. 1) a volley of bullets from the Ladies Gallery in the House of Representatives in Washington, D.C., during the morning session, wounding five Congressmen.

The Atomic Energy Commission conducted (Mar. 1, Mar. 26, Apr. 6) thermonuclear tests at Pacific Proving Grounds on Bikini Atoll, Marshall Islands. 31 Americans, 236 natives, and 23 Japanese fishermen in the area received injuries from radioactive particles during the first experiment. The United States offered Japan an indemnity of $800,000 for the harm to her nationals.

Rival longshoremen unions tied up (Mar. 5-Apr. 3) the port of New York in the longest strike in the city's history, resulting in a loss of $500,000,000 to the shipping industry.

In a unanimous decision, the nine judges of the United States Supreme Court ruled (May 17) racial segregation unconstitutional in public schools in the *Brown vs. Board of Education* case.

A spectacular air-raid drill with squadrons of airplanes dropping theoretical bombs involved (June 14) the United States, Hawaii, Alaska, Puerto Rico, the Virgin Islands and ten provinces of Canada in the world's largest demonstration of its kind.

Migratory labor became an acute problem in California and Texas as Mexican farm laborers illegally entered the United States in quest of the few available jobs. A roundup in June netted some 55,000 illegal aliens in California.

The Communist Control Act outlawed (Aug. 24) the Communist party in the United States.

Chinese Communist bombing planes, shelling Nationalist-controlled Formosa, killed (Sept. 3) two U.S. Army officers on Quemoy Island.

The Senate rebuked (Dec. 2) by a vote of 67 to 22, Republican Senator Joseph R. McCarthy of Wisconsin for his tactics and behavior as chairman of the public hearings (Apr. 22-June 27) by the Senate Permanent Investigating subcommittee of U.S. Army Department officials. His influence and "McCarthyism" waned following the Senate's vote.

Violent Caribbean hurricanes blazed paths of destruction and death across the Atlantic states. Then named exclusively for women, the hurricanes were called "Carol" (Aug. 30-31), "Edna" (Sept. 11), and "Hazel" (Oct. 15-16).

A 75-foot statue by sculptor Felix de Weldon, depicting the flag raising on Iwo Island in the Pacific during World War II, was dedicated (Nov. 10) in Arlington National Cemetery, in honor of the U.S. Marine Corps.

A controversy arose over the effects of cigarette-smoking as a possible cause of lung cancer.

Novelist Ernest Hemingway and his wife were injured (Jan. 24) in East Africa, when a rescue plane crashed on takeoff at Butiaba, on Lake Albert, after their own plane had crashed the day before near Murchson Falls.

McCall's magazine coined, in the editorial of its May issue, a new word, "togetherness."

The Cuban mambo was very popular with ballroom dancers. The dance, devised by bandleader Perez Prado, had been introduced in the United States in 1949.

The games of bingo and raffles were legalized (Apr. 20) in New Jersey.

Deaths of the year included historian and editor Frederick Lewis Allen (Feb. 13), botanist David Fiarchild (Aug. 6), football coach Glenn Scobey "Pop" Warner (Sept. 7), cartoonist Harry ("Mutt & Jeff") Fisher (Sept. 7), and actor Lionel Barrymore (Nov. 15).

In Print

Outstanding fiction included *Benton's Row*, by Frank Yerby; *Beyond This Place*, by A. J. Cronin; *Blue Hurricane*, by F. van Wyck Mason; *The Dollmaker*, by Harriet Arnow; *A Fable*, by William Faulkner (Pulitzer prize 1955); *Good Morning, Miss Dove*, by Frances Gary Patton; *Hadrian's Memoirs*, by Marguerite Yourcenar; *The High and the Mighty*, by Ernest Kellogg Gann; *High Water*, by Richard Bissell; *The Iron Maiden*, by Edwin Lanham; *Katherine*, by Anya Seton; *Lord Vanity*, by Samuel Shellabarger; *Love Is Eternal*, by Irving Stone; *Mary Anne*, by Daphne du Maurier; *No Time for Sergeants*, by Mac Hyman; *Not as a Stranger*, by Morton Thompson; *The Pride of the Peacock*, by Ruth Chatterton; *Reunion*, by Merle Miller; *The Royal Box*, by Frances Parkinson Keyes; *Sweet Thursday*, by John Steinbeck; and *The View from Pompey's Head*, by Hamilton Basso. *The Robe* (1953) continued to head the list as the best seller. Conspicuous among nonfiction books were *Call to Greatness*, by Adlai E. Stevenson; *The Mind Alive*, by Harry and Benaro Overstreet; *TNT, the Power Within You*, by Charles Myron Bristol; *Second Tree from the Corner*, by E. B. White; and *I'll Cry Tomorrow*, by Lillian Roth.

On Stage

Arturo Toscanini, 87, retired (Apr. 4) as conductor of the NBC Symphony Orchestra, closing a musical career of over 68 years.

The seventieth gala opening (Nov. 8) of the New York Metropolitan Opera House, comprising acts from four operas, was televised before paying audiences in 32 theaters in more than 25 cities.

On the Broadway stage, two outstanding musicals ended their runs: *South Pacific* (1949) with 1,925 performances on Jan. 16, and *The King and I* (1951) with 1,246 performances on Mar. 20. The plays produced included *The Caine Mutiny; King of Hearts; Anniversary Waltz; Bad Seed; Lunatics and Lovers; Witness for the Prosecution;* and *Anastasia.* New musicals included *By the Beautiful Sea; The Pajama Game; The Boy Friend; Fanny;* and *Mrs. Patterson.* Menotti produced a new opera, *The Saint of Bleecker Street* (Pulitzer prize 1955). Kurt Weill's *The Threepenny Opera* was revived in a small off-Broadway theater, the Theater de Lys, (Mar. 10).

Films

White Christmas, with Bing Crosby and Danny Kaye was the top-money film. Other pictures included: *The Caine Mutiny*, with Humphrey Bogart; *The Country Girl*, with Bing Crosby, Grace Kelly, and William Holden; *Desiree*, with Marlon Brando and Jean Simmons; *The Glen Miller Story*, with James Stewart and June Allyson; *The High and the Mighty*, with John Wayne; *Magnificent Obsession*, with Jane Wyman and Rock Hudson; *Rear Window*, with James Stewart and Grace Kelly; *Seven Brides for Seven Brothers*, with Jane Powell and Howard Keel; *A Star Is Born*, with Judy Garland and James Mason; *There's No Business Like Show Business*, with Ethel Merman, Donald O'Connor, and Marilyn Monroe; and *Three Coins in the Fountain*, with Clifton Webb and Dorothy McGuire. Two notable foreign films were *Ugetsu*, from Japan, and a screen version of Verdi's opera *Aida*, from Italy.

Television

Bing Crosby's first variety special, *The Bing Crosby Show*, aired (Jan. 3) on CBS, with Jack Benny as guest.

All four networks broadcast (Mar. 28) *The General Foods Anniversary Show* with a galaxy of stars including Mary Martin, Groucho Marx, Rosemary Clooney and Ed Sullivan.

ABC and DuMont began (Apr. 22) live coverage of the Army-McCarthy hearings.

Father Knows Best made its start on CBS, ABC's *Disneyland* won an Emmy for best variety series, and *I Love Lucy* was again the highest-rated program in television.

Music

All of You; Cara Mia; Cross Over the Bridge; Fanny; The Happy Wanderer; Hernando's Hideaway; Hey, There; The High and the Mighty; Home for the Holidays; I'm Walking Behind You; Joey; Let Me Go, Lover!; Make Yourself Comfortable; Mambo Italiano; The Man That Got Away; Mister Sandman; The Naughty Lady of Shady Lane; Papa Loves Mambo; Shake, Rattle and Roll; Sh-Boom; Steam Heat; Teach Me Tonight; This Ole House; Three Coins in the Fountain; Wanted; Young and Foolish; Young at Heart.

1955

$\mathcal{D}$r. Jonas Edward Salk, New York-born physician, perfected a vaccine against paralytic polio.

The Soviet Union expressed (June 25) regret over the firing by two of its MIG planes on a United States naval patrol plane on a routine flight (June 22) over the Bering Strait. (Seven crewmen were injured; Russia paid 50 percent of the damage, on Mar. 17, 1956.)

The People's Republic of China released (Aug. 3) eleven American airmen, shot down in 1953 near Antung, Manchuria.

President Eisenhower suffered (Sept. 24) a heart attack in Denver while vacationing in Colorado.

A time bomb, placed by a son in his mother's luggage with the intent to collect $37,000 insurance money, exploded (Nov. 1) in midair near Longmont, Calif., killing all 44 persons aboard the plane.

The A.F.L. and the C.I.O. ended (Dec. 5) a 20-year separation by merging.

Besides devastating tornadoes and floods in many sections of the country, two violent hurricanes from the Caribbean swept northward through the Atlantic states. They were called "Connie" (Aug. 8), and "Diane" (Aug. 19).

Deaths of the year included publisher Robert R. McCormick (Apr. 1); actress Theda Bara (Apr. 7); Dr. Albert Einstein, 76 (Apr. 18); poet James Agee (May 16); educator Mary McLeod Bethune (May 18); former Secretary of State Cordell Hull (July 23); and pitcher Cy Young (Nov. 4).

In Print

The 114-year-old New York newspaper *Brooklyn Eagle* ceased (Mar. 16) publication, following a 45-day strike of employees. (Walt Whitman had served as editor 1846-48.)

The year was well represented in top-selling fiction, with *Andersonville*, by MacKinlay Kantor (Pulitzer prize 1956); *Auntie Mame*, by Patrick Dennis; *Band of Angels*, by Robert Penn Warren; *Bonjour Tristesse*, by Francoise Sagan; *Cash McCall*, by Cameron Hawley; *The Man in the Gray Flannel Suit*, by Sloan Wilson; *Marjorie Morningstar*, by Herman Wouk; *The Prophet*, by Sholom Asch; *Sincerely, Willis Wayde*, by John Phillips Marquand; *Something of Value*, by Robert Ruark; *Ten North Frederick*, by John O'Hara; and *The Tontine*, by Thomas D. Costain. Nonfiction included *The Day Lincoln Was Shot*, by James

Bishop; *The Dead Sea Scrolls*, by Edmund Wilson; *Gift from the Sea*, by Anne Morrow Lindbergh; *How to Live 365 Days a Year*, by John A. Schindler; *Inside Africa*, by John Gunther; *Inspiring Messages for Daily Living*, by Norman Vincent Peale; *A Night to Remember*, by Walter Lord; *The Secret of Happiness*, by Billy Graham; and *Thinking Life Through*, by Fulton J. Sheen. From previous years, *The Power of Positive Thinking* (1951) and *A Man Called Peter* (1952) continued to head the list.

On Stage

Marian Anderson, noted American contralto, made (Jan. 7) her operatic debut at the New York Metropolitan Opera House in *Un Ballo in Maschera*, thereby becoming the first African-American to be engaged as a permanent member of the company.

Gershwin's opera *Porgy and Bess* was performed (Feb. 22) in Milan at La Scala by a Black American company on a goodwill tour. It was the first American opera to be given at the historic opera house and the first American company to appear there.

Carlisle Floyd's opera *Susannah* was premiered (Feb. 24) in Tallahassee, Fla., at Florida State University.

New to the New York stage were *Bus Stop; Cat on a Hot Tin Roof* (Pulitzer prize 1955); *Inherit the Wind; The Diary of Anne Frank* (Pulitzer prize 1956); *Will Success Spoil Rock Hunter; No Time for Sergeants; A Hatful of Rain;* and *The Matchmaker*. The outstanding musicals were: *Plain and Fancy; Silk Stockings; Damn Yankees;* and *Pipe Dream*. The company of the Paris Comedie-Francaise visited (Oct.) the United States for the first time.

Films

Cinerama Holiday grossed the most money. Other pictures included *Battle Cry*, with Van Heflin and Aldo Ray; *The Blackboard Jungle*, with Glenn Ford; *East of Eden*, with Julie Harris and James Dean; *Guys and Dolls*, with Marlon Brando, Jean Simmons, and Frank Sinatra; *I Am a Camera*, with Julie Harris; *Lady and the Tramp* (Walt Disney cartoon); *A Man Called Peter*, with Richard Todd; *Mister Roberts*, with Henry Fonda and James Cagney; *Not as a Stranger*, with Olivia de Haviland and Robert Mitchum; *Oklahoma!*, with Gordon MacRae and Shirley Jones; *Rebel Without a Cause*, with James Dean; *The Sea Chase*, with John Wayne and Lana Turner; *The Seven-Year Itch*, with Marilyn Monroe; *Strategic Air Command*, with James Stewart; *To Hell and Back*, with Audie Murphy; *20,000 Leagues under the Sea*, with James Mason; and *The View from Pompey's Head*, with Richard Egan and Dana Wynter.

Television

Steve Allen hosted (Mar. 7) the first coast-to-coast broadcast of the Emmy Awards, on NBC.

The network also presented (June 7) the first color telecast of a presidential appearance: President Eisenhower's speech to West Point graduates.

Lawrence Welk made his debut on ABC, *Gunsmoke* started on CBS, and Johnny Carson's CBS program was launched (and canceled) in the 1955-56 season.

The Colgate Variety Hour was canceled by NBC and was replaced by *The Steve Allen Show* the following year.

Television introduced (June) a new form of entertainment —the quiz show, with fabulous rewards, or "give-aways," as they were called, for the correct answers. *The $64,000 Question*, the first, continued until allegedly unethical practices of quiz shows came under investigation by the New York district attorney's office.

Phil Silvers won an Emmy for best actor in a continuing performance, and *The $64,000 Question* was rated number one in popularity.

Davy Crockett caps, inspired by the television program, were the rage among boys.

Music

Songs that hit the number one position on the charts included *(We're Gonna) Rock Around the Clock*, Bill Haley and His Comets; *The Yellow Rose of Texas*, Mitch Miller; *Love Is a Many Splendored Thing*, The Four Aces; *Autumn Leaves*, Roger Williams; and *Sixteen Tons*, Tennessee Ernie Ford.

This was a milestone year for American music, the beginning of rock and roll. Bill Haley's *(We're Gonna) Rock Around the Clock* would change the sound of American music though it wasn't the first rock and roll song. Although historians disagree, many suggest that the first was a song called *Rocket 88*, by Jackie Brenston. The author of the term "rock and roll" was disc jockey Alan Freed, who borrowed the phrase from the 1947 rhythm and blues hit by Wild Bill Moore.

Haley's song created riots in theaters, and Clare Booth Luce denounced it as degenerate. But a few months later, on July 9, when the song hit number one on Billboard's chart, American music had taken a new course. Not since the big band era had popular music had such a profound impact on American culture.

Although the song remains an icon of American popular music, Haley and his career did not flourish. Born on July 6, 1925, William John Clifton Haley Jr. succumbed to alcoholism and paranoia and died on Feb. 9, 1981 in Harlingen, Tex.

1956

*A*nti-American demonstrations broke out (Jan.) in Amman, Hebron, Nablus, and in the Jordanese sector of Jerusalem.

The launching by United States military authorities in West Germany of meteorological balloons, carrying camera equipment, brought protests to Washington from the Soviet Union (Feb. 5) and Hungary (Feb. 8), and to the United Nations by Albania, Bulgaria, and Czechoslovakia.

Nikita S. Khrushchev, head of the eight-man Communist party Secretariat, astonished (Feb. 14) the world by condemning, before the 20th Soviet Communist Party Congress in Moscow, the isolationist policies of Stalin and his "cult of personality." He thereby opened the Soviet Union to foreign trade, journalists, and a restricted number of tourists.

The Senate rejected (Mar. 27) a five-point proposal to change the electoral system in favor of nationwide popular elections.

New York newspaper labor columnist Victor Riesel was blinded (Apr. 5) in both eyes, while leaving a restaurant in the city's theater district, by an acid-throwing assailant.

The Association of University Professors, at a meeting in St. Louis, censured (Apr. 6-7) six universities, a medical school, and an agricultural college as violating academic freedom by the dismissal or suspension of faculty members who had invoked the Fifth Amendment or refused to sign loyalty oaths.

The international social event of the year was the wedding of blonde Hollywood actress Grace Kelly, 26, of Philadelphia, and Prince Rainier II, 32 of Monaco. The marriage took place on Apr. 18 in a civil ceremony in the throne room of the Grimaldi palace and was consecrated on Apr. 19 at a nuptial mass in the St. Nicholas Cathedral.

The New York Coliseum, costing $35,000,000, opened (Apr. 28) as the world's largest exhibitions building.

Two eastbound air liners, having left Los Angeles within three minutes of each other, collided and crashed (June 30) into the Grand Canyon in northern Arizona, in the worst commercial air disaster to date, killing 117 passengers and 11 crew members.

A strike of 650,000 United Steelworkers crippled (July 1-27) 90 percent of the country's steel output.

The transatlantic luxury liners, Italian SS *Andrea Doria* and the Swedish-American SS *Stockholm*, collided (July 25) forty miles off Nantucket; the Italian ship sank in eleven hours, with a loss of fifty lives.

An Army helicopter accomplished (Aug. 24) the first non-stop transcontinental flight, from San Diego, Ca. to Washington, D.C., in 37 hours, with a crew of five.

Widespread political demonstrations against Communist rule in Hungary led (Nov. 4) to a surprise invasion by Soviet armed forces, reckoned at 200,000 troops and 2,500 war tanks and armored cars. The Russians killed an estimated 32,000 persons; subsequently more than 25,000 Hungarians were deported to Siberia.

Patrick Air Force Base, Fla., fired (Dec. 8) the first American test rocket for sending a man-made satellite into orbit. The missile reached a height of 125 miles, traveling at a speed of 4,000 miles per hour.

At Yankee Stadium in New York, playing against the Brooklyn Dodgers, right-hand pitcher Don Larsen of the New York Yankees, achieved (Oct. 8) the first "perfect game" in World Series history, allowing no hits, no runs, and no man to reach first base.

In boxing, heavyweight world champion Rocky Marciano (Rocco Marchegiano), 31, undefeated in 49 professional bouts, gave up (Apr. 27), his title; 21-year-old Floyd Patterson and the 39-or-more-year-old Archie Moore fought (Nov. 30) in Chicago for the vacated honor, Patterson scoring a knockout victory in the fifth round, thus becoming the youngest fighter in history to succeed to the title.

The last known Union Army veteran, Albert Woolson, a drummer boy at seventeen, died (Aug. 2) at the age of 109 in Duluth, Minnesota.

In the November presidential elections, Dwight D. Eisenhower, Republican, was reelected to office, defeating the Democratic opponent Adlai E. Stevenson.

Deaths of the year included baseball great Connie Mack (Feb. 8), jazz musician Clifford Brown (June 27), sexologist Alfred Kinsey (Aug. 25), athlete Mildred "Babe" Didrikson Zaharias (Sept. 27), aviation pioneer William Boeing (Sept. 28), and jazz musician Art Tatum (Nov. 4).

In Print

Books of fiction included *A Certain Smile*, by Francoise Sagan; *Don't Go Near the Water*, by William Brinkley; *The Last Hurrah*, by Edwin O'Connor; *Peyton Place*, by Grace Metalious; and *A Single Pebble*, by John Hersey. Nonfiction included: *Deliver Us from Evil*, by Thomas A. Dooley; *The Nun's Story*, by Kathryn Hulme; *Profiles in Courage*, by John Fitzgerald Kennedy; and *The Search for Bridey Murphy*, by Morey Bernstein.

On Stage

Among plays new to Broadway were *Middle of the Night; Separate Tables; Auntie Mame; Long Day's Journey into Night;* and *The Happiest Millionaire.* Musicals were represented by *My Fair Lady* (running into 1962); *Mr. Wonderful; The Most Happy Fella; Li'l Abner; Bells Are Ringing;* and *Happy Hunting.*

The Central City Opera House premiered (July 7) Douglas Moore's opera *The Ballad of Baby Doe.*

Films

The Ten Commandments, with Charlton Heston and Anne Baxter and *Around the World in 80 Days* were the top-money films. Other pictures included *Anastasia,* with Ingrid Bergman and Yul Brynner; *The Conqueror,* with John Wayne and Susan Hayward; *The Eddy Duchin Story,* with Tyrone Power and Kim Novak; *Friendly Persuasion,* with Gary Cooper and Dorothy McGuire; *Giant,* with Elizabeth Taylor, James Dean, and Rock Hudson; *High Society,* with Bing Crosby and Grace Kelly; *I'll Cry Tomorrow,* with Susan Hayward; *The King and I,* with Deborah Kerr and Yul Brynner; *The Man in the Gray Flannel Suit,* with Gregory Peck and Jennifer Jones; *The Man Who Knew Too Much,* with James Stewart and Doris Day; *The Man with the Golden Arm,* with Frank Sinatra; *The Rainmaker,* with Burt Lancaster and Katharine Hepburn; *Seven Wonders of the World; The Teahouse of the August Moon,* with Marlon Brando and Glenn Ford; *Trapeze,* with Burt Lancaster; and *War and Peace,* with Audrey Hepburn and Henry Fonda.

Music

Songs that were number one on the charts included *Memories Are Made of This,* Dean Martin; *Rock and Roll Waltz,* Kay Starr; *Lisbon Antigua,* Nelson Riddle; *Poor People of Paris,* Les Baxter; *Heartbreak Hotel,* Elvis Presley; *The Wayward Wind,* Gogi Grant; *I Want You, I Need You, I Love You,* Elvis Presley; *My Prayer,* The Platters; *Don't Be Cruel/Hound Dog,* Elvis Presley; *Love Me Tender,* Elvis Presley; and *Singing the Blues,* Guy Mitchell.

1957

$\mathcal{P}$resident Dwight D. Eisenhower began his second term.

Three American military airplanes, giant B-52 Stratofortresses, circled (Jan. 16-18) the globe in a nonstop flight in the record time of 45 hours and 19 minutes.

Over a period of years, the "Mad Bomber" had planted 32 homemade bombs in New York City, of which 23 exploded and injured 15 people. A 16-year undercover police search ended when a mentally deranged electric company ex-employee was arrested this year (Jan. 22) in his Waterbury (Conn.) home.

A succession of seven earthquakes rocked (Mar. 22) San Francisco—the worst in 51 years.

New York's last electric passenger streetcar trolley, a service in operation since 1888, ran (Apr. 7) its final trip, over the Queensboro Bridge.

The U.S. Post Office suspended (Saturday, Apr. 13) regular mail delivery for one day due to "lack of funds."

The 30th anniversary of Charles A. Lindbergh's historic transatlantic solo airplane crossing in 1927 was commemorated (May 21) with a duplication of the flight by an Air Force Super Sabre jet, called *Spirit of St. Louis II*. It flew from McGuire Air Force Base, N.J., to Le Bourget Airport, Paris, in the identical time of 33 hours, 29 minutes, 30 seconds.

Nearly 337 years after the Mayflower sailed from England with its cargo of 102 Pilgrims and crew of 48, an exact replica of the small square rigger, named the Mayflower II and equipped with only one modern device, a wireless radio, crossed the Atlantic from Plymouth, England, to Plymouth, Mass., in 53 days (Apr. 20-June 13), fourteen less than the original voyage.

The crescent-shaped Harry S. Truman Library in Independence, Mo., erected at the cost of $1,750,000 by public subscription for the preservation of the former President's 3,500,000 official documents, was dedicated (July 6) and presented to the Federal Government.

A balloon, manned by an Air Force physician, set (Aug. 19-20) an altitude record of 102,000 feet, remaining in the air 32 hours; much valuable scientific data were obtained.

The movement to desegregate the public schools met with violent segregationist opposition in Little Rock, Ala., where Governor Orval Faubus called out (Sept. 2) the National Guard. On Presidential order, (Sept. 24) as rioting increased, Federal troops were sent in, armed with rifles and bayonets. Other disorders occurred in Nashville, Tenn. where a new $500,000 elementary school was dynamited (Sept. 9-10); and in Montgomery, Atlanta, New Orleans, and Wichita Falls, Tex.

The U.S. Coast Guard cutter *Spar* circumnavigated North America via the Panama Canal and the Northwest Passage—the first American vessel to accomplish the undertaking and to cross the top of the continent.

Soviet scientists launched (Oct. 4) into space the first artificial man-made earth-orbiting satellite, called *Sputnik I*; thirty days later, a second craft, bearing a small female dog named Laika, was fired (Nov. 3).

The $110,000,000, 45,000-ton battleship *Wisconsin*, commissioned in 1944, was withdrawn (Nov. 6) from service and consigned to the mothball fleet at Bayonne, N.J.

Captured operating a photographic studio in Brooklyn, N.Y., under the name of Emil R. Goldfus, Rudolf Ivanovich Abel, 53, a Soviet colonel working in counter-intelligence and espionage areas in the United States, was sentenced (Nov. 15) to 30 years in prison and a fine of $3,000. He was returned to Soviet authorities in exchange for U-2 pilot Francis Gary Powers on Feb. 10, 1962.

An eight-day strike of motormen crippled (Dec. 8-16) New York's subway traffic system.

Arturo Toscanini, aged 90, died (Jan. 16) in New York.

Fidel Castro led (Sept. 5) an uprising in Cienfuegos, Cuba, against the government of President Fulgencio Batista.

Deaths of the year included explorer Admiral Richard Byrd (Mar. 11), jazz musician Jimmy Dorsey, gangster Albert Anastasia (Oct. 25), and producer Louis B. Mayer (Oct. 29).

In Print

There was a marked increase of Civil War books in anticipation of its centenary. Fiction titles included *Below the Salt*, by Thomas B. Costain; *A Death in the Family*, by James Agee (Pulitzer prize 1958); *Fairoaks*, by Frank Yerby; *The Lady*, by Conrad Richter; *Letter from Peking*, by Pearl Buck; *By Love Possessed*, by James Gould Cozzens; *On the Beach*, by Nevil Shute; *Rally Round the Flag, Boys*, by Max Shulman; *Remember Me to God*, by Myron S. Kaufman; *The Scapegoat*, by Daphne du Maurier; *Sing Out the Glory*, by Gladys Hasty Carroll; and *The Town*, by William Faulkner. Nonfiction included *The Hidden Persuaders*, by Vance Packard.

On Stage

New plays included *A Visit to a Small Planet; The Tunnel of Love; Look Back in Anger; Romanoff and Juliet; Look Homeward, Angel* (Pulitzer prize 1958); *The Dark at the Top of the Stairs;* and the musicals *New Girl in Town; West Side Story; Jamaica;* and *The Music Man.*

Films

Heading top-money films was *The Bridge on the River Kwai*, with Alec Guinness, William Holden, and Jack Hawkins. Other movies included *Don't Go Near the Water*, with Glenn Ford and Gia Scala; *Les Girls*, with Gene Kelly and Mitzi Gaynor; *A Hatful of Rain*, with Eva Marie Saint and Don Murray; *Heaven Knows, Mr. Allison*, with Deborah Kerr and Robert Mitchum; *Island in the Sun*, with James Mason and Joan Fontaine; *Pal Joey*, with Rita Hayworth and Frank Sinatra; *The Pride and the Passion*, with Cary Grant and Frank Sinatra; *The Prince and the Showgirl*, with Sir Laurence Olivier and Marilyn Monroe; *Raintree County*, with Montgomery Clift and Elizabeth Taylor; *Sayonara*, with Marlon Brando; and *The Spirit of St. Louis*, with James Stewart. A French documentary, *Albert Schweitzer*, with English narration, also attracted nationwide interest.

Music

The number one songs of the year included *Too Much*, Elvis Presley; *Young Love*, Tab Hunter; *Party Doll*, Buddy Knox; *Round and Round*, Perry Como; *All Shook Up*, Elvis Presley; *Love Letters in the Sand*, Pat Boone; *(Let Me Be Your) Teddy Bear*, Elvis Presley; *Tammy*, Debbie Reynolds; *Diana*, Paul Anka; *That'll Be the Day*, The Crickets; *Honeycomb*, Jimmie Rodgers; *Wake Up Little Susie*, Everly Brothers; *Jailhouse Rock/Treat Me Nice*, Elvis Presley; *You Send Me*, Sam Cooke; and *April Love*, Pat Boone.

1958

Three months after the Soviet Union's launching of the first earth-orbiting man-made satellite in 1957, U.S. scientists, spurred by public censure, duplicated the Russian accomplishment: the Army released (Jan. 31) the first American satellite, *Explorer I*, at Cape Canaveral, Fla.; the Navy followed (Mar. 17) with *Vanguard I*; and the Air Force orbited (Dec. 18) an Atlas missile equipped with a radio which broadcast a Christmas message by President Eisenhower—the world's first talking satellite. In other developments, the Air Force conducted (Feb. 9-16) at Randolph Air Base, Tex., a seven-day simulated flight of an airman in a hermetically sealed steel chamber, and the Army experimented (Dec. 13) with a squirrel monkey as a passenger in a *Jupiter* intermediate range missile at Cape Canaveral. Four attempts to reach or circle the moon failed (Aug. 17, Oct. 11, Nov. 8, Dec. 6).

At sea, the American nuclear-powered submarines, the *Skate*, set (Feb. 24-Mar. 5) a new record for an underwater transatlantic crossing to England in 8 days 11 hours, making the return to Nantucket in 7 days 5 hours. The *Nautilus* crossed (Aug. 3) under the icecap of the North Pole in a trans-polar trip of 1,830 miles from the Pacific to the Atlantic, in the Arctic regions imagined 94 years before by Jules Verne in *20,000 Leagues under the Sea*. The *Seawolf* conducted (Aug. 7-Oct. 6) undersea operations for 60 days without surfacing, bettering an earlier record of the *Skate*.

The United States participated in the Brussels World's Fair (Apr.-Oct.); at the American Pavilion, performances were given of Rodgers and Hammerstein's musical comedy *Carousel*, Carlisle Floyd's opera *Susannah*, Gian Carlo Menotti's opera *Maria Golovin* (a world premiere), and Archibald MacLeish's allegory *J.B.*

East German police seized nine members of the U.S. Army's Third Armored Division when their helicopter landed (June 9) by error in Zwichau. After weeks of fruitless diplomatic exchanges, the International Red Cross obtained the release of the men on July 19 and the United States paid $1,748 for their upkeep while in custody.

The Cuban insurrectionist forces of Fidel Castro kidnapped (June 26-July 1) 29 United States sailors and marines, 18 American civilians and three Canadians near the U.S. Navy base at Guantanamo Bay.

During a storm Russian jet fighters shot down (June 27) an unarmed U.S. Air Force transport plane, which had lost its way and invaded Soviet air space on a flight from Turkey to Iran. The nine crewmen escaped death.

A five-mile suspension bridge, the longest in the world, across the turbulent Straits of Mackinac between Lake Michigan and Lake Huron, was opened (June 28) after four years of construction, at a cost of $80,000,000.

Vice President Richard M. Nixon undertook (Apr.-May) an eighteen-day goodwill tour of eight South American countries. He met with mixed reception and, in some places, with hostile demonstrations.

The day after "an urgent plea" by President Camille Chamoun of Lebanon, following the bloody overthrow (July 14) of the Iraqi government of 23-year-old King Faisal by rebels in Baghdad, 3,500 United States Marines were landed at Beirut to protect American lives and property. (Later reinforced by 2,000 British paratroopers, the number of U.S. Marine and Army forces reached a total of 14,300; their gradual withdrawal began on Aug. 17, after the local political situation stabilized.)

The U.S. Post Office increased (Aug. 1) 3-cent letter postage to 4 cents.

More than 250,000 members of the sect of Jehovah's Witnesses gathered (Aug. 3) from all parts of the world in New York's baseball parks, Yankee Stadium and Polo Grounds, and in the surrounding areas to climax an eight-day Divine Will International Assembly, the largest convention assemblage in the city's history.

A nationwide scandal, resulting from investigations by the district attorney's office in New York, caused the gradual cancellation of almost all quiz shows (1955) on network television, for allegedly unethical practices, particularly the giving of answers beforehand to selected contestants. (Ten of the twenty arraigned contestants pleaded guilty to charges of perjury on Jan. 17, 1962 before the Court of Special Sessions in New York and received suspended sentences in consideration of their "humiliation." The contestants won from $500 to a record $220,500.)

New York lost its two National League baseball clubs: the New York Giants to San Francisco, and the Brooklyn Dodgers to Los Angeles.

"Beatnik," "beat generation," and "angry young man," were new terms in common parlance; beards were the fashion of many young males of this group. The "beat" movement evolved a literature of its own, expressed by Jack Kerouac in his novels *On the Road* (1957), *The Subterraneans* (1958), *Maggie Cassidy* (1959), and *Lonesome Traveler* (1960), and his poems *Mexico City Blues* (1959). Poets of the category included, among others, Allen Ginsberg ("Kaddish," 1961) and Charles Olson ("The Maximus Poems," 1961).

William Christopher Handy, "father of the blues" (1912), died on Mar. 28 at 84, in New York.

Nikita S. Khrushchev was elected (Mar. 27) Premier of the Union of Soviet Socialist Republics.

Deaths of the year also included critic George Nathan (Apr. 8), psychiatrist John B. Watson (Sept. 28), actor Tyrone Power (Nov. 15), and inventor Charles F. Kettering (Nov. 25).

In Print

The Nobel prize in literature went to 68-year-old Russian writer and poet Boris Pasternak. He declined the award, thus drawing international attention to his novel *Doctor Zhivago*. The book was first published in 1957 in Italy and subsequently translated into twelve languages.

American fiction was represented by *Anatomy for a Murder*, by Robert Traver; *The Enemy Camp*, by Jerome Weidman; *Exodus*, by Leon M. Uris; *From the Terrace*, by John O'Hara; *Home from the Hills*, by William Humphrey; *Ice Palace*, by Edna Ferber; *Lolita*, by Vladimir Nabokov; *North from Rome*, by Helen MacInnes; *The Travels of Jamie McPheeters*, by Robert Lewis Taylor (Pulitzer prize, 1959); *The Winthrop Woman*, by Anya Seton; and *Women and Thomas Harrow*, by John P. Marquand. Nonfiction included *The Affluent Society*, by John Kenneth Galbraith; *The Edge of Tomorrow*, by Thomas A. Dooley; *Kids Say the Darndest Things!*, by Art Linkletter; and *Only in America*, by Harry Golden.

On Stage

New plays on the New York stage included *Two for the Seesaw; Sunrise at Campobello; Who Was the Lady I Saw You With; Say, Darling; A Touch of the Poet; The World of Suzie Wong; Once More with Feeling; The Pleasure of His Company; Make a Million; The Marriage-Go-Round; J.B.* (Pulitzer prize 1959); and *The Gazebo*. Among successful musicals were *La Plume de Ma Tante* and *Flower Drum Song*.

Twenty-three-year-old American pianist Van Cliburn, of Kilgore, Tex., a native of Shreveport, La., figured in front-page news when he won (Apr. 13) in Moscow the coveted Tchaikovsky prize, a gold medal and 25,000 rubles— $6,250 in official exchange.

Films

South Pacific, with Mitzi Gaynor and Rossano Brazzi earned top money. Other leading films included *Auntie Mame*, with Rosalind Russell; *The Big Country*, with Gregory Peck and Jean Simmons; *The Brothers Karamazov*, with Yul Brynner and Maria Schell; *Cat on a Hot Tin Roof*, with Elizabeth Taylor and Paul Newman; *A Farewell to Arms*, with Rock Hudson and Jennifer Jones; *Gigi*, with Leslie Caron and Maurice Chevalier; *No Time for Sergeants*, with Andy Griffith and Myron McCormick; *Peyton Place*, with Lana Turner and Hope Lange; *The Vikings*, with Kirk Douglas and Tony Curtis; *Windjammer*; and *Young Lions*, with Marlon Brando and Montgomery Clift.

Television

NBC's *Project 20* presented (Mar. 14) "The Twisted Cross," a documentary on Hitler narrated by Alexander Scourby.

The first of a series of science documentaries, "Our Mr. Sun," was aired (Nov. 19) by CBS's *Bell Science Series*, hosted by Dr. Frank Baxter.

CBS also sent (Nov. 30) the first videotaped news broadcast to its West Coast affiliates. The comic pianist Victor Borge starred (Dec. 11) in a one-man program on CBS.

The Lone Ranger, which had been launched in the 1949-50 season, was canceled. "Requiem For A Heavyweight," which had been broadcast on CBS's *Playhouse 90*, won the Emmy for best single program of the year.

Music

At the Hop (Danny and the Juniors), hit the number one position on the charts. Other top songs included *Don't/I Beg of You*, Elvis Presley; *Tequila*, The Champs; *Twilight Time*, The Platters; *Witch Doctor*, David Seville; *All I Have to Do Is Dream*, Everly Brothers; *The Purple People Eater*, Sheb Wooley; *Hard-Headed Woman*, Elvis Presley; *Poor Little Fool*, Ricky Nelson; *Volare (Nel Blu Dipinto Di Blu)*, Domenico Modugno; *Little Star*, The Elegants; *It's All in the Game*, Tommy Edwards; *It's Only Make Believe*, Conway Twitty; *Tom Dooley*, The Kingston Trio; *To Know Him Is to Love Him*, The Teddy Bears; and *The Chipmunk Song*, The Chipmunks with David Seville.

1959

$\mathcal{A}$dmitted to the Union as the 49th and 50th states, respectively, were Alaska (Jan. 3) and Hawaii (Aug. 21).

Soviet scientists released four missiles carrying dogs and a rabbit, and rocketed a missile that hit the moon 35 hours after launching (*Lunik II*, Sept. 18). The Army's *Pioneer IV*, launched (Mar. 3) at Cape Canaveral, Fla., was the first successful U.S. man-made satellite placed in orbit. The Navy orbited (Feb. 17) the world's first space-based weather station (May 28). It then launched a missile three hundred miles into the air which carried two small monkeys named Able and Baker. They were recovered alive in fifteen minutes off Antigua. The Navy also launched (Sept. 18) the twelfth U.S. earth satellite (*Vanguard III*). In an experimental test for the Post Office Department, the first to be conducted for the purpose, a guided missile, fired (June 8) from a submarine off the Florida coast, delivered 3,000 letters in 22 minutes to the naval airport at Jacksonville.

The nuclear submarine *Skate* set (Mar. 14-26) on its second submerged trip under the North Pole's icepack a new record of 12 days, bettering its own in 1958 by five days; the craft only surfaced (Mar. 17) to scatter the ashes of Sir Hubert Wilkins, British Polar explorer (d. Dec. 1, 1958), at the Pole, in accordance with his last wishes.

Serious prison riots broke out in Massachusetts (Mar. and Apr.), Montana (Apr.), Tennessee (May), and Missouri (June).

Cuban Premier Fidel Castro, whose guerrilla forces overthrew the government of Fulgencio Batista, came (Apr.) to the United States on an unofficial eleven-day goodwill speaking tour, visiting Washington, Princeton, New York, Boston, Montreal, Houston.

An unprecedented strike against seven major hospitals in New York by eleven hundred nurses' aides, cooks, orderlies, porters and housekeeping employees, lasted forty-five days (May 8-June 22).

At Groton, Conn., the Navy launched the nation's first ballistic-missile submarine (June 9)—the 380-foot, 5,400-ton, $100,000,000 *George Washington*, and at Quincy, Mass., its first nuclear-powered surface vessel (July 14)—the 725-foot, 14,000-ton cruiser *Long Beach*.

The 2,222-mile St. Lawrence Seaway, linking the Great Lakes with the Atlantic, a project in planning for 40 years, was formally dedicated

(June 26) by Queen Elizabeth II and President Eisenhower aboard the royal yacht *Britannia*.

As part of a cultural exchange program, the U.S.S.R presented (in New York's Coliseum) the Soviet Exhibition of Science, Technology and Culture, and the United States held (in Moscow's Sokolniki Park) the American National Exhibition which was opened July 24, by Vice President Richard M. Nixon. From a display of 8,000 books at the American exhibit, the Soviet Ministry of Culture ordered the removal of 100 volumes defined as objectionable in contents; 70 were later returned under plastic cover.

Reciprocating the previous year's visit of four American composers, six Soviet musicians—composers Dmitri Shostakovich, Dmitri Kabalevsky, General Secretary Tikhon Krennikov of the Composers' Union, Fikret Amirov, Konstantin Dankevich, and musicologist Boris Yarutovsky—paid a month's visit to this country (Oct. 22-Nov. 21).

A nationwide strike of 500,000 members of the United Steelworkers of America crippled industry for 116 days (July 15-Nov. 7), the longest walkout in the nation's steel history.

A series of earthquakes occurred (Aug. 17-18) at West Yellowstone, Mont., the first in this century, causing heavy landslides of rock and earth which trapped and killed many vacationers and damaged the Hebgen Dam on the Madison River.

Soviet Premier Nikita S. Khrushchev came to the United States on a 13-day visit (Sept. 15-27), which extended from Washington, D.C., and New York to Los Angeles and San Francisco. At Hyde Park, N.Y., he placed a wreath on the grave of former President Franklin D. Roosevelt. In Los Angeles, he engaged in a lively debate with the president of 20th Century-Fox film company and witnessed a special can-can performance ("A person's face is more beautiful than his backside," was his comment). In Des Moines, he examined a farm machinery factory and a meat packing house ("We have beaten you to the moon, but you have beaten us in sausage making," he declared). At Coon Rapids, Iowa, he inspected the farm of hybrid corn growers. He threatened twice to leave the country, the first time when he was denied a tour of Disneyland for security reasons and again when he resented remarks in the speech of the Los Angeles mayor. In San Francisco, he faced seven leaders of the AFL-CIO in a stormy labor discussion. He conferred with President Eisenhower at the Chief Executive's Camp David retreat in Maryland.

A mob of some 2,000 anti-U.S. Panamanian demonstrators attempted (Nov. 3) to seize the Canal Zone; repelled, they tore down the American flag at the U.S. Embassy in Panama, burned American citizens' automobiles, and stoned United States property.

Sixteen days before Thanksgiving, the Government health department revealed that certain cranberry crops had been contaminated by the weed-killer aminothiazole; the affected produce was destroyed.

President Eisenhower attended a Western Summit conference in Paris as part of a 19-day (Dec. 3-22) goodwill mission to nine European, Middle East and African countries—the longest trip yet made by a President in office.

Thin, transparent plastic bags for clothes came into use—bringing, during the first four months of the year, death by suffocation to at least twenty young children either while playing with the bags, or sleeping on them as mattress covers in their cribs.

After 31 years on radio and television, the *Voice of Firestone* concluded (June 1) its Monday night programs of light classic and operatic music. Howard Barlow had been the orchestra conductor since 1943.

Popular among the current dances was the cha-cha.

The world's heavyweight championship title went to Sweden, when Ingemar Johansson, European champion, defeated (June 26) the American title holder, Floyd Patterson, a 5-1 favorite, at Yankee Stadium, New York. Johansson won by a third-round knockout with his much vaunted right hand, having floored Patterson seven times before the referee halted the bout.

For the first time in baseball, a second All-Star game was played in a single season (Aug. 3, at Los Angeles Stadium).

Deaths of the year included singers Buddy Holly and Richie Valens (Feb. 3); comedian Lou Costello (Mar. 3); gourmet Duncan Hines (Mar. 15); author Raymond Chandler (Mar. 26); Ethel Barrymore, 79 (June 18), last of the famous Drew-Barrymore family of actors; actor Errol Flynn (Oct. 14); singer Mario Lanza (Oct. 15); and Walter Williams, 117 (Dec. 19), a soldier in General Hood's Texas Brigade and the last Confederate Army and Civil War veteran.

In Print

In American literary history, the year will be remembered for a judicial pronouncement: Federal Judge Frederick van Pelt Bryan ruled (July 21) unconstitutional the U.S. Post Office ban on the unexpurgated American edition (declared by the Postmaster General "an obscene and filthy work") of D. H. Lawrence's 1928 English novel *Lady Chatterley's Lover*—a decision which recalled a similar ruling in favor in James Joyce's *Ulysses* in 1933. Following the decree, stories with sexual contact multiplied in such numbers that outraged religious and civic leaders appealed to Congress for some restrictive legislation. Municipal authorities confiscated quantities of publications deemed pornographic.

Fiction of the year included *Advise and Consent*, by Allen Drury; (Pulitzer prize 1960); *Dear and Glorious Physician*, by Taylor Caldwell; *From the Terrace*, by John O'Hara; *Hawaii*, by James Michener; and *The Ugly American*, by William J. Lederer and Eugene Burdick. In nonfiction *Act One*, by Moss Hart; *Folk Medicine*, by Dr. DeForest Clinton Jarvis; *The House of Intellect*, by Jacques Barzun; *The Papers of Benjamin Franklin; The Status Seekers*, by Vance Packard; *Twixt Twelve and Twenty*, by Pat Boone; *The Years with Ross*, by James Thurber; *My Brother Was an Only Child*, by Jack Douglas; and *For 2 Cents Plain*, by Harry Golden.

On Stage

On the New York stage were seen, among other plays, *A Majority of One; Sweet Bird of Youth; A Raisin in the Sun; At the Drop of a Hat; The Miracle Worker; The Tenth Man;* and *Five Finger Exercise.* New musicals included: *Redhead; Destry Rides Again; Gypsy; Take Me Along; The Sound of Music; Fiorello* (Pulitzer prize 1960); and *Once upon a Mattress.*

Films

Released late in the year, *Ben Hur,* with Charlton Heston, Martha Scott, and Stephen Boyd, a new screen version of Lewis Wallace's 1880 novel, became the top box office attraction. Other pictures included: *Anatomy of a Murder,* with James Stewart, Lee Remick, Ben Gazzara, and Joseph N. Welch; *Hercules,* with Steve Reeves; *A Hole in the Head,* with Frank Sinatra, Edward G. Robinson, and Eddie Hodges; *Imitation of Life,* with Lana Turner and John Gavin; *North by Northwest,* with Cary Grant and Eva Marie Saint; *The Nun's Story,* with Audrey Hepburn, Peter Finch, and Edith Evans; *On the Beach,* with Gregory Peck, Ava Gardner, Anthony Perkins, and Fred Astaire; *Operation Petticoat,* with Cary Grant and Tony Curtis; *Pillow Talk,* with Doris Day, and Rock Hudson; *Porgy and Bess,* with Sidney Poitier, Dorothy Dandridge, and Sammy Davis; *Sleeping Beauty; Some Like It Hot,* with Marilyn Monroe, Joe E. Brown, and Jack Lemmon; and *They Came to Cordura,* with Gary Cooper, Van Heflin, and Rita Hayworth.

Television

ABC broadcast (June 28) *The Record Years,* a tribute to the recording industry hosted by Dick Clark.

Laurence Olivier made his U.S. television debut (Oct. 30) on NBC's production of *The Moon And Sixpence.* Olivier later won an Emmy for his performance.

CBS Reports broadcast (Dec. 18) "Iran: Brittle Ally," narrated by Edward R. Morrow and Winston Burdett.

Bonanza made its NBC debut in the 1959-60 season and *The Steve Allen Show,* which had moved to Mondays on NBC, was canceled. *Gunsmoke* was the most popular program for the third consecutive year.

Music

Songs that hit number one on the charts included: *Smoke Gets in Your Eyes,* The Platters; *Stagger Lee,* Lloyd Price; *Venus,* Frankie Avalon; *Come Softly to Me,* The Fleetwoods; *The Happy Organ,* Dave "Baby" Cortez; *Kansas City,* Wilbert Harrison; *The Battle of New Orleans,* Johnny Horton; *Lonely Boy,* Paul Anka; *A Big Hunk of Love,* Elvis Presley; *The Three Bells,* The Browns; *Sleep Walk,* Santo and Johnny; *Mack the Knife,* Bobby Darin; *Mr. Blue,* The Fleetwoods; *Heartaches by the Number,* Guy Mitchell; *Why,* Frankie Avalon.

1960

$\mathcal{I}$n protest against segregation at variety store lunch counters, Black students in Greensboro, N.C., staged (Feb. 1) a "sit-down" demonstration—an action which quickly spread to other Southern cities. Similar stores in New York were picketed in sympathy, and nationwide, more than 1,000 participants faced trial for the disturbances.

The training manuals of the U.S. Air Force came (Feb. 3) under criticism for statements like the one declaring that 30 of the 95 persons who revised the new Bible translation for the National Council of Churches were members of subversive groups.

President Eisenhower made two two-week goodwill tours: the first (Feb.) to Puerto Rico, Brazil, Argentina, Chile, and Uruguay—where he contracted an eye irritation from a tear gas bomb during an anti-American outburst in Montevideo; and the second (June) to South Korea, the Philippine Islands, Formosa, and Okinawa. In Okinawa 1,500 Leftists staged a derisive snake-dance. A contemplated visit to Japan was canceled because of mounting anti-U.S. demonstrations there.

During the President's visit to Brazil, 19 musicians of the U.S. Navy band and 42 other persons lost (Feb. 25) their lives in a collision of a U.S. Navy transport plane and a Brazilian airliner over Sugar Loaf Mountain near Rio de Janeiro—only three of the 64 aboard the planes were saved.

Communist China continued its periodic shelling of the off-shore island of Nationalist-held Quemoy and increased its bombardments during President Eisenhower's visit to Formosa.

The world's largest submarine, the nuclear-powered 7,750-ton USS *Triton*, circumnavigated the globe on a submerged voyage of 41,519 miles in 84 days (Feb. 26-May 10), following the general route of the sixteenth century Portuguese explorer Ferdinand Magellan.

A Soviet missile shot down (May 1) a U.S. Air Force U-2 spy plane which had flown into Soviet territory; the Russians characterized the flight as "an aggressive provocation aimed at wrecking the summit conference" scheduled that month by Great Britain, France, the United States, and Russia. Soviet Premier Nikita S. Khrushchev angrily denounced the United States and President Eisenhower, and rescinded his invitation to the Eisenhower to visit the U.S.S.R. As a result, the summit meeting was canceled. (Francis Gary Powers, pilot of the ill-fated U-2, was sentenced on Aug. 19, by a Moscow court, to 10 years' imprisonment for espionage. On February 10, 1962, Powers was exchanged for Soviet spy Colonel Rudolf Ivanovich Abel.)

A strike of 12,000 actors in New York caused (June 2-12) a ten-day blackout of the city's 22 Broadway theaters.

The 15th session of the UN General Assembly brought (Sept. 20-Oct. 13) to New York so large a concentration of foreign governmental representatives that their protection required the vigilance of the city's entire police, the FBI, and other secret agencies. Conspicuous were Soviet Premier Nikita S. Khrushchev and Cuban Premier Fidel Castro, both of whom fraternized familiarly on the streets and before news and television cameras. Khrushchev also appeared on the balcony of the Russian Embassy and answered questions directed at him by the public. At the UN, during a stormy debate, he twice angrily interrupted a speech by British Prime Minister Harold Macmillan; on another occasion, he signified his disapproval of the remarks by the Philippine delegate by removing his shoe and pounding on the podium with the heel.

The SS *Hope*, a privately financed floating hospital and medical school, sailed (Sept. 22) from San Francisco on a year's mission to carry medical knowledge and treatment to the people of Indonesia and South Vietnam.

The Post Office Department established its first automated post office in Providence, R.I., and issued (Oct. 20) a special postage stamp commemorating the event.

After 27 years on radio, *The Romance of Helen Trent*, a daytime soap opera, came (June 24) to an end with the 7,222th episode.

Floyd Patterson, 25-year-old boxer, became (June 20) the first and youngest man in boxing to regain the world's heavyweight championship, at the Polo Grounds, New York, with a fifth-round knockout of the defending title holder Ingemar Johansson of Sweden. Patterson had lost the title to Johansson in 1959.

Deaths of the year included: Oscar Hammerstein 2nd, 65 (Aug. 23); Emily Post, 86 (Sept. 25); Lawrence Tibbett, 63 (July 15); Clara Kimball Young, 70 (Oct. 15).

In the November elections, by a small popular majority, Democratic Senator John Fitzgerald Kennedy of Massachusetts beat his Republican opponent, Vice President Richard Milhous Nixon. During the campaign, they engaged in four nationally televised debates—a new political phenomenon.

The national population was 179,323,175 (or 183,300,000, including members of the Armed Forces and other Americans abroad).

In Print

Among the year's books of popular fiction were *The Constant Image*, by Marcia Davenport; *The Dean's Watch*, by Elizabeth Goudge; *The Leopard*, by Giuseppe de Lampedusa; *The Lovely Ambition*, by Mary Ellen Chase; and *To Kill a Mockingbird*, by Harper Lee (Pulitzer prize 1961). Readers of nonfiction bought *Arthritis and Folk Medicine*, by DeForest Clinton Jarvis; *Born Free*, by

Joy Adamson; *The Conscience of a Conservative,* by Barry Goldwater, Arizona's Republican Senator; *The Night They Burned the Mountain,* by Thomas A. Dooley; *Pictorial History of the Civil War,* by Bruce Catton; *The Rise and Fall of the Third Reich,* by William L. Shirer; *This Is My God,* by Herman Wouk; and *The Waste Makers,* by Vance Packard. Newly discovered diaries and memoirs increased the output of books about the Civil War for the coming centenary.

On Stage

The Broadway stage presented, among other plays, *Toys in the Attic; A Thurber Carnival; The Best Man; A Taste of Honey; Advise and Consent;* and *All the Way Home* (Pulitzer prize 1961). Popular among new musicals were *Bye, Bye, Birdie; The Fantasticks; Tenderloin; The Unsinkable Molly Brown; Camelot; Wildcat; Do Re Mi;* and *West Side Story.*

Films

The top picture, money-wise, was *Can-Can* with Frank Sinatra, Shirley MacLaine, Maurice Chevalier, and Louis Jourdan. Other films included *The Apartment,* with Jack Lemmon and Shirley MacLaine; *Butterfield 8,* with Elizabeth Taylor and Laurence Harvey; *Elmer Gantry,* with Burt Lancaster and Jean Simmons; *Exodus,* with Paul Newman and Eva Marie Saint; *From the Terrace,* with Paul Newman and Joanne Woodward; *G.I. Blues,* with Elvis Presley; *Journey to the Center of the Earth,* with Pat Boone and Arlene Dahl; *The Man in the Cocked Hat,* with Peter Sellers and Terry Thomas; *Please Don't Eat the Daisies,* with Doris Day and David Niven; *Psycho,* with Janet Leigh and Anthony Perkins; *Solomon and Sheba,* with Yul Brynner and Gina Lollobrigida; *Spartacus,* with Laurence Olivier, Kirk Douglas, and Charles Laughton; *Suddenly Last Summer,* with Elizabeth Taylor and Katharine Hepburn; and *The World of Suzie Wong,* with Nancy Kwan and William Holden. Two films dealt with England's great aesthete: *Oscar Wilde,* with Robert Morley and Phyllis Calvert and *The Trials of Oscar Wilde,* with Peter Finch and Yvonne Mitchell.

Television

CBS televised (Jan. 31) *The Fabulous Fifties,* a special hosted by Henry Fonda, with guests such as Dick Van Dyke, Mike Nichols and Elaine May, Jackie Gleason, and Eric Sevareid. CBS also broadcast (Aug. 26—Sept. 12) the Summer Olympics from Rome.

The first of the Nixon-Kennedy presidential debates was carried (Sept. 26) by all three networks.

Comedian Danny Kaye appeared (Oct. 30) on his first variety special, with Louis Armstrong as guest.

NBC presented (Dec. 8) *Peter Pan,* with Mary Martin, Cyril Ritchard and Maureen Bailey.

NBC White Paper aired (Dec. 20) "Sit-In," a report on desegregation.

Candid Camera made its debut in the 1960-61 season on CBS. *The Hallmark Hall Of Fame's* production of *Macbeth* won an Emmy for program of the year. For the fourth consecutive season, *Gunsmoke* was the top-rated program.

Music

The number one hits included: *El Paso*, Marty Robbins; *Running Bear*, Johnny Preston; *Teen Angel*, Mark Dinning; *Theme from: A Summer Place*, Percy Faith; *Stuck on You*, Elvis Presley; *Cathy's Clown*, Everly Brothers; *Everybody's Somebody's Fool*, Connie Francis; *Alley-Oop*, The Hollywood Argyles; *I'm Sorry*, Brenda Lee; *Itsy Bitsy Teenie Weenie Yellow Polka Dot Bikini*, Brian Hyland; *It's Now or Never*, Elvis Presley; *The Twist*, Chubby Checker; *My Heart Has a Mind of Its Own*, Connie Francis; *Mr. Custer*, Larry Verne; *Save the Last Dance for Me*, The Drifters; *I Want to Be Wanted*, Brenda Lee; *Georgia on My Mind*, Ray Charles; *Stay*, Maurice Williams and the Zodiacs; *Are You Lonesome Tonight*, Elvis Presley.

1961

 $\mathcal{J}$ ohn Fitzgerald Kennedy, Democrat, of Massachusetts, was inaugurated as the 35th President, and the rocking chair became a familiar article of presidential furniture.

Marking two years of declining relations with Cuba, the outgoing Eisenhower administration severed (Jan. 3) diplomatic relations in consequence of Castro's demand that the United States reduce its embassy in Havana to eleven persons.

It was the 100th anniversary of the Civil War, or "War between the States." A five-year centennial celebration opened (Jan. 8) with ceremonies at the tombs of Ulysses S. Grant in New York and Robert E. Lee in Lexington, Va. There was (Jan. 9) a reenactment in Charleston, S.C., of the bombardment of the *Star of Hope*, a Federal ship sent to reinforce the Union garrison at Fort Sumter.

The great scientific event of the year was the successful orbiting (Apr. 13) by the Soviet Union of the first man-carrying space missile around the earth, its passenger the cosmonaut Yuri Gagarin. The feat was duplicated on Aug. 7 by Gherman S. Titov. United States scientists at Cape Canaveral, Fla., launched (May 5) their first man-in-space missile, carrying astronaut Alan B. Shepard Jr. in a suborbital flight of fifteen minutes—a successful experiment repeated (July 21) with Virgil I. Grissom.

Forty-two American tourists on a Caribbean cruise, along with 565 other nationals and 350 crew members, were trapped aboard the Portuguese luxury liner *Santa Maria* when the vessel was seized (Jan. 22) at sea. The vessel finally landed (Feb. 2) at Recife, Brazil, after pursuit and capture by U.S. Navy planes and ships.

President Kennedy authorized (Mar. 1) the formation of the Peace Corps, men and women who volunteered for service in education, agriculture, and hygiene in undeveloped overseas areas.

There was an abortive attempt to overthrow the Castro regime in Cuba, launched (Apr. 17) by Cuban exiles on the marshy beaches of Las Villas province with U.S. military equipment. The Bay of Pigs incident involved the prestige of the United States and brought denunciation from abroad, due to the alleged participation of the U.S. Central Intelligence Agency. Premier Castro offered (May 17) to exchange captured invaders for American tractors, but the negotiations were abandoned after a five-week deadlock on terms.

The U.S. Department of Labor created (Apr. 30) an Office of Automation to study its effects on labor.

Four instances of hijacking American airliners occurred (May 1, July 24, Aug. 3, Aug. 9): in three cases the planes were diverted at gunpoint to Havana; in the fourth, the attempt was foiled by a landing in El Paso, Tex.

Anti-segregationists, forming a bi-racial passive resistance group called the Congress of Racial Equality (known as CORE), started a movement of Freedom Rides into the Deep South on interstate public busses. The riders encountered mob violence in Anniston, Ala. (May 14) and in Montgomery, Ala. (May 20). To maintain peace, President Kennedy ordered U.S. marshals to the areas until normal conditions were restored.

Ernest Hemingway, Nobel Prize-winning American author (1953), fatally shot himself (July 2) at his home in Ketchum, Idaho.

By invoking the Taft-Hartley Labor Act (1947), President Kennedy halted (July 3) a crippling 18-day tie-up of the nation's merchant fleet, which resulted from a jurisdictional dispute over American-owned, or so-called "runaway," ships under foreign registry.

The Soviet Union imposed (Aug. 12-13) drastic restrictions on travel between East and West Berlin in an effort to halt the flow of refugees from East Germany to the "free" world. The Russians erected a 25-mile concrete wall, along the dividing line, across which Western and Communist battle-armed units faced each other only a few yards apart. President Kennedy reinforced (Aug. 18) the 5,000-man U.S. garrison in West Berlin by the addition of 1,500 men.

The Soviet Union resumed (Sept. 1) nuclear testing, despite a Big Power moratorium, and, overriding protests from non-Communist nations and an appeal from the United States, exploded (Oct. 31) at its Arctic proving ground a bomb estimated from 62 to 90 megatons.

Hurricane Carla, described as the fiercest storm of the century, lashed (Sept. 10-11) the coastal regions of Louisiana and upper Texas; hurricane Esther swept (Sept. 19-21) the Atlantic coast from North Carolina to Cape Cod.

On an invitation extended by Vice President Lyndon B. Johnson during his visit to Karachi, a 40-year-old Pakistani camel driver toured (Oct. 15-21) the United States, as a guest of the People-to-People exchange program.

The Metropolitan Museum of Art, New York, acquired (Nov. 15) at a local public auction, Rembrandt's painting *Aristotle Contemplating the Bust of Homer* for the highest sum ever paid for any canvas—$2,300,000. The painter had received 500 florins, or about $7,800, in 1653.

To prevent the return to power by the slain Dominican dictator Rafael Trujillo's family, the United States intervened (Nov. 19) with a show of naval strength in the island's waters.

As a further step in the project to orbit a human astronaut, the Air Force flew (Nov. 29) a chimpanzee, named Enos, in two complete 17,500-mile-an-hour revolutions around the Earth in 3 hours 21 minutes, and safely recovered the capsule and the living animal in the Atlantic, 250 miles south of Bermuda.

Intense excitement was generated in baseball by the efforts of Mickey Mantle and Roger Maris, both playing with the New York Yankees, to equal or better Babe Ruth's 1927 record of 60 home runs in a 154-game season. The "M Boys," as they were called, didn't make it: Mantle hit 54 and Maris 59; however, the latter went on to set the new record of 61 for a season of 162 games.

Dancing couples favored, among new dances, The Twist and La Pachanga by Cuban composer and dancer Eduardo Davidson. Less popular were The Fish, The Pony, The Madison, The Mess Around, and The Bristol Stomp.

Deaths of the year included playwright George S. Kaufman, 71 (June 2); Dr. Lee De Forest, "the father of radio" and more than 300 other inventions, 87 (June 30); Ernest Hemingway, 61; baseball's great "Ty" (Tyrus Raymond) Cobb, known as the "Georgia Peach," 74 (July 17); Dag Hammarskjold, Swedish-born Secretary General of the United Nations, 56 (Sept. 18); James Thurber, 66 (Nov. 2); "Grandma Moses" (Anna Mary Robertson Moses), self-taught painter of American scenes, 101 (Dec. 13); and Moss Hart, 57 (Dec. 20).

In Print

The year's books of fiction included *The Agony and the Ecstasy,* by Irving Stone; *The Carpetbaggers,* by Harold Robbins; *Clock without Hands,* by Carson McCullers; *Daughter of Silence,* by Morris L. West; *The Edge of Sadness,* by Edwin O'Connor; *Franny and Zooey,* by J. D. Salinger; *God Must Be Sad,* by Fannie Hurst; *The Incredible Journey,* by Sheila Burnford; *The Judas Tree,* by A. J. Cronin; *Midcentury,* by John Dos Passos; *Mila 18,* by Leon M. Uris; *A New Life,* by Bernard Malamud; *Pomp and Circumstance,* by Noel Coward; *Spirit Lake,* by MacKinlay Kantor; *To Kill a Mockingbird,* by Harper Lee; *The White Rajah,* by Nicholas Monsarrat; *Wilderness,* by Robert Penn Warren; and *The Winter of Our Discontent,* by John Steinbeck. Nonfiction included: *Before I Sleep,* by Thomas A. Dooley; *Citizen Hearst,* by W. A. Swanberg; *Diary and Autobiography of John Adams,* first four volumes; *Living Free,* by Joy Adamson; *The Making of the President 1960,* by Theodore H. White; *A Nation of Sheep,* by William Lederer; and *Ring of Bright Water,* by Gavin Maxwell.

On Stage

New to the stage were the plays *Rhinoceros; Come Blow Your Horn; Mary, Mary; A Far Country;* and the musical *Carnival!.* Opening later in the season and continuing into 1962 were the plays *Purlie Victorious; The Caretaker; A Shot in the Dark; Write Me a Murder; Gideon; Take Her, She's Mine; Ross; The Night of the Iguana;* and the musicals *Sail Away; Milk and Honey; How to Succeed in Business Without Really Trying; The Gay Life;* and *Subways Are for Sleeping.* The Threepenny Opera closed after 2,611 performances, a run that began in 1954.

A bitter salary dispute between management and musicians threatened to prevent the opening of New York's Metropolitan Opera for its 77th season.

Nausicaa, an American opera by Australia-born composer Peggy Glanville-Hicks, received (Aug. 19) its world premiere in Athens, Greece, in the recently restored ancient open-air theater, Herodes Atticus, below the Acropolis.

The San Francisco Opera produced the first American performance of Benjamin Britten's new opera *A Midsummer Night's Dream* (Oct. 10).

Films

Among films, the top-money picture was *The Guns of Navarone*, with Gregory Peck, David Niven, and Anthony Quinn. Other motion pictures included *Come September*, with Rock Hudson and Gina Lollobrigida; *La Dolce Vita*, with Anita Ekberg and Marcello Mastroianni; *Flower Drum Song*, with Nancy Kwan and James Shigeta; *King of Kings*, with Jeffrey Hunter and Siobhan McKenna; *Splendor in the Grass*, with Natalie Wood and Warren Beatty; and *West Side Story*, with Natalie Wood and Richard Beymer. The shooting of films outside the United States caused American labor unions to seek restrictive legislation.

Television

The first live telecast of a presidential news conference was carried by all three networks as John Kennedy met the press shortly after his inauguration.

Walter Cronkite of CBS conducted (Oct. 12) the first of three interviews with Kennedy's predecessor on "Eisenhower on the Presidency."

CBS's *G.E. Theater* was canceled during the 1961-62 season. *The Garry Moore Show* on CBS won an Emmy for outstanding programming achievement in the field of variety, and NBC's *Wagon Train*, another Western, displaced *Gunsmoke* as the nation's most watched show.

Music

The number one charted songs included *Wonderland by Night*, Bert Kaempfert; *Will You Love Me Tomorrow*, The Shirelles; *Calcutta*, Lawrence Welk; *Pony Time*, Chubby Checker; *Surrender*, Elvis Presley; *Blue Moon*, The Marcels; *Runaway*, Del Shannon; *Mother-in-Law*, Ernie K-Doe; *Travelin' Man*, Ricky Nelson; *Running Scared*, Roy Orbison; *Moody River*, Pat Boone; *Quarter to Three*, Gary U.S. Bonds; *Tossin' and Turnin'*, Bobby Lewis; *Wooden Heart (Muss I Denn)*, Joe Dowell; *Michael*, The Highwaymen; *Take Good Care of My Baby*, Bobby Vee; *Hit the Road Jack*, Ray Charles; *Runaround Sue*, Dion; *Big Bad John*, Jimmy Dean; *Please Mr. Postman*, The Marvelettes; *The Lion Sleeps Tonight*, The Tokens.

1962

$\mathscr{D}$eteriorating relations with Cuba were the prime concern of the United States foreign policy during 1962. The U.S. State Department publicized (Jan. 3) a report that said Cuba represents "a bridgehead of Sino-Soviet imperialism and a base for Communist agitation and subversion within the inner defense of the Western Hemisphere." Late in the year, the United States and the Soviet Union were brought to a confrontation over Soviet atomic missile sites being built in Cuba.

The world was on the brink of war (Oct. 22) as President Kennedy imposed a quarantine, effective Oct. 24, against arms shipments to Cuba.

The Soviet Union challenged (Oct. 23) the United States right to quarantine.

The U.S. Navy was ordered (Oct. 24) to sink any ship that refused to obey the quarantine order. A fleet of 24 Soviet ships had been sighted en route to Cuba and the U.S. Navy stopped one (Oct. 25), but then allowed it to proceed since it was not carrying arms. The next day the United States and the Soviets agreed at the United Nations to avoid clashes at sea. Soviet Premier Khrushchev offered (Oct. 27) to withdraw Soviet offensive weapons from Cuba if the United States reciprocated in Turkey. President Kennedy rejected the proposal.

The Cuban crisis was resolved (Oct. 28) when the Soviet Union agreed to remove its rocket bases in Cuba in return for an American pledge not to invade Cuba.

The U.S. Defense Dept. set up (Feb. 8) a new military command in South Vietnam. President Kennedy said (Feb. 14) that United States troops in Vietnam training missions had been instructed only "to fire to protect themselves if fired upon."

In 1962 John H. Glenn, Jr., the first American in orbit, circled (Feb. 20) the earth three times in *Friendship* 7. M. Scott Carpenter in *Aurora* 7 also completed a three-orbit flight (May 24) and Walter M. Schirra completed (Oct. 3) six orbits of the Earth.

Century 21 Exposition in Seattle, the first World's Fair to be held in the United States in 22 years, opened Apr. 21 with a "space age" theme.

Prices on the New York Stock Exchange were hit (May 28) by the largest one-day drop since the "Black Tuesday" of Oct. 28, 1929. The Dow Jones index fell 34.95 points to 576.93. In the next few days, the stock market rebounded and recovered virtually all of the loss.

Adolf Eichmann, 56, former Gestapo officer convicted by an Israeli court of playing a major role in the Nazi extermination of Jews, was hanged (May 31).

Aviation's worst disaster to date involving a single plane occurred when an Air France Boeing-707 jet crashed (June 3) on takeoff from Paris, killing 130 persons.

The New York Yankees became world champions when they beat the San Francisco Giants in the seventh game (Oct. 16) of baseball's World Series.

James Meredith, 29, an Air Force veteran, became the first African-American to be enrolled at the University of Mississippi (Sept. 30) after a clash between state officials and the U.S. Justice Department. This clash led to a contempt citation against Mississippi Governor Ross Barnett in the Fifth U.S. Circuit Court in New Orleans.

Pope John XXIII opened the 21st Ecumenical Council of the Roman Catholic Church in Rome (Oct. 11).

Serious border clashes erupted (Oct. 20) on the Indian-Chinese border. India declared a national emergency and requested United States assistance. Communist China declared a unilateral cease-fire and withdrew its troops (Dec. 1) from the disputed area.

Former Vice President Richard M. Nixon was defeated (Nov. 6) by incumbent Democratic Governor Edmund G. Brown in the race for the California governorship. Nixon bitterly attacked the press for unfair reporting and said, "You won't have Nixon to kick around anymore."

Film star Marilyn Monroe, 36, died (Aug. 5). Though it was apparently suicide from an overdose of pills, there is still speculation on the cause of her death.

Mrs. Eleanor Roosevelt, 78, widow of President Franklin Delano Roosevelt, died (Nov. 7). Kirsten Flagstad, 67, the opera singer, died (Dec. 8).

A heavy fog over London from Dec. 3 to Dec. 10 was blamed for the death of at least 170 people.

In Print

The 1962 Pulitzer prize for fiction was awarded to William Faulkner for *The Reivers*.

On Stage

Paul Scofield in *A Man for All Seasons* and Margaret Leighton in *The Night of the Iguana* were cited for the best performances for the 1961-62 season in the Variety Poll of New York Drama Critics. Cited for outstanding performances in supporting roles were Sandy Dennis in *A Thousand Clowns* and Barbara Streisand in *I Can Get It for You Wholesale*. Peter Fonda in *Blood, Sweat Stanley Poole*, and Barbara Harris in *From the Second City*, were rated as most promising performers. The Pulitzer committee found no play worthy of the award.

Films

The Academy of Motion Picture Arts and Sciences' Oscars for 1962 were awarded to *Lawrence of Arabia*, best picture; Anne Bancroft in *The Miracle Worker*, best actress; and Gregory Peck in *To Kill a Mockingbird*, best actor.

Other major films of the year included: *The Wonderful World of the Brothers Grimm*, with Laurence Harvey and Claire Bloom; *Whatever Happened to Baby Jane?*, with Bette Davis and Joan Crawford; *Advise and Consent*, with Walter Pidgeon, Charles Laughton, Franchot Tone, Don Murray, Henry Fonda, and Gene Tierney; *Bird Man of Alcatraz*, with Burt Lancaster; *Divorce—Italian Style*, with Marcello Mastroianni; *Hatari*, with John Wayne; *The Longest Day*, with John Wayne, Robert Mitchum, and Robert Ryan; *The Music Man*, with Robert Preston and Shirley Jones; *Requiem for a Heavyweight*, with Anthony Quinn and Julie Harris; and *Sergeants Three*, with Frank Sinatra, Dean Martin, and Sammy Davis, Jr.

Two modestly scaled films, *David and Lisa* and *The Connection*, had profound impact on the moviemaking industry. Both were independently made at relatively low cost. They were harbingers of a cycle of films dealing boldly with contemporary themes and made outside the orbit of major studio control.

Television

Lt. Col. John Glenn's first orbital Mercury space flight was covered (Feb. 20) by all three networks.

CBS presented (June 11) "Julie and Carol At Carnegie Hall," starring Julie Andrews and Carol Burnett.

Telstar, an experimental communications satellite, successfully transmitted (July 10) transatlantic television signals for the first time.

NBC broadcast (Dec. 10) "The Tunnel," a documentary on the construction of a tunnel under the Berlin Wall.

CBS's *The Dick Van Dyke Show* won an Emmy for comedy, and the network's *The Beverly Hillbillies* made its debut and became the top-rated program.

Ten money winners on rigged television quiz shows received suspended sentences in New York Special Sessions Court (Jan. 17) after pleading guilty to perjury charges.

Music

Songs that topped the charts this year at the number one position included *Peppermint Twist-Part I*, Joey Dee and the Starliters; *Duke of Earl*, Gene Chandler; *Hey! Baby*, Bruce Channel; *Don't Break the Heart That Loves You*, Connie Francis; *Johnny Angel*, Shelley Fabares; *Good Luck Charm*, Elvis Presley; *Soldier Boy*, The Shirelles; *Stranger on the Shore*, Mr. Acker Bilk; *I Can't Stop Loving You*, Ray Charles; *The Stripper*, David Rose and His Orchestra; *Roses Are Red (My Love)*, Bobby Vinton; *Breaking Up Is Hard to Do*, Neil Sedaka; *The Loco-Motion*, Little Eva; *Sheila*, Tommy Roe; *Sherry*, The Four Seasons; *Monster Mash*, Bobby "Boris" Pickett and the Crypt-Kickers; *He's a Rebel*, The Crystals; *Big Girls Don't Cry*, The Four Seasons; *Telstar*, The Tornadoes.

1963

*J*ohn Fitzgerald Kennedy, the 35th President of the United States, was killed (Nov. 22) by an assassin in Dallas, Tex. A few hours later, police arrested Lee Harvey Oswald, 24, on charges of firing the fatal bullet from a building along the President's parade route.

Exactly 99 minutes after President Kennedy was pronounced dead, Lyndon Baines Johnson, the Vice President, was sworn in as President by Federal District Judge Sarah Hughes at the Dallas airport. In Washington, D.C., President Johnson said to the nation: "I will do my best. That is all I can do. I ask for your help and God's."

In full view of a nationwide television audience, Lee Harvey Oswald was fatally shot (Nov. 24) in the basement of the Dallas municipal building by Jack Ruby, a nightclub owner.

President Kennedy was buried at Arlington National Cemetery (Nov. 25) after a solemn ritual attended by an unprecedented number of world dignitaries.

An earthquake (Feb. 21-22) at Skopje, Yugoslavia, destroyed most of the town and killed 1,100 persons. Floods in Kentucky, West Virginia, Virginia and Tennessee (Mar. 13) left 18 dead and 30,000 homeless. Hurricanes and tidal waves killed 12,000 persons in East Pakistan (May 29). Hurricane Flora slammed into Haiti and caused 2,500 deaths (Oct. 3-4). A tidal wave (Oct. 9), caused by the collapse of a dam near Belluno, Italy, killed 1,800.

The United States and the Soviet Union announced (Jan. 7) an end to their negotiations on the Cuban crisis and declared the matter closed. Some 17,000 Russian troops remaining in Cuba were to be withdrawn. The two world powers agreed (Apr. 5) to establish a "hot line" between Washington and Moscow to speed communications in a crisis like the Cuban confrontation.

The U.S. navy nuclear submarine *Thresher* was lost (Apr. 10) in the North Atlantic with 129 aboard.

After large demonstrations and mass arrests, Black leaders and civic leaders in Birmingham, Ala., reached an agreement (May 6-7) to desegregate public facilities.

Astronaut Maj. L. Gordon Cooper, Jr., orbited the Earth 22 times in Mercury capsule *Faith 7*.

Pope John XXIII, 81, died (June 3) in Vatican City. The Sacred College of Cardinals elected (June 21) Giovanni Battista Montini as Pope of the Roman Catholic Church. He took the name Paul VI.

A rift between the U.S.S.R. and Red China deepened after ideological talks ended July 20 without an agreement.

A gang halted the Glasgow-to-London train on the outskirts of London (Aug. 15) and got away with a spectacular haul of $7,368,000. Within a few months, Scotland Yard rounded up nineteen persons in connection with the robbery, but only about 10 percent of the loot was recovered.

"March on Washington," a demonstration (Aug. 28) in behalf of civil rights legislation, drew over 250,000 persons in Washington, D.C.

A bomb explosion in a Negro church in Birmingham, Ala., killed four children (Sept. 15).

The 114-day strike against all of New York City's major newspapers ended Apr. 1. The cost of the settlement with the printers and other craft unions resulted in a decision by the Hearst Corporation to close the *Daily Mirror* (Oct. 15).

Konrad Adenauer retired (Oct. 16) as Chancellor of West Germany and was succeeded by Ludwig Erhard. Britain also had a change of command when Prime Minister Harold Macmillan was succeeded (Oct. 19) by Sir Alec Douglas-Home.

South Vietnamese President Ngo Dinh Diem was killed in an Army-led coup (Nov. 1-2).

Deaths of the year included Dick Powell, 58 (Jan. 2); Otto Harbach, 89 (Jan. 24); Clifford Odets, 57 (Aug. 15); Edith Piaf, 47 (Oct. 11); Adolphe Menjou, 73 (Oct. 29).

In Print

Best-selling fiction of the year included *The Group*, by Mary McCarthy; *The Glass Blowers*, by Daphne du Maurier; *Shoes of the Fisherman*, by Morris West; *Raise High the Roof Beam, Carpenters*, by J. D. Salinger. In the nonfiction category, leaders included *Happiness Is a Warm Puppy*, by Charles M. Schulz; *Ordeal of Power*, by Emmet J. Hughes; *The American Way of Death*, by Jessica Mitford; *The Fire Next Time*, by James Baldwin; *I Owe Russia $1,200*, by Bob Hope. A total of 25,784 titles was published, up from 21,904 in 1962.

The Pulitzer Prize committee found no 1963 works meriting awards in the categories of fiction, drama or music.

On Stage

The New York newspaper strike (Dec. 8, 1962, to Apr. 1, 1963) was a devastating blow to the Broadway stage. Theater attendance dropped sharply as long-running shows and new productions found it difficult to survive without reviews and publicity. Edward Albee's *Who's Afraid of Virginia Woolf?* was the biggest critical and box-office hit of the 1962-1963 season. Plays by several established writers had very brief lives. Among these were Tennessee Williams' *The Milk Train Doesn't Stop Here Anymore*; Sidney Kingsley's *Night Life*; Lillian Hellman's *My Mother, My Father and Me*; Garson Kanin's *Come on Strong*; and Irwin Shaw's *Children from Their Games*. Two hit musicals, *Oliver!* and *Stop the World—I Want to Get Off*, were British imports.

Films

Motion Picture Academy Oscars for 1963 were awarded to *Tom Jones*, best picture; Patricia Neal in *Hud*, best actress; Sidney Poitier in *Lilies of the Field*, best actor. Poitier's Oscar was the first in a major category to be given to a black actor. The late Hattie McDaniel had previously won an Oscar for her supporting role in *Gone with the Wind*.

Cleopatra, starring Elizabeth Taylor, Richard Burton and Rex Harrison, had its world premier on June 12 in New York City. Costing $37,000,000, it was the most expensive film in the history of the cinema. Seats for *Cleopatra* cost as much as $5.50. Other important films of the year included: *Dr. No*, with Sean Connery; Alfred Hitchcock's *The Birds; Charade*, with Cary Grant and Audrey Hepburn; *America, America; The Balcony; Days of Wine and Roses*, with Jack Lemmon, Lee Remick, and Charles Bickford; Federico Fellini's *8 ½*, with Marcello Mastroianni; *The Great Escape*, with Steve McQueen and James Garner; *How the West Was Won*, with James Stewart and Debbie Reynolds; *Irma La Douce*, with Jack Lemmon and Shirley MacLaine; *It's a Mad, Mad, Mad, Mad World*, with Sid Caesar, Buddy Hackett, Jonathan Winters, and Jimmy Durante; *Lord of the Flies; Mondo Cane; PT 109*, with Cliff Robertson; and *The Ugly American*, with Marlon Brando.

Television

Princess Grace hosted (Feb. 17) a CBS guided tour of the principality of Monaco. Another tour, this of the Kremlin, was offered (May 21) two months later by NBC, with Frank Bourgholtzer.

President Kennedy's assassination and the events in its immediate aftermath were covered (Nov. 22-15) by all three networks.

ABC aired (Dec. 29) "The Making Of The President, 1960," a documentary with commentary from, and based on the book by, Theodore H. White.

Jack Klugman won the Emmy for acting in a single performance for his role in "Blacklist" on CBS's *The Defenders*. *The Beverly Hillbillies* was again the nation's most watched show.

Music

The top-selling, number one songs included: *Go Away, Little Girl*, Steve Lawrence; *Walk Right In*, The Rooftop Singers; *Hey Paula*, Paul and Paula; *Walk Like a Man*, The Four Seasons; *Our Day Will Come*, Ruby and the Romantics; *He's So Fine*, The Chiffons; *I Will Follow Him*, Little Peggy March; *If You Wanna Be Happy*, Jimmy Soul; *It's My Party*, Lesley Gore; *Sukiyaki*, Kyu Sakamoto; *Easier Said Than Done*, The Essex; *Surf City*, Jan and Dean; *So Much in Love*, The Tymes; *Fingertips (Pt. II)*, Little Stevie Wonder; *My Boyfriend's Back*, The Angels; *Blue Velvet*, Bobby Vinton; *Sugar Shack*, Jimmy Gilmer and the Fireballs; *Deep Purple*, Nino Tempo and April Stevens; *I'm Leaving It Up to You*, Dale and Grace; *Dominique*, The Singing Nun.

1964

$\mathcal{T}$he Beatles, a rock and roll quartet from Liverpool, England, arrived in the United States early in the year and triggered the American outbreak of Beatlemania, a form of hysteria that gripped teen-age audiences wherever the Beatles performed. The Beatles included Paul McCartney, 23; John Lennon, 24; George Harrison, 22; and Ringo Starr, 24.

Pope Paul VI visited the Holy Land (Jan. 4-6), the first Roman Catholic pontiff to make the pilgrimage to the birthplace of Christianity.

Twenty-three persons were killed (Jan. 9-12) in the Panama Canal Zone in riots sparked by the raising of the United States flag by American high school students.

The ninth Winter Olympic Games were held (Jan. 29-Feb. 9) in Innsbruck, Austria. The Russians led the field with 11 gold medals.

The 24th amendment to the U.S. Constitution, banning the poll tax as a condition for voting in federal elections, became part of the Constitution when South Dakota became the 38th state to ratify the amendment (Jan. 23).

Cassius Marcellus Clay knocked out Sonny Liston, the 8-to-1 favorite, in the heavyweight championship fight (Feb. 25). Clay later adopted the name Muhammad Ali.

Jack L. Ruby was condemned (Feb. 14) to die in the electric chair for the murder of Lee Harvey Oswald, the alleged assassin of President Kennedy.

The most violent earthquake in North America in recent times killed some 131 persons in Alaska (Mar. 27).

The New York World's Fair opened (Apr. 22) at Flushing Meadows in Queens, N.Y.

Northern Dancer won the Kentucky Derby (May 2) in the record time of two minutes.

The Civil Rights Act of 1964 was signed (July 2) by President Johnson. It was the most comprehensive civil rights legislation since Reconstruction.

Riots in Harlem (July 18-23), in Jersey City (July 24-26) and in Philadelphia (Aug. 28-30) punctuated the "long, hot summer."

The Warren Commission report on the assassination of President Kennedy, filed (Sept. 24) with President Johnson, found that Lee Harvey Oswald acted alone in firing the fatal bullet. This conclusion has been challenged repeatedly.

Fifty-seven people fled East Germany and entered West Berlin through a secret tunnel, the largest such escape since the German Communist regime built the wall in 1961.

The St. Louis Cardinals beat the New York Yankees four games out of seven to win baseball's World Series (Oct. 7-15).

The XVIII Olympiad, the first to be held in Asia, ended Oct. 24 in Tokyo. American athletes dominated in track and field, swimming and basketball.

Nikita S. Khrushchev, Premier of the Soviet Union and Soviet Communist Party chief, was suddenly stripped of his power (Oct. 15) and replaced by Leonid I. Brezhnev, who became first secretary of the Communist Party, and Aleksei N. Kosygin who became Premier.

Communist China exploded its first atom bomb (Oct. 16).

Lyndon B. Johnson was elected (Nov. 3) the 36th President of the United States in a landslide victory over the Republican nominee, Senator Barry Goldwater.

Martin Luther King, Jr., leader of the non-violent movement for civil rights in the United States, received (Dec. 10) the Nobel Peace Prize.

Herbert Clark Hoover, 90, the 31st President of the United States, died Oct. 20.

General of the Army Douglas MacArthur, 84, a dominant American military figure of the 20th century, died (Apr. 5).

Jawaharlal Nehru, 75, Prime Minister of India since that country became independent in 1947, died (May 27).

Other deaths during 1964 included: Brendan Behan, 41 (Mar. 20); Eddie Cantor, 72 (Oct. 10); Rachel Carson, 56 (Apr. 14); Ian Fleming, 56 (Aug. 12); Ben Hecht, 70 (Apr. 18); Alan Ladd, 50 (Jan. 29); Harpo Marx, 70 (Sept. 28); Sean O'Casey, 84 (Sept. 18); Cole Porter, 71 (Oct. 16).

In Print

This year's fiction included *Herzog*, by Saul Bellow; *The Keeper of the House* (a 1965 Pulitzer prize winner), by Shirley Ann Grau; *The Rector of Justin*, by Louis Auchincloss; *Julian*, by Gore Vidal; *The President*, by R. V. Cassill; *Reuben, Reuben*, by Peter de Vries; *Little Big Man*, by Thomas Berger; *To an Early Grave*, by Wallace Markfield; and *The Loser*, by Borden Deal. Nonfiction books included *A Moveable Feast*, by Ernest Hemingway; *The Naked Society*, by Vance Packard; *The American Irish*, by William Shannon; and *The Italians*, by Luigi Barzini.

On Stage

The 400th anniversary of William Shakespeare's birth was celebrated with numerous productions of the Bard's plays, including *Hamlet* on Broadway, with Richard Burton starring and John Gielgud directing. Other plays of the season included *The Subject Was Roses* (Pulitzer prize winner); *The Deputy*; *Dylan*; *Any Wednesday*; and *Luv*. Hit musical productions were *Hello, Dolly!*, based on Thornton Wilder's *The Matchmaker*; *Funny Girl*, based on the life of Fanny Brice; and *Fiddler on the Roof*, adapted from the stories of Sholom Aleichem.

Films

Motion Picture Academy Oscars for 1964 were awarded to *My Fair Lady*, best picture; Julie Andrews in *Mary Poppins*, best actress; Rex Harrison in *My Fair Lady*, best actor.

The top money-making film of the year was *The Carpetbaggers* with George Peppard, Carroll Baker, and Alan Ladd. Other films of the year included: *The Americanization of Emily*, with Julie Andrews and James Garner; *Becket*, with Richard Burton and Peter O'Toole; *Behold a Pale Horse*, with Anthony Quinn, Gregory Peck, and Omar Sharif; *The Best Man*, with Henry Fonda and Cliff Robertson; *Dr. Strangelove*, with Peter Sellers, George C. Scott, and Sterling Hayden; *From Russia with Love*, with Sean Connery; *Goldfinger*, with Sean Connery; *Hamlet*, with Richard Burton; *A Hard Day's Night*, with the Beatles; *Marriage, Italian Style*, with Sophia Loren and Marcello Mastroianni; *The Night of the Iguana*, with Richard Burton, Deborah Kerr, and Ava Gardner; *The Pink Panther*, with David Niven and Peter Sellers; *Seven Days in May*, with Burt Lancaster, Kirk Douglas, Fredric March, and Edmund O'Brien; *Topkapi*, with Melina Mercouri, Peter Ustinov, and Maximilian Schell; *The Unsinkable Molly Brown*, with Debbie Reynolds and Harve Presnell; *What a Way to Go*, with Shirley MacLaine, Paul Newman, Robert Mitchum, and Dean Martin; and *Zorba the Greek*, with Anthony Quinn.

Television

ABC produced (Sept. 10) *Letters From Vietnam*, a report on an American helicopter unit.

CBS offered (Dec. 16) *Casals At 88*, a documentary on cellist Pablo Casals.

Dick Van Dyke, Alfred Lunt, Lynn Fontanne, Barbra Streisand and Leonard Bernstein received Emmys for outstanding individual achievement in entertainment.

NBC's *Bonanza* was the top-rated program.

Music

The number one songs of the year included: *There! I've Said It Again*, Bobby Vinton; *I Want to Hold Your Hand*, The Beatles; *She Loves You*, The Beatles; *Can't Buy Me Love*, The Beatles; *Hello, Dolly!*, Louis Armstrong; *My Guy*, Mary Wells; *Love Me Do*, The Beatles; *Chapel of Love*, The Dixie Cups; *A World Without Love*, Peter and Gordon; *I Get Around*, Beach Boys; *Rag Doll*, The Four Seasons; *A Hard Day's Night*, The Beatles; *Everybody Loves Somebody*, Dean Martin; *Where Did Our Love Go*, The Supremes; *The House of the Rising Sun*, The Animals; *Oh, Pretty Woman*, Roy Orbison; *Do Wah Diddy Diddy*, Manfred Mann; *Baby Love*, The Supremes; *Leader of the Pack*, The Shangri-Las; *Ringo*, Lorne Greene; *Mr. Lonely*, Bobby Vinton; *Come See About Me*, The Supremes; *I Feel Fine*, The Beatles.

1965

*P*resident Johnson outlined his program for a "Great Society" in the State of the Union message (Jan. 4) to the 89th Congress.

The United States expanded the war in Vietnam by bombing the northern zone (Feb. 7) after Vietcong attacks in South Vietnam.

Soviet cosmonaut Lt. Col. Aleksei A. Leonov became the first man to float in space outside of his spacecraft while orbiting the Earth (Mar. 18-19).

President Johnson proposed unconditional peace negotiations on Vietnam in a speech (Apr. 7) at Johns Hopkins University.

The Astrodome, the world's largest air-conditioned stadium, opened (Apr. 9) in Houston.

Civil war broke out in the Dominican Republic when the ruling junta was overthrown (Apr. 24) by rebels demanding the return of deposed President Juan Bosch. President Johnson ordered (Apr. 28) U.S. Marines to the area to protect American citizens, and in the President's words, "to prevent another Communist state in this hemisphere."

A national "teach-in" debate on the Vietnam war was held (May 15) on 100 college campuses.

The United States resumed air attacks on North Vietnam after a six-day suspension produced no progress toward peace negotiations.

Supreme Court Justice Arthur Goldberg was picked (July 20) to succeed Adlai Stevenson as U.S. Ambassador to the United Nations. Washington lawyer Abe Fortas was named (July 28) by President Johnson to succeed Goldberg on the Supreme Court.

The Medicare Bill to provide medical care for the aged was signed (July 30) by President Johnson.

The Watts district in Los Angeles, a Black slum area, was set aflame (Aug. 11-16) by rioting that resulted in 30 persons being killed.

The Indonesian army blocked (Sept. 30) a Communist-backed coup and launched a campaign of retaliation that resulted in the killing of at least 200,000 persons.

Sandy Koufax, the Los Angeles Dodgers star hurler, with four no-hit games to his credit, pitched two shutouts during the World Series to give the Dodgers a 4-3 victory over the Minnesota Twins.

Electric power failure blacked out parts of the northeastern United States and Canada for about 16 hours (Nov. 9-10).

Rhodesia declared (Nov. 11) its independence from Great Britain. England called the declaration unconstitutional and instituted economic counter-measures. The dispute grew out of the policy of Rhodesia's 220,000 whites to maintain political domination over the country's 4,000,000 blacks.

Lt. Col. Frank Borman and Comdr. James A. Lovell, Jr., completed (Dec. 18) a record 14-day, 206-orbit flight in their *Gemini 7* capsule.

The United States suspended air attacks (Dec. 24) on North Vietnam in a Christmas truce and began a major diplomatic peace offensive.

The world of literature mourned the death of the master storyteller, William Somerset Maugham, who died (Dec. 16) at the age of 91 at St. Jean-Cap-Ferrat, France.

Sir Winston Churchill, 90, England's great World War II leader, died (Jan. 24) in London.

Malcolm X, Negro nationalist leader, was slain (Feb. 21) by assassins in New York.

Adlai Stevenson, 65, collapsed on a London street and died (July 15).

Dr. Albert Schweitzer, 90, died (Sept. 4) in his jungle hospital at Lambarene, Gabon.

Other deaths during the year included Nat "King" Cole, 45 (Feb. 15); Judy Holliday, 42 (June 7); H. V. Kaltenborn, 86 (June 14); Stan Laurel (Arthur Stanley Jefferson), 74 (Feb. 23); David O. Selznick, 63 (June 22).

In Print

Among the year's books of fiction were *The Man*, by Irving Wallace; *The Source*, by James Michener; *Up the Down Staircase*, by Bel Kaufman; *The Ambassador*, by Morris West; *Hotel*, by Arthur Hailey; *The Looking Glass War*, by John Le Carre; *Those Who Love*, by Irving Stone; *The Green Berets*, by Robin Moore. Nonfiction books included *Markings*, by Dag Hammarskjold; *The Making of the President—1964*, by Theodore White; *Is Paris Burning?*, by Larry Collins and Dominique Lapierre; *Kennedy*, by Theodore Sorenson; *A Thousand Days* (a Pulitzer prize winner), by Arthur Schlesinger Jr.; *Yes, I Can*, by Sammy Davis, Jr.; *Games People Play*, by Eric Berne; and *A Gift of Prophecy*, by Ruth Montgomery.

On Stage

The most striking play of the season was German playwright Peter Weiss's *The Persecution and Assassination of Marat as Performed by the Inmates of the Asylum of Charenton Under the Direction of the Marquis de Sade*. Other productions launched during 1965 included: *The Odd Couple; On a Clear Day You Can See Forever; The Roar of the Greasepaint—The Smell of the Crowd; The Royal Hunt of the Sun; Man of La Mancha; Half a Sixpence;* and one-man shows by Maurice Chevalier, and Charles Aznavour. The Pulitzer Prize committee skipped the drama award for 1965.

Films

Motion Picture Academy Oscars for 1965 were awarded to *The Sound of Music*, best film; Julie Christie in *Darling*, best actress; Lee Marvin in *Cat Ballou*, best actor. Other major films released during the year included: *What's New, Pussycat*, with Peter Sellers and Peter O'Toole; *Shenandoah*, with James Stewart; *The Sandpiper*, with Elizabeth Taylor and Richard Burton; *Dr. Zhivago*, with Geraldine Chaplin, Julie Christie, Omar Sharif, and Rod Steiger; *Von Ryan's Express*, with Frank Sinatra and Trevor Howard; *The Yellow Rolls-Royce*, with Rex Harrison, Jeanne Moreau, George C. Scott, Ingrid Bergman, and Omar Sharif; *Help!*, with the Beatles; *Those Magnificent Men in Their Flying Machines*, with Stuart Whitman and Terry Thomas; *The Spy Who Came in from the Cold*, with Richard Burton, Claire Bloom, and Oskar Werner; *Thunderball*, with Sean Connery; *The Agony and the Ecstacy*, with Charlton Heston and Rex Harrison; *Lord Jim*, with Peter O'Toole and James Mason; and *The Cincinnati Kid*, with Steve McQueen and Edward G. Robinson.

Television

Mike Wallace hosted (May 24) *The National Driver's Test* on a CBS News Special.

ABC produced (Aug. 25) *The Agony of Vietnam* on the war's affect on the people. NBC presented (Nov. 24) *Frank Sinatra: A Man & His Music*, a solo turn by the singer which later won an Emmy.

CBS launched (Dec. 9 the first of the Peanuts specials, *A Charlie Brown Christmas*, which also earned an Emmy.

Perry Mason was canceled during the 1965-66 season. *The Fugitive* won an Emmy as the outstanding dramatic series, and Bill Cosby received one for his performance as a leading actor in *I Spy*. For the second consecutive year, NBC's *Bonanza* had the most viewers.

Music

There were many number one songs this year: *Downtown*, Petula Clark; *You've Lost That Lovin' Feelin'*, The Righteous Brothers; *This Diamond Ring*, Gary Lewis and the Playboys; *My Girl*, The Temptations; *Eight Days a Week*, The Beatles; *Stop! In the Name of Love*, The Supremes; *I'm Telling You Now*, Freddie and the Dreamers; *Game of Love*, Wayne Fontana and the Mindbenders; *Mrs. Brown You've Got a Lovely Daughter*, Herman's Hermits; *Ticket to Ride*, The Beatles; *Help Me Rhonda*, Beach Boys; *Back in My Arms Again*, The Supremes; *I Can't Help Myself (Sugar Pie, Honey Bunch)*, The Four Tops; *Mr. Tambourine Man*, The Byrds; *(I Can't Get No) Satisfaction*, The Rolling Stones; *I'm Henry VIII, I Am*, Herman's Hermits; *I Got You Babe*, Sonny and Cher; *Help!*, The Beatles; *Eve of Destruction*, Barry McGuire; *Hang on Sloopy*, The McCoys; *Yesterday*, The Beatles; *Get Off My Cloud*, The Rolling Stones; *I Hear a Symphony*, The Supremes; *Turn! Turn! Turn!*, The Byrds; *Over and Over*, The Dave Clark Five.

1966

$\mathcal{C}$harles de Gaulle began (Jan. 8) his second seven-year term as President of France.

Four hydrogen bombs aboard a U.S. B-52 bomber were lost (Jan. 17) over Polomares, Spain, after a mid-air collision with a jet tanker. Three of the four bombs were quickly recovered. The fourth was found intact (Apr. 7) in the Mediterranean Sea.

Mrs. Indira Gandhi, the only child of Jawaharlal Nehru, leader in India's emergence as an independent nation, was sworn in (Jan. 24) as Prime Minister of India. She succeeded Lai Bahadur Shastri, who died Jan. 11.

The United States resumed (Jan. 31) air raids over North Vietnam after a 37-day suspension.

Kwame Nkrumah, President of Ghana, was deposed (Feb. 24) by military leaders while he was on a mission to the Far East.

Astronauts Neil A. Armstrong and David R. Scott were forced to make an emergency landing near Okinawa after achieving the first docking in space (Mar. 16).

New York's old Metropolitan Opera House, a landmark for 83 years, closed (Apr. 16) after a gala program. Efforts to preserve the building as a landmark were unsuccessful. The company moved to new quarters in Lincoln Center for the Performing Arts.

Communist China's "cultural revolution," which sparked profound social and political upheaval, was launched early in May.

Unmanned U.S. spacecraft *Surveyor I* made a perfect soft landing on the moon (June 1) and transmitted 10,388 pictures of the lunar surface over a 12-day period.

In a historic ruling (June 13), in the case of *Miranda vs. Arizona*, the U.S. Supreme Court decreed that accused persons under arrest must be informed of their Constitutional rights against self-incrimination before police commence interrogation.

Large-scale rioting broke out (July 14-15) on Chicago's West Side and in Cleveland's Hough district (July 18-23).

Charles J. Whitman went berserk and shot 45 persons, 12 fatally, from the top of a 27-story tower in Austin, Tex. (Aug. 1). Earlier he had murdered both his mother and wife. The episode ended when police shot him to death.

An avalanche of coal-mining waste killed 144 children and 28 adults in the Welsh village of Aberfan (Oct. 21).

Baltimore beat the Los Angeles Dodgers four straight games to win the baseball World Series. The New York Yankees finished last in the American League for the first time since 1912.

Historic buildings and priceless art works were damaged in floods that engulfed Florence and Venice in November.

Attorney General Edward W. Brooke of Massachusetts was elected (Nov. 8) U.S. Senator on the Republican ticket. He became the first African American ever elected to the Senate by popular vote.

Deaths during the year included: Montgomery Clift, 45 (July 23); Walt Disney, 65 (Dec. 15); Minnie Guggenheimer (Mrs. Charles S.), 83 (May 23); Hedda Hopper, 75 (Feb. 1); Kathleen Norris, 85 (Jan. 18); Billy Rose (William Samuel Rosenberg), 66 (Feb. 10); Clifton Webb, 72 (Oct. 13); Ed Wynn (Isiah Edwin Leopold), 79 (June 19).

In Print

Among the year's top novels were *Valley of the Dolls*, by Jacqueline Susann; *Capable of Honor*, by Allen Drury; *The Fixer* (a Pulitzer prize winner), by Bernard Malamud; *Giles Goat-Boy*, by John Barth; *The Crying of Lot 49*, by Thomas Pynchon; *Any God Will Do*, by Richard Condon; *The Ninety and Nine*, by William Brinkley; *The Last Gentleman*, by Walder Perry; *The Diary of a Rapist*, by Evan S. Connell, Jr.; *Crazy February*, by Carter Wilson; *The Origin of the Brunists*, by Robert Coover; *All in the Family*, by Edwin O'Connor; *A Country of Strangers*, by Conrad Richter; and *The Embezzler*, by Louis Auchincloss. In the nonfiction category were *In Cold Blood*, by Truman Capote; *The Last 100 Days*, by John Toland; *The Last Battle*, by Cornelius Ryan; *With Kennedy*, by Pierre Salinger; *Rush to Judgment*, by Mark Lane; *Inquest: The Warren Commission and the Establishment of Truth*, by Edward Jay Epstein; and *Death of a President*, by William Manchester.

On Stage

Most successful musical productions of the Broadway season were *Mame*, starring Angela Lansbury in a comedy based on the Patrick Dennis novel *Auntie Mame*; *Cabaret*, an adaptation of Christopher Isherwood's *Berlin Stories*; and *Sweet Charity*, based on Federico Fellini's film *Nights of Cabiria*. Other production included Edward Albee's *A Delicate Balance*, a Pulitzer Prize winner; *I Do, I Do*, a musical based on Jan de Hartog's play, *The Fourposter*; *The Killing of Sister George*; *Philadelphia, Here I Come*; and *Don't Drink the Water*.

Films

The Motion Picture Association of America adopted a new production code in 1966 that distinguished between films suitable for children and those for adults only. The code was designed to permit bolder films to be made for adult audiences, such as the film adaptation of Edward Albee's play, *Who's Afraid of Virginia Woolf?*

Motion Picture Academy Oscars for 1966 went to *A Man for All Seasons*, best film; Elizabeth Taylor in *Who's Afraid of Virginia Woolf?*; Paul Scofield in *A Man for All Seasons*, best actor. Other major films of the year included: *Alfie*, with Michael Caine and Shelly Winters; *The Bible...In the Beginning*, with John Juston, Ava Gardner, Peter O'Toole, and Stephen Boyd; *Blow-up*, with David Hemmings and Vanessa Redgrave; *Born Free*, with Virginia McKenna and Bill Travers; *Fantastic Voyage*, with Stephen Boyd and Raquel Welch; *The Fortune Cookie*, with Jack Lemmon and Walter Matthau; *A Funny Thing Happened on the Way to the Forum*, with Zero Mostel and Phil Silvers; *Georgy Girl*, with Lynn Redgrave and James Mason; *Hawaii*, with Julie Andrews, Max Von Sydow, and Richard Harris; *How to Steal a Million*, with Audrey Hepburn and Peter O'Toole; *Is Paris Burning?*, with Gert Frobe and Leslie Caron; *Khartoum*, with Charlton Heston and Laurence Olivier; *A Man and a Woman*, with Anouk Aimee; *A Man for All Seasons*, with Paul Scofield; and *The Professionals*, with Burt Lancaster and Lee Marvin.

Television

A new production of *Death Of A Salesman*, starring Lee J. Cobb, was presented (May 8) by CBS.

The three major networks provided (Aug. 6) coverage of the White House wedding of Luci Baines Johnson and Patrick J. Nugent.

Shirley Booth, Barbara Loden, Pat Hingle and Hal Holbrook performed (Dec. 8) in a new version of *The Glass Menagerie* on CBS.

General William Westmoreland was interviewed (Dec. 27) in Saigon by Charles Collingwood and Morley Safer on a CBS News Special.

Mission: Impossible was launched during the 1966-67 season and won an Emmy.

Batman also made its television debut, while *Candid Camera* and *The Adventures Of Ozzie and Harriet* were canceled.

Among the Emmy winners were NBC's *The Monkees*, as the outstanding comedy series. Eli Wallach won for the outstanding performance by an actor in a supporting dramatic role. *Bonanza* was rated the most popular program for the third year in a row.

Music

Topping the charts: *The Sounds of Silence*, Simon and Garfunkel; *We Can Work It Out*, The Beatles; *My Love*, Petula Clark; *Lightnin' Strikes*, Lou Christie; *These Boots Are Made for Walkin'*, Nancy Sinatra; *The Ballad of the Green Berets*, S/Sgt. Barry Sadler; *(You're My) Soul and Inspiration*, The Righteous Brothers; *Good Lovin'*, The Young Rascals; *Monday, Monday*, The Mama and the Papas; *When a Man Loves a Woman*, Percy Sledge; *Paint It Black*, The Rolling Stones; *Paperback Writer*, The Beatles; *Strangers in the Night*, Frank Sinatra; *Hanky Panky*, Tommy James and the Shondells; *Wild Thing*, The Troggs; *Summer in the City,* The Lovin' Spoonful; *Sunshine Superman,* Donovan; *You Can't Hurry Love,* The Supremes; *Cherish,* The Association; *Reach Out, I'll Be There,* The Four Tops; *96 Tears,* ? (Question Mark) and the Mysterians; *Last Train to Clarksville,* The Monkees; *Poor Side of Town,* Johnny Rivers; *You Keep Me Hangin' On,* The Supremes; *Winchester Cathedral,* The New Vaudeville Band; *Good Vibrations,* The Beach Boys; *I'm a Believer,* The Monkees.

1967

*T*hree United States astronauts, Virgil I. Grissom, Edward H. White and Roger B. Chaffee, were killed (Jan. 27) in a flash fire in an Apollo spacecraft during a test at Cape Kennedy, Fla.

A tanker, the *Torray Canyon*, owned by the Union Oil Company of California, ran aground (Mar. 18) at the western channel of the English Channel. The ship broke apart, and its cargo of oil spilled and polluted the beaches of southwest Britain and Normandy in France.

North Vietnam President Ho Chi Minh rejected (Mar. 21) President Johnson's proposal for peace talks.

Svetlana Alliluyeva, only daughter of the late Soviet dictator Joseph Stalin, arrived (Apr. 21) in the United States after having broken her ties with Russia.

Soviet Cosmonaut Vladimir M. Komarov became the first casualty of an actual space mission when his spacecraft crashed to Earth (Apr. 24) during a re-entry maneuver.

The worst crisis in the Middle East since the outbreak of war in 1956 flared up in May when United Arab Republic President Nasser requested the withdrawal of United Nations peace-keeping troops from the Egyptian-Israel border. The U.A.R. closed the Gulf of Aqaba to Israeli shipping (May 22). Full-scale fighting began (June 5) between Israel and Egypt, Syria, and Jordan. There followed a "six-day war" in which Israel smashed the Arab forces and occupied the Sinai Peninsula, the Gaza Strip, Jordanian territory west of the Jordan River and the Golan Highlands of south-east Syria.

Thurgood Marshall, U.S. Solicitor General, became the first Black man to be appointed to the U.S. Supreme Court (June 13).

Fighting broke out (July 6) between Nigerian federal troops and secessionist forces seeking independence for the region of Biafra.

A total of 69 persons were killed in race-rioting in Newark (July 12-17) and Detroit (July 23-30).

Nguyen Van Thieu and Nguyen Cao Ky were elected (Sept. 3) President and Vice President of South Vietnam.

Che Guevara, right-hand man to Fidel Castro during the Cuban revolution, was captured and killed (Oct. 10) by the Bolivian army.

Opponents of American participation in the Vietnam war demonstrated (Oct. 21) in Washington, D.C. Marshalls and soldiers were used to block attempts to storm the Pentagon.

The world's first human heart transplant was performed (Dec. 3) by South African surgeon Dr. Christiaan N. Barnard. He replaced the damaged heart of a 53-year-old man with the heart of a 25-year-old woman who had died of brain injuries suffered in an automobile accident.

A suspension bridge over the Ohio River between Point Pleasant, W. VA, and Kanauga, Ohio, collapsed (Dec. 15), killing at least 46 persons.

Deaths during the year included Charles Bickford, 78 (Nov. 9); Primo Carnera, 60 (June 29); Nelson Eddy, 65 (Mar. 6); John Nance Garner, 98 (Nov. 7); Woody Guthrie, 55 (Oct. 3); Bert Lahr, 72 (Dec. 4); Jayne Mansfield, 34 (June 29); Paul Muni, 71 (Aug. 25); Elmer Rice, 74 (May 8); Francis Cardinal Spellman, 78 (Dec. 2); Spencer Tracy, 67 (June 10); Paul Whiteman, 77 (Dec. 29).

In Print

William Styron's novel *The Confessions of Nat Turner* won the Pulitzer award for fiction. His portrait of the leader of slave rebellions in the antebellum South generated sharp controversy among blacks and literary critics.

Other important novels of the year included *All the Little Live Things*, by Wallace Stegner; *Why Are We in Vietnam?*, by Norman Mailer; *Topaz*, by Leon Uris; *Washington, D.C.*, by Gore Vidal; *The Man Who Knew Kennedy*, by Vance Bourjaily; *Fathers*, by Herbert Gold; *When She Was Good*, by Philip Roth; *The Chosen*, by Chaim Potok; *Death Kit*, by Susan Sontag; *The Man Who Cried I Am*, by John A. Williams; *Under the Eye of the Storm*, by John Hersey; *The Eighth Day*, by Thornton Wilder; and *A Bad Man*, by Stanley Elkin. Nonfiction books included: *La Vida*, by Oscar Lewis; *Down These Mean Streets*, by Piri Thomas; *Death at an Early Age: The Destruction of the Hearts and Minds of Negro Children in the Boston Public Schools*, by Jonathan Kozol; *The New Industrial State*, by John Kenneth Galbraith; and *The Medium Is the Message*, by Marshall McLuhan (in collaboration with Quentin Fiore).

On Stage

British playwrights came to the rescue of the Broadway theater. Among the top plays of the season were Tom Stoppard's *Rosencrantz and Guildernstern Are Dead*, Harold Pinter's *The Homecoming* and John Bowen's *After the Rain*. *Hello Dolly!* turned up in an all-Black version starring Pearl Bailey and Cab Calloway. A Yiddish musical revue, *Hello, Solly!* ran for six weeks. Other productions of the season included: *Black Comedy; Little Murders; Spofford; You Know I Can't Hear You When the Water's Running; Hallelujah, Baby!; How Now, Dow Jones; Ilya, Darling;* and *Sherry!*

For the fourth time in six years, there was no drama award made by the Pulitzer Prize committee for 1967.

Films

Motion Picture Academy Oscars for 1967 were awarded to *In the Heat of the Night*, best film; Katharine Hepburn in *Guess Who's Coming to Dinner?* best actress; Rod Steiger *In the Heat of the Night*, best actor.

The Dirty Dozen with Lee Marvin, Ernest Borgnine, Charles Bronson, Jim Brown, and John Cassavetes was the year's top money-making film. Other big films at the box office were: *You Only Live Twice*, with Sean Connery; *Casino Royale*, with Peter Sellers and Ursula Andress; *Thoroughly Modern Millie*, with Julie Andrews; *Barefoot in the Park*, with Robert Redford and Jane Fonda; *To Sir with Love*, with Sidney Poitier, Judy Geeson, and Suzy Kendall; *Hombre*, with Paul Newman, Frederic March, Richard Boone, and Cameron Mitchell; *Bonnie and Clyde*, with Warren Beatty and Faye Dunaway; *Camelot*, with Richard Harris with Vanessa Redgrave; *The Comedians*, with Elizabeth Taylor, Richard Burton; *Cool Hand Luke*, with Paul Newman; *A Countess from Hong Kong*, with Sophia Loren and Marlon Brando; *Doctor Dolittle*, with Rex Harrison and Samantha Eggar; *Elvira Madigan*, with Pia Degermark and Thommy Berggren; and *Ulysses*, with Milo O'Shea.

Television

Both CBS and NBC covered (Jan. 15) Super Bowl I.

Hal Holbrook starred (Mar. 6) during CBS's production of *Mark Twain Tonight*.

NBC broadcast (Sept. 9) *Rowan and Martin's Laugh-In Special*.

I Spy was canceled during the 1967-68 season.

Barbara Anderson was awarded an Emmy for her supporting role as a dramatic actress in NBC's *Ironside*.

After a long run by Westerns, *The Andy Griffith Show* became the top rated program.

Music

Songs hitting the number one spot included: *King of a Drag*, The Buckinghams; *Ruby Tuesday*, The Rolling Stones; *Love Is Here and Now You're Gone*, The Supremes; *Penny Lane*, The Beatles; *Happy Together*, The Turtles; *Somethin' Stupid*, Nancy Sinatra and Frank Sinatra; *The Happening*, The Supremes; *Groovin'*, The Young Rascals; *Respect*, Aretha Franklin; *Windy*, The Association; *Light My Fire*, The Doors; *All You Need Is Love*, The Beatles; *Ode to Billie Joe*, Bobbie Gentry; *The Letter*, The Box Tops; *To Sir With Love*, Lulu; *Incense and Peppermints*, Strawberry Alarm Clock; *Daydream Believer*, The Monkees; *Hello Goodbye*, The Beatles.

1968

$\mathscr{D}$r. Christiaan N. Barnard performed the world's third heart transplant operation (Jan. 2). The patient, Dr. Philip Blaiberg, 58, a retired South African dentist, became the world's longest survivor of this surgical technique when he lived until Aug. 17, 1969.

A Strategic Air Command B-52 carrying four hydrogen bombs crashed near Thule, Greenland (Jan. 22). Radioactive material spread over a wide area, although there was no nuclear explosion.

A U.S. Navy electronic intelligence vessel, the USS *Pueblo*, was seized (Jan. 23) by North Korean patrol boats in the Sea of Japan. North Korea claimed that the ship had violated its territorial waters and demanded an apology before releasing the 83-man crew. A formal apology was made and the crew was released after nearly a year of imprisonment.

Communist forces in Vietnam opened devastating strikes (Jan. 30) on Saigon and 30 provincial capitals on the first day of the Tet, or New Year, truce. Fighting in the city of Hue continued until Feb. 24.

Alexander Dubcek was elected (Jan. 25) First Secretary of the Czechoslovakian Communist Party. He promised to liberalize the regime.

Minnesota Sen. Eugene J. McCarthy, running in the New Hampshire primary (Mar. 12) for the Democratic Presidential nomination, polled 42 percent of the vote against 48 percent for President Johnson. Senator Robert Kennedy's entry into the Presidential race came four days later.

The Reverend Dr. Martin Luther King, Jr., 39 leader of the non-violent civil rights movement, was killed (Apr. 4) by a sniper in Memphis. President Johnson proclaimed April 7 a day of mourning. Dr. King's burial in Atlanta (Apr. 9) was attended by 100,000 mourners including a host of political leaders. The assassin, James Earl Ray, an escaped convict, was captured (June 8) at a London airport; he was subsequently convicted and sentenced to 99 years.

The campus revolution was in full swing around the world. In the United States the problems of student alienation, administrative bureaucracy, the Vietnam war, the draft, and black protests against racism were seen as the prime causes of student unrest. "New Left" groups, headed by the Students for a Democratic Society (S.D.S.), occupied several buildings at Columbia University in New York late in April. The events at Columbia followed a pattern set at the Berkeley campus of the University of California in 1964. Large-scale student outbreaks also occurred for various reasons in France, West Germany, Poland, Czechoslovakia, and Japan.

Vice President Hubert H. Humphrey entered (Apr. 27) the race for the Democratic Presidential nomination.

Senator Robert F. Kennedy, 42, was shot (June 5) by an assassin at the Hotel Ambassador in Los Angeles, where he was celebrating his victory in the California primary election. He died the following day, less than five years after the assassination of his older brother, President John F. Kennedy. Sirhan Bishara Sirhan, a Jordanian Arab, was seized with gun in hand.

The Soviet Union directed more than 200,000 of its own allied troops to invade Czechoslovakia (Aug. 20-21) in an effort to halt the democratization process.

Vice President Humphrey was nominated for President at the Democratic Convention in Chicago (Aug. 26-29). Violence inside the convention hall and on the streets of Chicago plagued the Democratic meeting. Senator Edmund S. Muskie of Maine was chosen as the Vice Presidential nominee.

Mrs. Jacqueline Kennedy, widow of President John F. Kennedy, was married (Oct. 20) to Aristotle Onassis, Greek shipping magnate, on his private island of Skorpios off the coast of Greece.

Richard Milhous Nixon was elected (Nov. 5) 37th President of the United States by a narrow margin. He won 302 of the 538 electoral votes and 43.4 percent of the popular vote against Humphrey's 191 electoral votes and 42.7 percent of the popular vote. George Wallace, running on the American Independent Party ticket, received 9,906,000 popular votes and 45 electoral votes.

Yale University announced (Nov. 14) that it would admit women for the first time in its 267-year history.

On Stage

Theater productions of the year included *How to Be a Jewish Mother; Staircase; The Prime of Miss Jean Brodie; The Happy Time; I Never Sang for My Father; A Day in the Death of Joe Egg; Golden Rainbow; The Price; Plaza Suite; George M.; Hair; The Man in the Glass Booth* and Howard Sackler's *The Great White Hope.*

Films

Oliver! won the Motion Picture Academy award for best film of 1968. Katharine Hepburn, for her role in *The Lion in Winter*, and Barbra Streisand, for her role in *Funny Girl*, were named best actresses, the first tie in the Oscar competition since 1931. Cliff Robertson was named best actor for his role in *Charly. The Graduate*, with Anne Bancroft and Dustin Hoffman was the biggest money-maker of the films released during 1968. Other major films of the year included *The Odd Couple*, with Jack Lemmon and Walter Matthau; *Planet of the Apes*, with Charlton Heston; *Rosemary's Baby*, with Mia Farrow; *Yours, Mine and Ours*, with Lucille Ball and Henry Fonda; *The Green Berets*, with John Wayne; *2001: A Space Odyssey*, with Keir Dullea and Gary Lockwood; *The Fox*, with

Sandy Dennis and Keir Dullea; *The Thomas Crown Affair*, with Steve McQueen; *In Cold Blood*, with Robert Blake and Scott Wilson; *Charlie Bubbles*, with Albert Finney; *Rachel, Rachel*, with Joanne Woodward and Estelle Parsons; *The Valley of the Dolls*, with Barbara Parkins and Patty Duke; and *The Happiest Millionaire*, with Fred MacMurray and Tommy Steele.

Television

The war in Southeast Asia was the subject of another network documentary when a CBS News Special offered (Feb. 27) *Walter Cronkite In Vietnam*.

Bill Cosby starred (Mar. 18) in his first variety special on NBC.

Elvis Presley made his first TV appearance in several years on a Dec. 3 NBC special. CBS launched *60 Minutes* during the 1968-69 season, while *The Smothers Brothers*, *The Andy Griffith Show* and *Star Trek*, which had been introduced two years earlier, were all canceled. *The Dick Cavett Show* on ABC won an Emmy for outstanding achievement in a daytime program, and *Rowan & Martin's Laugh-In* on NBC was the nation's most popular show.

Music

The number one hits included *Judy in Disguise (With Glasses)*, John Fred and His Playboy Band; *Green Tambourine*, Lemon Pipers; *Love Is Blue*, Paul Mauriat; *(Sittin' On) The Dock of the Bay*, Otis Redding; *Honey*, Bobby Goldsboro; *Tighten Up*, Archie Bell and the Drells; *Mrs. Robinson*, Simon and Garfunkel; *This Guy's in Love With You*, Herb Alpert; *Grazing in the Grass*, Hugh Masekela; *Hello, I Love You*, The Doors; *People Got to Be Free*, The Rascals; *Harper Valley P.T.A.*, Jeannie C. Riley; *Hey Jude*, The Beatles; *Love Child*, Diana Ross and the Supremes; *I Heard It Through the Grapevine*, Marvin Gaye.

1969

$\mathscr{P}$resident Richard M. Nixon was inaugurated as the 37th President Jan. 20.

The world's first total artificial heart transplant on a human was performed (Apr. 4) by Dr. Denton A. Cooley in Houston.

The toll of Americans killed in the Vietnam conflict reached 33,641, more than died in the Korean War.

The British sent in troops (Apr. 20) as a result of clashes between Catholics and Protestants in Northern Ireland.

Charles de Gaulle resigned (Apr. 28) as president of France after defeat in a national referendum.

Charles Evers, Negro civil rights leader, was elected (May 13) mayor of Fayette, Miss.

Associate Justice Abe Fortas, under pressure arising from attacks on his relationship with convicted financier Louis Wolfson, resigned (May 15) from the U.S. Court of Appeals. Warren Burger was nominated (May 21) by President Nixon to become Chief Justice of the Supreme Court, succeeding Earl Warren, who had earlier announced his intention to retire.

The U.S. Navy destroyer *Frank E. Evans* was cut in two (June 2) by an Australian aircraft carrier in the South China Sea during practice maneuvers. Seventy-three American seamen were lost.

President Nixon announced (June 8) that 25,000 American soldiers would be withdrawn from Vietnam by the end of August. It was the opening step in his plan to "Vietnamize" the war.

Astronauts Neil Armstrong and Edwin E. Aldrin became (July 20) the first men to walk on the moon, fulfilling a pledge made by the late President Kennedy that Americans would succeed in making a manned lunar landing before the 1960's were over.

Film actress Sharon Tate and four other persons were found (Aug. 9) murdered and mutilated in a Los Angeles home rented by Miss Tate and her husband, Polish film director Roman Polanski. Late in the year, Charles Manson and members of his cult were arrested as the alleged killers.

Over 400,000 persons, most of them youngsters, gathered (Aug. 16) at Bethel, N.Y., for the start of the four-day Woodstock Music and Art Fair. Though there were traffic jams, minimal food and sanitary facilities, widespread marijuana smoking, nudity and public love-making, there were no serious incidents of violence and the occasion was filled with good spirit.

A United States jetliner, with 146 persons aboard, was hijacked (Jan. 3) to Cuba in the newest of many similar incidents. Plane hijacking also became a weapon in the conflict between Israel and Arab guerrilla forces. A spectacular hijacking took place (Oct. 31) when an armed U.S. Marine, Lance Corp. Raffaele Minichiello, commandeered a TWA jetliner between Los Angeles and San Francisco and forced it to fly to Rome. Minichiello was arrested by Italian police shortly after the plane landed.

Hurricane Camille hit (Aug. 17) with devastating impact along the Gulf Coast, leaving about 300 dead and thousands homeless in Mississippi, Louisiana and Alabama.

The first nationwide Moratorium Day (Oct. 15) in protest against the war in Vietnam was observed by millions of Americans of all political persuasions.

The New York Mets won the National League pennant and then the World Series, four games to one, against the Baltimore Orioles (Oct. 16). Early in the year (Jan. 12), the New York Jets beat the Baltimore Colts, 16-7, scoring the first victory for the American Football League in the Super Bowl. Jets quarterback "Broadway" Joe Namath completed 17 of 28 passes in that game and emerged as football's most glamorous star. The New York Knickerbockers dominated professional basketball in 1969 by setting a new record of 18 consecutive victories. In hockey, the New York Rangers also led their division at year's end.

Astronauts Charles Conrad, Jr., and Alan L. Bean completed (Nov. 24) the second round-trip flight from the Earth to the moon.

General of the Army Dwight David Eisenhower, 34th President of the United States, died (Mar. 28) at the age of 78 in Walter Reed Army Hospital, Washington, D.C., after a long illness.

Ho Chi Minh, 79, president of North Vietnam, died (Sept. 3) in Hanoi.

Other deaths during the year included Irene Castle, 75 (Jan. 25); Alaska; Sen. Everett McKinley Dirksen, 73 (Sept. 7); Judy Garland, 47 (June 22); Sonja Henie, 57 (Oct. 12); Boris Karloff, 81 (Feb. 2); Frank Loesser, 59 (July 28); Rocky Marciano, 45 (Aug. 31); Josh White, 61 (Sept. 5).

In Print

Fiction bestsellers included *Ada*, by Vladimir Nabokov; *The Andromeda Strain*, by Michael Crichton; *Bullet Park*, by John Cheever; *Except for Me and Thee*, by Jessamyn West; *The First Circle*, by Aleksandr L. Solzhenitsyn; *Force 10 from Navarone*, by Alistair MacLean; *The Godfather*, by Mario Puzo; *The Love Machine*, by Jacqueline Susann; *Portnoy's Complaint*, by Philip Roth; *Slaughterhouse-Five*, by Kurt Vonnegut, Jr.; *A Small Town in Germany*, by John Le Carre; and *A World of Profit*, by Louis Auchincloss. One of the year's fiction bestsellers, *Naked Came the Stranger*, turned out to be a literary hoax. Purportedly written by a Long Island housewife, Penelope Ashe, the book was actually hatched up by a group of 13 newspapermen, each of whom was assigned to write a chapter which, if found to have any literary merit, had to be rewritten.

Top nonfiction included *Anti-Memoirs*, by Andre Malraux; *The Arms of Krupp*, by William Manchester; *Grant Takes Command*, by Bruce Catton; *Instant Replay*, by Jerry Kramer; *Jennie*, by Ralph G. Martin; *The Joys of Yiddish*, by Leo Rosten; *The Peter Principle*, by Laurence J. Peter and Raymond Hull; and *The Valachi Papers*, by Peter Maas.

On Stage

Longest-running shows on Broadway at the end of the year were *Hello Dolly; Fiddler on the Roof; Man of La Mancha;* and *Mame*. Off-Broadway, the longest-running shows were: *The Fantasticks; This Was Burlesque; The Premise; You're a Good Man; Charlie Brown; Curley McDimple; Your Own Thing; Jacques Brel Is Alive and Well and Living in Paris;* and *The Boys in the Band*. Among the major new productions of the season were *In the Matter of J. Robert Oppenheimer; Red White and Maddox; We Bombed in New Haven; Hadrian VII;* and Nicole Williamson's version of *Hamlet*. Howard Sackler's *The Great White Hope* won the Pulitzer prize.

Films

The Love Bug with Dean Jones was the top money-making film of 1969. Other major films of the year were *Funny Girl*, with Barbara Streisand; *Bullitt*, with Steve McQueen; *Butch Cassidy and the Sundance Kid*, with Paul Newman and Robert Redford; *Romeo and Juliet*, with Leonard Whiting and Olivia Hussey; *True Grit*, with John Wayne; *Midnight Cowboy*, with Dustin Hoffman and Jon Voight; *Oliver*, with Mark Lester and Oliver Reed; *Goodbye Columbus*, with Richard Benjamin and Ali McGraw; *Chitty Chitty Bang Bang*, with Dick Van Dyke and Sally Anne Howes; *Easy Rider*, with Peter Fonda and Dennis Hopper; *Where Eagles Dare*, with Richard Burton and Clint Eastwood; *Winning*, with Paul Newman and Joanne Woodward; *Impossible Years*, with David Niven and Lola Albright; *Three in the Attic*, with Christopher Jones and Yvette Mimieux; *Finian's Rainbow*, with Fred Astaire and Petula Clark; *Support Your Local Sheriff*, with James Garner; *The April Fools*, with Jack Lemmon and Catherine Deneuve; *The Undefeated*, with John Wayne and Rock Hudson; *The Wild Bunch*, with William Holden and Ernest Borgnine; *Star*, with Julie Andrews; *Alice's Restaurant*, with Arlo Guthrie; *The Arrangement*, with Kirk Douglas, and Deborah Kerr; and *100 Rifles*, with Jim Brown and Raquel Welch. A Swedish film, *I Am Curious (Yellow)*, broke box office records and also broke prior standards for dealing with sex in films.

Television

The three commercial networks enabled millions of Americans and many people around the world to witness (July 20-21) the landing of *Apollo 11* on the moon.

CBS broadcast (Sept. 21) a Woody Allen special, with appearances by Candice Bergen and Billy Graham.

Vice President Agnew's speech attacking the media was covered (Nov. 13) by the networks.

The Carol Burnett Show made its debut and *Dragnet* was canceled during the 1969-70 season.

ABC's *Marcus Welby, M.D.* won an Emmy for outstanding dramatic series. *Rowan & Martin's Laugh-In*, for the second consecutive year, was the top-rated show.

Music

The hits this year included *Crimson and Clover*, Tommy James and the Shondells; *Everyday People*, Sly and the Family Stone; *Dizzy*, Tommy Roe; *Aquarius/Let the Sunshine In*, The Fifth Dimension; *Get Back*, The Beatles with Billy Preston; *Love Theme From "Romeo and Juliet"*, Henry Mancini; *In the Year 2525*, Zager and Evans; *Honky Tonk Women*, The Rolling Stones; *Sugar, Sugar*, The Archies; *I Can't Get Next to You*, The Temptations; *Suspicious Minds*, Elvis Presley; *Wedding Bell Blues*, The Fifth Dimension; *Come Together/Something*, The Beatles; *Na Na Hey Hey Kiss Him Goodbye*, Steam; *Leaving on a Jet Plane*, Peter, Paul and Mary; *Someday We'll Be Together*, Diana Ross and the Supremes.

1970

$\mathscr{J}$. Edgar Hoover, Director of the FBI, warned (Jan. 2) the nation against, "Extremist all-Negro hate-type organizations," such as the Black Panthers.

A Pan American Boeing 747 made (Jan. 12) the first transatlantic revenue flight of a jumbo jet from New York to London. The aircraft, twice as wide as the largest passenger aircraft then in service, entered regular commercial operation the following month.

Ross Perot returned (Jan.) from a 12-day trip on a chartered 707 airliner, called *Peace on Earth*, in a futile effort to deliver Christmas presents and gifts to American POWs in North Vietnam.

Scented advertisements for such products as shaving cream and perfumes were published in magazines, and the first scented newspaper ad appeared in January.

The Federal "Chicago 7" grand jury found (Feb. 18) all seven defendants not guilty of conspiracy to create riots at the 1968 Democratic National Convention, but indicted five of them for crossing state lines with intent to start riots.

The United States cast (Mar. 17) its first veto in the United Nations, against a resolution that would have condemned Great Britain for failing to use military force to topple the white minority government of Rhodesia.

The first major postal workers' strike in the nation's history began (Mar. 18) when more than 6,000 letter carriers in New York walked off the job. That action later shut down or curtailed service in more than 30 cities. A "sick out" by air traffic controllers snarled (Mar. 25) airline flights for two weeks.

President Richard Nixon signed (Apr. 1) a bill banning cigarette advertising on television.

The Senate rejected (Apr. 8) President Nixon's Supreme Court nomination of Judge G. Harrold Carswell. A week later, the President nominated (Apr. 14) Harry A. Blackmun to the Court.

Apollo 13, damaged by an exploding oxygen tank that nearly killed its three-man crew, returned (Apr. 27) safely to Earth.

U.S. troops were sent (Apr. 30) into Cambodia to attack Communist sanctuaries. In protests against the invasion, four students at Kent State University were killed (May 4) by Ohio National Guard troops.

The Army named (May 15) two colonels as the first women generals in U.S. history.

Labor Secretary George P. Shultz was named (June 10) as director of the new Office of Management & Budget, and was replaced by James Hodgson; Caspar Weinberger, the head of Federal Trade Commission, became deputy to Shultz.

The last U. S. troops were withdrawn (June 29) from Cambodia.

A survey found (July) that 17 percent of those questioned in Charlotte, N.C., believed that the 1969 *Apollo 11* moon landing was a Hollywood hoax.

Rev. Daniel J. Berrigan, wanted for burning draft records as a protest against the Vietnam war, was captured (Aug. 11) by the FBI.

President Nixon signed (Aug. 12) the Postal Reorganization Act to make the Postal Service an independent agency.

Vice President Spiro Agnew began (Aug. 23) an eight-day trip to five Asian nations. A California company sold more than 55,000 Spiro Agnew wristwatches, at $14.95 each, in their first two months on the market.

President Nixon offered (Oct. 7) a "cease-fire in place" and proposed an international peace conference to discuss the conflict in Southeast Asia and a timetable for troop withdrawals.

NASA announced (Oct. 29) a U.S.-Soviet accord for the standardization of spacecraft docking systems.

Black militant Angela Davis was indicted (Nov. 11) on charges of murder, kidnapping and conspiracy.

Fifty U.S. servicemen landed (Nov. 21) by helicopter in North Vietnam in a failed attempt to rescue 50 to 100 POWs thought to be held at the Sontay prison camp near Hanoi.

Walter J. Hickel was fired (Nov. 25) as Secretary of Interior, and succeeded by Rogers C. B. Morton, the chief of the Republican National Committee.

President Nixon signed (Dec. 31) the National Air Quality Control Act.

Democrat John Connally was nominated (Dec. 14) as Treasury Secretary to replace David M. Kennedy.

The World Trade Center was topped (Dec. 23) in New York City to become the tallest building in the world.

A first-class stamp cost six cents.

The U.S. Census Bureau estimated that the suburban population would reach 74 million in 1970, thereby outnumbering the 59 million people living in the nation's central cities and the 71 million residing outside metropolitan areas.

The psychedelic tie-dye look spread from the flower children of California into world of fashion.

In the world of sports, the Kansas City Chiefs defeated (Jan. 11) the Minnesota Vikings to win Super Bowl IV; pitcher Denny McLain of the Detroit Tigers was suspended from baseball for his 1967 involvement in a bookmaking operation; UCLA won (Mar. 21) its fourth consecutive NCAA basketball championship; and the Baltimore Orioles defeated (Oct. 15) the Cincinnati Reds in five games to win the World Series.

Deaths of the year included: quiz master Hal March, 49 (Jan. 19); author Erle Stanley Gardner, 80 (Mar. 11); author John O'Hara, 65 (Apr. 11); entertainer Gypsy Rose Lee, 56 (Apr. 27); union leader Walter P. Reuther, 62 (May 9); author John Gunther, 68 (May 29); coach Vince Lombardi, 57 (Sept. 3); rock guitarist Jimi Hendrix, 27 (Sept. 18); singer Janis Joplin, 27, (Oct. 4); and historian Richard Hofstadter, 54 (Oct. 24).

In Print

The top-selling books of the year were *Love Story*, by Eric Segal; *QB VII*, by Leon Uris; *Island in the Stream*, by Ernest Hemingway; *Passenger to Frankfurt*, by Agatha Christie; *Rich Man, Poor Man*, by Leon Uris; *The Child From the Sea*, by Elizabeth Goudge; *The Crystal Cave*, by Mary Stewart; *Caravan to Vaccares*, by Alistair MacLean; *God Is An Englishman*, by R. F. Delderfield; and *Doctor Cobb's Game*, by R. V. Cassill.

Notable nonfiction: *The Greening of America*, by Charles A. Reich; *Civilisation*, by Kenneth Clark; *The Sensuous Woman*, by "J"; *Everything You Always Wanted to Know About Sex*, by David R. Reuben; *Future Shock*, by Alvin Tofler; *Inside the Third Reich*, by Albert Speer; *A White House Diary*, by Lady Bird Johnson; *Khrushchev Remembers*, by Nikita Khrushchev; *Crime In America*, by Ramsey Clark; *Don't Fall Off The Mountain*, by Shirley MacLaine.

On Stage

On the Broadway stage, *Hello, Dolly!*, closed on Dec. 27, with 2,844 performances. Other notable plays that continued successful runs: *Fiddler On The Roof* (2,788 perf.) and *Man of La Mancha* (2,297 perf.). *Plaza Suite* closed (Oct. 3) with 1,097 performances, while *Hair* reached 1,294 performances.

The plays produced included: *Paris is Out*; *Sheep on the Runway*; *Charles Aznavour*; *Gloria and Esperanza*; *Child's Play*; *Harvey*; *Purlie*; *Minnie's Boys*; *Look to the Lilies*; *Borstal Boy*; *Applause*; *The Boy Friend*; *Inquest*; *Company*; *Bob and Ray—The Two and Only*; *Conduct Unbecoming*; *The Rothschilds*; *Two by Two*; *Paul Sills' Story Theater*; *Orlando Furioso*; *Sleuth*; *Les Blancs*; *Home*; *The Gingerbread Lady*; and *The Me Nobody Knows*.

The Tony award for Best Play went to *Borstal Boy*, written by Frank McMahon. Fritz Weaver won Best Actor for his role in *Child's Play*, and Tammy Grimes won Best Actress for her part in *Private Lives*. Best Musical was *Applause*, Best Actor, Cleavon Little in *Purlie*, and Best Actress Lauren Bacall in *Applause*.

Films

This year, 236 feature films were released.

The Academy Award for Best Picture of the Year was given to *Patton* (Best Actor, George C. Scott).

Other films included *Airport*, with Burt Lancaster, Dean Martin and Helen Hayes; *Five Easy Pieces*, with Jack Nicholson; *The Great White Hope*, with James Earl Jones and Jane Alexander; *Gimme Shelter*, featuring the Rolling

Stones; *Little Big Man*, with Dustin Hoffman and Faye Dunaway; *M*A*S*H*, with Donald Sutherland, Elliott Gould, and Sally Kellerman; *Where's Poppa?*, with George Segal; *Lovers and Other Strangers*, with Gig Young, Ann Jackson, Beatrice Arthur, Diane Keaton, and Richard Castellano; *Love Story*, with Ali McGraw and Ryan O'Neal; *Women In Love*, with Glenda Jackson, who was named Best Actress. A notable foreign film, from France, was *The Sorrow and the Pity*, a documentary about the French public's acquiescence to Nazi barbarity during the German occupation of France.

In 1950, there were 19,100 movie theaters in the United States and average weekly attendance was fifty-million. In 1970, there were 13,800 movie theaters and average weekly attendance had dropped to 18 million. Though the total number of movie theaters had declined slightly through the 1950s, this was balanced by the growth in multiplex theaters. By comparison, in 1945, an average of 82 million Americans had visited a movie theater in a typical week.

Television

ABC presented (Mar. 22) *Harry & Lena*, a musical special with Harry Belafonte and Lena Horne.

CBS broadcast (Sept. 8) *A Day in the Life of the United States*, a look at various events around the country on the day men first landed on the Moon.

A variety of Motown music performers appeared (Dec. 18) on ABC's special production of *The Smokey Robinson Show*.

NFL Monday Night Football and *The Mary Tyler Moore Show* made their debuts, and *The Ed Sullivan Show* was canceled during the 1970-71 season.

All in the Family earned an Emmy for outstanding comedy series, and *Marcus Welby, M.D.* was the nation's top ranked program.

Music

The number one songs this year included *Raindrops Keep Fallin' On My Head*, B. J. Thomas; *I Want You Back*, Jackson Five; *Venus*, Shocking Blue; *Thank You Falettinme Be Mice Elf Agin*, Sly & The Family Stone; *Bridge Over Troubled Water*, Simon & Garfunkel; *Let It Be*, the Beatles; *ABC*, Jackson 5; *American Woman*, Guess Who; *Everything is Beautiful*, Ray Stevens; *The Long and Winding Road*, Beatles; *The Love You Save*, Jackson 5; *Mama Told Me (Not To Come)*, Three Dog Night; *(They Long To Be) Close To You*, Carpenters; *Make it With You*, Bread; *War*, Edwin Starr; *Ain't No Mountain High Enough*, Diana Ross; *I'll Be There*, Jackson 5; *I Think I Love You*, Partridge Family; *The Tears Of A Clown*, Smokey Robinson & The Miracles; and *My Sweet Lord*, George Harrison.

Simon & Garfunkel dominated the Grammy Awards, winning Record of the Year, Album of The Year, and Song of the Year with *Bridge Over Troubled Waters*. Best Vocal Male Performance went to Ray Stevens for *Everything Is Beautiful*, and Best Vocal Female Performance was given to Dionne Warwick for *I'll Never Fall in Love Again*.

1971

$\mathcal{T}$he South Vietnamese Army, aided by U.S. aircraft, attacked (Feb. 8) portions of the Ho Chi Minh Trail in Laos. Army Lieutenant William L. Calley, Jr., was convicted (Mar. 29) of murdering 22 South Vietnamese civilians in My Lai on Mar. 16, 1968. President Nixon said (Apr. 7) the U.S. would withdraw 100,000 troops from Vietnam by Christmas.

The New York Times began (June 13) publication of portions of 47-volume "Pentagon Papers." After various restraining orders and court tests, the U.S. Supreme Court upheld (June 30) publication of the documents.

The Army announced (July 28) a crackdown on narcotics use by American troops in South Vietnam. The U.S. resumed (Dec. 26) bombing of North Vietnam.

In a statistical review of Richard Nixon's first two years as President, the White House announced he had traveled 185,000 miles, visited 17 foreign countries, signed 776 bills and hosted more than 13,000 guests at 132 dinners, not including an additional 4,000 people who attended various breakfasts, luncheons, teas, coffees and receptions.

The U.S., Great Britain, France and the Soviet Union signed (Aug. 23) an agreement for unrestricted passage through East Germany between West Berlin and West Germany.

Sen. Edward Kennedy was defeated (Jan. 21) in seeking re-election as Assistant Majority Leader.

The Supreme Court ruled (Apr. 20) that the use of busing to end racial segregation in public schools is constitutional. President Nixon named (Oct. 21) Lewis F. Powell and William H. Rehnquist to succeed Justices Hugo L. Black and John M. Harlan on the Supreme Court.

The price of a half-gallon of milk reached sixty-seven cents.

The 26th amendment to the Constitution, which lowered the voting age for all elections to 18, was ratified (June 30). Those new voters cast their first votes in the off-year elections. The House of Representatives failed to pass (Nov. 18) a proposed constitutional amendment that would have allowed voluntary prayers in public schools.

President Nixon called (Aug. 15) for a 90-day wage, price and rent freeze.

Apollo 14 landed (Feb. 5) on the Moon, becoming the third American manned mission to explore the lunar surface. *Apollo 15* began (July 31) a three-day visit to the Moon. *Mariner 9* became (Nov. 13) the first man-made object to orbit another planet following a five-and-a-half-month, 247 million mile trip.

President Nixon signed (Jan. 2) the Omnibus Crime Control Act authorizing Federal aid for state and local law enforcement. The Internal Revenue Service's official taxpayers guide advised "Bribes and kickbacks to non-governmental officials are deductible unless the individual has been convicted of making the bribe or has entered a plea of guilty or nolo contendere." William A. (Tony) Boyle, the president of United Mine Workers, was indicted (Mar. 2) for illegal campaign contributions and embezzlement. Nixon commuted (Nov. 13) former Teamster leader Jimmy Hoffa's 13-year sentence after he had served four years and nine months.

Charles Manson and three other defendants were sentenced (Mar. 29) to death after a nine-and-a-half month trial for the death of Sharon Tate and six others.

President Nixon announced (June 1) a massive "national offensive" against drug addiction.

A Navy deserter hijacked (July 2) an aircraft from San Antonio to Buenos Aires, flying 7,650 miles in the longest hijacking on record.

More than 1,000 N.Y. state troopers and police stormed (Sept. 13) Attica State Correctional Facility when 1,200 inmates held 38 guards; nine hostages and 28 convicts died in the attack.

The U.S. and Japan signed (June 17) a treaty returning Okinawa to Japanese rule; the Senate ratified (Nov. 10) the agreement. Emperor Hirohito met (Sept. 26) President Nixon in Anchorage, Alaska, for the first meeting between a Japanese monarch and an American president.

The American table tennis team began (Apr. 10) the first visit of a sports team to Communist China. President Nixon announced the suspension of the U.S. trade embargo with China four days later.

The National Railroad passenger Corporation (Amtrak) began (May 1) service.

The Kennedy Center opened (Sept. 8) in Washington with a performance of Leonard Bernstein's "Mass."

An earthquake in Southern California killed (Feb. 9) 65 people.

Vice President Agnew hit (Feb. 13) three spectators with a golf ball during the Bob Hope Desert Classic.

The National Emergency Warning Center mistakenly ran (Feb. 20) an emergency alert tape which was broadcast across the nation.

A two-room shack in Tupelo, Miss., birthplace of Elvis Presley, opened (July 1) as a tourist attraction.

The Baltimore Colts defeated (Jan. 7) the Dallas Cowboys to win Super Bowl V. The Pittsburgh Pirates defeated (Oct. 17) the Baltimore Orioles in seven games to win the World Series. Bobby Fischer became (Oct. 26) the first American to qualify for world chess championships.

Deaths of the year included: boxer Charles (Sonny) Liston, 38 (Jan. 5); former presidential candidate Thomas E. Dewey, 68 (Mar. 16); poet Ogden Nash, 68 (May 19); musician Jim Morrison, 27 (July 3); musician Louis Armstrong, 71 (July 6); and former Secretary of State Dean Acheson, 78 (Oct. 12).

In Print

Among the novels published were *Wheels*, by Arthur Hailey; *The Winds of War*, by Herman Wouk; *The Day of the Jackal*, by Frederick Forsyth; *The Exorcist*, by William Peter Blatty; *Message from Malaga*, by MacInnes; *Rabbit Redux*, by John Updike; *Our Gang*, by Phillip Roth; *Nemesis*, by Agatha Christie; *The Betsy*, by Harold Robbins; and *Bear Island*, by Alistair MacLean.

Nonfiction included *Bury My Heart at Wounded Knee*, by Dee Brown; *Tracy and Hepburn*, by Garson Kanin; *Honor Thy Father*, by Gay Talese; and *Wunnerful, Wunnerful*, by Lawrence Welk.

On Stage

Plays produced on Broadway included: *David's Metamorphoses; No, No, Nanette; A Midsummer Night's Dream; Four On a Garden; The School for Wives; And Miss Reardon Drinks a Little; Abelaid and Heloise; All Over; 70, Girls 70; Lenny; You're A Good Man Charlie Brown; The Philanthropist; How the Other Half Lives; The Trial of the Catonsville Nine; Jesus Christ Superstar; Ain't Supposed to Die a Natural Death; To Love Another Summer—To Pass Another Winter; On the Town; The Prisoner of Second Avenue; Twigs; The Two Gentlemen of Verona; Inner City;* and *Follies.*

Sleuth, written by Anthony Shaffer, won a Tony for Best Play. Best Actor went to Brian Bedford for his part in *The School for Wives*. Maureen Stapleton was awarded Best Actress for *Gingerbread Lady*. Steven Sondheim's *Company* was Best Musical of the year. Best Actress in a musical was Helen Gallagher in *No, No Nanette*, and Hal Linden was Best Actor in *The Rothschilds*.

Films

Outstanding motion pictures of the year included *The Anderson Tapes*, with Sean Connery and Dyan Cannon; *Bananas*, with Woody Allen and Louise Lasser; *Carnal Knowledge*, with Jack Nicholson, Candice Bergen, and Art Garfunkel; *A Clockwork Orange*, with Malcolm McDowell and Patrick Magee; *The Emigrants*, with Max von Sydow and Liv Ullman; *Fiddler On The Roof*, with Topol and Norma Crane; *The French Connection*, with Gene Hackman, Best Actor; William Friedkin, Best Director; and, Best Picture of the Year; *The Homecoming: A Christmas Story*, with Patricia Neal and Richard Thomas; *Klute*, with Jane Fonda and Donald Sutherland; *Kotch*, with Walter Matthau and Deborah Winters; *Macbeth*, with Jon Finch and Francesca Annis; *Plaza Suite*, with Walter Matthau and Elaine May; and *Summer Of '42*, with Jennifer O'Neill and Gary Grimes.

Foreign films of the year included *The Conformist* with Dominique Sanda and Jean-Louis Trintignant, directed by Bernardo Bertolucci. *The Garden of the*

Finzi-Continis with Dominique Sanda and Lino Capolicchio, directed by Vittorio DeSica, was a story about the effects of fascism on Italian Jews during World War II.

Television

CBS Reports broadcast (Feb. 23) *The Selling of the Pentagon*, a documentary on the Defense Department's public relations activities.

Walter Cronkite interviewed (June 23) Daniel Ellsberg in a *CBS News Special* on the Pentagon Papers case.

The first World Series night game was televised (Oct. 13) by NBC and drew a record audience for a World Series broadcast.

The *Masterpiece Theater* production of "Elizabeth R." won an Emmy for outstanding dramatic series, *The Carol Burnett Show* was named outstanding variety musical series, and "Brian's Song" was selected as the outstanding single program.

All in the Family was the number one show.

Music

The top selling songs were: *Knock Three Times*, Dawn; *One Bad Apple*, Osmonds; *Me and Bobby McGee*, Janis Joplin; *Just My Imagination (Running Away With Me)*, Temptations; *Joy to the World*, Three Dog Night; *Brown Sugar*, Rolling Stones; *Want Ads*, Honey Cone; *It's Too Late*, Carole King; *Indian Reservation*, Raiders; *You've Got a Friend*, James Taylor; *How Can You Mend a Broken Heart*, Bee Gees; *Uncle Albert/Admiral Halsey*, Paul & Linda McCartney, *Go Away Little Girl*, Donny Osmond; *Maggie May*, Rod Stewart; *Gypsys, Tramps & Thieves*, Cher; *Theme from "Shaft,"* Isaac Hayes, *Family Affair,* Sly & The Family Stone; *Brand New Key*, Melanie.

Carole King dominated the Grammys; her record, *It's Too Late*, was voted Record of the Year; her album, *Tapestry*, was Album of the Year, and she also won Song of The Year for *You've Got a Friend*, and Best Female Vocal Performance for *Tapestry*. James Taylor won Best Male Vocal Performance for *You've Got a Friend*.

1972

*P*resident Richard Nixon approved (Jan. 5) a six-year, $5.5 billion program to develop the Space Shuttle.

Commerce Secretary Maurice H. Stans resigned (Jan. 27) his post to work full-time on the Nixon re-election campaign and was succeeded by Peter G. Peterson.

The Federal Government mandated (Feb. 5) the screening of airline passengers and luggage to deter airplane hijacking.

Readers Digest celebrated (January) its golden anniversary.

A Sacramento County Clerk rejected (February) at least 20 voter registration applications because female applicants insisted on using the "Ms." prefix as a substitute for Mrs. or Miss.

Attorney General John Mitchell resigned (Feb. 15) his position to direct the Nixon presidential campaign and was replaced by Richard Kleindienst.

With more than 15 million sales, the Volkswagen Beetle outsold (Feb. 17) the total sales of the Ford Model T.

The trial of Rev. Philip Berrigan and six other antiwar activists began (Feb. 21) in Harrisburg on charges of plotting to kidnap Henry Kissinger and other crimes.

President Nixon arrived (Feb. 21) in Peking for an eight-day visit to China, including a banquet for 700 people in the Great Hall of the People and a trip to the Great Wall.

The *Pioneer 10* spacecraft was launched (Mar. 2) on a 21-month trip to Mars and Jupiter.

Clifford Irving admitted (Mar. 13) that his Howard Hughes biography was a fabrication and pleaded guilty to conspiring to defraud McGraw-Hill of $750,000.

The Senate approved (Mar. 22) the proposed Constitutional amendment barring discrimination based on sex and sent the measure to the states. (It did not receive ratification by the states.)

North Vietnamese forces launched (Mar. 30) a massive attack across the South Vietnamese border.

Congress passed (Apr. 7) the Federal Election Campaign Act to limit campaign financing.

The U.S. launched (Apr. 15) heavy raids against North Vietnam.

The Chinese pandas Ling-ling and Hsing-hsing arrived (Apr. 16) at the National Zoo in Washington, D.C.

The *Apollo 16* astronauts visited (Apr. 20-23) the Moon and carried back 214 pounds of rocks and soil samples.

President Nixon ordered (May 8) the mining of North Vietnam's Haiphong Harbor.

Arthur Bremer shot (May 15) and seriously wounded Alabama Governor George C. Wallace during a presidential primary campaign appearance in Laurel, Maryland.

Treasury Secretary John B. Connally Jr. resigned (May 16) and George P. Shultz was named as his successor.

President Nixon began (May 22) the first visit of an American president to the Soviet Union. He and Leonid Brezhnev discussed arms limitation and the avoidance of military conflict, and signed an arms reduction pact on May 29.

Sally Priesand was ordained (June 3) in Cincinnati as the first woman rabbi in the nation.

Washington, D.C., police apprehended (June 17) five men in the attempted bugging of the Democratic National Committee offices in the Watergate Building.

John Mitchell resigned (July 1) as chairman of President Nixon's re-election organization.

Jean Westwood was named (July 14) chairman of the Democratic National Committee, the first woman to head a major U.S. party.

Senator George McGovern announced (July 31) the withdrawal of Senator Thomas F. Eagleton as his running mate on the Democratic presidential ticket because of revelations about his past emotional problems. R. Sargent Shriver was named to replace him.

The Senate approved (Aug. 3) a strategic arms limitation agreement treaty restricting the number of anti-ballistic missile sites.

Bobby Fischer, 29, of Brooklyn, N.Y., became (Sept. 1) the first American to win the World Chess Championship following a two-month contest with Boris Spassky.

San Francisco opened (Sept. 11) the nation's first new rapid transit system in 50 years.

Seven men were indicted (Sept. 15) in Washington on burglary, conspiracy and wiretapping charges in the Watergate case.

Congress overrode (Oct. 15) President Nixon's veto to enact the Water Pollution Control Act.

The Dow Jones Industrial Index closed (Nov. 14) above 1000 for the first time ever.

George Romney resigned (Nov.) as Secretary of Housing & Urban Development, Elliot L. Richardson shifted from the Department of Health, Education and Welfare to the Department of Defense after the resignation of Melvin R. Laird, and Caspar W. Weinberger moved to HEW.

UN Ambassador George Bush was named (Dec. 11) chairman of the Republican Party.

The U.S. resumed (Dec. 18) heavy B-52 bombing of North Vietnam.

After 36 years, *Life* magazine suspended (Dec. 29) publication.

The Dallas Cowboys defeated the Miami Dolphins to win Super Bowl VI; the nation's first major league baseball strike delayed (Apr. 1) the start of the season by ten days; and the Oakland Athletics defeated the Cincinnati Reds in seven games to win the World Series.

The year's deaths included: poet John Berryman, 57 (Jan. 7); columnist Walter Winchell, 74 (Feb. 20); baseball player and manager Gil Hodges, 47, (Apr. 2); FBI Director J. Edgar Hoover, 77 (May 2); actor William Boyd, 74 (Sept. 12); baseball player Jackie Robinson, 53 (Oct. 24); helicopter pioneer Igor Ivanovitch Sikorsky, 83 (Oct. 26); muscle building expert Charles Atlas, 79 (Dec. 24); and former President Harry Truman, 88 (Dec. 26).

In Print

Best selling fiction for the year included *Jonathan Livingston Seagull*, by Richard Bach; *The Odessa File*, by Frederick Forsyth; *Semi-Tough*, by Dan Jenkins; *August 1914*, by Alexander Solzhenitsyn; *The Persian Boy*, by Mary Renault; *The Camerons*, by Michael Crichton; *The Winds of War*, by Herman Wouk; *On the Night of the Seventh Moon*, by Victoria Holt; *The Eiger Sanction*, by Trevanian; and *Two From Galilee*, by Marjorie Holmes.

Nonfiction included *I'm O.K.—You're O.K.*, by Thomas A. Harris; *The Best and the Brightest*, by David Halberstam; *Supermoney*, by Adam Smith; *Dr. Atkins Diet Revolution*, by Robert C. Atkins; *The Peter Prescription*, by Lawrence E. Peter; *Eleanor: The Years Alone*, by Joseph P. Lash; *"Johnny We Hardly Knew Ye"*, by Kenneth P. O'Donnell and David F. Powers, with Joe McCarthy; *Journey to Ixtlan*, by Carlos Castaneda; and *The Joy of Sex*, by Alex Comfort.

On Stage

Plays produced included *Man of LaMancha; Vivat! Vivat Regina; Night Watch; Sticks and Bones; The Country Girl; A Funny Thing Happened On The Way To The Forum; Sugar; Grease; Neil Diamond One Man Show; Night Watch; That Championship Season; Jacques Brel is Alive and Well and Living In Paris; 6 Rms Riv Vu; Pippin; Butley; Much Ado About Nothing; The Last of Mrs. Lincoln; Purlie; The Secret Affairs of Mildred Wild; Sticks and Bones;* and *The Sunshine Boys.*

Two awards were given in the Tony's Best Musical category this year: Best Score went to *Two Gentlemen of Verona*, and Best Music and Lyrics to Steven Sondheim's *Follies*. Phil Silvers took Best Actor for his work in the revival of *A Funny Thing Happened On The Way To The Forum*, and Alexis Smith won Best Actress for her work in *Follies*. David Rabe's *Sticks and Bones* won the Tony Award for best play, while Cliff Gorman took Best Actor for his role in *Lenny*. Best Actress went to Sada Thompson in *Twigs*.

Films

Earning $86.3 million this year, the Academy Award's Best Film of the year was *The Godfather*. Marlon Brando won the Best Actor award, which he refused in a political protest. James Caan and Robert Duvall were nominated for Best Supporting Actors, and the film won Best Screenplay, for its adaptation from Mario Puzo's novel. The film also starred Diane Keaton, Al Pacino, and John Cazale.

Other motion pictures released included *Cabaret*, with Liza Minelli, Joel Grey, and Michael York; *Deliverance*, with Burt Reynolds and Jon Voight; *The Groundstar Conspiracy*, with George Peppard and Michael Sarrazin; *The Heartbreak Kid*, with Charles Grodin, Cybill Shepherd, and Eddie Albert; *The Hot Rock*, with Robert Redford and George Segal; *Junior Bonner*, with Steve McQueen, Robert Preston, and Ida Lupino; *Lady Sings the Blues*, with Diana Ross, Billy Dee Williams, and Richard Pryor; *Sounder*, with Cicely Tyson and Paul Winfield; *Travels With My Aunt*, with Maggie Smith and Alec McCowen; *Up the Sandbox*, with Barbra Streisand and David Selby; and *What's Up, Doc?*, with Ryan O'Neal, Barbra Streisand, and Madeline Kahn.

Television

Walter Cronkite interviewed (Jan. 27) former President Johnson on CBS's production of *LBJ: Lyndon Johnson Talks Politics*. All three networks covered (Feb. 17) President Nixon's trip to China. Four days later, PBS broadcast *The Politics—And Comedy—Of Woody Allen*.

ABC aired (Aug. 12-15) a six-and-a-half-hour, four-part version of *War And Peace*.

M*A*S*H was introduced, and *Bonanza* and *Mission: Impossible* were canceled during the 1972-73 season.

CBS's *The Waltons* received an Emmy for outstanding drama series. *All in the Family* again was the nation's most popular program.

Music

The most popular music included *American Pie*, Don McLean; *Let's Stay Together*, Al Green; *Without You*, Harry Nillson; *Heart of Gold*, Neil Young; *A Horse With No Name*, America; *The First Time Ever I Saw Your Face*, Roberta Flack; *Oh Girl!*, Chi-Lites; *I'll Take You There*, Staple Singers; *The Candy Man*, Sammy Davis Jr.; *Song Sung Blue*, Neil Diamond; *Lean on Me*, Bill Withers; *Alone Again, Naturally*, Gilbert O'Sullivan; *Brandy (You're a Fine Girl)*, Looking Glass; *Black & White*, Three Dog Night; *Baby Don't Get Hooked on Me*, Mac Davis; *Ben*, Michael Jackson; *My Ding-A-Ling*, Chuck Berry; *I Can See Clearly Now*, Johnny Nash; *Papa Was a Rolling Stone*, Temptations; *I Am Woman*, Helen Reddy; *Me and Mrs. Jones*, Billy Paul.

Roberta Flack won Record of Year for *The First Time Ever I Saw Your Face*. Ewan McColl was the composer and won Song of The Year for his effort. Helen Reddy received the Best Female Vocal Performance award for *I Am Woman*. Best Male Vocal Performance was given to Harry Nillson for *Without You*, and Album of the Year went to *Concert for Bangladesh* with George Harrison, Ravi Shankar, Bob Dylan, et al.

1973

$\mathscr{T}$he U.S. halted (Jan. 15) bombing attacks on North Vietnam less than a month after massive Christmas air raids on Hanoi.

Juan Carona, 38, was convicted of 25 counts of murder in Yuba City, Calif.

Richard Nixon began (Jan. 21) his second term as President. The cost of the Inaugural Ball was $4 million—compared to $4 a couple for the nation's first such event, James Madison's, in 1809.

The U.S. Supreme Court ruled in *Roe v. Wade* that state laws prohibiting abortions before the third month are unconstitutional.

President Nixon announced (Jan. 23) a Vietnam cease-fire agreement to go into effect in five days. The United States, North Vietnam, South Vietnam, and the Vietcong signed (Jan. 27) a peace agreement in Paris.

G. Gordon Liddy and James W. McCord were convicted of the Watergate break-in after five other defendants pleaded guilty earlier in the month.

The first 142 American POWs were released (Feb. 12) in Hanoi and arrived in California two days later.

L. Patrick Gray III was named (Feb. 17) successor to J. Edgar Hoover as FBI director.

Native Americans took (Feb. 27) hostages at Wounded Knee, and ended their take-over on May 10.

The last U.S. troops departed (Mar. 29) South Vietnam after nearly a decade of American involvement.

H. Rap Brown, former head of the Student Non-Violent Coordinating Committee, was convicted (Mar. 29) in New York City of armed robbery and assault with a deadly weapon, and was sentenced to a term of 5 to 15 years.

Nixon aides H. R. Haldeman, John D. Ehrlichman, and John W. Dean and Attorney General Richard G. Kleindienst resigned (Apr. 30) over the growing Watergate scandal.

The newly completed Sears Tower in Chicago became (May 3) the tallest building in the world.

CIA Director James Schlesinger was named (May 4) to replace Elliot Richardson as Defense Secretary.

The *Washington Post* won (May 7) the Pulitzer Prize for Bob Woodward and Carl Bernstein's Watergate reporting. All charges of espionage, theft, and conspiracy were dismissed (May 11) against Daniel Ellsberg and Anthony J. Russo, Jr., in the Pentagon Papers trial.

The *Skylab* orbiting space station was launched (May 14).

The U.S. Senate Select Committee on Presidential Campaign Activities, chaired by North Carolina Democrat Sam J. Ervin and Tennessee Republican Howard H. Baker, began (May 17) hearings on Watergate. Archibald Cox was named (May 18) Special Watergate Prosecutor by new Attorney General Eliot Richardson.

Thomas Bradley defeated (May 29) Sam Yorty to become the first black mayor of Los Angeles.

Soviet leader Leonid I. Brezhnev visited (June 16–25) the United States, and the two countries signed a series of agreements, including one to avoid military confrontations.

Nixon aide Alexander P. Butterfield disclosed (July 16) the existence of the White House taping system.

Vice President Spiro Agnew announced (Aug. 6) that he was under Justice Department investigation for receiving kickbacks and income tax evasion while serving as governor of Maryland. He resigned Oct. 10 before pleading no contest to the charges.

Henry Kissinger was nominated, Secretary of State; he was confirmed by the Senate on Sept. 21.

Maynard Jackson was elected (Oct. 16) as the first black mayor of Atlanta.

Attorney General Richardson resigned (Oct. 20), and Deputy Attorney General William D. Ruckelshaus and Special Prosecutor Cox were fired in the "Saturday Night Massacre" over their handling of the disputed Watergate tapes.

William B. Saxbe was named (Nov. 1) President Nixon's fourth Attorney General, and Leon Jaworski was nominated as the new Watergate Special Prosecutor. Nixon told (Nov. 17) a press conference: "People have got to know whether or not their President is a crook—well, I'm not a crook."

President Nixon signed (Nov. 16) the Alaska Pipeline Act authorizing construction of a 789-mile pipeline from the North Slope to Valdez.

The White House disclosed (Nov. 21) the existence of an 18 $\frac{1}{2}$-minute gap in the tape of a Nixon-Haldeman conversation.

The Neiman-Marcus Christmas catalog offered an $80,000 "contemplative environment," a self-contained room complete with film screens, bar, exercise equipment, water bed and other features.

Gerald Ford was sworn in (Dec. 6) as the 40th Vice President, replacing Spiro Agnew. He was the first to take office under the terms of the 25th Amendment.

In sports news, the Miami Dolphins defeated the Washington Redskins to win Super Bowl VII; the American League adopted a rule allowing the designated hitter; Billie Jean King beat Bobby Riggs in straight sets in a nationally televised tennis match; and the Oakland Athletics defeated the New York Mets in seven games to win the World Series.

Deaths of the year included: former President Lyndon B. Johnson, 64 (Jan. 22) actor Edward G. Robinson, 79 (Jan. 26); author Pearl S. Buck, 80 (Mar. 6); musical actress Betty Grable, 56 (July 2); comedian Joe E. Brown, 80 (July 6); World War I ace and businessman Edward Rickenbacker, 79 (July 23); director John Ford, 78 (Aug. 31); and drummer Gene Krupa, 64 (Oct. 16).

The population in the United States was 206,827,000.

In Print

Gore Vidal's *Burr* topped the list of best-selling fiction. Other best-sellers were *The Honorary Consul*, by Graham Green; *The Hollow Hills*, by Mary Stewart; *Come Nineveh, Come Tyre*, by Allen Drury; *Theophilus North*, by Thornton Wilder; *Postern of Fate*, by Agatha Christie; *The First Deadly Sin*, by Lawrence Sanders; *Beulah Land*, by Lonnie Coleman; *The Salamander*, by Morris West; and *World Without End*, by Jimmy Breslin.

Heading the nonfiction list were *Alistair Cooke's America*, by Alistair Cooke; *How to Be Your Own Best Friend*, by Mildred Newman and Bernard Berkowitz with Jean Owen; *Upstairs at the White House*, by J. B. West with Lynn Kotz; *In One Era and Out the Other*, by Sam Levenson; *The Best of Life*, by David E. Scherman; *Pentimento*, by Lillian Hellman; *Cosell*, by Howard Cosell; *Portrait of a Marriage*, by Nigel Nicolson; and *Real Lace*, by Stephen Birmingham.

On Stage

Three notable revivals were produced: *A Streetcar Named Desire*; *A Moon for the Misbegotten*; and *The Pajama Game*.

Two Neil Simon plays closed: *The Prisoner of Second Avenue* and *The Sunshine Boys*. Other closings were: *The River Niger*; *Jesus Christ Superstar*; and *Sugar*.

Plays produced included *A Little Night Music*; *The Jockey Club Stakes*; *Finishing Touches*; *Gigi*; *The Changing Room*; *Irene*; *Seesaw*; *The Women*; *The Play's the Thing*; *Cyrano*; *Raisin*; and *Good Evening*.

Jason Miller (who would play a feature role in *The Exorcist* this year) was awarded Best Play for writing *That Championship Season*. Best Actor was Alan Bates in *Butley*, and Julie Harris was Best Actress in *The Last of Mrs. Lincoln*. For the third year in a row Steven Sondheim was awarded Best Musical this year for *A Little Night Music*. Ben Vereen took Best Musical Actor in *Pippin*, and Glynis Johns Best Musical Actress in *A Little Night Music*.

Films

The Exorcist grossed $88.5 million, followed by *The Sting* (which was named Best Picture) at $79 million.

Down from 296 in 1972, 219 feature films were released.

Many memorable motion pictures were produced: *American Graffiti*, with Richard Dreyfuss and Ron Howard; *A Touch of Class*, with Glenda Jackson,

George Segal, and Paul Sorvino; *The Effect of Gamma Rays on Man-in-the-Moon Marigolds*, with Joanne Woodward and Judith Lowry; *The Exorcist*, with Ellen Burstyn, Max von Sydow, Linda Blair, Jason Miller, and Lee J. Cobb; *The Ice-man Cometh*, with Lee Marvin, Fredric March, and Robert Ryan; *Paper Moon*, with Ryan O'Neal, Tatum O'Neal, Madeline Kahn, and Randy Quaid; *Papil-lon*, with Steve McQueen, Dustin Hoffman, and Anthony Zerbe; *Save the Ti-ger*, with Jack Lemmon and Jack Gilford; *Serpico*, with Al Pacino and Tony Roberts; *Sleeper*, with Woody Allen and Diane Keaton; *Sleuth*, with Laurence Olivier and Michael Caine; *The Sting*, with Paul Newman, Robert Redford, Robert Shaw, Charles Durning, Ray Walston, and Eileen Brennan; and *The Way We Were*, with Barbra Streisand, Robert Redford, Patrick O'Neal, and Bradford Dillman.

Television

CBS produced (Feb. 11) *Duke Ellington...We Love You Madly*, an all-star tribute to the musician, with appearances by Count Basie, Ray Charles, Miles Davis, and Sarah Vaughan. Lily Tomlin starred (Mar. 16) in a CBS comedy special. The nation watched (May 15–Nov. 15) pooled live coverage by all three networks and PBS taped highlights of the Watergate hearings. ABC broadcast (Sept. 20) live Billie Jean King's successful tennis match against Bobby Riggs. Katharine Hepburn made her television debut in ABC's pro-duction of *The Glass Menagerie. Upstairs, Downstairs* on PBS's *Masterpiece Theater* won an Emmy as outstanding drama series.

All in the Family was the most watched show for the third consecutive year.

Music

Again, Roberta Flack was at the forefront of the Grammys. Her *Killing Me Softly with His Song* won Record of the Year, and Best Female Vocal Perform-ance. Stevie Wonder's *You Are the Sunshine of My Life* took Best Male Vocal Per-formance, and his *Innervisions* was Album of the Year. The top song went to composers Norman Gimbel and Charles Fox for *Killing Me Softly with His Song*.

Best-selling songs of the year included *You're So Vain*, Carly Simon; *Su-perstition*, Stevie Wonder; *Crocodile Rock*, Elton John; *Killing Me Softly with His Song*, Roberta Flack; *Love Train*, O'Jays; *The Night the Lights Went Out in Georgia*, Vicki Lawrence; *Tie a Yellow Ribbon 'Round the Ole Oak Tree*, Dawn; *You Are the Sunshine of My Life*, Stevie Wonder; *Frankenstein*, Edgar Winter Group; *My Love*, Paul McCartney & Wings; *Give Me Love (Give Me Peace on Earth)*, George Harrison; *Will It Go Round in Circles*, Billy Preston; *Bad, Bad Leroy Brown*, Jim Croce; *The Morning After*, from the film *The Poseidon Adventure*, sung by Maureen McGovern; *Touch Me in the Morning*, Diana Ross; *Brother Louie*, Sto-ries; *Let's Get It On*, Marvin Gaye; *Delta Dawn*, Helen Reddy; *We're an American Band*, Grand Funk; *Half Breed*, Cher; *Angie*, Rolling Stones; *Midnight Train to Georgia*, Gladys Knight & the Pips; *Keep on Truckin'*, Eddie Kendricks; *Photo-graph*, Ringo Starr; *Top of the World*, Carpenters; *The Most Beautiful Girl*, Charlie Rich; and *Time in a Bottle*, Jim Croce.

1974

$\mathcal{T}$he largest airport in the world opened (Jan. 13) outside of Dallas.

Heiress Patricia Hearst, 19, granddaughter of William Randolph Hearst, was kidnapped by members of the Symbionese Liberation Army (SLA).

The House approved (Feb. 6) a resolution to begin an impeachment inquiry against President Richard Nixon.

The *Skylab 3* astronauts returned (Feb. 8) to Earth after 85 days, the longest manned spaceflight to date.

The Civil War ironclad USS *Monitor*, which sank in 1862, was found (Mar. 7) off the coast of Hatteras, N.C.

After selling 650,000 jukeboxes in the U.S. since 1933, the Wurlitzer Co. announced (Mar.) that it would stop production in April.

The *Mariner* spacecraft photographed (Mar. 24) the planet Mercury.

Some 350 people were killed (Apr. 3) in wide-ranging tornadoes from Georgia to Canada.

The House Judiciary Committee began (May 9) impeachment hearings against President Nixon and voted three articles of impeachment on July 27 and July 30.

Six members of the SLA were killed (May 17) in a shootout with police in Los Angeles.

President Nixon released (Aug. 5) excerpts from White House tapes that revealed he had impeded the Watergate investigation. He announced his resignation three days later, and Vice President Gerald Ford was sworn (Aug. 9) as the 38th President.

The price of a first-class stamp was 10 cents.

President Ford named (Sept. 4) George Bush as the nation's first envoy to the People's Republic of China.

In a controversial step, President Ford pardoned (Sept. 8) former President Nixon unconditionally for any acts he may have committed while in office.

President Ford proposed (Sept. 16) a conditional amnesty for Vietnam draft evaders and deserters willing to work up to two years in public service jobs.

Mary Louise Smith became (Sept. 16) the first woman to head the Republican National Committee.

The Franklin National Bank failed (Oct. 8), the largest U.S. bank collapse to date.

The Army announced (Nov. 8) that First Lt. William L. Calley would be paroled after serving one-third of his 10-year prison term for his role in the My Lai massacre in Vietnam.

Karen Silkwood died (Nov. 12) in an unexplained car crash while investigating irregularities at the Kerr McGee nuclear fuel plant.

The U.S. government filed (Nov. 20) an antitrust suit against American Telephone & Telegraph.

Congress passed (Nov. 21) the Freedom of Information Act to broaden public access to government records.

Congressman Wilbur D. Mills of Arkansas resigned (Dec. 10) as chairman of the House Ways and Means Committee following an involvement with burlesque dancer Fanne Fox.

Gov. Jimmy Carter of Georgia announced (Dec. 12) his candidacy for President.

Nelson A. Rockefeller was sworn in (Dec. 19) as the 41st Vice President, the second man to assume the post without a public vote.

In sports news, the Miami Dolphins defeated (Jan. 13) the Minnesota Vikings to win Super Bowl VIII; Atlanta Braves outfielder Hank Aaron hit (Apr. 8) his 715th home run to surpass Babe Ruth's record; Frank Robinson signed (Oct. 3) with the Cleveland Indians to become the first black manager in the majors; and the Oakland Athletics defeated the Los Angeles Dodgers in five games to win the World Series.

Deaths of the year included: cowboy singer Tex Ritter, 68 (Jan. 2); newscaster Chet Huntley, 62 (Mar. 20); comedian Bud Abbott, 78 (Apr. 24); musician Duke Ellington, 75 (May 24); former Chief Justice Earl Warren, 83 (July 9); baseball player Jay Hanna "Dizzy" Dean, 63 (July 17); actor Walter Brennan, 80 (Sept. 21); and TV host Ed Sullivan, 73 (Oct. 13).

In Print

Novels of the year included: *Centennial*, by James Michener; *Something Happened*, by Joseph Heller; *The Seven-Per-Cent Solution*, by Nicholas Meyer; *The Pirate*, by Harold Robbins; *Tinker, Tailer, Soldier, Spy*, by John LeCarré; *The Ebony Tower*, by John Fowles; *Harlequin*, by Morris West; *The Dogs of War*, by Frederick Forsyth; *Lady*, by Thomas Tryon; and *Jaws*, by Peter Benchley.

Nonfiction included: *All Things Bright and Beautiful*, by James Herriot; *The Palace Guard*, by Dan Rather; *The Bermuda Triangle*, by Charles Berlitz; *Strictly Speaking*, by Edwin Newman; *Tales of Power*, by Carlos Castaneda; *A Bridge Too Far*, by Cornelius Ryan; *All the President's Men*, by Carl Bernstein and Bob Woodward; *The Woman He Loved*, by Ralph G. Martin; and *Helter Skelter*, by Vincent Bugliosi with Curt Gentry.

On Stage

Plays produced during the year included: *Gypsy; Cat on a Hot Tin Roof; Mack and Mabel; Absurd Person Singular; Equus; Sherlock Holmes; All Over Town; Of Mice and Men; Find Your Way Home; Lorelei; Noel Coward in Two Keys; Over*

Here!; The Island; Candide; My Fat Friend; Thieves; Words and Music; Jumpers; Sizwe Banzai Is Dead; Sgt. Pepper's Lonely Hearts Club Band; God's Favorite; and *Clarence Darrow* (a one man show with Henry Fonda, it ran for 22 performances).

Best Play went to Joseph A. Walker's *The River Niger*. Michael Moriarty was Best Actor in *Find Your Way Home*, and Colleen Dewhurst was Best Actress for her role in a revival of *A Moon for the Misbegotten*. Best Musicals were *Raisin*, and *Gigi* for best score. Best Actor was Christopher Plummer in *Cyrano*, and Best Actress was Virginia Capers in *Raisin*.

Films

The Godfather, Part II was named Best Picture.

Other motion pictures of the year included *Alice Doesn't Live Here Anymore*, with Ellen Burstyn, Kris Kristofferson, Diane Ladd, and Jodie Foster; *The Apprenticeship of Duddy Kravitz*, with Richard Dreyfuss, Jack Warden, and Randy Quaid; *Chinatown*, with Jack Nicholson, Faye Dunaway, and John Huston; *The Conversation*, with Gene Hackman, John Cazale, and Teri Garr; *The Front Page*, with Jack Lemmon, Walter Matthau, and Carol Burnett; *Harry and Tonto*, with Art Carney and Ellen Burstyn; *Monty Python and the Holy Grail*, with Graham Chapman, John Cleese, and Terry Gilliam; *Murder on the Orient Express*, with Albert Finney, Ingrid Bergman, Sean Connery, Lauren Bacall, Martin Balsam, and Jacqueline Bisset; *The Parallax View*, with Warren Beatty, Paula Prentiss, and Hume Cronyn; *The Sugarland Express*, with Goldie Hawn and William Atherton; *That's Entertainment!*, with Fred Astaire, Bing Crosby, and countless stars from MGM's golden years; and *Young Frankenstein*, with Gene Wilder, Marty Feldman, Teri Garr, Peter Boyle, Cloris Leachman, and Madeline Kahn.

Television

Cicely Tyson starred (Jan. 31) in *The Autobiography of Miss Jane Pittman* on CBS. The networks covered (July 24–30) the debates and voting by the House Judiciary Committee on the impeachment of President Nixon. A week later, the President appeared (Aug. 8) on national television to announce his resignation. *ABC Theater* presented *The Missiles of October*, a reenactment of the Cuban missile crisis. *Gunsmoke*, first broadcast on Sept. 10, 1955, and the longest running Western, was canceled during the 1974–75 season. *The Hollywood Squares* won an Emmy as outstanding daytime game or audience participation show. And for the fourth straight year, *All in the Family* had the most viewers in America.

Music

Popular songs included *The Joker*, Steve Miller Band; *Show and Tell*, Al Wilson; *You're Sixteen*, Ringo Starr; *The Way We Were*, Barbra Streisand; *Love's Theme*, Love Unlimited Orchestra; *Seasons in the Sun*, Terry Jacks; *Dark Lady*, Cher; *Sunshine on My Shoulders*, John Denver; *Hooked on a Feeling*, Blue Swede;

Bennie and the Jets, Elton John; *TSOP—The Sound of Philadelphia*, MFSB featuring The Three Degrees; *The Loco-Motion*, Grand Funk; *The Streak*, Ray Stevens; *Band on the Run*, Paul McCartney & Wings; *Billy, Don't Be a Hero*, Bo Donaldson & The Heywoods; *Sundown*, Gordon Lightfoot; *Rock the Boat*, Hues Corporation; *Rock Your Baby*, George McCrae; *Annie's Song*, John Denver; *Feel Like Makin' Love*, Roberta Flack; *The Night Chicago Died*, Paper Lace; *You're Havin' My Baby*, Paul Anka; *I Shot the Sheriff*, Eric Clapton; *Can't Get Enough of Your Love, Babe*, Barry White; *Rock Me Gently*, Andy Kim; *I Honestly Love You*, Olivia Newton-John; *Nothing from Nothing*, Billy Preston; *Then Came You*, Dionne Warwick & Spinners; *You Haven't Done Nothin'*, Stevie Wonder; *You Ain't Seen Nothing Yet*, Bachman-Turner Overdrive; *Whatever Gets You Through the Night*, John Lennon with the Plastic Ono Nuclear Band; *I Can Help*, Billy Swan; *Kung Fu Fighting*, Carl Douglas; *Cat's in the Cradle*, Harry Chapin; and *Angie Baby*, Helen Reddy.

It was a successful year for Olivia Newton-John. *I Honestly Love You* earned her Record of the Year and Best Female Vocal Performance. Other big winners included: Stevie Wonder's *Fullfillingness' First Finale* for Album of the Year and Best Male Vocal Performance.

1975

*J*ohn Mitchell, H. R. Haldeman, John Ehrlichman, and Robert C. Mardian were convicted (Jan. 1) of all charges in connection with the Watergate cover-up.

President Gerald Ford appointed (Jan. 4) Vice President Nelson Rockefeller to head a commission to investigate alleged domestic spying by the CIA. The Senate started a similar probe on Jan 27.

Guy Madison Brock, a retired North Carolina wholesale grocer, wrote (January) a $1,000 check to help pay off the $493 billion national debt. Brock was not alone; in the prior fiscal year the U.S. Treasury had received total of $417,000 in similar personal contributions.

The U.S. Labor Department announced (Feb. 7) that unemployment reached 8.2 percent in January, the highest level since 1941.

President Ford named (Feb. 13) Carla Hills Secretary of Housing & Urban Development; she was confirmed by the Senate on Mar. 5.

The U.S. signed (Feb. 14) an agreement making the Marianas Islands a U.S. Commonwealth.

William E. Miller began (February) appearing in American Express "Do You Know Me?" TV commercials. He was the 1964 Republican Vice Presidential candidate.

An Air Force C-5A transport crashed (Apr. 4) in Saigon, killing 200 Vietnamese refugees aboard.

Cambodia's capital, Phnom Penh, was occupied (Apr. 17) by insurgent Khmer Rouge forces, toppling the U.S. supported government of Lon Nol.

The Government of South Vietnam surrendered (Apr. 30) to Communists troops following the departure of the last Americans from Saigon.

U.S. *Apollo* and Soviet *Soyuz* spacecraft docked (July 17) in space as part of a joint test program.

The Senate approved (July 22) a resolution to return U.S. citizenship to Confederate General Robert E. Lee.

Former Teamster president James Hoffa disappeared (July 31) outside a Detroit motel, and the FBI joined the search three days later.

President Ford escaped two assassination attempts in a little more than two weeks; the first by Lynette Alice "Squeaky" Fromme on Sept. 5 and the second by Sara Jane Moore on Sept. 22.

Elizabeth Ann Bayley Seton was canonized (Sept. 14) by Pope Paul VI as the first native-born American saint.

Patricia Hearst was found (Sept. 18) after a year and a half with the SLA, and a San Francisco court refused to grant her bail on bank robbery charges.

The Presidential Clemency Board closed (September) operations after a year's existence. During that time, only 21,000 of the nation's 108,000 convicted Vietnam draft evaders and deserters applied to the panel for conditional pardons.

Nelson Rockefeller disclosed (Nov. 3) that he would not seek the Vice Presidential spot in 1976. President Ford, meanwhile, named Donald H. Rumsfeld as Defense Secretary to replace James Schlesinger, George Bush as the new Director of Central Intelligence, Elliot Richardson as Commerce Secretary and Brent Scowcroft as Assistant for National Security Affairs.

Ronald Reagan announced (Nov. 21) his candidacy for President.

President Ford nominated (Nov. 28) John Paul Stevens to succeed William O. Douglas on the Supreme Court.

The President traveled (Dec. 1-5) to China to meet with Mao Tse-tung, and later visited Indonesia and The Philippines.

In sports news, the Pittsburgh Steelers defeated (Jan. 12) the Minnesota Vikings to win Super Bowl IX, and the Cincinnati Reds defeated the Boston Red Sox in seven games to win the World Series.

Among the year's deaths were: comedian Larry Fine, 73 (Jan. 24), of The Three Stooges; entertainer Ozzie Nelson, 68 (June 3); and baseball manager Casey Stengel, 85 (Sept. 30).

In Print

Curtain by Agatha Christie, *The Greek Treasure* by Irving Stone, and *Ragtime* by E. L. Doctorow topped the best-seller list. Others novels included *The Choirboys*, by Joseph Waumbaugh; *In the Beginning*, by Chaim Potok; *Looking for Mr. Goodbar*, by Judith Rossner; *Humboldt's Gift*, by Saul Below; *The Eagle Has Landed*, by Jack Higgins; *Shogun*, by James Clavell; and *The Moneychangers*, by Arthur Hailey.

On the nonfiction list: *Bring on the Empty Horses*, by David Niven; *The Relaxation Response*, by Herbert Benson; *Sylvia Porter's Money Book*, by Sylvia Porter; *Angels*, by Billy Graham; *Power*, by Michael Korda; *The Age of Napoleon*, by Will and Ariel Durant; *The Ascent of Man*, by Jacob Bronowski; *My Life*, by Golda Meir; *The New Yorker Album of Drawings, 1925-1975;* and *Winning Through Intimidation*, by Robert J. Ringer.

Saul Bellow won the Pulitzer Prize for his novel *Humboldt's Gift.*

On Stage

Grease, which opened on Feb. 14, 1972, continued running, with 1,763 performances by June. Two other holdovers dominated the season: *Pippin* with 1,512, and *Raisin* with 847 performances.

Plays produced included: *Chicago; The First Breeze of Summer; A Chorus Line; Lampost Reunion; Treemonisha; Me and Bessie; Kennedy's Children; Hello, Dolly* (revival); *A Musical Jubilee; Habeas Corpus; Angel Street; Same Time Next Year; Sweet Bird of Youth* (revival); *The Royal Family; Travesties; The Wiz; The Ritz; Dance With Me; Seascape;* and *Bette Midler's Clams on the Half Shell Revue.*

There was one performance of *Home Sweet Home* (Jan. 4), which starred Yul Brynner.

Peter Shaffler's *Equus* won Best Play. Best Actor award went to John Kani in *Sizwe Banzi is Dead,* and Winston Ntshona in *The Island.* Best Actress was Ellen Burstyn in *Same Time Next Year.* The Best Musical for the year was *The Wiz.* Best Actor in a musical was John Cullum, *Shenandoah.* Angela Lansbury's role in *Gypsy* earned her Best Actress.

Films

Milos Forman's *One Flew Over the Cuckoo's Nest,* Best Picture, dominated the year's outstanding movies. It starred Jack Nicholson, Best Actor, Louise Fletcher, Best Actress, Will Sampson, Danny DeVito, and Christopher Lloyd. Forman was named Best Director.

Other popular films included: *Barry Lyndon,* with Ryan O'Neal and Marisa Berenson; *Dog Day Afternoon,* with Al Pacino, John Cazale, and Charles Durning); *The French Connection II,* with Gene Hackman and Fernando Rey; *Love and Death,* with Woody Allen and Diane Keaton; *The Man Who Would Be King,* with Sean Connery, Michael Caine, and Christopher Plummer; *Nashville,* with Lily Tomlin and Geraldine Chaplin; *The Prisoner of Second Avenue,* with Jack Lemmon and Anne Bancroft; *The Sunshine Boys,* with George Burns, Walter Matthau, and Richard Benjamin. The year's outstanding foreign film was Lina Wertmuller's *Swept Away,* starring Giancarlo Giannini and Mariangela Melato.

Jaws grossed $133.4 million.

Television

ABC Theater presented (Jan. 12) a drama on the court-martial of Army Lieutenant William Calley, who was tried for his role in the My Lai massacre. The war in Vietnam also was the subject of an NBC News Special broadcast (Apr. 29) which looked back at the U.S. role in the war.

Jason Robards and Colleen Dewhurst starred (May 27) in *ABC Theater's* production of *A Moon for the Misbegotten. NBC's Saturday Night Live* earned an Emmy for outstanding comedy, variety or musical series. The most watched program for the fifth consecutive season was *All in the Family.*

Music

The number one songs of the year included *Lucy in the Sky With Diamonds,* Elton John; *Mandy,* Barry Manilow; *Please, Mr. Postman,* Carpenters; *Laughter in the Rain,* Neil Sedaka; *Fire,* Ohio Players; *You're no Good,* Linda Ronstadt; *Pick Up the Pieces,* AWB; *Best of My Love,* Eagles; *Have You Never Been*

Mellow, Olivia Newton-John; *Black Water*, Doobie Brothers; *My Eyes Adored You*, Frankie Valli; *Lady Marmalade*, Labelle; *Lovin' You*, Minnie Ripperton; *Philadelphia Freedom*, Elton John Band; *(Hey, Won't You Play) Another Somebody Done Somebody Wrong Song*, B. J. Thomas; *He Don't Love You (Like I Love You)*, Tony Orlando & Dawn; *Shining Star*, Earth, Wind & Fire; *Before the Next Teardrop Falls*, Freddy Fender; *Thank God I'm a Country Boy*, John Denver; *Sister Golden Hair*, America; *Love Will Keep Us Together*, Captain & Tennille; *Listen to What the Man Said*, Wings; *The Hustle*, Van McCoy & The Soul City Symphony; *One of These Nights*, Eagles; *Jive Talkin'*, Bee Gees; *Fallin' in Love*, Hamilton, Joe Frank & Reynolds; *Get Down Tonight*, K.C. & The Sunshine Band; *Rhinestone Cowboy*, Glen Campbell; *Fame*, David Bowie; *I'm Sorry*, John Denver; *Bad Blood*, Neil Sedaka; *Island Girl*, Elton John; *That's the Way (I Like It)*, K. C. & The Sunshine Band; *Fly, Robin, Fly*, Silver Convention; *Let's Do it Again*, Staple Singers.

It was a diverse year for musical awards. Record of the Year went to the Captain & Tennille for *Love Will Keep Us Together*. Paul Simon won Album of The Year and Best Male Vocal performance for his *Still Crazy After All These Years*. Stephen Sondheim won Song of The Year for his poignant *Send in the Clowns*, and Janis Ian won Best Female Vocal Performance for *At Seventeen*.

1976

$\mathcal{I}$n a poll (Jan.) of nine Democratic presidential candidates by the National Organization For Reform of Marijuana Laws, only George Wallace was absolutely opposed to the decriminalization of pot.

Daniel P. Moynihan resigned (Feb. 2) as U.S. ambassador to the United Nations.

According to a survey (Feb.) by the MIT/Harvard University Joint Center For Urban Studies, Americans defined the "good life" as an income of $25,000 a year, a seven-room house in the suburbs, two cars and three weeks of vacation.

Aerospace giant Lockheed disclosed (Feb. 6) that it had bribed Dutch Prince Bernhardt.

Sen. Lloyd Bentsen withdrew from the Democratic presidential contest, followed by Birch Bayh, Milton Shapp and Sargent Shriver (Feb.–Nov.).

The U.S. Environmental Protection Agency banned (Feb. 18) the production of almost all pesticides containing mercury.

President Gerald Ford disclosed (Feb.) that he had earned $135,000 and had a bank account of only $1,239. The President's limited savings were partly the result of his paying all or most of the expenses of his four grown children, including the educational costs of three of them.

Patricia Hearst was convicted (Mar.) of a 1974 bank robbery along with Symbionese Liberation Army members who had abducted her.

Conrail began (Apr. 1) operating as a federally funded corporation to manage six failed railroads in the Northeast.

Congressman Wayne Hayes of Ohio told (May 25) the House that he had a personal relationship with Elizabeth Ray, a staff aide. He resigned his seat on Sept. 1.

The U.S. and the Soviet Union approved (May 28) a nuclear test agreement to allow the inspection of test sites.

The SR-71A reconnaissance aircraft set (June 28) a world speed record of 2,193.1 mph near Beale Air Force Base, Calif.

Americans, including a gathering of six million people in New York City to see Operation Sail, celebrated (July 4) the nation's bicentennial.

Scientists at Yale University discovered (July 18) Lyme arthritis, a new strain of the ailment.

After a one billion-mile trip, *Viking 1* became (July 20) the first spacecraft to land successfully on Mars and send back photographs.

The U.S. removed (July 20) its last forces from Thailand.

Ronald Reagan named (July 26) Sen. Richard Schweiker as his running mate for the Republican presidential nomination. The GOP, however, selected (Aug. 16-19) President Ford and Sen. Robert Dole to oppose Jimmy Carter and Sen. Walter Mondale. The Democratic candidates defeated (Nov. 2) their Republican opponents by a narrow margin.

A pound of pork chops cost $1.84.

The U.S. vetoed (Nov. 15) Vietnam's ambassador to the U.N. because Hanoi had failed to give an accounting of some 800 American servicemen still listed as missing in action from the war in Southeast Asia.

The Pittsburgh Steelers defeated (Jan. 18) the Dallas Cowboys to win Super Bowl X and the Cincinnati Reds defeated the New York Yankees in four games to win the World Series.

The year's notable deaths included: singer/actor Paul Robeson, 77 (Jan. 23); musical film director Busby Berkeley, 80 (Mar. 14); historian Samuel Eliot Morison, 88 (May 15); tycoon J. Paul Getty, 83 (June 6); artist Alexander Calder, 77 (Nov. 11); and Chicago mayor Richard Daley, 74 (Dec. 20).

In Print

Topping the best sellers was *Trinity*, by Leon Uris, which remained on the best seller list for 43 weeks. Other outstanding fiction included *Sleeping Murder*, by Agatha Christie; *Storm Warning*, by Jack Higgins; *Raise the Titanic!*, by Clive Cussler; *Slapstick*, by Kurt Vonnegut; *The Crash of '79*, by Paul S. Erdman; *Ceremony of The Innocent*, by Taylor Caldwell; *Blue Skies, No Candy*, by Gael Greene; *The Users*, by Joyce Haber; and *Touch Not the Cat*, by Mary Stewart.

Roots, by Alex Haley, was the number one book on the general reading list when the year ended. The book was the basis for a later miniseries, one of the most highly watched programs in TV viewing history.

Gail Sheehy's book, *Passages*, had been on the best seller list for thirty weeks. Other nonfiction included: *Blind Ambition*, by John Dean; *Your Erroneous Zones*, by Wayne W. Dyer; *The Grass is Always Greener Over the Septic Tank*, by Erma Bombeck; *The Hite Report*, by Shere Hite; *Adolf Hitler*, by John Toland; *Blood and Money*, by Thomas Thompson; *The Right and the Power*, by Leon Jaworski; *To Jerusalem and Back*, by Saul Bellow.

On Stage

Plays produced included: *California Suite; Godspell;* a revival of *Guys and Dolls; Four Colored Girls Who Have Considered Suicide/When the Rainbow Is Enuf; Porgy and Bess* (revival); *Comedians; Your Arms Too Short to Box With God; Pacific Overtures; A Matter of Gravity; Knock Knock; Bubbling Brown Sugar; Monty Python Live!; Shirley MacLaine at the Palace; The Robber Bridegroom;* and *An Evening With Diana Ross.*

Tom Stoppard, who wrote *Travesties*, won a Tony Award for Best Play, and John Wood took Best Actor for his role in the play. Best Actress went to Irene Worth for her performance in a revival of *Sweet Bird of Youth*. Best Musical was *A Chorus Line*. Best Actor in a musical was won by George Rose in *My Fair Lady*, and Best Actress went to Donna McKenchie in *A Chorus Line*.

Films

The Academy Award for Best Motion Picture went to *Rocky*, which starred Sylvester Stallone and Talia Shire. Although he had been acting and writing for many years, *Rocky* would be the start of a very successful career for Mr. Stallone. Richard Avildsen, the film's director, also won an Oscar for Best Director.

Other films of the year included: *All The President's Men*, with Robert Redford, Dustin Hoffman, and Jason Robards; *The Bad News Bears*, with Walter Matthau and Tatum O'Neal; *Bound For Glory*, with David Carradine; *The Front*, with Woody Allen, Zero Mostel, and Herschel Bernardi; *The Last Tycoon*, with Robert DeNiro, Jeanne Moreau, and Jack Nicholson; *The Man Who Fell to Earth*, with David Bowie; *Marathon Man*, with Dustin Hoffman, Laurence Olivier, Roy Schieder, and William Devane; *Network*, with William Holden, Faye Dunaway, Peter Finch, and Ned Beatty; *Robin and Marian*, with Sean Connery, Audrey Hepburn, and Robert Shaw; *The Seven Percent Solution*, with Alan Arkin, Nicol Williamson, Laurence Olivier, and Robert Duvall; *The Shootist*, with John Wayne, Lauren Bacall, and Ron Howard; and *Taxi Driver*, with Robert DeNiro, Cybill Shepherd, and Jodie Foster.

This year, the average budget for a feature film was $4 million.

Television

Jane Alexander and Edward Herrmann co-starred (Jan. 11-12) on *ABC Theater's* presentation of "Eleanor & Franklin."

Presidential politics took center stage when all networks covered (Sept. 23) the first of three debates between Gerald Ford and Jimmy Carter.

ABC aired (Dec. 14) Barbara Walters's first special, featuring interviews with Jimmy Carter and Barbara Streisand.

The Mary Tyler Moore Show ended its run in the 1976-77 season, and James Garner, star of *The Rockford Files*, received an Emmy as outstanding actor in a dramatic series.

Happy Days on ABC displaced *All in the Family* as the top-rated program.

Music

The number one songs included: *Saturday Night*, Bay City Rollers; *Convoy*, C. W. McCall; *I Write The Songs*, Barry Manilow; *Theme From "Mahogany" (Do You Know Where You're Going To)*, Diana Ross; *Love Rollercoaster*, Ohio Players; *50 Ways To Leave Your Lover*, Paul Simon; *Theme From S.W.A.T.*, Rhythm Heritage; *Love Machine (Part 1)*, Miracles; *December, 1963 (Oh, What a Night)*, Four Seasons; *Disco Lady*, Johnnie Taylor; *Let Your Love Flow*, Bellamy Brothers; *Welcome Back*, John Sebastian; *Boogie Fever*, Sylvers; *Silly Love Songs*, Wings; *Love Hangover*, Diana Ross; *Afternoon Delight*, Starland Vocal Band; *Kiss and Say Goodbye*, Manhattans; *Don't Go Breaking My Heart*, Elton John & Kiki Dee; *You Should be Dancing*, Bee Gees; *Shake, Shake, Shake, Shake Your Booty*, KC & The Sunshine Band; *Play That Funky Music*, Wild Cherry; *A Fifth of Beethoven*, Walter Murphy & The Big Apple Band; *Disco Duck (Part 1)*, Rick Dees & His Case of Idiots; *If You Leave Me Now*, Chicago; *Rock'n Me*, Steve Miller; *Tonight's the Night (Gonna Be Alright)*, Rod Stewart.

Record of the Year went to George Benson for *This Masquerade*. Album of the Year was Steve Wonder's *Songs in the Key of Life*. Song of the Year was *I Write the Songs*. Best Male Vocal was given to Stevie Wonder for *Songs in the Key of Life*. Linda Ronstadt received a Grammy for Best Female Performance in *Hasten Down the Wind*.

1977

*J*acqueline Means became (Jan. 1) the first woman Episcopal priest in the U.S.

Following restoration of the death penalty, Gary Gilmore was executed (Jan. 17) by firing squad in Utah State Prison.

Federal scientists announced (Jan. 19) that they had discovered the germ that caused Legionnaires' Disease, which had killed 29 people in Philadelphia in July 1976.

On his last full day in office, President Gerald Ford pardoned (Jan. 19) "Tokyo Rose," who had been convicted of making propaganda broadcasts to American forces during World War II.

Former Governor Jimmy Carter was inaugurated (Jan. 20) as the 39th President. Carter pardoned Vietnam War draft resistors the next day.

Larry Flynt, editor of *Hustler*, was convicted (Feb. 8) in Cincinnati of engaging in organized crime and pandering obscenity.

Bad weather in the form of heavy snow and ice prompted (Feb.) a half-percentage point reduction in the nation's economic growth rate for the year's first quarter.

President Carter cut off (Feb. 24) aid to Argentina, Uruguay, and Ethiopia for violations of human rights.

In the nation's first dial-a-President radio program, some 9 million Americans attempted (Mar. 12) to call President Carter. Only 42 reached the Oval Office.

President Carter delivered (Mar. 17) a human rights message to the United Nations.

A KLM Boeing 747 and a Pan Am 747 collided (Mar. 27) on a runway in the Canary Islands, killing 547.

In a national address, the President called (Apr. 18) for limits on energy use.

After climbing up New York's 110-story World Trade Center building, daredevil George Willig was fined (May 26) $1.10—a penny a floor.

Nine million people in New York City and Westchester County were blacked out (July 13) after a violent electrical storm. The Department of Energy was created (Aug. 4).

Oldsmobile introduced (Sept. 13) the first American car fueled by diesel.

Columbia University revolt leader Mark Rudd surrendered (Sept. 14) to authorities after evading arrest for seven and half years.

Bert Lance resigned (Sept. 21) as Director of the Office of Management and Budget following a controversy over his financial affairs.

Richard Helms, who headed the CIA in 1966-1973, was fined (Nov. 4) $2,000 and given a two-year suspended sentence for false testimony to a Senate Committee investigating covert operations in Chile.

The last installment of the *L'il Abner* comic strip was published (Nov. 13).

The Concorde began (Nov. 22) service to New York eight years after its first flight and more than a year after the start of transatlantic flights to Washington.

Although the FBI released (Dec. 7) 40,000 pages of material from its investigation of John Kennedy's assassination, there were few new facts in the 200 volumes of information made available to the public.

The Oakland Raiders defeated the Minnesota Vikings to win Super Bowl XI, and the New York Yankees defeated the Los Angeles Dodgers in six games to win the World Series.

Among the prominent deaths of the year were: jazz pianist Errol Garner, 53 (Jan. 2); director of Selective Service System Gen. Lewis Hershey, 83 (May 20); actor Alfred Lunt, 84 (Aug. 3); singer Elvis Presley, 42 (Aug. 16); comedian Groucho Marx, 86 (Aug. 20); singer Bing Crosby, 73 (Oct. 14); and band leader Guy Lombardo, 75 (Nov. 5).

The U.S. population had reached 219,760,000.

In Print

Best fiction was: *The Silmarillion*, by J.R.R. Tolkien; *The Thorn Birds*, by Colleen McCullough; *The Honourable Schoolboy*, by John Le Carre; *Illusions*, by Richard Bach; *Beggarman, Thief*, by Irwin Shaw; *The Book of Merlyn*, by Terence H. White; *Dreams Die First*, by Harold Robbins; *The Immigrants*, by Howard Fast; *The Black Marble*, by Joseph Wambaugh; *Dynasty*, by Robert S. Elegant; *Daniel Martin*, by John Fowles; *Delta of Venus*, by Anais Nin; *The Second Deadly Sin*, by Lawrence Sanders; *The Women's Room*, by Marilyn French; and *KG 200*, by J. D. Gilman & John Clive.

On the nonfiction side: *All Things Wise and Wonderful*, by James Herriot; *The Book of Lists*, by David Wallechinsky, Irving Wallace & Amy Wallace; *The Amityville Horror*, by Jay Anson; *The Complete Book of Running*, by James F. Fixx; *Gnomes*, text by Wil Huygen, illustrated by Rien Poortvliet; *Looking Out for Number One*, by Robert J. Ringer; *The Second Ring of Power*, by Carlos Castaneda; *The Dragons of Eden*, by Carl Sagan; *Even Big Guys Cry*, by Alex Karras and Herb Gluck; and *Six Men*, by Alistair Cooke.

On Stage

Beatlemania opened on May 31. It was a review of the songs of John Lennon, Paul McCartney and George Harrison.

Other plays produced this year included: *The Act; Miss Margarida's Way; The Gin Game; An Almost Perfect Person; Jesus Christ Superstar* (revival); *Chapter Two; A Touch of The Poet; The Trip Back Down; Otherwise Engaged; A Party With*

Betty Comden and Adolph Green; American Buffalo; Lily Tomlin "Appearing Nitely";
Mummenschanz; The Shadow Box; Anna Christie; I Love My Wife; Side by Side by
Sondheim; Annie; The Basic Training of Pavlo Hummel; and *Cold Storage.*

The Tony Award for Best Play went to Michael Cristofer's *The Shadow Box.* Al Pacino, in *The Basic Training of Pavlo Hummel,* took Best Actor. Dorothy Loudon provided a memorable performance in *Annie,* which won her a Tony. The show was also the Best Musical of the year. Barry Bostwick, appearing in *The Robber Bridegroom,* won Best Actor.

Films

Box office receipts were $2.376 billion.

Annie Hall, Woody Allen's film, earned three Academy Awards: Best Picture; Best Director, Woody Allen; and Best Actress, Diane Keaton.

Other outstanding films were: *Close Encounters of the Third Kind,* with Richard Dreyfuss, Francois Truffaut, and Teri Garr; *The Goodbye Girl,* with Marsha Mason and Richard Dreyfuss; *Julia,* with Jane Fonda, Vanessa Redgrave, and Jason Robards; *MacArthur,* with Gregory Peck and Ed Flanders; *The Spy Who Loved Me,* with Roger Moore and Barbara Bach; *Star Wars,* with Mark Hamill, Carrie Fisher, Harrison Ford, Alex Guinness, and Peter Cushing; and *Three Women,* with Sissy Spacek and Shelley Duvall.

Star Wars grossed over $185 million, and *Close Encounters of The Third Kind* earned $77 million. *Star Wars* cost $11 million ($1 million over budget); *Casablanca* cost $878,000 to make in 1943.

Television

CBS Reports produced (Mar. 22) *The Fire Next Door,* a report by Bill Moyers on arson in The Bronx.

Richard Pryor's first comedy special was offered (May 5) by NBC, with guests John Belushi and Maya Angelou.

CBS presented (Nov. 25) a 10th anniversary special for *Rolling Stone* magazine.

NBC brought (Nov. 27) viewers an animated special, *Doonesbury,* based on Garry Trudeau's cartoon series.

The Carol Burnett Show was canceled in the 1977-78 season, and Dave Powers was awarded an Emmy for outstanding directing in a comedy, variety or musical series for his work on *The Carol Burnett Show.*

ABC's *Laverne and Shirley* was the most watched program.

Music

Number one songs included: *You Don't Have to Be a Star (To Be In My Show),* Marilyn McCoo & Billy Davis Jr.; *You Make Me Feel Like Dancing,* Leo Sayer; *I Wish,* Stevie Wonder; *Car Wash,* Rose Royce; *Torn Between Two Lovers,* Mary MacGregor; *Blinded by the Light,* Manfred Mann's Earth Band; *New Kid In Town,* Eagles; *Love Theme from "A Star Is Born" (Evergreen),* Barbra Streisand; *Rich Girl,* Daryl Hall & John Oates; *Dancing Queen,* Abba; *Don't Give*

Up on Us, David Soul; *Don't Leave Me This Way*, Thelma Houston; *Southern Nights*, Glen Campbell; *Hotel California*, Eagles; *When I Need You*, Leo Sayer; *Sir Duke*, Stevie Wonder; *I'm Your Boogie Man*, KC & The Sunshine Band; *Dreams*, Fleetwood Mac; *Got to Give it Up*, Marvin Gaye; *Gonna Fly Now (Theme from "Rocky")*, Bill Conti; *Undercover Angel*, Alan O'Day; *Da Doo Ron*, Shaun Cassidy; *Looks Like We Made It*, Barry Manilow; *I Just Want to be Your Everything*, Andy Gibb; *Best Of My Love*, Emotions; *Star Wars Theme/Cantina Band*, Meco; *You Light Up My Life*, Debbie Boone; *How Deep is Your Love*, Bee Gees.

The Eagles' *Hotel California* won the Grammy award for Record of The Year. Song of The Year went to Paul Williams and Barbara Streisand for *Evergreen*. Barbara Streisand also won Best Female Vocal Performance for *Evergreen*.

1978

*A*ttorney General Griffin Bell nominated (Jan. 19) William H. Webster as Director of the FBI.

To help shrink the nation's $625 million annual deficit, the U.S. Postal Service began testing (Jan.) a smaller 13-cent stamp.

The Desert Empire Bank near Palm Springs, Calif., offered a Rolls-Royce Silver Shadow worth $55,000 to any customer who deposited $1 million for six years. Twenty people made inquiries but none took the offer.

A research chemist in Missouri warned (Feb.) that snowflakes were potentially hazardous because the lead content of the flakes he tested was six times higher than the federal clean water standard.

The longest coal strike in American history ended (Mar. 25) after 110 days.

The President signed (Apr. 6) a bill to raise the mandatory retirement age from 65 to 70.

Former acting FBI director L. Patrick Gray and two other ex-Bureau officials were indicted (Apr. 10) on conspiracy charges.

After a heated national debate, the Senate voted (Apr. 18) to give the Panama Canal to Panama on Dec. 31, 1999.

David ("Son of Sam") Berkowitz received (June 12) a life sentence for each of six murders.

King Hussein of Jordan married (June 15) American Elizabeth Halaby in Amman.

The Government reported (July 28) that consumer prices rose at an 11.4 percent annual rate in the year's second quarter.

President Carter declared (Aug. 7) the Love Canal section near Niagara Falls a disaster area because of accumulated toxic waste in the ground.

Three Americans became (Aug. 17) the first travelers to successfully cross the Atlantic in a balloon.

New York City health inspectors checked (Sept. 7) Garment District air conditioners and water supplies for the source of Legionnaires' Disease that had killed two people.

President Carter sponsored a Middle East summit at Camp David during which Egyptian President Anwar Sadat and Israeli Prime Minister Menachem Begin signed (Sept. 17) a peace agreement.

William and Emily Harris were sentenced (Oct. 3) to ten years-to-life for abducting Patricia Hearst.

The airline industry was deregulated as Congress voted (Oct. 15) to phase out federal control of airline routes and fares. That same day, Congress passed the National Energy Act to regulate natural gas prices and set fuel efficiency standards.

Nine hundred and eleven members of the Rev. Jim Jones's cult, the People's Temple, committed suicide (Nov. 19) in Guyana.

The *Pioneer Venus 1* spacecraft began (Dec. 5) orbiting Venus and probing the planet's atmosphere and surface with radar. *Pioneer Venus 2* sent (Dec. 9) four probes to the surface; one probe survived and sent data for an hour.

President Carter announced (Dec. 15) that the U.S. and China would establish full diplomatic relations on Jan. 1, 1979.

Cleveland became (Dec. 15) the first major American city to default on loan obligations since the Depression.

The House Select Committee on Assassinations reported (Dec. 30) that President John Kennedy and the Rev. Martin Luther King probably had been killed as the result of conspiracies.

In the world of sports, the Dallas Cowboys defeated (Jan. 15) the Denver Broncos to win Super Bowl XII; Czech tennis player Martina Navratilova defected (Sept. 9) to the West and requested U.S. political asylum; and the New York Yankees defeated the Los Angeles Dodgers in six games to win the World Series.

Notable deaths in 1978 included: former Vice President Hubert Humphrey, 66 (Jan. 13); actress Peggy Wood, 86 (Mar. 18); cat Morris, 17 (July 7); philanthropist John D. Rockefeller III, 72 (July 10); historian Bruce Catton, 78 (Aug. 28); ventriloquist Edgar Bergen, 75 (Sept. 30); artist Norman Rockwell, 84 (Nov. 8); and anthropologist Margaret Meade, 76 (Nov. 15).

In Print

Richard Bach's *Illusions* remained on the best seller list for its 78th week, and J.R.R. Tolkien's *The Silmarillion* continued for its 61st consecutive week.

The remainder of the list was dominated by books by well-known authors. Among them: *Chesapeake*, by James A. Michener; *War and Remembrance*, by Herman Wouk; *Fools Die*, by Mario Puzo; *Second Generation*, by Howard Fast; *The Far Pavilions*, by M. M. Kaye; *Evergreen*, by Belva Plain; *The Stories of John Cheever*, by John Cheever; *The Coup*, by John Updike; *Wifey*, by Judy Blume; *Prelude to Terror*, by Helen McGuinness; *Eye of the Needle*, by Ken Follet; and *The Stand*, by Stephen King.

Similarly, the nonfiction list was also dominated by the work of well-known authors: *Mommie Dearest*, by Christina Crawford; *A Distant Mirror*, by Barbara W. Tuchman; *If Life is a Bowl of Cherries—What Am I Doing in the Pits*, by Erma Bombeck; *American Caesar*, by William Manchester; *Faeries*, described and illustrated by Brian Froud and Alan Lee; *In Search of History*, by Theodore H. White; *Tutankhamun: The Untold Story*, by Thomas Hoving; *The Buchwald*

Stops Here, by Art Buchwald; and *Robert Kennedy and His Times*, by Arthur Schlesinger.

On Stage

The American Dance Machine, The Best Little Whorehouse In Texas, and *Eubie!* were among plays produced on Broadway this year. Others included: *The Crucifer of Blood; First Monday in October; King of Hearts; Platinum; The Kingfisher; On the Twentieth Century; Deathtrap; Timbuktu!; Hello, Dolly!* (revival); *Dancin'; Ain't Misbehavin'; Working;* and *Ballroom*. A revival of *Stop the World—I Want to Get Off* starred Sammy Davis Jr. and ran for thirty performances.

Da, a play written by Hugh Leonard received two Tonys: Best Play; and Best Actor, which went to Barnard Hughes. Jessica Tandy took Best Actress for her role in *The Gin Game*.

Best Musical was won by *Ain't Misbehavin'*; Best Score, *On the Twentieth Century*. John Cullum, appearing in *On the Twentieth Century*, was given the Tony for Best Actor. Liza Minelli won Best Actress for her role in *The Act*.

Films

The Deer Hunter was named Best Picture. It starred Robert DeNiro and Meryl Streep.

Other outstanding films of the year: *California Suite*, with Maggie Smith, Alan Alda, Richard Pryor; *Grease*, with John Travolta, Olivia Newton-John, and Stockard Channing; *Coming Home*, with Jane Fonda, Jon Voight, and Bruce Dern; *Days of Heaven*, with Brook Adams, Richard Gere, and Sam Shepard; *Heaven Can Wait*, with Warren Beatty, Julie Christie, James Mason, Dyan Cannon, and Jack Warden; *Interiors*, with Diane Keaton, Geraldine Page, E.G. Marshall, and Maureen Stapleton; *National Lampoon's Animal House*, with John Belushi, Tim Matheson, and Donald Sutherland; *Superman*, with Christopher Reed, Margot Kidder, Gene Hackman, Marlon Brando, Susannah York, and Ned Beatty; and *An Unmarried Woman*, with Jill Clayburgh, Alan Bates, Michael Murphy, and Cliff Gorman.

Grease earned $96.3 million.

Television

Paul Winfield and Cicely Tyson starred (Feb. 12-14) on NBC's drama on Martin Luther King, Jr. The following month, NBC also offered (Mar. 26) a *Tribute to "Mr. Television,"* Milton Berle.

The 1978-79 season marked the end of the road for the celebrated *All in the Family* series.

Another situation comedy, ABC's *Taxi*, won an Emmy as outstanding comedy series, while *Roots: The Next Generation* was honored as outstanding limited series.

Three's Company became the top-rated program.

Music

Billy Joel's *Just the Way You Are* took the Grammy Awards' Record of The Year and Song of The Year. Other winners were: *Saturday Night Fever*, Album of The Year (various artists); Barry Manilow's *Copacabana*, Best Male Vocal Performance; *You Needed Me*, Best Female Vocal Performance, sung by Anne Murray.

The top selling songs were: *Baby Come Back*, Player; *Stayin' Alive*, Bee Gees; *(Love Is) Thicker Than Water*, Andy Gibb; *Night Fever*, Bee Gees; *If I Can't Have You*, Yvonne Elliman; *With a Little Luck*, Wings; *Too Much, Too Little, Too Late*, Johnny Mathis/Deniece Williams; *You're the One That I Want*, John Travolta & Olivia Newton-John; *Shadow Dancing*, Andy Gibb; *Miss You*, Rolling Stones; *Three Times A Lady*, Commodores; *Grease*, Franki Valli; *Boogie Oogie*, Taste Of Honey; *Kiss You All Over*, Exile; *Hot Child in the City*, Nick Gilder; *You Needed Me*, Ann Murray; *MacArthur Park*, Donna Summer; *You Don't Bring Me Flowers*, Barbra Streisand & Neil Diamond; *Le Freak*, Chic.

The Compact Disc (CD) was introduced by Philips; it would be re-introduced again in 1982. After its second introduction, the CD challenged the LP and cassette as a recording medium.

1979

The United States established (Jan. 1) full diplomatic relations with China.

Former Attorney General John Mitchell, the last of the Watergate prisoners, was released (Jan. 19) on parole after serving 19 months of a two-and-a-half-to-eight-year sentence in a federal prison. As a result of the Watergate scandal, 25 men served jail terms.

Patricia Hearst was released (Jan. 29) from prison after three years following President Jimmy Carter's commutation of her seven-year sentence.

The Congressional Joint Committee on Printing determined (Jan.) that the government would save several millions of dollars if it changed the size of its stationery from 8 x 10, the standard adopted in 1921, to 8 x 11 and ordered the change to be made by year's end.

A 2,500 year old Greek statue, valued at $250,000, was stolen (Feb. 9) from the Metropolitan Museum of Art, the first major theft in the institution's 110 year history.

The U.S. Ambassador to Afghanistan was kidnapped (Feb. 14) in Kabul.

Barbara Tuchman became (Feb. 27) the first woman President of the American Academy and Institute of Arts & Letters.

The *Voyager I* spacecraft made (Mar. 5) its closest approach to Jupiter—172,000 miles.

The Supreme Court ruled (Mar. 5) unconstitutional laws requiring alimony payments by divorced husbands but not by wives.

The House voted (Mar. 19) to allow live television coverage of its proceedings for the first time.

President Anwar Sadat of Egypt and Prime Minister Menachem Begin of Israel signed (Mar. 26) a formal peace treaty in a Washington ceremony.

The cooling system of a pressurized water atomic reactor at the Three Mile Island power plant near Harrisburg, Penn., malfunctioned (Mar. 28) causing the nation's worst nuclear accident. Thousands of people had to leave their homes.

Mayor Lern Larisey of Cloud Lake, Fla., refunded (May) $22.61 of federal aid when the government mistakenly designated his 136-person town as a "major disaster area."

A federal grand jury indicted (May 23) Bert Lance, former Director of the Office of Management and Budget, and three business associates on conspiracy charges.

In the nation's worst aviation tragedy to date, an American Airlines DC-10 crashed (May 25) shortly after take-off from Chicago, killing all 272 aboard and three on ground.

President Carter authorized (June 7) the development of the MX strategic missile.

American Bryan Allen won (June 12) a $185,000 prize by pedaling an aircraft across the English Channel.

The Sioux Nation was awarded (June 13) $17.5 million for North Dakota land taken from them in 1877.

President Carter and Soviet President Leonid Brezhnev signed (June 18) the SALT II strategic arms agreement in Vienna.

American life was disrupted (June) by a major oil shortage leading to long lines of cars at gas stations.

The *Skylab* orbiting laboratory broke up (July 11) over the Indian Ocean and some debris hit Australia as the spacecraft reentered the atmosphere after six years in space.

Following 10 days of seclusion at Camp David, President Carter addressed (July 15) the nation and called the energy crisis an American "crisis of confidence."

In July Charles Duncan Jr. replaced James Schlesinger as Secretary of Energy; Patricia Harris succeeded Joseph Califano as Secretary of Health, Education & Welfare; William Miller took over from W. Michael Blumenthal as Secretary of Treasury; Benjamin Civiletti followed Griffin Bell as Attorney General; and Neil Goldschmidt replaced Brock Adams as Secretary of Transportation.

Andrew Young resigned (Aug. 15) as the U.S. Ambassador to the United Nations after disclosing that he had made unauthorized contacts with the Palestine Liberation Organization.

The *Pioneer 2* spacecraft flew (Sept. 1) past Saturn to discover new rings around the planet and its 11th moon.

Congress approved (Sept. 27) the creation of the Department of Education as the 13th Cabinet level department of the executive branch.

President Carter announced (Oct. 11) increased U.S. surveillance of Cuba.

The deposed Shah of Iran arrived (Oct. 22) in the U.S. for cancer treatment from his exile in Mexico. Some 500 Iranian militants seized (Nov. 4) the U.S. embassy in Teheran and about 90 people, including 65 Americans, were taken hostage. Seventeen days later, a U.S. Marine was killed as a mob besieged the American embassy in Islamabad, Pakistan. A mob later attacked (Dec. 2) the U.S. embassy in Libya and damaged two floors.

The General Accounting Office reported (Nov. 24) that thousands of U.S. troops had been sprayed with the toxic herbicide, Agent Orange, while serving in Vietnam.

Two U.S. sailors were killed (Dec. 3) and 10 were wounded when a Navy bus in which they were riding was ambushed by a Puerto Rican nationalist group near San Juan.

Congress authorized (Dec. 21) federal assistance to the troubled Chrysler Corp. by providing $1.5 billion in loan guarantees.

The Pittsburgh Steelers defeated (Jan. 21) the Dallas Cowboys to win Super Bowl XIII, and the Pittsburgh Pirates defeated the Baltimore Orioles in seven games to win the World Series.

Deaths in 1979 included: former Vice President Nelson Rockefeller, 70 (Jan. 26); actor Al (Captain Video) Hodge, 66 (Mar. 19); actor John Wayne, 72 (June 11); conductor Arthur Fiedler, 84 (July 10); catcher Thurman Munson, 32 (Aug. 2); publisher Samuel Newhouse, 84 (Aug. 29); cartoonist Al Capp, 70 (Nov. 5); television preacher Archbishop Fulton J. Sheen, 84 (Dec. 9); and composer Richard Rodgers, 77 (Dec. 30).

In Print

John Cheever's *The Stories of John Cheever* won the Pulitzer Prize for fiction.

At the end of the year, *Sophie's Choice* by William Styron had been on the best seller list for 30 consecutive weeks, and Herman Wouk's *War and Remembrance* for 63 weeks.

Other big sellers on the fiction list included *Jailbird*, by Kurt Vonnegut; *Smiley's People*, by John Le Carre; *Triple*, by Ken Follett; *The Last Enchantment*, by Mary Stewart; *The Executioner's Song*, by Norman Mailer; *Memories of Another Day*, by Harold Robbins; *The Dead Zone*, by Stephen King; *The Establishment*, by Howard Fast; *The Top of the Hill*, by Irwin Shaw; *The Green Ripper*, by John D. MacDonald; *The Third World War: 1985*, by General Sir John Hackett and Other top-ranking NATO Generals and Advisors; *There's No Such Place as Far Away*, by Richard Bach; and *Shadow Of The Moon*, by M. M. Kaye.

On the nonfiction side: *Aunt Erma's Cope Book*, by Erma Bombeck; *The Brethren*, by Bob Woodward and Scott Armstrong; *White House Years*, by Henry Kissinger; *Cruel Shoes*, by Steve Martin; *James Herriot's Yorkshire*, by James Herriot; *The Americans*, by Alistair Cooke; *The Right Stuff*, by Tom Wolfe; *Serpentine*, by Thomas Thompson; *Sylvia Porter's New Money Book for the 80's*, by Sylvia Porter; *The Pritikin Program*, by Nathan Pritikin; *With No Apologies*, by Barry M. Goldwater; *Anatomy of an Illness*, by Norman Cousins; *The Windsor Story*, by J. Bryan III and Charles J. V. Murphy; and *Connections*, by James Burke.

On Stage

Productions that opened this year included: *The Madwoman of Central Park*; *The Price*; *Father's Day*; *Live From New York*; *Peter Pan, or the Boy Who Wouldn't Grow Up* (revival); *On Golden Pond*; *Evita*; *The 1940's Radio Hour*; *Sugar Babies*; *The Grand Tour*; *Sarava*; *Wings*; *They're Playing Our Song*; *A Kurt Weil Cabaret*; *Sweeney Todd: The Demon Barber of Fleet Street*; *Bedroom Farce*; *Whose Life is it Anyway?*; and *The Elephant Man*.

Tonys went to *Sweeney Todd*, with words and music by Stephen Sondheim, for Best Musical. Best Actor was Len Cariou, and Best Actress was Angela Lansbury, all in the same musical. The Best Play of the year was *The*

Elephant Man. Tom Conti won a Tony for his role in *Whose Life is it Anyway?*, and Constance Cummings took Best Actress for her part in *Wings.*

Films

Four films dominated the year: Frances Ford Coppola's *Apocalypse Now,* with Martin Sheen, Marlon Brando, Robert Duvall, Frederic Forrest, Sam Bottoms, and Dennis Hopper; *The China Syndrome,* with Jack Lemmon, Jane Fonda, and Michael Douglas; *Kramer vs. Kramer,* with Dustin Hoffman, Meryl Streep, and Jane Alexander; and *Norma Rae,* with Sally Field, Beau Bridges, Ron Leibman, and Pat Hingle. *Kramer vs. Kramer* was named Best Picture.

Other outstanding pictures were: *Being There,* with Peter Sellers, Shirley MacLaine, and Melvyn Douglas; *Breaker Morant,* with Edward Woodward and Jack Thompson; *Breaking Away,* with Dennis Christopher and Dennis Quaid; *Hair,* with John Savage, Treat Williams, and Beverly D'Angelo; *La Cage Aux Folles,* with Michael Serrault and Ugo Tognazzi; *Manhattan,* with Woody Allen, Mariel Hemingway, and Diane Keaton; *Moonraker,* with Roger Moore and Richard Kiel; *The Muppet Movie,* with Charles Durning, Bob Hope, James Coburn, Dom DeLuise, Mel Brooks, and Steve Martin; and *The Tin Drum,* with David Bennet, Angela Winkler, and Charles Aznavour.

Superman—The Movie grossed $82.5 million.

Television

PBS presented (Apr. 15) *Baryshnikov At The White House,* portions of the dancer's White House appearance two months earlier.

NBC broadcast (Oct. 1) a live special marking the 17th anniversary of *The Tonight Show Starring Johnny Carson.*

Lou Grant on CBS earned an Emmy as outstanding drama series, and the long reign of sitcoms was broken when *60 Minutes* moved into the top rating spot.

Music

The top songs of the year included *Too Much Heaven,* Bee Gees; *Do You Think I'm Sexxy,* Rod Stewart; *I Will Survive,* Gloria Gaynor; *Tragedy,* Bee Gees; *What a Fool Believes,* Doobie Brothers; *Knock On Wood,* Amil Stewart; *Heart of Glass,* Blondie; *Reunited,* Peaches & Herb; *Hot Stuff,* Donna Summer; *Love You Inside Out,* Bee Gees; *Ring My Bell,* Anita Ward; *Bad Girls,* Donna Summer; *Good Times,* Chic; *My Sharona,* The Knack; *Sad Eyes,* Robert John; *Don't Stop 'til You Get Enough,* Michael Jackson; *Rise,* Herb Alpert; *Pop Muzik,* M; *Heartache Tonight,* Eagles; *No More Tears (Enough is Enough),* Barbra Streisand/Donna Summer; *Babe,* Styx; *Escape (The Pina Colada Song),* Rupert Holmes.

Record of the Year went to The Doobie Brothers for *What a Fool Believes.* Album of The Year was given to Billy Joel for *52nd Street.* Kenny Loggins and Michael McDonald received the Grammy for Song of The Year for *What a Fool Believes.* Best Male vocal went to Billy Joel for *52nd Street;* Female Vocal went to Dionne Warwick for *I'll Never Love This Way Again.*

1980

$\mathscr{P}$resident Jimmy Carter advised the Senate that it should delay ratification of the SALT strategic arms treaty until the Soviets withdrew from Afghanistan. He also announced a U.S. boycott of the Summer Olympics in Moscow in retaliation for the Soviet intervention in Afghanistan.

After logging 161,331 miles and spending $35,000, James Vardaman became (Jan.) the first American to spot 698 different species of birds in North America in one year.

In the broadest investigation of political corruption undertaken by the FBI for 25 years, the Bureau disclosed (Feb. 3) that its Operation Abscam had implicated 31 public officials, including a U.S. senator and seven congressmen.

CBS television anchorman Walter Cronkite announced (Feb. 15) his retirement.

The Department of Transportation reported (Feb. 28) that all 79 foreign cars and most American-made autos tested in 35 mph crashes had failed to protect their occupants.

President Carter signed (Mar. 31) a law to deregulate the banking industry and raise the limit on federally insured accounts to $100,000.

The U.S. broke (Apr. 7) diplomatic relations with Iran because of the hostage crisis. American forces failed (Apr. 24) in an attempt to rescue the hostages. Eight military personnel were killed and five injured in the futile operation. Cyrus Vance resigned as Secretary of State four days later over Carter's decision to launch the raid, and Senator Edmund Muskie was named to replace him.

Dr. George Nickopoulous was indicted (May 16) in Memphis on 14 counts of excessive drug prescriptions to 11 patients, including singers Elvis Presley and Jerry Lee Lewis.

Race riots in Miami killed (May 17) 14 people following the acquittal of four white policemen charged with fatally beating a Black man.

In an eruption 500 times more powerful than the Hiroshima atomic bomb, Mt. St. Helens erupted (May 18) and spewed volcanic ash over 120 miles of Washington state.

The first women graduated (May 28) from West Point.

On two different days, the North American defense network computer system in Colorado Springs sent out (June) erroneous reports that the Soviets had launched an ICBM attack against the U.S.

Billy Carter, the President's brother, registered (July 14) as a Libyan government agent and received $220,000 in loans from Tripoli.

In response to efforts by Vietnam veteran Jan Scruggs, President Carter authorized (July 14) the provision of government land in Washington, D.C., to be used for a memorial to honor Americans who died in Southeast Asia. Scruggs began the effort with $2,500 that he had raised himself.

Rep. Michael Joseph Myers of Pennsylvania was expelled (Oct. 2) from the House after a bribery conviction in the Abscam case, the first Congressman ousted since 1861.

Hollywood film actors ended (Oct. 23) a 94-day strike.

Ronald Reagan defeated (Nov. 4) Jimmy Carter.

The *Voyager 1* spacecraft flew (Nov. 12) within 77,000 miles of Saturn.

In the sports arena, the Pittsburgh Steelers defeated (Jan. 26) the Los Angeles Rams to win Super Bowl XIV; the U.S. hockey team won the gold medal at the Winter Olympics in Lake Placid, N.Y.; and the Philadelphia Phillies defeated (Oct. 21) the Kansas City Royals in six games to win the World Series.

Prominent deaths included: former Supreme Court justice William O. Douglas, 81 (Jan. 10); labor leader George Meany, 85 (Jan. 11); comedian Jimmy Durante, 86 (Jan. 29); director Alfred Hitchcock, 80 (Apr. 29); actor Jay (Tonto) Silverheels, 62 (May 5); author Henry Miller, 88 (June 7); felon Willie Sutton, (Nov. 2); actor Steve McQueen, 50 (Nov. 7); and singer John Lennon, 40 (Dec. 8).

In Print

Topping the year's best-seller fiction was James A. Michener's *The Covenant*. Other novels included *The Key to Rebecca*, by Ken Follett; *Firestarter*, by Stephen King; *Loon Lake*, by E. L. Doctorow; *Unfinished Tales*, by J.R.R. Tolkien; *Masquerade*, by Kit Williams, *Answer as a Man*, by Taylor Caldwell; *The Fifth Horseman*, by Larry Collins and Dominique Lapierre; *Come Pour the Wine*, by Cynthia Freeman; *Rage of Angels*, by Sidney Sheldon; *The Origin*, by Irving Stone; *The Tenth Commandment*, by Lawrence Sanders; *The Hidden Target*, by Helen MacInnes; *Manchu*, by Robert Elegant; and *The Clan of the Cave Bear*, by Jean M. Auel.

Nonfiction: *Cosmos*, by Carl Sagan; *Crisis Investing*, by Douglas R. Casey; *Side Effects*, by Woody Allen; *Peter the Great*, by Robert K. Massie; *The Sky's the Limit*, by Wayne Dyer; *Goodbye, Darkness*, by William Manchester; *The Coming Currency Collapse*, by Jerome F. Smith; *American Dreams*, by Studs Terkel; *Ingrid Bergman: My Story*, by Ingrid Bergman and Alan Burgess; *Free to Choose*, by Milton and Rose Friedman; *Betty Crocker's International Cookbook*, a collection of recipes; *Craig Claiborne's Gourmet Diet*, by Craig Claiborne and Pierre Franey; *A Field Guide to the Birds*, by Roger Tory Peterson; *Swanson on Swanson*, by Gloria Swanson; and *Number 1*, by Billy Martin.

In December, Random House had eight best-sellers on *The New York Times* list. The previous month, it had eleven.

Tom Wolfe's, *The Right Stuff*, a book about NASA's first astronauts, won the National Book Award. The same prize for fiction went to William Styron for *Sophie's Choice*. Norman Mailer's *The Executioner's Song*, won the Pulitzer Prize for fiction.

On Stage

Ira Levin's *Deathtrap* reached 1,361 performances.

A revival of *Camelot*, starring Richard Burton, opened on July 8, ran for 56 performances, and closed on August 23.

Other plays produced this year included: *Amadeus*; *42nd Street*; *The Suicide*; *Brigadoon* (revival); *A Life*; *Fifth of July*; *Lunch Hour*; *Watch on the Rhine*; *Betrayal*; *Filumena*; *West Side Story* (revival); *Whose Life is it Anyway* (return engagement); *Children of a Lesser God*; *A Day in Hollywood/A Night in the Ukraine*; *Barnum*; *Nuts*; and *Blackstone!*.

The Best Play was *Children of a Lesser God*, with John Rubinstein, Best Actor, and Phyllis Frelich, Best Actress. Andrew Lloyd Weber's *Evita* won Best Musical, Jim Dale was Best Actor in *Barnum*, and Best Actress was awarded to Patti LuPone for her performances in *Evita*.

Films

Ordinary People won the award for Best Picture. It starred Mary Tyler Moore and Timothy Hutton.

Other notable films of the year included *Airplane!*, with Robert Hays, Julie Hagerty, Robert Stack, Lloyd Bridges, Leslie Nielsen, and Peter Graves; *All God's Children*, with Richard Widmark, Ned Beatty, and Ossie Davis; *Atlantic City*, with Burt Lancaster and Susan Sarandon; *The Blues Brothers*, with John Belushi, Dan Aykroyd, Aretha Franklin, John Candy, Ray Charles, and Cab Calloway; *Coal Miner's Daughter*, with Sissy Spacek and Tommy Lee Jones; *The Elephant Man*, with John Hurt, Anthony Hopkins, Anne Bancroft, and John Gielgud; *The Empire Strikes Back*, with Mark Hamill, Harrison Ford, Carrie Fisher, and Billy Dee Williams; *The Last Metro*, with Catherine Deneuve and Gerard Depardieu; *Melvin and Howard*, with Jason Robards and Mary Steenburgen; *Raging Bull*, with Robert DeNiro, Cathy Moriarty, and Joe Pesci; *Stir Crazy*, with Gene Wilder and Richard Pryor; *The Shadow Box*, with Joanne Woodward, Christopher Plummer, and Valerie Harper; *The Shining*, with Jack Nicholson, Shelley Duvall, and Scatman Cruthers; *The Stunt Man*, with Peter O'Toole, Steve Railsback, and Barbara Hershey; and *Superman II*, with Christopher Reeve, Margot Kidder, Gene Hackman, Terence Stamp, and Ned Beatty.

The average admission price to a movie theater was $2.69. The number of screens in America was 17,500, and average weekly attendance was 20,000. Americans would pay $2.750 billion at the box office.

The Empire Strikes Back, the sequel to *Star Wars*, grossed $134.2 million. The worldwide gross for *Star Wars* at the end of this year had reached $510 million.

Television

A six-hour adaptation of *The Martian Chronicles* was offered (Jan. 27-29) by NBC.

Henry Fonda, Jose Ferrer and John Houseman were in the cast of the *Hallmark Hall of Fame's* broadcast (Apr. 30) of *Gideon's Trumpet*.

PBS aired (June 2) *Picasso—A Painter's Diary*.

Hill Street Blues made its debut on NBC and won an Emmy for outstanding drama series.

Shogun, also on NBC, was recognized as the outstanding limited series, and Michael Leeson won an Emmy for outstanding writing in a comedy for his work on ABC's *Taxi*.

Dallas was the top-ranked television show.

Music

The top songs of the year included: *Please Don't Go*, KC & The Sunshine Band; *Rock With You*, Michael Jackson; *Do That to Me One More Time*, Captain & Tennille; *Crazy Thing Called Love*, Queen; *Another Brick in the Wall (Part II)*, Pink Floyd; *Call Me*, Blondie; *Funkytown*, Lipps, Inc.; *Comin' Up (Live at Glasgow)*, Paul McCartney & Wings; *It's Still Rock and Roll to Me*, Billy Paul; *Magic*, Olivia Newton-John; *Sailing*, Christopher Cross; *Upside Down*, Diana Ross; *Another One Bites the Dust*, Queen; *Woman in Love*, Barbra Streisand; *Lady*, Kenny Rogers; and *(Just Like) Starting Over*, John Lennon.

This was Christopher Cross' year: he won Record of the Year for *Sailing*, Album of the Year for *Christopher Cross*, and Song of the Year for *Sailing*. Best Male Vocal went to Kenny Loggins for *This is It*. Bette Midler won Best Female Vocal for *The Rose*.

1981

$\mathcal{R}$onald Reagan was inaugurated (Jan. 20) as the 40th President. (He was born in Tampico, Illinois, on Feb. 6, 1911.) That same day, 52 American hostages were released by Iran after 444 days of captivity.

A survey of high school students showed (Feb. 18) a leveling off in the use of illegal drugs by young people in 1980, the first such plateau in five years.

A nine-year-old boy surrendered (March) to the FBI for the theft of $118 from a bank in Manhattan. The nation's youngest bank robber had avoided apprehension because, at 4 feet five inches, he was too short to be filmed by security cameras.

President Reagan and three other men were wounded in Washington, D.C. (Mar. 30), by six shots fired by John Hinckley Jr., 25, from a .22 caliber pistol.

NASA successfully launched (April 12) *Columbia*, the nation's first Space Shuttle.

According to a survey (May) by a trade magazine, the popularity of apple pie had slipped. The survey found that the desert appeared in the menus of only 64 percent of America's restaurants, down from 88 percent in 1971.

Former Agriculture Secretary Earl Butz pled (May 22) guilty to filing a false income tax return in 1978.

In an apparent serial murder case, the number of missing and murdered young black men in Atlanta was reported (May 25) to have reached 30 victims.

Sandra Day O'Connor was nominated (July 7) by President Reagan as the first female Supreme Court Justice; she was confirmed on Sept. 21.

A suspended overhead walkway in the new Hyatt Regency Hotel in Kansas City collapsed (July 17), killing 111 people.

California undertook (July-Sept.) a spraying campaign to eradicate the Mediterranean fruit fly.

The nation's federal air traffic controllers began (Aug. 3) a strike.

A 65 million year old Tyrannosaurus Rex skeleton was discovered (Aug. 17) in Haystack Butte, S.D.

Two Navy F-14 fighters shot down (Aug. 19) two Libyan fighters off Libya's coast.

Mark David Chapman, who murdered John Lennon in 1980, was sentenced (Aug. 24) to 20 years in prison.

Pablo Picasso's painting, *Guernica*, was returned (Sept. 10) to Spain after four decades in the Museum of Modern Art in New York.

Simon & Garfunkel were reunited (Sept. 19) after 11 years in a concert for 400,000 people in New York's Central Park.

Warner Communications, owner of the Superman trademark, sued (Oct.) students of Richard J. Daley College in Chicago for calling their school paper the *Daley Planet*.

The White House announced (Nov. 13) a Justice Department investigation of a $1,000 cash payment from Japanese magazine to the President's national security advisor, Richard Allen.

In sporting news, the Oakland Raiders defeated (Jan. 25) the Philadelphia Eagles to win Super Bowl XV; a players strike against major league baseball ended (July 31) after seven weeks; and the Los Angeles Dodgers defeated the New York Yankees in six games to win the World Series.

Notable deaths in 1981 included: actor Richard (Paladin) Boone, 63 (Jan. 11); singer Bill Haley, 55 (Feb. 9); General Omar Bradley, 88 (April 8); boxer Joe Lewis, 66 (April 12); writer William Saroyan, 72 (May 18); singer Harry Chapin, 38 (July 16); playwright Paddy Chayefsky (Aug. 1); writer Lowell Thomas, 89 (Aug. 30); historian Will Durant, 96 (Nov. 8); actor William Holden, 63 (Nov. 16); actor Jack Albertson, 74 (Nov. 25); and actress Natalie Wood, 43 (Nov. 29).

The United States population was 229,637,000.

In Print

The best-seller list included *An Indecent Obsession*, by Colleen McCullough; *The Hotel New Hampshire*, by John Irving; *Nobel House*, by James Clavell; *Cujo*, by Stephen King; *No Time for Tears*, by Cynthia Freeman; *Spring Moon*, by Bette Bao Lord; *Remembrance*, by Danielle Steel; *Gorky Park*, by Martin Cruz Smith; *Rabbit is Rich*, by John Updike; *The Cardinal Sins*, by Andrew M. Greeley; *Go Slowly, Come Back Quickly*, by David Niven; *The Legacy*, by Howard Fast; and *Masquerade*, by Kit Williams.

Nonfiction best-sellers included *A Light in the Attic*, by Shel Silverstein; *The Lord God Made Them All*, by James Herriot; *Cosmos*, by Carl Sagan; *A Few Minutes With Andy Rooney*, by Andy Rooney; *Never-Say-Diet Book*, by Richard Simmons; *The Walk West*, by Peter & Barbara Jenkins; *Pathfinders*, by Gail Sheehy; *The Best of Dear Abby*, by Abigail Van Buren; *Laid Back in Washington*, by Art Buchwald; *Miss Piggy's Guide to Life*, by Miss Piggy, as told to Henry Beard; *From Bauhaus to Our House*, by Tom Wolfe; *Elvis*, by Albert Goodman; *Teenage Romance*, by Delia Ephron; *Elizabeth Taylor: The Last Star*, by Kitty Kelley; and *How to Make Love to a Man*, by Alexandra Penney.

On Stage

A Chorus Line hit 2,825 performances.

Plays produced: Jules Feiffer's *A Taste of Honey*; *Crimes of the Heart*; *The Dresser*; *Piaf*; *The Pirates of Penzance*; *Mass Appeal*; *Sophisticated Ladies*; *Woman of the Year*, *Fools*; *A Talent for Murder*. Revivals were: *Fiddler on the Roof*, *My Fair Lady*; and *Camelot*. *The Life & Adventures of Nicholas Nickleby*, an 8-hour production with 42 actors in 138 speaking roles, it was presented in two parts — the first had one intermission, the second two.

Best Musical was *42nd Street*. Best Score went to *Woman of The Year*, which starred Lauren Bacall; she earned Best Actress for her role. Kevin Kline was awarded Best Actor for his performance in *The Pirates of Penzance*.

Two Tony awards went to *Amadeus*: Best Play and Ian McKellen, Best Actor. Best Actress for the year was given to Jane Lapotaire in *Piaf*.

Films

Chariots of Fire won the award for Best Picture.

Notable films included: *Absence of Malice*, with Paul Newman and Sally Field; *Arthur*, with Dudley Moore, Liza Minnelli, John Gielgud, Geraldine Fitzgerald, and Jill Eikenberry; *Body Heat*, with William Hurt, Kathleen Turner, Richard Crenna, Ted Danson, J. A. Preston, and Mickey Rourke; *The Cannonball Run*, with Burt Reynolds, Roger Moore, Farrah Fawcett, Dom DeLuise, Dean Martin, and Sammy Davis Jr.; *Das Boot* (*The Boat*), with Jurgen Prochnow; *Diva*, with Wilhelmenia W. Fernandez; *Excalibur*, with Nicol Williamson and Nigel Terry; *Gallipoli*, with Mel Gibson and Mark Lee; *On Golden Pond*, with Henry Fonda, Jane Fonda, and Katharine Hepburn; *Prince of the City*, with Treat Williams, Jerry Orbach, and Lindsay Crouse; *Ragtime*, with Harold Rollins Jr., James Cagney, Elizabeth McGovern, and Mary Steenburgen; *Raiders of the Lost Ark*, with Harrison Ford, Karen Allen, Paul Freeman, and John Rhys-Davies; *Reds*, with Warren Beatty, Diane Keaton, Maureen Stapleton, and Jack Nicholson; *Stripes*, with Bill Murray, Harold Ramis, Warren Oates, Sean Young, John Candy, and John Larroquette; *The Road Warrior*, with Mel Gibson and Bruce Spence; and *Whose Life is It Anyway?*, with Richard Dreyfuss, John Cassavetes, and Christine Lahti.

Americans paid $115.6 million to see *Raiders of the Lost Ark*.

In 1959, the number of theaters — called "drive-ins" — where you could watch a movie, sit in your car and have a 'burger and a Coke had peaked at 4,800. This year, the number had fallen to 3,600.

Television

All networks covered (Mar. 30) the attempted assassination of President Reagan. Four months later, they broadcast (July 29) the wedding of Prince Charles and Lady Diana Spencer.

Danny Kaye played (Nov. 7) a serious role in CBS's production of *Skokie*, a drama on the neo-Nazi movement in an Illinois town.

Mork & Mindy and *Lou Grant* were canceled during the 1981-82 season.

Sir Laurence Olivier received an Emmy as outstanding supporting actor in a limited series or special for his role in *Brideshead Revisited* on PBS.

Dallas again was the most popular program.

Music

America's most popular songs included: *The Tide is High*, Blondie; *Celebration*, Kool & The Gang; *9 to 5*, Dolly Parton; *I Love a Rainy Night*, Eddie Rabbitt; *Keep on Loving You*, REO Speedwagon; *Rapture*, Blondie; *Kiss on My List*, Daryl Hall & John Oates; *Morning Train (Nine to Five)*, Sheena Easton; *Bette Davis Eyes*, Kim Carnes; *Stars on 45 Medley*, Stars on 45; *The One That You Love*, Air Supply; *Jessie's Girl*, Rick Springfield; *Endless Love*, Diana Ross & Lionel Richie; *Arthur's Theme, Best That You Can Do*, Christopher Cross; and *Private Eyes*, Daryl Hall & John Oates; *Physical*, Olivia Newton-John.

The Grammy Awards were diverse this year: Record of the Year went to Kim Carnes for *Bette Davis Eyes*. John Lennon & Yoko Ono received Album of the Year for *Double Fantasy*. Dona Weiss and Jackie DeShannon received Song of the Year for writing *Bette Davis Eyes*. Best Male Vocal went to Al Jarreau for *Breakin' Away*, and Lena Horne received Best Female Vocal for *Lena Horne: The Lady and Her Music Live on Broadway*.

1982

$\mathcal{T}$he White House announced (Jan. 1) that Richard Allen, President Ronald Reagan's national security adviser, would be replaced by William P. Clark.

A federal judge in Arkansas reversed (Jan. 5) a state law requiring public school instruction in both creationism and evolutionism.

President Reagan announced (Jan. 7) his decision to continue the registration of young men for the draft.

To settle an eight-year antitrust suit by the Justice Department, American Telephone & Telegraph agreed (Jan. 8) to divest itself of 22 Bell System regional operating companies.

An Air Florida 737 aircraft struck (Jan. 13) Washington, D.C.'s, 14th Street Bridge and plunged into the Potomac River, killing 78 people, including four victims traveling across the bridge in cars.

State officials in Michigan introduced (Jan.) legislation requiring farmers to brand and register their cattle and other livestock following a sharp increase in rustling from ranches and farms because of the recession.

The U.S. imposed (Mar. 10) economic sanctions against Libya in retaliation for its role in international terrorism.

The Department of the Interior reported (Mar. 10) that certain bird populations that had been considered close to extinction—including the bald eagle, osprey, and brown pelican—were now increasing in number.

Jim Princeton returned (Apr. 6) $37.1 million in negotiable bearer certificates that he found outside a Wall Street building.

Leavenworth, Kans., home of a federal maximum security prison, announced (Apr.) plans to acquire the Richard Nixon Library after Duke University declined.

Braniff International became (May 13) the first major U.S. airline to declare bankruptcy.

Stevie Wonder, Jackson Browne, Bob Dylan, Linda Ronstadt, and others appeared (June 6) at an antinuclear rally at the Rose Bowl in Pasadena, Calif.

Graceland, Elvis Presley's home in Memphis, opened (June 7) to the public for the first time.

John Hinckley was found (June 21) not guilty by reason of insanity in the 1981 attempted assassination of President Reagan.

Alexander Haig resigned (June 25) as Secretary of State and was replaced by George P. Shultz.

The Equal Rights Amendment failed (June 30) to achieve ratification by the required 38 states within 10 years after Congress passed the measure.

The Rev. Moon married (July 21) 4,000 people in New York City.

San Francisco became (July 28) the first U.S. city to ban the sale and possession of hand guns.

President Reagan ordered (Aug. 20) 800 Marines into Beirut as part of multinational peacekeeping force.

A quart of milk cost $1.10.

Authorities in Chicago reported (Oct. 2) seven victims of cyanide-filled Tylenol capsules. A subsequent nationwide alert resulted in the recall of 264,000 bottles of the medication. The federal government later issued (Nov. 4) regulations requiring tamper-resistant packages for over-the-counter medicines.

John Delorean, chairman of the Delorean Motor Co., was arrested (Oct. 19) in Los Angeles on cocaine possession charges.

President Reagan announced (Oct. 26) a record $110 billion deficit for fiscal year 1982.

In a seven-and-a-half-hour operation at the Utah Medical Center in Salt Lake City, Barney Clark of Des Moines received (Dec. 2) an artificial heart.

Charles Brooks, an inmate at Fort Worth Prison in Texas, became (Dec. 7) the first American executed by lethal injection.

In sports news, the San Francisco 49ers defeated (Jan. 24) the Cincinnati Bengals to win Super Bowl XVI; the St. Louis Cardinals defeated (Oct. 20) the Milwaukee Brewers in seven games to win the World Series; and the longest, most expensive strike in sports to date ended after nearly two months when football players reached agreement with the NFL owners and resumed playing on Nov. 21.

The year's deaths included: radio disc jockey Murray ("The K") Kaufman, 60 (Feb. 2); jazz pianist Thelonious Monk, 64 (Feb. 17); acting teacher Lee Strasberg, 80 (Feb. 17); comedian John Belushi, 33 (Mar. 5); author and philosopher Ayn Rand, 77 (Mar. 6); Supreme Court justice Abe Fortas, 71 (April 5); poet Archibald MacLeish, 89 (April 20); pitcher Satchel Paige, 75 (June 8); author John Cheever, 70 (June 19); TV host Dave Garroway, 69 (July 21); actor Henry Fonda, 77 (Aug. 12); Princess Grace of Monaco, 54 (Sept. 14); union leader David Dubinsky, 80 (Sept. 17); and New York State Appellate Court Justice Vincent A. Lupiano, 74, (Sept. 15).

In Print

Outer space occupied the top three best-seller slots for the year: *Space*, by James Michener, *2010: Odyssey Two*, by Arthur C. Clarke, and *E.T. The Extra-Terrestrial Storybook*, by William Kotzwinkle.

Best-selling fiction included *The Valley of Horses*, by Jean M. Auel; *Mistral's Daughter*, by Judith Kranz; *Foundation's Edge*, by Isaac Asimov; *Master of the Game*, by Sidney Sheldon; *Different Seasons*, by Stephen King; *Life, The Universe and Everything*, by Douglas Adams; *Deadeye Dick*, by Kurt Vonnegut; *Crossings*, by Danielle Steel; *The Parsifal Mosaic*, by Robert Ludlum; *Goodbye, Mickey Mouse*, by Len Deighton; *Life Sentences*, by Elizabeth Forsythe Hailey; and *Second Heaven*, by Judith Guest.

Nonfiction: *And More by Andy Rooney*, Andrew A. Rooney; *Living, Loving & Learning*, Leo Buscaglia; *Megatrends*, John Naisbitt; *Growing Up*, Russell Baker; *Keeping the Faith*, Jimmy Carter; *A Light in the Attic*, Shel Silverstein; *When Bad Things Happen to Good People*, Harold S. Kushner; *The Fall of Freddie the Leaf*, Leo Buscaglia; *The One Minute Manager*, Kenneth Blanchard & Spencer Johnson; *Life Extension*, Durk Pearson & Sandy Shaw; *The Path to Power: The Years of Lyndon Johnson*, Robert A. Caro; *Miracle at Midway*, Gordon W. Prange; *Having it All*, Helen Gurley Brown; and *Atlantic High*, William F. Buckley Jr.

Rabbit Is Rich, written by John Updike, won both the National Book Award for fiction and the Pulitzer Prize.

On Stage

Plays produced included: *Cats*; *Waltz of the Stork*; *Joseph and the Amazing Technicolor Dreamcoat*; *Medea*; *Pump Boys and Dinettes*; *Come Back to the 5 & Dime Jimmy Dean, Jimmy Dean*; *Encore*; *Nine*; *84 Charing Cross Road*; *Foxfire*; *Torch Song Trilogy*; and *Agnes of God*.

Nine was picked as the Best Musical at the Tony Awards. Ben Harney and Jennifer Holiday were Best Actor and Actress in *Dreamgirls*. Best Play was *Nicholas Nickleby*; Roger Rees won Best Actor in the same play. Zoe Caldwell earned Best Actress for her work in *Medea*.

Films

Gandhi received the award for Best Picture. Ben Kingsley took an Oscar for Best Actor for his work in the film.

This year's outstanding feature films included: *An Officer and a Gentleman*, with Richard Gere, Debra Winger, Louis Gossett Jr., David Keith, and Robert Loggia; *Blade Runner*, with Harrison Ford, Rutger Hauer, Sean Young, Daryl Hannah, and Edward James Olmos; *E.T.—The Extra Terrestrial*, with Dee Wallace, Henry Thomas, Peter Coyote, and Drew Barrymore; *Fitzcaraldo*, with Klaus Kinski and Claudia Cardinale; *48 Hours*, with Nick Nolte and Eddie Murphy; *Missing*, with Jack Lemmon, Sissy Spacek, and John Shea; *Poltergeist*, with JoBeth Williams and Craig T. Nelson; *Sophie's Choice*, with Meryl Streep and Kevin Kline; *The Best Little Whorehouse in Texas*, with Burt Reynolds, Dolly Parton, Dom DeLuise, and Charles Durning; *Tootsie*, with Dustin Hoffman, Jessica Lange, Teri Garr, Bill Murray, Dabney Coleman, and Charles Durning; and *The Verdict*, with Paul Newman, Charlotte Rampling, Jack Warden, and James Mason.

In 1915 the film, *The Birth of a Nation*, grossed $10 million. This year, *E.T.—The Extra Terrestrial* grossed $228.4 million.

Television

CBS Reports broadcast (Jan. 23) *The Uncounted Enemy: A Vietnam Deception* on the falsification of intelligence data during the war. General William Westmoreland later sued CBS for libel.

A televised *Night of 100 Stars*, an Actors' Fund benefit from the Radio City Music Hall, was shown (Mar. 8) on ABC.

Ed McMahon and Tim Conway hosted (May 25) *Television's Greatest Commercials* on NBC.

St. Elsewhere and *Cheers* made their debuts on NBC in the 1982-83 season, while *M*A*S*H* and *Taxi* were canceled.

Tyne Daly earned an Emmy as outstanding actress in a drama series for her work in CBS's *Cagney & Lacey*.

60 Minutes returned to the number one program spot.

Music

Daryl Hall & John Oates had two number one songs this year: *I Can't Go for That (No Can Do)*, and *Maneater*. Other hits included: *Centerfold*, J. Geils Band; *I Love Rock 'n Roll*, Joan Jett & The Blackhearts; *Chariots of Fire*, Vangelis; *Ebony and Ivory*, Paul McCartney/Stevie Wonder; *Don't You Want Me*, Human League; *Eye of the Tiger*, Survivor; *Abracadabra*, Steve Miller Band; *Hard to Say I'm Sorry*, Chicago; *Jack & Diane*, John Cougar; *Who Can it Be Now*, Men At Work; *Up Where We Belong*, Joe Cocker & Jennifer Warnes; *Truly*, Lionel Richie; and *Mickey*, Toni Basil.

The musical group Toto, took two Grammys: Record of the Year for *Roseanna*, and Album of the Year for *Toto IV*. Song of the Year was awarded to Johnny Christopher, Mark James and Wayne Carson for *Always on My Mind*. Best Male Vocal Performance went to Lionel Richie for *Truly*, and Melissa Manchester earned Best Female Vocal Performance for *You Should Hear How She Talks About You*.

1983

*P*resident Ronald Reagan declared (Jan. 3) Times Beach, Mo., a federal disaster area because of the threat posed by the release of dioxin, a highly toxic chemical.

Elizabeth Dole was nominated (Jan. 5) by the President to replace Drew Lewis as Secretary of Transportation; she was sworn in on Feb. 7.

U.S. unemployment reached (Jan. 7) 12 million.

President Reagan nominated (Jan. 12) Margaret Heckler to replace Richard Schweiker as Secretary of Health and Human Services; she was sworn in on Mar. 9.

General Motors announced (Feb. 14) an agreement to produce sub-compact cars for the U.S. market in a joint venture with Toyota Motor Corp. of Japan.

The Selective Service System sent (Feb. 17) the names of 5,154 men to the Justice Department for prosecution for failure to register for the draft.

The White House announced (Mar. 3) that the number of U.S. advisers in El Salvador had increased from 35 to 55.

Anne McGill Burford resigned (Mar. 9) as administrator of the Environmental Protection Agency following charges of mismanagement and political favoritism. William Ruckelshaus was sworn in as her replacement on May 18.

In a national address, President Reagan challenged (Mar. 23) scientists to develop an effective antiballistic missile defense ("Star Wars") to counter the Soviet nuclear threat.

Nicaragua charged (Mar. 23) that 2,000 contra rebels backed by the U.S. had invaded the country from Honduras.

Dr. Barney Clark died (Mar. 23), 112 days after becoming the first human to receive a permanent artificial heart.

NASA launched (Apr. 4) the space shuttle *Challenger* from Cape Canaveral with four astronauts aboard; they returned safely five days later.

Harold Washington was elected (Apr. 12) as the first black Mayor of Chicago.

The U.S. embassy in Beirut was badly damaged (Apr. 18) by a car bomb explosion that killed 47 people, including 17 Americans.

The Dow-Jones Industrial Average closed (Apr. 22) above 1,200 for the first time.

A severe earthquake rocked (May 2) California, the state's strongest in 12 years.

President Reagan announced (May 4) U.S. support of the contras.

Diana Ross reunited (May 16) with two other Supremes in a celebration of Motown Records' 25th anniversary.

The U.S. Department of Health and Human Services announced (May 24) that the agency's number one priority was to find the cause of acquired immune deficiency syndrome (AIDS).

Leaders of seven Western industrial democracies were hosted (May 28) by President Reagan at a summit conference in Williamsburg, Va.

Jerry Lee Lewis married (June 7) his fifth wife, Shawn Michelle Stevens.

The Supreme Court reaffirmed (June 15) the 1973 *Roe v. Wade* decision that gave women unrestricted rights to abortions in the first trimester.

Sally Ride became (June 18) the first American woman in space when she and four male astronauts were launched on a six-day mission aboard *Challenger.*

President Reagan named (June 18) Paul A. Volcker to a second term as chairman of the Federal Reserve Board.

In a landmark decision, the Supreme Court voided (June 23) congressional attempts to exercise legislative veto over decisions by federal regulatory agencies.

The Justice Department announced (June 30) that the FBI would conduct a formal investigation of the 1980 Reagan campaign's acquisition of briefing books belonging to the staff of former President Jimmy Carter.

The gross national product (GNP) rose at an 8.7 percent annual rate in the second quarter, compared to 2.6 percent in the first quarter. Unemployment fell in June to 9.8 percent.

The state of Washington's Public Power Supply System declared (July 22) itself unable to pay off debts for two canceled nuclear power plants, the largest U.S. municipal default in history.

Lt. Col. Guion Bluford became (Aug. 30) the first black astronaut in a flight aboard *Challenger*.

Soviet fighter aircraft shot down (Sept. 1) a Korean Airlines 747 airliner after it strayed into Soviet airspace, killing all 269 people aboard.

Interior Secretary James G. Watt resigned (Oct. 9) following controversy over his remarks describing the Coal Advisory Commission as "a black, a woman, two Jews and a cripple." William P. Clark was sworn in as his successor on Nov. 21.

As a result of a suicide truck-bomb attack, 241 U.S. Marines and Navy personnel were killed (Oct. 23) in Beirut; 58 French military were killed in a separate attack.

U.S. military forces, together with troops from six Caribbean states, invaded (Oct. 25) the island of Grenada to end an "atmosphere of violent uncertainty" said to have prevailed since an Oct. 13 coup; 18 U.S. troops were killed before the last 190 American combat troops were withdrawn on Dec. 15.

A two-day international conference began (Oct. 31) in Washington, D.C., and heard studies suggesting that even limited nuclear war could produce an extended "nuclear winter" leading to the possible extinction of human life.

President Reagan signed (Nov. 2) a bill designating the third Monday in January as a national holiday celebrating the birthday of Rev. Martin Luther King, Jr.

The President began (Nov. 8) a seven-day visit to Japan and South Korea, including a visit to U.S. troops near the Korean demilitarized zone.

The Cabbage Patch doll was created (Nov. 12) in Haywood, Calif.

Former EPA official Rita Lavelle was convicted (Dec. 1) in federal court on four counts of perjury and obstructing a congressional inquiry related to corruption and mismanagement at EPA.

U.S. Navy carrier-based aircraft attacked (Dec. 4) Syrian positions in Lebanon in response to Syrian attacks on unarmed U.S. reconnaissance aircraft the day before.

In a series of bomb attacks at U.S. and French embassies and elsewhere in Kuwait, seven people were killed (Dec. 12) and 66 injured.

Former President Gerald Ford appeared (Dec. 18) on the TV program *Dynasty*.

The Administration acknowledged (Dec. 20) that construction of new concrete security barriers around the White House and other federal buildings was a precaution against terrorist attacks.

The U.S. formally announced (Dec. 28) its intention to withdraw from the UN Educational, Scientific and Cultural Organization to protest increasing politicization of the agency's functions.

A first-class stamp cost 20 cents.

In sports news, tennis star Bjorn Borg retired (Jan. 22) at age 26; the Washington Redskins defeated (Jan. 30) the Miami Dolphins to win Super Bowl XVII; the U.S. Football League opened (Mar. 6) its first season; the U.S. lost (Sept. 26) the America's Cup for the first time in 132 years when *Australia II* beat *Liberty*; and the Baltimore Orioles defeated the Philadelphia Phillies in five games to win the World Series.

Deaths of the year included playwright Tennessee Williams, 71 (Feb. 25); TV and radio host Arthur Godfrey, 79 (Mar. 16); swimmer and actor Buster Crabbe, 75 (Apr. 23); choreographer George Balanchine, 79 (Apr. 30); boxer Jack Dempsey, 87 (May 31); lyricist Ira Gershwin, 86 (Aug. 17); and singer Dennis Wilson, 39 (Dec. 28).

In Print

Books at the top of the fiction list included: *Poland*, by James A. Michener; *Pet Sematary*, by Stephen King; *The Name of the Rose*, by Umberto Eco; and *Who Killed the Robbins Family?*, by Bill Adler and Thomas Chastain. Other best-selling novels included: *The Wicked Day*, by Mary Stewart; *The Robots of*

Dawn, by Isaac Asimov; *Changes*, by Danielle Steel; *Moreta: Dragonlady of Pern*, by Anne McCaffrey; *The Saga of Baby Devine*, by Bette Midler; *Return of the Jedi*, adapted by Joan D. Vinge; *The Neverending Story*, by Michael Ende; *Berlin Game*, by Len Deighton; *Hollywood Wives*, by Jackie Collins; and *The Auerbach Will*, by Stephen Birmingham.

On the nonfiction best seller list: *Motherhood*, by Erma Bombeck; *The Best of James Herriot*, by James Herriot; *In Search of Excellence*, by Thomas J. Peters; *While Reagan Slept*, by Art Buchwald; *On Wings of Eagles*, by Ken Follett; *Megatrends*, by John Naisbitt; *Vietnam: A History*, by Stanley Karnow; *Tough Times Never Last, But Tough People Do!*, by Robert H. Schuller; *The Human Body*, by Jonathan Miller; *One Brief Shining Moment*, by William Manchester; *Blue Highways*, by William Least Heat Moon; *Approaching Hoofbeats: Horsemen of The Apocalypse*, by Billy Graham; *A Light in the Attic*, by Shel Silverstein; *A Hero For Our Time*, by Ralph G. Martin; and *The Kingdom of the Sea*, by Paul Theroux.

Alice Walker's *The Color Purple* earned her the Pulitzer Prize.

On Stage

New plays produced this year included Neil Simon's *Brighton Beach Memoirs*; *Five-Six-Seven-Eight...Dance!*; *La Cage aux Folles*; *Zorba*; *My One and Only*; *American Buffalo*; *Doonesbury*; *Baby*; *Noises Off*; *Torch Song Trilogy*; and *The Tap Dance Kid*.

Cats, Andrew Lloyd Webber's extravagant production, was Musical of the Year. Tommy Tune won a Tony for *My One and Only*, and Best Actress went to Natalia Makarova in *On Your Toes*. Harvey Fierstein's *Torch Song Trilogy* was Best Play, and for which he also won a Tony for Best Actor. Jessica Tandy, who starred in *Foxfire*, won Best Actress.

Films

Terms of Endearment was named Best Picture. It starred Shirley MacLaine, who won a Best Actress award, and Debra Winger.

This year's other memorable films included *The Big Chill*, with Tom Berenger, Glenn Close, William Hurt, Kevin Kline, and Jeff Goldblum; *Flashdance*, with Jennifer Beals; *Return of the Jedi*, with Mark Hamill, Harrison Ford, Carrie Fisher, Billy Dee Williams, Alec Guiness, and Anthony Daniels; *The Right Stuff*, with Sam Shepard, Scott Glenn, Dennis Quaid, Ed Harris, Barbara Hersey, and Fred Ward; *Risky Business*, with Tom Cruise, Rebecca DeMornay, and Joe Pantoliano; *Scarface*, with Al Pacino, Michelle Pfeiffer, and Robert Loggia; *Sudden Impact*, with Clint Eastwood, Sondra Locke, Pat Hingle, and Bradford Dillman; *Tender Mercies*, with Robert Duvall and Tess Harper; *Trading Places*, with Eddie Murphy, Dan Aykroyd, Jamie Lee Curtis, Ralph Bellamy, Don Ameche, and Denholm Elliott; *Under Fire*, with Nick Nolte, Gene Hackman, Joanna Cassidy, Ed Harris, and Jean-Louis Trintignant; *War Games*, with Matthew Broderick, Dabney Coleman, and Ally Sheedy; and *Zelig*, with Woody Allen and Mia Farrow.

Qualifying as one of the top ten biggest grossing films of all time was *Return of the Jedi*—it earned $168 million.

Television

ABC presented (Nov. 20) *The Day After*, a movie simulating the destruction of a Kansas town by a nuclear attack. That same evening, NBC began presenting a seven-hour miniseries on John Kennedy's presidency, with Martin Sheen playing JFK. *Happy Days* was canceled in the 1983–84 season. John Ford Noonan won an Emmy for outstanding writing in a drama series for a *St. Elsewhere* script. *Dallas* was rated the country's most-watched show.

Music

Toto came back this year with a number one hit, *Africa*. Men at Work also spent some time at the top spot with *Down Under*, and Lionel Richie gained the number one position again with *All Night Long (All Night)*, while Michael Jackson had two number one sellers—*Beat It* and *Billie Jean*.

Other number one hits included *Baby, Come to Me*, Patty Austin and James Ingram; *Come on Eileen*, Dexys Midnight Runners; *Let's Dance*, David Bowie; *Flashdance...what a Feeling*, Irene Cara; *Every Breath You Take*, Police; *Sweet Dreams (Are Made of This)*, Eurythmics; *Maniac*, Michael Sembello; *Tell Her About It*, Billy Joel; *Total Eclipse of the Heart*, Bonnie Tyler; *Islands in the Stream*, Kenny Rogers; and *Say Say Say*, Paul McCartney and Michael Jackson.

Michael Jackson took three Grammy awards: His *Beat It* was Record of the Year, *Thriller* was Album of the Year, and he earned Best Male Vocal Performance for the single *Thriller*. Sting was given Song of the Year for *Every Breath You Take*, and Best Female Vocal Performance was won by Irene Cara for *Flashdance...What a Feeling*.

1984

$\mathscr{A}$fter a break of 117 years, the U.S. restored (Jan. 10) full diplomatic relations with the Vatican. American astronauts became the first to walk (Feb. 7) untethered in space.

Following orders from President Ronald Reagan, 1,400 U.S. Marines completed their withdrawal (Feb. 29) from Beirut, Lebanon.

The U.S. Central Intelligence Agency began mining (Feb.) harbors in Nicaragua.

Astronauts from the space shuttle *Challenger* repaired (Apr. 10) the damaged Solar Maximum Mission satellite, the first time in history that an orbiting satellite was fixed on a "house call."

A Philadelphia radio station broadcast (Apr. 27) a "No Michael Jackson" weekend.

President Reagan completed (May 1) a visit to China.

The Supreme Court ruled (May 22) that the awarding of partnerships by law firms on the basis of sex, race, or religion is illegal.

President Reagan participated (June 6) in ceremonies in France commemorating the 40th anniversary of the World War II D-Day landings.

A casualty from the Vietnam War was laid to rest (June) at the Tomb of the Unknown Soldier in Arlington National Cemetery.

News media reported (June) that Charles Z. Wick, director of the U.S. Information Agency, had spent $32,000 in USIA funds for security devices for his home, and that prior to a trip that month to Japan, he had requested a bulletproof limo, a police escort, and transportation for four armed guards.

Jesse Jackson negotiated (June 26) with Cuban President Fidel Castro for the release of 22 jailed Americans.

Vanessa Williams became (July 23) the first Miss America to resign her crown.

The space shuttle *Discovery* was launched (Aug. 30) on its maiden flight and returned to Earth after a five-day mission.

A suicide bomber killed (Sept. 20) two Americans and 38 others in a truck bomb explosion at the U.S. embassy in Beirut.

In his first personal meeting with a senior Soviet official, President Reagan welcomed (Sept. 28) Foreign Minister Andrei Gromyko to the White House.

A 28-year-old Chicago printer won (Sept.) the $40 million Illinois state lottery, joining 1,114 Americans who had become millionaires over the prior 20 years by winning state lotteries.

Labor Secretary Raymond Donovan was indicted (Oct. 2) on 137 counts of fraud.

Richard Miller became (Oct. 3) the first FBI agent charged with espionage.

Dr. Kathryn Sullivan walked (Oct. 11) in space during the sixth flight of *Challenger*, the first American woman to work outside an orbiting spacecraft.

Doctors in California implanted (Oct. 26) a baboon's heart in two-week old "Baby Fae."

Ronald Reagan and George Bush were reelected (Nov. 6), defeating Walter Mondale and Geraldine Ferraro, the first female vice presidential candidate of a major party.

A statue of three servicemen was unveiled (Nov. 9) at Washington's Vietnam Veterans Memorial, and the memorial became a national monument.

U.S. astronomers announced (Dec. 10) the discovery of a planet outside the solar system.

New York "Subway Vigilante" Bernard Goetz shot (Dec. 22) four teenagers after they harassed him and one of them asked for $5.00.

In sports news, the Los Angeles Raiders defeated (Jan.) the Washington Redskins to win Super Bowl XIII; President Reagan opened (July 28) the XXIII Olympiad in Los Angeles; and the Detroit Tigers defeated (Oct. 14) the San Diego Padres in five games to win the World Series.

Deaths of the year included: actor Johnny (Tarzan) Weissmuller, 79 (Jan. 20); singer Marvin Gaye, 44 (Apr. 1); photographer Ansel Adams, 82 (Apr. 22); jazz pianist Count Basie, 79 (Apr. 26); restaurateur Ray Kroc, 81 (June 19); bandleader Fred Waring (July 29); author Truman Capote, 59 (Aug. 25); and baseball manager Walter Alston, 72 (Oct. 1).

In Print

The Pulitzer Prize for fiction was won by William Kennedy for *Ironweed*.

Stephen King and Peter Straub's *The Talisman* topped this year's best-selling fiction, followed by: *The Sicilian*, by Mario Puzo; *Love and War*, by John Jakes; *The Life and Hard Times of Heidi Abramowitz*, by Joan Rivers; *So Long, and Thanks for All the Fish*, by Douglas Adams; *Nutcracker*, by E. T. A. Hoffman; *The Fourth Protocol*, by Frederick Forsyth; *...And Ladies of the Club*, by Helen Hooven Santmyer; *Lincoln*, by Gore Vidal; *God Knows*, by Joseph Heller; *Strong Medicine*, by Arthur Hailey; *Life Its Ownself*, by Dan Jenkins; *Jitterbug Perfume*, by Tom Robbins; *Illusions of Love*, by Cynthia Freeman; and *The Butter Battle Book*, by Dr. Seuss.

The life story of Lee Iacocca, *Iacocca: An Autobiography* by Lee Iacocca with William Novak, was at the top of the nonfiction list. Other best-selling nonfiction included: *Pieces of My Mind*, by Andrew A. Rooney; *Loving Each Other*, by Leo Buscaglia; *The Good War*, by Studs Terkel; *Hey, Wait a Minute, I Wrote a Book!*, by John Madden with Dave Anderson; *Dr. Burns' Prescription for*

Happiness, by George Burns; *Moses the Kitten*, by James Herriot; *The Bridge Across Forever*, by Richard Bach; *Heritage*, by Abba Ebban; *Elvis Is Dead and I Don't Feel So Good Myself*, by Lewis Grizzard; *A Light in the Attic*, by Shel Silverstein; *The Brain*, by Richard M. Restak; *Son of the Morning Star*, by Evan S. Connell; *The Weaker Vessel*, by Antonia Fraser; and *One Writer's Beginnings*, by Eudora Welty.

On Stage

By midyear, *A Chorus Line* was the longest-running show in Broadway history, with 4,086 performances. Other holdovers with more than a thousand performances included *Oh! Calcutta!* with 3,777 performances; *42nd Street*, 1,990; *Dreamgirls*, 1,439; *Torch Song Trilogy*, 1,222; and *Cats*, 1,106.

Plays produced included *Alone Together*; *Death of a Salesman*; *Glengarry Glen Ross*; *Hurly Burly*; *Ma Rainey's Black Bottom*; *Much Ado About Nothing*; *The Real Thing*; *Sunday in the Park with George*; *Alone Together*; *The Wiz*; *Doug Henning and His World of Magic*; and *Whoopi Goldberg*, a one woman show starring the actress that ran for 148 performances.

Three of the season's top awards went to *The Real Thing*: Best Play; Best Actor, Jeremy Irons; and Best Actress, Glenn Close. *La Cage Aux Folles* won Best Musical, with George Hearn as Best Actor. Best Actress in a musical was awarded to Chita Rivera in *The Rink*.

Films

The number of films produced this year was less than previous years; the top grossing films of the year were *Beverly Hills Cop*, with Eddie Murphy and Judge Reinhold and *Indiana Jones and the Temple of Doom*, with Harrison Ford and Kate Capshaw.

Amadeus won Best Picture; F. Murray Abraham took the Best Actor award.

Other films included *Ghostbusters*, with Dan Aykroyd, Bill Murray, Harold Ramis, Sigourney Weaver, Rick Moranis, and Annie Potts; *Gremlins*, with Zack Galligan and Hoyt Axton; *Greystroke: The Legend of Tarzan, Lord of the Apes*, with Christopher Lambert, Andie McDowell, Ian Holm, and Ralph Richardson; *The Killing Fields*, with Sam Waterston, Haing S. Ngor, John Malkovich, Julian Sands, and Craig T. Nelson; *A Passage to India*, with Judy Davis, Victor Banerjee, and Alec Guiness; *Places in the Heart*, with Sally Field; *Police Academy*, with Steve Guttenberg, Kim Cattrall, and Bubba Smith; *Romancing the Stone*, with Michael Douglas, Kathleen Turner, and Danny DeVito; *Star Trek III: The Search for Spock*, with William Shatner, Leonard Nimoy, DeForrest Kelley, and Christopher Lloyd; and *Splash*, with Tom Hanks, Daryl Hannah, and John Candy.

Television

Farrah Fawcett starred (Oct. 8) in *The Burning Bed* on NBC. The production was the highest rated single program of the 1984–85 season. Hollywood actor George C. Scott played (Dec. 17) Scrooge in CBS's new version of *A Christmas Carol*, sponsored exclusively by IBM.

Miami Vice made its NBC debut in the 1984–85 season.

Among the Emmy winners this year were *The Cosby Show* for outstanding comedy series; Edward James Olmos for outstanding supporting actor in a drama series for his role on *Miami Vice*; and Betty Thomas of *Hill Street Blues* for outstanding actress in a drama series. *Dynasty* was the most popular program on television.

Music

This year was a mix of familiar names and new groups and individuals achieving the number one position. The number one songs included *Owner of a Lonely Heart*, Yes; *Karma Chameleon*, Culture Club; *Jump*, Van Halen; *Footloose*, Kenny Loggins; *Against All Odds (Take a Look at Me Now)*, Phil Collins; *Hello*, Lionel Richie; *Let's Hear It for the Boys*, Deniece Williams; *Time After Time*, Cyndi Lauper; *The Reflex*, Duran Duran; *When Doves Cry*, Prince; *Ghostbusters*, Ray Parker Jr.; *What's Love Got to Do with It*, Tina Turner; *Missing You*, John Waite; *Let's Go Crazy*, Prince; *I Just Called to Say I Love You*, Stevie Wonder; *Caribbean Queen, No More Love on the Run)*, Billy Ocean; *Wake Me Up Before You Go-Go*, Wham!; *Out of Touch*, Daryl Hall and John Oates; and *Like a Virgin*, Madonna.

Tina Turner's *What's Love Got to Do with It* won three Grammys this year: Record of the Year, Best Female Vocal Performance, and Song of the Year. Album of the Year went to Lionel Richie for *Can't Slow Down*, and Best Vocal Male Performance was awarded to Phil Collins for *Against All Odds (Take a Look at Me Now)*.

1985

$\mathcal{I}$n an unusual step, President Ronald Reagan announced (Jan. 8) that White House Chief of Staff James Baker and Treasury Secretary Donald Regan would exchange jobs. Two weeks later, on Jan. 21, the President's second inaugural ceremony was relocated to inside the Capitol Building because of bad weather.

A dozen eggs cost 96 cents.

A New York City grand jury determined (Jan. 25) that "Subway Vigilante" Bernard Goetz would not have to face trial on charges of shooting four black youths. Instead he was indicted for illegal possession of handguns.

The Department of Education called on the Justice Department for assistance as the federal tab on defaulted student loans reached (Feb.) $4.5 billion, and nearly 10 percent of all student borrowing had become bad debts.

Edwin Meese III was confirmed (Feb. 23) by the Senate as Attorney General 13 months after his nomination.

Labor Secretary Raymond Donovan, the first cabinet officer to be indicted while in office, resigned (Mar. 15) his post, and President Reagan nominated (Mar. 20) William Brock to replace him.

Sen. Jake Garn of Utah flew (Apr. 12) aboard the space shuttle *Discovery* and became the first member of Congress to ride into space.

Rep. Silvio Conte of Massachusetts launched (Apr.) a campaign to rid Capitol Hill of one trillion cockroaches.

During a visit to Germany, President Reagan laid (May 5) a wreath in a cemetery at Bitburg containing the graves of some Nazi *Waffen-SS* members.

John Walker, Jr., was arrested (May 20) by the FBI in one of the most serious espionage cases since World War II.

A jury found (June 10) Claus von Bulow not guilty of attempting to murder his wife, Sunny.

Terrorists seized (June 14) TWA flight 847 with 153 people aboard. The hijackers later killed one of the passengers, an American sailor, and released the final 39 hostages on June 30.

David Stockman resigned (July 9) as director of the Office of Management and Budget, and was replaced by James Miller.

Three months after launching a new version of Coke, the Coca-Cola Co. announced (July 10) it was going to continue producing the original, 99-year-old formula soft drink.

The Live Aid concert raised (July 13) $70 million for victims of famine in Africa.

Actor Rock Hudson was admitted (July 25) to the hospital suffering from AIDS.

U.S. unemployment fell (Sept. 6) to a five-year low of 6.9 percent.

An American-French team found (Sept. 1) the wreckage of the sunken liner *Titanic*.

Palestinian terrorists hijacked (Oct. 7) the Italian cruise ship *Achille Lauro* with more than 400 passengers aboard and killed one of them, wheelchair-bound Leon Klinghoffer, an American. Three days later, U.S. Navy fighter aircraft forced an Egyptian airliner carrying four of the hijackers to land in Sicily.

President Reagan met (Nov. 21) in Geneva with General Secretary Mikhail Gorbachev for a "fireside summit" and the first discussions between the heads of the U.S. and Soviet Union in six years.

In the largest civil judgment in U.S. history, a state jury in Houston awarded (Nov. 19) damages of $10.53 billion to Pennzoil Co. in its case against Texaco, Inc.

American scholar Gary Taylor discovered (Nov. 23) a previously unknown poem by Shakespeare in an Oxford University library.

Robert McFarlane resigned (Dec. 4) as President Reagan's assistant for national security affairs.

The President signed (Dec. 12) the Gramm-Rudman bill requiring a balanced budget.

Mother Teresa dedicated (Dec. 24) an AIDS hospice in New York City.

Five Americans were killed (Dec. 27) during a terrorist attack at the Rome Airport.

In sports news, the San Francisco 49ers defeated (Jan. 20) the Miami Dolphins to win Super Bowl XIX; baseball owners and players settled (Aug. 7) a two-day strike; New York Yankee Don Baylor was hit (Aug. 29) by a pitch for a record 190th time; and the Kansas City Royals defeated (Oct. 27) the St. Louis Cardinals in seven games to win the World Series.

Deaths of the year included: former Ambassador Henry Cabot Lodge, 82 (Feb. 27); former Sen. Sam Ervin, 88 (Apr. 23); cartoonist Chester Gould, 84 (May 11); actor Rock Hudson, 59 (Oct. 2); actor Yul Brynner, 65 (Oct. 10); and baseball player Roger Maris, 51 (Dec. 14).

In Print

The number one book was Jean Auel's *The Mammoth Hunters*. Other popular fiction entries: *Lake Wobegon Days*, by Garrison Keillor; *Texas*, by James Michener; *Contact*, by Carl Sagan; *Secrets*, by Danielle Steel; *Skeleton Crew*, by Stephen King; *Galapagos*, by Kurt Vonnegut; *The Polar Express*, by Chris Van Allsburg; *The Secrets of Harry Bright*, by Joseph Wambaugh; *World's Fair*, by E. L. Doctorow; *The Cat Who Walks Through Walls*, by Robert A. Heinlein; *What's Bred in the Bone*, by Robertson Davies; *The Accidental Tourist*, by Anne Tyler;

London Match, by Len Deighton; *Lucky*, by Jackie Collins; and *The Vampire Lestat*, by Anne Rice.

On the nonfiction side, Lee Iacocca's *Iacocca: An Autobiography* had been on the best-selling list for 62 consecutive weeks. Following in the number two slot, another autobiography, *Yeager*, by Chuck Yeager and Leo Janos, the story of the first man to fly faster than sound, spent half the year on the bestseller list. *A Light in the Attic*, by Shel Silverstein continued for 148 consecutive weeks.

Other best-selling books written by well-known people included *I Never Played the Game*, by Howard Cosell; *On the Road with Charles Kuralt*, by Charles Kuralt; *Dancing in the Light*, by Shirley MacLaine; and *Elvis and Me*, by Priscilla Beaulieu Presley with Sandra Harmon.

Other nonfiction included: *House*, by Tracy Kidder; *You Can Fool All of the People All of the Time*, by Art Buchwald; *Shoot Low, Boys—They're Ridin' Shetland Ponies*, by Lewis Grizzard; *Ansel Adams*, by Ansel Adams with Mary Street Alinder; *Only One Woof*, by James Herriot; *Made in America*, by Peter Ueberroth; *Comet*, by Carl Sagan; *Charles & Diana*, by Ralph G. Martin; *The Be (Happy) Attitudes*, by Robert Schuller; *Fit for Life*, by Harvey Diamond and Marilyn Diamond; *The Frugal Gourmet*, by Geoff Smith; *Jane Brody's Good Food Book*, by Jane E. Brody; and *Webster's Ninth New Collegiate Dictionary*.

The Good War: An Oral History of World War II, by Studs Terkel, won the National Book Award for nonfiction.

On Stage

Dream Girls achieved 1,522 performances. A number of Broadway shows continued with stunning longevity: *Cats* with 1,521 performances; *Brighton Beach Memoirs*, 1,530; and *La Cage aux Folles*, 1,161.

Plays produced included: *Dancing in the End Zone*; *I'm Not Rappaport*; *The King and I*; *Strange Interlude*; *Joe Egg*; *Biloxi Blues*; *Leader of the Pack*; *Big River: The Adventures of Huckleberry Finn*; *Aren't We All*; *As Is*; *Doubles*; *The Odd Couple*; *Singin' in the Rain*; *Song and Dance*; *The Search for Signs of Intelligent Life in the Universe*; *The Iceman Cometh*; *Tango Argentino*; *Mayor*; *The Mystery of Edwin Drood*; *Blood Knot*; *Jerry's Girls*; and *Much Ado About Nothing*.

Best Play of the season was *As Is*. Derek Jacobi earned Best Actor in *Much Ado About Nothing*, and Stockard Channing Best Actress in *Joe Egg*. Best Musical was *Big River: The Adventures of Huckleberry Finn*.

Films

Sydney Pollack's *Out of Africa*, with Robert Redford, Meryl Streep, and Klaus Maria Brandauer earned him Best Director, as well as an Oscar for Best Picture.

Other films included: *Back to the Future*, with Michael J. Fox, Christopher Lloyd, and Crispin Glover; *Brazil*, with Jonathan Pryce, Kim Greist, Robert DeNiro, Ian Holm, and Michael Palin; *Cocoon*, with Don Ameche, Wilfred Brimley, Hume Cronyn, Jessica Tandy, and Steve Guttenberg; *The Color Pur-*

ple, with Whoopi Goldberg, Danny Glover, and Oprah Winfrey; *My Beautiful Launderette*, with Gordon Warnecke and Daniel Day-Lewis; *My Life as a Dog*, with Anton Glanzelius and Tomas von Bromssen; *National Lampoon's European Vacation*, with Chevy Chase and Beverly D'Angelo; *The Natural*, with Robert Redford, Robert Duvall, Glenn Close, Kim Basinger, Wilford Brimley, and Richard Farnsworth; *Prizzi's Honor*, with Jack Nicholson, Kathleen Turner, and Anjelica Huston; *Rambo: First Blood, Part II*, with Sylvester Stallone and Richard Crenna; *Ran*, with Tatsuya Nakadai and Satoshi Terao; *The Trip to Bountiful*, with Geraldine Page, John Heard, and Rebecca DeMornay; and *Witness*, with Harrison Ford and Kelly McGillis.

Television

HBO broadcast (Apr. 13) *The Second City 25th Anniversary Show*, a tribute to a unique comedy ensemble from Chicago. A new version of *Death of a Salesman* was presented (Sept. 15) by CBS. *The Love Boat* was canceled by ABC during the 1985–86 season.

Red Skelton received the Governors' Award at the Emmy presentations. The NBC *Hallmark Hall of Fame*'s production of *Love Is Never Silent* won for outstanding drama/comedy special. *The Cosby Show* was the highest-rated show.

Music

We Are the World was recorded by a wide range of performers, called USA for Africa; the proceeds were donated to starving children in Africa. The song was composed by Michael Jackson and Lionel Richie, and their effort earned them a Grammy for Song of the Year. The song was recorded, and simultaneously videotaped, and shown extensively on MTV.

Phil Collins's album *No Jacket Required* won a Grammy for Album of the Year and Best Male Vocal Performance. Whitney Houston earned Best Female Vocal Performance for *Saving All My Love for You*.

The number one sellers for the year included: *I Want to Know What Love Is*, Foreigner; *Careless Whisper*, Wham!; *Can't Fight This Feeling*, REO Speedwagon; *One More Night*, Phil Collins; *Crazy for You*, Madonna; *Don't You, Forget About Me*, Simple Minds; *Everything She Wants*, Wham!; *Everybody Wants to Rule the World*, Tears for Fears; *Heaven*, Bryan Adams; *Sussudio*, Phil Collins; *A View to a Kill*, Duran Duran; *Everytime You Go Away*, Paul Young; *Shouts*, Tears for Fears; *The Power of Love*, Huey Lewis & The News; *St. Elmo's Fire, (Man in Motion)*, John Parr; *Money for Nothing*, Dire Straits; *Oh Sheila*, Ready for the World; *Take on Me*, A-Ha; *Saving All My Love for You*, Whitney Houston; *Part-Time Lover*, Stevie Wonder; *Miami Vice Theme*, Jan Hammer; *We Built This City*, Starship; *Separate Lives*, Phil Collins & Marilyn Martin; *Broken Wings*, Mr. Mister; and *Say You, Say Me*, Lionel Richie.

1986

$\mathscr{P}$resident Ronald Reagan imposed (Jan. 3) economic sanctions against Libya to retaliate against terrorist attacks in Rome and Vienna.

The *Voyager 2* spacecraft flew (Jan. 14) within 50,625 miles of Uranus. Just two weeks later, the space shuttle *Challenger* exploded (Jan. 28) on its 10th flight, killing seven astronauts, including high school teacher Christa McAuliffe. An investigation revealed that NASA had relaxed safety standards to speed up the launch date.

Robert Penn Warren was named (Feb. 20) the first poet laureate of the U.S.

Former Philippine President Ferdinand Marcos arrived (Feb. 26) in Hawaii after resigning his office. Within the first month of his exile, Marcos had spent $19,971 for long-distance telephone calls; $18,952 for clothing; $10,555 for toothpaste, soap, and beauty aids; and $2,552 for shoes, none of them for Mrs. Marcos. These expenditures did not include the $450,813 spent by the U.S. government to transport Marcos and his party to Hawaii.

The *New England Journal of Medicine* reported (Mar. 6) that moderate exercise could significantly reduce the risk of death from many causes.

The House rejected (Mar. 20) a $100 million aid bill for the Nicaraguan contras.

Four Americans were killed (Apr. 2) when a terrorist bomb exploded aboard a TWA jet flying from Rome to Athens.

Actor Clint Eastwood was elected (Apr. 8) Mayor of Carmel, Calif.

After a nine-year absence, the electric news headline sign over Times Square resumed (Apr. 14) service. The sign had been first lit on Nov. 6, 1928, and had reported all major news events.

U.S. Air Force and Navy aircraft attacked (Apr. 15) ground targets in Libya following the death of an American Army sergeant in the terrorist bombing of a West Berlin disco.

A hospital in Cleveland announced (Apr. 16) the first U.S. surrogate birth of a test tube baby.

The Agriculture Department approved (Apr. 22) the release of the first genetically altered virus into the environment.

Six million people joined (May 25) to make a "Hands Across America" chain across the country to raise money for the homeless.

Following an elaborate "facelift," the Statue of Liberty celebrated (July 4) its 100th birthday, with President Reagan in attendance.

The Senate confirmed (Sept. 17) William Rehnquist as the nation's 16th Chief Justice and Antonin Scalia as an Associate Justice of the Supreme Court.

Congress voted (Sept. 23) to designate the rose as the country's official flower.

Reporter Nicholas Daniloff was freed (Sept. 29) by the Soviet Union after being jailed for a month on espionage charges and following U.S. agreement to drop similar charges against Soviet diplomat Gennadi Zukharov.

A cargo plane carrying arms to the contras was shot down (Oct. 5) over Nicaragua. The sole surviving American crewman was captured and revealed CIA connections to the mission.

Ronald Reagan and Mikhail Gorbachev held (Oct. 10–12) a summit meeting in Iceland and nearly concluded a major arms reduction agreement.

A Lebanese magazine, *Al-Shiraa*, disclosed (Nov. 3) that the U.S. had secretly sold arms to Iran. Three weeks later, Attorney General Edwin Meese announced (Nov. 25) the diversion of funds from the arms sales to the contras. The President announced the resignation of national security assistant Adm. John Poindexter and the dismissal of Marine Lt. Col. Oliver North.

General Motors removed (Dec. 1) H. Ross Perot from its board of directors after he continued to criticize the company's chairman, Roger Smith.

In sports news, the Chicago Bears defeated (Jan. 26) the New England Patriots to win Super Bowl XX, and the New York Mets defeated the Boston Red Sox in seven games to win the World Series.

Deaths of the year included: author Bernard Malamud, 71 (Mar. 18); actor James Cagney, 86 (Mar. 30); author Theodore White, 71 (June 17); jazz musician Benny Goodman, 77 (June 13); lyricist Alan Jay Lerner, 67 (June 14); singer Kate Smith, 79 (June 17); former Gov. W. Averell Harriman, 94 (July 26); lawyer Roy Cohn, 59 (Aug. 2); actor Gary Grant, 82 (Nov. 29); and bandleader Desi Arnaz, 69 (Dec. 2).

In Print

E. L. Doctorow, author of *World's Fair*, won the National Book Award for fiction.

Another year ended with a Stephen King horror story in the top ten: *It* was number one and had been on the bestseller list for 17 consecutive weeks. Other fiction included *Whirlwind*, by James Clavell; *Red Storm Rising*, by Tom Clancy; *A Taste for Death*, by P. D. James; *Hollywood Husbands*, by Jackie Collins; *The Prince of Tides*, by Pat Conroy; *The Flight of the Intruder*, by Stephen Coonts; *Wanderlust*, by Danielle Steel; *The Polar Express*, by Chris Van Allsburg; *Foundation and Earth*, by Isaac Asimov; *Last Breed*, by Louis L'Amour; *The Golden Cup*, by Belva Plain; *Through a Glass Darkly*, by Karleen Koen; *Perfume*, by Patrick Suskin; and *A Perfect Spy*, by John Le Carre.

Nonfiction included: *Fatherhood*, by Bill Cosby; *His Way*, by Kitty Kelley; *McMahon!*, by Jim McMahon and Bob Verdi; *A Day in the Life of America*; *Word for Word*, by Andrew A. Rooney; *James Herriot's Dog Stories*, by James Herriot; *One Knee Equals Two Feet*, by John Madden; *The Christmas Day Kitten*, by James

Herriot; *You're Only Old Once!*, by Dr. Seuss; *Across China*, by Peter Jenkins; *One More Time*, by Carol Burnett; *Pat Nixon: The Untold Story*, by Julie Nixon Eisenhower; *A Season on the Brink*, by John Feinstein; *Life: The First Fifty Years;* and *The Reckoning*, by David Halberstam.

Larry McMurty's view of the old west, *Lonesome Dove*, was awarded the Pulitzer Prize for fiction. (It would later be made into a highly acclaimed, much-watched TV movie, starring Robert Duvall and Anjelica Huston.)

On Stage

This season's plays included: *Broadway Bound; Corpse!; Fences; Jerome Kern Goes to Hollywood; Uptown...It's Hot!; Execution of Justice; Jackie Mason's "The World According to Me"; The Life and Adventures of Nicholas Nickleby; Mummenschanz; Precious Sons; So Long on Lonely Street; Big Deal; Social Security; The Petition; Sweet Charity; Long Day's Journey into Night;* and *Me and My Gal*.

Two Tonys went to *I'm Not Rappaport*: Best Play and Best Actor to Judd Hirsch. Lily Tomlin won Best Actress for her role in *The Search for Intelligent Life in the Universe*. Best Musical was *The Mystery of Edwin Drood*, and George Rose won Best Actor in the same musical. Best Actress was Bernadette Peters in *Song and Dance*.

Films

Aliens, with Sigourney Weaver, Michael Biehn, Paul Reiser, and Bill Paxton, depicted the adventures of a group of intergalactic Marines in the sequel to the very popular 1979 film. *Platoon*, with Tom Berenger, William Dafoe, Charlie Sheen, and Forest Whitaker was Oliver Stone's account of a young soldier's year-long duty near the Cambodian border.

Other popular films included: *Children of a Lesser God*, with William Hurt, Marlee Matlin, and Piper Laurie; *The Color of Money*, with Paul Newman, Tom Cruise, Mary Elizabeth Mastrantonio, Helen Shaver, and John Turturro); *Cobra*, with Sylvester Stallone and Brigitte Nielsen; *Crocodile Dundee*, with Paul Hogan; *Down and Out in Beverly Hills*, with Nick Nolte, Bette Midler, and Richard Dreyfuss; *Ferris Bueller's Day Off*, with Matthew Broderick, Mia Sara, and Jennifer Grey; *The Great Mouse Detective; Hannah and Her Sisters*, with Mia Farrow, Michael Caine, Dianne Wiest, and Barbara Hershey; *Legal Eagles*, with Robert Redford, Debra Winger, Daryl Hannah, and Brian Dennehy; *The Mission*, with Robert DeNiro and Jeremy Irons; *A Room with a View*, with Helen Bonham Carter, Maggie Smith, Denholm Elliott, Julian Sands, and Daniel Day-Lewis; *Star Trek IV: The Voyage Home*, with William Shatner, Leonard Nimoy, and DeForest Kelley; and *Top Gun*, with Tom Cruise, Kelly McGillis, Val Kilmer, and Tom Skerritt).

A Japanese import was well received: *Tampopo*, with Ken Watanabe, was the story of a truck driver helping a widow turn her failing noodle restaurant into a success.

In 1933, the first year such figures were recorded, the average movie ticket cost 23 cents; this year, the average ticket was up to $3.67.

Television

HBO carried (Mar. 29) *Comic Relief*, a three-hour benefit for the homeless, starring Billy Crystal, Whoopi Goldberg, and Robin Williams. Geraldo Rivera hosted (Apr. 21) the unproductive opening of a sealed underground room that had allegedly been Al Capone's vault. Five days later, PBS made the first televised broadcast of Garrison Keillor's *A Prairie Home Companion* radio program. *L.A. Law* made its debut on NBC, and *Hill Street Blues* was canceled during the 1986-87 season. Bruce Willis received an Emmy as outstanding lead actor in a drama series for his role on ABC's *Moonlighting*. *The Cosby Show* was once again the top-rated program.

Music

Thirty songs hit the number position this year, the most since 1975. They included: *That's What Friends Are For*, Dionne & Friends; *How Will I Know*, Whitney Houston; *Kyrie*, Mr. Mister; *Sara*, Starship; *These Dreams*, Heart; *Rock Me Amadeus*, Heart; *Kiss*, Prince & The Revolution; *Addicted to Love*, Robert Palmer; *West End Girls*, Pet Shop Boys; *Greatest Love of All*, Whitney Houston; *Live to Tell*, Madonna; *On My Own*, Patti LaBelle and Michael McDonald; *There'll Be Sad Songs (To Make You Cry)*, Billy Ocean; *Holding Back the Years*, Simply Red; *Invisible Touch*, Phil Collins; *Sledgehammer*, Peter Gabriel; *Glory of Love*, Peter Cetera; *Papa Don't Preach*, Madonna; *Higher Love*, Steve Winwood; *Venus*, Bananarama; *Take My Breath Away*, Berlin; *Stuck with You*, Huey Lewis & The News; *When I Think of You*, Janet Jackson; *True Colors*, Cyndi Lauper; *Amanda*, Boston; *Human*, Human League; *You Give Love a Bad Name*, Bon Jovi; *The Next Time I Fall*, Peter Cetera with Amy Grant; *The Way It Is*, Bruce Hornsby & The Range; and *Walk Like an Egyptian*, Bangles.

The Big Grammy winner was Steve Winwood: His *Higher Love* took Record of the Year and Best Male Vocal Performance. Paul Simon's *Graceland* took Album of the Year. Barbra Streisand won Best Female Vocal Performance for her album *The Broadway Album*.

1987

$\mathscr{P}$resident Ronald Reagan submitted (Jan.) the first trillion-dollar budget in U.S. history, with a projected deficit of $107.8 billion.

The Dow Jones Industrial Average closed (Jan. 8) at 2002.25, the first time it had surpassed the 2000 level.

Three American Beirut University faculty members were captured (Jan. 24) by Muslim terrorists.

Thousands of tourists traveled (Jan.) to Shrewsbury, Vt., to watch a lovesick moose pursue a cow named Jessica around a pasture. The moose gave up the futile courtship after 76 days.

John Demjanjuk, a former autoworker who lived for 40 years in the U.S., was placed (Feb. 16) on trial in Jerusalem as "Ivan the Terrible," accused of murdering hundreds of Jews at Treblinka, a Nazi death camp.

President Reagan removed (Feb. 19) trade sanctions against Poland after its Communist government released political prisoners.

The Tower Commission issued (Feb. 26) its report concluding that the President's top advisers were responsible for the situation that led to the Iran-contra affair. The report also asserted that President Reagan was largely out of touch with the operations undertaken by his National Security Council staff. The story would continue to occupy headlines for years thereafter.

Television evangelist Jim Bakker was forced (Mar. 19) to resign from the PTL network and his ministry after confessing sexual adventures.

The government approved (Mar. 20) the use of AZT to treat AIDS patients.

A report by the Legal Action Center for the Homeless indicated (Apr.) that of a sample of 500 people who ate at soup kitchens, less than 10 percent were women and more than 80 percent were black or Hispanic. A majority could not find jobs or were too disabled to work, nearly one-third slept on the street, and 40 percent consumed one meal or less a day.

The government announced (Apr. 16) that new forms of animal life created through genetic splicing could be patented by their inventors.

Austrian President and former UN Secretary-General Kurt Waldheim was banned (Apr. 27) from entering the U.S. because of his activities with the German army during World War II.

Televised public hearings began (May 5) before the Senate and House committees investigating the Iran-contra affair. Oliver North began six days of testimony on July 7. The hearings ended Aug. 3 after more than 250 hours of testimony from 28 witnesses.

Gary Hart withdrew (May 8) from the presidential race following allegations of infidelity.

An Iraqi air-launched missile hit (May 17) the U.S. frigate *Stark*, killing 37 men.

Robert Bork was nominated (July 1) by President Reagan to fill the Supreme Court vacancy created by the retirement of Justice Lewis F. Powell, Jr. The Senate rejected the nomination on Oct. 23.

Commerce Secretary Malcolm Baldrige was killed (July 25) when a horse fell on him.

Adm. John Poindexter resigned (Sept. 29) from the Navy over his role in the Iran-contra affair.

An earthquake registering 6.1 on the Richter scale shook (Oct. 1) Los Angeles for 20 seconds, killed 7 and injured more than 100.

Wall Street suffered (Oct. 19) the worst day in its history when the Dow Jones Average dropped a record 508.32 points (22.6 percent) and wiped out $500 billion in the value of shares.

A first volume of the Gutenburg Bible sold (Oct. 22) for $5.39 million in a New York City auction.

A deer hunter discovered (Oct. 22) an unmanned aircraft in trees in Star Lake, N.Y., after it had flown 65 miles without a pilot and had run out of fuel.

Douglas Ginsburg withdrew (Nov. 1) as President Reagan's latest nominee for a Supreme Court seat because of allegations that he had used marijuana.

Caspar Weinberger resigned (Nov. 5) as Secretary of Defense, and the President nominated Frank Carlucci as his successor.

A man serving 17 years for murder in California sued (Nov. 8) a juror for $24 million, claiming that the juror's dozing through much of his trial contributed to his wrongful conviction.

Van Gogh's *Irises* was sold (Nov. 11) to the Getty Museum at Sotheby's in New York City for $53.9 million.

Ivan Boesky agreed (Nov. 14) to pay a penalty of $100 million to the government for illegal insider trading activities.

President Reagan and Canadian Prime Minister Brian Mulroney signed (Dec. 2) a free trade agreement.

The President and Soviet leader Mikhail Gorbachev signed (Dec. 8) the Intermediate Range Nuclear Forces (INF) treaty in Washington, D.C., and agreed to dismantle all 2,611 medium and short range nuclear-armed missiles based in Europe.

The U.S. population had risen to 243,419,000.

Former Reagan aide Michael Deaver was convicted (Dec. 15) of perjury.

In sports news, the New York Giants defeated (Jan.) the Denver Broncos to win Super Bowl XXI; *Stars and Stripes* regained (Feb. 4) the America's Cup from Australia; Greg LeMond became (July 27) the first American to win the

Tour de France bike race; NFL football players ended (Oct. 15) a 24-day strike without achieving their goals; and the Minnesota Twins defeated the St. Louis Cardinals in seven games to win the World Series.

Deaths of the year included: pianist Liberace, 67 (Feb. 4); artist Andy Warhol, 58 (Feb. 21); comedian Danny Kaye, 74 (Mar. 3); former CIA Director William Casey, 74 (May 6); dancer Fred Astaire, 88 (June 22); comedian Jackie Gleason, 71 (June 24); film director John Huston, 81 (Aug. 28); former Gov. Alf Landon, 100 (Oct. 13); Chicago Mayor Harold Washington (Nov. 25); and author James Baldwin, 63 (Nov. 30).

In Print

At the end of the year a Stephen King novel, *The Tommyknockers*, was the number one seller. Another Stephen King book, *Misery*, which would be made into a motion picture, had been on the bestseller list for 29 consecutive weeks.

Other bestsellers this year included *Kaleidoscope*, by Danielle Steel; *The Bonfire of the Vanities*, by Tom Wolfe; *Leaving Home*, by Garrison Keillor; *The Polar Express*, by Chris Van Allsburg; *Patriot Games*, by Tom Clancy; *Presumed Innocent*, by Scott Turow; *2061: Odyssey Three*, by Arthur C. Clarke; *Heaven and Hell*, by John Jakes; *Beloved*, by Toni Morrison; *Sarum*, by Edward Rutherfurd; *Winters' Tales*, by Jonathan Winters; *Legacy*, by James A. Michener; *Bluebeard*, by Kurt Vonnegut; and *Winter*, by Len Deighton.

The previous year, a Bill Cosby book finished in the number one position on the nonfiction list. This year was a repeat for Cosby with his *Time Flies*. Other nonfiction included *Trump: The Art of the Deal*, by Donald J. Trump; *The Cat Who Came for Christmas*, by Cleveland Amory; *Family: The Ties That Bind...and Gag!*, by Erma Bombeck; *Seven Stories of Christmas Love*, by Leo Buscaglia; *A Day in the Life of America; Man of the House: The Life and Political Memoirs of Speaker Tip O'Neal*, by Tip O'Neal with William Novack; *A Day in the Life of the Soviet Union; Chronicle of the 20th Century*, edited by Clifton Daniel; *Free to Be...A Family*, edited by Marlo Thomas with Christopher Cerf and Letty Cotton Pogrebin; *Spycatcher*, by Peter Wright; *Perestroika*, by Mikhail Gorbachev; *The National Geographic Society*, by C. D. B. Bryan; *I Think I Don't Remember*, by Art Buchwald; and *Thriving on Chaos*, by Tom Peters.

On Stage

A *Chorus Line* continued to make theatrical history: By June, it hit 5,338 performances, followed closely by *Oh! Calcutta*, with 5,319.

Produced plays included *Dreamgirls; Sherlock's Last Case; Cabaret; Into the Woods; Teddy and Alice; Breaking the Code; Burn This; Stardust; Les Miserables; Starlight Express;* and *The Nerd*.

Best Play was *Fences*, in which James Earl Jones earned Best Actor. Best Actress was Linda Lavin in *Broadway Bound*. Best Musical went to *Les Miserables*. Robert Lindsay was Best Actor in a musical for *Me and My Gal*, Best Actress was split between Bernadette Peters for *Song and Dance* and Maryann Plunkett's role in *Me and My Gal*.

Films

The Last Emperor won the award for Best Picture.

Other films produced this year included *Au Revoir, Les Infants*, with Gaspard Manesse; *Babette's Feast*, with Stephane Audran; *Broadcast News*, with William Hurt, Holly Hunter, and Albert Brooks; *The Dead*, with Anjelica Huston and Donald McCann; *Empire of the Sun*, with Christian Bale and John Malkovich; *Fatal Attraction*, with Michael Douglas, Glenn Close, Ann Archer, and Fred Gwynne; *Full Metal Jacket*, with Matthew Modine, Adam Baldwin, and Vincent D'Onofrio; *Hope and Glory*, with Sarah Miles and David Hayman; *Hotel Terminus: The Life and Times of Klaus Barbie*; *House of Games*, with Lindsay Crouse, Joe Montegna, and J. T. Walsh; *Matewan*, with Chris Cooper and Will Oldham; *Moonstruck*, with Cher, Nicolas Cage, Olympia Dukakis, Danny Aiello, and Vincent Gardenia; *Radio Days*, with Mia Farrow, Dianne Wiest, and Julie Kavner; *Swimming to Cambodia*, with Spalding Grey; and *Wall Street*, with Michael Douglas, Charlie Sheen, Daryl Hannah, Hal Holbrook, Terrence Stamp, and Martin Sheen.

Television

CBS presented (Apr. 21) *Carnegie Hall: The Grand Reopening* with Leonard Bernstein, Frank Sinatra, Zubin Mehta, Yo-Yo Ma, and Lena Horne. *Seven Days in the Soviet Union*, a report on everyday activities in the former USSR, was broadcast (June 24) by a CBS News Special. *Thirtysomething* made its ABC debut and promptly won an Emmy, while *St. Elsewhere* was canceled. John Larroquette earned his fourth consecutive Emmy for outstanding supporting actor for his work on NBC's *Night Court*. HBO's *Dear America: Letters Home from Vietnam* received an Emmy for outstanding informational special. And *The Cosby Show* was still the top-ranked program.

Music

Music produced during the year included: *Shake You Down*, Gregory Abbott; *At This Moment*, Billy Vera and The Beaters; *Open Your Heart*, Madonna; *Livin' on a Prayer*, Bon Jovi; *Jacob's Ladder*, Huey Lewis and The News; *Lean on Me*, Club Nouveau; *Nothing's Gonna Stop Us Now*, Starship; *I Knew You Were Waiting (For Me)*, Aretha Franklin and George Michael; *(I Just) Died in Your Arms*, Cutting Crew; *With or Without You*, U2; *You Keep Me Hangin' On*, Kim Wilde; *Always*, Atlantic Star; *Head to Toe*, Lisa Lisa and Cult Jam; *I Wanna Dance with Somebody (Who Loves Me)*, Whitney Houston; *Alone*, Heart; *Shakedown*, Bob Seger; *I Still Haven't Found What I'm Looking For*, U2; *Who's That Girl*, Madonna; *La Bamba*, Los Lobos; *I Just Can't Stop Loving You*, Michael Jackson and Siedah Garrett; *Didn't We Almost Have It All*, Whitney Houston; *Here I Go Again*, Whitesnake; *Lost in Emotion*, Lisa Lisa and Cult Jam; *Bad*, Michael Jackson; *I Think We're Alone Now*, Tiffany; *Mony Mony*, Billy Idol; *(I've Had) The Time of My Life*, Bill Medley and Jennifer Warnes; *Heaven Is a Place on Earth*, Belinda Carlisle; *Faith*, George Michael; and *So Emotional*, Whitney Houston.

Grammys were given to Paul Simon for *Graceland*. Album of the Year was given to U2 for *The Joshua Tree*. Best Male Performance went to Sting for *Bring on the Night*. Best Female Vocal Performance was Whitney Houston in *I Wanna Dance with Somebody*.

The best-selling soundtrack from *Saturday Night Fever* had sold (May) over 26.5 million albums. *Whitney Houston*, the debut album by Whitney Houston released in 1985, had sold over 14 million copies (May). On June 30, North American sales of Bing Crosby's recording of *White Christmas* (Irving Berlin) had reached 170,884,207. To date, this was the biggest-selling single.

1988

$\mathcal{F}$ears about AIDS infection led to a sharp increase (Jan.) in demand for latex examining gloves used by medical professionals.

An unsuccessful opera singer committed suicide (Jan. 29) by hurling himself from the balcony of the Metropolitan Opera House during a performance of Verdi's *Macbeth*.

The Senate confirmed (Feb. 3) the nomination of Anthony Kennedy for a seat on the Supreme Court.

Panamanian strongman Manuel Noriega was indicted (Feb. 4) by a Miami grand jury on charges he had received more than $4.5 million in payoffs from drug dealers.

Arizona Gov. Evan Mechan was impeached (Feb. 5) for high crimes, misdemeanors, and malfeasance.

Television evangelist Jimmy Swaggart was banned (Feb. 25) from preaching for a year by the elders of his church for sexual improprieties.

Writers of television soap operas went on strike (Mar. 8) for better terms of employment.

Eugene Mariho of Atlanta became (Mar. 15) the first black Catholic archbishop in the U.S.

The price of a first-class stamp was 25 cents.

Harvard University was awarded (Apr. 12) the first patent for a higher form of life—a genetically altered mouse.

President Ronald Reagan's former Deputy Press Secretary, Larry Speakes, revealed (Apr.) that he had invented or borrowed statements attributed to the President.

More than 9,000 pounds of cocaine, valued at $2 billion, was seized (May 3) in Florida by drug enforcement officers.

Nearly 1.4 million illegal aliens applied for amnesty before the government's May 4 deadline.

President Reagan visited (May 29–June 2) the Soviet Union and formally signed the 1987 INF treaty. He and Mrs. Reagan then visited Queen Elizabeth II in London.

David Stern blew (June 6) the world's biggest bubble, 50 feet in length, in New York City.

Eugene McCarthy, who had not won elective office since a 1964 Senate race, announced (June) plans to again be a presidential candidate after three prior futile campaigns.

The Supreme Court upheld (June 20) a law requiring the admission of women to private clubs.

The U.S. Navy cruiser *Vincennes* shot down (July 3) an Iranian airliner over the Persian Gulf, killing 290 passengers and crew.

Gov. Michael Dukakis and Sen. Lloyd Bentsen were nominated (July 19–20) by the Democratic National Convention as presidential and vice presidential candidates. During the primary season, Dukakis had competed against Al Gore, Gary Hart, Paul Simon, Richard Gephardt, Bruce Babbitt, and Jesse Jackson.

The nation's last Playboy Club, in Lansing, Mich., closed (July 31).

The federal government approved (Aug. 7) the first hair-growing drug for general use.

George Bush and Dan Quayle were nominated (Aug. 17–18) by the Republican National Convention as the GOP's presidential and vice presidential candidates. Other Republican contenders had included Alexander Haig, Robert Dole, and Pat Robertson.

Thousands of Americans applied (Sept. 16) for the Elvis Presley credit card, which allowed a credit maximum of $3,500.

Lauro Cavazos was named (Sept. 20) Secretary of Education, the first Hispanic member of the Reagan cabinet.

Barbara Harris became (Sept. 24) the first American woman Anglican bishop.

The space shuttle *Discovery* was launched (Sept. 29) successfully, the first U.S. manned spaceflight since the *Challenger* disaster.

George Bush carried 40 states (Nov. 8) to defeat Michael Dukakis and win election as the country's 41st President.

In one of the largest business deals to date, Kohlberg, Kravis, Roberts & Co. paid (Nov. 30) $25.07 billion to acquire RJR Nabisco.

Pan Am flight 103's 747 was blown up (Dec. 21) in midair and the wreckage crashed in Lockerbie, Scotland, killing all 259 aboard and 11 on the ground.

In sports news, the Washington Redskins defeated (Jan.) the Denver Broncos to win Super Bowl XX; the first night baseball game in history at Wrigley Field was called (Aug. 8) after four innings due to rain; and the Los Angles Dodgers defeated the Oakland A's in five games to win the World Series.

Deaths of the year included: sculptor Louise Nevelson, 88 (Apr. 17); inventor Frank Zamboni, 87 (July 28); Robin (The Boy Wonder), 49 (Nov. 1.); and singer Roy Orbison, 52 (Dec. 6).

The U.S. population was 245,807,000.

In Print

Two major awards this year went to Richard Rhodes's book *The Making of the Atomic Bomb*—the Pulitzer Prize and the National Book Award.

The best-selling fiction of the year included *The Sands of Time*, by Sidney Sheldon; *The Cardinal of the Kremlin*, by Tom Clancy; *Alaska*, by James A. Michener; *The Polar Express*, by Chris Van Allsburg; *One*, Richard Bach; *Dear Mili*, by Wilhelm Grimm; *The Queen of the Damned*, by Anne Rice; *Anything for Billy*, by Larry McMurty; *Final Flight*, by Stephen Coonts; *Mitla Pass*, by Leon Uris; *Breathing Lessons*, by Anne Tyler; *Zoya*, by Danielle Steel; *The Shell Seekers*, by Rosamunde Pilcher; and *Love in the Time of Cholera*, by Gabriel Garciá Márquez.

Best-selling nonfiction included: *All I Really Need to Know I Learned in Kindergarten*, by Robert Fulghum; *Gracie*, by George Burns; *A Brief History of Time*, by Stephen W. Hawking; *Child Star*, by Shirley Temple Black; *Seven Stories of Christmas Love*, by Leo Buscaglia; *The Last Lion*, by William Manchester; *Don't Bend Over in the Garden Granny, You Know Them Taters Got Eyes*, by Lewis Grizzard; *Christmas in America*; *Chronicle of the 20th Century*, edited by Clifton Daniel; *Talking Straight*, by Lee Iacocca with Sonny Kleinfield; *The Home Planet*, by Kevin W. Kelley; *Goldwater*, by Barry M. Goldwater; *The First Salute*, by Barbara W. Tuchman; and *Press On!*, by Chuck Yaeger and Charles Leerhsen.

On Stage

Plays produced included *Checkmates*; *Michael Feinstein in Concert: Isn't It Romantic*; *Rumors*; *Black and Blue*; *Sarafina*; *Our Town*; *The Phantom of the Opera*; *A Walk in the Woods*; *M. Butterfly*; *The Gospel at Colonus*; *Oba Oba*; *Mail*; *Romance Romance*; *Legs Diamond*; *Eastern Standard*; and *Shirley Valentine*.

M. Butterfly won a Tony for Best Play. Ron Silver earned Best Actor and Joan Allen Best Actress, both in *Burn This*. This year *Phantom of the Opera* was given Best Musical, and Michael Crawford won Best Actor as the star of the show. Joanna Gleason took Best Actress for *Into the Woods*.

Films

Barry Levinson's film *Rain Man* earned Levinson a Best Director award, as well as awards for Best Picture and Best Actor (Dustin Hoffman).

Other prominent films this year included *A Fish Called Wanda*; *The Accidental Tourist*, with William Hurt, Kathleen Turner, Geena Davis, Amy Wright, and Ed Begley Jr.; *The Accused*, with Jodie Foster, Kelly McGillis, and Bernis Coulson; *Bird*, with Forest Whitaker and Diane Venora; *A Cry in the Dark*, with Meryl Streep, Sam Neill, and Bruce Myles; *Dangerous Liaisons*, with John Malkovich, Glenn Close, Michelle Pfeiffer, Swoosie Kurtz, and Keanu Reeves; *Dead Ringers*, with Jeremy Irons and Genevieve Bujold; *Die Hard*, with Bruce Willis, Bonnie Bedelia, Reginald VelJohnson, Alan Rickman, and Alexander Godunov; *Heathers*, with Winona Ryder and Christian Slater; *The Last Temptation of Christ*, with Willem Dafoe, Harvey Keitel, Barbara Hershey, Harry Dean Stanton, and David Bowie; *Mississippi Burning*, with Gene Hackman and Willem Dafoe; *The Naked Gun*, with Leslie Nielsen, Priscilla Presley, Ricardo Montalban, George Kennedy, and O. J. Simpson; *The Navigator,* with Bruce Lyons and Chris Haywood; *Talk Radio*, with Eric Bogosian and Alec Baldwin; *The Thin Blue Line*, with documentary directed by Errol Morris; *The Unbearable Lightness of Being*, with Daniel Day-Lewis, Juliette Binoche, and Lena Olin; *Who Framed Roger Rabbit?*, with Bob Hoskins, Christopher Lloyd, and Joanna Cassidy; and *Women on the Verge of a Nervous Breakdown*, with Carmen Maura and Antonio Banderas.

Television

Lindsay Wagner starred (May 2) in *The Taking of Flight 847: The Uli Derickson Story*.

ABC's *Roseanne* and CBS's *Murphy Brown*, two sitcoms featuring strong female characters, made their debuts in the 1988–89 season, while *Miami Vice* was canceled. NBC's *L.A. Law* was awarded an Emmy as outstanding drama series; Fox's *The Tracy Ullman Show* won as outstanding variety, music, or comedy program; and *Lonesome Dove* was recognized for Simon Wincer's direction in a miniseries or special. *The Cosby Show* was number one for the fourth consecutive year.

Music

Top music of the year included: *Got My Mind Set on You*, George Harrison; *The Way You Make Me Feel*, Michael Jackson; *Need You Tonight*, INXS; *Could've Been*, Tiffany; *Seasons Change*, Expose; *Father Figure*, George Michael; *Never Gonna Give You Up*, Rick Astley; *Man in the Mirror,* Michael Jackson; *Get Outta My Dreams, Get Into My Car,* Billy Ocean; *Where Do Broken Hearts Go*, Whitney Houston; *Wishing Well,* Terrence Trent D'Arby; *Anything for You*, Gloria Estefan and Miami Sound Machine; *One More Try*, George Michael; *Together Forever,* Rick Astley; *Foolish Beat*, Debbie Gibson; *Dirty Diana*, Michael Jackson; *The Flame*, Cheap Trick; *Hold On to the Nights*, Richard Marx; *Roll with It*, Steve Winwood; *Monkey*, George Michael; *Sweet Child o' Mine*, Guns N' Roses; *Don't Worry, Be Happy*, Bobby McFerrin; *Love Bites*, Def Leppard; *Red Red Wine*, UB40; *Groovy Kind of Love*, Phil Collins; *Kokomo*, Beach Boys; *Wild, Wild West*, The Escape Club; *Bad Medicine*, Bon Jovi; *Baby, I Love Your Way/Freebird Medley (Free Baby)*, Will to Power; *Look Away*, Chicago; and *Every Rose Has Its Thorn*, Poison.

Grammy winners this year included: Bobby McFerrin's *Don't Worry, Be Happy*, which took Record of the Year, Song of the Year and Best Male Vocal Performance. Album of the Year was earned by George Michael for *Faith*, and Tracy Chapman's *Fast Car* earned her Best Female Vocal Performance.

1989

$\mathcal{T}$wo U.S. Navy F-14 fighters shot down (Jan. 14) a pair of Libyan MiG-23s over the Mediterranean Sea as they approached the U.S. carrier *John F. Kennedy* with apparent hostile intent.

George Bush was inaugurated (Jan. 20) as the nation's 41st President.

Ronald Brown was elected (Feb. 10) Chairman of the Democratic National Committee and became the first African American to head a major political party.

The U.S. Census Bureau forecasted (Feb.) that the country's population would peak at 302 million in 50 years and then begin a slow decline before stabilizing at 292 million in 2080.

Law enforcement officials announced (Feb. 16) that the 1988 crash of Pan American flight 103 at Lockerbie, Scotland, resulted from a bomb explosion.

Oliver North's Iran-contra trial began (Feb. 21) in Washington, D.C. North was convicted (May 4) of three of the 12 charges against him, and sentenced (July 5) to a $150,000 fine and a suspended prison term.

A convicted murderer in South Carolina who had successfully appealed his electric chair sentence was accidentally electrocuted (Mar. 7) while sitting on the toilet wearing earphones.

John Tower's nomination as Secretary of Defense was rejected (Mar. 9) by the Senate. President Bush then nominated Dick Chaney to the post.

The nation's unemployment rate fell (Mar. 10) to 5.1 percent, the lowest since May 1974.

Congress renewed (Mar. 24) a $40 million aid program for the Nicaraguan contra rebels.

Two scientists, including Stanley Pons of the University of Utah, claimed (Mar. 24) to have found the secret of low-temperature nuclear fusion.

The 987-foot tanker *Exxon Valdez* ran aground (Mar. 24) in Alaska's Prince William Sound and spilled 11 million gallons of crude oil, the largest oil spill in history.

Space Services, Inc., of Texas became (Mar. 29) the first private company to achieve a commercial space launch.

Rep. Jim Wright resigned (May 31) as Speaker of the House following an investigation of financial improprieties. Tom Foley was elected (June 6) as his successor.

The Supreme Court ruled (June 21) that burning the American flag is a legal form of political expression.

Following police charges against a Dallas merchant for selling records to a minor, a chain of 119 record stores in the Southwest required (June) that its customers furnish proof of age (18 or above) to buy certain sexually explicit records.

The Supreme Court placed (July 3) new restrictions on women's rights to abortion.

President Bush began (July 9) a visit to Europe with a stop in Poland and a meeting (July 11) with Lech Walesa, founder of Solidarity.

Muslim extremists claimed (July 31) to have killed Marine Lt. Col. William Higgins following his Feb. 1988 abduction.

Pictures of Neptune, including shots of Triton, the largest of Neptune's eight moons, were transmitted (Aug. 25) back to Earth by *Voyager 2*.

Hurricane Hugo, the worst storm of the decade, slammed (Sept. 21) into the East Coast and devastated Georgia and South Carolina.

A divorced Tennessee woman was awarded (Sept. 21) temporary custody of seven frozen embryos that had been fertilized by her former husband. The husband had argued that he did not want to become a father without his consent.

Northern California was rocked (Oct. 17) by a severe earthquake that killed more than 60, injured several thousand, and caused $5.6 billion in damage.

Television evangelist Jim Bakker was sentenced (Oct. 24) to 45 years in prison and a $500,000 fine for defrauding his PTL followers.

L. Douglas Wilder became (Nov. 8) the first black governor of Virginia.

Mikhail Gorbachev and President Bush met (Dec. 3) aboard a Soviet cruise ship in Malta and announced agreements to cut nuclear forces by half and to reduce their conventional forces in Europe.

Leona Helmsley, co-owner of the Helmsley Palace Hotel in New York City, was fined (Dec. 12) $7 million and sentenced to four years in prison for tax evasion.

U.S. forces invaded (Dec. 20) Panama, removed Manuel Noriega as president, and installed a new government led by Guillermo Endara.

In sports news, the San Francisco 49ers defeated (Jan.) the Cincinnati Bengals to win Super Bowl XXIII; Cincinnati Reds manager Pete Rose was suspended (Aug. 24) for life by baseball commissioner A. Bartlett Giamatti for alleged gambling infractions; and the Oakland A's defeated the San Francisco Giants in four games to win the World Series.

Deaths of the year included: historian Barbara Tuchman, 77 (Feb. 6); activist Abbie Hoffman, 52 (Apr. 12); boxer Sugar Ray Robinson, 67 (Apr. 12); comedian Lucille Ball, 76 (Apr. 26); comedian Gilda Radner, 42 (May 20); comedian Mel Blanc, 81 (July 10); baseball commissioner A. Bartlett Giamatti, 51 (Sept. 1); songwriter Irving Berlin, 101 (Sept. 22); ice cream merchant Tom Carvel (Oct. 21); broadcast executive William Paley (Oct. 26); pianist Vladimir Horowitz, 85 (Nov. 5); choreographer Alvin Ailey, 58 (Dec. 1); and baseball manager Billy Martin, 61 (Dec. 25).

In Print

The year ended with a Stephen King book, *The Dark Half*, once again in the number one spot. Other books on the best seller list included: *Daddy*, by Danielle Steel; *Clear and Present Danger*, by Tom Clancy; *Caribbean*, by James A. Michener; *Foucault's Pendulum*, by Umberto Eco; *Tales from Margaritaville*, by Jimmy Buffett; *The Polar Express*, by Chris Van Allsburg; *Jimmy Stewart and His Poems*, by Jimmy Stewart; *Straight*, by Dick Francis; *The Eleventh Hour*, by Graeme Base; *California Gold*, by John Jakes; *The Pillars of the Earth*, by Ken Follett; *The Joy Luck Club*, by Amy Tan; and *Spy Line*, by Len Deighton.

On the nonfiction list, the top two bestsellers were written by Robert Fulghum: *It Was on Fire When I Lay Down on It* and *All I Really Need to Know I Learned in Kindergarten*. Roseanne Barr's *Roseanne* and Nancy Reagan's *My Turn* finished in second and third place. respectively. Other notable nonfiction included *Education of a Wandering Man*, by Louis L'Amour; *All My Best Friends*, by George Burns with David Fisher; *Liar's Poker*, by Michael Lewis; *Drive*, by Larry Bird with Bob Ryan; *Chronicle of America*, edited by Clifton Daniel; *Chili Dawgs Always Bark at Night*, by Lewis Grizzard; *The Tempting of America*, by Robert H. Bork; *Among Schoolchildren*, by Tracy Kidder; *I Want to Grow Hair, I Want to Grow Up, I Want to Go to Boise*, by Erma Bombeck; and *Bo*, Bo by Schembechler and Mitch Albom. *A Brief History of Time* by Stephen W. Hawking, had been on the bestseller list for 90 weeks by the end of the year.

On Stage

This year's plays produced on Broadway included: *City of Angels*; *Dangerous Games*; *Eastern Standard*; *A Few Good Men*; *Ghetto*; *Grand Hotel*; *Gypsy*; *The Heidi Chronicles*; *Hizzoner!*; *Jerome Robbins Broadway*; *Lend Me a Tenor*; *Mandy Patinkin in Concert: Dress Casual*; *Mastergate*; *Metamorphosis*; *Orpheus Descending*; *Prince of Central Park*; *Run for Your Wife!*; *Sid Caesar & Company*; *Shenandoah*; *Shirley Valentine*; *Starmites*; *Sweeney Todd*; *Tru*; *The Tenth Man*; *Threepenny Opera*; and *Welcome to the Club*.

Best Play was *The Heidi Chronicles*. Phillip Bosco won Best Actor in *Lend Me a Tenor*, and Pauline Collins earned Best Actress in *Shirley Valentine*. Best Musical went to *Jerome Robbins Broadway*.

Films

Batman's earnings this year were $251,188,924.

Driving Miss Daisy was named Best Picture. Jessica Tandy was named Best Actress for her role in the film.

Other outstanding films of the year included: *The Bear*; *The Adventures of Baron Munchausen*, with John Neville, Eric Idle, Jonathan Pryce, Oliver Reed, and Uma Thurman; *Born on the Fourth of July*, with Tom Cruise, Raymond J. Barry, and Willem Dafoe; *Cinema Paradiso*, with Philippe Noiret and Jacques Perin; *Cousins*, with Ted Danson, Isabella Rossellini, Sean Young, and Lloyd Bridges; *Dead Poets Society*, with Robin Williams and Robert Sean Leonard; *Do the Right Thing*, with Danny Aiello, Ossie Davis, Ruby Dee, Richard Edson, and Giancarlo Esposito; *Drugstore Cowboy*, with Matt Dillon and Kelly Lynch; *A Dry White Season*, with Donald Sutherland, Marlon Brando, Susan Sarandon, and Jurgen Prochnow; *Enemies, a Love Story*, with Ron Silver, Anjelica Huston, Lena Olin, and Alan King; *Field of Dreams*, with Kevin Costner, Amy Madigan, Ray Liotta, and James Earl Jones; *Glory*, with Matthew Broderick, Denzel Washington, and Morgan Freeman; *Lethal Weapon 2*, with Mel Gibson, Danny Glover, and Joe Pesci; *The Little Mermaid*; *My Left Foot*, with Daniel Day-Lewis and Brenda Fricker; *Romero*, with Raul Julia and Richard Jordan; *True Love*, with Annabella Sciorra and Ron Eldard; *The War of the Roses*, with Michael Douglas, Kathleen Turner, and Danny DeVito; *When Harry Met Sally*, with Billy Crystal, Meg Ryan, Carrie Fisher, and Bruno Kirby; and *Roger & Me* (documentary, directed by Michael Moore).

Television

NBC rebroadcast (Mar. 24) its original 1960 production of *Peter Pan*. Andrew Dice Clay appeared (Sept. 6) on *The 1989 MTV Music Awards*. The three commercial networks, along with all-news CNN, provided (Oct. 17) coverage of the San Francisco earthquake. ABC offered (Oct. 29) *The Final Days*, a dramatization of a book of that title about the end of Richard Nixon's presidency. Julie Andrews and Carol Burnett reprised (Dec. 13) their 1962 duo performance in ABC's *Julie & Carol: Together Again*. *Roseanne* was America's top-rated show.

Music

My Prerogative, Bobby Brown; *Two Hearts*, Phil Collins; *When I'm with You*, Sheriff; *Straight Up*, Paula Abdul; *Lost in Your Eyes*, Debbie Gibson; *The Living Years*, The Mechanics; *Eternal Flame*, Bangles; *The Look*, Roxette; *She Drives Me Crazy*, Fine Young Cannibals; *Like a Prayer*, Madonna; *I'll Be There for You*, Bon Jovi; *Forever Your Girl*, Paula Abdul; *Rock On*, Michael Damian; *Wind Beneath My Wings*, Bette Midler; *I'll Be Loving You, Forever)*, New Kids on the Block; *Satisfied*, Richard Marx; *Baby Don't Forget My Number*, Milli Vanilli; *Good Thing*, Fine Young Cannibals; *If You Don't Know Me by Now*, Simply Red; *Toy Soldiers*, Martika; *Batdance*, Prince; *Right Here Waiting*, Richard Marx; *Cold Hearted*, Paula Abdul; *Hangin' Tough*, New Kids on the Block; *Don't Wanna Lose You*, Gloria Estefan; *Girl I'm Gonna Miss You*, Milli Vanilli; *Miss You Much*, Janet Jackson; *Listen to Your Heart*, Roxette; *When I See You Smile*, Bad English; *Blame It on the Rain*, Milli Vanilli; *We Didn't Start the Fire*, Billy Joel; and *Another Day in Paradise*, Phil Collins.

Grammys this year went to: Bette Midler's *Wind Beneath My Wings*, which took Record of the Year and Song of the Year. Album of the Year and Best Female Vocal Performance were awarded to Bonnie Rait for *Nick of Time*. Michael Bolton earned Best Male Vocal Performance for *How Am I Supposed to Live Without You*.

1990

$\mathscr{M}$arion Barry, Mayor of Washington, D.C., was videotaped (Jan. 19) as he smoked cocaine in a motel room and was arrested.

In an article in the *Journal of the American Medical Association*, two medical researchers wrote (Mar. 16) that the AIDS epidemic in the U.S. had peaked.

Imelda Marcos, former first lady of the Philippines, went on trial (Mar. 20) in New York City for fraud.

Prof. Robert Polhill was released (Apr. 23) after 39 months as a hostage in Beirut.

The shuttle *Discovery* launched (Apr. 25) the Hubble Space Telescope. Two months later, NASA announced (June 27) that the spacecraft's mirror was incorrectly shaped and that it was not expected to function any better than a ground-based telescope. (It would later be repaired in a special mission of the space shuttle.)

A Japanese businessman bid (May 16) a record $82.5 million for van Gogh's *Portrait of Dr. Gachet* at an auction at Christie's in New York City.

The Bush Administration advised (May 23) Congress that the savings and loan industry bailout could cost as much as $130 billion, double the previous projection.

Mikhail Gorbachev met (May 31–June 3) with President George Bush in a Washington summit.

South African black leader Nelson Mandela visited the U.S. He received (June 20) a ticker-tape parade in New York City and met (June 25) with President Bush in the White House.

President Bush issued (June 26) a statement listing "tax revenue increases" as part of a budget deficit reduction plan, despite his "read my lips" campaign promise not to raise taxes.

The northern spotted owl was added (June) to the federal list of endangered species, potentially threatening the logging industry in certain areas.

Oliver North's three felony convictions were suspended (July 20) by the Federal Court of Appeals.

Justice William Brennan announced (July 20) his retirement from the Supreme Court, and Judge David Souter was nominated (July 23) to replace him.

The U.S. announced (Aug. 7) that it was sending military forces to Saudi Arabia in response to Iraq's invasion (Aug. 1) of Kuwait. The number of deployed American service personnel in Operation Desert Shield rose to 527,000.

Four New York City children were killed (Aug.) by random gunshots in separate incidents.

Charles Keating, owner of the Lincoln Savings and Loan Association, was indicted (Sept. 18) on 42 charges of criminal fraud.

Elizabeth Dole, the first Bush Cabinet member to leave the administration, resigned (Oct. 24) as Labor Secretary.

Ivana Trump filed (Nov. 2) for divorce from millionaire real estate developer Donald Trump.

"Junk bond king" Michael Milken was sentenced (Nov. 21) to 10 years in prison for violating federal tax and securities laws. He also agreed to pay a $200 million fine and $400 million in restitution.

President Bush agreed (Dec. 12) to provide $1 billion in food aid to the Soviet Union.

In sports news, the San Francisco 49ers defeated (Jan.) the Denver Broncos to win Super Bowl XXIV; the Cincinnati Reds defeated the Oakland A's in four games to win the World Series; and NFL Commissioner Paul Tagliabue fined (Nov. 27) the New England Patriots and three players $72,500 for harassing a female reporter in the locker room.

Deaths of the year included: radio and TV host Arthur Godfrey, 81 (Jan. 19); social critic Lewis Mumford (Jan. 26); entertainer Sammy Davis, Jr., 64 (May 16); puppeteer Jim Henson, 53 (May 16); boxer Rocky Graziano, 71 (May 22); singer Pearl Bailey, 72 (Aug. 17); broadcaster Douglas Edwards, 73 (Oct. 13); conductor and composer Leonard Bernstein, 72 (Oct. 14); psychologist B. F. Skinner, 86 (Aug. 18); hockey coach Fred Shero, 65 (Nov. 24); editor Norman Cousins, 75 (Nov. 30); composer Aaron Copland, 90 (Dec. 2); and football coach George Allen, 72 (Dec. 31).

In Print

The year ended with Jean Auel's *The Plains of Passage* in the top spot. Stephen King's *Four Past Midnight* finished second, not quite continuing his string of consecutive number one bestsellers. The year's other best-selling fiction included *The Witching Hour*, by Anne Rice; *The Polar Express*, by Chris Van Allsburg; *Memories of Midnight*, by Sidney Sheldon; *Dazzle*, by Judith Krantz; *Jurassic Park*, by Michael Crichton; *The Burden of Proof*, by Scott Turow; *Possession*, by A. S. Byatt; *Longshot*, by Dick Francis; *The Stand*, by Stephen King; *Lady Boss*, by Jackie Collins; *Carl's Christmas*, by Alexandra Day; *Oh, the Places You'll Go!*, by Dr. Seuss; and *The General in His Labyrinth*, by Gabriel Garcia Marquez.

The nonfiction list had a mix of repeat titles from the previous year, some notable authors, and new names: *A Life on the Road*, by Charles Kuralt; *The Civil War*, by Geoffrey C. Ward with Ric Burns and Ken Burns; *Bo Knows Bo*, by Bo Jackson and Dick Schaap; *Millie's Book*, "as told to" Barbara Bush; ; *Iron John*, by Robert Bly; *The Cat and the Curmudgeon*, by Cleveland Amory; *An*

American Life, by Ronald Reagan; *Get to the Heart*, by Barbara Mandrell with George Vecsey; *Friday Night Lights*, by H. G. Bissinger; *Suddenly*, by George F. Will; *It Was on Fire When I Lay Down on It*, by Robert Fulghum; *If I Ever Get Back to Georgia, I'm Gonna Nail My Feet to the Ground*, by Lewis Grizzard; and *You Just Don't Understand*, by Deborah Tannen. *All I Really Need to Know I Learned in Kindergarten* by Robert Fulghum had been on the bestseller list for 95 consecutive weeks. An illustrated gift edition was also issued this year.

On Stage

Plays produced included: *Accomplice; Aspects of Love; Buddy: The Buddy Holly Story; Cat on a Hot Tin Roof; The Cemetery Club; Change in the Heir; Evening with Harry Connick Jr. and His Orchestra; Fiddler on the Roof; The Grapes of Wrath; Jackie Mason—Brand New; Junon and Avos—The Hope; Lettice and Lovage; Michael Feinstein in Concert—Piano and Voice; The Miser; Miss Margarida's Way; Oh, Kay!; Once on This Island; Peter Pan; The Piano Lesson; Prelude to a Kiss; Shadowlands; Shogun: The Musical; Six Degrees of Separation; Some Americans Abroad; The Sound of Music; Stand-Up Tragedy; Those Were the Days; Truly Blessed*; and *Zoya's Apartment*.

Best Musical was *City of Angels*, and James Naughton, in the same musical, earned Best Actor. Best Actress in a Musical went to Tyne Daly in *Gypsy*. Best Play of the Year was *The Grapes of Wrath*. Robert Morse won Best Actor in *Tru*.

Films

Kevin Costner won a Best Picture award for his film *Dances With Wolves*. Costner was also named Best Director.

Other of the year's notable films included *Alice*, with Mia Farrow, Alec Baldwin, William Hurt, Cybill Shepard, Bernadette Peters, and Keye Luke; *Cyrano de Bergerac*, with Gerard Depardieu, Anne Brochet, and Vincent Perez; *Ghost*, with Patrick Swayze, Demi Moore, and Whoopi Goldberg; *The Godfather, Part III*, with Andy Garcia, Al Pacino, Diane Keaton, Talia Shire, Eli Wallach, and George Hamilton; *Goodfellas*, with Robert DeNiro, Ray Liotta, Joe Pesci, Lorraine Bracco, Paul Sorvino, and Angela Pietropinto; *Green Card*, with Gerard Depardieu and Andie McDowell; *The Grifters*, with Anjelica Huston, John Cusak, Annette Benning, and Pat Hingle; *The Hunt for Red October*, with Sean Connery, Alec Baldwin, Scott Glenn, and James Earl Jones; *Miller's Crossing*, with Gabriel Byrne, Albert Finney, and Marcia Gay Harden; *Misery*, with James Caan; Kathy Bates, Richard Farnsworth, Frances Sternhagen, and Lauren Bacall; *Pacific Heights*, with Michael Keaton, Melanie Griffith, and Matthew Modine; *Presumed Innocent*, with Harrison Ford, Brian Dennehy, Raul Julia, Bonnie Bedelia, Paul Winfield, and Greta Scacchi; *Q & A*, with Nick Nolte, Timothy Hutton, Armand Assante, and Patrick O'Neal; *Reversal of Fortune*, with Glenn Close, Jeremy Irons, Ron Silver, Annabella Sciorra, Uta Hagen, and Fisher Stevens; *Vincent and Theo*, with Tim Roth and Paul Rhys; *Welcome Home, Roxy Carmichael*, with Winona Ryder and Jeff Daniels; and

White Hunter, Black Heart, with Clint Eastwood, Jeff Fahey, and George Dzundza.

Television

ABC broadcast (Feb. 4) *Sammy Davis Jr.'s 60th Anniversary Celebration*. *Law and Order* and *Beverly Hills 90210* made their debuts in the 1990–91 season. *Murphy Brown* won an Emmy as outstanding comedy series. Fox's *In Living Color* was named outstanding variety, music or comedy series. Patricia Wettig was named outstanding actress in a drama series for her work on *thirtysomething. Cheers* was the top-ranked program.

Music

How Am I Supposed to Live Without You, Michael Bolton; *Opposites Attract*, Paula Abdul w/ The Wild Pair; *Escapade*, Janet Jackson; *Black Velvet*, Alannah Myles; *Love Will Lead You Back*, Taylor Dayne; *I'll Be Your Everything*, Tommy Page; *Nothing Compares 2 U*, Sinead O'Connor; *Vogue*, Madonna; *Hold On*, Wilson Phillips; *It Must Have Been Love*, Roxette; *Step by Step*, New Kids on the Block; *She Ain't Worth It*, Glenn Medeiros f/Bobby Brown; *Vision of Love*, Mariah Carey; *If Wishes Came True*, Sweet Sensation; *Blaze of Glory*, Jon Bon Jovi; *Release Me*, Wilson Phillips; *(Can't Live Without Your) Love and Affection*, Nelson; *Close to You*, Maxi Priest; *Praying for Time*, George Michael; *I Don't Have the Heart*, James Ingram; *Black Cat*, Janet Jackson; *Ice Ice Baby*, Vanilla Ice; *Love Takes Time*, Mariah Carey; *I'm Your Baby Tonight*, Whitney Houston; and *Because I Love You (The Postman Song)*, Stevie B.

Another Day in Paradise by Phil Collins earned Record of the Year at the Grammys. Quincy Jones took Album of the Year for *Back on the Block*. Song of the Year went to Julie Gold for *From a Distance*. Best Male Vocal Performance was earned by Roy Orbison for *Oh Pretty Woman*, and Best Female Vocal Performance was awarded to Mariah Carey for *Vision of Love*.

1991

$\mathcal{P}$an American World Airways filed (Jan. 8) for bankruptcy and ceased operations on Dec. 4.

Two days after the expiration of a UN deadline for withdrawal of Iraqi forces from Kuwait, U.S. and Coalition aircraft and sea-launched missiles attacked (Jan. 17) Baghdad, launching Operation Desert Storm. Some 200,000 Coalition troops began a ground offensive on Feb. 24, and the first U.S. units entered Kuwait City three days later. The same day (Feb. 27), President George Bush suspended all military operations and announced the liberation of Kuwait.

White Los Angeles police officers were videotaped (Mar. 3) beating Rodney King, a black construction worker.

The nation's unemployment rate reached (Mar. 8) 6.5 percent, the highest in four years.

The price of a first-class stamp was 29 cents.

Albania and the U.S. restored (Mar. 15) full diplomatic relations after a 52-year break.

Congress voted (Mar. 21) a savings and loan association bailout package of $78 billion.

President Bush ordered (Apr. 5) U.S. aircraft to drop supplies to Kurdish refugees in northern Iraq.

Cpl. Freddie Stowers became (May) the first Black soldier to win the Medal of Honor for service in either world war. He originally had been recommended for the medal on Sept. 28, 1918.

Some 14,500 American military and civilian personnel and dependents evacuated (June 10) Clark Air Force Base and moved to Subic Bay Naval Base in the Philippines after the eruption of Mt. Pinatubo.

The remains of Zachary Taylor, the nation's 12th President, were removed (June 17) from a Louisville, Ky., grave to ascertain whether he had died of arsenic poisoning. No trace of arsenic was found.

Justice Thurgood Marshall announced (June 27) his retirement from the Supreme Court. President Bush nominated (July 1) Clarence Thomas to succeed him.

Woodstock, N.Y., the town that had hosted the legendary Woodstock concert in 1969, ran up (July) an $8.5 million debt to the local sewer district resulting from its growing popularity as a weekend retreat.

President Bush began (July 29) a visit to the Soviet Union. He cited (July 30) Mikhail Gorbachev for "instituting reforms that changed the world," and signed (July 31) a treaty to reduce nuclear weapons inventories.

A woman in Texas was found guilty (Sept. 3) of conspiring to kill the mother of her daughter's rival for a place on the school cheerleading squad.

The Federal Reserve seized (Sept. 11) the U.S. assets of Ghaith Pharon and fined him $37 million for his role in the Bank of Credit and Commerce International scandal.

Negotiations for an international treaty on climate change and greenhouse gases failed (Sept. 21) when the U.S. refused to set limits on carbon dioxide emissions. Five days later, eight people entered the Biosphere, a huge, airtight greenhouse in Arizona, for a two-year stay.

President Bush proposed (Sept. 28) additional cuts in nuclear weapons.

Arkansas Gov. Bill Clinton entered (Oct. 3) the race for the Democratic presidential nomination.

Anita Hill, a University of Oklahoma law professor, charged (Oct. 6) that she had been sexually harassed by Clarence Thomas, Supreme Court justice nominee. Her testimony before televised hearings of the Senate Judiciary Committee touched off a national debate on sexual harassment in the workplace. The full Senate confirmed Thomas four days later.

Imelda Marcos ended five years of exile in the U.S. when she returned (Nov. 4) to the Philippines.

The U.S. Court of Appeals overturned (Nov. 15) the conviction of John Poindexter in the Iran-contra case.

John Sununu resigned (Dec. 3) as President Bush's Chief of Staff and was replaced by Transportation Secretary Samuel Skinner.

Joseph Cicippio, Alan Steen, and Terry Anderson, the last three Americans held hostage in Lebanon, were released (Dec.).

Actress and activist Jane Fonda married (Dec. 21) businessman and Atlanta Braves owner Ted Turner.

The U.S. population of the United States was 252,076,000.

In sports news, the New York Giants defeated (Jan.) the Buffalo Bills to win Super Bowl XXV; the Minnesota Twins defeated the Atlanta Braves in seven games to win (Oct.) the World Series; and Magic Johnson announced (Nov. 7) his retirement from professional basketball after testing positive for the HIV virus that causes AIDS.

Deaths of the year included: football player Red Grange, 87 (Jan. 28); political tactician Lee Atwater, 40 (Mar. 29); pianist Rudolf Serkin, 86 (May 8); jazz saxophonist Stan Getz, 64 (June 6); author Isaac Bashevis Singer, 87 (July 25); newscaster Harry Reasoner, 68 (Aug. 6); actress Colleen Dewhurst, 67 (Aug. 22); jazz trumpeter Miles Davis, 65 (Sept. 28); baseball manager Leo Durocher, 86 (Oct. 7); comedian Redd Foxx, 68 (Oct. 11); singer Tennessee Ernie Ford, 72 (Oct. 17); author Theodor Seuss Geisel, 87 (Nov. 24); and actor Ralph Bellamy, 87 (Nov. 29).

In Print

Again a Stephen King book, *Needful Things*, finished the year in second place. The number one book was *Scarlett* by Alexandra Ripley, a sequel to *Gone with the Wind*.

Other widely read fiction included *No Greater Love*, by Danielle Steel; *The Sum of All Fears*, by Tom Clancy; *Night over Water*, by Ken Follett; *The Doomsday Conspiracy*, by Sidney Sheldon; *The Polar Express*, by Chris Van Allsburg; *The Jolly Christmas Postman*, by Janet Ahlberg and Allan Ahlberg; *The Firm*, by John Grisham; *WLT*, by Garrison Keillor; *Disney's Beauty and the Beast*; *Comeback*, by Dick Francis; *Gone with the Wind* (reissued), by Margaret Mitchell; *Remember*, by Barbara Taylor Bradford; and *Oh, the Places You'll Go*, (92 weeks on the bestseller list), by Dr. Seuss.

The top nonfiction book of the year was Katharine Hepburn's memoirs, *Me: Stories of My Life*. Following were: *Uh-Oh*, by Robert Fulghum; *Memories*, by Ralph Emery with Tom Carter; *Den of Thieves*, by James B. Stewart; *Under Fire*, by Oliver L. North; *The Jordan Rules*, by Sam Smith; *Childhood*, by Bill Cosby; *The World Is My Home*, by James A. Michener; *When You Look Like Your Passport Photo, It's Time to Go Home*, by Erma Bombeck; *Brother Eagle, Sister Sky: A Message from Chief Seattle*, illustrated by Susan Jeffers; *Prairyerth*, by William Least Heat-Moon; *Parliament of Whores*, by P. J. O'Rourke; *Molly Ivins Can't Say That, Can She?*, by Molly Ivins; *Annie Leibovitz: Photographs, 1970–1990*, and *Backlash*, by Susan Faludi.

In the fiction category, John Updike received the National Book Award for his *Rabbit at Rest*. The Newberry Medal, presented by the American Library Association, is awarded annually to an author of the most distinguished contribution to American literature for children published in the United States during the previous year. This year the prize went to Jerry Spinelli's *Maniac Magee*.

On Stage

Plays produced on Broadway included: *Assassins*; *André Heller's Wonderhouse*; *The Big Love*; *Catskills on Broadway*; *A Christmas Carol*; *The Crucible*; *Dancing at Lughnasa*; *Getting Married*; *The Homecoming*; *I Hate Hamlet*; *La Bête*; *Lost in Yonkers*; *Lucifer's Child*; *Miss Saigon*; *Mule Bone*; *Nick & Nora*; *On Borrowed Time*; *Our Country's Good*; *Park Your Car in Harvard Yard*; *Penn & Teller: The Refrigerator Tour*; *Secret Garden*; *The Speed of Darkness*; *Taking Steps*; and *The Will Rogers Follies*.

Neil Simon's *Lost in Yonkers* earned Best Play of the Year. Best Actor was Nigel Hawthorne in *Shadowlands*. Best Actor went to Jonathan Price in *Miss Saigon*, and Best Actress was earned by Lea Salong in the same musical.

Films

Two exceptionally popular films were released this year: one, Jonathan Demme's thriller *The Silence of the Lambs* took top honors: Best Picture; Best Director; Best Actress, Jodie Foster; and Best Actor, Anthony Hopkins. The other was Ridley Scott's *Thelma and Louise*, a tale of two women liberating themselves and trying to outrun the law, with Susan Sarandon, Geena Davis, Christopher McDonald, Brad Pitt, and Harvey Keitel.

Other films included *Barton Fink*, with John Turturro and John Goodman; *Boyz 'N the Hood*, with Cuba Gooding, Jr., Ice Cube, and Larry Fishburne; *City Slickers*, with Billy Crystal, Jack Palance, Helen Slater, Daniel Stern, and Bruno Kirby; *Dead Again*, with Kenneth Branagh, Emma Thompson, Derek Jacobi, Andy Garcia, and Robin Williams; *The Doctor*, with William Hurt, Christine Lahti, Elizabeth Perkins, and Mandy Patinkin; *Europa, Europa*, with Marco Hofschneider and Julie Delpy; *Guilty by Suspicion*, with Robert DeNiro, Annette Bening, George Wendt, Sam Wanamaker, and Patricia Wettig; *Jungle Fever* (Wesley Snipes, Annabella Sciorra, Ossie Davis, Ruby Dee, Anthony Quinn); *Madonna: Truth or Dare*, with Madonna; *Mortal Thoughts*, with Demi Moore, Bruce Willis, Glenne Headly, and Harvey Keitel; *Paris Is Burning* (documentary, directed by Jennie Livingston); *Terminator 2: Judgment Day*, with Arnold Schwarzenegger, Linda Hamilton, and Edward Furlong; and *What About Bob?*, with Bill Murray, Richard Dreyfuss, and Julie Hagerty.

Television

The three networks and CNN provided coverage (Jan. 16–17) of Operation Desert Storm, the 100-hour land battle to expel Iraqi forces from Kuwait. CNN became a primary international news medium as a result of its around-the-clock reporting. *L.A. Law* won an Emmy for outstanding dramatic series, and Jonathan Winters received a statue for his work as a supporting actor in *Davis Rules*. *60 Minutes* returned to the number one ranking.

Music

Justify My Love, Madonna; *Love Will Never Do (Without You)*, Janet Jackson; *The First Time*, Surface; *Gonna Make You Sweat (Everybody Dance Now)*, C + C Music Factory; *All the Man That I Need*, Whitney Houston; *Someday*, Mariah Carey; *One More Try*, Timmy T; *Coming Out of the Dark*, Gloria Estefan; *I've Been Thinking About You*, Londonbeat; *You're in Love*, Wilson Phillips; *Baby Baby*, Amy Grant; *Joyride*, Roxette; *I Like the Way (The Kissing Game)*, Hi-Five; *I Don't Wanna Cry*, Mariah Carey; *More Than Words*, Extreme; *Rush Rush*, Paula Abdul; *Unbelievable*, EMF; *(Everything I Do) I Do It for You*, Bryan Adams; *The Promise of a New Day*, Paula Abdul; *I Adore Mi Amor*, Color Me Badd; *Good Vibrations*, Marky Mark and the Funky Bunch f/Loleatta Holloway; *Emotions*, Mariah Carey; *Romantic*, Karyn White; *Cream*, Prince and The New Power Generation; *When a Man Loves a Woman*, Michael Bolton; *She Adrift on Memory Bliss*, P. M. Dawn; and *Black or White*, Michael Jackson.

This was Natalie Cole's year for outstanding achievement. Her album *Unforgettable* won Record of the Year, Album of the Year, and Song of the Year. The album was a collection of songs her father, Nat "King" Cole—he died on

Feb. 15, 1965—had recorded during the 1950s and '60s. In the song *Unforget-table*, Cole's voice was mixed with her father's earlier version.

Best Male Vocal Performance was awarded to Michael Bolton for *When a Man Loves a Woman*, and Best Female Vocal Performance went to Bonnie Rait for *Something to Talk About*.

1992

*D*uring a visit to Asia on international trade matters, President George Bush became nauseated and collapsed (Jan. 8) while dining at Japanese Prime Minister Kiichi Miyazawa's residence.

R. H. Macy & Co., with 251 retail stores across the country, including the celebrated flagship store on 34th Street in Manhattan, filed (Jan. 27) for bankruptcy.

Trans World Airways filed (Jan. 31) for bankruptcy.

Following allegations of sexual misconduct, Sen. Brock Adams of Washington announced (Mar. 1) that he would not seek reelection.

The House Ethics Committee reported (Mar. 5) that 355 current and former House members had written nearly 20,000 overdrafts at the House bank in 39 months.

Texas businessman H. Ross Perot said (Mar. 18) that he would seek the presidency on an independent ticket if volunteers placed him on all 50 state ballots. He withdrew from the race on July 16 and reentered it on Oct. 2.

Crime boss John Gotti was convicted (Apr. 2) in New York City of murder, extortion, and obstruction of justice. A week later (Apr. 9), Gen. Manuel Noriega of Panama was convicted in Miami of racketeering, drug trafficking, and money laundering.

Following the acquittal (Apr. 29) of four white police officers on all but one count in the beating of Rodney King, a black construction worker, Los Angeles was ravaged by riots, looting, and arson.

Fictional TV newswoman Murphy Brown was criticized (May 19) by Vice President Dan Quayle for having an illegitimate child, "mocking the importance of fathers...and calling it just another 'lifestyle choice.'"

More than a million Americans voted (June 4) on which of two likenesses of Elvis Presley should go on a postage stamp; the younger version won 3–1. Four months later, the Postal Service announced (Oct. 6) that, in addition to Elvis, 29-cent stamps would carry the images of Ritchie Valens, Buddy Holly, Bill Haley, and other singers.

Former Defense Secretary and presidential counselor Clark Clifford was indicted (July 29) by two grand juries for bribery and other infractions associated with the Bank of Credit and Commerce International (BCCI) scandal.

President Bush named (Aug. 13) Secretary of State James Baker White House Chief of Staff and overall manager of his faltering presidential campaign.

One of the worst natural disasters in American history, Hurricane Andrew, slammed (Aug. 24) into Florida with winds of up to 165 mph. The storm killed 30 people, damaged or destroyed 85,000 homes, and caused as much as $20 billion in damage.

A Florida court supported (Sept. 25) the petition of a 12-year-old boy to end his natural mother's parental rights and allow him to be adopted by his foster parents.

President Bush vetoed (Sept. 29) a bill that would have restricted China's trade with the U.S. pending improvements in China's performance on human rights, free trade, and arms proliferation.

The Senate approved (Oct. 2) the Strategic Arms Limitation Treaty, which sharply reduced the number of long-range nuclear weapons held by the U.S. and four former Soviet republics. The Senate also overrode a presidential veto of legislation removing the ban on abortion counseling at federally financed family planning clinics.

A 22-pound meteorite crashed (Oct. 9) into a parked car in Peekskill, N.Y. Six days later, the International Astronomical Union warned (Oct. 15) that the Swift-Tuttle comet could strike Earth on Aug. 14, 2126, with sufficient power to end civilization. The likelihood of such a catastrophe was rated at 1 in 10,000. Scientists later invalidated (Dec. 28) that forecast, and, instead, postponed the possibility of a very close brush or direct hit by the comet to 3044.

CIA officials told (Oct. 10) Congress that, responding to Justice Department pressure, they misled prosecutors in Atlanta about their knowledge of a multi-million-dollar bank fraud involving illegal loans to Iraq.

The Louisiana Supreme Court ruled (Oct. 19) that forcing a convicted prisoner to take drugs that might make him sane enough to be executed would violate his right to protection against cruel and unusual punishment and infringe on his privacy.

Following complaints from dozens of female civilian employees, the U.S. Army began (Oct. 29) an investigation of sexual harassment at two St. Louis military facilities.

Gov. Bill Clinton of Arkansas was elected (Nov. 3) the 42nd President.

The next day, the *Quayle Quarterly*, a 20-page newsletter devoted to the "positions, gaffes, opinions and gaffes" of Vice President Quayle, stopped publication.

A Dearborn, Mich., police corporal was suspended (Nov. 6) and ordered to undergo a psychiatric evaluation because he consistently wrote the numeral 7 with a horizontal line through the downstroke.

A federal judge in Florida ordered (Nov. 16) the city of Miami to create "safe zones" where the homeless could cook, eat, sleep, and bathe without fear of arrest.

The last U.S. forces departed (Nov. 24) Subic Bay Naval Base and ended nearly a century of American military presence in the Philippines.

Watt Espy, an historian of capital punishment, determined (Nov.) that 2,636 U.S. convicts awaited execution—more than any time before—and documented 18,482 executions since 1608.

Some 1,800 U.S. Marines and Navy SEALs landed (Dec. 9) in Mogadishu, Somalia, as the first stage of Operation Restore Hope.

President Bush pardoned (Dec. 24) former Defense Secretary Caspar Weinberger and five other officials in the Reagan Administration of one conviction, three guilty pleas, and two pending cases related to the Iran-contra affair.

The White House announced (Dec. 29) the completion of the START II nuclear arms treaty with Russia to eliminate multiple warhead missiles and reduce total strategic warheads by about two-thirds.

In sports news, the Washington Redskins defeated (Jan.) the Buffalo Bills to win Super Bowl XXVI; Larry Bird, one of basketball's greatest players, retired (Aug. 18); Fay Vincent resigned (Sept. 7) as commissioner of major league baseball; and the Toronto Blue Jays defeated (Oct. 24) the Atlanta Braves in six games to become the first non-U.S. team to win the World Series.

Deaths of the year included: actor Jose Ferrer, 80 (Jan. 26); television host Bert Parks, 77 (Feb. 2); author Alex Haley, 70 (Feb. 10); scholar S. I. Hayakawa, 85 (Feb. 27); author Isaac Asimov, 72 (Apr. 6); football player Lyle Alzado, 43 (May 14); band leader Lawrence Welk, 89 (May 17); diplomat Philip Habib, 72 (May 25); broadcaster Eric Sevareid, 79 (July 9); Judge John Sirica, 88 (Aug. 14); baseball announcer Red Barber, 84 (Oct. 22); writer, producer and director Hal Roach, 100 (Nov. 2); Superman, 54 (Nov. 18); singer Roy Acuff, 89 (Nov. 23); and panda Ling-Ling, 23 (Dec. 30).

In Print

When the year ended, *Dolores Claiborne*, a Stephen King novel, was the number one seller, continuing King's string of holding either the number one or two position. *Gerald's Game*, another King novel, was in the ninth position. The number two spot was occupied by *Mixed Blessings* by Danielle Steel, an author also consistently on the bestseller lists, as is James Michener, whose *Mexico* was in the number three position.

Other notable fiction included *The Pelican Brief*, by John Grisham; *The Tale of the Body Thief*, by Anne Rice; *The Bridges of Madison County*, by Robert James Waller; *The Stars Shine Down*, by Sidney Sheldon; *Sabine's Notebook*, by Nick Bantock; *The General's Daughter*, by Nelson DeMille; *Griffin & Sabine*, by Nick Bantock; *Mostly Harmless*, by Douglas Adams; *Where Is Joe Merchant?*, by Jimmy Buffet; *Dinotopia*, by James Gurney; and *Driving Force*, by Dick Francis.

The outspoken and popular radio talk show host Rush Limbaugh's book, *The Way Things Ought to Be*, took the number one spot on the nonfiction list. Following was General H. Norman Schwarzkopf's autobiography, *It Doesn't Take a Hero*. Others on the nonfiction list included: *Every Living Thing*, by James Herriot; *Truman*, by David McCullough; *Women Who Run with the Wolves*, by Clarissa Pinkola Estes; *I Can't Believe I Said That*, by Kathie Lee Gifford with Jim Jerome; *The Te of Piglet*, by Benjamin Huff; *JFK: Reckless Youth*, by

Nigel Hamilton; *Genius,* by James Gleick; *My Life,* by Earvin "Magic" Johnson with William Novak; *Young Men & Fire,* by Norman Maclean; *Dave Barry Does Japan,* by Dave Barry; *Hang Time,* by Bob Greene; and *I Haven't Understood Anything Since 1962,* by Lewis Grizzard. *Sex,* by Madonna, was more than an erotic book, it was an event. One bookstore in New York City offered patrons a one minute peek at the book for one dollar, a bargain since the book cost $49.95.

On Stage

Shows produced included: *Anna Karenina; As You Like It; Boseman and Lena; The Comedy of Errors; Conversations with My Father; Crazy for You; Death and the Maiden; The Destiny of Me; Falsettos; Five Guys Named Moe; Flaubert's Latest; Four Baboons Adoring the Sun; Guys and Dolls; Jake's Women; Jelly's Last Jam; Metro; The Most Happy Fella; Remembrance; Salome; The Seagull; Search and Destroy; A Small Family Business; Someone Who'll Watch over Me; A Streetcar Named Desire; 3 from Brooklyn; Two Shakespearean Actors; Two Trains Running; The Visit;* and *Weird Romance.*

Best Play was *Dancing at Lughnasa.* Judd Hirsh won Best Actor for his role in *Conversations with My Father.* A Tony for Best Musical went to *Crazy for You.* Gregory Hines took a Tony for his role in *Jelly's Last Jam,* and Faith Prince won Best Actress in *Guys and Dolls.*

Films

Unforgiven was named Best Picture.

One of the most popular films of the year was *Basic Instinct,* starring Michael Douglas and Sharon Stone. Another memorable picture, *The Player,* with Tim Robbins, Greta Scacchi, Fred Ward, and Peter Gallagher, took ambition and paranoia to new heights. Directed by Hollywood veteran Robert Altman, the film also featured many real movie personalities as themselves in bit parts.

Other films included: *A Brief History of Time; The Addams Family,* with Anjelica Huston, Christopher Lloyd, and Raul Julia; *Alien 3,* with Sigourney Weaver and Charles Dance; *A Few Good Men,* with Tom Cruise, Jack Nicholson, Demi Moore, Kevin Pollack, Kiefer Sutherland, J. T. Walsh, and Christopher Guest; *A River Runs Through It,* with Tom Skerritt, Craig Sheffer, and Brad Pitt; *A League of Their Own,* with Geena Davis and Tom Hanks; *Batman Returns,* with Michael Keaton, Michelle Pfeiffer, and Danny DeVito; *Beauty and the Beast; Bob Roberts,* with Tim Robbins, Gore Vidal, Susan Sarandon, James Spader, Fred Ward, Peter Gallagher, and Alan Rickman; *Boomerang,* with Eddie Murphy; *The Bodyguard,* with Kevin Costner and Whitney Houston; *Cape Fear,* with Robert DeNiro, Nick Nolte, and Jessica Lange; *Death Becomes Her,* with Meryl Streep and Goldie Hawn; *Glengarry Glen Ross,* with Jack Lemmon, Al Pacino, Alan Arkin, Ed Harris, Kevin Spacey, Alex Baldwin, and Jonathan Pryce; *The Hand That Rocks the Cradle,* with Rebecca DeMornay, Annabella Sciorra, and Ernie Hudson; *Hero,* with Dustin Hoffman, Geena Davis, and Andy Garcia; *Home Alone 2: Lost in New York,* with Macaulay

Culkin, Joe Pesci, and Daniel Stern; *Honey, I Blew Up the Kid*, with Rick Moranis and Marcia Strassmen; *Honeymoon in Vegas*, with Nicholas Cage, James Caan, Sarah Jessica Parker, and Angela Pietropinto; *Howard's End*, with Anthony Hopkins, Emma Thompson, Helena Bonham Carter, and Samuel West; *Husbands and Wives*, with Woody Allen, Mia Farrow, Sydney Pollack, and Judy Davis; *The Last of the Mohicans*, with Daniel Day-Lewis, Madeleine Stowe, and Wes Studi; *Lethal Weapon 3*, with Mel Gibson, Danny Glover, and Joe Pesci; *My Cousin Vinny*, with Joe Pesci, Marisa Tomei, Ralph Macchio, and Fred Gwynne; *Malcolm X*, with Denzel Washington; *The Mambo Kings*, with Armand Assante and Antonio Banderas; *Of Mice and Men*, with Gary Sinise and John Malkovich; *Patriot Games*, with Harrison Ford, Anne Archer, Patrick Bergin, and James Earl Jones; *Passenger 57*, with Wesley Snipes and Bruce Payne; *Single White Female*, with Bridget Fonda and Jennifer Jason Leigh; *Sister Act*, with Whoopi Goldberg and Maggie Smith; *Sneakers*, with Robert Redford, Dan Aykroyd, and Ben Kingsley; *Under Siege*, with Steven Seagal, Tommy Lee Jones and Gary Busey; *Unlawful Entry*, with Kurt Russell, Madeleine Stowe, and Ray Liotta; *Wind*, with Matthew Modine and Jennifer Grey; *Wayne's World*, with Dana Carvey and Mike Myers; and *White Men Can't Jump*, with Wesley Snipes and Woody Harrelson.

Television

Johnny Carson retired (May 22) after 29 years as host of *The Tonight Show*; about 55 million viewers tuned in to NBC to see his farewell appearance. Jay Leno, a longtime substitute host, took over. David Letterman, on at 1:30 a.m. each night following Carson, accepted a three-year, $43 million offer from CBS, to move his show to 11:30 p.m. opposite Leno. Alistair Cooke, a television personality since 1952 and longtime host of *Masterpiece Theater*, concluded (Nov. 29) his last appearance with a simple "So goodnight and good-bye."

Northern Exposure on CBS won an Emmy for outstanding dramatic series; a writing Emmy went to Elaine Pope and Larry Charles for their work on NBC's *Seinfeld*; and *The Tonight Show Starring Johnny Carson* won as outstanding variety, music, or comedy program.

There were 92.1 million American households with television.

Music

Top songs included: *All 4 Love*, Color Me Badd; *Don't Let the Sun Go Down on Me*, George Michael and Elton John; *I'm Too Sexy*, Right Said Fred; *To Be with You*, Mr. Big; and *Save the Best for Last*, Vanessa Williams.

Dr. Arthur B. Lintgen, of Rydal, Pa., has a unique and proven ability to identify music on phonograph records purely by visual inspection without hearing a note.

1993

*A*ircraft from the United States, France and Britain attacked (Jan. 13) Iraqi missile sites. Four days later, U.S. Navy warships launched 40 cruise missiles at an industrial complex outside of Baghdad.

The Space Shuttle *Endeavor* was launched (Jan. 13) on the 53rd shuttle mission and returned to Earth six days later.

The first American troops, a contingent of Marines, withdrew (Jan. 19) from Somalia.

Bill Clinton was inaugurated (Jan. 20) as the nation's 42nd President.

The President withdrew (Jan. 22) his nomination of Zoe Baird as Attorney General following controversy surrounding her hiring of illegal aliens. Judge Kimba Wood withdrew (Feb. 5) her name as nominee for the post after a similar difficulty. The President subsequently nominated (Feb. 11) Janet Reno for the position and she was confirmed (March 11) a month later.

Five people were killed (Feb. 26) and hundreds were injured when a bomb exploded in New York City's World Trade Center.

Four law enforcement officers were killed (Feb. 28) and 14 were injured as they attempted to arrest Branch Dividian cult leader David Koresh in his fortified compound outside of Waco, Tex. After a two-month siege, Federal officers attacked (Apr. 19) the compound, during which a fire destroyed the main building and killed Koresh and about 80 of his followers.

President Clinton met (April 3-4) with Russian President Boris Yeltsin in Vancouver, B.C., and pledged $1.6 billion in U.S. aid.

A Federal jury found (April 17) two Los Angeles police officers guilty of violating Rodney King's civil rights; two other officers were acquitted.

Defense Secretary Les Aspin announced (April 27) an order to drop most restrictions against the participation of women in air and naval warfare. The President unveiled (Jul. 19) a compromise proposal for easing restrictions against homosexuals in the armed forces.

A ship loaded with hundreds of illegal Chinese immigrants ran aground (June 6) in the surf off Queens, N.Y.

The United States launched (June 28) a missile attack on Baghdad in retaliation against Iraq's attempted assassination of former President George Bush during a visit to Kuwait.

Floods in the Midwest were estimated (Aug. 9) to have caused more than 50 deaths, left more than 70,000 people homeless and produced $12 billion in damages.

During fighting in Somalia, 12 GIs were killed (Oct. 3). President Clinton promised four days later to have all U.S. personnel out of the country within six months.

More than 6,500 firefighters battled (Nov. 4) more than 12 major fires in California.

The U.S. House of Representatives enacted (Nov. 17) the North American Free Trade Agreement.

Astronauts aboard the Shuttle *Endeavor* returned (Dec. 13) to Earth following successful repairs of the Hubble Space Telescope while in orbit.

Forbes magazine published (Sept. 27) a list of the ten highest paid entertainers, estimating their earnings for 1992 and 1993: Oprah Winfrey, TV host, producer, $98 million; Steven Spielberg, movie director, $72 million; Bill Cosby Jr., actor, comedian, $66 million; Guns N' Roses, rock group, $53 million; Prince, pop singer, $49 million; Charles Schulz, cartoonist, $48 million; Kevin Costner, actor, $48 million; U2, rock group, $47 million; Garth Brooks, country singer, $47 million; David Copperfield, magician, $46 million.

In sports, the Dallas Cowboys defeated the Buffalo Bills (Jan. 31) in Super Bowl XXVII; Marge Schott, owner of the Cincinnati Reds baseball team, was suspended (Feb. 3) for a year and fined $25,000 for making ethnic slurs; Michael Jordan retired (Oct. 6) from basketball; and the Toronto Blue Jays beat (Oct. 23) the Philadelphia Phillies in six games to win their second World Series.

Included among the year's most famous obituaries were: trumpet virtuoso Dizzy Gillespie, 75 (Jan. 6); lyricist Sammy Cahn, 79 (Jan. 15); actress Audrey Hepburn, 63 (Jan. 20); Supreme Court Justice Thurgood Marshall, 84 (Jan. 24); tennis champion Arthur Ashe, 49 (Feb. 6); actress Helen Hayes, 92 (Mar. 17); novelist John Hersey, 78 (Mar. 24); singer Marian Anderson, 96 (Apr. 8); union organizer Cesar Chavez, 66 (Apr. 23); catcher Roy Campanella, 71 (June 26); actor George (Spanky) McFarland, 64 (June 30); World War II flyer General James Doolittle, 96 (Sept. 27); actor Vincent Price, 82 (Oct. 25); former Nixon chief of staff H. R. Haldeman, 66 (Nov. 12); TV host Garry Moore, 78 (Nov. 29); businessman and ambassador Thomas J. Watson, Jr., 79 (Dec. 31); and canine friend Loopy, 9 (July 21).

In Print

The year ended with a mixture of familiar authors and some new names topping the best seller list. Best sellers for the year included: *The Bridges of Madison County*, Robert James Walker; *The Client*, John Grisham; *Slow Waltz at Cedar Bend*, Robert James Walker; *Without Remorse*, John Clancy; *Nightmares and Dreamscapes*, Stephen King; *Vanished* Danielle Steel; *Lasher*, Anne Rice; *Pleading Guilty*, Scott Turow; *Like Water for Chocolate*, Laura Esquivel; *The Scorpio Illusion*, Robert Ludlum; *The Golden Mean*, Nick Bantock; *A Dan-*

gerous Fortune, Ken Follett; *I'll Be Seeing You*, Mary Higgins Clark; *Mr. Murder*, Dean Koontz; *Gai-Jin*, James Clavell.

Nonfiction best sellers were: *See I Told You So*, Rush Limbaugh; *Private Parts* Howard Stern; *Seinlanguage*, Jerry Seinfeld; *Embraced By the Light*, Betty J. Eadie with Curtis Taylor; *Ageless Body, Timeless Mind*, Deepak Chopra; *Stop the Insanity*, Susan Powter, *Women Who Run with the Wolves*, Clarissa Pinkola Estes; *Men Are from Mars, Women Are from Venus*, John Gray; *The Hidden Life of Dogs*, Elizabeth Marshall Thomas; *And If You Play Golf, You're My Friend*, Harvey Penick with Bud Shrake; *The Way Things Ought to Be*, Rush Limbaugh; *Beating the Street*, Peter Lynch with John Rothchild; *Harvey Penick's Little Red Book*, Harvey Penick with Bud Shrake; *Wouldn't Take Nothing for my Journey Now*, Maya Angelou; and *Further Along the Road Less Traveled*, M. Scott Peck, M.D.)

On Stage

Tony Kushner's epic play *Angels in America: Millennium Approaches* was the most prominent dramatic hit of the Broadway season. Kushner's work won the Tony for Best Play.

Films

Movie going audiences of all ages had much to pick from. The year was a goldmine of memorable films. *The Firm* (Tom Cruise, Ed Harris, Holly Hunter, Hal Holbrook) earned over $151 million by the end of September, followed by *The Fugitive* (Harrison Ford, Tommy Lee Jones) with reported box office earnings of more than $147 million.

Schindler's List, Steven Spielberg's drama about German industrialist Oskar Schindler's effort to save 1,000 Jews from death during the Nazi Holocaust, was Oscar night's big winner for 1993. The film was nominated for 12 Oscar's and earned seven awards, including Best Picture, Best Director for Mr. Spielberg, and Best Screenplay for Steven Zaillin.

The year's blockbuster was Steven Spielberg's *Jurassic Park*, with Sam Neill, Laura Dern, and Jeff Goldblum. Other noteworthy films were *In the Line of Fire*, with Clint Eastwood, John Malkovich, and Rene Russo; *Sleepless in Seattle*, with Tom Hanks and Meg Ryan, *Rising Sun*, with Sean Connery and Wesley Snipes; *What's Love Got to Do With It*, with Angela Bassett and Laurence Fishburne; *Dave*, with Kevin Kline and Sigourney Weaver; *The Piano*, with Holly Hunter; and *Philadelphia*, with Tom Hanks.

Television

On September 19th, at its 45th annual prime-time Emmy Awards, The Academy of Television Arts and Sciences presented its picks for the year's top TV shows:

Best Drama Series: *Picket Fences* (CBS). Best Actor, Drama Series: Tom Skerritt, *Picket Fences* (CBS). Best Actress, Drama Series: Kathy Baker, *Picket Fences* (CBS). Best Comedy Series: *Seinfeld* (NBC). Actor, Comedy Series:

Ted Danson, *Cheers* (NBC). Best Actress, Comedy Series: Roseanne Arnold, *Roseanne* (ABC).

Music

Whitney Houston, ever present on the pop music scene, continued her success with another Grammy for Record of the Year, *I Will Always Love You*, and Top Female Vocal for the same song.

Song of the Year: *A Whole New World* (Aladdin's Theme), Alan Menken and Time Rice.

Album of the Year, *The Bodyguard.*

Top Male Pop Vocal, *If Ever I Lose My Faith in You*, Sting.

Index